EUROPEAN CONSUMER PROTECTION

This volume analyses the theory and practice of European consumer protection in the context of consolidation initiatives seen, *inter alia*, in the revision of the consumer *acquis*, the Draft Common Frame of Reference and the proposal for an EU Consumer Rights Directive. The issues addressed are all the more significant given the passage of the Consumer Rights Directive, the appointment of an Expert Group on a Common Frame of Reference, the Commission's 2010 Green Paper on progress towards a European Contract Law and the proposal for a Common European Sales Law. The contributions to this volume point to the arrival of a contested moment in EU consumer protection, questioning the arrival of the 'empowered' consumer and uncovering the fault lines between consumer protection and other goals. What emerges is a model of polycontextual EU consumer protection law, a model that challenges the assumptions in both the 2010 Green Paper and more recent initiatives.

JAMES DEVENNEY is Professor of Commercial Law at the Law School, University of Exeter.

MEL KENNY is Reader in Commercial Law at Leicester Law School.

EUROPEAN CONSUMER PROTECTION

Theory and Practice

Edited by

JAMES DEVENNEY

and

MEL KENNY

CAMBRIDGE UNIVERSITY PRESS
Cambridge, New York, Melbourne, Madrid, Cape Town,
Singapore, São Paulo, Delhi, Mexico City

Cambridge University Press
The Edinburgh Building, Cambridge CB2 8RU, UK

Published in the United States of America by Cambridge University Press, New York

www.cambridge.org
Information on this title: www.cambridge.org/9781107013018

First published 2012

A catalogue record for this publication is available from the British Library

Library of Congress Cataloguing in Publication Data

European consumer protection : theory and practice / edited by
James Devenney, Mel Kenny.
p. cm.
ISBN 978-1-107-01301-8 (Hardback)
1. Consumer protection–European Union countries. I. Devenney, James. II. Kenny, Mel.
HC240.9.Z9.C63E96 2012
381.3′4094–dc23

2011039824

ISBN 978-1-107-01301-8 Hardback

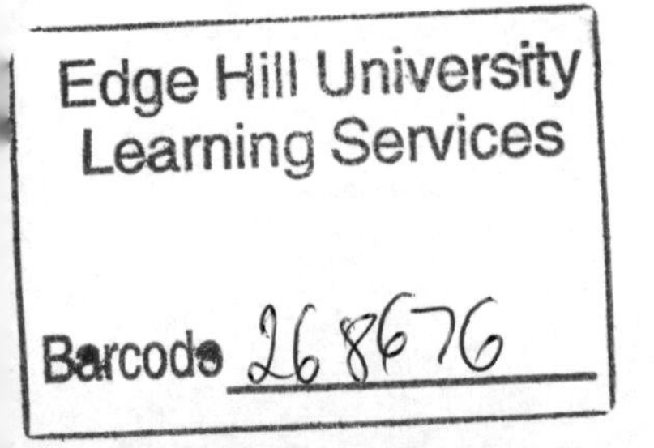

CONTENTS

Preface ix

PART I **Consumer protection strategies and mechanisms in the EU** 1

1 From minimal to full to 'half' harmonisation 3
NORBERT REICH

2 Comment: the future of EU consumer law – the end of harmonisation? 6
CHRISTIAN TWIGG-FLESNER

3 Two levels, one standard? The multi-level regulation of consumer protection in Europe 21
VANESSA MAK

4 A modernisation for European consumer law? 43
CRISTINA PONCIBÒ

5 Effective enforcement of consumer law: the comeback of public law and criminal law 64
PETER ROTT

6 E-consumers and effective protection: the online dispute resolution system 82
IMMACULADA BARRAL-VIÑALS

7 Unfair terms and the Draft Common Frame of Reference: the role of non-legislative harmonisation and administrative cooperation? 99
JAMES DEVENNEY AND MEL KENNY

PART II **Conceptualising vulnerability** 121

8 The definition of consumers in EU consumer law 123

BASTIAN SCHÜLLER

9 Recognising the limits of transparency in EU consumer law 143

CHRIS WILLETT AND MARTIN MORGAN-TAYLOR

10 The best interests of the child and EU consumer law and policy: a major gap between theory and practice? 164

AMANDINE GARDE

11 Protecting consumers of gambling services: some preliminary thoughts on the relationship with European consumer protection law 202

ALAN LITTLER

PART III **Contextualising consumer protection in the EU** 237

12 Consumer protection and overriding mandatory rules in the Rome I Regulation 239

CHRISTOPHER BISPING

13 Determining the applicable law for breach of competition claims in the Rome II Regulation and the need for effective consumer collective redress 257

LORNA GILLIES

14 Horse sales: the problem of consumer contracts from a historical perspective 282

WARREN SWAIN

15 The role of private litigation in market regulation: beyond 'legal origins' 300

AXEL HALFMEIER

16 Advertising, free speech and the consumer 313

PAUL WRAGG

17 Are consumer rights human rights? 336

MONIKA JAGIELSKA AND MARIUSZ JAGIELSKI

18 Consumer protection in a normative context: the building blocks of a consumer citizenship practice 354

JIM DAVIES

19 Recommended changes to the definitions of 'auction' and 'public auction' in the proposal for a directive on consumer rights 378

CHRISTINE RIEFA

20 Consumer law regulation in the Czech Republic in the context of EU law: theory and practice 397

BLANKA TOMANČÁKOVÁ

21 Resistance towards the Unfair Terms Directive in Poland: the interaction between the consumer *acquis* and a post-socialist legal culture 412

RAFAŁ MAŃKO

PART IV **Conclusions** 435

22 European consumer protection: theory and practice 437

MEL KENNY AND JAMES DEVENNEY

Index 450

PREFACE

This book emanates from a duo-colloquium – Consumer Protection in Europe: Theory and Practice – hosted by the Centre for European Law and Legal Studies at Leeds University, in association with the Institute of Commercial and Corporate Law at Durham University, in December 2009. That conference, which has also given rise to a second edited collection (*Consumer Credit, Debt and Investment in Europe* (Cambridge University Press, 2012)), explored consumer protection in Europe in the context of the then proposed Consumer Rights Directive,[1] efforts to consolidate the consumer *acquis*[2] and the Draft Common Frame of Reference.[3] The issues explored by that conference are even more relevant today given, for example, the passage of the Consumer Rights Directive, the Commission's appointment of an Expert Group on a Common Frame of Reference in the area of European contract law,[4] the Commission Green Paper on policy options for progress towards a European Contract Law for consumers and businesses,[5] and the proposal for a Common European Sales Law (CESL).

The conference was the second in a series of events organised within the work programme 'Credit and Debt: Protecting the Vulnerable in Europe', a project placing special emphasis on vulnerability in financial transactions and then based at the Centre for European Law and Legal Studies at Leeds Law School. The project owes its genesis to work originally organised under the umbrella of the Commission's Sixth Framework Programme (FP6) on the protection of vulnerable family

[1] Available at http://ec.europa.eu/consumers/rights/docs/COMM_PDF_COM_2008_0614_F_EN_PROPOSITION_DE_DIRECTIVE.pdf.

[2] On which see, for example, B. Heiderhoff and M. Kenny, 'The Commission's 2007 Green Paper on the Consumer *Acquis*: Deliberate Deliberation?' (2007) 32 *ELR* 740.

[3] See C. von Bar and E. Clive, *Principles, Definitions and Model Rules of European Private Law: Draft Common Frame of Reference (DCFR)*, (Oxford University Press, 2010).

[4] See Commission Decision 2010/233/EU; [2010] OJ L 105/109.

[5] See European Commission, Green Paper from the Commission on policy options for progress towards a European Contract Law for consumers and businesses, COM (2010) 348 final.

sureties. This was an ambitious transfer of knowledge project coordinated by Dr Aurelia Colombi Ciacchi, who was then at the Centre for Law and Politics at Bremen University, and Professor Stephen Weatherill at the Institute of European and Comparative Law at Oxford. It was only logical to develop some of the ideas which can be traced to that original research in Bremen – with the valuable collaboration of Professor Gert Brüggemeier (Bremen), Professor Gerry McCormack (Leeds) and Professor Sjef van Erp (Maastricht) – in this project.

The collection is divided into three parts. Part I casts a critical light over consumer protection strategies and mechanisms in the EU, with particular emphasis on the rationales (and bases) for EU consumer protection law, effective enforcement, the modernisation agenda in European private law, the post-Lisbon policy matrix and the constitutionalisation of consumer protection. Part II deals with concepts of vulnerability in the context of consumer protection and critically explores responses to vulnerability in this context. This part poses, illuminates and seeks to resolve key questions about the proper scope of European consumer protection law. Part III contextualises various aspects of European consumer protection law. This part integrates perspectives from private international law, historical analysis of consumer protection in action, critical analysis of the role of private litigation in market regulation, public law influences on consumer protection standards, and the citizenship implications of consumer protection. Thus intriguing insights are offered as to aspects of consumer protection in individual Member States.

This collection, and the conference from which it emanates, would not have been possible without the generous support it has received from Marie Curie research funds through the European Commission (European Reintegration Grant 223605) within the Seventh Framework Programme (FP7). In Brussels we are grateful to the assistance and support of Pascale Dupont, Chantal Huts and Laurent Correia, our FP7 project officers. We are also indebted at an institutional and material level to the Institute of Corporate and Commercial Law at Durham and to the Centre for European Law and Legal Studies at Leeds. In this regard our special thanks are due to Professor Dagmar Schiek at the Centre for European Law and Legal Studies for her support of this event.

We are also indebted to all those who submitted proposals, held papers, chaired sessions and made contributions to the conference and to this volume. In particular we are grateful to Dr Orkun Akseli

(Durham), Professor Cristina Amato (Brescia), Dr Rodica Diana Apan (Baia Mare), Professor Immaculada Barral-Vinals (Barcelona), Christopher Bisping (Leicester), Dr Sarah Brown (Leeds), Andrew Campbell (Leeds), Dr Olha Cherednychenko (Amsterdam), Jim Davies (Northampton), Karen Fairweather (Queensland), Marine Friant-Perrot (Nantes), Dr Amandine Garde (Durham), Dr Lorna Gillies (Leicester), Professor Axel Halfmeier (Leuphana University Lüneburg), Professor Roger Halson (Leeds), Professor Geraint Howells (Manchester), Dr Monika Jagielska (Katowice), Dr Mariusz Jagielski (Katowice), Howard Johnson (Cardiff), Professor Andrew Keay (Leeds), Dr Alan Littler (Tilburg), Dr Vanessa Mak (Tilburg), Martin Morgan-Taylor (De Montfort), Dr David Pearce (Leeds), Sarah Nield (Southampton), Dr Chiara Perfumi (Brescia), Dr Cristina Poncibò (Turin), Catherine Garcia Porras (Rotterdam), Norbert Reich (Bremen), Dr Christine Riefa (Brunel), Professor Peter Rott (Copenhagen), Professor Dagmar Schiek (Leeds), Bastian Schüller (Oslo), Professor Christian Twigg-Flesner (Hull), Dr Warren Swain (Queensland), Blanka Tomančáková (Palacky), Professor Chris Willett (Essex), Dr Paul Wragg (Leeds), Professor Willem van Boom (Rotterdam).

We are also grateful to Palgrave Macmillan for allowing reproduction of Chapter 5 of Jim Davies's book *The European Consumer Citizen in Law and Policy*, published 2011 (Palgrave Macmillan), reproduced with permission of Palgrave Macmillan.

Any conference and any project relies on the cooperation and dedication of many otherwise unsung members of the support staff; we would like to take the opportunity to thank Amanda Hemingway, Lindsey Hill and Karen Houkes at Leeds Law School for their patience and help. We would also like to thank Harriet Boatwright, John Gibson and Susan Lacey at University of Leeds, Conference and Events, for the highly professional delivery of a truly memorable event. We are also grateful for the assistance provided by a small team of post- and undergraduates in Leeds who assisted in all aspects of conference organisation and in compiling the conference report: Anna Dachowska, Naeem Hirani, Sophie Hobson, Sophie Leslie, Erica Robinson, Bijan Varahram, Andrew Vernon, Ourania Vrondou, Alexandra Weatherdon, Abigail Webb and Sacha Wooldridge, deserve our particular thanks. Crucial support has also been given by the highly dedicated staff at Cambridge University Press; in particular we would like to thank Daniel Dunlavey, Kim Hughes, Finola O'Sullivan and Richard Woodham for their ongoing support and efficient management of the production process. Editorial assistance to the project was enthusiastically delivered by Claire Devenney.

Since the organisation of this conference and the publication of this collection, we have both moved to new pastures: Mel to found the Research Group on Credit, Debt and Consumer Protection at Leicester University and James to a Chair in Commercial Law at the University of Exeter. Information on the ongoing work and forthcoming events under the project can be obtained from the editors.

This collection is dedicated to our parents.

Mel Kenny and *James Devenney*
Marie Curie Credit and Debt Project: FP7 ERG 223605

PART I

Consumer protection strategies and mechanisms in the EU

1

From minimal to full to 'half' harmonisation

NORBERT REICH

This short chapter, based on a longer version in German,[1] discusses the new tendency in EU consumer law towards full harmonisation in contrast to the earlier minimum harmonisation approach. Under the latter, Member States were free to increase the extent and intensity of consumer protection; however, they had to guarantee effective implementation and enforcement of the minimum standards prescribed by EU directives *inter alia* on doorstep and distance selling, unfair terms and consumer sales. The only exception in the case law remained the Product Liability Directive which precluded an extension of the strict liability regime beyond its scope of application, for example to retailers.

Since about 2000, in implementing a more aggressive internal market strategy, the Commission has opted for a full harmonisation approach which would prevent Member States from maintaining or adopting more protective consumer protection provisions in the harmonised field (doctrine of 'preemption'). The Commission justifies its new policy with the argument that consumer confidence requires a uniform set of rules, and with the experience that minimum harmonisation had led to a fragmentation of Member State laws which had created additional impediments to cross-border marketing, especially in e-commerce. The new strategy, which seems to be to some extent supported by recent case law, has been implemented in directives in the area of distance marketing of financial services, unfair commercial practices, consumer credit and timeshare agreements. A recent proposal on a Consumer Rights Directive of 8 October 2008,[2] as a follow-up of a general policy to review the consumer *acquis*, is the most ambitious and at the same time the most controversial step in this

Emeritus, Universität Bremen, Braudel Senior Fellow, EUI Florence (1 January to 31 May 2009).

[1] N. Reich, Von der Minimal- zur Voll- zur Halbharmonisierung (2010) *ZEuP* 7–39.

[2] COM (2008) 614 final. For a critique H. Micklitz and N. Reich, 'Cronica de una muerta anunciada: the Commission Proposal on a Directive of Consumer Rights' (2009) *CMLRev* 471–519; the state of the consumer *acquis* has been analysed in H. Micklitz, N. Reich and P. Rott, *Understanding EU Consumer Law* (Antwerp: Intersentia, 2009).

direction, and includes a redrafting of the directives on doorstep contracts (to be renamed 'off-premises contracts'), distance selling, unfair terms and the sale of consumer goods, which is also to contain a fully harmonised general pre-contractual information obligation. This contrasts to some extent with the newly adopted Regulation 593/2008 (Rome I)[3] on conflict-of-law provisions in consumer contracts which seeks to ensure that the consumer who is directed into contracting at his/her habitual residence always enjoys the protection of the home legislation, notwithstanding any considerations relating to party autonomy.

The chapter criticises the Commission's 'new approach' on both empirical and theoretical grounds. The consumer confidence argument cannot simply be turned on its head to require full harmonisation; it has never been corroborated as such. The scope of the full harmonisation principle remains unclear and may lead to negative and unpredictable spill-over effects into the different laws of Member States. There is a general tendency to 'downgrade' consumer protection objectives, despite a great deal of Commission rhetoric to the contrary; the chapter gives several examples in this direction. Finally, the chapter questions the authority of the EU to fully harmonise areas which belong to the key competence of Member States, where it must respect the principle of proportionality according to Article 5(3) EC (now Article 5(4) TEU).

As a compromise, the author proposes a theory of 'half harmonisation' which would allow uniform standards where justified from an internal market perspective, most notably concerning the marketing, information and quality related to products and services. Yet it would limit legislation to minimum harmonisation, or exclude it altogether, in all areas where there is no such need, and where different constitutional traditions must be respected under the principle of proportionality, for example, by providing for effective (but different!) remedies for breach of pre-contractual information duties, as well as for the enforcement of product and/or service standards, prescriptions on language, lists of unfair clauses in consumer contracts, etc. Preemption of Member State law should not go beyond what is necessary to achieve Treaty objectives, which expressly include consumer protection.

In the meantime there seems to be a widely shared consensus among EU lawyers that the scope of the full harmonisation clause of Article 4 of the above-mentioned proposal is definitely going

[3] [2008] OJ L 176/6.

too far.[4] This overwhelmingly critical consensus has been subscribed to and elaborated in Opinions by the ECOSOC,[5] the Committee of Regions,[6] and, more recently, by the rapporteur of the European Parliament, Mr Schwarz.[7] In her speech before the Madrid Consumer Day Conference on 15 March 2010, the competent Commissioner, Viviane Reding, proposed a new approach toward harmonisation which would distinguish between online and offline transactions; only the first should be caught by full harmonisation. This author has criticised a demarcation which cannot reasonably be maintained in practice. On the other hand, an optional instrument (blue button) could be developed for cross-border transactions based on the Draft Common Frame of Reference.[8]

[4] P. Rott and E. Terryn, 'The Proposal for a Directive on Consumer Rights – No Single Set of Rules' (2009) *ZEuP* 456; B. Gsell and C. Herresthal (eds.), *Vollharmonisierung im Privatrecht* (Tübingen: Verlag Mohr, 2009; H. Micklitz, 'The Targeted Full Harmonisation Approach: Looking Behind the Curtain', in G. Howells and E. Schulze (eds.), *Modernising and Harmonising Consumer Contract Law* (Munich: Sellier, 2009), 47ff.; see also G. Howells and E. Schulze, 'Overview of the proposed Consumer Rights Directive', in the same volume, 6–8; C. Huguenin, M. Hermann and Y. Benhamou, 'Konsumenten-vertragsrecht in der Gesetzgebung' (2009) *GPR* 159; M. Artz, 'Die "vollständige Harmonisierung" des Europäischen Verbraucherprivatrechts' (2009) *GPR* 171; Jud and C. Wendehorst (eds.), *Neuordnung des Verbraucherprivatrechts in Europa* vitnna: MANZ'sche Verlag, 2009; C. Twigg-Flesner and D. Metcalf, 'The Proposed Consumer Rights Directive: Less Haste, More Thought?' (2009) *European Review of Contract Law* 368; Martiin W. Hesselink, 'The Consumer Rights Directive and the CFR: Two Worlds Apart?' (2009) *European Review of Contract Law* 290; Martiin W. Hesselink, 'Towards a Sharp Distinction between B2B and B2C?' (2010) *ERPL* 57; S. Whittaker, 'Unfair Terms and Consumer Guarantees: the Proposal for a Directive on Consumer Rights and the Significance of "Full Harmonisation"' (2009) *European Review of Contract Law* 223; J. Smits, 'Full Harmonisation of Consumer Law? A Critique of the Draft Directive on Consumer Rights', in *Festskript till Thomas Wilhelmsson* (Helsinki: JFT 2009) and (2010) *ERPL* 5; more positive (with the exception of unfair terms): E. Hondius, 'The Proposal for a European Directive on Consumer Rights: a Step Forward' (2010) *ERPL* 103.

[5] [2009] OJ C 317/54. [6] [2009] OJ L 200/76.

[7] European Parliament Working Document of 3 March 2010 (PE 439.177v02–00).

[8] Outline edition Sellier 2009; *re* blue button-proposal: H. Schulte-Nölke, 'EC Law on the Formation of Contract – from the CFR to the "Blue Button"' (2007) *European Review of Contract Law* 332 at 348; H. Beale, 'Pre-contractual Obligations: the General Contract Law Background' (2008) *Juridica Int.* 42; St Grundmann, 'The Optional European Code on the Basis of the Acquis' (2004) *ELR* 698; J. Basedow, 'Ein optimales Europäisches Vertragsgesetz – Opt-in, Opt-out, wozu überhaupt' (2004) *ZEuP* 12; N. Reich, 'Der CFR und Sonderprivatrechte im Europäischen Privatrecht' (2007) *ZEuP* 161 at 175.

The final version of the Consumer Rights Directive 2011/83/EU of 25 October 2011 ([2011] OJ L 304/64) has come up with implementing the 'half harmonisation' concept in its Article 4: 'Full harmonisation' is limited to consumer information and withdrawal rights for distance and off-premises contracts, while consumer information other than distance or off-premises contracts (Article 5 (4)), unfair terms (Article 32) and consumer sales (Article 33) – with some exceptions concerning delivery (Article 18), fees for the use of means of payment (Article 19), passing of risk (Article 20), and additional payments (Article 22) – remain under the minimum harmonisation principle.

2

Comment: the future of EU consumer law – the end of harmonisation?

CHRISTIAN TWIGG-FLESNER

The development of EU consumer law has reached an important watershed. After decades of piecemeal harmonisation of selected aspects, it seems the moment has been reached where the future of EU consumer law may lie somewhere other than in further harmonisation of national law. The trigger has been the shift in responsibility for much of EU consumer law from DG SANCO to DG Justice following the appointment of a new Commission in 2009, and Commissioner Reding's willingness to open a debate as to where the priorities for EU consumer law should lie.[1] Furthermore, after a period of uncertainty, it now seems that the work on the Common Frame of Reference (CFR) on European contract law has resumed in earnest, and, more importantly, that this has once again been linked with the future development of EU consumer law. The Commission opened a broad debate about this in a Green Paper on policy options for progress towards a European Contract Law for consumers and businesses in July 2010.[2] This contribution will first take stock of the current situation regarding EU consumer law before moving on to examine the various policy choices put forward in the Green Paper. It will be suggested that the overall focus for the future development of EU consumer law should be on cross-border transactions, and that further harmonisation of national consumer laws should be stopped.

Professor of Commercial Law, University of Hull (UK).

[1] V. Reding, An Ambitious Consumer Rights Directive: Boosting Consumers' Protection and Helping Businesses, 15 March 2010, SPEECH/10/91.

[2] COM (2010) 348 final, 1 July 2010.

A brief history of EU consumer law

Before turning to the potential future direction of EU consumer law, a brief account of its evolution is necessary.[3] EU consumer law is largely the result of harmonisation of national laws. There have been two dominant arguments for this approach:

1. Each transaction – whether domestic or cross-border – is subject to one national law, but in the cross-border context, two national laws (those of the consumer and the trader) collide. One law has to govern that transaction. The complication in identifying which law this might be is that consumer law is usually regarded as 'mandatory law', i.e. it will apply irrespective of the terms of the specific contract, and it cannot be displaced by choosing a law from another jurisdiction as applicable to the transaction. Differences between consumer laws of the various Member States could deter traders and consumers from dealing across borders, because traders, in particular, may not be aware of the different levels of protection their customers might enjoy. In order to promote the development of the border-free internal market, it was thought necessary to harmonise the key areas of consumer law so as to remove, or at least reduce, this perceived obstacle to cross-border consumer transactions within the EU.
2. It is argued that consumers do not engage in cross-border shopping because the differences in consumer law mean that consumers are not confident enough that they will be adequately protected when buying goods or services abroad (the 'consumer confidence' argument). The strength of this argument is in some doubt,[4] because other factors, such as linguistic difficulties or practical difficulties (e.g. transport) could be more significant obstacles to cross-border shopping – although these are not (as) susceptible to legislative intervention.

Much of EU consumer law is therefore tied to the internal market, not least because the EC Treaty (now the Treaty on the Functioning of the European Union (TFEU)) did not provide a formal legal basis for consumer protection measures until the Maastricht Treaty 1992 became law. Initially, the then Article 100 (subsequently Article 94 EC, now Article 115 TFEU) was utilised, but once the Single European Act

[3] For a fuller account see e.g. H. Micklitz, N. Reich and P. Rott, *Understanding European Consumer Law* (Antwerp: Intersentia, 2009).

[4] Seminally, T. Wilhelmsson, 'The Abuse of the "Confident Consumer" as a Justification for EC Consumer Law' (2004) 27 *Journal of Consumer Policy* 317–37.

entered into effect, the then Article 100a (subsequently Article 95 EC, now Article 114 TFEU) became the legal basis for all subsequent consumer law directives. Article 114 TFEU is used for the adoption of measures approximating national rules which have the object of the establishment and functioning of the internal market. Any harmonisation measure has to have a link to the operation of the internal market,[5] although once the provision is engaged, action is not limited to harmonisation at a low level; rather, in the context of consumer protection (among other things), a high level of protection should be pursued.[6] By developing EU consumer law on the basis of this article, it became inevitable that the approach would be one of harmonising *national* laws, rather than creating free-standing EU rules. No distinction was made between cross-border and domestic consumer transactions, and the harmonised rules apply to all types of consumer transaction.

Most EU consumer law is based on directives, which require that the national laws of the Member States ensure that the outcomes stated by a particular directive are achieved in national law. A string of directives was adopted between 1985 and 2002, dealing with doorstep selling (85/577/EEC), package travel (90/314/EEC), unfair terms (93/13/EEC), timeshare (94/47/EC, since replaced), distance selling (97/7/EC), sale of consumer goods and guarantees (99/44/EC) and the distance marketing of financial services (2002/65/EC). All but the last of these directives adopted a minimum harmonisation standard, which permitted Member States to adopt or retain rules which were more favourable to consumers. Directives are not free-standing measures, but will only take effect once transposed into national law. The burden is on each Member State to ensure the effective transposition of a directive. This does not require a verbatim, or 'copy-out', transposition,[7] and Member States have some choice in deciding how to achieve the outcomes required by a directive, using suitable legal concepts and terminology.[8] Furthermore, directives only address selected aspects of the law – directive-based rules slot into existing national law. And in the case of minimum harmonisation directives, corresponding national legislation (either pre-existing or adopted to transpose a directive) may go further than the directive; indeed, minimum harmonisation has allowed Member States to implement a directive by

[5] C-376/98, *Germany* v. *Parliament and Council (Tobacco Advertising)* [2000] ECR I-8419.
[6] Art. 95(3) EC; Art. 114(3) TFEU.
[7] E.g. Case C-59/89, *Commission* v. *Germany* [1991] ECR I-2607, para. 18.
[8] E.g. Case 363/85, *Commission* v. *Italy* [1987] ECR 1733.

retaining existing national law without major change if that already matched, or exceeded, the minimum standard demanded by a directive.

The upshot of this approach is that there is not one consistent body of consumer law which is truly European; rather, there are now twenty-seven national rules on doorstep selling, distance selling and so on. National consumer laws have become a mix of pointillist[9] EU measures and existing national law (some of which is specifically concerned with consumer protection, the remainder the general law applicable to all transactions alike). While action so far has resulted in greater approximation of national laws and a reduction of differences, in reality, it has only adjusted the degree of diversity between the national laws of the Member States, making the overall picture more rather than less complex.

In order to get a better understanding of the state of EU consumer law, the Commission undertook an exercise which has become known as the *Acquis* review. This included the so-called EC Consumer Law Compendium and Database (the Compendium project), which analysed the transposition of eight consumer law directives[10] into the national laws of the twenty-seven EU Member States. This project comprised a database which detailed how each provision from a directive had been transposed into the laws of each of the twenty-seven Member States,[11] and a comparative analysis[12] which identified continuing discrepancies in areas already harmonised. There were three key reasons for these: (1) incoherence and ambiguity within the existing *acquis*, including inconsistencies between the different language versions of particular directives; (2) regulatory gaps in the directives tackled in differently by the Member States; and (3) reliance on minimum harmonisation clauses by the Member States.[13]

A Green Paper on the review of the consumer *acquis* was published in 2007.[14] This put forward a range of policy options regarding the future development of EU consumer law. Although it seemingly invited comments on a change of approach, such as limiting future legislation to cross-border transactions or even distance contracts only, or shifting

[9] W. H. Roth, 'Transposing "Pointillist" EC Guidelines into Systematic National Codes: Problems and Consequences' (2002) 6 *Eur. Rev Priv L* 761–76.

[10] Those on doorstep selling (85/577/EEC), distance selling (97/7/EC), sales (99/44/EC), unfair terms (93/13/EEC), package travel (90/314/EEC), timeshare (94/47/EC), unit pricing (98/6/EC) and injunctions (98/27/EC).

[11] Available at http://www.eu-consumer-law.org/.

[12] Published as H. Schulte-Nölke, C. Twigg-Flesner and M. Ebers (eds.), *EC Consumer Law Compendium* (Munich: Sellier, 2008).

[13] *Ibid.*, 497–504. [14] COM (2006) 744 final.

to full/maximum harmonisation, much of the Green Paper expressed a thinly disguised bias in favour of particular options.[15] The Green Paper was duly followed by a proposal for a Directive on Consumer Rights,[16] which – if adopted – would adopt a full harmonisation standard, removing the possibility for Member States to maintain or introduce more favourable rules than those specified in the directive. The proposal met with quite severe criticism of both its scope and substance,[17] and significant changes are expected to be made during the legislative stages. However, if this proposal were to become law, then two fundamental features of EU consumer law – harmonisation of national law and the use of directives – would be maintained. Somewhat unexpectedly, however, the involvement of a new Commissioner and the transfer of responsibility for the reform of EU consumer law to DG Justice both seem to have been the catalyst for thinking again about the best way forward in EU consumer law. Although work on the Consumer Rights Directive will continue for the time being, it seems that a change of direction may be on the cards.

A change of direction?

On 1 July 2010, the European Commission published a Green Paper on policy options for progress towards a European Contract Law for consumers and businesses (the 2010 Green Paper).[18] The purpose of this Green Paper is to reinvigorate the development of a CFR on EU contract law, and to explore potential future action in the field of contract law. The genesis of the CFR is well known and there is no need to go into detail here.[19] It suffices to say that a pan-European research network prepared the so-called Draft Common Frame of Reference (DCFR)[20] and submitted

[15] Cf. B. Heiderhoff and M. Kenny, 'The Commission's 2007 Green Paper on the Consumer Acquis: Deliberate Deliberation' (2007) 35 *ELR* 740–51.

[16] COM (2008) 614 final. See G. Howells and R. Schulze (eds.), *Modernising and Harmonising Consumer Contract Law* (Munich: Sellier, 2009).

[17] M. Faure, 'Towards Maximum Harmonization of Consumer Contract Law ?!?' (2008) 15 *Maastricht Journal* 433–45; P. Rott and E. Terryn, 'The Proposal for a Directive on Consumer Rights: No Single Set of Rules' (2009) 17 *ZEuP* 456–88 at 458–65; T. Wilhelmsson, 'Full Harmonisation of Consumer Contract Law?' (2008) 16 *ZEuP* 225–9. H. Micklitz and N. Reich, 'Crónica de una muerte annunciada: the Commission Proposal for a "Directive on Consumer Rights"' (2009) 46 *CMLRev*, 471–519.

[18] COM (2010) 348 final.

[19] See e.g. C. Twigg-Flesner, *Europeanisation of Contract Law* (London: Routledge-Cavendish, 2008), ch. 5.

[20] C. von Bar, E. Clive and H. Schulte-Nölke (eds.), *Principles, Definitions and Model Rules of European Private Law: Draft Common Frame of Reference* (Munich: Sellier, 2009).

this to the Commission at the end of 2008. At that point, there was some uncertainty as to whether the Commission would take any further action in this regard. However, in April 2010, the Commission established an Expert Group to use the DCFR as basis for studying the feasibility of some kind of instrument on European contract law.[21]

The 2010 Green Paper considers both business-to-consumer and business-to-business contracts, but for present purposes, the focus will be on business-to-consumer contracts. It is stated in the Green Paper that the differences in national consumer laws have the effect of deterring both consumers and traders from engaging in cross-border transactions,[22] although it is also acknowledged that linguistic and other practical barriers are equally problematic.[23] This recognition marks a change from past practice, which focused primarily on the legal framework. It is also conceded that that the proposed Consumer Rights Directive would not overcome the problem of legal diversity, especially because the negotiations over the proposal 'have highlighted that there are limits to an approach based on full harmonisation'.[24] So some other action may be necessary to ensure that a framework suitable for supporting the operation of the internal market is created.

The overall policy question put for consultation in the Green Paper is what the legal nature of any potential instrument on European contract law might be. A total of seven options is presented:

1. It is suggested that the text to be prepared by the Expert Group could become a 'source of inspiration'[25] for European and national legislators when developing new legislation, and also a part of higher education and professional training to promote a better understanding of contract law in the EU. Perhaps somewhat optimistically, it is suggested that this might result in the voluntary convergence of national contract laws. It is also noted that such a non-formal text would have little impact on the current diversity of contract laws.
2. The text presented by the Expert Group could be given the status of an official toolbox for the legislator, binding either the Commission only when proposing new legislation, or – by virtue of an inter-institutional agreement between the Commission, Council and Parliament – binding on all of the EU institutions. Although this might prove beneficial for

[21] Commission Decision setting up the Expert Group on a Common Frame of Reference in the area of European Contract Law [2010] OJ L 105/109.
[22] The 2010 Green Paper, p. 5. [23] *Ibid.*, p. 4. [24] *Ibid.*, p. 5. [25] *Ibid.*, p. 7.

future legislation in so far as its overall coherence is concerned, it would not remove divergences which currently exist, at least not immediately.

3. The Commission could adopt a recommendation, suggesting to the Member States that they might, over time, adopt an agreed set of EU contract rules as part of their national legal systems. This might either replace national contract law rules, or be an optional alternative to existing national law. This, too, might not deal with present divergences, and also bears the risk of incomplete or incoherent adoption of the recommended text.
4. Going one step further, the much-discussed 'optional instrument' on EU contract law could be adopted by means of a regulation, to operate alongside national laws as an alternative to using one particular national law. As far as consumer contracts are concerned, it is pointed out that confidence in them would depend on the level of protection enshrined in such an optional instrument. One difficulty would be the existence of national mandatory rules on consumer protection, which would have to be displaced by the rules contained in the optional instrument if it were to achieve its objective of providing a clear single set of rules for the internal market.
5. Instead of a regulation, there could be a directive on European contract law, harmonising national contract laws. Interestingly, the Green Paper suggests that this would be of a minimum standard, allowing Member States to retain more protective rules. This is not regarded as a positive aspect because of the diversity that would pertain. Moreover, past experience shows that directives do not always result in uniform rules and uniform interpretation of those rules. Consequently, directives might not provide the degree of legal certainty required by business.
6. Rather than having an optional instrument, a regulation establishing one European Contract Law to replace all the national laws could be adopted. This would produce one single text applicable throughout the EU. However, it is noted in the Green Paper that such action might be difficult to justify on the basis of proportionality and subsidiarity, especially if it applied to domestic as well as cross-border transactions.
7. Finally, the idea of a European Civil Code is raised. This would have the advantage of covering the entirety of the law of obligations, and consequently provide even greater legal certainty across the EU.

In addition to these broad options, the Commission also raises two questions of scope. First, it is queried whether whatever approach is adopted should apply to both business-to-business and business-to-consumer transactions, or to one of these only. Secondly, it is asked whether the instrument should apply to both domestic and cross-border contracts, or to cross-border contracts only. While consumers might find the existence of two regimes confusing, the Green Paper suggests that 'an instrument covering cross-border contracts only, capable of resolving the problems of conflicts of laws could make an important contribution to the smooth functioning of the internal market'.[26]

The remarkable feature of this Green Paper is that a broad range of options is presented for consultation. In some instances, the Commission identifies drawbacks for the internal market, particularly with regard to the less-interventionist options. However, the starting point no longer seems to be the desire to defend established practice, in contrast to the 2007 Green Paper on the review of the consumer *acquis*. This means that the possibility of action limited to cross-border transactions and the use of a regulation are both now serious alternatives to further harmonisation of national laws by directive. I have argued elsewhere[27] that the time has come to abandon harmonisation and to proceed instead with a detailed regulation applicable to cross-border transactions only. In the following section, I will restate the main elements of my argument.

The case for a cross-border-only regulation for consumer transactions

The starting point for arguing in favour of a different approach is the experience of harmonising aspects of national consumer laws by directives. Although this has undoubtedly resulted in the general raising of consumer protection across the EU by the creation of a guaranteed minimum level of protection, it has also created new problems. The implementation of directives into national law is a far from straightforward task, and while it may seem desirable to allow individual countries to adapt their national law to meet the requirements of a directive in whichever way they see fit, it does not provide the clarity and transparency which one might expect from a legal framework for consumer transactions. Directives do not operate as free-standing legislation, but only as rules of national law,[28] and if

[26] *Ibid.*, p. 12.

[27] C. Twigg-Flesner, 'Time to do the Job Properly: the Case for a New Approach to EU Consumer Legislation' (2010) 33(4) *Journal of Consumer Policy* 355–375.

[28] With the exception of circumstances where directives can be directly effective, but it is another well-established principle of EU law that directives cannot have direct effect in purely private relationships (horizontal direct effect).

consumers really wanted to discover what their legal rights might be in a particular cross-border transaction, they would still have to look to relevant national measures. This is exacerbated by the fact that directives leave some matters unregulated, and national law has to step in to fill those gaps. To the extent that such gap-filling rules are not regarded as mandatory rules, they may in some instances, under the Rome I Regulation, be those of the country where the trader is based.[29] This undoubtedly creates a rather confusing picture.

The alternative would be to create a free-standing EU measure which would deal with all those difficult cross-border cases. My argument in favour of such an approach is based on a number of factors, which are set out below.

Constitutional considerations: EU consumer law measures have largely been based on Article 114 TFEU (ex Article 95 EC), the internal market article. The alternative legal basis, Article 169 TFEU (ex Article 153 EC), is limited to 'measures which support, supplement and monitor the policy pursued by the Member States' (Article 169(2)(b) TFEU). Article 114 TFEU is concerned with the harmonisation ('approximation') of national laws, unlike Article 169(2)(b) TFEU which could be the basis for an EU measure which does not seek to harmonise national laws. So there is a legal basis for action other than harmonisation, especially where this would 'supplement' Member State action by providing a measure dedicated to cross-border transactions.

Whatever action is taken has to comply with the principles of conferral, proportionality and subsidiarity (Article 5 TEU). The principle of conferral limits EU action to the competences conferred on it by the Treaties (Article 5(2) TEU). Both consumer protection (Article 4(2)(f) TFEU) and the internal market (Article 4(2)(a) TFEU) are areas of shared competence. In that context, the principle of subsidiarity found in Article 5(3) TEU is engaged, which permits EU action 'only if and in so far as the objectives of the proposed action cannot be sufficiently achieved by the Member States, either at central level or at regional and local level, but can rather, by reason of the scale or effects of the proposed action, be better achieved at Union level'. Member States are obviously able to adopt legislation to deal with domestic consumer protection issues, but cannot legislate individually to regulate cross-border consumer transactions. Although the exact scope of the subsidiarity principle is unclear,[30]

[29] This would be the case if the law applicable to the contract were that of the trader, rather than the consumer, which is still possible.

[30] In C-491/01, *The Queen* v. *Secretary of State for Health ex parte British American Tobacco (Investment) Ltd and others* [2002] ECR I-11543, the Court said that subsidiarity in the

it does seem plausible to argue that it would limit detailed action in the field of consumer law to the cross-border dimension only.

In addition, the proportionality principle requires that the 'content and form of Union action' does not exceed what is necessary to achieve a particular objective. Harmonisation of national laws, which is both intrusive and disruptive to national legal systems, might be open to challenge for being disproportionate.[31] Admittedly, the ECJ has held[32] that the EU legislature has 'broad discretion in areas which involve political, economic and social choices on its part' (*IATA* (C-344/04), paragraph 18), meaning that only a 'measure [which] is manifestly inappropriate having regard to the objective which the competent institution is seeking to pursue' (*ibid.*) would be regarded as disproportionate. Nevertheless, if one were able to work out the cost of harmonising national laws and compare this to the cost of operating with a separate cross-border regime, one might just discover that the latter might bring greater benefits to consumers and businesses alike. Detailed evidence on this point is needed.

Regulation rather than directive: as already mentioned, the need to transpose directives into national law tends to have the effect of undermining the objective of harmonisation, which is to create a common legal framework applicable to all transactions within the EU. Directives do not have to be transposed verbatim – the form and method is left to the Member States (Article 288 TFEU (ex Article 249 EC)). The end result is still diverse national laws, often utilising legal language or concepts which differ from those used in the corresponding directive. Harmonisation by directive does not do away with the need for consumers and traders to seek information about which national legislation

context of Article 114 TFEU (Art. 95 EC) applied 'inasmuch as that provision does not give it exclusive competence to regulate economic activity on the internal market, but only a certain competence for the purpose of improving the conditions for its establishment and functioning' (para. 179). The Court did not consider whether this might mean that the principle might preclude legislation beyond the cross-border context.

[31] Cf. H. Schulte-Nölke. The Way Forward in European Consumer Contract Law: Optional Instrument instead of Further Deconstruction of National Private Laws, in C. Twigg-Flesner (ed.), *Cambridge Companion to European Union Private Law* (Cambridge University Press, 2010).

[32] C-344/04, *The Queen on the Application of International Air Transport Association, European Low Fares Airline Association* v. *Department for Transport* [2006] ECR I-403, para. 80.

is applicable to their contract, especially once there is a dispute and legal action is likely.

The fact that harmonisation by directives has its limits is starting to be recognised at the European level. The alternative would be a regulation, which would be directly applicable and would not require implementation into national law (Article 288 TFEU). The Commission has noted that 'replacing directives with regulations can, when legally possible and politically acceptable, offer simplification as they enable immediate application and can be directly invoked before courts by interested parties'.[33] It is clearly 'legally possible' to use a regulation for future EU consumer law measures, even on the basis of Article 114 TFEU, because this is not limited to approximation by directives – national rules can be 'approximated' through a regulation which would replace relevant national laws. Legislating by regulation would remove many of the difficulties of having to transpose directives. Once adopted, all national measures within the scope of a regulation would simply be repealed. There would still be difficulties, of course: for example, a regulation would be based on terminology and concepts distinct from national ones. One the other hand, a regulation could make the task of interpreting and applying the law easier for national courts, because it would be immediately obvious that EU law was applicable, and that relevant interpretative techniques would have to be used. With national legislation implementing directives, this could be far less obvious (especially if existing law was deemed to comply with a directive), and could increase the likelihood of divergent interpretation.

As far as the question of 'political unacceptability' is concerned, it seems unlikely that the use of a regulation would be so unacceptable that it should be rejected. For a start, using a regulation would make the contribution of the EU to consumer protection much more obvious. Moreover, it would be easier for both consumers and traders to discover the applicable legal framework. Admittedly, if the regulation applied to both domestic and cross-border transactions, there could be political difficulties, because it would be obvious that every consumer transaction was governed by European, rather than domestic, rules. In the context of harmonisation, national legislatures could use the European route to push through reforms of domestic law which might otherwise not happen, while at the same time claiming to take action for consumers'

[33] Commission of the European Communities, A Europe of Results – Applying Community Law. COM (2007) 502 final, n. 12.

interests. But if the EU regulation applied to cross-border transactions only, this obstacle would be removed.

Cross-border-only application: the case for shifting from harmonisation by directive to the use of a regulation, possibly only of cross-border application, emerges from the foregoing discussion. It has already been noted that the principles of subsidiarity and proportionality provide support for the suggestion that action should be confined to the cross-border context. In the Green Paper on the review of the consumer *acquis*, the idea of a cross-border-only measure did not receive much support. The key objection was that a measure applicable to cross-border transactions only would result in legal fragmentation as different legal frameworks would apply to domestic and cross-border transactions. While there may be a risk that those consumers who shop across borders might be confused by the existence of two separate legal regimes with – potentially – different degrees of protection, it seems possible that appropriate consumer education might overcome this sufficiently. Moreover, the bulk of consumer transactions will surely remain domestic ones, and in light of the EU's diversity, necessitate divergent strategies at the domestic level. Continuing with the harmonisation of national consumer laws by directive towards a one-size-fits-all framework for all consumer transactions seems not only unnecessary, but likely to be detrimental to the majority of consumers. A cross-border-only measure would establish a clear framework for such transactions, and be of use to those consumers and traders engaged in transacting across borders.

In order to encourage cross-border transactions, a clear legal framework for such transactions is needed, but it does not follow that harmonisation of national laws is the best way of achieving this. It seems that thinking has hitherto been too fixed on existing ways of dealing with legal issues touching on more than one jurisdiction, notably traditional conflicts-of-law rules. Cross-border transactions on a large scale need a different approach, which the kind of regulation advocated in this contribution would provide.

Of course, there is the difficulty of coming to an appropriate definition of 'cross-border transaction' to demarcate clearly the respective responsibilities of domestic and EU law. This is not a new challenge, and it has already been debated extensively in the field of transnational commercial law. For example, the UN Convention on the International Sale of Goods 1980 (CISG) applies where the (commercial) parties to a contract for the sale of goods have their respective places of business in different states (Article 1 (1) CISG). Taking a similar approach, a transaction which occurred in the Member State where the consumer resided and the trader had his place of business would be a domestic transaction. In contrast, a transaction concluded e.g. over the internet between a consumer residing in one Member State, and the trader having his place of business in another, would be a cross-border contract. Both seem straightforward enough. The difficult cases might be consumers living in a border region shopping regularly in the neighbouring country, and consumers purchasing something while travelling, or being on holiday, in another Member State. Although there is a cross-border element here to the extent that the consumer has his residence in one country and the trader his place of business in another, both consumer and trader will be present in the same Member State when the transaction occurs. It might therefore seem reasonable to assume that the relevant legal framework should be that of the Member State in which the transaction takes place.

Overall, therefore, the way forward should be a regulation which is applicable to cross-border transactions only. Admittedly, this would not entirely remove the need for domestic law, but the extent to which domestic law did still have a role to play would depend on the breadth of such a regulation's coverage. The normal rules of private international law would apply to identify the national law which would act as a 'gap-filler'. However, in one crucial respect, the current rules found in the Rome I Regulation (593/2008/EC) would need to be amended: national mandatory rules within the scope of the cross-border consumer regulation should be disapplied so as to ensure that one single framework applied throughout the EU. This necessity also means that the level of consumer protection in such a regulation needs to be high one.

Furthermore, this regulation should be applicable automatically, rather than on an opt-in basis. If left as an optional regulation, then consumers and traders alike might still be deterred from cross-border transactions because of the uncertainty as to whether a particular transaction would be subject to national law or the EU regulation. Making the EU regulation applicable automatically would provide greater legal certainty.

If this idea had been put forward two or three years ago, it would not have got very far. The Green Paper on the *acquis* review had a clear bias against the use of a regulation and a restriction to the cross-border sphere, and the proposal for a Consumer Rights Directive similarly rejected alternatives to the further harmonisation of nation law. But since then, the discussion has moved on. Not only has the proposal for a Consumer Rights Directive run into some difficulties because of its 'full harmonisation' approach, but there has also been a greater desire to think again about how best to regulate the internal market. The shift towards using regulations has, for example, been advocated by Professor Monti in his report *A New Strategy for the Single Market.*[34] He notes that:

> Currently, 80% of the single market rules are set out through directives. These have the advantage of allowing for an adjustment of rules to local preferences and situations. The downsides are the time-lag between adoption at EU level and implementation on the ground and the risks of non implementation or goldplating at national level . . . There is thus a growing case for choosing regulations rather than directives as the preferred legal technique for regulating the single market. Regulation brings the advantages of clarity, predictability and effectiveness. It establishes a level playing field for citizens and business and carries a greater potential for private enforcement. However, the use of regulation is not a panacea. Regulations are appropriate instruments only when determined legal and substantial preconditions are satisfied.[35]

He then goes on to say that:

> Harmonisation through regulations can be most appropriate when regulating new sectors from scratch and easier when the areas concerned allow for limited interaction between EU rules and national systems. In other instances, where upfront harmonisation is not the solution, it is worthwhile exploring the idea of a 28th regime, a EU framework alternative to but not replacing national rules. The advantage of the 28th regime is to expand options for business and citizens operating in the single market: if the single market is their main horizon, they can opt for a standard and single legal framework valid across Member States; if they move in a predominantly national setting, they will remain under the national regime. An additional benefit of this model is that it provides a reference point and an incentive for the convergence of national regimes . . . It should be examined further . . . in the area of commercial contracts where a reference framework for commercial contracts could remove obstacles to cross-border transactions.[36]

However, there seems to be no reason why the same approach should not also be considered when reforming areas in which there is existing legislation. Indeed, the argument for a twenty-eighth regime on commercial contracts also has relevance to the need for a better legal framework for *consumer* transactions. Monti's vision seems to be that

[34] M. Monti, *A New Strategy for the Single Market: at the Service of Europe's Economy and Society* (Brussels, 2010) (available at http://ec.europa.eu/bepa/pdf/monti_report_final_10_05_2010_en.pdf; last accessed 26 July 2010).

[35] *Ibid.*, p. 93. [36] *Ibid.*

of an 'optional instrument' (Option (4) in the 2010 Green Paper), whereas my argument is in favour of a non-optional cross-border-only measure. This is largely a matter of degree, because both approaches assume that it is not necessarily appropriate for domestic transactions to be subject to EU law. If that basic point were to become the foundation for future action, then EU law might make a much more valuable contribution to consumer law as a whole.

Concluding comment

The time has come to rethink from scratch the way EU consumer law is created. The harmonisation model has run its course and can now be safely consigned to the scrapheap. Instead, the EU should develop a coherent legal framework, adopted as a regulation, dealing with cross-border transactions only. As well as benefiting consumers and businesses in Europe, such a regulation could also serve as a template for the development of a transnational consumer law, reaching beyond the borders of the EU. The 2010 Green Paper provides a unique opportunity to develop a new approach to EU consumer law – it is to be hoped that this chance will not be missed.

POSTSCRIPT

Since this chapter was written, two developments have occurred: (1) the Consumer Rights Directive has been adopted,[37] but it only deals with various information duties and the right of withdrawal – no changes have been made to the directives on consumer sales and unfair terms; and (2) a proposal for an optional Common European Sales Law (CESL) was presented in October 2011.[38] The latter reflects a step away from further harmonisation towards the use of a regulation for EU consumer law. However, while the CESL would be limited to cross-border transactions, its focus is not solely on consumer transactions; also, it would be optional, rather than automatically applicable. So while this proposal is a welcome development, it is suggested that a lot more still needs to be done.[39]

[37] Directive 2011/83/EU on Consumer Rights (2011) OJ L 304/64.

[38] COM (2011) 635 final.

[39] For a fuller consideration of the arguments in this chapter, see C. Twigg-Flesner, *A Cross-Border-Only Regulation for Consumer Transaction in the EU: A New Approach to EU Consumer Law* (New York: Springer, 2012).

3

Two levels, one standard? The multi-level regulation of consumer protection in Europe

VANESSA MAK

Introduction

With the nomination of European private law as a 'multi-level system',[1] including private law rules of national and of EU origin, the image was created that European private law could be regarded as a *system*. In other words, it was suggested that the continuing development of private law instruments by the EU had slowly reached a point where, in its interaction with national private laws, a new private law system had come to emerge. That system, if we consider the existing body of EU law in the area of private law, would encompass rules as diverse as contract law, company law, property law and, prominently at its core, consumer law.

Even though the notion of a multi-level system does justice to the fact that EU private law has grown into an important regulatory layer for private transactions in Europe alongside and in interaction with national laws, the degree of 'systematisation' must at this point still be downplayed, as it must also in consumer law. Although consumer law appears to have become one of the most developed and most settled areas of European private law, even here significant inconsistencies remain. In particular, a tension can be observed between positive harmonisation through directives and negative harmonisation through the four freedoms of the EU Treaty (on which more below, see next section). There is, therefore, a lack of coherence in the standard of consumer protection that is applied throughout EU legislation in the field of consumer law. This has knock-on effects in national laws and therefore poses a threat to legal certainty.

D.Phil. (Oxon), M.Jur. (Oxon), LL.M. (Rotterdam); Associate Professor of Private Law, Tilburg University.

[1] Cf. Mauro Bussani, '"Integrative" Comparative Law Enterprises and the Inner Stratification of Legal Systems' (2000) 8 *ERPL* 85, at 93.

Coherence may nevertheless be pursued in different ways. The Commission's push for a greater degree of harmonisation of EU consumer law through directives continues, most recently through the Consumer Rights Directive. Bringing together four existing directives, albeit to differing degrees, this new instrument aims for further integration of the European retail market 'by decreasing the fragmentation, tightening up the regulatory framework and providing consumers with a high common level of consumer protection and adequate information about their rights and how to exercise them'.[2] Although a laudable initiative for polishing up the existing EU consumer *acquis*, these objectives – as well as the content of the directive – show that the Commission's proposal does not touch upon the most fundamental problems in the existing, multi-level framework of regulation. In particular, great emphasis is placed on the fragmentary nature of the existing *acquis*, the negative effects of which the proposal seeks to counter by imposing a degree of maximum harmonisation. Article 4 states to this effect: 'Member States may not maintain or introduce, in their national law, provisions diverging from those laid down in this Directive, including more or less stringent provisions to ensure a different level of consumer protection unless otherwise provided for in this Directive.'[3]

Whether the *standard* of consumer protection in EU consumer law is adequate for all types of transactions taking place in Europe is, however, not a question that the Commission seems concerned with: that while the standard, as said, remains unsettled and as a result threatens to harm the coherence (and legal certainty) of national laws. A reorientation is called for, therefore, to address problems in the underlying framework of EU consumer law. In this chapter, I will focus on financial services, where particular problems arise in the regulation of cross-border and domestic transactions. With the upheavals in financial markets throughout the world the need for adequate regulation in this field has once again come to the fore. My main interest is in the way in which the failure of financial markets – which is in essence a problem of public

[2] Proposal for a Directive of the European Parliament and of the Council on Consumer Rights COM (2008) 614 final, p. 2. Directive 2011/83/EU of the European Parliament and of the Council on Consumer Rights [2011] OJ L 304/64 has now been adopted. The deadline for transposition is 13 December 2013.

[3] The phrase 'unless otherwise provided for in this Directive' was added to restrict the scope of maximum harmonisation in the directive; see Inter-institutional File 2008/0196 (COD). Commissioner Viviane Reding has indicated that she will consider 'the option of more targeted harmonization where it is practical'; Speech/10/91, 'An ambitious Consumer Rights Directive: boosting consumers' protection and helping businesses' (Madrid, 15 March 2010).

law regulation – affects the way in which consumer protection should be given shape through contract law. Many British and Dutch consumers, for example, lost significant sums of money with the demise of the Icelandic Landesbanki; other examples relate to the extent to which credit agreements can be fulfilled when financial markets break down. Remedies were in some cases available through public regulation (e.g. in the form of a minimum guarantee for bank deposits), but such measures are restricted in scope and amount and cannot cover all losses suffered by consumers. Private remedies, therefore, remain important. But how should they be regulated in the multi-level system of European private law?

My argument is in favour of greater systematisation in this area, in order to ensure greater coherence and, through this, legal certainty. This does not mean, however, that a uniform standard should be imposed, for example through maximum harmonisation. Instead, a case will be made for distinguishing between cross-border and purely domestic financial services. They are of a different nature, but may be regulated on the basis of one standard of consumer protection, with the possibility for adjustment where there is justification for it – an approach similar to EU free movement regulation and focusing on what is admissible under the *Cassis de Dijon* test. For cross-border services, a case will be made for a higher standard of protection than for purely domestic transactions on the ground that consumers are likely to have less insight into the stability of foreign financial markets and hence be unable sufficiently to estimate the risk that they take when entering into a service agreement (e.g. for a bank deposit or for credit) with a foreign supplier.

The chapter has three sections. First, the tension between free movement regulation and consumer law will be explored in order to clarify how it has come to distort the standard of consumer protection in EU consumer law. Secondly, I will consider the position and aims of financial services law within the political and doctrinal structure of the multi-level system of European private law. Should financial services be regulated through harmonised rules throughout the European Union, or does it make sense to differentiate between cross-border and domestic transactions? Moreover, should a degree of maximum harmonisation be adopted? To answer these questions, the rules and objectives of the financial services directives will be evaluated against the background of the EU's framework for financial market regulation. Thirdly, I will look at the substantive question: who is the 'reference consumer' in financial services law? Which standard should be adopted to ensure a coherent approach between internal market regulation through the four freedoms and positive harmonisation through directives? Drawing these lines together, this chapter will conclude with some observations on systematisation in EU consumer law and the possible lessons that could be taken on board in future review projects in the field.

The double-headed standard of consumer protection

Directives aimed at harmonisation of the national laws of the Member States (positive harmonisation) should operate within the boundaries set by the free movement provisions of the Treaty (negative harmonisation). The Commission envisaged such an approach in its response to the *Cassis de Dijon* case law,[4] stating that instruments of positive harmonisation would focus on those areas which were admissible under the test laid down by the Court.[5] Nevertheless, practice since then has reflected a different approach. Given the diverging consumer concepts adopted in both strands a tension between free movement regulation and positive harmonisation has become apparent. The concept of the 'average consumer' who is reasonably circumspect sets the standard for the free movement regulation under the Treaty; protective measures in national law are in that light soon regarded as unjustified barriers to trade.[6] At the same time, positive harmonisation pursues a 'high level' of consumer protection and directives are persistently applied in a pro-consumer manner, sometimes even excessively so.[7]

With knock-on effects in national laws, this tension leads to inconsistencies in legislation and case law, thereby creating a highly complex and uncertain legal environment for businesses and consumers to interact in. Such uncertainty in turn raises the potential for unfair outcomes in the application of consumer law between individual consumers and businesses

[4] Case 120/78, *Rewe-Zentrale AG* v. *Bundesmonopolverwaltung für Branntwein (Cassis de Dijon)* [1979] ECR 649.

[5] Communication of 3 October 1980 [1980] OJ C 256/2. See also Hannes Unberath and Angus Johnston, 'The Double-Headed Approach of the ECJ Concerning Consumer Protection' (2007) 44 *CMLRev* 1237, at 1240–1.

[6] *Ibid.* Compare also Stephen Weatherill, *EC Consumer Law and Policy* (Cheltenham: Edward Elgar 2005), 39–40.

[7] Compare Art. 169(1), (3) of the Treaty on the Functioning of the European Union (TFEU) (formerly Art. 153(1), (3) EC) and Art. 114(3) TFEU (formerly Art. 95(3) EC). The only exception appears to be in relation to misleading advertising, where the consumer notion is linked to aspects of 'consumer confusion' applied in intellectual property cases; compare Case C-210/96 *Gut Springenheide GmbH and Rudolf Tusky* v. *Oberkreisdirektor des Kreises Steinfurt – Amt für Lebensmittelüberwachung* [1998] ECR I-4657. Also, Unberath and Johnston, 'The Double-Headed Approach', n. 227.

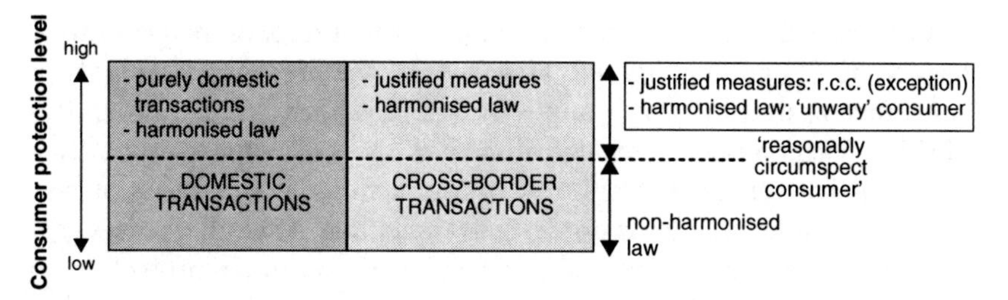

Figure 3.1 Consumer protection and market interests in the EU

in the internal market.[8] For example, one may wonder why the same consumer who is deemed capable of assessing the quality of products on the basis of their labelling has no need for reading skills when it comes to unfair terms in contracts: according to the case law of the ECJ national courts are obliged to test the fairness of a contractual term even if the consumer has omitted to plead its unfair character.[9]

The picture that emerges of the respective positions of consumer protection and market interests in European consumer law, therefore, could look something like Figure 3.1.

In this figure the dotted line represents the boundary set by EU free movement regulation. Higher standards for consumer protection can either be grounded on measures that are justified under the *Cassis de Dijon*-criteria, or on measures of harmonised law (mostly in the form of directives). For domestic transactions, it should be noted, the influence of EU law is limited to harmonised law; purely domestic transactions can be subject to any level of consumer protection presuming the applicable regulation has no bearing on the entry of foreign parties into the domestic market and therefore does not form a barrier to trade in the internal market. Transactions concluded between private parties residing in the same Member State and which are purely domestic in every other respect can thus be regulated at that – the national – level.[10]

[8] In more detail, Vanessa Mak, 'A Shift in Focus: Systematisation in European Private Law through EC law', available at http://papers.ssrn.com/sol3/papers.cfm?abstract_id=1511624.

[9] Compare Case C-168/05, *Elisa María Mostaza Claro* v. *Centro Móvil Milenium SL* [2006] ECR I-10421; Case C-243/08, *Pannon* [2009] ECR I-4713; Case C-40/08, *Asturcom Telecomunicaciones SL* v. *Nogueira* [2009] ECR I-9579; Case C-358/01, *Commission* v. *Spain* [2003] ECR I-13145.

[10] One can debate about what qualifies as a 'cross-border' and what as a 'purely domestic' transaction. For the sake of clarity, I will limit 'purely domestic' to the definition given here. This could lead to foreign consumers receiving better protection than national consumers, e.g. when opening a bank account during a short stay in another Member

Visualised like this, two problems in the current regulation of consumer law in the EU are highlighted. First, we see the diverging standards of consumer protection which apply in free movement regulation and in positive harmonisation through directives. As said, this is primarily a problem that relates to cross-border transactions. Nevertheless, it also indirectly influences purely domestic transactions. After all, the fact that there is uncertainty about the philosophy of consumer protection in EU law – in particular in determining who the average consumer is – has effects also in national laws and can lead to uncertainty there. It can therefore have a much wider impact on the way in which national regulators will approach consumer protection and the standard that they will choose to apply. This point will be returned to in the final section of the chapter. Secondly, besides this indirect influence, there is a direct interference of EU law with transactions of a purely domestic nature, through harmonised law. This may be unnecessary: for these types of transactions it could be preferable to leave it to the Member States to regulate according to local needs.[11] In this light, at least, the European Commission's push for maximum harmonisation would need to be reconsidered. That is the point to which we now turn.

Two levels

In the light of the twin objectives of EU consumer law, the promotion of the internal market and the strengthening of consumer protection, it is not surprising that a degree of harmonisation is being pursued between the laws of the Member States. This helps further the goal of creating wider consumer choice within a more competitive market.[12] However, one question that has been pushed to the background in the discussion on harmonisation of European consumer law and also, more specifically, of financial services law is that of the territorial scope of harmonising

State. This would not be the first time in EU regulation, however; for example, in some Member States (e.g. Germany and Italy) the implementation of Reg. 2560/2001 on Cross-Border Payments in 2002 meant that consumers with foreign bank cards could withdraw cash without charge from any bank, whereas national consumers were charged if they used cash machines from a bank other than their own. Particular problems relating to online transactions will have to be left aside due to considerations of space.

[11] See further below. Note also that the balance between the two categories of transaction may change should a greater degree of harmonisation be realised, resulting in more cross-border transactions, in which case the category of 'purely domestic transactions' will naturally decrease.

[12] Compare House of Lords, *Consumer Credit in the European Union: Harmonisation and Consumer Protection* (2006), [81].

rules. In particular, should EU rules aimed at harmonisation apply to cross-border transactions only or should they also extend to domestic transactions?

There may be an excuse for this neglect when it is looked at it in light of the most recent developments relating to the review of the consumer *acquis*. With the adoption of a new standard of maximum harmonisation – as suggested in the proposal for a Consumer Rights Directive – the point would become more or less irrelevant. In that event, rules so introduced would be mandatory and Member States would not be allowed to diverge from them either upwards or downwards.[13] More importantly, for the objectives of maximum harmonisation to succeed that standard would have to apply to *all* types of transaction, whether of a cross-border or domestic nature. These objectives, after all, are to facilitate internal market transactions by laying down rules that apply equally throughout the EU area and, so it is thought, remove barriers to trade that might exist because of differences in laws. In particular from the perspective of businesses, that goal would only be achieved if laws were similar for each type of transaction. Only then would sellers and suppliers be able to market their products freely throughout the EU – either directly or through local stores within the Member States – without encountering complications resulting from different laws applying to cross-border and local transactions.

Nevertheless, whether the standard of maximum harmonisation is the right one and whether it should be adopted for the Consumer Rights Directive (and if so, for which rules exactly) are questions that require careful consideration. The likelihood that maximum harmonisation is becoming the new standard may be increasing, seeing the intention expressed by the Commission 'to review and reform existing EU consumer protection directives, to bring them up-to-date and progressively adapt them from minimum harmonisation to full harmonisation measures'.[14] However, in the current economic climate, and also in the light of the constitutional crises that the EU has experienced in recent years, it is not surprising to hear voices pleading in favour of a more cautious approach of the European legislature.[15] The EU would be welcomed to take a step back in issues that are felt to belong to the national sphere of

[13] Art. 4 of the proposed Consumer Rights Directive.

[14] The Commission's Consumer Policy Programme for 2002–2006 COM (2002) 208; also, Consumer Policy Strategy 2007–2013 COM (2007) 99 final, p. 16.

[15] Compare H. Micklitz and Norbert Reich, 'Crónica de una muerte anunciada: the Commission Proposal for a Directive on Consumer Rights' (2009) 46 *CMLRev* 471, at 478–80.

regulation and to leave these to the Member States to deal with. In this way, due consideration could be given to local interests.[16] It remains to be seen how the European legislature and the ECJ will respond to these developments.

In financial services law a reconsideration of the degree of harmonisation does, in any event, seem appropriate. EU financial services law has in recent years introduced some measures of maximum harmonisation in relation to financial services marketed to consumers through the Consumer Credit Directive and the Distance Marketing of Financial Services Directive.[17] The process was not altogether painless and the results that came out are not as far-reaching as envisaged in the initial proposals, with maximum harmonisation limited to a select range of topics.[18] One explanation for this could be that numerous financial dealings in the retail market are conducted within the domestic market; consumers do not shop for credit in other countries but rather walk into the nearest branch office of their local bank.[19] Hence, local regulation suffices. Of course one could counter that these directives could be used as means to *stimulate* consumers to explore cross-border credit options. However, even then it is questionable whether maximum harmonisation would be the appropriate standard to pursue. Local interests – in the current economic climate in particular relating to the stability of financial markets and the certainty of services contracts (e.g. credit agreements) being fulfilled – seem to demand an approach that takes heed of domestic circumstances and, therefore, a degree of harmonisation that enables regulation at the domestic level. UK law, for example, reflects such a notion in its sensitivity towards vulnerable consumers as expressed in consumer credit law.[20]

[16] At the same time, in order to sustain the market economy, the EU should not feel hindered from taking more steps where these are needed. For example in financial supervision, currently the topic of heated debate, a move towards stricter EU regulation could help balance the interests of private parties where the market fails to come up with satisfactory solutions. Compare Simon Deakin and Alain Supiot (eds.), *Capacitas: Contract Law and the Institutional Preconditions of a Market Economy* (Oxford: Hart, 2009).

[17] Directive 2008/48/EC of the European Parliament and of the Council on credit agreements for consumers and repealing Council Directive 87/102/EEC [2008] OJ L 133/66. The deadline for implementation of the directive was 11 June 2010. Directive 2002/65 of the European Parliament and of the Council concerning the distance marketing of consumer financial services [2002] OJ L 271/16.

[18] See further below.

[19] House of Lords (n. 12) [86]–[92].

[20] Cf. Sarah Brown, 'European Regulation of Consumer Credit: Enhancing Consumer Confidence and Protection from a UK Perspective?' (paper presented at the Leeds Conference).

With these interests in mind, it seems that the strategy of maximum harmonisation in financial services law needs to be abandoned. Instead the European legislature should rather opt for minimum harmonisation; and it should even consider separating the regulation of cross-border transactions from the regulation of domestic financial services where these have no relation to the internal market. The latter approach, it is submitted, could serve market integration objectives while at the same time allowing room for local interests in consumer protection to be taken into account. Support for that view can be found in the framework of EU law itself: in the competence distribution in the Treaty, in supplementary regulation of financial markets, in legislation, and in case law.

Legislative competence

First, there is no way around the fact that competence distribution in EU consumer law is linked to internal market policy much more than to consumer protection policy. The Treaty stipulates that the competence of the EU in this area is not absolute but is shared with the Member States (see Article 169(3) TFEU; formerly Article 153(3) EC). Article 114 TFEU (formerly Article 95 EC) often offers a more favourable basis, therefore, as it allows the EU to act alone, but has the downside that the competence attributed to the EU is specifically related to the integration of the internal market, rather than to ensuring consumer protection. The latter is only an ancillary goal. In other words, on the basis of these provisions the EU is only able to act in the context of the internal market and therefore restricted to situations where actual barriers to trade exist which disfavour a cross-border activity directly.[21] Although that does not mean that the EU legislature will never be able to use this competence in relation to consumer protection, it does face two important restrictions: (1) the need for a barrier to trade to exist; and (2) the internal market element that will colour the substance of the instrument adopted, in particular the level of consumer protection.

The fact that competence is linked to market integration in this manner lends support to the view that EU regulation in consumer financial services law needs to stay away from purely domestic transactions. The competence to harmonise, whether to a minimum degree or in the form of maximum harmonisation, is lacking for these types of

[21] Case C-376/98, *Tobacco Advertising* [2008] ECR-I 8419 also Maduro, Opinion in Case C-58/08, *Vodafone* [2009] at [23].

transaction:[22] what is contained within the domestic sphere cannot be made subject to the legislative competence of the European legislature. Moreover, it should not, for the national legislature is sufficiently able to regulate at this level. That observation is also in accordance with the principles of subsidiarity and proportionality laid down in the EU Treaty.[23]

It is of course true that a different approach can be observed in the existing *acquis*, in which domestic transactions have been affected by European legislation. The European legislature has assumed competence for minimum harmonisation in the majority of consumer directives, some of which also affect financial services (e.g. the Unfair Terms Directive); and furthermore, the Consumer Credit Directive has introduced maximum harmonisation in the field, albeit with many optional provisions for the Member States. Although strong arguments can be made in favour of such approaches – mainly along the line that these strategies strengthen the position/confidence of consumers by providing a minimum level of consumer protection throughout the EU – that does not take away the fact that the intervention of the EU legislature here seems stretched beyond what is necessary for market integration purposes. After all, purely domestic transactions have no direct bearing on the internal market. The more convincing argument to justify this approach is that it ensures legal certainty, because consumers will be assured of a minimum set of rules applicable to the type of transaction in issue (e.g. consumer credit). In other words, whichever credit institution they approach in their jurisdiction (or in other EU Member States), there is a minimum standard of protection that applies. While that is certainly a strong argument, nevertheless it cannot on its own account for the level of regulation that is chosen. That decision must always be balanced with wider, competition law arguments in EU law: for instance, a deregulatory approach in relation to domestic transactions may increase consumer choice in credit products.[24] Of course, it is then the duty of the Member States to ensure an appropriate level of protection for such transactions.[25]

Naturally, such issues of competence may become less relevant depending on the way in which the financial services market develops

[22] Cf. Vanessa Mak, 'Review of the Consumer Acquis: towards Maximum Harmonisation?' (2009) 17 *European Review of Private Law* 55, at 63–4.

[23] Art. 5(2) and (3) EC Treaty; copied in Art. 5(3) and (4) of the Treaty on European Union (TEU).

[24] Cf. House of Lords (n. 12).

[25] See also below.

in the future. If, for example, the cross-border market for consumer credit expands because of its stimulation through measures of (minimum) harmonisation the volume of purely domestic transactions is likely to decrease. Consumers who would look for credit on the domestic market will instead obtain it through a cross-border transaction. In that case – which is not an unlikely scenario in the light of the ongoing integration of the European market – the domestic market could become so small that it was eventually overtaken by the cross-border market. Competence would then no longer be at issue but would fall to the European legislature as the guardian of free movement regulation in the internal market.

The regulatory framework of the EU financial market

Secondly, responses to the financial crisis that reached Europe in the autumn of 2008 and the subsequent economic recession suggest a shift in regulation. The reregulation of financial supervision law at national level appears to have gained political favour in this economic climate.[26] This is important to note, because the regulation of financial markets and supervision creates the background against which EU financial services law is given shape: the regulatory side determines the general framework within which businesses can undertake financial risks and operate in different markets with sufficient stability, while within this framework financial services law goes on to provide standards for (consumer) transactions with the aim of furthering market integration in Europe.

The policies that are being pursued within these contexts – financial stability and legal certainty on the one hand and market integration policy on the other – are, however, not always compatible and may give rise to friction. An example can be found in payments related to internet trading. EU financial services regulation through the free movement provisions seeks to facilitate such transactions as much as possible, clearly with an eye to removing barriers to trade in the internal market.[27]

[26] The UK in particular has lobbied for a solution in which supervision stays within the power of national authorities; see Economic and Financial Affairs Council, press release 16838/09 (2 December 2009).

[27] Compare Directive (EC) 2000/31 of the European Parliament and of the Council of 8 June 2000 on certain legal aspects of information society services, in particular electronic commerce, in the internal market [2000] OJ L 178/1; Directive (EC) 2000/35 of the European Parliament and of the Council of 29 June 2000 on combating late payment in commercial transactions [2000] OJ L 200/35.

From the regulatory perspective, however, the main concern is with the *safety* of settlement and custody arrangements. Although different tactics may be chosen, this remains the central focus; safety may for example be ensured through disclosure of activity and transparency of operations, or alternatively through authorisation and supervision of settlement institutions requiring a lesser need of information supply to regulators.[28] While these strands may be compatible when the economy is doing well – and safety arrangements may boost the internal market – problems are likely to arise when bad times hit. The natural response of national regulators will be to sharpen security arrangements in order to stabilise their domestic market, even when such actions hamper trade within the internal market. Recent experience confirms this protectionist trend, with governments developing elaborate support schemes for their domestic banks, and overall reverting to more nationally oriented economic strategies.

Against this background, it seems likely that greater emphasis will be placed on legal certainty in financial transactions in relation to market integration policy. The tension that occurs then is between the goal of giving effect to directives aimed at certainty in financial relations (such as Directive 97/5 on cross-border credit transfers),[29] and that of market integration in the free movement regulation, where measures of this kind would normally be set aside as barriers to trade.[30] The EU could provide effective counter-measures at the transnational level to further integration and boost the European financial market in this respect, although the level of consumer protection in that context remains to be determined.[31] Otherwise, however, it seems appropriate to leave the regulation of internal transactions to the Member States, which have better and more direct insight into their domestic markets, and to reject the idea of maximum harmonisation.

[28] J. H. Dalhuisen, 'Financial Liberalization and Re-regulation' in Mads Andenas and Wulf-Henning Roth (eds.), *Services and Free Movement in EU Law* (Oxford University Press, 2002), 279, at 292.

[29] Directive (EC) 97/5 of the European Parliament and of the Council on cross-border credit transfers [1997] OJ L 43/1997.

[30] Compare Case C-33/74, *Van Binsbergen* v. *Bestuur van de Bedrijfsvereniging voor de Metaalnijverheid* [1974] 1299; Case C-398/95 *SETTG* v. *Ypourgos Ergasias* [1997] ECR I-3091, at [22]–[23]. Also, Despina Mavromati, *The Law of Payment Services in the EU: the EC Directive on Payment Services in the Internal Market* (The Hague: Kluwer Law International, 2008), 24ff.

[31] See further below.

Limitations of the acquis *in financial services law*

Regardless of the economic climate, however, the existing *acquis* in financial services law already gives cause for reflection on the appropriate level of regulation for cross-border and domestic transactions. Most recently, this came to the fore in the revision of the Consumer Credit Directive. In this review process, the Commission initially proposed wide-ranging measures aimed at laying down uniform rules for credit transactions throughout the EU, with a degree of maximum harmonisation. After consultations with stakeholders and Member State representatives, however, these initial ambitions had to be downplayed. The proposal was found to be overly protective and hence was thought to create unacceptable burdens for the banking industry, in particular due to some relatively far-reaching provisions introducing a principle of 'responsible lending'.[32] Although, in hindsight, stronger emphasis on such a principle could have been beneficial for banks and consumers alike – for if such a principle had been adopted in time, it might have softened the blow of the credit crunch for Europe[33] – it makes sense, on other grounds, to question the need for a far-reaching measure such as proposed by the initial review. In particular, as was stressed by several respondents, including the House of Lords Sub-committee on the European Union, financial markets are very much shaped by local factors.[34] Therefore, the majority of products and services offered and the associated risks are closely connected to this local setting. That factor currently appears to outweigh internal market policy objectives – with market integration pushed aside in favour of stability, as indicated just now – and it lends support to a restrained approach with less scope for maximum harmonisation. That is, effectively, also what happened with the Consumer Credit Directive in its final version. The provisions of the directive that aim for a degree of maximum harmonisation are much narrower in scope than originally envisaged.[35]

[32] Cf. Peter Rott, *Consumer Credit*, in H. Micklitz, Norbert Reich and Peter Rott, *Understanding EU Consumer Law* (Antwerp: Intersentia, 2009), 185.

[33] The financial crisis was triggered by a rise in mortgage defaults and foreclosures in the United States. For an analysis, see Robert Skidelsky, *Keynes: The Return of the Master* (Penguin, 2010), ch. 1.

[34] House of Lords (n. 12) [86]–[92].

[35] They cover pre-contractual and contractual information duties, as well as calculation of the annual percentage rate of charge (APR) and the consumer's rights in respect to early repayment of an agreement.

The ECJ: law-maker or deal-breaker?

Finally, an important factor to be taken into account is the intermediary role played by the ECJ in the interaction between EU law and national laws. In relation to financial services, the case law of the Court has created a tension between those two levels which goes to the heart of the regulatory question. At issue was to what extent the consumer's right of cancellation under the Doorstep Selling Directive could have consequences for the consumer's position in relation to linked contracts.[36] Linked contracts, in that context, are, for example, credit agreements where the loan is intended to be used for the purchase of land.[37] The ECJ ruled in *Heininger* that the right of cancellation laid down in the Doorstep Selling Directive (1) applied to credit agreements secured by a charge on land and (2) that this right was unlimited in time, and national laws were therefore precluded from imposing a time limit.[38] In *Schulte* that ruling was extended even further to protect the interests of consumers. The Court held in that case that '[t]he Member States must therefore ensure that ... a bank which has not complied with its obligation to inform the consumer [in accordance with the Doorstep-selling Directive] bears the consequences of the materialisation of those risks so that the obligation to protect consumers is safeguarded'.[39] Effectively, the result of that approach would seem to be that consumers who are entitled to withdraw from a credit agreement under the Doorstep Selling Directive also have the right to cancel the associated contract for, for example, the purchase of land.[40] Such an outcome is incredibly favourable to consumers and may be criticised as extending protection beyond what is reasonable.[41] More important to note, however, is that the ECJ through this extensive interpretation imposes a standard of consumer protection on the Member States that goes much further than is customary in their national laws. In many jurisdictions the fact

[36] Council Directive 85/577/EEC to protect the consumer in contracts negotiated away from business premises [1985] OJ L 372/31.

[37] Note that the Consumer Credit Directive explicitly excludes such contracts from its scope; see Art. 2(2)(b) of the directive.

[38] Case C-481/99 *Heininger* v. *Bayerische Hypo- und Vereinsbank AG* [2001] ECR I-9945 at [40] and [48].

[39] Case C-350/03, *Schulte* v. *Bausparkasse Badenia* [2005] ECR I-9215 at [100].

[40] *Ibid.* at [97].

[41] E.g. because it relates to the *use* that the consumer makes of the money obtained under the credit agreement, rather than the subject matter of the information that the seller failed to supply. Compare Unberath and Johnston, 'The Double-Headed Approach', 1260–1.

that the purchase contract was agreed before the loan agreement would make it very hard for the consumer to prove a causal link between the failure to inform and the investment risk taken.[42] Cancellation of the linked contract would then not be an option. Should *Schulte* be interpreted as placing a duty on the Member States to ensure that such remedies *are* available, it would therefore impose protection not deemed necessary by the Member States for domestic transactions. Local interests, therefore, do not seem to be served by this judgment from the ECJ.

When applied to cross-border transactions, nevertheless, some merit may be found in a solution of this kind and the idea might even be entertained of extending this kind of risk transfer to other types of credit agreement than those sold at the doorstep. After all, the cross-border credit market will for a range of transactions usually be less transparent to consumers than their domestic markets, e.g. with regard to the stability of foreign markets, and such transactions will therefore carry with them a greater degree of risk. Not only may this raise questions with regard to the information that should be supplied at the conclusion of credit agreements to ensure a sufficient level of consumer protection, in particular, it brings up the question of which remedies should be available in case things go wrong.[43] The European Commission has so far not taken a stance on this issue, apart from deciding to leave it outside the scope of the Consumer Credit Directive on the ground that 'such consequences seem inappropriate in a directive on credit agreements only'.[44] Affirmative action could have substantial benefits, nevertheless, for it could open up the European credit market for consumers to an extent that has failed to happen so far.

Therefore, it would make sense to streamline coordination of the financial market in Europe along these two separate levels: at the EU level when matters of regulation or services law are at stake with a cross-border element to them; and left to national laws when matters are purely domestic in nature. That approach may of course be turned around if (or when) the two levels of regulation grow closer together in the future. For example, if the practical differences that divide international and national consumer markets diminish, cross-border and domestic transactions could become more alike and the standard for consumer protection adopted at both levels could then also be adjusted to accommodate both types.

[42] *Ibid.* [43] Further below. [44] COM (2004) 747 final, p. 5.

One standard?

Even if it is accepted that maximum harmonisation is not the way forward and that a distinction should be made between cross-border and domestic transactions, there is another question to be answered. Which level of consumer protection should be pursued at either level of regulation? To answer that question, we need to return to the tension between free movement regulation and positive harmonisation set out above,[45] and determine whether a satisfactory answer can be found to the question of: who the 'reference consumer' is in financial services law.

The idea that one standard for the 'average consumer' could be adequate, as would be the case if maximum harmonisation became the standard, seems illusory. Bearing in mind the grounds for differentiation between the regulation of domestic and cross-border transactions proposed earlier in this chapter, it is useful to make a brief further enquiry into the features that distinguish both types of transaction. This can not only clarify the grounds on which it makes sense not only to regulate at two levels but also why it seems appropriate to apply different standards of consumer protection. Which standard that should be is another question. If domestic transactions are left to the domain of national regulation, that standard will in any case vary greatly between local markets according to their specific interests.[46] For cross-border credit transactions, on the other hand, the framework should be similar across Europe; the paradigm transaction will be one between a consumer domiciled in an EU Member State and a credit provider operating from another Member State. The position of consumers entering foreign markets in this way appears fairly similar across Europe – for example in terms of limitations encountered with regard to risk assessment in foreign markets, on which more below – and it seems possible therefore to try and determine a common standard of consumer protection that could be adopted in this regulatory framework.

Consumer interests in domestic and cross-border contexts

What makes the cross-border consumer dissimilar to the domestic consumer? One can think of a number of factors that place them in

[45] See below.

[46] An overview of those markets has to be left outside the scope of this chapter for practical reasons relating to the size of such an enquiry. Observations made on national regulation will therefore remain general in nature.

different positions – even though they can physically be the same person. When a consumer deals with a financial service provider in another Member State, several elements stand out:

1. The stability of the financial market in the supplier's Member State influences the 'safety' of the agreement and hence the risk that the consumer takes by entering into the agreement.
2. The consumer will generally not be in a position to assess that risk solely on the basis of the pre-contractual, contractual and post-contractual information that existing legislation requires the supplier to give.[47]
3. Protection can be given in several ways, e.g. through regulatory measures, such as a 'safety' accreditation from a national financial services authority,[48] or through independent advice before the conclusion of contract or through other forms of information provision.
4. Protection can also take the form of remedies in the post-contractual phase, e.g. a right of withdrawal.
5. The level of protection prescribed through measures of positive harmonisation needs to be balanced against the boundaries set by the free movement regulation; at the moment, an inconsistent standard is applied for the 'reference consumer' in these two areas.

The idea, in short, is that the safety of financial services depends for a large part on the stability of the financial market in which these services are offered.[49] Although consumers will normally have relatively good insight into the stability of that market in their home countries, the same cannot be said for foreign markets. The Icesave case is an example of that, where many consumers were enticed to deposit savings at the Landesbanki despite knowing next to nothing about the stability of the Icelandic financial system.[50] Similar situations may arise where credit agreements fall through because of an unexpected collapse of a credit-providing institution in another jurisdiction; possible consequences could be that consumers who were bound contractually to take delivery of a house and to settle payment for it on a specified date were unable to

[47] The question of how to assess and to create safeguards against systemic risk is, in essence, a regulatory question, and one that regulators themselves are struggling with. See, for example, Stephen Schwarcz, 'Systemic Risk' (2008) 97 *Georgetown Law Journal* 193.

[48] For example, the safety accreditation of the Nederlandsche Bank; see www.dnb.nl.

[49] As explained above.

[50] Although Iceland is not currently a Member State of the EU, the example fits *mutatis mutandis* the claims that this chapter seeks to make.

fulfil these obligations and as a result became liable for breach of contract. Therefore, it makes sense to adjust the level of consumer protection in accordance with these complexities (here listed under points (1) and (2)). In order to do that, the elements listed under points (3), (4) and (5) provide the framework for determining an appropriate level of protection.

The 'reference consumer' in cross-border financial services transactions

Taking the status quo as a starting point, it can be seen that the level of consumer protection is substantively influenced by the *means* of protection. Brought down to its essence, the regulation of consumer transactions in Europe seems to focus on two elements of contract law in particular, namely information provision to consumers (corresponding with point (3) and protection in the post-contractual phase, for example through the prescription of a 'cooling-off' period within which the consumer is entitled to exercise a right to withdraw from an agreed deal (corresponding with point (4)).[51] These are balanced out differently depending on the standard adopted for the 'reference consumer' (point (5)).

Effectively, the result is that in free movement cases particular emphasis is put on the first element. The ECJ relies on the capacity of consumers to make informed choices about available products and services based on the information provided. On that ground, national measures that impose stricter protection are often struck down as barriers to trade, for they suppress products where information provision might have offered sufficient consumer protection.[52] Consumer directives, on the other hand, place much more significance on the post-contractual protection of the consumer. While information requirements are imposed on the seller of goods or provider of services, these alone are not deemed to be sufficient; on top, the consumer is protected by cooling-off periods,[53] contractual remedies, and increasingly also by obligations on national judges to test of their own motion the compatibility of terms in consumer contracts against EU consumer law.[54]

[51] Cf. Weatherill, *EC Consumer Law*, 84.

[52] Compare Case C-70/03, *Commission* v. *Spain* [2004] ECR I-7999.

[53] For example, Consumer Credit Directive; Doorstep Selling Directive; Package Travel Directive.

[54] See Joined Cases C-240/98 to C-244/98 *Océano Grupo Editorial SA* v. *Rocío Murciano Quintero* and *Salvadat Editores SA* v. *José M Sánchez Alcón Prades and others* [2000] ECR I-4941; Case C-473/00 *Cofidis SA* v. *Jean-Louis Fredout* [2002] ECR I-10875; Case C-168/05

This divergence of standards, and the reflection of it in the means of consumer protection, creates uncertainty for consumers (which rights do they have in different types of transaction?) and for businesses (which mandatory consumer rights do they have to take into account in designing standard form contracts?). Which level of protection is pursued by EU legislation, other than generally a 'high level', also remains unclear in the proposed Consumer Rights Directive.[55] It is vital, therefore, to address this question – admittedly a point coloured by policy decisions – of who the 'reference consumer' is. The answer to that question would seem to give the only relevant guidance to the further development of EU consumer law that the Commission seeks to achieve. To promote the twin objectives of market integration and consumer protection, therefore, a tidying up of the 'reference consumer' standard is needed – and hence a rebalancing of the available means of protection.

Arguably, such a rebalancing should lean towards the free movement standard for the 'reference consumer' rather than a less 'circumspect' consumer. That standard corresponds with the internal market objectives of the EU reflected in the provisions of the Treaty, and coincides with the competence attribution to the EU legislature in relation to consumer protection measures. In this sense, it is a solution that fits the idea of a systematisation of financial services law, as proposed in this chapter. It stresses that the regulatory function of the EU has its origins in internal market policy and continues to do so, even after the entry into force of the Lisbon Treaty. In that light, the integration of the market is the main goal with which the European legislature should be concerned. Consumer protection, of course, is also of high importance and should still be pursued – but as an ancillary policy alongside the policy of market integration.

This approach does not diminish the EU's responsibility with regard to consumer interests. What it does is to alter the *object* of the protective measures, shifting the focus from the consumer to the nature of the transaction in order to determine the interests that need to be protected. A forceful case can still be made for a higher level of consumer protection for cross-border financial services than for other cross-border transactions regulated by the free movement provisions – their complexity requires it. Even a 'reasonably circumspect consumer' has a limited capacity to process

Elisa María Mostaza Claro v. *Centro Móvil Milenium SL* [2006] ECR I-10421; Case C-243/08 *Pannon* [2009]; Case C-40/08 *Asturcom* v. *Rodríguez Nogueira* [2009].

[55] Evidenced also by the continuing discussion on the content of the directive; see for the latest draft www.consilium.europa.eu.

the large quantities of complex information that are needed to assess the risk assumed when entering into a financial deal such as a credit agreement. The threshold for assessing that risk, moreover, lies even higher because of the unfamiliar context of dealing in a foreign financial market. Therefore, a higher level of protection seems appropriate.

It needs to be borne in mind, however, that a higher level of consumer protection is not always automatically favourable to consumers. As economic theory shows, too high a level of protection can backfire on consumers, for example through a price increase for products or through a decrease in choice of available services.[56] To determine the appropriate level of protection, therefore, further research (for example through market studies) is needed.[57]

Inspiration can of course already be found in existing law. The notion of a high level of protection for financial services – though based on a wholly different consumer concept – is also adopted in the existing *acquis*, namely in the Distance Marketing of Financial Services Directive. The emphasis, nevertheless, is very strongly placed on information provision in the pre-contractual phase. It may be doubted whether that is the most appropriate means of consumer protection in this context, seeing that the consumer is likely to be faced with an overload of information.[58] The introduction of a standard form, the Standard European Consumer Credit Information form (SECCI), goes some way towards solving that problem; but it still requires consumers to consider an impressive amount of information, in particular in the case of one-off transactions. More appropriate, therefore, could be to extend protection through more powerful remedies in the post-contractual phase. One could think not only of a right of withdrawal in cases where information duties have been ignored, but also of remedies for mistake or non-disclosure. Facts unknown to either or both of the parties, such as the instability of a financial market, could in such a scheme be regarded as grounds for avoidance of the contract and/or a claim in damages.

In this respect, regulation of financial services could become a *lex specialis* of the general rules on mistake and non-disclosure that have – to

[56] For example, with regard to intermediaries in financial services, see *Financieel Dagblad*, 17 November 2009, 'Consument wordt dupe van toezicht'.

[57] Useful insights may also be derived from studies in behavioural economics; see for example the paper by Bastian Schüller on 'The Definition of Consumers in EC Consumer Law' presented at the Leeds conference.

[58] Cf. economic literature; for example, Omri Ben-Shahar, 'The Myth of the "Opportunity to Read" Contract Law' (2009) 5 *European Review of Contract Law* 1.

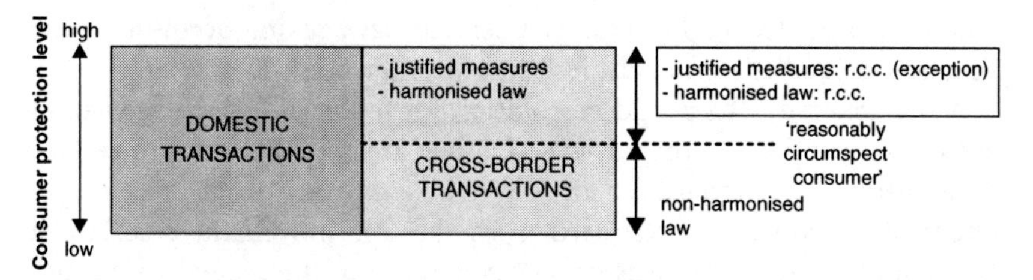

Figure 3.2 Consumer protection and market interests in the EU after readjustment

an extent – emerged in European contract law. A common core of rules on information duties and remedies can be identified from legal systems in Europe and principles and model rules covering these issues have been included in the Draft Common Frame of Reference.[59] Although these rules are already of a fairly protective nature, they are not intended specifically to apply to consumers and they do not cover withdrawal rights in the way proposed here. Following the arguments put forward above, it seems appropriate to adopt measures that are similar in nature (e.g. information duties and related withdrawal rights) but more protective for consumers in the context of financial services contracts, and, in that light, to regard these as a *lex specialis.*

Should the regulatory framework for cross-border financial services be readjusted to give effect to this approach, the picture would then become as shown in Figure 3.2.

Conclusion

In conclusion, the case of financial services shows that improvements could be made to the regulation of EU consumer law by adopting a 'systematised' approach in which the multi-level aspects of such regulation were reorganised against the background of wider regulation in the EU. In relation to retail financial services (such as consumer credit agreements), it has been argued, it would be appropriate to adopt a double-layered approach, tailored separately to domestic and to cross-border services. Effectively, this means that purely domestic transactions could be regulated at national level, in accordance with the EU law principles of subsidiarity and proportionality. For cross-border transactions, a higher level of protection than is customary for consumer contracts

[59] Hugh Beale, 'The Draft Common Frame of Reference: Mistake and Duties of Disclosure' (2008) 4 *European Review of Contract Law* 317.

could be provided in EU financial services law, taking account of the unfamiliar (and therefore riskier) cross-border market.

More generally, the proposed solution for financial services law could serve as a model for the review of other areas of EU consumer law. By adjusting the standard for the 'reference consumer' to the 'reasonably circumspect consumer' standard from the free movement case law, a step could be made towards greater coherence in the regulatory framework for financial services. At the same time, this approach would still enable the European legislature to secure high levels of consumer protection where they were deemed appropriate. It would be worthwhile to pursue further research in EU consumer law to see whether similar progress could be made to develop a systematised regulatory framework that suited the needs of businesses and consumers in the European consumer market.

4

A modernisation for European consumer law?

CRISTINA PONCIBÒ

European consumer law between state and market

In the late 1990s European competition law underwent a process of modernisation.[1] This complex and fundamental process addressed both substantive issues and enforcement law and has evidently enhanced the role of private actors in effectively enforcing EU competition law in the Member States.[2] The aim of this chapter is to discuss whether European consumer law is now following a similar path by enhancing the role played by private actors (e.g. consumers' and traders' associations) to harmonise, implement and enforce the rules set out by EU consumer directives. In particular, the chapter discusses the cases of co-regulation and private enforcement by examining two examples: the representation of consumer interests before European standardisation organisations (ESOs) and the emergence of collective private enforcement in the Member States. In addition, in the fourth section of this chapter we consider the impact of networking in consumer matters by sketching some considerations about the network of public authorities established by the Consumer Protection Cooperation Regulation.[3]

In this section the chapter tries to outline some reflections about the EU model of consumer protection between state (i.e. greater harmonisation of consumer contract law) and market. On the one hand, the Commission has adopted the directive on consumer rights dealing with the 'hardcore' of consumer protection, namely consumer contracts.[4] The directive aims to

Lecturer, Faculty of Law, University of Turin, Italy.

[1] I. Van Bael and J. F. Bellis, *Competition Law of the European Community* (The Netherlands: Kluwer Law International, 2009), 1–5.

[2] Council Regulation no. 1/2003, [2002] OJ L 1/13.

[3] Council Regulation (EC) no. 2006/2004 on cooperation between national authorities responsible for the enforcement of consumer protection laws [2004] OJ L 364/1.

[4] Council Directive 2011/83/EU on consumer rights, amending Council Directive 93/13/EEC and Council Directive 1999/44/EC and repealing Council Directive 85/577/EEC and Council Directive 97/7/EC [2011] OJ L 304/64–88.

merge four consumer directives, concerning the sale of consumer goods and guarantees (Directive 99/44), unfair contract terms (Directive 93/13), distance selling (Directive 97/7) and doorstep selling (Directive 85/577), into a single horizontal instrument to regulate the common aspects of these directives in a systematic way by simplifying and updating the existing rules, while removing the inconsistencies and closing the gaps.[5]

The Commission's directive immediately attracted the attention of private law scholars who have generally adopted a sceptical view towards the measure from different points of view.[6] The most controversial aspect of the proposal is the shift from the minimum to exhaustive harmonisation approach followed in the four existing directives to embrace a full harmonisation approach. Consequently, the level of consumer protection for the transactions which fall within the scope of the four directives will be fixed by the directive with no room left for regional or national variation (Article 4: 'Member States shall not maintain or introduce, in their national law, provisions diverging from those laid down in this Directive, including more or less stringent provisions to ensure a different level of consumer protection unless otherwise provided for in this Directive').

In doing so, the directive will have to slot into the legal framework created by national general contract law. But national contract laws still differ *inter se* and one of the advantages of the minimum harmonisation approach has been the possibility of retaining existing provisions unless they were not always consumer-specific rules. According to the literature, the principle of full harmonisation could thus produce a rather strange result. General contract law in the Member States could turn out to be more favourable in some respects than the legislation transposing the directive, leading to the paradox that it may be better for an individual not to be a consumer.

[5] G. Howells and R. Schulze, *Modernising and Harmonizing Consumer Contract Law* (Munich: Sellier, 2009); H. Schulte-Nölke, C. Twigg-Flesner and M. Ebers, *EC Consumer Law Compendium* (Munich: Sellier, 2008).

[6] J. M. Smits, 'Full Harmonisation of Consumer Law? A Critique of the Draft Directive on Consumer Rights', 1 March 2009, TICOM Working Paper on Comparative and Transnational Law 2009/2; C. Poncibò, 'Some Thoughts on the Methodological Approach to EC Consumer Law Reform' (2009) 21(3) *Loyola Consumer Law Review* 353–71; R. Sefton-Green and J. Rutgers, 'Revising the Consumer Acquis: (Half) Opening the Doors of the Trojan Horse' (2008) 3 *ERPL* 427–42; S. Whittaker, 'Form and Substance in the Reception of EC Directives' (2007) 4 *ERCL*, 381–409; M. B. M. Loos, 'The Influence of European Consumer Law on General Contract Law and the Need for Spontaneous Harmonisation' (2007) 4 *ERPL* 515–31.

To summarise, some adjustment as a result of any harmonisation measure is inevitable, but legal scholars underline that, far from ensuring that consumers recognise the benefit of the internal market, consumers might instead come to resent the erosion of national consumer rights as a result of the directive. In the light of these critiques, the directive has found very little consent in private law scholarship.[7]

On the other hand, while the Commission has recently striven for greater harmonisation, it has also shown a sort of 'market orientation'. The Commission has under certain circumstances adopted an approach based on the belief that an information-seeking, self-reliant consumer can be adequately protected by an effectively operating market.[8] According to the EU, empowered consumers have the capacity to understand and process the information available to them; moreover, they know and exercise their rights and seek redress when these rights are violated.[9]

Central to this view is the notion of the average consumer elaborated by the European Court of Justice (ECJ)[10] and then included in the Unfair Commercial Practices Directive (UCPD) which gives this notion statutory authority, standing and permanence.[11] The UCPD is intended to harmonise fully disparate Member State measures which seek to curb unfair commercial practices harmful to the economic interests of the consumer. It has the twofold aim of contributing to the smooth functioning of the internal market and providing consumers with a high level of protection. The UCPD protects the *benchmark* consumer: 'the reasonably well-informed and reasonably observant and circumspect consumer, taking into account social, cultural, and linguistic factors, as interpreted by the Court of Justice (recital 18)'. Consequently, it does not protect the consumer who is distracted or uninformed about the goods or services which are the subject matter of a commercial practice. Nor does it protect those consumers who naively allow themselves to be convinced by deceptive exaggerations in advertising.

In more detail, the UCPD employs a general clause which is designed to preclude unfair commercial behaviour by traders, with a few exceptions,

[7] *Ibid.*

[8] K. J. Cseres, *Competition Law and Consumer Protection* (The Hague: Kluwer Law International, 2005).

[9] Commission Staff working document, Second Consumer Markets Scoreboard, Brussels, 28 January 2009, SEC (2009), 76, Part 3, 1.

[10] Case C-210/96, *Gut Springenheide GmbH, Rudolf Tusky* v. *Oberkreisdirektor des Kreises Steinfurt-Amt fur Lebensmittel überwachung* [1998] ECR I-4657, at §31.

[11] Council Directive 2005/29/EC concerning unfair business-to-consumer commercial practices in the internal market [2005] OJ L 149/22.

and which divides questionable practices into two categories: those which are misleading and those which are aggressive (Article 5). A practice is found to be unfair when it both fails to respect the professional standards of accuracy and disclosure required, or that would be customary in a given field and influences significantly the economic behaviour of the *average* consumer, precluding him or her from dispassionately using the pertinent information to evaluate a commercial proposal, thereby inducing the consumer to take an economic decision that he or she might not have otherwise taken. Both misleading and aggressive practices are defined relative to the perceptions of the *benchmark* consumer.

Self and co-regulation in consumer protection

In the market-oriented model for consumer protection introduced in the previous section there is space for hybrid solutions to protect consumers' interests: instruments that combine governmental and non-governmental actors and create new patterns of interaction to enable social actors to organize themselves. I think of the examples of self-regulation and, particularly, co-regulation that are gaining in influence to pursue some important goals that are discussed in the next sections and that include the harmonisation of product safety standards in the internal market and the implementation and enforcement of the rules set forth in the consumer directives.

Legal scholars are quite sceptical about self-regulation in consumer issues, primarily because private initiatives only work if it is assumed that the consumer is well informed, empowered and confident. They note that 'for the time being [i.e. 2003] we should be cautious about over reliance on these methods, not least because their effectiveness has yet to be demonstrated'.[12] Notwithstanding these concerns, these tools are often used at EU and national levels, and there is some evidence that self-regulation and co-regulation are gaining influence in consumer matters. For example, in England and Wales we encounter varieties of self-regulation in the codes of practice associated with the Office of Fair Trading (OFT), co-regulation of advertising by the Advertising Standards Authority, the OFT and OFCOM, private groups and standards in consumer safety, a banking code of practice and internet codes.

[12] G. Howells and T. Wilhelmsson, 'EC Consumer Law: Has it Come of Age ?' (2003) 28 *ELR* 370–88 at 370.

More importantly, the final report concerning *Self-regulation Practices in SANCO Policy Areas*, published in 2008, describes a variety of private initiatives in this area and, in considering a number of cases, shows that consumer protection 'standards' are quite often provided by large sellers across the internal market instead of being imposed by the Member States. The document examines a number of self-regulation activities within consumer affairs, public health and food safety to analyse evidence of impediments to effective self-regulation in terms of the effectiveness of these experiences. With respect to consumer affairs the report focuses on the following areas: selling (i.e. direct marketing, direct selling, distance selling), informing consumers (i.e. labelling), advertising and standardisation. From the analysis it is clear that self-regulatory practices differ in the extent to which they are compulsory or voluntary. Some codes of practice or guidelines are purely voluntary and there is no monitoring and no complaint handling; these practices are just meant to help companies, and are more a kind of advice or guideline which may be followed. But some self-regulatory practices emerge that are compulsory for the members of the self-regulatory scheme; these practices are in certain cases heavily monitored and sanctioned (e.g. the Code of Ethics and alternative resolution scheme of the OTE (Organisation for Timeshare in Europe) includes a part about complaints handling and sanctions, including suspension and expulsion from membership). The examples indicated in the report show that the picture is rapidly changing and, in certain cases, self-regulation is not limited to providing guidelines, but also includes complaint procedures and sanctions for non-compliance.

This chapter specifically examines the case of co-regulation and argues that this tool should be conceived as *something different* from pure self-regulation. Legal scholars conceive of co-regulation as a mixture of hard law and private initiatives and as an instrument for dealing differently with old problems, such as the harmonisation and the regulation of European contract law. In the context of EU law, co-regulation is usually regarded rather as an implementing mechanism, presupposing the prior adoption of a piece of European legislation.[13] Consequently, co-regulation assumes the direct involvement of a public actor in this regulatory process, which is usually not the case with self-regulation.

[13] E. Hondius, 'The future of self-regulation in consumer matters on a European level', Working Paper presented at the European University Institute, 25 October 2003; G. Howells, 'The Function of Soft Law in EC Consumer Law', in P. Craig and C. Harlow (eds.), *Law Making in the European Union* (The Hague: Kluwer Law International, 1998), 310–31.

For this reason, this instrument can be said to situate itself somewhere between legislation and 'pure self-regulation' by constituting some form of 'conditioned self-regulation'.[14]

In this respect it is possible to see a parallel to the experience with competition law where the process of modernisation has included a shift towards self-regulation by undertakings in relation to their compliance with the prohibition concerning anti-competitive agreements; undertakings evaluate their agreements under Article 101 TFEU in its entirety and decide whether an agreement falls within the provision and, if it does, whether or not it can qualify for exemption. But such self-assessment occurs in the shadow of the law, with the potentially significant consequences of failing to assess correctly. In such cases the agreement is rendered void and unenforceable. As a consequence, the undertakings could be subject to large fines, while, in some Member States, individuals could face fines and/or imprisonment or could be banned from holding directorships for up to five years. Furthermore, the undertakings could face private actions for damages.

From a functional perspective, it should be noted that both self-regulation and co-regulation are, at present, used to reach three fundamental goals relevant for the protection of the consumers' interests. The goals include:

1. the implementation of certain consumer directives in the Member States;
2. the enforcement of consumer rights; and
3. the harmonisation of product safety standards.

The latter point will be carefully examined in the next section.

With respect to the first point, certain directives in consumer protection leave specific issues of regulation to private actors by asking for their cooperation and by sponsoring their initiatives in the transposition of the principles set forth in the directive.[15] Thus the codes of conduct have become an integral feature of the EU legal landscape. A number of industries have moved to adopt codes of conduct, for example, the directive on misleading advertising states that:

> This Directive does not exclude the voluntary control of misleading advertising by self-regulatory bodies and recourse to such bodies by the

[14] L. Senden, 'Soft Law, Self-Regulation and Co-Regulation in European Law: Where Do They Meet ?' (2005) 9(1) *EJCL*, 111–13; D. M. Trubek and L. G. Trubek, 'Hard and Soft Law in the Construction of Social Europe: the Role of the Open Method of Coordination' (2005) 11 *ELJ* 343–56.

[15] K. Armstrong and C. Kilpatrick, 'Law, Governance, or New Governance? The Changing Open Method of Coordination' (2007) 12 *Columbia Journal of European Law* 649–50.

> persons or organisations referred to in Art. 4 if proceedings before such bodies are in addition to the court or administrative proceedings referred to in that Article (Article 5).[16]

The later directive takes an even more encouraging stance:

> This Directive does not exclude the voluntary control, which Member States may encourage, of misleading or comparative advertising by self-regulatory bodies and recourse before such bodies are in addition to the court of administrative proceedings referred to in that Article.[17]

The Directive on Electronic Commerce provides that the codes of conduct shall be used as an aid to implement Articles 5 and 16, comprising fair commercial practices, but also contractual provisions (Articles 9 and 10).[18] Moreover, within the framework of the UCPD,[19] self-regulation plays a role in defining what constitutes a misleading practice. The responsibilities are normally clear when a binding code of conduct is in place and a general principle is introduced: when a firm has committed itself to a code of conduct, non-compliance will be considered a misleading practice if the commitment is firm and verifiable and the trader has indicated in its commercial practice that it is bound by the code.

As regards the second point, it should be noted that co-regulation is relevant to the enforcement of consumer rights. The Communication concerning the enforcement of the consumer *acquis*, published in 2009, stresses that new forms of enforcement are emerging in the Member States to ensure compliance with the consumer *acquis* and indicates among them alternative dispute resolution (ADR) and out-of-court settlement mechanisms. Accordingly, they can be an expedient and attractive alternative for consumers who have been unsuccessful in informally resolving their dispute with a trader.[20]

In the same Communication, the Commission specifically encourages businesses, in collaboration with Member States and consumer

[16] Council Directive 84/450/EEC on the approximation of the laws, regulations and administrative provisions of the Member States concerning misleading advertising, [1984] OJ L 250/17–20.

[17] Council Directive 97/55/EC amending Directive 84/450/EEC concerning misleading advertising so as to include comparative advertising [1997] OJ L 290/18–23.

[18] Council Directive 2000/31/EC on certain legal aspects of information society services, in particular electronic commerce, in the internal market [2000] OJ L 178/1–16.

[19] Council Directive 2005/29/EC concerning unfair business-to-consumer commercial practices in the internal market [2005] OJ L 149/22.

[20] Commission Communication of 2 July 2009 to the European Parliament, the Council, the European Economic and Social Committee and the Committee of the Regions on the enforcement of the consumer *acquis*, COM (2009) 330 final.

organisations, to develop self-regulatory measures in the form of a code of conduct to set up complaint handling systems which are credible and work efficiently. This position is based on the idea that co-regulation and self-regulatory measures, which include monitoring mechanisms and complaint handling procedures, can reinforce industry's commitment in securing a high level of compliance and work as an alternative, or better, as a complement to formal legislation. The Commission indicates the examples of the 'Toy Safety Pact' and the 'Citizen's Energy Forum'.

In the proposed approach public enforcement actions and enforcement actions by self-regulatory bodies complement one another, the former providing a supportive legal and judicial context and the latter extra resources for straightforward cases. Again, the UCPD is a good example of this because it maintains the view that self-regulation can support judicial and administrative enforcement and clarifies the role that code owners can play in enforcement. Member States may rely on self-regulatory dispute settlements to enhance the level of consumer protection and maximise compliance with the legislation. But the UCPD also clarifies that self-regulation cannot replace judicial or administrative means of enforcement. It reinforces the effectiveness of codes of conduct by requiring Member States to enforce the self-regulatory rules against traders who have undertaken to be bound by the codes. As a result, the bodies that police self-regulatory codes can maximise the impact of limited resources provided they meet the criteria of efficacy, legitimacy, accountability and consistency.

The new legislative framework

The most interesting example of co-regulation relevant in protecting the interests of consumers concerns product safety standardisation and, particularly, the 'New Legislative Framework' (NLF) which entered into force in January 2010.[21] It is well known that the revitalisation of the single market in the 1980s required not only reform in the legislative process, which was achieved through the Single European Act 1986, but also a new approach to harmonisation to facilitate the passage of these measures; traditional Community harmonisation techniques were slow and generated excessive uniformity.

[21] Council Regulation (EC) no. 764/2008 laying down procedures relating to the application of certain national technical rules to products lawfully marketed in another Member State and repealing Decision no. 3052/95/EC.

A new regulatory technique and strategy was laid down by the Council Resolution on the new approach to technical harmonisation and standardisation (1985).[22] Under the new approach, directives specify only the essential elements for safe products, while optional technical requirements for compliance are specified in the harmonised standards developed by the non-profit ESO. By adopting such techniques 'the ECCommission apparently found in the 1980s a magic tool to reach the goal of a common market: private standards'.[23]

The NLF for products extends the principles of the new approach to almost all products areas from January 2010. Evidently, this is a fundamental development for European standardisation.[24] The NLF aims to bring together into a single legislative package all the legislative instruments needed for ensuring the placing on the market of safe products and for providing effective surveillance of the market and control of products from third countries.

Thus, the package brings together provisions on accreditation of conformity assessment bodies, on market surveillance, competence criteria and selection process (notification), definitions, obligations for economic operators, consolidated conformity assessment procedures and rules for their use, as well as provisions on marketing. In the field of market surveillance the new framework sets out some very clear obligations on Member States and national authorities to intervene on non-conforming or dangerous products in the areas covered by European harmonisation legislation for the first time. In particular, national authorities must have the power, authority and means to withdraw, or have withdrawn, from the market dangerous or non-conforming products. They must even have the authority to have a product destroyed if necessary.

The regulation in its relations with existing legislation attempts to put into place a seamless system for all products and therefore does not make any distinction between consumer and non-consumer products. An important element in the new framework is that it brings together, into one single legislative environment, market surveillance and the control of products from third countries; in many Member States today they are not necessarily brought together and yet they are complementary pillars

[22] Council Resolution of 7 May 1985 on a New Approach to Technical Harmonisation and Standards, OJ 1985 C136.

[23] G. Spindler, 'Market Processes, Standardisation, and Tort Law', (2008) 4:3 *European Law Journal* 316–336 at 316.

[24] H. Schepel, *The Constitution of Private Governance: Product Standards in the Regulation of Integrating Markets* (Oxford: Hart Publishing, 2005).

of the edifice for safe products. The new framework will entail putting into place new communication channels between national authorities and the Commission. For example, the 2009 Communication on the enforcement of the consumer *acquis*[25] specifies that the General Product Safety Directive and the NLF require the establishment of an EU market surveillance framework to assist Member States' authorities in monitoring products and establishes a rapid alert system (Rapex) between market surveillance authorities through which Member States have to inform each other when measures are taken against consumer products posing a serious risk to consumers' health and safety.

The NLF will be developed gradually, but, according to the opinion of the Secretary General of the European Association for the Coordination of Consumer Representation in Standardisation (ANEC), the consequence of its adoption will be that 'more and more European product legislation will rely on supporting European standards to provide easiest means of achieving compliance with the law' and, thus, the NLF places 'new demands on the European standardisation system'.[26]

Legal scholars have always tended to criticise the paralegal structure of private standards;[27] in particular, Schepel has published a first comprehensive study on the production of product standards and has described such processes as a case of 'private governance'.[28] Schepel notes that against the ongoing process of globalisation, the state generally loses its centrality in the activity of government; accordingly, the law derives from different sources not necessarily limited to parliamentary law-making and extends its validity beyond the nation state.

With respect to this framework, the literature has often underlined that consumers' interests should be involved in the standards-making process.[29] The European Commission has stated this on numerous occasions and this is also the position of the European standardisation bodies. ANEC advances the European consumer voice in standardisation by representing and defending consumer interests in such a process.[30] The organisation is composed of national representatives (one from each of

[25] Commission, Communication on the enforcement of the consumer acquis, 2 July 2009, COM (2009) 330 final.

[26] ANEC, GA Open Session, 11 June 2009, Secretary's General Statement at 4.

[27] Spindler, 'Market Processes' at 328.

[28] Schepel, *The Constitution of Private Governance*, 11.

[29] Howells and Wilhelmsson, 'EC Consumer Law', 386–87.

[30] J. Davies, 'Entrenchment of New Governance in Consumer Policy Formulation: a Platform for European Consumer Citizenship Practice ?', (2009) 32 *Journal of Consumer Policy* 245–67, 257.

the EU and EFTA Member States) chosen by the national consumer organisations recognized by the EU Commission and EFTA.

There is therefore evidence that the representation of consumers' interests in the process of standardisation is quite limited, given that it finds the obstacles discussed below.[31] My point here is that the substantive legitimacy of the NLF, and not only its formal legitimacy, should be assessed. The legitimacy of the NLF will depend on the capability of the standardisation process effectively to include all the interests involved, and specifically, the interests of the consumers. Moreover, the 'battle for standards' is not limited to the ESOs but has a global dimension.[32] The situation is similar to that at the International Standardisation Organisation (ISO) and the ESOs are obliged to follow up the ISO norms and to incorporate them formally into their own projects.

Unfamiliarity of consumer organisations

The ESOs have a specialized vocabulary and 'jargon' and the perception is that standards are for industry. ANEC Strategy states that consumer interests are only marginally represented in many countries.[33] Moreover, the consumer voice in the European Committee for standardisation (CEN) and the European Committee for Electrotechnical Standardisation (CENELEC) is represented through national delegations and ANEC underlines the need to establish a truly effective platform of European interests alongside the traditional grounding on national delegations.

Lack of awareness

The lack of awareness by consumers and their associations of how standards ensure consumer protection is one of the biggest hurdles. In many countries, consumer organisations work to influence their governments to pass and enforce laws to protect them. However, this might not be the only answer. The following examples show the ways in which standards can support legislation: consumers' representatives, by appointment to a technical committee, subcommittee or working group developing a standard or standards in a particular field, could shape and

[31] C. Poncibò, 'The Challenges of EC Consumer Law', European University Institute, Max Weber Program Working Paper no. 2007/24.

[32] M. Blair, A. Williams and L.-W. Lin, 'The Roles of Standardization, Certification and Assurance Services in Global Commerce', May 2008, CLPE Research Paper no. 12/2008.

[33] ANEC, Strategy 2008–2013, 11 June 2009.

influence the standard at issue in the interest of the consumers (i.e. better, safer, or more environmentally friendly products).[34] Standards can also provide a valuable indicator for minimum criteria to protect vulnerable markets; it is easy to forget that some consumer protection laws may be increasingly difficult to enforce due to market deregulation and globalisation of trade. The 'dumping' of substandard products across borders is one unfortunate result in these cases.

Consumer organisations that are not yet organised

Consumer organisations may realise the value of standards – but are not yet organised effectively for this work. On the one hand, they need to interact either with the national standards body, or with regional or international consumer organisations, on standards issues. On the other hand, they need to organise and brief the people who will be dealing with the standards activity.

Evidently, in such a context, technical expertise is needed and, according to available data, ANEC can rely on approximately two hundred volunteer experts engaged in the technical committees and working groups of the European standards organisations. Nevertheless, consumers' representatives involved at the national level in standardisation usually have both a low commitment to the process and insufficient knowledge. But even when a consumer representative is willing and able to participate, an obstacle may be insufficient training and briefing available for the representative to make an effective impact. Providing support in this area is normally the shared responsibility of national standards bodies and consumer associations.

Insufficient recognition by national standards bodies

According to the ANEC strategy as outlined above, there is often insufficient recognition by national standards bodies of the value of consumer participation. A national standards body needs to ensure that adequate consumer representation happens at various levels. Consumer representatives may also have an impact on European standardisation by participating in policy or technical groups that decide national

[34] Examples of 'consumer friendly' standards are ISO 8317, Child-resistant packaging – Requirements and testing procedures for reclosable packages; ISO10002, Customer Satisfaction – Guidelines for complaints handling; ISO 22000:2005, Food safety management systems – Requirements for any organisation in the food chain.

priorities, and which set overall work programmes, and related policy, to be advanced at EU level.

Funding

Some of the most frequent obstacles which consumer organisations encounter are limited financial resources and human resources with appropriate expertise. Consumer representatives often rely on national standards bodies themselves to help defray the costs of attending meetings, while other sources of support are government agencies or outside donor agencies. This problem, which will be more evident in the NLF, has been confirmed by ANEC. And while ANEC is trying to find alternative funding solutions, such as establishing partnerships, it has recognised that it 'must build alliances in order to achieve its mission of improving consumer protection and welfare. We have to recognise that we do not have the resources – either in terms of money or people – to go it alone. We literally cannot afford to be a lone voice.'[35]

Collective private enforcement

This chapter tries to pursue a unitary perspective and, thus, it includes two sections on enforcement law. The idea is that EU consumer law should be considered *in relation to the consistency* of consumer law enforcement.

In this regard collective redress refers to the means by which individuals are able to group together to use a single (judicial or non-judicial) mechanism to claim monetary or non-monetary compensation arising from an event in which each member of the group has similar interests. This ought not to be seen exclusively through litigation; it is a much wider concept, and policy-making and law-making ought to see it as such. Redress, and also collective redress, can be provided using public enforcement mechanisms, litigation, alternative dispute resolution (ADR) mechanisms, tribunals, compensation schemes and funds (both statutory and voluntary) and other voluntary mechanisms.

There has, over the past year, been an active debate as to how best to promote revised collective redress procedures across the Union, particularly in the area of competition claims. In particular, private enforcement before national courts to protect subjective rights under Community

[35] ANEC Strategy.

law, especially 'by awarding damages to the victims of infringements' (recital 7), is explicitly mentioned in the Regulation no. 1/2003 (the Competition Modernisation Regulation). The Commission has expressly issued the Green Paper on Damages actions for breach of the EC antitrust rules.[36] These proposals were then published in April 2008 by way of a White Paper.[37]

Collective redress has, then, become a live issue in EU consumer law that again takes the same path previously taken by competition law. The Green Paper on consumer collective redress was published on 27 November 2008 to put forward four options, ranging from no action to a court-based collective action, while contemplating some role for ADR and oversight of reparation by public regulatory authorities.[38] Then, the Commission produced a follow-up to its Green Paper on consumer collective redress (8 May 2009). The new consultation presented the first look at the impact of the policy options, drafted on the basis of the responses to the Green Paper. The responses indicated that no single option provided in the Green Paper was satisfactory for achieving the objectives of improving access to effective means of redress for mass consumer claims in the EU, and improving the functioning of the internal market by making it more competitive. Rather, a common trend emerging from the responses was that a combination of several instruments was the best way forward. In August 2009 the Commission published a feedback statement summarising the responses to the consultation on consumer collective redress.

My point here is that central to the debate between academics, practitioners, consumer associations and the industry is the possibility of developing a judicial group action procedure.[39]

Recently, a number of mechanisms have proliferated in the Member States establishing a form of national experimentalism in the absence of

[36] Commission, Green Paper on damages actions for breach of the EC antitrust rules, 19 December 2005, COM (2005) 672, 19.

[37] Commission, White Paper on damages actions for breach of the EC antitrust rules, 2 April 2008, COM (2008) 165.

[38] Commission, Consultation Paper for discussion on the follow-up to the Green Paper on consumer collective redress, May 2009, at 15. Commission (EC), Green Paper on consumer collective redress, COM (2008) 794, 27 November 2008.

[39] A. Stadler, 'Group Actions as a Remedy to Enforce Consumer Interests', in F. Cafaggi and H. Micklitz (eds.), *New Frontiers of Consumer Protection: the Interplay between Private and Public Enforcement* (Antwerp: Intersentia, 2009); F. Cafaggi and H.-W. Micklitz, 'Administrative and Judicial Enforcement in Consumer Protection: the Way Forward', in Cafaggi and Micklitz, *New Frontiers*.

a common European framework.[40] It is well known that such experiments take three main forms: the test case (England and Wales, Germany); the model of action provided by the Injunctions Directive with some improvements (Italy, Spain and France) and, finally, the class action model with some modifications (Sweden).[41]

If we examine the responses to the consultation two positions are of particular interest in the discussion of judicial group action: the European Consumers' Organisation (BEUC) and the OFT. BEUC gave its full support to the creation of a new, judicial group action procedure. It argued that this should permit claims on an opt-out basis, have as wide a scope as possible, be open and creative when it comes to compensating consumers, apply to both domestic and cross-border litigation and be accompanied by efficient funding mechanisms. However, BEUC did recognise the need to give courts discretion over the admissibility of any particular claim – a gate-keeping function of the sort already described.[42]

This pro-reform position has also been articulated by regulators such as the OFT, the UK's consumer and competition authority. I note that, in its response, the OFT stated its support for a 'binding, effective system that delivers redress to consumers, a Europe-wide legal process accessible by consumers and consumer groups'. It suggested that such a procedure should permit some claims (those brought by designated representative groups) to be brought on an opt-out basis. It should be possible for consumers to claim against multiple defendants at a time, but the mechanism should be limited to cross-border disputes for an initial period. The OFT also suggested limiting defendants' ability to recover their legal costs if they won, to prevent vulnerable and other consumers being deterred by the fear of having a defendant's legal costs imposed on them, while representative bodies should be able to recover their costs in full on any successful claim.

At this stage, the Commission is considering the responses to the Green Paper and will probably proceed in the next few months. This phenomenon represents a fundamental shift from the traditional

[40] Poncibò, 'Some Thoughts'; R. D. Kelemen, 'American-Style Adversarial Legalism and the European Union', European University Institute, RSCAS Working Paper No. 2008/37; R. Alderman, 'The Future of Consumer Law in the United States – Hello Arbitration, Bye-Bye Courts, So-Long Consumer Protection', 19 September 2007, University of Houston Law Center Working Paper No. 2008-A-09; C. Hodges, *Multi-Party Actions* (Oxford University Press, 2001).

[41] Poncibò, 'Some Thoughts'.

[42] Stakeholders' responses at: http://ec.europa.eu/consumers/redress_cons/response_GP_collective_redress_en.htm (last accessed 1 February 2010).

European consumer protection that in many countries has been developed from above, by the states, and not from below by consumer activism and, sometimes, consumer litigation.[43] The Commission itself states that 'The traditional view of enforcement of consumer protection has been that public authorities apply hard law. Today, alternatives exist where consumers may directly seek redress.'[44]

Enforcement networks

According to the literature,[45] one of the most distinctive features of the reformed institutional architecture of EU competition law is the European Competition Network (ECN) that has been established to facilitate cooperation between the competition authorities of the Member States and to protect the consistent enforcement of competition policy. At this stage, the ECN has received some preliminary but generally positive comments by the scholars.[46]

Interestingly, a network of public authorities has also been established to manage the increasing number of cross-border consumer complaints in the single market by the Consumer Protection Cooperation (CPC) Regulation (also CPC and CPC Network).[47] The 2009 Communication on the enforcement of the consumer *acqu*is expressly mentions the CPC Network.[48] The idea of network governance has attracted the attention of the legal scholars who note that, while networks have been a feature of governance for a long time, the scope, range and intensity of governmental networks have expanded and that this expansion is what is new.

One commentator has analysed the way in which networks have transformed the global political order, explaining how networks are a prevalent feature of that order, ranging from the environment to security, from financial regulation to international trade and from policing to

[43] Cafaggi and Micklitz, 'Administrative and Judicial Enforcement'.

[44] Commission, Communication on the enforcement of the consumer *acquis*, 2 July 2009, COM (2009) 330 final.

[45] I. Maher, 'Regulation and Modes of Governance in EC Competition Law: What's New in Enforcement?' (2008) 31 *Fordham International Law Journal* 1713–40.

[46] F. Cengiz, 'The European Competition Network: Structure, Management and Initial Experiences of Policy Enforcement', European University Institute Max Weber Programme Papers no. 2009/05.

[47] Council Regulation (EC) no. 2006/2004 of 27 October 2004 on cooperation between national authorities responsible for the enforcement of consumer protection laws [2004] OJ L 364/1.

[48] Commission Communication on the enforcement of the consumer *acquis*.

macroeconomic policy.[49] In particular, Slaughter adopts a broad view of the network, using it to capture 'all the different ways that individual government institutions are interacting with their counterparts either abroad or above them'. She defines a network as a 'pattern of regular and purposive relations among like government units working across the borders that divide countries from one another and that demarcate the "domestic" from the "international" sphere'.

For our purposes, one may distinguish different types of network, while recognising that some networks may have more than one role. For example, there are enforcement networks, designed to render enforcement more efficacious across international boundaries; information networks, aimed at the exchange of information between governmental agencies or the like, on matters as diverse as security, the environment, policing, and health; and harmonisation networks, designed to foster closer uniformity in regulatory standards.

Relevant in the perspective of this contribution is, for instance, the International Consumer Protection and Enforcement Network (ICPEN), a membership organisation consisting of the trade practices law enforcement authorities of more than three dozen countries, most of which are members of the OECD. The mandate of ICPEN is to share information about cross-border commercial activities that may affect consumer interests, and to encourage international cooperation between law enforcement agencies.[50]

Networks of national officials play an important role in the development of Community policy.[51] On some occasions it has been the Member States, acting through the Council, that have driven such developments, while on other occasions the Commission has been the driving force. The best-known example of national network influence on Community policy-making is the comitology system.[52] The most formal networks exist where there is the strongest EU incentive for effective enforcement across national borders. The Commission will normally be in the driving seat and will press for measures that enhance the

[49] A. M. Slaughter, *A New World Order* (Princeton University Press, 2004), 548.

[50] ICPEN is a network of governmental organisations involved in the enforcement of fair trade practice laws and other consumer protection activities.

[51] P. Craig, 'Shared Administration and Networks: Global and EU Perspectives', paper presented at the workshop on comparative administrative law held at Yale Law School, 7–9 May 2009.

[52] C. Bergstrom, *Comitology: Delegation of Powers in the European Union and the Committee System* (Oxford University Press, 2005).

enforcement capacities of the relevant national agencies to render the Community regulatory regime more effective.

For the purposes of this chapter I will focus on the three networks that the EU Commission has specifically adopted at various stages to enforce consumers' rights: the European Consumer Centres Network (ECC-Net), the FIN-Net and, more important and recent, the Enforcement Network.

The ECC-Net is an EU-wide network with local contact points launched by the EU Commission in 2005 and designed to promote consumer confidence by advising citizens on their rights as consumers and providing easy access to redress, particularly in cases where the consumer has made a cross-border purchase.[53] The aim of the ECC-Net is to provide consumers with a wide range of services, from providing information on their rights to giving advice and assistance with their complaints and the resolution of disputes. It is present in all the Member States and it is located in host organisations (i.e. public or non-profit-making bodies designated by the Member State and agreed by the EU Commission). The ECC-Net has the task of advising on out-of-court-settlement procedures for consumers throughout Europe and on cooperating with each other and with other European networks. Similar to the ECC-Net is the FIN-Net launched by the EU Commission in 2001 which provides a financial dispute resolution network of national out-of-court complaints schemes across the European Economic Area countries.[54]

The most important mechanism is the network established under the Consumer Protection Cooperation Regulation or CPC Network[55] which brings together national public authorities responsible for the enforcement of the EU consumer *acquis*. This CPC Network, which gives authorities the means to prevent businesses undertaking cross-border activities that are harmful to consumers, sets out a common framework under which these authorities are to work together and provides for minimum investigative and enforcement powers.[56] Precisely, it partially harmonises the authorities' investigative and enforcement powers and lays down the mechanisms for exchanging relevant information and/or

[53] ECC-Net was created by merging two previously existing networks: the European Consumer Centres or Euroguichets, which provided information and assistance on cross-border issues, and the European Extra-Judicial Network or EEJ-Net which helped consumers to resolve their disputes through alternative dispute resolution schemes using mediators or arbitrators.

[54] FIN-Net at http://ec.europa.eu/internal_market/finservices-retail/finnet/index_en.htm.

[55] Commission Communication on the enforcement of the consumer *acquis*.

[56] Davies, 'Entrenchment of New Governance'.

taking enforcement action to stop infringements in cross-border situations. It obliges Member States to act upon mutual assistance requests addressed to them and to ensure that adequate resources are allocated to the network's authorities to meet those obligations.

The CPC Regulation further provides a broader framework for the development of administrative cooperation initiatives for which the Commission provides funding. The obligation of the watchdogs to engage in mutual assistance, including the possible exercise of investigative and/or enforcement powers, applies when there are intra-Community infringements of the national laws transposing the consumer *acquis* and as listed in the annex of the regulation. It includes fourteen directives and one regulation, including the Doorstep Selling Directive[57] and the Air Passengers Regulation;[58] as with any list-based system, it must be constantly updated as legislation is adopted (e.g. the UCPD).[59]

The Commission has issued a report to analyse the initial years of operations under the CPC Network for the years 2007 and 2008.[60] The report underlines that, following a relatively slow start, its activity quickly accelerated to reach a total of 719 mutual assistance requests in two years. The majority of the cases are requests for information (39 per cent of the total number) and requests to take enforcement measures to stop a confirmed breach of legislation (37 per cent of the total number). In addition, the CPC Network has carried out two joint market surveillance and enforcement exercises which took the form of internet inquiries; one on websites selling airline tickets in 2007 and one on websites offering ring tones for mobile phones in 2008. The majority of infringements concerned misleading advertising provisions (close to a third of the total number of cases) and online commercial practices (e.g. internet and mailings). In terms of sectors, the two EU sweeps contributed to increasing the number of mutual assistance requests in

[57] Council Directive 85/577/EEC to protect the consumer in respect of contracts negotiated away from business premises [1985] OJ L 372/31.

[58] Council Regulation (EC) no. 261/2004 of 11 February 2004 establishing common rules on compensation and assistance to passengers in the event of denied boarding and of cancellation or long delay of flights, and repealing Regulation (EEC) no. 295/91 [2004] OJ L 46/1.

[59] Art. 16 of the Directive 2005/29 amends the 2004 Regulation to add itself to the list.

[60] Commission (EC), Report from the Commission to the European Parliament and to the Council on the application of Regulation (EC) no. 2006/2004 of the European Parliament and of the Council of 27 October 2004 on cooperation between national authorities responsible for the enforcement of consumer protection laws, Brussels, SEC (2009).

the sectors where the authorities carried out their inquiries, namely transport and communication.

In consideration of the above, such an instrument, if carefully designed, could represent a positive force to improve the current unsatisfactory level of enforcement of consumer rights in cross-border cases.

Conclusion

The expression 'modernising European consumer law' has appeared in the White Paper *A Better Deal for Consumers* issued by the UK government.[61] This chapter pointed out that, although we are not facing the enforcement turbulence which has visited EU competition law, the picture is also changing with respect to EU consumer law. These two areas of European law, often indicated by legal scholars as 'two wings of the same house', enjoy a common destiny that consists, primarily, in reliance on the role that private actors can play, the emergence of the private enforcement and the adoption of new instruments such as the ECN and the CPC Networks.[62] Moreover, this chapter has tried to show that co-regulation is used as a means to implement consumer directives, to harmonise standards and enforce rules. In the landscape here described the consumer is conceived of as an active, empowered consumer rather then a 'victim' who needs to be protected. This new role for the consumer raises practical issues: is the model of the empowered consumer credible if we consider behavioural science studies in consumer decision-making?[63]

Finally, the chapter adopts a unitary perspective to include enforcement law. This approach aims to underline that the confidence of the consumer depends primarily on the possibility of obtaining an effective protection of the rights granted by EU consumer law. In consideration of these developments, this chapter stresses the need to reconsider and strengthen the representation of the consumers' interests when using co-regulation and to develop the private collective enforcement of consumer rights.[64]

[61] HM Government, *A Better Deal for Consumers: Delivering Real Help Now and Change for the Future*, 2 July 2009.

[62] Cseres, *Competition Law*.

[63] C. Poncibò and R. Incardona, 'The Average Consumer, the Unfair Commercial Practices Directive, and the Cognitive Revolution' (2007) 30 *Journal of Consumer Policy* 21–38.

[64] R. Van den Bergh and L. Visscher, 'The Preventive Function of Collective Actions for Damages in Consumer Law' (2008) 1(2) *Erasmus Law Review* 5–30.

Although the quasi-public standards of the new approach and the NLF seem to be a very good tool for achieving the goal of European integration, this chapter underlines that the institutional governance of such organisations has to incorporate consumers' interests in the process of enacting standards. There is a growing awareness of the fact that standards overcome the boundary between merely technical issues and normative definitions of risks and safety and, thus, that we have to seek institutional designs that keep the advantages of standard setting while ensuring a sort of democratic control. Such an important process cannot be limited to a unilateral approach. Moreover, an effective (collective) private enforcement of consumer rights could contribute to forcing organisations into adopting 'adequate standards'. Furthermore, it may also play a dual role by providing incentives against organisations disregarding the consumer's interests and, even though it is problematic to contest such standards before the courts, by providing a measure of indirect judicial control over them.

Unless the legal effects attributed by the directives to the standards of CEN and the other ESOs are more 'powerful' than 'normal' voluntary standards the point here is that they should be subject to judicial control. This contribution does not say that the process of modernisation envisaged here would be necessarily good for consumers, but these developments deserve more attention. Consumer law at EU level has certainly not come of age,[65] but it is entering a new phase. We should be sensitive to the complexity of the regulation of consumer markets and expand our horizons.

[65] Howells and Wilhelmsson, 'EC Consumer Law'.

5

Effective enforcement of consumer law: the comeback of public law and criminal law

PETER ROTT

Introduction

While substantive consumer law has undergone thorough Europeanisation through the activities of the EU, and the influence of the EU is ever increasing, regulation of enforcement issues has remained largely in the competence of the Member States, and the Member States have taken different approaches towards enforcement. Germany has traditionally emphasised the enforcement of individual rights by individuals, complemented by collective private law action. Unlike in France and Belgium, where criminal law complements private enforcement, or in the United Kingdom and Scandinavia, where public bodies such as the Office of Fair Trading or the Consumer Ombudsmen play an important role and criminal law sanctions are also used,[1] criminal law and public law have rarely ever been used in Germany for the protection of consumers. Some protective mechanisms that had been in place were removed, in part with explicit reference to the new private law mechanisms. This concerns, in particular, an earlier prohibition on the conclusion of doorstep credit contracts (see former §56 paragraph 1 no. 6 *Gewerbeordnung* (Trading Act; GewO; abolished with effect from 1 January 1991)), which was designed to protect, in particular, vulnerable persons from imprudent

Peter Rott is Associate Professor of European Private Law at the University of Copenhagen. He wrote this chapter while doing research in the excellence centre 'Foundations of European Law and Polity' at the University of Helsinki. The chapter draws, in particular, from research done for an expert study commissioned by the European Commission; see Civic Consulting, Evaluation of the effectiveness and efficiency of collective redress mechanisms in the European Union, available at http://ec.europa.eu/consumers/redress_cons/collective_redress_en.htm.

[1] For the UK, see P. Cartwright, *Consumer Protection and the Criminal Law* (Cambridge University Press, 2001).

loan agreements.[2] Its abolition has made possible the infamous 'junk property' cases that led to the ECJ judgments in *Heininger*, *Schulte* and *Crailsheimer Volksbank*.[3] Another field is the control of gas prices by public authorities, which was abolished in 1998 with a view to the liberalisation of the gas market. Germany has recently faced mass litigation in the civil courts over gas price increases.[4]

Most authors nowadays discuss the potential of private law mechanisms, and in particular collective redress mechanisms such as class actions or group actions, to act as a second means of enforcement, standing next to public law enforcement. This has been, for example, the explicit objective of German legislation concerning model claims in the field of capital market law.[5] This chapter takes the opposite perspective. By looking at the development of consumer law enforcement in Germany, it explores the limitations of individual and collective private law mechanisms and demonstrates how, in recent years, public law mechanisms have been, although very carefully, introduced in consumer law. Furthermore, criminal law is now beginning to play its role, in particular in the field of fraudulent practices on the internet. Bringing ECJ case law and the German experience together, the chapter makes an attempt to develop criteria for the extent to which public law sanctions, and perhaps even criminal law sanctions, are necessary to meet the EU standards of effective enforcement.

[2] See, for example, *Oberlandesgericht* Hamburg, 28/2/1962 (OLG) (1962) *Neue Juristische Wochenschrift* (*NJW*) 1123. A contract that was nevertheless concluded at the doorstep was initially held to be invalid due to illegality, see BGH, 22 May 1978 (1978) *NJW* 1970, at 1971. After the adoption of the Doorstep Selling Act, the BGH reconsidered this opinion and decided that the consumer was sufficiently protected by his right of withdrawal under doorstep selling law: see BGH, 16 January 1996 (1996) *NJW* 926, at 928.

[3] Case C-481/99, *Georg Heininger and Helga Heininger* v. *Bayerische Hypo– und Vereinsbank AG* [2001] ECR I–9945; Case C-350/03, *Elisabeth Schulte, Wolfgang Schulte* v. *Deutsche Bausparkasse Badenia AG* [2005] ECR I-9215; Case C-229/04, *Crailsheimer Volksbank eG* v. *Klaus Conrads, Frank Schulzke und Petra Schulzke-Lösche, Joachim Nitschke* [2005] ECR I-9273; on which see P. Rott, 'Linked Contracts and Doorstep Selling: Case Note on ECJ, Judgments of 25 October 2005, Cases C-350/03 – *Schulte* and C-229/04 – *Crailsheimer Volksbank*', (2006) *Yearbook of Consumer Law* 403ff. For critique of the abolition of §56 para. 1 no. 6 GewO, see K.-J. Schmelz, 'Verbesserung des Verbraucherschutzes im Konsumentenkreditrecht?' (1991) *NJW* 1219ff.

[4] See, for example, P. Derleder and P. Rott, 'Die rechtlichen Grenzen von Gaspreiserhöhungen – Von der Monopolkontrolle zur Äquivalenzkontrolle bei den Leistungen der Daseinsvorsorge' (2005) *Wohnungswirtschaft und Mietrecht* (*WuM*) 423ff.; K. Markert, 'Zur Kontrolle von Strom- und Gaspreiserhöhungen nach § 307 und § 315 BGB' (2008) *Zeitschrift für Neues Energierecht* (*ZNER*) 44ff.

[5] See the explanations of the German government, *Bundestagsdrucksache* 15/5091, at 16.

Why enforcement of EU consumer law?

There is a formal and a substantive answer to this. Formally, the Member States have to ensure the enforcement of consumer law of EU origin because EU law requires them to do so. Substantively, there is of course a deeper reason, which is the EU's idea of a certain type of marketplace.

The formal argument: the principle of effectiveness

For many years the ECJ has emphasised that the Member States are not entirely free in determining the way in which consumers or citizens in general can enforce their rights as conferred by EU law. National enforcement provisions, be they of substantive law or of procedural law, have increasingly come under scrutiny, especially as regards the principle of the effective enforcement of EU law. This principle was first developed by the ECJ in 1976, in the cases of *Rewe* and *Comet*.[6] In its negative form, the principle of effectiveness prohibits Member States from framing the conditions for the enforcement of individual rights in such a way that they make it virtually impossible or excessively difficult to obtain redress.[7] In its positive form, which is perhaps of greater importance today, the principle of effectiveness has been codified in secondary law, including EU consumer law. For example, under Article 7(1) of the Unfair Contract Terms Directive 93/13/EEC, Member States must ensure that, in the interests of consumers and of competitors, adequate and effective means exist to prevent the continued use of unfair terms in contracts concluded with consumers by sellers or suppliers. More recent directives refer to 'sanctions' or 'penalties'. Under Article 11(1) of Directive 2002/65/EC on the distance marketing of financial services, Member States must provide for appropriate sanctions in the event of the supplier's failure to comply with national provisions adopted pursuant to this directive. According to Article 11(3), these penalties must be effective, proportional and dissuasive. Despite the leeway granted through the open wording of these formulae, the ECJ has demonstrated its willingness to exercise control over their implementation.

[6] Case 33/76, *Rewe-Zentralfinanz eG and Rewe-Zentral AG* v. *Landwirtschaftskammer für das Saarland* [1976] ECR 1989, at para. 5, and Case 45/76, *Comet BV* v. *Produktschap voor Siergewassen* [1976] ECR 2043, at paras. 11–18.

[7] Case C-261/95, *Rosalba Palmisani* v. *Istituto nazionale della previdenza sociale (INPS)* [1997] ECR I-4025, at para. 27, with further references.

The substantive argument: the EU-type of marketplace

Behind the requirement of effective enforcement of consumer law is the wish for a particular type of marketplace where fair competition prevails. Consumer law does not simply serve the individual consumer but is also a means for disciplining the market. This was, for example, emphasised by the ECJ in the unfair contract terms case of *Océano Grupo*:

> the court's power to determine of its own motion whether a term is unfair must be regarded as constituting a proper means both of achieving the result sought by Article 6 of the Directive, namely, preventing an individual consumer from being bound by an unfair term, and of contributing to achieving the aim of Article 7, since if the court undertakes such an examination, that may act as a deterrent and contribute to preventing unfair terms in contracts concluded between consumers and sellers or suppliers.[8]

One other example is the Unfair Commercial Practices Directive 2005/29/EC which generally prohibits unfair commercial practices in the EU.

The relationship between private law, public law and criminal law

EU law, and in particular the principle of effectiveness, leaves it by and large to the Member States to develop the appropriate mix of sanctions for the breach of, *inter alia*, EU consumer law. As the ECJ held in *Berlusconi and others*, the Member States can, for example, combine sanctions provided for by criminal law, public law and private law,[9] as long as the particular sanction or combination of sanctions is effective, dissuasive and proportionate.[10] The Court has never obliged the Member States to adopt criminal penalties. In fact, AG Mazár stated in the case of *Commission* v. *Council* concerning criminal sanctions in the case of ship-source pollution:

> [W]hat is the contribution of criminal penalties to the effectiveness of a law? Criminological debate continues as to which way and in which matters criminal penalties represent the best means of ensuring the effective enforcement of the law. It may be too simple to assume that criminal law is always the appropriate remedy for a lack of effectiveness.[11]

[8] Joined Cases C-240/98 to C-244/98, *Océano Grupo* v. *Murciano Quintero and others* [2000] ECR I-4941, at para. 28.

[9] See Joined Cases C-387/02, C-391/02 and C-403/02, *Silvio Berlusconi, Sergio Adelchi, Marcello Dell'Utri and others* [2005] ECR I-3565, at para. 65, with further references.

[10] See AG Kokott, *ibid.*, at para. 121.

[11] AG Mazár, Case C-440/05, *Commission* v. *Council* [2007] ECR I-9097, at para. 117.

Consequently, the non-availability of specific types of sanction does not indicate that the national sanctions system is ineffective. This has to be proven by the party that challenges the effectiveness of the system, which is usually the Commission.[12] However, the EU has also made it plain that in certain cases the use of public law or criminal law may be necessary in order to effectively pursue the goals of EU law. Relevant judgments concerned the competence of the EU to require Member States to introduce criminal law sanctions in certain areas of law. In the case of *Commission* v. *Council* on the introduction of criminal sanctions for the violation of EC environmental law, AG Ruiz-Jarabo Colomer said:

> In some instances it is sufficient to restore the situation existing prior to the contravention. That outcome, however, which is not a punishment in the strict sense and which is usually referred to as a 'civil penalty', frequently requires, in order to attain the deterrent objectives referred to, the addition of punishments in the true meaning of the word, which must be more or less severe according to the importance of the legal interest under threat and the degree of social disapproval of the infringing behaviour.[13]

This was confirmed by the ECJ in the above-mentioned case of *Commission* v. *Council* concerning criminal sanctions in the case of ship-source pollution,[14] although the ECJ clarified in this judgment that the determination of the type and level of the criminal penalties to be applied did not fall within the Community's sphere of competence.[15] In environmental law, insufficient enforcement by private actors is of course obvious, and the range of public fines is also limited in some Member States. The problem of insufficient private enforcement, however, also exists in other fields of law, including consumer law, as will be shown below.

The limits of enforcement through private law mechanisms

The limits of individual litigation

It has long been recognised that there are a number of situations in which a consumer will not be able to or is highly unlikely to take individual

[12] See Case C-478/99, *Commission* v. *Sweden* [2002] ECR I-4147, at paras. 22ff., and AG Sharpston, Case C-32/05, *Commission* v. *Luxembourg* [2006] ECR I-11323, at para. 60.

[13] AG Ruiz-Jarabo Colomer, Case C-176/03, *Commission* v. *Council* [2005] ECR I-7879, at para. 46.

[14] Case C-440/05, *Commission* v. *Council* [2007] ECR I-9097, at paras. 66ff.

[15] *Ibid.*, at para. 70. For more extensive discussion of this latter issue see AG Mazár, Case C-440/05, at paras. 103ff.

action against a trader who has breached consumer law provisions. The extent to which individual redress is likely to be pursued obviously depends upon many factors that vary among the Member States, including the legal framework, business attitudes and also the cultural attitudes of individuals in respect of litigation. Also, the availability of effective out-of-court settlement schemes plays a major role in this. Generally, one may distinguish the following situations.

Situations in which no individual claims are possible

First of all, there are situations in which no individual claims exist at all even though individuals may be harmed. This may be the case in unfair competition law where the Unfair Commercial Practices Directive 2005/29/EC does not envisage individual remedies for consumers, an approach that Germany has explicitly followed.[16] An unfair commercial practice, for example misleading advertising, may be actionable under contract law but is not necessarily so.[17]

Lapse of time and lack of evidence

There are situations in which the breach of law and the related harm to consumers only come to light after many years, which is typical of competition law cases. One example would be the coffee cartel of Tchibo, Melitta and Dallmayr which had been in operation since 2000:[18] no consumer would be able to present convincing evidence on how much 'cartel coffee' he or she had consumed and to quantify the individual damage, suffered, as a result. The same applies to items such as petrol, since consumers do not usually collect their petrol bills, even though the petrol companies have long been suspected of anti-competitive behaviour.

Low-value claims

While the first two situations relate to impossible or nearly impossible claims, the situation with low-value claims is different. Here, the reasonable consumer will weigh the potential gains on one hand and the effort, expense and potential risk on the other and then decide whether it is worth bringing the claim. The variables differ from one country to the

[16] See F. Weiler, 'Ein lauterkeitsrechtliches Vertragslösungsrecht des Verbrauchers?' (2003) *Wettbewerb in Recht und Praxis* (*WRP*) 423 ff.

[17] See H. Apostolopoulos, 'Neuere Entwicklungen im europäischen Lauterkeitsrecht: Problematische Aspekte und Vorschläge', *WRP* (2004), 841, at 846.

[18] See http://www.bundeskartellamt.de/wDeutsch/download/pdf/Presse/091221_PM_Kaffeeroester.pdf.

next, and from one claim to the next, and estimates as to the value of the claim that justifies litigation are difficult.[19] Obviously, the likelihood of success is one factor, but so also are the particularities of the court system, including the court fees, the requirement to be represented by a lawyer, lawyers' fees, the availability (by law and in practice) of contingency fees, the existence of the loser-pays principle, the availability of legal insurance and so on. Small claims courts certainly facilitate access to the court system in low-value claims cases in that, normally, court fees are significantly lower and no legal representation is needed. Even then, however, a (reduced) threshold remains below which a consumer would not normally go to court.

In Germany the threshold for a more or less clear-cut case could be relatively low. In fact, in 2005, 264,000 claims that were decided in the first instance courts had a value of less than 300 euro, representing approximately 2.7 per cent of the totality of civil law lawsuits decided in Germany.[20] Many consumers have legal insurance that would cover such claims. Still, there is a threshold below which not even German consumers would litigate. In the expert study commissioned by the European Commission, interviewees estimated this threshold in a range between 50 and 250 euro.

High-value high-risk claims

A similar assessment exercise can be made with regard to high-value claims. Here, it is less the effort and time a consumer has to invest but rather the litigation risk that will influence the consumer's decision for or against litigation. Types of claims that include high litigation risk are capital market claims and product liability claims. In these cases litigation costs are usually high, although they still differ greatly between Member States. Frequently, these cases go through three instances, which increases litigation costs drastically. Therefore, the availability of limitations to litigation costs through caps on court fees and lawyers' fees or contingency fees plays an important role in the consumer's decision whether to litigate or not. German court fees are modest in comparison with other

[19] The EC Commission refers to data according to which 20 per cent of all consumers would not go to court for less than 1,000 euro, whereas 50 per cent of all consumers would not take legal action in cases below 200 euro. See the Commission's Green Paper on collective redress mechanisms, COM (2008) 794 final, at 4.

[20] See *Statistisches Bundesamt*, series 10, 2.1, *Rechtspflege – Zivilgerichte 2005*, published in 2007.

countries. Lawyers' fees are freely negotiable, but competition is stiff on the German market for legal services, and clients can always find lawyers who will work for the fee that is laid down in a fee table and in which the relevant fee depends upon the value of the claim. Contingency fees have only been allowed since July 2008,[21] after the previous total prohibition had been ruled unconstitutional by the German Constitutional Court,[22] and they are still severely restricted. Third-party financing is also only in its infancy on the German market.[23]

Psychological barriers

Beyond the above-mentioned situations in which a reasonable consumer may, after weighing the potential benefits, costs and risks of individual litigation, decide against legal action, psychological barriers against individual litigation exist. One is the perceived shame or embarrassment at having been ripped off; for example, of having been unwise enough to purchase woollen blankets on a bus tour. This may be aggravated in cases where the relationship between the consumer and the trader was of a dubious nature anyway, for example, if the consumer was frustrated within the ambit of a contract related to pornographic content.[24] But even if no such 'shameful' experience was perceived, many consumers may simply shy away from going to court. Consumer attitudes in this respect vary greatly between Member States. In some Member States, it is the sheer and almost legendary length of court proceedings that acts as a deterrent to individual litigation.[25] Germany, however, certainly ranks among the more litigious societies in the EU.

[21] New §49b para. 2 Federal Lawyers Act (*Bundesrechtsanwaltsordnung*, BRAO) and §4a Lawyers' Fees Act (*Rechtsanwaltsvergütungsgesetz*, RVG).

[22] Constitutional Court, 12 December 2006 (2007) *NJW* 979.

[23] See in particular the activities of Cartel Damage Claims (CDC), a company that has collected claims against a cement cartel worth 114 million euro and has brought them before the LG Düsseldorf. Concerning the admissibility of this action see LG Düsseldorf, 21 February 2007 (2007) *Betriebs-Berater* (*BB*) 847; OLG Düsseldorf, 14 May 2008 (2008) *Wirtschaft und Wettbewerb* (*WuW*) 847; BGH (2009) *WRP* 745. For third-party financing of capital market law cases see A. Halfmeier, P. Rott and E. Feess, *Kollektiver Rechtsschutz im Kapitalmarktrecht* (Frankfurt School Verlag, 2010), 41.

[24] Although, for example, telephone sex litigation has been brought in Germany and has made its way to the highest civil court; see for example BGH, 9/6/1998 (1998) *NJW* 2895; BGH, 22 November 2001 (2002) *NJW* 361.

[25] Italy was found on numerous occasions in the European Court of Human Rights liable for overly lengthy court proceedings; see for example ECtHR, 28 July 1999, *Bottazzi* v. *Italy*, *Reports of Judgments and Decisions* 1999-V. The issue is also salient, for example, in Portugal.

The availability of alternative dispute resolution mechanisms

Alternative dispute resolution (ADR) mechanisms can reduce both the barriers to taking action in low-value claims and the psychological barriers to initiating claims. Successful ADR schemes exist, for example, in the Scandinavian countries. It should, however, be noted that few ADR mechanisms are free of charge, and that ADR mechanisms are not available in all Member States and in all sectors. In addition, some ADR schemes are dominated by business interests and therefore do not command consumer confidence. Some schemes are only accessible for claims of a particular minimum or maximum value.[26] Furthermore, ADR is usually unsuitable in cases of difficult questions of law and fact, for example, in product liability cases and capital market cases. And finally, ADR does not work with rogue traders since they would not submit themselves to ADR. Thus, the improvement of the availability of ADR schemes can mitigate the lack of individual litigation but does not solve the problem entirely. In Germany, there are some two hundred ADR bodies, some specially designed for business/consumer conflicts, some of a more general nature, but they are of limited relevance in practice, as compared to in-court litigation. Although the number of consumers who resort to ADR schemes such as the ADR scheme for e-commerce or the ADR scheme of the banking ombudsman is increasing, it is still small.

The limits of collective litigation

Collective litigation can mitigate some of the above-mentioned limitations of individual litigation, and collective redress mechanisms have been introduced by a number of Member States, with variable success.[27] They have also attracted the attention of the EU Commission, which has not only commissioned a study on the evaluation of the effectiveness and

[26] For an excellent overview see Centre for Consumer Law of the Katholieke Universiteit Leuven, *An Analysis and Evaluation of Alternative Means of Consumer Redress other than Redress through Ordinary Judicial Proceedings* (2007), available at http://ec.europa.eu/consumers/redress_cons/adr_en.htm.

[27] See the country reports in M. Casper, A. Janssen, P. Pohlmann and R. Schulze (eds.), *Auf dem Weg zu einer europäischen Sammelklage?* (Munich: Sellier European Publishers, 2009). See also P. Rott, 'Collective Redress Mechanisms in European Consumer Law', in V. Reddy (ed.), *Consumer Law: Globalisation, Poverty and Development* (New Delhi: LexisNexis forthcoming 2010).

efficiency of national collective redress mechanisms[28] but has also subsequently published a Green Paper on such mechanisms.[29]

In particular, collective mechanisms may reduce litigation costs and therefore the litigation risk in high-value claims as much as in mass low-value claims, and it may also overcome the psychological barriers. They can also facilitate investigations into the trader's conduct. However, there remain areas in which even collective litigation is impossible or unlikely to be resorted to. The first area is claims where no material damage exists but where other issues are at stake, in particular the molestation of the consumer. This would apply to cases of cold calling. Here, the only relevant type of collective action is a collective action in the collective interest of consumers, where a consumer association sues for damages (on its own account), to be used for its future work, such as the French collective action under Article L. 421–1 of the *Code de la consommation.*[30] In Germany, the legislator has introduced a skimming-off procedure in the field of unfair competition law,[31] under which consumer organisations can skim off the unlawful profits from the trader. These profits, however, have to be paid into the public purse, not to the consumer organisation. This procedure has not been very effective until now, in particular since the consumer organisation has to prove the trader's intentional breach of the law of unfair competition, and it also has to calculate the unlawful profits gained from that breach.[32] It has, however, recently been used successfully in one action against a company which engaged in subscription traps.[33] The second area is fraudulent practices where consumers are intimidated and

[28] See Civic Consulting.

[29] COM (2008) 794 final. In parallel to this, the Commission explores collective mechanisms in the field of competition law; see the Commission's White Paper on damages actions for breach of the EC antitrust rules, COM (2008) 165 final.

[30] See, for example H. Beuchler, 'Frankreich', in H. Micklitz and A. Stadler (eds.), *Das Verbandsklagerecht in der Informations- und Dienstleistungsgesellschaft* (Landwirtschaftsverlag, 2005), 57ff.

[31] The legal basis is §10 *Gesetz gegen den unlauteren Wettbewerb* (Unfair Competition Act) (UWG).

[32] For detailed analysis of the few cases that have been brought until now, see P. Rott, 'Kollektive Klagen von Verbraucherverbänden in Deutschland' in M. Casper *et al.*, *Auf dem Weg*, 259ff. A similar claim was introduced in 2005 for cartel law cases, in §§34, 34a of the Competition Act (*Gesetz gegen Wettbewerbsbeschränkungen*, GWB) but has not yet been tested in court.

[33] See OLG Frankfurt, 4 December 2008 (2009), *Verbraucher und Recht* (*VuR*) 151. See also O. Meyer-van Raay and J. Deitermann, 'Gefangen in der (Internet-)Kostenfalle?' (2009) *VuR* 335, at 339ff.

therefore do not dare to engage in litigation at all, regardless of whether litigation is individual or collective.[34]

In all other cases, the extent to which collective mechanisms can mitigate the limitations of individual litigation very much depends on their particular design and attractiveness to the relevant actors. The above-mentioned survey of currently existing collective mechanisms of the Member States has demonstrated the operation of many practical obstacles to those mechanisms. In Germany there seems to be some distrust of private actors, including consumer organisations, being empowered with effective or even deterrent instruments, with industry lobbying heavily against anything that could come close to an American-style class action. The existing mechanisms have been designed in such a way that they are not particularly attractive to consumer organisations or to law firms. One type of action where consumer organisations can sue on the behalf of individual consumers (*Sammelklage*) has gained some relevance, after a somewhat slow start, but this is due to the litigation risk and the administrative burdens on the consumer organisation. Furthermore, the *Sammelklage* is, in practice, limited in its ambit to medium-value claims of up to 1,000 euro per consumer and to groups of between 20 and 100 consumers.[35]

Finally, company law may constitute an impediment to private law enforcement. Typically, fraudulent practices are exercised by a company. Should indeed the company then be sued and found liable, it frequently disappears immediately, and a new company is established.[36] Unlike, for example, English law where an injunction would prevent the directors of a company from following precisely this sort of strategy, such mechanisms are not available in German private law.

German experience and recent developments

German experience discloses a mixed picture. On the one hand, the number of private law cases that go to court certainly ranks among the highest in Europe, the main reason being fairly easy access to the courts. German court procedures are rather cheap and comparatively fast. In addition, many consumers hold legal insurance which takes the

[34] S. Ernst, 'Schärfere Verbrauchergesetze als Schutz vor "Online-Abzocke"?' (2009) *VuR* 321.

[35] For detailed analysis of case law, see Rott, 'Kollektive Klagen'.

[36] For the purpose of illustration, see the overview of actions by the German federal consumer association *vzbv* against the operators of internet subscription scams at http://www.vzbv.de/mediapics/kostenfallen_im_internet.pdf.

litigation risk from them and acts as an incentive to litigate. On the other hand, certain practices in breach of consumer legislation have not stopped or even decreased, even after more than thirty years of consumer legislation. Examples include unfair contract terms[37] where the current system of collective enforcement is just not sufficiently deterrent,[38] cold calling[39] and spamming, and all sorts of internet fraud. While in the field of unfair contract terms more effective collective mechanisms would seem to be possible, cold calling, spamming and internet fraud are areas in which this does not appear to be the case. It is these areas in which we can see a move towards public law and criminal law enforcement.

Public law sanctions

Public law sanctions have of course always been present in health-related fields of law, i.e. in foodstuff law, pharmaceuticals law and so on. However, they have now also entered the field of non-health-related consumer law. One example is premium telecommunications services. Here, the legislator has introduced some protective mechanisms, such as price caps and a time limit of sixty minutes,[40] and breaches are sanctioned by public law fines.[41]

The most recent field in which public sanctions have been introduced, following constant demands by consumer associations, was indeed the field of cold calling where the legislator explicitly recognised that the enforcement of the pre-existing prohibition under the law of unfair competition was difficult.[42] In August 2009, the Act against unfair telephone advertising (*Gesetz zur Bekämpfung unlauterer Telefonwerbung und zur Verbesserung des Verbraucherschutzes bei besonderen Vertriebsformen*)

[37] The *vzbv* has achieved 1,500 injunctions against traders between 1977 and 2008.

[38] For details, see P. Rott, *Effektivität des Verbraucherrechtschutzes: Rahmenfestlegungen des Gemeinschaftsrechts* (2006), available at http://download.ble.de/04HS033.pdf, at 119 ff.

[39] Around 60,000 consumer complaints reach the consumer organisations per year, which is estimated to be only a small percentage of the actual cold calls. Between 2000 and March 2009, the *vzbv* has initiated eighty-four successful actions against traders (litigation and undertakings). See also the report by the German Ministry of Justice at http://www.bmj.de/files/-/2306/Bericht%20des%20BMJ%20zum%20Thema%20unerw%C3%BCnschte%20Werbeanrufe.pdf.

[40] §66d and §66e Telecommunications Act (*Telekommunikationsgesetz*, TKG); on which see A. Ditscheid, 'Der neue Telekommunikationskundenschutz' (2007) *MultiMedia und Recht* (*MMR*) 210ff.

[41] See §149 no. 13a to 13j TKG.

[42] See the explanations of the German government, *Bundestagsdrucksache* 16/10734, at 1.

was passed. It brought changes to contract law[43] but it also introduced fines of up to 50,000 euro for intentional or negligent breach of the prohibition of cold calling.[44] The responsible agency is the *Bundesnetzagentur* (Federal Network Agency), which is the regulator for telecommunications, postal services, energy supply and railway services. In a first step, the *Bundesnetzagentur* merely shut down telephone numbers used for cold calling and fax spamming.[45] More recently, in December 2009 and January 2010, it has started to impose fines of a total of 500,000 euro on call centres and their customers who engaged in cold calling.[46]

Criminal law sanctions

In the past, German criminal courts were only rarely involved in consumer law cases that amounted to fraud. The only consumer-law-specific criminal law provision could be found in the law of unfair competition. According to §16 of the Unfair Competition Act, it is a criminal offence to make false statements in advertisements to the public with the intention of giving the impression of a particular lucrative offer. One rare example where this provision was actually applied was a bus tour case that made its way to the Federal Civil Court (*Bundesgerichtshof*, BGH). In several cases, the trader had, among other things, promised that participants would get a delicious lunch, while they were then handed out a can of soup or beans. The trader also mentioned that the addressee had won a prize of around 500 deutschmarks (approximately 250 euro) which he now had to collect. In fact, the participants only received between 3 and 10 deutschmarks in cash, and in one case only shampoo worth 2.80 deutschmarks. The BGH held that the trader's announcement amounted to a criminal offence.[47]

Clearly, certain commercial practices are not only unfair but fraudulent, which triggers the question of whether the trader can be sentenced for

[43] In particular, the exemptions for contracts on the sale of newspapers, periodicals and magazines and on gaming and lottery services from the right of withdrawal under distance selling law do not apply any longer if the contract was concluded over the telephone; see new §312d para. 4 BGB.

[44] New §20 of the UWG.

[45] See the overview at http://www.bundesnetzagentur.de/media/archive/17034.pdf. The legal basis is §67 TKG.

[46] See the press statement at http://www.bundesnetzagentur.de/media/archive/18111.pdf.

[47] BGH (2002) *NJW* 3415; on which see S. Pluskat, 'Die Tücken von "Kaffeefahrten"' (2003) *WRP* 18ff. The OLG Oldenburg as appeal court had only treated the promise of delicious lunch as a criminal offence but not the promise of a prize.

fraud in the terms of §263 of the German Criminal Code (*Strafgesetzbuch*, StGB). In that provision fraud is defined as follows:

> Whoever, with the intent of obtaining for himself or a third person an unlawful material benefit, damages the assets of another, by provoking or affirming a mistake by pretending that false facts exist or by distorting or suppressing true facts, shall be punished with imprisonment for not more than five years or a fine.

The sentences are higher if the fraudster acted as a member of a gang, or if he acted professionally. Attempted fraud is also a criminal offence, according to §263 paragraph 2 StGB. Certain unfair commercial practices are now at least considered by prosecutors and sometimes, although not always, brought to trial as cases relating to misleading pricing. Typical examples are outlined below.

Offers disguised as bills

A common practice, in particular by traders selling advertisements, is to send 'offers' that are made up as bills. In earlier case law, the courts rejected the idea that this could be a criminal offence since the character of an offer was recognisable from the small print at the bottom or on the back of the page.[48] In 2001, the BgH again had the opportunity to deal with a case in which a trader had sent 'offers' to his victims that had actually been designed as bills, in particular since they displayed the payment date in a prominent manner. This time, the court held this to be fraud under §263 StGB, since the character of an offer was only recognisable from the small print at the bottom of the page. Although the statements were objectively true, the BGH recognised the trader's intention to cause the addressee to make a mistake by paying a non-existent bill.[49] This is an important case, with potentially significant impact on other scams in the area of consumer law.

Provoking premium calls

In February 2009, the *Landgericht* (LG) Offenburg[50] convicted two men who had lured consumers into calling expensive premium numbers,

[48] See BGH, 27 February 1979 (1997) *Neue Zeitschrift für Strafrecht* (*NStZ*), 186. See also OLG Frankfurt, 17 August 1994 (1997) *NStZ* 187. For critical comments see the prosecutors H.-J. Mahnkopf and A. Sonnberg, 'Anmerkung' (1997) *NStZ* 187ff.

[49] See BGH, 26 April 2001 (2001) *NJW* 2187. See also BGH, 4 December 2003 (2004), *Neue Zeitschrift für Strafrecht – Rechtsprechungs-Report* (*NStZ-RR*) 110. For critique see S. Ernst, 'Scheinrechnungen und Betrug – Keine Schutzbedürftigkeit der Nachlässigkeit und Gutgläubigkeit bei Unternehmen' (2004) *MultiMedia und Recht* (*MMR*) 243.

[50] LG Offenburg, 9 February 2009 – 2 KLs 16 Js 674/03 2 AK, unreported.

expecting to have won a prize. The men were convicted of fraud with one year and six months' jail on probation. Unfortunately, the court was not in a position also to seize their unlawfully acquired profits since the law that applied at the time of the fraudulent activities only allowed such a seizure if the harmed individuals did not have claims in damages – even if none of them had ever claimed damages, as in the instant case. The law was changed with effect from 1 January 2007, reflecting a remarkably realistic perspective on consumer behaviour. The law now allows the courts to determine the unlawful profits and to seize them for a period of three years. During this period, individual claims can be met from this amount. After three years, the remaining unlawful profits are paid into the public purse.[51]

Another fraudulent practice that has become frequent is to call mobile phone users randomly and to hang up after the first ring. If the users think that they have missed a call, they call the respective number, which is of course an expensive premium number. While the LG Hildesheim has held that this method was fraud in terms of the Criminal Court,[52] the prosecutor at the LG Hanover has denied any criminal law relevance of such activities, arguing that the mere call did not imply a request to be called back.

Subscription traps

The damage caused by fraudulent internet pages facilitating long-term subscription traps on unsuspecting customers is estimated by consumer associations to amount to several million euro per year.[53] In one case, three students had defrauded about a thousand customers of about 130,000 euro. They had collected the victims' internet addresses from a database and sent the victims e-mails asking them to open a particular webpage. They then sent the victims bills of over 86 euro, which many victims actually paid. The students were sentenced by the LG Göttingen to jail between fifteen and eighteen months on probation.[54]

[51] See §111i paras. 2, 3 and 5 of the Criminal Procedural Code (*Strafprozessordnung*, StPO).

[52] See LG Hildesheim, 10 February 2004, 26 KLs 16 Js 26785/02, available at http://www.kanzlei-richter.com/images/stories/entscheidungen/zivilrecht/bezirk_olg_celle/bezirk_lg_hildesheim/lg_hildesheim/2004–02–10_lg_hildesheim_-_26_kls_16_js_26785–02.pdf. The prosecution at the LG Augsburg argued similarly.

[53] On such 'business models' and their economic success see B. Klas and P. Schwarz, 'Kostenfallen im Internet' (2009) *VuR* 341ff.

[54] See http://www.heise.de/newsticker/meldung/Abofallen-Betreiber-zu-Haftstrafen-verurteilt-751729.html.

Fraud also has a civil law dimension in that it is a tort under §823 paragraph 2 BGB. In an important judgment of August 2009, the *Amstgericht* (AG) Karlsruhe held that an infamous lawyer by the name of Katja Günther had committed the tort of assistance to attempted fraud in sending debt collection letters to victims of subscription traps. She was therefore held liable for the litigation costs of a targeted victim who had sued her.[55] However, the courts are by no means united in their approach. The LG Düsseldorf has, in a similar case, rejected a consumer association's claim for an injunction under the Unfair Competition Act.[56] The consumer association had argued that it was an unfair commercial practice to charge consumers in circumstances where they had not realised that they were entering into a contract since that was only mentioned in small print at the bottom of the webpage.

Consumer fraud?

Interestingly, the opposite situation of fraud by consumers has also been considered in academic writing. Rettenmaier and Kopf have argued that a consumer who purchases an item by distance selling, although he or she merely intends to use the item for a short while and to withdraw from the contract thereafter, might commit fraud.[57] Of course, this would seem to be difficult to prove.

Limitations of fraud

One limitation of fraud under §263 StGB is that it requires damage to be incurred by the victim. In the above-mentioned bus tour case, for example, the victims had not paid money for nothing. For the money they had actually spent, they had received bus transport, and if they had bought anything on that tour, they had also obtained the goods (although they were overly expensive).[58] In a recent case in which a trader of secondhand cars had held himself out to be a consumer, thereby trying

[55] AG Karlsruhe, 12/8/2009, 9 C 93/09, available at http://www.telemedicus.info/urteile/Wettbewerbsrecht/Abmahnungen/869-AG-Karlsruhe-Az-9-C-9309-Abofallen-Inkasso-als-Beihilfe-zum-versuchten-Betrug.html. See also Klas and Schwarz, (2009) *VuR* 341, at 343ff.

[56] LG Düsseldorf, 28 August 2009, 38 O 24/09, unreported. In contrast, the prosecutor at the same court had classified the same activity as fraud and had already frozen the trader's bank account of 670,00 euro; see http://www.netzwelt.de/news/80663-abofallen-landgericht-entscheidet-gegen-verbraucherschuetzer.html.

[57] See F. Rettenmaier and O. Kopf, 'Der unlautere Abschluss und Widerruf von Fernabsatzverträgen – Betrug gemäß §263 Abs. 1 StGB?' (2007) *Juristische Rundschau* (*JR*) 226ff.

[58] See S. Pluskat (2003) *WRP* 18 at 22.

to avoid mandatory consumer sales law and excluding his liability for defects, the OLG Cologne held that there was only fraud if the car was not actually worth the purchase price.[59] However, the trader's conduct should still amount to attempted fraud, which is also a criminal offence, since the trader had aimed to prevent the consumer from making claims if defects had come to light within the otherwise applicable prescription period, a matter which the court had failed to consider.

The relationship between criminal law and unfair competition law

The decision of the BGH was criticised in academic writing, in particular since the BGH explicitly stated that the victim's credulity did not preclude the perpetrator's potential conviction for fraud.[60] *Scheinfeld* argues that this approach is in conflict with the EU's image of the average consumer, as enshrined, in particular, in Article 5(2) of the Unfair Commercial Practices Directive 2005/29/EC. Thus, commercial practices that are not unfair under this directive (since the average consumer would not be misled) could at the same time be sanctioned under German criminal law, which appears to be contradictory.[61] Of course, one could also argue that such scams are truly addressed to overly credulous consumers in any case, so that this is the target group that is to be considered under Article 5(2) of Directive 2005/29/EC.

Whatever the position under the law of unfair commercial practices is, it should be clearly distinguished from the position under criminal law (as long as criminal law is not used to sanction the breach of unfair commercial practices law). First of all, as a formal argument, the EU lacks the competence to regulate criminal law, such as the prerequisites and sanctions of fraud. Secondly, fraud as defined in §263 StGB requires the trader's intention to cause a mistake by the victim in order to gain unlawful benefits, which directs the perspective to the relationship between the trader and his individual victim, as opposed to the activities of the trader in the marketplace in general. Surely it was not the intention of the European legislator to support such practices by protecting the trader through the law of unfair competition? In fact, the full harmonisation approach of Directive 2005/29/EC is meant to ensure that a trader

[59] OLG Cologne, 2 December 2008 (2009) *NStZ-RR* 176.

[60] BGH, 4 December 2003 (2004) *NStZ-RR* 110.

[61] See J. Scheinfeld, 'Betrug durch unternehmerisches Werben?' (2008) *Zeitschrift für Wirtschafts- und Steuerstrafrecht* (wistra) 167ff.

who acts in good faith is not inhibited in his cross-border activities by divergent standards of the national laws of unfair competition, but not to lower standards in such a way that fraud would be permitted.

Perspectives on public enforcement of EU consumer law

Although the German legislator has explicitly rejected the idea that EU law requires the introduction of public law fines for cold calling, there seem to be situations where this, or even criminal law sanctions,[62] is the only way to protect consumers effectively, unless one wants to increase the powers of consumer associations dramatically, for example with powers to bring sufficiently deterrent claims for the compensation of damage done to the collective interests of consumers. This is not likely to happen, given the general scepticism against this form of private enforcement. Then, the principle of effectiveness would indeed require the state to take action, as is already common practice in a number of EU Member States, where public law fines would normally seem to be sufficient. It is probably the almost complete lack of public law sanctions in German consumer law that has required prosecutors and courts to resort to criminal law, which is, however, unspecific to consumer law and therefore uncertain in its potential for the protection of consumers. This can be traced through the divergent approaches taken by different prosecutors and different courts.

Therefore, the way forward seems to be for each Member State, under consideration of its specific jurisdictional impediments to individual enforcement and collective enforcement by private law mechanisms, to identify the remaining enforcement gaps and to fill them with public and/or criminal law sanctions. Evaluations of the current systems have already been commissioned and completed in a number of Member States and also by the EU, so that there remains little room for Member States to hide behind any alleged lack of data. As to the usefulness of public and/or criminal law sanctions, it should be possible to draw conclusions from the experience in those countries which have applied these for a long time. One aspect that deserves particular attention is the institutional setting. It may be expected that institutions such as competition authorities or prosecutors, which have no or little experience in the enforcement of consumer law and where consumer law is only one out of many areas to deal with, will not be overly devoted to this task. Certainly, specialised consumer authorities, agencies or ombudsmen are preferable.

[62] See the report of the German Ministry of Justice, at 4.

6

E-consumers and effective protection: the online dispute resolution system

IMMACULADA BARRAL-VIÑALS

Introduction

E-commerce is a new domain for contracting with consumers but it is not an unregulated area. Nevertheless, traditional solutions to this new form of contracting can be useless; e-consumers may fall outside the scope of application of the legal framework. Another important issue is how to enforce the rights of these e-consumers, who are not especially confident about the fairness of the internet. For this reason, the EU is paying attention to the forms of exchange that are emerging on the internet. The Future Challenges paper 2009–2014[1] focuses on these new issues and asks for different regulations for online consumer behaviour because it differs a lot from the usual offline practices. Do we need different regulations for the consumer depending on the type of contract? Would it not be more effective to have a general understanding of the nature of e-commerce when trying to solve the problems as they arise in this specific context?

Having that approach in mind this chapter focuses on two main areas: first, that the idea of the e-consumer seems to be wider than the concept of the offline consumer, and, second, the extent to which online dispute resolution systems (ODR) succeed in achieving consumer redress. For this purpose we have selected two central sets of issues.

Professor in Civil Law, Faculty of Law, University of Barcelona, ibarral@ub.edu

[1] Accessible at: http://ec.europa.eu/dgs/health_consumer/events/future_challenges_paper.pdf (last accessed on 21 January 2010). More precise guidelines can be found at the Communication on EU consumer policy strategy 2007–2013: Empowering consumers, enhancing their welfare, effectively protecting them, 13 March 2007, COM (2007) 99 final. Accessible at http://ec.europa.eu/consumers/overview/cons_policy/doc/EN_99.pdf, last visited 21 January 2010.

The first set of issues concerns the consumer protection tools used in e-commerce: that is to say analysis of the extent and effects of information requirements on this new contracting platform. In this context, a core point of consumer protection in e-commerce is that the pre-contractual information is extended to all parties, whether or not they are 'traditional' consumers; thus the e-consumer is not necessarily a weaker party but may be any contractor in a 'click and wrap' agreement. This means that the traditional, narrow definition of the consumer is not very useful in this new context. The objective is to try to find an integrated solution for practices which challenge our traditional understanding of consumer relations. The second set of issues concern EU policies on the enforcement of consumer protection and consumers' access of justice in the context of ODR. This chapter stresses that consumer protection on the internet cannot be understood without bearing in mind the ways in which electronic platforms offer efficient and novel dispute resolution systems which build 'e-confidence'.

Consumers and e-consumers: mass contracting and nonexperts on the web

E- consumers and the new information requirements: widening the consumer concept

The EU consumer *acquis* uses a rather strict concept of the consumer, which is based on a natural person who is acting for purposes which are outside his trade, business or profession. This narrow concept frustrates the expectations, for example, of small enterprises or farmers who may feel themselves to be in essentially the same position as such a 'traditional' consumer. This chapter will not deal with this issue,[2] rather, it addresses the complexity of the consumer definition issues which become even more acute, outside traditional, offline contracts, in the online contracting context.

Reflection on the extent of information requirements shows us how problems increase when we try to apply the narrow consumer definition in contracts entered into online, that is to say when e-consumers are considered as consumers. We will not discuss what an electronic contract

[2] On the concept of the consumer: I. Barral-Viñals, 'Consumers and new technologies: a step beyond', (2009) 27 (3–4) *Penn State International Law Review* 609. This paragraph is using that analysis to conclude the conceptual autonomy of e-consumer and the need of an integral approach.

is, as the Directive 2000/31 is rather clear on this definition and a lot of work has been done in the Member States to transpose this concept into domestic law. This chapter stresses that the legal framework applying to e-contracts widens the scope of consumer protection outside the traditional concept of the consumer in offline transactions.

Our starting point is that contracts communicated electronically emphasise the imbalance in the relationship between the parties and, because of this, the normal consumer remedies, such as pre-contractual information, apply to non-consumers in the traditional sense. In this context, we will see how information requirements are being used in the context of those who would traditionally be regarded as non-consumers in the Directive 2000/31/EC.[3]

Information requirements are relied on in the regulation of e-contracts to ensure consumer protection. These requirements seek to empower the weaker party faced with the complexity of the internet. The result is to protect the consumer, but also the professional or the trader who is also in this context, for the first time, recognised as a non-expert.

The main effect of Directive 2000/31/EC is to create a unique legal system of information requirements that is applied to both business to consumer (B2C) and business to business (B2B) transactions and thus extends consumer protection to all kinds of contractor. For that reason, Article 10 prescribes some pre-contractual information requirements based on the idea that we are dealing with instantaneous or 'click' agreements.[4] This means that as the will of the contractor is not express, the legal system must confer contractual security and certainty.

The directive validates the acceptance of an offer on the internet if the service provider has met its information obligations. Those articles state two particular information duties for acceptance of e-contracts to be effective:

1. The contractor, whether consumer or not, needs to know how to agree to the offer. So the service provider must inform as to the different technical steps that need to be followed in order to conclude the contract (Article 10(1)(a)); and the technical means for identifying and correcting input errors prior to the placing of the order (Article 10(1)(c)). The law deals with these two elements differently

[3] Directive 2000/31/EC of 8 June 2000 (Directive on Electronic Commerce).

[4] We are focusing on the prior information at the moment of the offer being accepted; for that reason we are not referring to Arts. 5 or 6, Directive 2000/31 which are about general information about the services provider or the electronic communications.

but they have a common explanation: both trying to ensure the effective acceptance of the offer. As Cavanillas Múgica[5] stresses, the contractor needs to be informed of the technical environment of the contract so as to avoid divergence arising between the parties on what was finally agreed. Moreover, the rule on silence applies all the more in the e-contract (see Article 7).

2. The service provider must also give information on documentation: about whether the concluded contract will be held on file and will be accessible (Article 10(b)). The contracting party has to know how and where the contract is going to be stored so that it can be reproduced at a later date. The reference to the languages used to contract is only a method by which to obtain the effectiveness of this obligation (Article 10(1)(d)). Similarly, contract terms and general conditions provided to the recipient must be made available in a way that allows the recipient to store and reproduce them.[6]

So, when an e-contract is offered to a consumer, it must satisfy all the relevant information prescriptions, that is to say, it must comply with Article 4, Distance Selling Directive. Moreover, it has to contain all the information requirements set down in the E-commerce Directive, especially Article 10. If the contractor is not a consumer, only the second part of this information is required. In this second case, contractors unfamiliar with the new contracting platform need further information about the contracting process and the proof of the contract to re-establish the imbalance between the parties.

In the context of e-commerce information requirements are thus less to do with the content of the contract than with the new way of entering into online contracts. Furthermore, the information requirements in Article 10 are not especially drawn up to protect the consumer, but relate to the way to conclude the electronic contract. In e-commerce, prior information requirements are a tool for consumer protection that has been extended to any contractor; in an electronic exchange, there is a weaker party that has to be informed and the weaker party may be any

[5] A. Cavanillas Múgica, 'Informática y teoría del contrato', in J. Dávara (ed.), *X años de encuentros sobre Informática y Derecho, 1996–1997* (Madrid: Publicaciones de la Universidad Pontifica de Comillas, 1997), 270.

[6] *See* I. Barral-Viñals, 'La "contratación por vía electrónica": adaptación del marco jurídico mediante los principios de equivalencia funcional", I, 107ff., and M. R. Llacer Matacás, 'Obligaciones vinculadas a la formación del contrato y codificación del derecho de consumo: información y documentación', II, 149 both in E. Llamas Pombo, *Estudios de derecho de obligaciones*, 2 vols. (Madrid: Wolters Kluwer-La Ley, 2006).

contractor whether or not s/he is a consumer in a traditional, offline sense. The imbalance between the electronic services provider and the other contractor may result in the same legal problem as in a consumer contract: there is a party that can be defined as a non-expert, who needs legal guidance by means of prior information requirements.[7]

The difference between the two cases is that when the weaker party is not a consumer, the information requirements can be excluded. So, the consumer is presumed to be a non-expert without exception; the non-consumer can decide the exact level of information requirement wanted. Similarly, these requirements apply only to mass contracts; they do not apply to contracts concluded exclusively by exchange of electronic mail or by equivalent individual communications (e.g. chats or videoconferences) because in such cases the imbalance between the parties does not exist.

Mass-contracting and non-experts: the new rationales in e-consumer protection

The broader concept of the consumer in e-commerce is based on the idea of protecting the weaker party, and this is any party that can be considered as a non-expert in a contract. In this context Weatherill,[8] referring to the scope of application of the Unfair Contract Terms Directive, refers to what he calls a 'irrational limitation': the remedies for contracts concluded between economically imbalanced parties could also be applied to small businesses, as the power differential which they confront may be a good deal wider than that between small trader and consumer.

Information requirements are cited in EU legislation as the main agent of consumer protection. In fact, information is aimed at complementing the market mechanism from the point of view of the weaker party, its function being to adjust the interaction of supply and demand in favour of demand. This re-establishes a certain degree of equilibrium between resources and realigns the respective power of companies and consumers. EU legislation has its own logic for information requirements

[7] This information is a common point in other international texts: Art. 14 of United Nations Convention on use of Electronic Communication in International Commerce approved by General Assembly Resolution 60/21, 23 November 2005; Art. 10 Uniform Electronic Transactions (UETA), Model Law approved in 1999 by National Conference of Commissioners on Uniform State Laws.

[8] S. Weatherill, *Regulating the Substance of Consumer Transactions: EU Consumer Law and Policy* (E Northampton: Elgar 2005), 117.

when one of the parties is legally defined as a consumer. This differential treatment is justified by evidence of the imbalance between the parties, which leads to the need for solutions favouring the 'weaker' party.[9] So EU consumer protection relies on a non-expert qualification weighted towards consumers as compared to professionals or enterprises. Consumers are protected when they are not experts.[10] Consequently, normal consumer remedies, such as information requirements, are able to apply to non-consumers in the legal sense when they are not experts, for example when the contract process is communicated electronically.

The second main feature of the EU approach to consumer protection is that we are dealing with cases of mass contracting, an approach which leads to the standardisation of contracts.[11] On the other hand, mass contracting is a process led by a class of experts with technical knowledge. In such cases, the imbalance between the parties comes from the proposition that only one party leads the bargaining process and has the necessary information to impose some conditions:[12] that is why the control of the standard contract terms is limited to the terms that have not been individually negotiated, because there is a suspicion of 'mass-produced' contracts that cannot be fair to the other party.[13] Therefore we need to reconceptualise the consumer from the narrow concept given in EU legislation.[14]

[9] See V Roppo, 'From Consumer Contracts to Asymmetric Contracts: a Trend to European Contract Law?' (2009) 5(3) *European Journal of Contract Law* 32.

[10] In that sense, see the previous work of I. Barral-Viñals, 'Del consumidor- destinatari final al consumidor – no expert en la contractació en massa' (2007) 2 *Revista Catalana de Dret Privat* 59ff.

[11] See L. Díez-Picazo Ponce de León, *Derecho y masificación social, tecnología y derecho (Dos esbozos)* (Madrid, 1987) 42ff., 50ff. and 95ff.

[12] For the rationales of these ideas see F. Kessler, 'Contracts of Adhesion: some Thoughts about Freedom of Contract' (1943) 34 *Col LR* 629ff.

[13] In this sense see Weatherill, *Regulating the Substance*, 118.

[14] The step beyond the one described in the last paragraph seems not to be the last. In fact, this extension of information requirements widens the concept of non-experts to include non-consumers is using traditional consumer tools, so the effect is rather limited. But, besides this, one can see another important main change that we should expect in the near future related to formal web-based consumer to consumer (C2C) selling. This can arise in the file sharing in peer-to-peer platforms; and online auctions such as e-bay.

First of all, we have to stress that in these cases, and formally, we have a C2C contract that does not enter the application of Directive 2000/31 or related national laws. But we must be aware that seller and buyer are using a third-party system that generates legal relationship between the three of them at different levels: it is a contract between the users, and a contract of every one of the users with the service provider: only this second aspect is clear in the field of application of the Directive 2000/31.

Enforcing e-consumer protection beyond alternative dispute resolution (ADR): the ODR

E-confidence

For some time now the EU has been interested in creating a climate of confidence on the web as far as consumers and small and medium-sized businesses are concerned.[15] Confidence in online transactions is the key to achieving the complete immersion of the European consumer in the internal market as provided for in the e-Europe action plan launched by the Commission in 2002 subsequently in e-Europe 2005.[16] Confidence in the web, as far as consumers are concerned, is measured in terms of security: consumers will only be able to evaluate the advantages that e-commerce offers over traditional sales methods if they know the medium and understand how it works, and so it is of the utmost importance to provide the consumer with the necessary tools to avoid or resolve possible disputes that may arise from electronic transactions, especially if they are cross-border.[17] Many things can be done to increase this confidence, but the Commission has focused on the development of tools to simplify the claims process. The rationale for this approach is that only fast, simple, inexpensive methods of redress will be able to persuade the consumer to take on the risk of the business failing to carry out its promise or carrying it out unsatisfactorily.[18] For that reason, in

[15] See the analysis of this issue in the differents ODRs made by Z. Tang, 'An Effective Dispute Resolution System for Electronic Consumer Contracts' (2007) 23 *Computer Law and Security Report* 42–52.

[16] See: *e-Europe: An information society for all*, Communication on a Commission initiative for the special Council at Lisbon, 23–4 March 2002, 18: ADR and ODR are basic tools to promote consumer confidence in e-commerce: http://europa.eu.int/information_society/eeurope/news_library/pdf_files/initiative_en.pdf). The next action plan e-Europe 2005 is dealing with the implementation of ODR as a way of increase e-confidence, pp. 14 and 15. See Communication *e-Europe 2005: An information society for all: An Action Plan*, Seville European Council, 21/22 June 2002, COM (2002) 263 final, http://europa.eu.int/information_society/eeurope/2005/all_about/action_plan/index_en.htm.

[17] Point 1 of preamble to recital 98: one of the interests of the DG Health and Consumers is 'to boost consumer confidence in the functioning of the internal market and consumers' scope for taking full advantage of the possibilities offered by the internal market, including the possibility for consumers to settle disputes in an efficient and appropriate manner through out-of-court or other comparable procedures'.

[18] This question has been repeated in documents on e-commerce since the first e-Europe plan in 2002. Most recently in the report on cross-border e-commerce in the EU, SEC (2009) 283 final, of March 2009, compiled by the Commission Working Group. This reports that 21 per cent of individuals do not use the internet for shopping because they are worried about problems in the way complaints may be handled or failures on the part

the field of individual claim resolution efficiency, the use of ADR systems to deal with complaints is considered an important instrument for generating confidence in e-commerce. So, the specific legal framework built in the EU in the late 1990s to deal with consumer complaints, is used in the development of e-confidence.

We then turn to analyse the legal framework in the EU for exercising ADR in consumer complaints, far before the regulation of ADR in private law such as in the Directive 2008/45/EC,[19] and see how it changes from the ADR to ODR.

The specific legal framework: the access of consumers to justice

Methods of ADR for consumer complaints are bound by a specific legal system which predates the general regulation of civil mediation within the EU; the system is, however, based on the same principles. A general regulation of ADR for civil matters is driven by Directive 2008/52/EC.[20] In fact point 11 of the preamble of this directive indicates that this area of consumer ADR is outside the scope of the directive; however, it is simply said that 'consumer complaint systems' are excluded, i.e. any conflict resolution mechanism, whether or not it involves mediation, according to its area of application: consumer complaints.[21] In accordance with this idea, consumer complaints *en bloc* are excluded as these have their own general ADR system laid down in two sets of regulations at Community level.

The first is Commission Recommendation 98/257/EC, on the principles applicable to the bodies responsible for out-of-court settlement of consumer disputes,[22] which only regulated ADRs involving the intervention

of the businesses. See http://ec.europa.eu/consumers/strategy/docs/com_staff_wp2009_en.pdf, last accessed, 25 January 2010.

[19] For the development of trust in e-commerce as a business strategy see M. A. Patton and A. Jøsang, 'Technologies for Trust in Electronic Commerce' (2004) 4 *Electronic Commerce Research*, 9–21.

[20] Directive 2008/52/EC of the European Parliament and of the Council on certain aspects of mediation in civil and commercial matters [2008] OJ May L 136/3–8.

[21] Point 11 of the preamble: 'This Directive should not apply to pre-contractual negotiations or to processes of an adjudicatory nature such as certain judicial conciliation schemes, *consumer complaint schemes*, arbitration and expert determination or to processes administered by persons or bodies issuing a formal recommendation, whether or not it be legally binding as to the resolution of the dispute.'

[22] Commission Recommendation 98/257/EC of 30 March 1998 on the principles applicable to the bodies responsible for out-of-court settlement of consumer disputes [1998] OJ L 115/31–4.

of a third party who proposed or imposed a solution. It did not include the procedures defined in Article 1 of the Recommendation, which simply seeks to bring the parties concerned together to convince them to find a solution by common consent, this being the essence of mediation.

The second is Commission Recommendation 2001/310/CE of 4 April on the principles for out-of-court bodies involved in the consensual resolution of consumer disputes,[23] which applies precisely to all those procedures, regardless of their appellation, that attempt to resolve a dispute by bringing the parties together to convince them to find a solution by common consent (Article 1). In Spain, these procedures are known as 'mediation' within the 'consumer arbitration system' set up by the 231/2008 Act[24] and constitute an initial stage in the procedure (Articles 37 and 38), though with a certain amount of conceptual autonomy.

The exclusion of 'consumer complaint systems' from the scope of Directive 2008/52 sometimes led to the omission of certain systems of dispute resolution in consumer law which traditionally fell within the categories of ADR. Clearly, the conduct of mediation or negotiation of consumer complaints may vary radically from mediation in family, community or multicultural conflicts, but these may be suited to the scheme provided for by Directive 2008/52 for mediation. Under the directive, the main problems relating to the quality of mediation (Article 4), the application of confidentiality (Article 5), and an appropriate enforcement mechanism (Article 6) can be treated as a whole in any mediation process, even when mediating in consumers' affairs.

At this point, the question seems to be why, in consumer law, the legislature has opted for ADR, even before extending the ADR system to all matters of private law generally? To answer this question we have to link it to 'consumer access to justice' as discussed below.

The 'consumer access to justice': the logic of the regulatory framework for consumer ADR

The previous and specific legislative approach to ADRs in consumer complaints stems from the actions initiated by the Green Paper on consumer access to justice in the internal market in 1993,[25] which sought

[23] Commission Recommendation of 4 April 2001 on the principles for out-of-court bodies involved in the consensual resolution of consumer disputes [2001] OJ L 109/56–61.

[24] *Real Decreto* (RD) *231/2008, de 15 febrero, por el que se regula el Sistema arbitral de consumo*, BOE 25, 02, 08.

[25] COM (93) 576 final, 76.

to design a regulatory framework to ensure the effectiveness of the regulatory framework for consumer protection. The Green Paper noted the proliferation of consumer ADR mechanisms in the Member States to meet the demand for efficient dispute resolution processes, an efficiency beyond the reach of the court system. The Green Paper tried to promote a comprehensive approach; next to the conclusions that affect the development of ADR and in particular of consumer arbitration, we find proposals on collective actions, or entitlement to legal aid. However, the value of this first text is to highlight the existence of ADR in some countries, including Spain, under the umbrella of consumer arbitration.[26]

The development of ADR in consumer matters is thus linked to consumer access to justice and the package of measures aimed at strengthening their rights to redress. This led to the Commission's Communication of 14 February 1996 concerning a plan of action on consumer access to justice and the settlement of consumer disputes which opted for ADRs.[27] 'Consumer access to justice' presents a variety of instruments, but emphasises that such access does not always mean access to the courts and that such access may occur by means of ADR. Moreover, the development of ADR is prioritised and promoted by the EU in the field of consumer protection.[28] This is reinforced in the Communication of 4 April 2001,[29] which states that ADR in consumer complaints is the best way to support consumers' claims and the necessary element to ensure the protection of their rights.

Interestingly, Communication 161/2001, and the characteristics of the ADR process, blend two of the central objectives in the expansion of e-commerce: the generation of trust and the promotion of new

[26] The findings that affect ADR are intensification of contacts between different consumer arbitration bodies in order to carry out a mutual exchange on the subject; in this context, it is recommended to further investigate the role of certain bodies (e.g. chambers of commerce and industry) in the creation of voluntary arbitration regimes, sectoral or regional (see the chapters relating to court procedures in Germany, Spain and Portugal).

[27] COM (96) 13 final. Similarly to the Commission Communication of 30 March 1998 on the judicial settlement of consumer disputes COM (1998) 198 final, it pretends to find a standard among the different types of ADR that Member States have created. Major differences can be found, for example, between the Scandinavian ombudsmen and the Spanish consumer arbitration system.

[28] For the different systems: the Study Centre for Consumer Law – Centre for European Economic Law, Katholieke Universiteit Leuven, Belgium, *An Analysis and Evaluation of Alternative Means of Consumer Redress other than Redress through Ordinary Judicial Proceedings: Final report*, 2007, http://ec.europa.eu/consumers/redress/reports_studies/comparative_report_en.pdf. Last accessed, 26 January 2010.

[29] See n. 16 for full references.

technologies. From now on the development of ADR in the EU will proceed along these two axes.[30]

Online dispute resolution: new categories

Consumer ADR is thus the choice promoted by the Commission.[31] In this approach, the EU is especially concerned about cross-border consumer contracts since these constitute the clearest embodiment of the internal market and therefore the prime focus of EU consumer law. The internet offers a radical means by which to promote market integration, requiring the adoption of the new practices of e-commerce alongside alternative methods of dispute resolution. This explains the change from ADRs to ODRs.

Indeed the intersection of ADRs and ODRs has already been remarked in Communication 161/2001 on improving consumer access to alternative dispute resolution mechanisms.[32] Moreover, this Communication underlines the great opportunity to use information technologies in consumer ADR. This intersection shows how dispute resolution systems may play a role in enhancing e-confidence; e-commerce will only grow if consumers have confidence in it. The true value of consumer ODRs lies in the system's efficiency.

[30] Spanish consumer arbitration, as seen in Communication 2001/161, predates the momentum of ADRs by the Community legislature: Law 22/1984 of 19 July, relates to the creation of a dispute resolution system with 'binding and enforceable on both parties'. As noted by C. J. Maluquer de Motes, this mandate, in turn, is within the ambit of Art. 51 EC which calls for the protection of consumers by 'effective procedures' to safeguard their health, safety and the protection of their rights. Finally, RD 636/1993, materialised this issue by opting for a system of institutional arbitration in a process bringing together consecutive phases of mediation and arbitration and, therefore, combines the two processes. This question is even more evident in the new regulation, RD 231/2008, which governs the 'consumer arbitration system', which provides mediation as a first phase of the process (Arts. 37 and 38), but with enough conceptual autonomy, and able to enforce the parties' agreement at any time. See C. J. Maluquer de Motes Bernet, 'Commentary to Art. 1', in J. Guilarte Gutiérrez (ed.), *Comentarios prácticos a la Ley de arbitraje* (Valladolid: Lex Nova, 2004) 224, 56, and C. J. Maluquer de Motes, 'El arbitraje de consumo como instrumento de calidad al servicio del consumidor y del empresario', in C. Florensa Tomas (ed.), *El arbitraje de consumo* (Valencia: Tirant Lo Blanch, 2004).

[31] In this context, Spanish consumer ADR has developed a rather special and effective 'consumer arbitration system' that split the process between mediation and arbitration. Moreover, the system is organised as a part of the public, institutional administration. Furthermore, it should be noted that consumer arbitration is one way, in fact, only resolves consumer disputes with an employer and, moreover, the consumer can only initiate consumer arbitration processes (Arts. 33(1) and 34(1)).

[32] See n. 23 for full reference.

However, despite the best intentions in policy-making, the real thrust of the ODR will depend on the effective development of confidence in e-commerce.[33] Confidence in the operation of the digital environment is the key to integration of the European consumer market and this may prove a key factor that succeeds in binding and expanding the EU economic space.[34]

E-confidence is measured in terms of trust: this will exist only if the consumer fully understands the environment and the advantages of electronic commerce. But besides an appropriate regulatory framework, for example, to the regulation of electronic signatures[35] or the protection of personal data, e-confidence also relies on a responsive system of dispute resolution, to an even greater extent than in offline relationships. The ability to offer consumers tools for resolving disputes that arise in electronic transactions, especially cross-border transactions, is crucial for generating confidence in e-commerce.[36] Only where consumers have access to simple, fast and inexpensive systems of redress will they be prepared to engage in e-commerce. Although DG SANCO has launched many programmes aimed at increasing confidence since 2002,[37] recent

[33] E-confidence is also linked to self-regulation shemes and to governance; new texts after 2004 focus on trustmarks and auto-regulation especially by means of best practices codes. This underlines the need for a simple regulatory framework. Nevertheless, the Commission links ADR/ODR to the general programme of protection of consumers and individual redress. See Commission staff working document, Consumer confidence in e-commerce: lessons learned from the e-confidence initiative, 8 November 2004, SEC (2004) 1390 http://ec.europa.eu/consumers/cons_int/e-commerce/e-conf_working_doc.pdf, last accessed 28 January 2010.

[34] See J. López Sánchez, 'Comercio electrónico y acceso de los consumidores a la Justicia' (2003) *Actualidad Jurídica Aranzadi*, 571, Aranzadi, Pamplona, 203, p. 40. A. Montesinos Garcia, 'El arbitraje de consumo virtual', in L. Cotino Hueso (ed.), *Consumidores y usuarios ante las nuevas tecnologías* (Valencia: Tirant lo Blanch, 2008), 264.

[35] This idea has been supported from the beginning of development of e-commerce in the EU, yet, at first, e-confidence relies on the use of asymmetric cryptographic techniques such as digital signatures: see Communication of 15 April 1997, A European initiative in electronic commerce, COM (1997) 157 final, para. 35. We have worked in the special issue: I. Barral, 'La seguridad en Internet: la firma electrónica', in *La regulación del comercio electrónico* (Madrid, Dykinson, 2003), 83ff.

[36] See Recommendation 98/257/CE, preamble, point 1:

> Whereas the Council, in its conclusions approved by the Consumer Affairs Council of 25 November 1996, emphasised the need to boost consumer confidence in the functioning of the internal market and consumers' scope for taking full advantage of the possibilities offered by the internal market, including the possibility for consumers to settle disputes in an efficient and appropriate manner through out-of-court or other comparable procedures.

[37] Cited above in n. 16.

studies of consumer behaviour in cross-border transactions have shown that perceptions of trust remain low. Therefore, the current strategy for consumer protection 2009–2014 again insists on increasing consumer confidence in the face of these new technological challenges.[38] In short, the development of ODR is no longer a question of consumer access to justice, but the generation of confidence in the new medium.

Nevertheless, as Hörnle underscores, ODR is of added value because it can be adapted to every type of claim.[39] Regarding consumer disputes in e-commerce, the role of ADR is emphasised in two important pieces of regulation: Article 17, Directive 2001/31/EC[40] and the Joint Declaration by the Council and the Commission on the Brussels I Regulation on jurisdiction and the recognition and enforcement of judgments in civil and commercial matters.[41] Both of them spell out the advantages of ODR in e-commerce. On 29 November 2011, the Commission proposed a Regulation on ODR in terms that will bring certainty to this question but cannot be analysed at the time of editing this chapter.[42]

In examining whether an efficient system of ODR has been established we thus turn to analysing two central issues: how consumer redress is currently linked to ODRs; and how the regulatory framework is going to adapt to them.

The ODR in consumer complaints: typology

The concept of ODR emphasises the fact that dispute resolution takes place online. But from this almost tautological statement, there is a wide range of variants. However, most of them can be traced back to the 2001/161 Communication announcing: 'If consumers have more choices

[38] See Communication on EU Consumer Policy Strategy 2007–2013: Empowering consumers, enhancing their welfare, effectively protecting them, 13 March 2007, COM (2007) 99 final. Accessible at http://ec.europa.eu/consumers/overview/cons_policy/doc/EN_99.pdf, last visited 21 January 2010.

[39] J. Hornle, 'Online Dispute Resolution in Business to Consumer E-commerce Transactions' (2002) 2 *JILT*, http://elj.warwick.ac.uk/jilt/02–2/hornle.html. Last accessed 25 February 2010.

[40] Directive 2000/31/EC concerning certain judicial aspects of the services of the information society, and in particular electronic commerce, within the internal market (2000) OJ L 178.

[41] Joint declaration of the Council and the Commission concerning Articles 15 and 73 of the Regulation in the minutes of the Council Meeting of 22 December 2000 which adopted this regulation.

[42] See proposal for a Regulation of the European Parliament and of the Council on online dispute resolution for consumer disputes [2011] L 794/2.

and benefit from greater flexibility, especially with the development of electronic commerce and communications technologies'.[43]

In fact, e-confidence has become the basis of ODR development in the EU and so, the value of consumer ODR lies in the effectiveness of the system. Thus the search for efficiency has made the classic ADR adapt to the online environment.

None the less, ODR cannot be considered simply as an online adaptation of ADR. In fact, ODR can be wider than ADR as the online context also allows cybercourts, which are not seen as an 'alternative' way of resolving disputes.[44] ODR therefore has to be analysed bearing in mind its conceptual autonomy; information and communication technology (ICT) allowing a technical approach that is simply not possible in the offline world. This is why we distinguish below between two concepts: the use of ICT in dispute resolution and the generation of new ODR platforms mediated by technical advances, in particular the advent of interoperability.

Use of ICT in ADR

The first level of ODR is the adaptation of traditional ADRs to the new environment: most visibly in methods of e-arbitration. This is the most formal type of ADR, in which the parties submit to the decision of a third-party arbitrator. The possibility of e-arbitration exists, as do initiatives such as the E-Global ADR Tribunal and e-arbitration-t, where software development has designed online arbitration provided through electronic mail and videoconferencing. The same instruments are used for mediation or negotiation.

These mechanisms increase the ability to resolve disputes between parties by 'electronic means'. In legal terms, this framework requires a dual legal consideration:

- implementation of the provisions derived from the technological processes applied: safety, traceability, confidentiality of data, etc. In this case, the use of electronic signatures allows resolution of the issues of the parties' identities and the integrity of mixed messages on the web. For its part, the enforcement of data protection in electronic communications addresses the most glaring problems of confidentiality;
- implementation of standards related to the specific dispute resolution techniques used.

[43] Communication 2001/161, Introduction para. 2. See n. 23 for full reference.
[44] G. Kaufmann-Kohler and T. Schultz, *Online Dispute Resolution: Challenges for Contemporary Justice* (The Hague: Kluwer Law International, 2004), 5–10.

New forms of ADR

The versatility of new technology means that mediation and negotiation procedures can be offered online together. The emphasis here is on the technical means for developing dialogue between the parties rather than on the intervention of a third party. The first step is normally a negotiation process, but if no result is obtained the next step is to assign a mediator. This is how the Electronic Consumer Dispute Resolution (ECODIR) mediation room works. It also appears in automated business systems such as eBay SquareTrade.

In this environment, ODRs tend to offer technological platforms for dialogue between the parties, with or without third-party intervention, as consecutive procedures. On a legal level this framework calls for three aspects to be considered:

1. those directly connected to the technological processes applied: security, traceability, data protection, etc.;
2. those connected to the specific dispute resolution technique used, i.e. negotiation, mediation, ombudsman. The fact that this concerns ODRs does not exclude the application of whichever specific dispute resolution technique is involved;
3. those deriving from the fact that the online environment makes it easy for the various ADRs to converge in a single technical mechanism, the form of which needs to be analysed so as to provide them with a suitable legal framework.

A particular case: automated negotiation systems

Full automation of the processes of ADR provides the tangible proof of what new technology can do when applied to dispute management on the web. In this case technology is used right from the start in order to design a process equivalent to a traditional ODR, in this case negotiation. Those processes known as 'automatic negotiation systems' are therefore procedures carried out without human intervention. This is the great innovation of ODRs. They are used especially in monetary claims where the only thing in dispute is the amount of compensation the consumer should receive.[45] This involves providing the necessary software to enable the parties to submit sealed offers. When the offers from both parties reach a certain percentage ratio, agreement is established automatically at the average of both. As can be imagined, this system is extremely fast and

[45] The first experience was Cybersettle; see *ibid.*, 17.

inexpensive, although the lack of human intervention may mean that some of the decisions are not the best possible. This is the prime example of the connection between new technology and ODR.

The Green Paper on alternative methods for resolving disputes under civil and commercial law excludes these automated negotiation systems because they lack the crucial characteristic of those ODRs in which a third party participates either as facilitator (mediation) or by imposing a solution (arbitration): impartiality. The 2001 Resolution also excludes 'customer complaint mechanisms operated by a business and concluded directly with the consumer, and such mechanisms carrying out such services operated by or on behalf of a business' (Article 1(2)).

However, the focus of these regulations does not fully take into account the structure of many ODRs. It is, in fact, often a third party who provides this instrument and whose actions are limited to overseeing the negotiations.[46] Indeed, electronic complaint platforms are mechanisms whose purpose is to help the consumer formulate a specific complaint and request the relevant compensation and, therefore, if these complaints are dealt with exclusively by electronic means, this implies the existence of an online law centre. It is this idea that gives them maximum potential when they are offered to deal with e-commerce disputes involving small sums.

In reality this is more a question of offering consumers good after-sales service rather than providing them with a means of resolving disputes, because the party generating the transaction avoids mechanisms that are too complex.

Automated negotiation systems organised by businesses and online complaint centres both clearly lack the impartiality that is usually required when third parties intervene in the dispute resolution process. However, it is clear that when complaints are dealt with appropriately this can enhance e-confidence just as much as mediation procedures.

[46] Green Paper on alternative dispute resolution in civil and commercial law, COM (2002) 196 final, n. 1: excluded from the scope of the document are complaint handling systems made available to consumers by professionals. These procedures are not conducted by third parties, but by one of the parties to the dispute. And 'automated negotiation systems', which do not involve any human intervention, which are offered by providers of IT services. These systems are not dispute resolution procedures conducted by third parties but technical instruments designed to facilitate direct negotiations between the parties to the dispute. Nevertheless, the recent study on ADR types on the different EU countries reserves a chapter to the 'direct negotiation'. See the Study Centre for Consumer Law – Centre for European Economic Law, Katholieke Universiteit Leuven, Belgium, 'An analysis and Evaluation of Alternative Means of Consumer Redress', 44ff.

Therein lies the paradox. ODRs are efficient, speedy and cheap; and such platforms will be successful. In this case a legal framework to regulate ODRs, outside the framework of traditional ADRs, is needed.

Conclusion

E-commerce as a new method of contracting requires an integrated regulatory approach. There are two main aspects which need to be addressed within this regulatory framework: fleshing out the concept of the e-consumer and ensuring the effectiveness of his or her rights through ODR. This approach faces two problems in securing answers to these challenges: the information available during the contracting process and the possibility of seeking redress after a contract is concluded.

For this reason, e-consumers demand a high level of legal protection because the internet has created new types of transactions in which a broader class of consumers is involved – consumers that require information and protection. Only a comprehensive understanding of this problem, of the broader concept of the consumer in e-contract formation, can lead to a fair regulation of mass contracting on the internet.

Moreover, full protection of e-consumers needs to build e-confidence and improve the effectiveness of individual redress by means that are fast, inexpensive and opportune. ODR satisfies these requirements and its development can be seen as a cornerstone in ensuring the effectiveness of e-consumer protection in the EU.

7

Unfair terms and the Draft Common Frame of Reference: the role of non-legislative harmonisation and administrative cooperation?

JAMES DEVENNEY AND MEL KENNY

Introduction

In late 2009 the final version, with notes and commentary, of *Principles, Definitions and Model Rules of European Private Law: Draft Common Frame of Reference* (DCFR) was published.[1] The magnitude of this work is immediately apparent: it is published in six volumes, spanning ten 'books' and includes provisions on general contract,[2] non-contractual obligations,[3] unjustified enrichment[4] and trusts.[5] It also includes provisions in relation to specific contracts such as sales contracts[6] and contracts relating to personal security.[7] The ultimate purpose of the DCFR has been the subject of much controversy,[8] although its authors were keen to stress:

> that what is referred to today as the DCFR originates in an initiative of European legal scholars. It amounts to the compression into rule form of decades of independent research and co-operation by academics with expertise in private law, comparative law and European Community law. The independence of the Groups and of all the contributors has been maintained and respected unreservedly at every stage of the labours ... The Study Group and the Acquis Group alone, however, bear responsibility

The first author is Professor of Commercial Law, University of Exeter; the second is Reader in Commercial Law, University of Leicester.

[1] See C. von Bar and E. Clive, *Principles, Definitions and Model Rules of European Private Law: Draft Common Frame of Reference (DCFR)* (Oxford University Press, 2010).
[2] See, in particular Books II and III. [3] See, for example, Book VI.
[4] See Book VII. [5] See Book X.
[6] See Book IV, Part A. [7] See Book IV, Part G.
[8] See S. Vogenauer, 'Common Frame of Reference and UNIDROIT Principles of International Commercial Contracts: Coexistence, Competition, or Overkill of Soft Law?' (2010) 6 *European Review of Contract Law* 143, at 149.

> for the content of these volumes. In particular, they do not contain a single rule or definition or principle which has been approved or mandated by a politically legitimated body at European or national level (save, of course, where it coincides with existing EU or national legislation). It may be that at a later point in time the DCFR will be carried over at least in part into a CFR, but that is a question for others to decide.[9]

In April 2010 the European Commission set up an Expert Group on a Common Frame of Reference in the area of European contract law,[10] the 'group's task . . . [being]. . . to assist the Commission in the preparation of a proposal for a Common Frame of Reference in the area of European contract law, including consumer and business contract law'.[11] At this point three important observations can be made. First, the DCFR is a hugely significant document in the future direction of EU consumer law. Secondly, it seems that the scope of any Common Frame of Reference (CFR) will be much narrower than that of the DCFR.[12] Thirdly, there is some support for a CFR in the form of an optional instrument although the precise form of such an instrument is still not entirely clear.[13]

This chapter builds on the final point and, through the prism of the unfair terms provisions in the DCFR, considers some of the challenges for a legislative CFR. In particular, it explores the (perhaps supporting) role of non-legislative harmonisation and judicial convergence. It also considers the impact of the procedural environment within which a CFR might operate, and underlines the role of administrative cooperation.

The Draft Common Frame of Reference: a brief overview of the unfair terms provisions

Chapter 9, Book II of the DCFR deals with the policing of 'unfair terms' in three situations: II. – 9:403 deals with unfair terms in contracts between consumers and businesses; II. – 9:404 deals with unfair terms between non-business parties; and II. – 9:405 deals with unfair terms in contracts between businesses. For present purposes we will focus on in II. – 9:403, which provides:

[9] See von Bar and Clive, *Principles, Definitions and Model Rules*, 3.

[10] See Commission Decision 2010/233/EU; [2010] OJ L 105/109.

[11] *Ibid.*, Art. 2. [12] See Vogenauer, 'Common Frame of Reference', 147.

[13] See the web pages connected to the Expert Group: http://ec.europa.eu/justice/policies/consumer/policies_consumer_intro_en.htm.

> In a contract between a business and a consumer, a term [which has not been individually negotiated] is unfair for the purposes of this Section if it is supplied by the business and if it significantly disadvantages the consumer, contrary to good faith and fair dealing.[14]

This test is supplemented by II. – 9:407 and a 'grey list' of unfair terms has been formulated.[15] The effect of a finding that a term is unfair is stated in II. – 9:408:

> (1) A term which is unfair under this Section is not binding on the party who did not supply it.
> (2) If the contract can reasonably be maintained without the unfair term, the other terms remain binding on the parties.

The test of unfairness

As is acknowledged by the authors of the DCFR,[16] this test of an unfair term between a business and a consumer finds some resonance with the test of unfairness in Article 3, Council Directive on Unfair Terms in Consumer Contracts ('the directive').[17] Yet the nature of the test in Article 3 of the Unfair Terms Directive has presented a number of challenges for the harmonisation agenda. In particular, that (minimum harmonisation) directive only sought 'to fix *in a general way* the criteria for assessing the unfair character of contract terms';[18] and the test of unfairness appears to be loaded with social, economic and behavioural norms.[19] Thus, in *Director General of Fair Trading* v. *First National Bank*

[14] In relation to the words in parenthesis, the authors of the DCFR note:

> It is a highly controversial issue whether in business to consumer relations, the 'content control' should only apply to terms which have not been individually negotiated or whether it should also cover individually negotiated terms. In the Acquis Principles prepared by the Acquis Group (which have been used as the model for these rules) the scope of the unfairness test is limited to non-negotiated terms. Thus, strictly speaking, the Acquis Group has only drafted rules on an unfairness test for non-negotiated terms, and has taken no position with regard to an unfairness control of individually negotiated terms. However, the majority of Study Group members wanted to extend this unfairness test to individually negotiated terms. Therefore, in the current version of the Article the words 'which has not been individually negotiated' are put in square brackets.

[15] See II. – 9:410.

[16] See von Bar and Clive, *Principles, Definitions and Model Rules*, 634.

[17] Directive 93/13/EEC [1993] OJ L 95/221. [18] Recital 15 (emphasis added).

[19] See J. Devenney and M. Kenny, 'Unfair Terms, Surety Transactions and European Harmonisation: a Crucible of Europeanised Private Law?' [2009] *Conveyancer and Property Lawyer* 295.

plc,[20] in the context of the predecessor of Regulation 5(1), Unfair Terms in Consumer Contracts Regulations 1999 ('the Regulations'),[21] Lord Bingham famously stated: 'Good faith in this context is not an artificial or technical concept; nor, since Lord Mansfield was its champion, is it a concept wholly unfamiliar to British lawyers. *It looks to good standards of commercial morality and practice*.'[22]

The key point for present purposes is that, as we have argued elsewhere,[23] such a test is built upon social, economic and behavioural norms and there are clear differences in such norms throughout the EU. Thus, as one example, one might refer to the marked differences in the operation of the doctrine of undue influence, in the context of non-professional surety protection, when comparing, on the one hand, the Republic of Ireland with, on the other hand, England and Wales.[24] One might, of course, look for EU jurisprudence on unfairness in relation to contractual terms;[25] yet the signs, as we have already suggested,[26] are far from encouraging.[27] For example, it has been noted that different Member States use:

[20] [2002] UKHL 52.

[21] Regulation 5(1) provides: 'A contractual term which has not been individually negotiated shall be regarded as unfair if, contrary to the requirement of good faith, it causes a significant imbalance in the parties' rights and obligations arising under the contract, to the detriment of the consumer.'

[22] [2002] UKHL 52 at [17].

[23] M. Kenny and J. Devenney, 'The Fallacy of the Common Core: Polycontextualism in Surety Protection: a Hard Case in Harmonisation Discourse', in M. Andenæs and C. Andersen (eds.), *The Theory and Practice of Harmonisation* (forthcoming Edward Elgar Publishing, 2012).

[24] See P. O'Callaghan, 'Protection from Unfair Suretyships in Ireland', in A. Colombi Ciacchi (ed.), *Protection of Non-Professional Sureties in Europe: Formal and Substantive Disparity* (Nomos, 2007); J. Mee, 'Undue Influence and Bank Guarantees' [2002] 37 *Irish Jurist* 292.

[25] In *Director General of Fair Trading* v. *First National Bank plc*, *supra*, Lord Steyn, for example, argued (at [32]) that 'the concepts of the Directive must be given autonomous meanings so that there will be uniform application of the Directive so far as is possible'. Although cf. C. Twigg-Flesner, *The Europeanisation of Contract Law* (London: Routledge-Cavendish, 2008), 124.

[26] See Devenney and Kenny, 'Unfair Terms', 295.

[27] See, for example, the European Commission's Report on Directive 93/13/EEC on unfair terms in Consumer Contracts (COM (2000) 248 final) at 32 rather optimistically noted that: 'An analysis of CLAB shows that already 4.4% of the judgments handed down by national courts in the field covered by the Directive refer to the Community text. At the current stage of European construction this is a figure to be proud of and reflects the progressive impact of Community law on the national legal orders.' At p. 34 it is noted that:

> National courts could have referred many cases to the Court of Justice for a preliminary ruling and it would have been very useful if the judgments of Court of Justice had been able to cast light on the scope of some of the Directive's more

> different benchmarks ... when reviewing contractual terms ... Accordingly, traders cannot use a contractual clause which is valid across the EU, but must instead formulate different clauses for each member state. Hence, considerable obstacles to the functioning of the internal market exist. Providers can only perform pre-formulated contracts across borders with considerable transaction costs.[28]

It is, of course, true that the concept of an unfair term in the DCFR is, to some extent, tighter than under the Unfair Terms Directive: 'The parties may not exclude the application of the provisions in this Section or derogate from or vary their effects';[29] the relationship between the transparency requirements and the test of unfairness has been clarified;[30] there has been some evolution of factors relevant to the unfairness test;[31] and a 'grey list' of unfair terms has been formulated.[32] Nevertheless, the difficulties related to the role of social, economic and cultural norms in individual Member States remains.

The key point for present purposes is that a purely legislative response to harmonisation is likely to be insufficient.[33] More thought needs to

> obscure provisions. Indeed the doctrine reveals the reluctance of the national courts to refer cases to the Court of Justice in this legal field.

See also *Freiburger Kommunalbauten GmbH Baugesellschaft & Co KG* v. *Hofstetter* [2004] ECR-I 3403 at [22] where the ECJ noted that it 'may interpret general criteria used by the Community legislation in order to define the concept of unfair terms. However, it should not rule on the application of these general criteria to a particular term'.

[28] H. Schulte-Nölke, *EC Consumer Law Compendium: Comparative Analysis* (2008) at p. 348, available at: http://ec.europa.eu/consumers/rights/docs/consumer_law_compendium_comparative_analysis_en_final.pdf.

[29] See II. – 9:401. [30] See II. – 9:402.

[31] II. – 9:407 provides:

> (1) When assessing the unfairness of a contractual term for the purposes of this Section, regard is to be had to the duty of transparency under II. – 9:402 (Duty of transparency in terms not individually negotiated), to the nature of what is to be provided under the contract, to the circumstances prevailing during the conclusion of the contract, to the other terms of the contract and to the terms of any other contract on which the contract depends. (2) For the purposes of II. – 9:403 (Meaning of 'unfair' in contracts between a business and a consumer) the circumstances prevailing during the conclusion of the contract include the extent to which the consumer was given a real opportunity to become acquainted with the term before the conclusion of the contract.

[32] See II. – 9:410.

[33] See M. Kenny, J. Devenney and L. Fox O'Mahony, 'Conceptualising Unconscionability in Europe: in the Kaleidoscope of Private and Public Law', in M. Kenny, J. Devenney and L. Fox O'Mahony, *Unconscionability in European Private Financial Transactions: Protecting the Vulnerable* (Cambridge University Press, 2010), 377.

be given to, for example, the place of non-legislative harmonisation;[34] and, in particular, the role of judicial convergence in European private law.[35] This is not to suggest that we should, for example, strive for the harmonisation of social, economic and cultural norms within every Member State. Yet, if, as seems to be a distinct possibility,[36] any CFR will only apply to cross-border transactions, there is an opportunity to, incrementally, develop in this context pan-European concepts of, for example, 'good faith' underpinned by 'EU' norms. Of course, the success of such a project depends on a number of factors, just two of which will be mentioned here. First, it depends upon the willingness, and ability, of the judiciary of individual Member States to participate in such an endeavour; and, at least in England and Wales, the existing record in relation to the interpretation and application of the Regulations is less than encouraging. It is, of course, true that, at times, the courts of England and Wales have taken what seems like a quintessentially EU approach to interpreting the Regulations.[37] Thus in *R. (on the application of Khatun)* v. *Newham LBC*,[38] in the context of the question of whether or not the Regulations applied to land transactions, Laws LJ confidently concluded:

> As for the bite of the various materials . . . I consider that the OFT had the better of the argument. First, Mr Underwood's seemingly strong point on the language – that 'goods and services' does not include land – is effectively demolished by the impact of the other language texts. 'Biens' and its cognates in Italian, Spanish and Portuguese refer to immovables as readily as movables. This alone undercuts a good deal of what Mr Underwood had to say. But more than this: I think, with respect to Mr Underwood, that other aspects of his submissions on this part of the case place an implicit but illegitimate reliance on the large divide in the law of England between real and personal property. He submitted that the Directive should be interpreted as only applying to 'contracts for goods and

[34] See, for example, A. Colombi Ciacchi, 'Non-Legislative Harmonisation of Private Law under the European Constitution: the Case of Unfair Suretyships' [2005] 13 *ERPL* 285. Cf. J. H. M. van Erp, 'European Private Law: Post-modern Dilemmas and Choices' (1999) 3 *Electronic Journal of Comparative Law*, www.gcl.org; A. I. Ogus 'Competition between National Legal Systems: a Contribution of Economic Analysis to Comparative Law' (1999) 48 *ICLQ* 405.

[35] *Ibid.*

[36] See: http://ec.europa.eu/justice/policies/consumer/policies_consumer_intro_en.htm.

[37] See J. Devenney, 'Gordian Knots in Europeanised Private Law: Unfair Terms, Bank Charges and Political Compromises' (2011) 62 *NILQ* 33, at 40.

[38] [2004] EWCA Civ 55.

> services as an English lawyer would understand those terms'. There is plainly no general principle to support such a proposition. Quite the contrary: European legislation has to be read as a single corpus of law binding across the member states. And the proposition leads to absurdity. A licence of land, which transfers no estate, might be covered by the Directive (as the provision of a service), but a lease or tenancy would not. The sale of a fixture, which by English law is treated as part of the land, would be excluded, but the sale of an identical object – say a statue – which was not fixed to the land would be included. In our domestic law these distinctions have a long history and a present utility. In the context of a Europe-wide scheme of consumer protection, they could be nothing but an embarrassing eccentricity.[39]

However, overall, the approach to the interpretation of the Regulations by the courts in England and Wales is rather mixed.[40] Take, for example, the case law in England and Wales on the vexed issue of whether or not the Regulations can apply to non-professional surety transactions.[41] The issue is part of the much wider debate as to whether or not, under the Regulations, the consumer must be the *recipient of goods or services*;[42] more specifically one of the difficulties with applying the Regulations to such transactions is that it is the non-professional surety *who supplies the service* whereas the creditor, as beneficiary of the agreement, will usually be acting in the course of business.[43]

Some support for the view that the Regulations can apply to surety transactions can be located in the Opinion of the European Court of Justice (ECJ) in *Bayerische Hypothetken* v. *Dietzinger.*[44] In that case the Court had to consider the applicability of Council Directive 85/577/EEC (on contracts negotiated away from business premises), which applies where 'a trader supplies goods or services to a consumer',[45] to surety transactions. In a judgment which has generated much discussion[46] the ECJ stated that:

[39] *Ibid.* at [78]. [40] See, generally, Devenney, 'Gordian Knots', 33.

[41] See G. McCormack, 'Protection of Surety Guarantors in England: Prophylactics and Procedure', in Colombi Ciacchi, *Protection of Non-Professional Sureties in Europe*, 172–3.

[42] Cf. H.G. Beale (ed.), *Chitty on Contracts*, 30th edn (London: Sweet & Maxwell, 2008) at para. 15–032.

[43] See also J. O'Donovan and J. Phillips, *The Modern Contract of Guarantee* (London: Sweet & Maxwell, 2003), 223.

[44] Case C-45/96, [1998] ECR I-1199. [45] Art. 1.

[46] See M. Kenny, 'Standing Surety in Europe: Common Core or Tower of Babel' (2007) *MLR* 175 at 180.

> it is apparent from the wording of Article 1 of Directive 85/577 and from the ancillary nature of guarantees that the directive covers only a guarantee ancillary to a contract whereby, in the context of 'doorstep selling', a consumer assumes obligations towards the trader with a view to obtaining goods or services from him. Furthermore, since the directive is designed to protect only consumers, a guarantee comes within the scope of the directive only where, in accordance with the first indent of Article 2, the guarantor has entered into a commitment for a purpose which can be regarded as unconnected with his trade or profession.[47]

The ECJ also noted that nothing in that directive required that 'the person concluding the contract under which goods or services are to be supplied be the person to whom they are supplied'[48] and that surety agreements were merely ancillary to the main contract.[49] The key point, for present purposes, is that *Dietzinger* arguably gives us a glimpse of how the ECJ might approach this issue in the context of the Unfair Terms Directive;[50] and in *Barclays Bank Plc* v. *Kufner*[51] Field J, relying heavily on *Dietzinger*,[52] held that surety transactions were not excluded from the scope of the Regulations.[53] By contrast, and in direct conflict, in *Bank of Scotland* v. *Singh*[54] Judge Kershaw QC, (seemingly) operating closer to the actual wording of the Regulations, held that the Regulations did not apply to surety transactions; and this view has subsequently been described as both 'compelling'[55] and 'convincing'.[56]

The ability to incrementally develop, in the context of a CFR applying to cross-border transactions, pan-European applications of the regulation of unfair terms also seems to require a robust and efficient reference process to the European Court of Justice to act as a compass; yet, it seems that the reference process has not always been perceived to have

[47] Case C-45/96 at [20]. Although cf. *Berliner Kindl Brauerei AG* v. *Andreas Siepert* [2000] ECR 1–1741 at [25]–[26] where the ECJ, in considering Council Directive 87/102/EEC for the approximation of the laws, regulations and administrative provisions of the Member States concerning consumer credit, noted: 'the scope of the Directive cannot be widened to cover contracts of guarantee solely on the ground that such agreements are ancillary to the principal agreement whose performance they underwrite, since there is no support for such an interpretation in the wording of the Directive . . . or in its scheme and aims'.

[48] *Ibid.* at [19]. [49] *Ibid.* at [18].

[50] See Beale, *Chitty on Contracts*, at paras. 44–139. [51] [2008] EWHC 2319 (Comm).

[52] Case C-45/96 [1998] ECR I-1199. [53] At [28].

[54] QBD, unreported, 17 June 2005.

[55] *Manches LLP* v. *Carl Freer* [2006] EWHC 991 at [25] *per* Judge Philip Price QC.

[56] *Williamson* v. *Governor of the Bank of Scotland* [2006] EWHC 1289 at [46] *per* George Bompas QC, sitting as a Deputy Judge.

such qualities.[57] Thus in *Page* v. *Combined Shipping and Trading Co. Ltd*[58] famously Staughton LJ stated:

> We have been shown the French, German and Italian versions all of which use the word 'normal/normale' instead of 'proper'. That does not necessarily mean the same as 'normal' in English; similarities in language can be deceptive. It seems to me, in short, that we ought to conclude that Mr Page has a good arguable case for recovering a substantial sum. It may well be that when this comes to trial we shall have to refer the problem to the European court, and it will take another two years after that before a decision emerges as to what the regulation really means. Maybe the parties will think there are better methods of spending their time and their money than disputing that for a long period of time. But for the present it is enough for us to say, I think, that there is a good arguable case.[59]

Indeed, even when operating with an efficient reference procedure, there still needs to be sufficient judicial engagement with it in order to facilitate (incremental) non-legislative harmonisation of the relevant concepts. Yet, in England and Wales, there seems to have been some reluctance to use the reference procedure in the context of the Regulations. Most recently the Supreme Court in *Office of Fair Trading* v. *Abbey National Plc*[60] refused to refer an issue related to Article 4(2), Unfair Terms Directive, to the European Court of Justice. As is well known, that case concerned the charges levied by banks on personal account holders in respect of unauthorised overdrafts (and related charges);[61] and, more specifically, whether such charges were capable of challenge under the Regulations. It quickly became clear that a key issue related to whether Regulation 6(2) circumscribed any claim that the charges were unfair for the purposes of the Regulations. The existence of Regulation 6(2), of course, can be traced to Article 4(2) of the directive which provides:

> Assessment of the unfair nature of the terms shall relate neither to the definition of the main subject matter of the contract nor to the adequacy of the price and remuneration, on the one hand, as against the services or goods supplies [sic] in exchange, on the other, in so far as these terms are in plain intelligible language.

[57] Cf. C. Turner and R. Munoz, 'Revisiting the Judicial Architecture of the European Union' (1999/2000) 19 *YEL* 1.

[58] [1996] CLC 1952. [59] *Ibid.* at 1956. [60] [2009] UKSC 6.

[61] See, for example, Office of Fair Trading (OFT), *Personal Current Accounts in the UK* (OFT 918, April 2007) at 2, which was followed by, *inter alia*, Office of Fair Trading, *Personal Current Accounts in the UK: a Market Study* (OFT 1005, July 2008).

At first instance,[62] and in the Court of Appeal,[63] it was held (albeit for differing reasons) that Regulation 6(2) did not prevent the relevant charges from being characterised as unfair under the Regulations. Nevertheless a further appeal by the banks was subsequently allowed by the Supreme Court,[64] which held that Regulation 6(2) did circumscribe claims that the charges were unfair for the purposes of the Regulations.

As noted elsewhere,[65] the Supreme Court – when considering Article 4(2) of the directive – was faced with an ambiguous 'compromise' provision in a directive; the purpose(s) of the directive was debatable; the ECJ had not considered the relevant provision; and the provision has been transposed in different ways throughout the EU.[66] In these circumstances it is strongly arguable that an interpretative reference to the ECJ was desirable, and indeed required, in *Abbey*.[67] However the Supreme Court controversially[68] felt that it was unnecessary to make such a reference. At the forefront of this decision was the view of Lord Walker[69] (which was broadly supported by Lord Mance[70] and Lady Hale[71]) that the issue was *acte clair*. Yet, as even Lord Walker came close to acknowledging,[72] such a view is difficult to sustain given the differing views of 'very experienced'[73] judges in the course of this litigation; and, one might add,[74] the views of judges in other cases (and, indeed, in *Abbey* Lord Phillips (supported to some extent by Lord Neuberger[75]) did not find the issue *acte clair*).[76]

An alternative argument was advanced by Lords Walker and Mance for not referring the matter to the ECJ; essentially they argued, with some legitimacy,[77] that the *construction* of Article 4(2) was a matter for EU law whereas its *application* was a matter for domestic law.[78] More specifically, they argued that *even if* the Court of Appeal construed Article 4(2) correctly, it was incorrect in its application of that construction to the facts.[79] Accordingly, so the argument went, the correct interpretation of Article 4(2) was not key to the determination of the

[62] [2008] EWHC 875 (Comm). [63] [2009] EWCA Civ 116. [64] [2009] UKSC 6.
[65] Devenney, 'Gordian Knots', 33.
[66] Schulte-Nölke, *EC Consumer Law Compendium*, 345.
[67] Cf. P. Davies, 'Bank Charges in the Supreme Court' (2010) 69 *CLJ* 21, at 23.
[68] *Ibid.* [69] At [48]–[50]. [70] At [115]–[117].
[71] At [92]. [72] At [49]. [73] *Ibid.*
[74] See Devenney, 'Gordian Knots', 33. [75] At [120]. [76] At [91].
[77] Cf. *Freiburger Kommunalbauten GmbH Baugesellschaft & Co. KG* v. *Ludger Hofstetter and Ulrike Hofstetter* [2004] ECR-I 3403 at [22] where the ECJ noted that it 'may interpret general criteria used by the Community legislation in order to define the concept of unfair terms. However, it should not rule on the application of these general criteria to a particular term.'
[78] At [50] and [116] respectively. [79] *Ibid.*

appeal and, therefore, a reference to the ECJ would not be necessary. Such reasoning is, of course, not without merit; but it is not clear that this reasoning entirely separates questions of law from questions of fact. More specifically, the conclusion that the Court of Appeal wrongly applied their interpretation of Article 4(2) is dependent on a *particular view* of the core/ancillary terms dichotomy which, surely, is partly a question of law.[80]

Yet, whatever the 'formal' reasons for refusing to refer to the ECJ it seems that there were wider factors at play.[81] First, the Supreme Court seemed concerned by the delay which a reference might entail,[82] again underlining the need for a robust and efficient reference process. Secondly, and arguably more importantly, as noted elsewhere,[83] the Supreme Court ruled on the *Abbey* appeal in the immediate aftermath of the banking crisis; and one does not have to be a conspiracy theorist to wonder whether or not a (perhaps perceived) vulnerability on the part of banks[84] (and the associated impact on the economy)[85] in any way affected (not necessarily illegitimately) the Supreme Court's ruling in *Abbey*.[86] For example, Lord Walker noted that in one year (2006) the banks made approximately £2.56 billion from these charges[87] (which equated to approximately one-third of the revenue made on current accounts);[88] and 'many thousands'[89] of cases against banks on this issue were stayed in the county courts pending a decision in *Abbey* when, presumably, the limitation clock would only begin to tick once the Supreme Court delivered its judgment![90]

[80] See Devenney, 'Gordian Knots', 51. [81] *Ibid.*
[82] See, for example, at [50] *per* Lord Walker (with whom Lady Hale and Lord Neuberger agreed).
[83] J. Devenney, 'Gordian Knots', 33.
[84] See Kenny *et al.*, 'Conceptualising Unconscionability in Europe', 377 at 378.
[85] Cf. M. Chen Wishart, 'Transparency and Fairness in Bank Charges' (2010) 126 *LQR* 157 at 158.
[86] *Ibid.* [87] At [36]. [88] At [47].
[89] *Office of Fair Trading* v. *Abbey National plc* [2009] UKSC 6 at [17] *per* Lord Walker.
[90] See Limitation Act 1980, s. 32(1) and *Kleinwort Benson Ltd* v. *Lincoln CC* [1999] 2 AC 349. Indeed one is reminded of the words of Lord Browne-Wilkinson in *Kleinwort Benson Ltd* v. *Lincoln CC* [1999] 2 AC 349 at 363:

> Much commercial . . . activity occurs on the basis of law which is not laid down by judicial decision. Such 'law' consists of the practice and understanding of lawyers skilled in the field. If, before payment, the payer had sought advice in some cases he would have been told that the law was dubious: if having received such advice he paid over, he must have taken the risk that the law was otherwise and cannot subsequently recover what he has paid. In other cases, he would have been told that the law was clear and he could safely act on it. If in this latter case the payer

Of course the Supreme Court was careful not to state that the charges in question could *never* be challenged under the Regulations:

> I do not believe any challenge to the fairness of the Relevant Terms has been made on the basis that they cause the overall package of remuneration paid by those in debit to be excessive having regard to the package of services received in exchange. In these circumstances the basis on which I have answered the narrow issue would seem to render that issue academic. It may be that, if and when the OFT challenges the fairness of the Relevant Terms, issues will be raised that ought to be referred to Luxembourg. That stage has not yet been reached.[91]

Yet any such challenge would probably, in some way, need to challenge the type of cross-subsidy which banks employ in the United Kingdom's largely 'free if in credit' banking system; and it is submitted that it would be a brave court that would categorise such an ingrained system as 'unfair'. The key point is, again, that social, cultural and economic norms affect the application and development of concepts such as unfairness.

Law and interfaces

A related point relates to law and interfaces. We have already noted[92] that the coverage of any CFR is likely to be significantly less comprehensive

> acted on the law as so advised and subsequently a court held that the law was not as advised, can the payer recover his payment as moneys paid under a mistake of law? In the ordinary case, the payer's adviser will just have given wrong legal advice: as a result the payment will have been paid under a mistake of law and will be recoverable. But in a limited number of cases, of which this may be one, it is not really possible to say that the legal adviser made a mistake in advising as he did ... It used to be said that the practice of conveyancers of repute was strong evidence of real property law: see *In re Hollis' Hospital Trustees and Hague's Contract* [1899] 2 Ch. 540, 551 ... [and] Denning L.J. said in *In re Downshire Settled Estates; Marquess of Downshire v. Royal Bank of Scotland* [1953] Ch. 218, 279: 'The practice of the profession in these cases is the best evidence of what the law is; indeed, it makes law.' ... I doubt whether today anyone would claim that a uniform practice of the profession makes the law. But in the present context it does have a significant impact. In holding that money paid under a mistake of law is recoverable, an essential factor is that the retention of the money so paid would constitute an unjust enrichment of the payee ... If, at the date of payment, it was settled law that payment was legally due, I can see nothing unjust in permitting the payee to retain moneys he received at a time when all lawyers skilled in the field would have advised that he was entitled to receive them and the payer was bound to pay them.

[91] See [91] *per* Lord Phillips. [92] See above at 100.

than the DCFR. It is not the purpose of this chapter to argue that any CFR should be as, or even more, comprehensive than the DCFR; nevertheless it seems clear to us that the interface between any CFR and existing domestic/EU law presents challenges for any harmonisation agenda. There would seem to be, at least, two relevant considerations. First, background (non-harmonised) rules may impact on the test of unfairness. Indeed the European Commission has noted that:

> the application of the same general criterion in two Member States may give rise to very different decisions, as a result of the divergences between the rules of substantive law that apply to different contracts. Hence harmonisation under the Directive is more apparent than real.[93]

Thus, and for example, in *Director General of Fair Trading* v. *First National Bank plc* the House of Lords – in considering a credit agreement term which provided that interest, at the contractual rate, would continue to accrue 'after as well as before any judgment (such obligation to be independent of and not to merge with the judgment)' – held that the term was not unfair on the ground, *inter alia*, that the problem related to the relevant background legislation. By contrast, in *UK Housing Alliance (North West) Ltd* v. *Francis*[94] the protection that could be offered by a court in possession proceedings contributed to a finding that a term in a sale and leaseback arrangement was not unfair under the Regulations. The key point, again, is that there is a need to incrementally develop EU conceptions of fairness in any CFR applicable to cross-border transactions. This is not to argue that there should be a much more extensive harmonisation of the area including relevant background rules; yet there is a need to unpack, and find consensus, on the type of characteristics of 'background' rules which contribute to a finding that a particular term is either 'fair' or 'unfair'.

The second point we wish to make about the interface between any CFR and existing domestic/EU law relates to legal fragmentation (especially as it seems that any CFR will not cover all legal aspects of cross-border transactions).[95] Essentially we would argue that judges play an important

[93] Report on Directive 93/13/EEC on unfair terms in Consumer Contracts (COM (2000) 248 final) at 30.

[94] [2010] EWCA Civ 117.

[95] See above at 100; B. Markesinis, 'Why a Code is Not the Best Way to Advance the Cause of European Legal Unity' (1997) 5 *ERPL* 519–24; P. Legrand, 'European Legal Systems are Not Converging' (1997) 45 *ICLQ* 52; P. Legrand, 'Against a European Civil Code' (1997) 60 *MLR* 44; P. Legrand, 'The Impossibility of Legal Transplants' (2003) 4 *Maastricht Journal of European and Comparative Law* 111, and most spectacularly P. Legrand,

role in minimising such fragmentation and in developing the resulting (combined) law in a coherent manner.[96] This is, perhaps, one of the regrettable aspects about the recent case of *RÖHLIG (UK) Ltd* v. *Rock Unique Ltd*[97] where Moore-Bick LJ stated:[98]

> Mr. Bompas submitted that when making his findings about the requirement of reasonableness the judge should have had regard to the provisions of the Unfair Terms in Consumer Contracts Regulations 1999 ('the 1999 Regulations') in order to ensure harmony between the two sets of legislative requirements. For that purpose he sought to place particular reliance on paragraphs (b) and (q) of Schedule 2 to the Regulations, which identify as terms that may be considered unreasonable clauses that inappropriately exclude or limit the customer's legal rights (including rights of set-off) or which exclude the right to take legal action or exercise other legal remedies . . . The 1999 Regulations were made to implement Directive 93/13/EEC, which is concerned with unfair terms in consumer contracts. A 'consumer' is defined for these purposes as a natural person acting for purposes outside his trade, business or profession. The scope of the 1999 Regulations is therefore narrower in some respects than that of the Unfair Contract Terms Act, which in many cases applies to business contracts as well as consumer contracts, but the principles that are to be applied are broadly the same: in each case it is necessary to judge the reasonableness of the term in question at the time the contract is made by reference to all the surrounding circumstances. I doubt very much whether the extended list of terms that may be regarded as unfair which is set out in schedule 2 to the Regulations adds much of substance to schedule 2 to the 1977 Act. Indeed, as one can see from *Granville Oil* v. *Davis Turner*, in a case such as the present the court will consider the effect on the parties' interests of terms such as clauses 21(A) and 27(B) when deciding whether they satisfy the requirement of reasonableness. In my view no assistance is to be gained in the present case from the 1999 Regulations.

A multidimensional view of consumer protection

It is clear that an effective evaluation of the control of standard terms in any system of law requires a holistic approach. In other words, it is necessary to consider not only those substantive provisions aimed

'Antivonbar' (2006) 1 *Journal of Comparative Law* 1; M. W. Hesselink, 'The Politics of European Contract Law: Who has an Interest in What Kind of Contract Law for Europe?' (2002) 2 *Global Jurist Frontiers*; and, generally, on legal pluralism: G. Teubner, 'The Two Faces of Janus: Rethinking Legal Pluralism' (1992) 13 *Cardozo Law Review* 1443 at 1445–8.

[96] See M. Kenny, 'Orchestrating Sub-Prime Consumer Protection in Retail Banking: Abbey National in the Context of Europeanised Private Law' (2011) 43 *European Review of Private Law* 43 at 68–9.

[97] [2011] EWCA Civ 18. [98] At [24]–[25].

directly at the policing of such terms but also of any substantive provisions which may indirectly police such terms. The point can be illustrated with reference to suretyship contracts.[99] As is well known a surety usually assumes secondary[100] and accessory liability.[101] It is also well established that a surety may be discharged from liability in certain situations:[102] for example, the creditor in a suretyship arrangement is under an equitable duty not to release any security held in respect of the principal debt;[103] prima facie the surety will be discharged if the creditor does so.[104] As a result it is commonplace[105] to find a term in suretyship agreements which purports to allow creditors to release such securities.[106] However, as we have seen, it remains a vexed question whether such terms, and indeed others, are subject to the controls found in the Unfair Terms in Consumer Contracts Regulations 1999. Yet, putting to one side the Regulations, it is clear that standard terms in contracts of suretyship are, to some extent, controlled through other mechanisms: perhaps through disclosure requirements,[107] interpretative techniques,[108] formalities[109] and even the doctrine of undue

[99] See J. Devenney, L. Fox-O'Mahony and M. Kenny, 'Standing Surety in England and Wales: the Sphinx of Procedural Protection' [2008] *Lloyds Maritime and Commercial Law Quarterly* 527.

[100] See J. Devenney, 'Aspects of Property, Security and Guarantees', in M. Furmston and J. Chuah (eds.), *Commercial and Consumer Law* (London: Pearson Publishing, 2010) at 24.

[101] *Ibid.* [102] *Ibid.*

[103] See, for example, *Skipton Building Society Ltd* v. *Stott* [2001] QB 261.

[104] See *Re Darwen & Pearce* [1927] 1 Ch. 176, but cf. *Carter* v. *White* (1883) 25 Ch. D 666.

[105] See *Barclays Bank plc Kufner* [2008] EWHC 2319 (Comm) at [16].

[106] See McCormack, 'Protection of Surety Guarantors in England', 172–73.

[107] See, for example, *London General Omnibus Co. Ltd* v. *Holloway* [1912] 2 KB 72, *Levett* v. *Barclays Bank plc* [1995] 1 WLR 1260, *Crédit Lyonnais Bank Nederland* v. *Export Credit Guarantee Department* [1996] 1 *Lloyd's Rep* 200, and *Royal Bank of Scotland* v. *Etridge (No. 2)* [2001] UKHL 44.

[108] Traditionally, for example, the English courts strictly interpreted terms which sought to exclude a surety's right to be discharged in circumstances where a surety would normally be discharged: see *Trafalgar House Construction (Regions) Ltd* v. *General Surety & Guarantee Co. Ltd* [1996] 1 AC 199. Of course the Courts now need to consider the impact of more 'modern' approaches to the interpretation of contracts as set out in, for example, *Investors Compensation Scheme Ltd* v. *West Bromwich Building Society* [1998] 1 WLR 896. Nevertheless, in *Liberty Mutual Insurance Co. (UK) Ltd* v. *HSBC Bank plc* [2002] EWCA Civ 691 at [56] Rix LJ argued that: 'the reasonable man does not expect fundamental principles of law, equity and justice, such as rights of set-off or of subrogation to be excluded unless the contract clearly says so'.

[109] In *J. Pereira Fernandes SA* v. *Mehta* [2006] EWHC 813 (Ch) at [16] Judge Pelling QC expressed the view that the purpose of such provisions 'is to protect people from being held liable on informal communications because they may be made without sufficient

influence.[110] Indeed we have also argued that insolvency provisions can affect the scope and effectiveness of standard-term regulation.[111] The key point for present purposes is that the substantive control of standard terms may be multidimensional and it is, therefore, necessary to review the cumulative effect of the provisions of the DCFR on the control of such terms.

Indeed surety transactions[112] illustrate another, wider point. Surety transactions are polycontextual in nature; they transcend traditional legal boundaries. Therefore, the protection of non-professional sureties may be located in different areas of law. Indeed, while most EU Member States have sought to increase the protection afforded to non-professional sureties there is marked diversity in the nature of the protection so afforded.[113] More specifically, as we have argued elsewhere, the protection afforded to non-professional sureties in individual Member States often involves different complex, context-specific orchestrations of various legal fields, concepts and mechanisms including, for example, (aspects of) contract law, consumer law, family law, property law and (even) constitutional law.[114] Thus to focus, solely by way of vertical legislative harmonisation measures, on particular aspects of those orchestrations may have different consequences in different Member States. Indeed it may even result in suretyship transactions becoming less attractive to banks[115] and an associated narrowing in access to credit.[116]

consideration or expressed ambiguously or because such communication might be fraudulently alleged against the party to be charged'.

[110] See *Dunbar Bank plc* v. *Nadeem* [1998] 3 All ER 876 discussed in Devenney *et al.*, 'Protection of Non-Professional Sureties', 156–7.

[111] See M. Kenny and Devenney, 'The Fallacy of the Common Core'.

[112] Cf. 105 above.

[113] See A. Colombi Ciacchi, 'Non-legislative Harmonisation of Private Law under the European Constitution: the Case of Unfair Suretyships' (2005) 13 *European Review of Private Law* 297.

[114] Kenny and Devenney, 'The Fallacy of the Common Core'.

[115] See M. Kenny, 'Standing Surety in Europe: Common Core or Tower of Babel' (2007) *MLR* 175 at 195–6.

[116] In *Royal Bank of Scotland* v. *Etridge (No. 2)* [2001] UKHL 44 at [34]–[35] Lord Nicholls reflected on the importance of such transactions:

> The problem considered in O'Brien's case and raised by the present appeals is of comparatively recent origin. It arises out of the substantial growth in home ownership over the last 30 or 40 years and, as part of that development, the great increase in the number of homes owned jointly by husbands and wives. More than two-thirds of householders in the United Kingdom now own their own homes. For most home-owning couples, their homes are their most valuable asset. They must surely be free, if they so wish, to use this asset as a means of raising money, whether for the purpose of the husband's business or for any

The key point is the vital role which non-legislative, incremental judicial harmonisation will play; and the emphasis will again be on judges to minimise fragmentation, and possibly unevenness in protection, when developing the resulting (combined) law in a coherent manner.

Effective enforcement

As noted above, an effective evaluation of the control of standard terms in any system of law requires a holistic approach to reviewing substantive provisions. Yet the cumulative effect of substantive provisions is only one part of the picture; procedural provisions also affect the shape, and effectiveness of, the control of such terms.[117] For example, the extent to which collective proceedings are available is an example of how procedural law may affect the nature of any substantive regulation of standard terms.[118] Of course the justifications for collective proceedings as a means of controlling the use of standard terms is, certainly in the consumer sphere, well rehearsed:[119] more specifically, many consumers may not have the information, resources and/or inclination to challenge

other purpose. Their home is their property. The law should not restrict them in the use they may make of it. Bank finance is in fact by far the most important source of external capital for small businesses with fewer than ten employees. These businesses comprise about 95 percent of all businesses in the country, responsible for nearly one-third of all employment. Finance raised by second mortgages on the principal's home is a significant source of capital for the start-up of small businesses. If the freedom of home-owners to make economic use of their homes is not to be frustrated, a bank must be able to have confidence that a wife's signature of the necessary guarantee and charge will be as binding upon her as is the signature of anyone else on documents which he or she may sign. Otherwise banks will not be willing to lend money on the security of a jointly owned house or flat.

[117] For an interesting historical account of the impact of procedural law on an area of substantive law see W. Swain, 'Usury and the Judicial Regulation of Financial Transactions in Seventeenth and Eighteenth Century England', in Kenny *et al.*, *Unconscionability in European Private Financial Transactions.*

[118] See T. Pfeiffer and J. Devenney, 'Control of Standard Terms (Collective Proceedings)', in G. Dannemann and S. Vogenauer, *The Common Frame of Reference for European Contract Law and its Interaction with English and German Law* [working title] (in preparation, Oxford University Press).

[119] See H. Beale, 'Legislative Control of Fairness: the Directive on Unfair Terms in Consumer Contracts', in J. Beatson and D. Friedmann (eds.), *Good Faith and Fault in Contract Law* (Oxford: Clarendon Press, 1995), 251.

'unfair' standard terms in the courts;[120] and, indeed, the seller or supplier may seek to settle out of court before, from their perspective, an unwelcome precedent is established.[121] Such concerns, of course, were reflected in Article 7 of the EC Council Directive on Unfair Terms in Consumer Contracts:

> Member States shall ensure that, in the interests of consumers and of competitors, adequate and effective means exist to prevent the continued use of unfair terms in contracts concluded with consumers by sellers or suppliers . . . The means . . . shall include provisions whereby persons or organizations, having a legitimate interest under national law in protecting consumers, may take action according to the national law concerned before the courts or before competent administrative bodies for a decision as to whether contractual terms drawn up for general use are unfair, so that they can apply appropriate and effective means to prevent the continued use of such terms.[122]

On the other hand, Goldberg notes that '[N]ot all consumers will benefit equally from the agent's efforts. Indeed, in most instances some consumers are likely to be worse off, receiving protection from a clause that affected them little or not at all in exchange for a higher price.'[123]

The DCFR makes no provision for collective proceedings in respect of 'unfair' terms. Some may have viewed this with concern: indeed we have already suggested that the effective substantive regulation of 'unfair' terms may be undermined by an insufficient procedural infrastructure; and this could, *inter alia*, be a significant obstacle in the political battle to

[120] See, for example, European Commission, Report from the Commission on the Implementation of Council Directive 93/13 EEC of 5 April 1993 on Unfair Terms in Consumer Contracts (COM (2000) 248 final).

[121] See A. Leff, 'Unconscionability and the Crowd: Consumers and the Common Law Tradition' (1970) 31 *University of Pittsburgh Law Review* 349, at 356–7.

[122] In *Océano Group Editorial SA* v. *Murciano Quintero* C-244/98 to C-244/98 the ECJ used, at [26]–[28], Art. 7 as part of its justification for the view that national courts could unilaterally raise the issue of unfairness:

> the court's power to determine of its own motion whether a term is unfair must be regarded as constituting a proper means both of achieving the result sought by Article 6 of the Directive, namely, preventing an individual consumer from being bound by an unfair term, and of contributing to achieving the aim of Article 7, since if the court undertakes such an examination, that may act as a deterrent and contribute to preventing unfair terms in contracts concluded between consumers and sellers or suppliers.

[123] V. Goldberg, 'Institutional Change and the Quasi-Invisible Hand' (1974) 17 *JL & Econ* 461, at 489.

gain support for the DCFR/CFR from, for example, consumer interest bodies. Indeed, II. – 9:401, which states that '[t]he parties may not exclude the application of the provisions in this Section or derogate from or vary their effects', *might* be taken as excluding such proceedings altogether. On the other hand, the provisions on unfair terms in the DCFR could relatively easily be tied in with existing EU provisions on collective proceedings, injunctions, etc.; and there are a number of signs that it was not the intention of DCFR to exclude collective proceedings. First, the commentary to II.-9:408, makes reference to the decision of the ECJ in *Océano Group Editorial SA* v. *Murciano Quintero*[124] and it is stated that:

> a consumer has to be protected, even if he ... fails to raise the unfair nature of the term, either because unaware of available rights or because deterred from enforcing them. Therefore, if the consumer does not take an explicit decision as to whether to be bound to the term or not, courts have to decide on their own accord about the consequences of unfairness.

This passage seems to accept that the effectiveness of the provisions contained therein may be undermined if, for example, too much emphasis is placed on the consumer challenging the term(s) in question. Secondly, the commentary to II. – 9:406 makes a brief reference to collective proceedings: 'In the case of terms which are insufficiently transparent, an informed market decision has not been made so that it is appropriate to apply judicial control. Furthermore, there is an interest to eliminate terms lacking transparency in collective proceedings.' Thus we would argue that II. – 9:401 does not exclude the possibility of collective proceedings and that would seem to accord with the desire of the Commission in other areas;[125] and, therefore, the provisions of the

[124] C-244/98 to C-244/98.

[125] For example, Art. 38 of the (original) proposed Consumer Rights Directive provided:

> Member States shall ensure that, in the interests of consumers and competitors, adequate and effective means exist to prevent the continued use of unfair terms in contracts concluded with consumers by traders ... In particular, persons or organisations, having a legitimate interest under national law in protecting consumers, may take action before the courts or administrative authorities for a decision as to whether contract terms drawn up for general use are unfair ... Member States shall enable the courts or administrative authorities to apply appropriate and effective means to prevent traders from continuing to use terms which have been found unfair ... Member States shall ensure that the legal actions referred to in paragraph 2 and 3 may be directed either separately or jointly depending on national procedural laws against a number of traders from

DCFR should be read alongside existing EU provision on collective proceedings, injunctions, etc.

Yet the existing EU collective proceedings and injunctions regime in this area is not without problem; it is important to highlight some issues with this regime, some of which underline the need for greater cooperation, and (to an extent) ensuring consistency, in quasi-judicial regulation of 'unfair' terms.[126] We will limit ourselves to three points. First, particularly in the consumer arena, collective proceedings (or the threat thereof) may be the main battleground in relation to 'unfair' terms.[127] Nevertheless, in the light of the fairly general tenor of Article 7, this presents risks for any harmonisation agenda, and a case can be made for further unpacking of the collective proceedings regime(s) necessary to support, for example, the objectives of the directive.[128] Secondly, collective proceedings in respect of standard terms often require 'an abstract review'[129] of the relevant term(s).[130] This may require, for example, the use of the notion of a 'typical consumer'.[131] Conceptions of the 'typical consumer' and of issues such as vulnerability may, of course, vary[132] and the directive provides little guidance on this issue.[133] The key point is that conceptions of a 'typical consumer', etc. may, to some extent, shape the substantive regulation of standard terms.[134] Thirdly, given the foregoing and the chameleon-like rationalisations of EU legislation in the consumer arena (establishing an internal market, preventing the distortion of competition promoting consumer confidence, etc.),[135] there is a real risk of differences between the enforcement practices of bodies empowered to bring collective proceedings under (the transpositions of) Article 7; and this may result in an unevenness of protection across the EU.[136] In short a case can be made for, *inter alia*,

the same economic sector or their associations which use or recommend the use of the same general contract terms or similar terms.

[126] See Pfeiffer and Devenney, 'Control of Standard Terms'.

[127] See, for example, C. Willett, *Fairness in Consumer Contracts: the Case of Unfair Terms* (Ashgate, 2007), 173–4.

[128] Cf. Schulte-Nölke, *EC Consumer Law Compendium*, 343.

[129] I. Ramsay, *Consumer Law and Policy*, 2nd edn, (Oxford: Hart Publishing, 2007) at p. 195.

[130] *Ibid.*

[131] See, for example, *Office of Fair Trading* v. *Foxtons Ltd* [2009] EWCA Civ 288.

[132] See generally Kenny *et al.*, 'Conceptualising Unconscionability in Europe', 377.

[133] Cf. Consumer Protection from Unfair Trading Regulations 2008, Regulation 2(2)–(6).

[134] See, for example, The Law Commission of England and Wales, *Unfair Terms in Contracts: a Consultation Paper* (no. 119) at 3.63.

[135] See Devenney, 'Gordian Knots', 33.

[136] *Ibid.*

greater coordination, and cooperation, of the enforcement activities of such bodies across the EU.[137]

Conclusions

The DCFR is a hugely significant document in the future direction of EU consumer law.[138] Yet, towards the end of the Introduction, the editors note that:

> It is still unclear whether or not the CFR, or parts of it, might at a later stage be used as the basis for one or more optional instruments, i.e. as the basis for an additional set of legal rules which parties might choose to govern their mutual rights and obligations. In the view of the two Groups such an optional instrument would open attractive perspectives, not least for consumer transactions.[139]

As noted above, there is, it seems, at least some support for a CFR in the form of an optional instrument although the precise form of such an instrument is still not entirely clear. Moreover it seems that any such instrument would be much narrower in scope than the DCFR. The purpose of this chapter has not been to discuss either of these two (possible) outcomes; rather the purpose of this chapter has been to explore some of the challenges for a *legislative* CFR through the prism of its provisions relating to unfair terms. In particular, it has been argued

[137] Cf. the the EC Directive on Injunctions for the Protection of Consumers' Interests ([1998] OJ. L 166/51 – see now Directive 2009/22/EC of the European Parliament and of the Council of 23 April 2009 on Injunctions for the Protection of Consumers' Interests (Codified Version)) and Regulation 2006/2004 on Cooperation Between National Authorities Responsible for the Enforcement of Consumer Protection Laws. Yet, perhaps unsurprisingly, the emphasis in, for example, Regulation 2006/2004 appears to be on mechanisms for pan-European enforcement rather than, for example, the need to develop a jurisprudence on quasi-judicial unfair terms regulation: see, for example, Art. 1, Regulation 2006/2004 but cf. for example Art. 16(2):

> The competent authorities may exchange competent officials in order to improve cooperation. The competent authorities shall take the necessary measures to enable exchanged competent officials to play an effective part in activities of the competent authority. To this end such officials shall be authorised to carry out the duties entrusted to them by the host competent authority in accordance with the laws of its Member State.

[138] See European Commission, Green Paper from the Commission on policy options for progress towards a European Contract Law for consumers and businesses, COM (2010) 348 final.

[139] See von Bar and Clive, *Principles, Definitions and Model Rules*, 23.

that the extent of the success of any such endeavour will be shaped by two key factors: the supporting role played by non-legislative harmonisation and judicial convergence; and the procedural environment – and more specifically the (cooperative) administrative infrastructure – within which a CFR might operate. We hope that these factors will be given due consideration as we move from a DCFR to a (possible) CFR.

POSTSCRIPT

On 11 October 2011 the European Commission published a proposal for an optional instrument on Sales Law (the Common European Sales Law (Com (2011) 635 final)) and on 25 October 2011 Directive 2011/83/EU on Consumer Rights was adopted. See further p. 20 above.

PART II

Conceptualising vulnerability

8

The definition of consumers in EU consumer law

BASTIAN SCHÜLLER

With the dawn of a new Consumer Rights Directive and the approach of full harmonisation, it is time to discuss the definitions within the upcoming framework. At the core of consumer law lies the legal definition of consumers; prima facie a very trivial and unproblematic legal definition for the scope of consumer law. But given the pace of merging EU consumer directives, each aspect must be discussed. The chapter discusses the limitation within the legal definition of a 'consumer' as a natural person. This politically laden limitation is normally a minor point of interest in analysing the draft, but under closer scrutiny, this limitation causes major incoherences within the EU consumer law approach.

This chapter discusses, in the first section, the problems for the legal definition of the consumer caused by the clash of different legal rationales. We can divide the EU consumer law approach into an 'economic' and a more recent 'political' rationale. Whereas the first is in line with the standard judicial definition of consumers as natural persons (by reference to the same basic assumptions as those underlying contract law), the second expands consumer law to the sphere of citizenship.

The second part discusses the compatibility of the normative legal definition of 'consumer' with the insights of other scientific fields into consumer behaviour. It challenges the method of defining a consumer as a natural person given that the actual act of buying consumer goods alone defines the consumer. Consumers are not defined by their nature, but by their acts and behaviour. The need for protection results from the specific situation and the specific behaviour involved in the sale of consumer goods. Focusing on the act as the key to defining consumers, the last part of the chapter discusses the possible advantages of using behavioural studies of consumers as the main source of inspiration for a deeper rationale of EC consumer law.

Institute of Private Law, Oslo University.

EU consumer definition

The current EU consumer legislation has no uniform definition of consumers;[1] the actual wording varies from directive to directive but they all share a common core,[2] that a consumer is:

- a natural person,
- who is acting for purposes which are outside his business, trade or profession.

This chapter is mostly about the first part of the definition, the consumer as a natural person. But a look at the different consumer definitions among European countries shows that there is plenty of variation in the way a consumer is legally defined. The definition ranges, in the area affected by the draft, from including legal persons to a very strict understanding of natural persons. In Denmark, for example, the definition of consumers in consumer sales (*Forbrugerkøbloven*) refers only to the kind of act, whereas Norway[3] has implemented the directives strictly in line with their wording. This fragmentation of the consumer definition will come to an end with the maximum harmonising approach of the EU. But quite aside from the different legal definitions of consumers, different national interpretations of a natural person will remain. The legal concepts of natural and legal persons in contract law depend on the legal system; some legal systems interpret 'natural person' more broadly than others. And there is no uniform definition or interpretation of a natural person at the EU level.

EU consumer law approach

The question then is why the consumer is still defined as a natural person in the new draft if it is highly probable that this will not lead to the desired harmonisation? This chapter states that, above and beyond judicial reasoning, there are political reasons behind recent development

[1] The recent proposal COM (2008) 614/3 final combines the Directives 2005/29/EC, 85/577/EC, 97/7/EC, and 99/44/EC in order to, *inter alia*, standardise the wording of the legal definitions.

[2] Directive 90/314 contains a very different definition of consumer: a consumer is a person 'who takes or agrees to take the package ("the principal contractor"), or any person on whose behalf the principal contractor agrees to purchase the package ("the other beneficiaries") or any person to whom the principal contractor or any other beneficiaries transfers the package ("the transferee")'.

[3] Norway, as an EFTA member, also implements the EU consumer directives.

of EU consumer law. The Commission is trying to reconnect the European Union, via consumer law, to its 'citizens'. There is a danger then that the Commission may accept certain incoherences and gaps in the consumer protection regime in order to achieve these ends.

The narrow consumer definition can be justified on two grounds: judicial grounds and political grounds.

The judicial argument

In *Idealservice*[4] the European Court of Justice (ECJ) stated clearly that, following the wording of Article 2 of the Directive 93/13 on unfair contract terms in consumer contracts, only natural persons could be consumers. The Court's decision is in line with the Commission's opinion that the term consumer relates exclusively to natural persons.[5] This opinion seems to be confirmed in *Océano*[6] where the ECJ noted that the system of protection is based on the idea that the consumer is in a weak position *vis-à-vis* the seller as regards his bargaining power and his level of knowledge. The idea of protection must be seen as an exception to contractual freedom and must be strictly interpreted. Therefore, only a specific category of person should be granted protection as the weaker party, here the consumer, who is acting for purposes which are outside his trade, business or profession. Legal persons and companies are not seen as weaker parties, because they are deemed to be economically stronger, more experienced in legal matters, more powerful and better organised, and thus need no protection. In addition, the ECJ, in its case law relating to Article 13 of the Convention of 27 September 1968 on jurisdiction and the enforcement of judgments in civil and commercial matters, interpreted the term consumer as meaning a private final consumer.[7] Advocate General Mischo used this fact in his opinion on the *Idealservice* case to conclude that the term consumer refers to 'an individual, which necessarily implies that a natural person is concerned'.[8]

[4] ECJ, 22 November 2001, Case C-541/99, *Cape Snc* v. *Idealservice Srl* [2001] ECR I-9049.

[5] See Opinion of the Advocate-General, 14 June 2001, Case C-541/99, *Cape Snc* v. *Idealservice Srl* [2001] ECR I-9049.

[6] ECJ, 27 June 2000, Case C-240/98, *Océano Grupo Editorial SA* v. *Roció Murciano Quintero* [2000] ECR I-4941.

[7] ECJ, 19 January 1993, Case C-89/91 *Shearson Lehmann Hutton Inc.* v. *TVB Treuhandgesellschaft für Vermögensverwaltung und Beteiligungen mbH* [1993] ECR I-139.

[8] See Opinion of the Advocate-General, 14 June 2001, Case C-541/99, *Cape Snc* v. *Idealservice Srl* [2001] ECR I-09049; 17.

It is very reasonable to see a protection regime in contract law as an exception to the rule of contractual freedom, and therefore to win for only a limited category of persons this protection. Exactly this was done by the ECJ in the *Océno* case by highlighting the difference between consumers and in the purposes of transacting between consumers and businesses.

The dogmatism of the ECJ seems clearly to show the difficulties in arguing for this narrow understanding of consumers. The Advocate General struggles with his legal argumentation and was reasonably not followed by the court. The main issue here is that the consumer is not a genuine legal but an economic construct, which has evolved over time from buyer to customer and finally to consumer and was imbued with the assumption of the 'economic man', i.e. rationality and self-interest.[9]

The political argument

A brief review of the Programmes, Green Papers, Strategies and Communications of the Commission on consumer policy reveals the development in the understanding of consumers and consumer policy. In the Programme for consumer protection and information policy of 1975,[10] the Commission recognised the consumer as the weaker party in the context of the shift from small local markets to mass markets. Consumers had, it seemed, lost their role as the balancing factor in the economic system, and their economic interests needed to be protected. Consumers required detailed information to enable them to better use their resources, to make free choices and so influence prices and products. It was accepted that the context demanded the enactment of five basic consumer rights:

1. the right to protection of health and safety;
2. the right to protection of economic interests;
3. the right of redress;
4. the right to information and education;
5. the right of representation;

and deeper knowledge of consumer behaviour and attitudes.

[9] K.-E. Wärneryd, 'The Consumer Image over the Centuries', in Klaus G. Grunert and John Thøgersen (eds.), *Consumers, Policy and the Environment: a Tribute to Folke Ölander*, (Boston, MA: Springer Science+Business Media Inc., 2005), 37–63.

[10] [1975] OJ C 092, 25 April.

The Programme of 1975 proposed, on the one hand, the end of the equality of contracting parties in consumer sales, so intervening in the basic principles of contract law, and on the other hand, reaffirmed the paradigm of the rational consumer who requires adequate information (and no more) to fulfil her role in the market.

In the second Programme of 1981,[11] the Commission deepened and confirmed the approach adopted in the first Programme, but also recognised consumer law as a means of fulfilling the goals of the common market.

The Green Paper of 2001[12] follows the same line of argument, and in addition, the Commission recognises that 'a fully functioning consumer internal market could play an important part in the strategy to bring the EU closer to its citizens, by dispelling the myth that internal market is a corporate business project and delivering tangible economic benefits to their daily life'[13]. This new aspect of consumer law is further encouraged by the equating of citizens with consumers in the Consumer Policy Strategy 2002–2006,[14] which also demands basic rights for consumers.

The EU Consumer Policy Strategy 2007–2013[15] represents the Commission's current understanding of consumers and their place in the modern market economy. Its main characteristics are to reconnect the citizens with the EU, to empower the European consumer through the provision of accurate information and market transparency, and to restore consumer confidence by effectively protecting basic rights, in order to fulfil the goals of the common market.

If we look at the development of EU consumer policy, it is clear that alongside the 'economic' rationale of consumer sovereignty (empowering the consumer as rational actor with free choices as balancing factor and driving force for the common market), a more 'political' rationale of embedding citizens/consumers into the European project underlies the Commission's approach. The economic rationale gives no reason to limit the consumer definition; on the contrary, the exclusion of non-professional legal persons is likely to have the opposite effect. On the other hand, the limitation of consumers makes perfect sense from a political perspective. Consumer law as an instrument for reconnecting European citizens with the European project needs to provide a clear and visible link (at least from the citizen's point of view). The consumer as natural person provides this link; only natural persons can be citizens and consumer law provides special rights exclusively for them.

[11] [1981] OJ C 133, 3 June. [12] COM (2001) 531. [13] COM (2001) 531, 10.
[14] COM (2002) 208. [15] COM (2007) 99.

By following these two different rationales for consumer law, the Commission creates inconsistencies within its own consumer approach. On the one hand, consumers should be defined as widely as possible to create confidence among consumers (all possible kinds of consumer); on the other hand, the definition has to be narrowed to reconnect the citizens with the EU. This ambivalence characterises the consumer definition: the first part refers to the political approach, and the second part refers to the economic approach. The limitation of consumers to natural persons is a constant within the different EU consumer directives and was used before the dawn of the political rationale. Initially however, the economic rationale was the sole driving force behind EU consumer policy and it coincided with the judicial justification for the definition of a consumer. Both approaches use the basic principles of contract law; economic reasoning and legal reasoning (in contract law) share the same philosophical roots and assumptions about individual freedom of choice. The shared roots allow the combined development of economic and legal reasoning in limited and connected areas. This effect can be observed at the national level where consumers are sometimes defined in accordance with the socio-economic environment.[16] Shifting the focus away from an economic to a political rationale, with strong reference to citizenship, dissolves the connection between economic and legal reasoning. This leads to even greater differences between the EU approach and the approach of the Member States.

EU vs. national approach

The shift towards full harmonisation can lead to problems for national consumer law regimes, because Member States have their own understanding of the scope of the consumer definition. In the main, Member States develop their consumer laws in accordance with their national legal systems, which are embedded in a national socio-economic environment. The focus on reconnection will consolidate the definition of consumers as natural persons without considering the need for national legal systems to adjust their definitions. The Member States, which have no need to reconnect with their citizens, adjust consumer law according to consumer awareness in their own culture. Even if we can describe some national consumer law regimes as 'civic' rights-based,[17] this does

[16] Especially in the Scandinavian countries.
[17] E.g. consumer law regimes in Scandinavia.

not entail the same approach as in the EU. States can establish some kind of consumer governance, i.e. a broad approach to consumer matters, and not just legal rules. The effectiveness of such approaches depends largely on cultural and socio-economic factors that are unique to particular Member States. But a crucial part of each of these approaches is the definition of consumers. As shown above, there is no universal understanding of the scope of the consumer definition, and with full harmonisation there will be no room left for adjustment in what is a crucial part of any consumer law regime.

Insights from behavioural studies

General remarks on consumer behaviour

The act of buying consumer goods can be highly complex from a scientific point of view, and how one approaches such acts depends on the scientific methods used. We can discern two different approaches to consumer behaviour: an approach which concentrates on decision procedures and the different methods adopted (rational choice); and an approach which concentrates on the chronological order of acts and their emotional effects (psychological approach). The first approach is mainly used in the social sciences and sees consumer behaviour as individual problem solving. It assumes that the individual has given preferences and uses rational methods to reach a decision. The second approach focuses more on the emotional condition of the individual before, during, and after the decision and its effect on the decision process. There are, in recent works on rational choice, efforts to combine these two approaches[18] in order to formulate a more coherent theory of individual behaviour. These approaches broaden the standard rational choice assumptions and are very helpful for predicting and understanding consumer behaviour. Characteristic of these recent theories is the effort to combine empirical psychological insights into the decision process with normative decision theory. H. Simons's 'bounded rationality'[19] thus increasingly becomes 'intended rationality', i.e. the individual actor tries to be rational but often fails because of psychological biases within the decision process. We can distinguish general biases that are present in all decision processes and

[18] Jon Elster (ed.) *Explaining Social Behavior: More Nuts and Bolts for the Social Sciences* (Cambridge University Press, 2007).

[19] H. A. Simon, 'A Behavioral Model of Rational Choice' (1955) 69(1) *The Quarterly Journal of Economics* 99–118.

cannot be overcome by legal measures from more specific (for consumer matters) biases that must be taken into consideration by the legislator because they may affect the practice of a legal rule by the actors.

The highly unknown species of 'consumers' and their behaviour is mainly analysed by social scientists and psychologists. Social scientists, mainly behavioural economists, in particular can provide valuable insights into consumer behaviour and its relation to the law. All those approaches to consumption, consumers, and consumer behaviour have one thing in common; they do not refer to consumers explicitly as natural persons. Consumers are not defined by their nature, but by their actions and behaviour. Consumption is not tied to the physical form of the acting agent or agency; it is an act. But the EU approach suggests that this expanded consumer definition is not recognised at the European level. It suggests that consumers can only be natural persons, and that only natural persons require consumer protection. But buying consumer goods bears no relation to the nature of the acting entity. It is not a question of one's nature but of the kind of action one engages in. Only the actual act, or the purpose of the act, matters. The act of buying is always in fact done by a natural person (physical entity) even in the case of a legal person. Both legal theory and social science assume consumers to behave rationally by satisfying their preferences and both are aware of specific difficulties in assuming that the consumer behaves rationally in reality. But it seems that the legal approach may not be as adequate or up to date as the social sciences. This can lead to ineffective laws and undermine the goal of consumer protection.

Researches in the field of heuristics offer many valuable results for discussing consumer behaviour and its effect on consumer legislation.

The bounded consumer

The heuristics (rules of thumb) and biases presented here are more of a general nature and can appear in the most decision processes. But they are a good starting point for the investigation of the consumer's rationality. The main discussion of consumer 'irrationality' is found in the field of law and economics and tries to combine Posner's normative economic approach[20] to law with the descriptive findings of psychology.

[20] R. A. Posner, 'Rational Choice, Behavioral Economics, and the Law' (1997–8) 50 *Stanford Law Review* 1551–75, defending his approach against critics from behavioural economists, especially Jolls, Sunstein and Thaler (see below).

The most important deviation from standard economic theory is the notion of bounded rationality (which is also acknowledged nowadays by nearly all economists), bounded willpower and bounded self-interest.[21]

Bounded rationality describes the limited capacity of the human mind to evaluate every possible alternative and calculate the corresponding results, unlike the assumptions in standard economic theory. The first economist who introduced the concept of bounded rationality in a broad manner was Herbert Simon, and this was the starting point for the psychological research regarding human decision-making. Consumers often make not unbiased judgments, a fact which can be exploited by business. Consumers also violate the expected utility assumption of standard economic theory, and consumer behaviour can be better described by the prospect theory (see below).

Bounded willpower describes the fact that most consumers act sometimes against their long-term interests. Especially when tempted by emotions consumers forget their long-term interest and focus instead only on their short-term interest. The famous and perhaps also one of the earliest description of this phenomena is the story of Ulysses' journey to the sirens; he demanded to be bound to the mast in order to enjoy the songs of the sirens while his comrades had to put wax in their ears to prevent them from steering the boat into the cliffs. Like Ulysses, most consumers cannot avoid acting against their own long-term interests on their own and may regret their choices afterwards, and therefore need some kind of institution to prevent them from doing so. Withdrawal rights as 'cooling-off periods' can be seen as such kind of institution to manage the bounded willpower of consumers.

The fact of bounded self-interest plays a role in the broader picture of consumer protection and policy; individuals are not only focused on their own well-being but have also a sense of that of others and their fair share. Consumers tend to act 'more nicely' (compared to predictions of classical economic theory) in bargaining processes as long as they feel treated fairly, and vice versa. The feeling of being treated unfairly can lead to spiteful behaviour; this may lead to acts to punish unfair behaviour at a financial cost to oneself.[22] Bounded self-interest is a very good example of the social factor in human behaviour. Individual

[21] C. Jolls, C. R. Sunstein and R. Thaler, 'A Behavioral Approach to Law and Economics', and 'A Behavioral Approach to Law and Economics', in Cass R. Sunstein (ed.), *Behavioral Law and Economics* (Cambridge University Press, 2007) 1476–80 and 13–58.

[22] See for a brief introduction D. Kahneman, J. L. Knetsch, and R. H. Thaler, 'Fairness and the Assumptions of Economics' (1986) 59(4) *The Journal of Business* 285–S300, and

behaviour is not only bounded by the mental incapacities which stop decision-making from being fully rational, but also by social manners and norms which have a huge impact on the individual. But on the other hand, social manners and norms are deeply dependent on particular cultures and can vary across different nations.[23]

The representativeness heuristic

The representativeness heuristic is a rule of thumb used to determine the probability that if A belongs to B, that A is representative of B. 'For example, when A is highly representative of B, the probability that A originates from B is judged to be high. On the other hand, if A is not similar to B, the probability that A originates from B is judged to be low.'[24] A common illustration of the problems with this heuristic is highlighted by the answers given when individuals are asked to guess which of two possible jobs a person has based on some given information about her qualities, for example, the question of whether a shy person is more likely to be a librarian or a salesman.[25] Researchers have shown that most people, confronted with such questions, reply in a way that suggests that the probability of having one job is the same as the probability that the given information about the person matches the stereotype of the job.[26] Most people will answer that a shy person is more likely to be a librarian than a salesman. But this answer ignores the more important influences on probability like prior probability. This bias can be described as insensitivity to prior probabilities, or base-rate frequency of outcomes.[27] In the case of the librarian or salesman, most people forget to count into their estimation the base-rate frequency of librarians and salesmen in the overall population. In fact the probability that a person is a shy salesman is higher than the

C. Camerer, and R. H. Thaler, 'Anomalies: Ultimatums, Dictators and Manners' (1995) 9(2) *The Journal of Economic Perspectives* 209–19.

[23] A. E. Roth *et al.* 'Bargaining and Market Behavior in Jerusalem, Ljubljana, Pittsburgh, and Tokyo: an Experimental Study' (1991) 81(5) *The American Economic Review* 1068–95.

[24] A. Tversky and D. Kahneman, 'Judgment under Uncertainty: Heuristics and Biases' (1974) 185 *Science* 1124–31.

[25] R. H. Frank, 'Rethinking Rational Choice', in Roger Friedland (ed.), *Beyond the Marketplace: Rethinking Economy and Society* (New York: Aldine de Gruyter, 1990), 53–87 at 73–74.

[26] Tversky and Kahneman, 'Judgment under Uncertainty', 1124–31.

[27] *Ibid.* at 1124.

probability that she is a shy librarian, because there are more salesmen than librarians among the population.[28]

In another experiment,[29] people were given brief personality descriptions of several individuals, taken randomly from a group with a known percentage of two occupations. The result was the same: people neglected prior probability and were mainly influenced by the given descriptions. Even when the description had no information value, prior probabilities were ignored. Only when there were no descriptions at all did people use prior probabilities and correctly estimate the likelihood that one individual belonged to one of the given occupations. So Kahneman and Tversky concluded, that '[e]vidently, people respond differently when given no [information] and when given worthless [information]. When no specific [information] is given, prior probabilities are properly utilized; when worthless evidence is given, prior probabilities are ignored.'[30] Another bias within representativeness can be described as the illusion of validity.[31] As seen above, people's confidence depends on the quality of the match between the selected outcome and the input information, with little respect for factors that limit accuracy. The unwarranted confidence that results from a fit between the predicted outcome and the input is called the illusion of validity. This bias is often seen when input information is highly redundant or strong correlated. '[P]eople tend to have great confidence in predictions based on redundant input variables ... Thus, redundancy among inputs decreases accuracy even as it increases confidence, and people are often confident in predictions that are quite likely to be off the mark.'[32]

The biases of the representative heuristic are very important for consumer behaviour and consumer law. In contrast to the standard economic and rationality paradigm, which states that all possible information is needed to arrive at the optimal solution, the findings of Kahneman and Tversky show that too much information can lead to suboptimal solutions for individuals. To avoid these consequences, it is important to find the proper information, i.e. the appropriate amount and the right kinds of information. The proper information depends, in consumer matters, on the kind of product, the situation and the individual consumer.

[28] Frank, 'Rethinking Rational Choice', 74 for a numerical example.
[29] Tversky and Kahneman, 'Judgment under Uncertainty', 1124–5. [30] *Ibid.* at 1125.
[31] *Ibid.* at 1126. [32] *Ibid.*

The availability heuristic

The availability heuristic is used when people estimate the probability or the frequency of an event or class with the help of experience and imagination. But this heuristic can lead to major biases because availability is not affected only by frequency. The so-called biases due to the retrievability of instances[33] occur because people take the more familiar and salient information into account and process it more than other information. In the same way, recent occurrences or information are more available than earlier ones. 'Economically, the availability bias is important because we often have to estimate the relative performance of alternative economic options.'[34] Further, there are biases due to the effectiveness of a search set[35] that occur because people tend to use the easiest way of searching for information. But the easiest means can also be the faultiest. Thus most people respond to the question 'Are there more (English) words starting with "r" or words with "r" as the third letter?', that there are more words starting with 'r'. This happens because it is easier to imagine all the words starting with 'r' (by imagining a dictionary, for example) than to think of all words containing 'r' as their third letter.[36] There are also biases of imaginability[37] that lead to an overestimation of the likelihood of foreseeable occurrences over those that are less foreseeable. Likewise, risks can be underestimated if possible dangers are difficult to conceive. The last bias within the heuristic of availability is the so-called bias of illusory correlation.[38] The frequency that two events co-occur is judged by the strength of the associated bond between them. The illusory correlation means that people see correlations although there are strong contradictory data or even, objectively, negative correlations. This bias prevents people from recognising the factual relationship between two events. So Kahneman and Tversky conclude:

> man has at his disposal a procedure (the availability heuristic) for estimating the numerosity of class, the likelihood of an event, or the frequency of co-occurrences, by the ease with which the relevant mental operations of retrieval, construction, or association can be performed. However, ... this valuable estimation procedure results in systematic errors.[39]

[33] *Ibid.* at 1127. [34] Frank, 'Rethinking Rational Choice', 72–6.
[35] Tversky and Kahneman, 'Judgment under Uncertainty', 1127.
[36] Frank, 'Rethinking Rational Choice', 73.
[37] Tversky and Kahneman, 'Judgment under Uncertainty', 1127.
[38] *Ibid.*, 1128. [39] *Ibid.*

The availability heuristic is interesting for consumer matters, because it points out the problems of generating information from past experience. Even if consumers are used to a buying situation or a consumer product, they may draw the wrong conclusions due to biases. This is important in cases of risky and long-term contracts, like consumer credit, where consumers have to imagine future developments in order to estimate the usefulness of the contract.

Anchoring and adjustment

Another heuristic which was described by Kahneman and Tversky is the adjustment and anchoring[40] heuristic. This heuristic is a common strategy of estimation where people choose an initial value, like an anchor, and adjust it with each additional piece of information to make estimations. But different anchors yield different estimates because of several biases within the anchor heuristic. One is the insufficient adjustment[41] bias which occurs when people use completely unrelated information as an anchor or, if the information is related, they adjust too little from it. Further there are biases in the evaluation of conjunctive and disjunctive events[42] which means that people tend to overestimate the probability of conjunctive events and underestimate the probability of disjunctive events. These biases have an important impact on economic issues where it is necessary to estimate the probability of success or failure of a venture or action. The last bias within the anchoring heuristic is the anchoring in the assessment of subjective probability distribution[43] which leads people to be overconfident about their subjective probability distribution, despite the fact that such certainty is not justified by their knowledge about the issue.

Prices of goods and services are one very interesting example of the anchoring effect. Consumers use prices, knowingly or unknowingly, to estimate the value of items they want to purchase.[44] Companies use this fact to mislead consumers about the 'true' value of an item. They price goods and services higher than usual and give sales discounts in order to reinforce the consumer's image of the item's higher value. Even if advanced information is available, consumers tend to estimate the value of goods based solely on the prices given.

[40] *Ibid.*, 1128–1130 and Frank, 'Rethinking Rational Choice', 75–6.
[41] Tversky and Kahneman, 'Judgment under Uncertainty', 1128.
[42] *Ibid.*, 1128–9. [43] *Ibid.*, 1129–30.
[44] S. Plous, *The Psychology of Judgment and Decision Making* (New York: Mcgraw-Hill, 2007), 147–9.

Many different experiments show that the anchoring heuristic and its biases are very pervasive and robust. Unfortunately, it is very difficult to avoid the biases, because the anchors often go unnoticed by the individuals. This gives companies plenty of scope to abuse the anchoring heuristic and to steer consumer behaviour.

Overconfidence

Overconfidence can help to explain the behaviour of individuals in overestimating the probability that positive events will happen and underestimating the probability that negative events will happen. This bias of extreme optimistic thinking is partly a result of the representativeness and the availability heuristics. Unrealistic optimism can occur due to the stereotypical thinking described within the representativeness heuristic; individuals connect many events with distinctive stereotypes and compare themselves to those stereotype. If the stereotypes do not fit they will conclude that the event may not happen to them, but they ignore the base rates. Due to the availability heuristic personal experience increases the likelihood of people believing that their own chances are greater than average.[45]

The overconfidence bias is for example crucial in the consumer credit market where most consumers underestimate the likelihood of not being able to repay their debt, due to illness or unemployment. For policymakers the overconfidence bias can have importance in designing rules and legal incentives for individual behaviour.[46]

Context matters

The most important result of behavioural studies for consumer policy and law is the importance of the context of choice situations. For classical economic theory, the context does not matter at all: rational individuals and consumers choose the best alternative in line with their preferences, unaffected by the actual situation. One mild anomaly of the classical rationality paradigm is mental accounting, which describes the effect of having different mental accounts. Consumers have different mental accounts for different situations of decision-making and

[45] N. D. Weinstein, 'Unrealistic Optimism About Future Life Events' (1980) 39 (5) *Journal of Personality and Social Psychology* 806–20 for a general study on unrealistic optimism.

[46] R. B. Korobkin and T. S. Ulen, 'Law and Behavioral Science: Removing the Rationality Assumption from Law and Economics' (2000) 88 (4) *California Law Review* at 1051.

because of this they treat alternatives in different ways. A well-known thought experiment by Tversky and Kahneman illustrates this phenomenon by asking individuals to imagine (a) that they were on the way to a play which costs $10 and they realised that they just lost $10 on the way to the play, and (b) that they had already purchased the ticket for $10 and, on the way to the play, they realised that they just lost the ticket. The respondents to both questions were asked if they would willing to buy a (in the case of (a)) or to buy another (in the case of (b)) ticket for the play. In classical economic theory, the two different choice situations should not matter for the actual decision of purchasing a ticket, but the results of the studies show that the majority in the first case would be willing to buy the ticket whereas the majority in the second case would not buy another ticket.[47] The expense for the individual is in both cases $20, but it matters how the expense is assembled. This study is an illustration of the mental accounting of individuals who have different 'mental accounts' for different categories of goods and services.[48] The phenomenon of mental accounting helps to understand the sunk costs fallacy which describes the fact that most people are influenced by their irreversible past decisions. Past expenses should not matter for a rational actor – they should be treated as sunk costs, i.e. costs which do not affect any future decision-making. But normally most people take those sunk costs into consideration and their decision behaviour depends on those sunk costs. One explanation might be that most people want to act in a consistent way and therefore pay heed to sunk costs. Korobkin and Ulen see in consumer contracts which are based on a monthly payment, but which can be cancelled by stopping the payment or returning the merchandise at any time, a conscious attempt to take advantage of the sunk cost fallacy. Most people, once they have paid the first monthly payment, are unlikely to cancel the contract, even if the utility of the merchandise received is lower than that of cancelling the contract.[49]

One answer to the problem of context-dependence in consumer behaviour can be found in the prospect theory which includes some of the most famous context fallacies, like framing and the endowment effect.

[47] A. Tversky and D. Kahneman, 'The Framing of Decisions and the Psychology of Choice' (1981) 211 *Science* 453–8.

[48] C. Jolls, 'Behavioral Economics Analysis of Redistributive Legal Rules' (1998) 51 *Vanderbilt Law Review* 1653–78, at 1669.

[49] Korobkin and Ulen, 'Law and Behavioral Science', 1126.

Prospect theory

Prospect theory is an alternative theory to the standard expected-utility approach of economics and consumer law. In their work, Tversky and Kahneman[50] propose that individuals will not evaluate and consider absolute utility as in the standard utility function but, rather, will consider relative changes to wealth in a 'value function'. Furthermore, an important characteristic of this value function is that the function is more pronounced in the case of losses rather than gains. This means that a gain does not have the same value as an equivalent loss. The prospect theory considers different known problems of rational behaviour that can affect consumer behaviour.

The relative change in wealth from a reference point (reference dependence) takes into account framing effects. Framing can change the reference point and lead to preference reversal. The framing of the problem can have a major influence on which solution will be chosen by an individual. A medical cure with a survival rate of 90 per cent will be selected over a medical cure with a death rate of 10 per cent. Even though the solution and the outcome is the same in both cases, individuals in their decision process are strongly affected by the presentation of the problem.

Prospect theory considers the endowment effect because the theory treats gains and losses differently, i.e. losses weigh more than gains (loss aversion). The theory uses an s-shaped value-function to describe the effects of gains and losses for an individual. The value function is bent at the reference point and runs concave for gains and convex for losses. This bend at the reference point describes the risk-averse behaviour for gains and the risk-seeking behaviour for losses of individual actors. Empirical studies show that individuals tend to weight losses twice as much as gains.[51] This loss-aversion behaviour explains the status quo bias and the endowment effect. The status quo bias describes the behaviour of individuals who tend to conserve the status quo and to avoid all solutions which might change it, even if the possible alternative is highly likely to improve the status of the individual. The endowment effect

[50] Tversky and Kahneman, 'Judgment under Uncertainty'; D. Kahneman and A. Tversky, 'Prospect Theory: an Analysis of Decision under Risk' (1979) 47 (2) *Econometrica* 263–91; D. Kahneman, 'A Perspective on Judgment and Choice: Mapping Bounded Rationality' (2003) 58 *American Psychologist* 697–720, and Frank, 'Rethinking Rational Choice', n. 25.

[51] D. Kahneman, J. L. Knetsch and R. Thaler, 'Experimental Tests of the Endowment Effect and the Coase Theorem', in Cass R. Sunstein (ed.), *Behavioral Law and Economics* (Cambridge University Press, 2007), 211–31.

describes the empirical findings of differences of willingness to pay (WTP) for an entitlement and the compensation demanded for the same entitlement (willingness to accept, WTA).[52] Those findings are in direct contradiction to the Coase theorem and throw light on the question of distributing rights between individual actors.

The theory also considers non-linear responses to probabilities, i.e. overweighting of small probabilities and underweighting of moderate and high probabilities.

Prospect theory, because of its descriptive character, can help to explain consumer behaviour in a more realistic way than the normative assumptions of classical economic theory and law. It can provide law with valuable insights into the individual decision process and can inspire lawmakers in their effort to establish an effective legal consumer regime.

Discussion

The results of behavioural studies are commonly and widely accepted, even among the most 'hardcore' rational-choice economics; but how to interpret those insights and how to include those biases into economic theory is still under discussion. It starts with the question of how serious and dangerous those rationality errors for consumers are or whether the market will not correct all irrational behaviour. Market forces and the effect of learning from one's own mistakes and the exchange of knowledge between different consumers may extinguish the most biases in the decision process.[53] On the other hand, the effects of learning and market forces are questioned by many authors, and they find some evidences of taking advantage of consumer behaviour by firms,[54] especially by the bundling of goods and services,[55] and in

[52] E. Hoffman, and M. L. Spitzer, 'Willingness to Pay vs. Willingness to Accept: Legal and Economic Implications' (1993) 71 *Washington University Law Quarterly* 59–114.

[53] R. A. Epstein, 'Behavioral Economics: Human Errors and Market Corrections' (2006) 73 *University of Chicago Law Review* 111–32.

[54] See J. D. Hanson, and D. A. Kysar, 'Taking Behavioralism Seriously: the Problem of Market Manipulation' (1999) 74 *New York University Law Review* 630–749 for a comprehensive description of behavioural research and the possible manipulation of consumers.

[55] O. Bar-Gill, 'Bundling and Consumer Misperception' (2006) 73 *University of Chicago Law Review* 33–62; see the exchange between Bar-Gill and Epstein: O. Bar-Gill, 'The Behavioral Economics of Consumer Contracts' (2007) 92 *Minnesota Law Review* 749–802 and R. A. Epstein, 'The Neoclassical Economics of Consumer Contracts' (2007) 92 *Minnesota Law Review* 803–35 for a general discussion about behavioural economics vs. neoclassical economics in consumer contracts.

the credit market.[56] The strongest critique against behavioural economics is its lack of methodological coherence. Behavioural economics, in contrast to neoclassical economics, has no comprehensive theory of human behaviour, and nor can one predict future individual actions with behavioural economics.[57] But, on the other hand, behavioural economics is a descriptive science and it tries not to make normative predictions such as neoclassical theory. This is perhaps also the reason why legal scholars find it sometimes hard to see any use in behavioural science. The advantages of neoclassical economic theory for law is its claim to give, more or less,[58] a precise prediction of individual behaviour and how it will be influenced by legal incentives.[59] For most economics and legal scholars, behavioural science is just a conglomeration of rationality biases and fallacies, but without any theory of how to predict or weight the different phenomena.[60] But this is perhaps the basic misunderstanding in the whole discussion; behavioural economics is not a new paradigm which can replace the old rationality paradigm, but it is like a toolbox[61] which can help to explain deviations from predicted rational behaviours; and at the same time it is a warning not to follow the predictions of neoclassical theory blindly. Other fields which can enrich the understanding of consumers and help to set the 'right' incentives can be found in the sociology of consumption[62] and the psychological analyses of the emotional side of consumer

[56] O. Bar-Gill, and E. Warren, 'Making Credit Safer' (2008) 157 (1) *University of Pennsylvania Law Review* 1–102.

[57] Epstein, cited above n. 53 at 121: 'the behavioral critique loses much of its bite, because it can no longer predict any *systematic* direction to the market errors'.

[58] The level of precision and the usefulness of the predictions in neoclassical economics has been subject to heavy criticism since the outbreak of the financial crises.

[59] S. Issacharoff, 'Can There Be a Behavioral Law and Economics?' (1998) 51 *Vanderbilt Law Review* 1729–46, at 1731.

[60] Epstein, cited above n. 53 at 122:

> In dealing with any compound probability it is possible either to overweight the individual event (representativeness or availability) or overweight the background estimation of probability (anchoring) ... There is little reason to deny that these effects have some impact in individual cases. But it is hard to make policy recommendations in the absence of information as to which effect is likely to be most profound in any given setting.

[61] Not every cognitive bias or fallacy occurs in every kind of decision-making; one has to pick the corresponding fallacy to enrich predictions adequately.

[62] Sociology of consumption focuses on the social effects and influences on consumers, such as social class and status, and distinguishes between different consumer models depending on the product, the situation and the individual consumer.

decisions.[63] All those approaches have in common that they help to overcome the reductionist assumptions of human behaviour in neoclassical theory and to broaden the understanding of consumer behaviour.

Conclusion

Behavioural studies and their results can help us to understand consumers and their behaviour and to protect them. But, as the above-mentioned biases imply, consumers are not the simple *homo oeconomicus* traditionally assumed by EU consumer law. Consumers may not have given or stable preferences and they may not be able to decide in a rational manner, as suggested by theory. Further, it is not only consumers, but professionals too, who suffer from biases, so why should there be any special kind of protection for consumers? Consumers, unlike professionals, are not aware of the obstacles in finding a satisfying decision. Thus, consumers are the weaker party, not because they are natural persons, but because consumers do not have the resources to analyse and overcome their biases. In order to protect consumers adequately, consumer law must consider consumer behaviour throughout the decision process. Given the findings of behavioural studies, the mantra of giving consumers all the information they need to act as a market balancing factor is very questionable. An important influence on consumer behaviour is the situation, i.e. the kind of goods, the kind of purchases, the consumer's experience and the cultural environment. The situation affects the involvement of consumers, which defines the relationship between consumers and a product or service. The level of involvement frames the decision process for consumers: the more involvement on the part of consumers, the more they will search for information and use it in a critical and rational decision process and vice versa. Effective consumer protection has to differentiate between different consumer situations in order to find a balance between consumer protection and unnecessary costs for business. Behavioural studies can support the legal system in its task of establishing an effective consumer protection law, because asymmetries in contract relations and the consumer's bounded and limited rationality both have to be considered.

[63] D. A. Statt, *Understanding the Consumer: a Psychological Approach* (London: Macmillan, 1997). Consumer behaviour is interpreted in the light of the entire consumer experience – buying is just a small part of consumer activity.

In recent papers on consumer protection, the Commission mentions the need for a better understanding of consumer behaviour.[64] But it seems that only certain findings of behavioural studies about consumers have been taken into account in the actual EC consumer law regime. The differentiation between different consumer goods and kinds of purchases indicates an awareness that the situation matters. Cooling-off periods and defaults can be seen as answers to some of the problems that behavioural studies have reveal, namely bounded willpower and framing. Minimum harmonisation can be understood as recognising the cultural effect on consumer behaviour, but with the dawn of full harmonisation the Commission is losing sight of this important factor in consumer behaviour. Instead, the Commission uses consumer law as an instrument for its own political purposes, the reconnection of the citizen/consumer with the European project and the creation of a common market. This can lead to conflicts with national consumer law legislation, which has no need to reconnect the state with its citizens via consumer law. Another point of using consumer law for such political purposes is that it connects the consumer status with the natural status of the actor. But consumers are solely defined by the nature of their acts and their behaviour. The focus on the natural status of consumers will hamper effective consumer protection in the long run. If the Commission looks more closely at the findings of behavioural science, it will gain deeper insight into consumers and their weaknesses. In this way, an adequate approach to consumers in the legal system may be found, starting with an adequate definition of consumer which is focused on actual behaviour instead of using the consumer for 'higher' political goals.

[64] See OJ C 25, COM (2005) 115, COM (2007) 99.

9

Recognising the limits of transparency in EU consumer law

CHRIS WILLETT AND MARTIN MORGAN-TAYLOR

Basic arguments

This chapter deals with the issue of transparency operating as a legitimising factor, notwithstanding some other feature of a term or practice that might be viewed as unfair. First, it is suggested that, apart from being of general practical and theoretical importance, this is a particularly important question for a number of reasons related to the future development of EU and domestic consumer law. Partly, this is because of the sheer scale of harmonisation that now exists. With such large areas of the law harmonised around European standards, it is important to ensure that national courts and governments understand the level of protection that is required as a minimum under these standards. However, the increased use of 'full harmonisation' means that the *upper* level of protection allowed also becomes potentially very important. Clarity on key issues (such as when there is a legitimising role for transparency) is also important if genuine assimilation of laws is to be feasible.

Second, there is an explanation as to what transparency actually is. This is followed by a discussion of an 'assisted informed consent' model (under which transparency is viewed as a legitimising factor). There is then a discussion of the more protective approach that does not view transparency as a legitimising factor. The thinking behind this approach may be that transparency does not actually produce more informed decisions, enable broader procedural fairness or generate market discipline; and that, in any case, it is appropriate to take an approach with a strong solidarity ethic that directly protects against unfair substantive consequences, matters of informed consent notwithstanding.

The first author is Professor of Consumer Law at University of Essex and the second author is Principal Lecturer, at De Montfort Law School.

Third, it is argued that the position (i.e. as to whether transparency can legitimise) is insufficiently certain; and that the law might send clearer signals on this. (Here, the main 'case study' is on the unfair contract terms regime, although this is supported by a brief discussion of the rules on commercial practices.) Finally, it is suggested that there might be an important role for regulators to play in producing the rigorous, research-based arguments that demonstrate why the rules should often be interpreted so as to reject transparency as a legitimising factor.

Background

The role and limits of transparency in consumer law have been much discussed in recent years;[1] and it continues to be of importance to consider what legitimising force transparency has. First, it is of significant practical importance for consumers. Are they protected from substantively unfair terms and practices even when these are clear? Secondly, it is of theoretical importance to understand the roles played by transparency as it speaks to the values that the law applies to the consumer market. Is the model one of (assisted) informed choice? Alternatively, is it one in which there is more of an ethic of solidarity and protection?[2]

However, the question as to the role and limits of transparency in European consumer law has particular importance in current circumstances. In part, this is because of the acute Europeanisation that has taken place, which makes questions as to the 'ethic' of EU consumer law (including this question as to the role of transparency) especially important.

A key part of the current Europeanisation picture is the regime on unfair contract terms. Currently this is contained in the Unfair Terms in

[1] See, for example, D. Kennedy, 'Distributive and Paternalist Motives in Contract and Tort Law with Special Reference to Compulsory Terms and Unequal Bargaining Power' (1982) *Maryland Law Review* 563; S. Grundman, W. Kerber and S. Weatherill (eds.), *Party Autonomy and the Role of Information in the Internal Market* (De Gruyter, 2001); S. Weatherill, *EU Consumer Law and Policy* (Cheltenham: Elgar, 2005), ch. 4; S. Smith, *Atiyah's Introduction to the Law of Contract* (Oxford University Press, 2005), 319–29 and 323; G. Howells, 'The Potential and Limits of Consumer Empowerment by Information' (2005) 32 (3) *Journal of Law and Society* 349; C. Willett, *Fairness in Consumer Contracts* (Aldershot: Ashgate, 2007), 2.4.3.4–5, 3.44, 6.4.2 and 6.5; and C. Willett, 'The Functions of Transparency in Regulating Contract Terms: UK and Australian Approaches' (2011) 60 *ICLQ* 355–385.

[2] For a very recent analysis of the tension in EU law between a social-justice, consumer-need-based approach and a more free-market, self-reliant consumer approach (which is likely to incline to greater focus on transparency as a legitimising factor) see H. Micklitz, 'Jack is out of the Box: the Efficient Consumer-Shopper' (2009) 3–4 *Juridiska Föreningen i Finland*, 417–436.

Consumer Contracts Directive (UTCCD)[3] implemented in the UK by the Unfair Terms in Consumer Contracts Regulations (UTCCR) 1999.[4] This applies horizontally to the vast majority of important goods and services transactions; including those, such as mortgages and tenancy agreements, that might not traditionally be thought of as goods or services.[5] It contains a 'general clause' on unfairness, which is based around whether a term causes significant imbalance to the detriment of the consumer and violates the requirement of good faith.[6] The directive is 'minimum' in character, so that Member States can choose to set a higher level of protection than that provided for under this general clause. The initial draft of the Consumer Rights Directive would have applied the 'full harmonisation' approach to unfair terms.[7] However the final directive does not cover unfair terms.[8] So the standards set would have represented not only the minimum that Member States must do to protect consumers but also the maximum that they are *permitted* to do. So it could have been especially important to decide on the role of transparency. Even in the absence of full harmonisation the proper interpretation of the general clause, and the proper role for transparency, remain important.

There has also been a very significant further Europeanisation of (regulatory) trade practices law under the Unfair Commercial Practices Directive (UCPD). Again, this new European regime is especially significant, not only because it sets *minimum* standards but also, vitally, because being a 'full harmonisation' measure it also sets the *ceiling*, in terms of the protection that can be provided.[9] So it becomes especially important to assess to what extent the fairness concepts are supposed to be interpreted so that practices are fair so long as they are transparent. If this is the case, Member States are not allowed to offer a higher level of protection, i.e. they must allow a practice so long as these transparency requirements are satisfied.

It is important, at this stage, to make something of a qualifying point about the extent to which Member States (and their courts) are, in practice, bound to any 'EU paradigm' as to the legitimising (or otherwise)

[3] Directive 93/13/EEC. [4] SI 2083.
[5] UTCCD, Art. 2; UTCCR, Regs. 3 and 4(1); and Willett, *Fairness in Consumer Contracts*, 3.2.
[6] UTCCD, Art. 3(1); UTCCD, Reg. 5(1).
[7] COM (2008) 614 final; on unfair terms see ch. 5 and see Art. 4. [8] 2011/83/EU.
[9] Art. 4; although some sectors, including financial services, are exempt from full harmonisation (Art. 3).

role of transparency. The point is that, under the UTCCD, the ECJ has taken the view that it is generally for national courts to apply the general clause on unfairness to the term in question within the relevant national legal context.[10] (Of course, this is assuming that the national court is interpreting the basic meaning of the test correctly.) So it may be that the ECJ will often leave it to national courts to decide, within the national legal context, whether transparency does or does not legitimise any unfairness in substance that exists. It is possible that the ECJ will take a similar sort of approach under the UCPD, leaving it to national courts to apply the test to the facts within the national legal context. This might mean that, in practice, national courts have a fair degree of latitude in deciding whether to treat transparency as a factor that legitimises a practice.

Nevertheless, the question of the extent to which transparency is intended to be viewed as a legitimising factor remains important. For one thing, we cannot be sure exactly how the ECJ will develop its approach in relation to either terms or practices. Indeed, we shall see below that the freedom allowed to national courts by the ECJ seems to depend on whether there is a 'benefit' for the consumer.[11] However, it is uncertain precisely what this means in terms of the relationship between transparency and fairness in substance.

Further, the potential pressures of full harmonisation are only one part of the picture. Even if there is ample scope generally for national courts to decide on the role of transparency, the question is how they will approach this issue. If the correct approach is not clear, national courts may vary in their approaches. As we shall see below, the tendency in the UK may be for approaches that favour treating transparency as a legitimising factor, while this may not be the case in other Member States. Such differences in national approaches are a matter of concern in terms of the aims of the directives. The UTCCD and UCPD seek to integrate the single market by eradicating competitive distortions.[12] For this to be successful, the regimes must be understood in as similar a manner as possible across Europe. This poses a difficult challenge in the case of many directives, given differing national traditions. There is an inevitable risk that rules will be approached and interpreted with strong reference to the pre-existing (and divergent) national legal, social and cultural contexts (e.g. differences in rules, doctrines, principles, regulatory

[10] Joined cases, *Océano Grupo Editorial* and *Salvat Editores* [2000] ECR I-4941, C-240/98 and C-244/98; and *Freiburger Kommunalbauten GmbH Baugesellschaft & Co. KG*, C-237/02.

[11] *Ibid.* [12] UTCCD, preamble, recital 2; UCPD, preamble, recital 3.

policy, judicial reasoning, lawyer attitudes, legal argument, the 'region' of the legal system that the rule is inserted into, etc.). So it is important to seek to develop a reasonably nuanced notion as to the nature and level of protection. This must include the extent to which transparency can legitimise terms and practices.

Finally, the transparency issue is of importance due to another aim of the directives. They aim at achieving a 'high level of consumer protection'.[13] The extent to which transparency can legitimise terms and practices is clearly relevant to whether we can say that such a high level of protection is granted.

The alternative philosophies on transparency as a legitimising factor

Meaning of transparency

Transparency can be defined as involving:

1. an obligation to disclose (or not omit) certain information deemed needed by consumers to improve informed decision making;
2. (possibly) a cancellation period allowing further time for reflection after a commitment is made. It should be emphasised that we are not referring simply here to statutory cancellation rights that might apply to the contract in question (e.g. the cancellation rights routinely applicable in doorstep and distance selling).[14] Of course, such statutory cancellation rights are intended to offer scope for reflection on the relevant risks. In addition, however, further scope for reflection on risks might be available due to cancellation rights that were voluntarily provided by traders when certain terms or practices were used. The effect of this would be to effectively provide cancellation rights in contracts where there was no statutory cancellation right and to lengthen the cancellation period in those cases such as doorstep and distance selling where one exists in any case;
3. for the above sort of information and for information (e.g. in standard terms) voluntarily provided by traders, certain standards of clarity.

[13] See UTCCD, Preamble; UCPD, Preamble; TFEU, Art. 114.

[14] See Directives 97/7/EC (distance selling), Art. 4 and 85/577/EEC (doorstep selling), Art. 4; in the UK, respectively, the Consumer Protection (Distance Selling) Regulations 2000, SI 2334, Regs. 10 and 11; and the Cancellation of Contracts Made in a Consumer's Home, Work etc. Regulations 2008, SI 1816, Reg. 7.

This clarity would involve, for example, requirements that contract terms be available at the point of contract; that information required to be disclosed should be disclosed at some other particular point, e.g. the provision of notice before interest rate increases or enforcement action; a reasonable opportunity to become acquainted with contract terms; clear, jargon-free language; decent-sized print; that sentences, paragraphs and overall contract are well structured; and that appropriate prominence is given to particularly important risks, whether these risks are contained in a term or are related to a practice (whether these are risks in the sense of significant reductions in the rights of consumers or the imposition of significant burdens on consumers).

These are the sort of criteria that tend to be insisted upon in relation to transparency in existing or proposed legislative measures and by courts and regulators.[15]

Assisted informed consent

On this model,[16] consumers are helped (by transparency) to better understand terms; and, if they agree to them, they are bound on the basis that they have made an informed choice. They are informed about trader practices; and, as a response to trader coercion, pressure, etc. (which might undermine informed decision-making), they are given information and time to reflect. Again, the conditions for informed decision-making have now been restored, so the problem has been solved.

This approach is based on the idea that consumers do not necessarily have the information-processing and search abilities to get to grips with terms and practices that lack transparency, or to search out information that is not provided. Therefore information must be given. However, the protection stops at this point. It is the least protective approach possible, involving the smallest relative deviation from a traditional freedom of contract approach. Traders can use the terms or practices in question, notwithstanding that the terms may be substantively detrimental or that the practice may be in some sense aggressive or have unfair substantive consequences. So long as the appropriate information is provided in

[15] *First National Bank* v. *Director General of Fair Trading* [2001] 3 WLR 1297, Lord Bingham, at 1308; Office of Fair Trading, Unfair Contract Bulletin, No. 4, 1997; Office of Fair Trading, Unfair Contract Terms Guidance, 2001, Analysis of Terms Breaching Regulation 7– Plain English and Intelligible Language, para. 19; Willett, *Fairness in Consumer Contracts*, 2.4.2.2, 2.4.3.4 and 6.4.2.

[16] See Willett, 'The Functions of Transparency in Regulating Contract Terms'.

the appropriate form, consumers are treated as free to choose how to proceed, whether this is to agree to what is proposed, bargain for a change or go elsewhere.

Rejection of transparency as a legitimising factor

On this model transparency does *not* necessarily legitimise terms that cross a certain threshold of substantive detriment.[17] Equally, poor performance practices, trader pressure, coercion, etc., is not necessarily legitimised by transparency.

In the context of contract terms, this approach is based, in part, on the argument that transparency is not usually capable of genuinely informing consumers, because consumers are unlikely to read terms even when they are transparent. There are a number of reasons for this. First of all, there may be a large quantity of information to be processed prior to the decision to enter the contract,[18] meaning that consumers focus only on the core aspects of the transaction. Further, consumers may suffer from over optimism and an inclination to discount future risks.[19] This may be because of factors such as the very positive general marketing messages; prior psychological commitment to purchases;[20] the way in which certain risks and benefits are 'framed';[21] and the 'normal' experience of routine, non-problematic performance by both parties, with terms (and their possibly negative consequences) not usually coming into play.[22] Also, consumers will know that traders will be unlikely to agree to any changes in any case, and may even believe that the terms have a legal sanction and represent 'the law'.

[17] For the purposes of this chapter we are assuming (as is usually, but not always the case) that no alternative (and substantively fairer) terms are offered by the trader in question or by other traders. If the term under scrutiny is sufficiently transparent and there *is* a transparent, accessible and fairer alternative, the question arises as to whether the law should and/or does uphold the term under scrutiny even although it crosses a certain threshold of unfairness in substance. However, in the absence of this possible justification for upholding the term, we return to the question as to whether transparency alone is sufficient. On the issue of alternatives see Willett, *Fairness in Consumer Contracts*, 2.4.2.2 and 2.3.4(v).

[18] On quantity, in particular, see Better Regulation Executive and the National Consumer Council, *Warning: Too Much Information Can Harm* (Interim Report), (London: NCC, 2007).

[19] So called 'hyperbolic discounting', on which see S. Frederick, G. Lowenstein and T. O'Donoghue, 'Time Discounting and Time Preference: a Critical Review' (2002) 40 *Journal of Economic Literature* 351.

[20] Willett, *Fairness in Consumer Contracts*, 2.4.2.2.

[21] See I. Ramsay, *Consumer Law and Policy* (Oxford: Hart, 2007) 73–4.

[22] Willett, *Fairness in Consumer Contracts*, 2.4.2.2.

All of these factors make it unlikely that consumers will attempt to get to grips with the terms even when they are transparent. As such, transparency of terms cannot be viewed, in practice, as producing the level of pre-contractual understanding that would make for real informed freedom of choice. This perspective is increasingly supported by behavioural economics research.[23]

In relation to practices, there is a similar way of justifying a rejection of transparency as a factor that always legitimises. Believing that transparency can achieve informed decision-making even where there has been, for instance, aggressive action by the trader tends to ignore:

1. the information-processing difficulties highlighted by behavioural economics research (summarised above) which are likely to be faced by consumers when dealing with standardised literature from traders;
2. the fact that these information-processing difficulties are likely to be exacerbated by any harassment, coercion or pressure. These difficulties will usually exist in routine transactions, i.e. where there has not been any actual aggression, but are likely to be made worse by aggressive practices. Such practices may make it even less likely that consumers will focus on, and digest, any standardised explanations;
3. the empirical research as to the limited impact of cancellation periods. There is no space here to develop this, but evidence suggests that, even where there is no positive evidence of an unfair selling tactic, for instance, cancellation periods are often not taken advantage of.[24] So, it may be unlikely that consumers would actually make use of a cancellation period to assess more fully the risks of the transaction.

So far we have outlined reasons why transparency is often unlikely to improve informed decision-making. However, even if there *is* sufficient transparency to produce a degree of informed consent, this is usually unlikely, in itself, to empower individuals or the broader market to force traders to provide fairer terms or practices. Individuals will tend to lack the bargaining power. The broader market *may* exert discipline that forces traders to make terms and practices fairer. However, while this may be

[23] See Ramsay, *Consumer Law and Policy*, 71–85; Frederick *et al.* 'Time Discounting'; J. Lee and J. M. Hogarth, 'The Price of Money: Consumers' Understanding of APRs and Contract Interest Rates' (1999) 18(1) *Journal of Public Policy and Marketing* 66–76; and T. A. Durkin, 'Credit Card Disclosures, Solicitations and Privacy Notices: Survey Results of Consumer Knowledge and Behaviour' (2006) August, *Federal Reserve Bulletin* A109-A121.

[24] Ramsay, *Consumer Law and Policy*, 345–6.

a reasonable prospect where core issues are concerned, it becomes less likely in the case of ancillary matters that do not routinely affect the active margin of consumers.

In the case of both terms and practices, rejection of transparency as a legitimising factor can also be rationalised in terms of a desire to have a strong solidarity ethic. In other words, the reasoning is that, whether or not there is informed consent, this solidarity ethic requires that parties, such as consumers, should be protected from terms and practices that impose unacceptable substantive risks and burdens. Such burdens are unacceptable in the context of activities undertaken in the private sphere of life and not for profit, and have the capacity to seriously affect the private sphere of life, especially where the most vulnerable are concerned. This can also be put in terms of protection of certain 'irreducible rights'.[25]

There is also a 'certainty' argument for rejecting transparency as a legitimising factor. In short, the argument is that effective consumer protection needs to be straightforward, to draw bright lines as to unacceptable terms and practices and to avoid debates as to the degree of transparency that might legitimise a term or practice.

Transparency as a legitimising factor in relation to contract terms

'Always unfair' terms

It is clear enough that transparency does *not* legitimise terms that are 'blacklisted'. UK domestic law has taken this approach to certain terms since the Unfair Contract Terms Act (UCTA) 1977. The terms in question are those that exclude or restrict liability for death or injury caused by negligence;[26] and (in consumer sale and supply of goods contracts) terms excluding or restricting the implied terms as to description, quality and fitness for particular purpose.[27]

Under the Sales Directive, there can be no exclusion or restriction[28] of the conformity obligations[29] (broadly reflecting the UK implied terms as

[25] This is a phrase used by Hugh Beale in this context in H. Beale, 'Legislative Control of Fairness', in J. Beatson and D. Freidmann, *Good Faith and Fault in Contract* (Oxford University Press, 1995), 232 at 245. Insisting on a certain level of fairness in substance has also been referred to as being about creation of a 'social market', within which certain basic social rights are guaranteed even within a market exchange (see H. Collins, 'Good Faith in European Contract Law' (1994) 14 *OJLS* 228, at 246).

[26] UCTA, s. 2(1). [27] UCTA, ss. 6(2) and 7(2).

[28] 99/44/EC, Art. 7. [29] See 99/44/EC, Art. 2.

to description, quality and fitness) or of the remedies (repair, replacement, price reduction and rescission)[30] available in cases of breach. The original Consumer Rights Directive proposal would have also blacklisted terms excluding or restricting liability for death or injury.[31] This proposal would also have blacklisted terms by which traders deny responsibility for commitments undertaken by their agents.[32] There would also have been bans on terms that in varying ways interfere with consumer access to justice,[33] seemingly reflecting the fundamental right to access to justice. However, as indicated above, all of the unfair terms elements were dropped from the final Directive. As such, such terms must be assessed as normal, with all other terms, under the general clause on unfairness. This re-emphasises the importance of questions as to the role of transparency under the general test.

The threshold question of core terms and the bank charges issue

On terms, the question as the legitimising force of transparency arises, first, in relation to the inability, in so far as a term is plain and intelligible, to make an assessment of fairness which relates to: 'the adequacy of the price and remuneration as against the services or goods supplied in exchange'.[34]

In short, transparency legitimises, in that if there is transparency (at least in the form of plain language), the substantive fairness of the price cannot be reviewed. However, the point is that the test above actually leaves open precisely what the 'price' is; so, in this sense, it leaves open exactly what is legitimised by transparency. This uncertainty has caused a problem in the UK. The Supreme Court chose to give the broadest possible legitimising role to transparency by taking the decision that 'price' covers virtually any charge (including those in question) that is formally expressed as a primary obligation.[35] This approach was applied to terms providing for very high bank charges to be levied

[30] See 99/44/EC, Art. 3.

[31] Consumer Rights Directive, Annex II, para. (b). [32] Para. (b).

[33] Excluding or hindering the right to take legal action or exercise a legal remedy, particularly by requiring consumers to take disputes exclusively to arbitration not covered by legal provisions (para. (c)); restricting the evidence available to the consumer or imposing on him a burden of proof that, under the applicable law, would lie with the trader (para. (d)); and giving the trader the right to determine whether the goods or services are in conformity or the exclusive right to interpret any term of the contract (para. (e)).

[34] UTCCD, Art. 4(2); UTCCR, Reg. 6(2)(b).

[35] *OFT* v. *Abbey National and others* [2009] UKSC 6.

when, for instance, consumers exceeded agreed overdraft limits. These charges were viewed by the Supreme Court as the 'price' for the purposes of this provision. This places the Supreme Court firmly in the 'assisted informed consent' camp. It ignores the fact that there are limited prospects of real informed consent with such charges, which are surely, in reality, very distant from what would affect the average consumer's mind as something payable in the normal performance of the contract. (Even if there was any meaningful form of informed consent, consumers would not have the bargaining power to have such terms deleted.) It also ignores the fact that such charges were unlikely to have been subjected to market discipline, because it is not the sort of matter that would have had a routine impact on the active margin of consumers.[36] As a result, there was rarely any significant choice for consumers all banks using terms allowing for these charges. Finally, the Supreme Court fails to read into the rule any sort of solidarity ethic. Such a solidarity ethic would surely hold that the charges were disproportionately high (£30, £40, etc.) for even the smallest and shortest-term unauthorised borrowing. Based on such an ethic, one might choose a narrow interpretation of 'price', so as to ensure that the charges would not be classed as the 'price' and would be subject to direct control under the unfairness test.

The broader point is that it would surely be better if the directive made it clearer how 'price' was to be understood for the purposes of this rule. This would be one way of making it clearer whether or not transparency can legitimise terms. In fact an indirect clarification may come with the Consumer Rights Directive. The final version does not deal with unfair terms as such (as mentioned several times above). However there is provision for specific consumer consent to be given to charges that are not paid in exchange for the trader's 'main' obligation.[37] The obvious intention here seems to be to distinguish between remuneration given for the trader's main obligation; and that (bank

[36] Interestingly, since the decision, there does now appear to be some competition over such charges between banks. For example, banks, including Santander, are advertising 'no fees' for unauthorised borrowing. However, this was not the case before, i.e. during the period when the charges being challenged were being used and when many customers were affected by them (these being customers who may expect to be told that they cannot claim back the charges in private law, because the charges were core price terms (despite the lack of competition over them when these consumers agreed to them)). An open question is why there is now competition – greater public awareness and anger? Political pressure?

[37] 2011/83/EU, Art. 22.

charges, for example) remuneration paid in exchange for other subsidiary 'services' (in the case of the bank charges, the 'service' is allowing the unauthorised borrowing to go ahead). This might suggest that a similar distinction is intended under the UTCCD. However it would obviously be better if the UTCCD itself was amended to make it absolutely clear that subsidiary charges are not price terms; and are therefore subject to the general test of unfairness.

The unfairness test

The next question in relation to terms is whether, in *applying* the test of unfairness, transparency can always, or at least very readily, legitimise, notwithstanding unfairness in substance.

In some respects, the sense might be that the answer must be in the negative. After all, there *is* currently a long 'indicatively unfair' list describing seventeen types of term;[38] regulatory practice tends to view these terms as unfair, transparency notwithstanding.[39] The Consumer Rights Directive would have moved further to strengthen the notion that this is correct by providing that terms on the list are 'presumed to be unfair'.[40] But, as we have seen, the unfair terms provisions are not in the final Directive.

But the stability of this position in relation to these terms, and more generally, is ultimately dependent on the precise language of the unfairness (significant imbalance/violation of good faith) test itself,[41] and how it is interpreted by the courts. In order for a term to be unfair it must cause a significant imbalance in rights and obligations to the detriment of the consumer; *and* it must violate the requirement of good faith. The open-textured nature of the 'good faith' limb of the test (which includes the

[38] UTCCD, Art. 3(3) and Annex; UTCCR, Reg. 5 (2) and Schedule 2.

[39] See discussion by Willett, *Fairness in Consumer Contracts* at 6.3.3 and 6.5. It is true, of course, that terms such as exemption clauses come in that huge variety of forms and some will be much less unfair in substance than others. However, even in the context of exemption clauses, it is clear that the OFT views many as unfair, however they are presented. So, for instance, the OFT generally views terms as unfair where they completely exclude a particular liability that would otherwise arise; or significantly *limit* liability (e.g. limitation of the damages claimable so as not to cover consequential losses) (Unfair Contract Terms Guidance, 2001, paras. 1.3, 2.2.2, 2.3.1 and 2.3.3).

[40] CRD, Art. 35 (of course, this is a separate list from the new blacklist that would be added by the CRD – see above at n. 31 and related text.

[41] UTCCD, Art. 3(1); UTCCR, Reg. 5(1).

issue of transparency)[42] leaves open the possibility of transparency not only being a necessary requirement, but also being a legitimising factor, i.e. a factor that can prevent there being a violation of good faith. If there is no violation of good faith, there is no unfairness, given that terms must cause significant imbalance *and* violate the good faith requirement in order to be unfair.

The position of the ECJ is unclear. The Court has said that it is generally for national courts to apply the general clause on unfairness to the term in question within the relevant national legal context.[43] However, it seems that the Court *will* step in and decide that a term is definitely unfair where there is no 'benefit' at all for the consumer.[44] This may refer to there being no countervailing *substantive* benefit, i.e. that there is no price advantage or other favourable term that might be said to counterbalance the unfairness of the term under scrutiny.[45] If this is what the ECJ is referring to, then this effectively means that transparency cannot legitimise terms that are unduly unfair in substance and which are not balanced out by a substantively favourable provision. This would mean that Member States were required to protect consumers from terms that were sufficiently unfair in substance, and should not allow transparency as a 'defence' in such cases. Certainly, the ECJ has said that an 'exclusive jurisdiction' clause[46] offered no benefit to the consumer and was, therefore, unfair.[47] However, no argument seems to have been made in the case as to the term being transparent. So it remains unclear whether, if a term is sufficiently transparent, this can count as a 'benefit'. It therefore also remains unclear whether, for the ECJ, transparency can legitimise a term that is substantively unfair. Indeed, it is not inconceivable that the 'benefit' concept might be developed by the ECJ to the point where (for the ECJ) a 'benefit' (in the form of transparency) was always taken to be sufficient to defeat a finding of unfairness.

[42] Good faith certainly involves a consideration of procedural fairness (as well as fairness in substance); the preamble referring to good faith as an 'overall evaluation of the different interests involved' (recital 16). This certainly seems to include transparency (see Willett, *Fairness in Consumer Contracts*).

[43] Joined cases, *Océano Grupo Editorial* and *Salvat Editores* and *Freiburger Kommunalbauten GmbH Baugesellschaft & Co. KG*, n. 10.

[44] *Ibid.*

[45] See *Freiburger* case, n. 10; and Willett, *Fairness in Consumer Contracts*, 3.5.4.

[46] This is a clause requiring the consumer to take action only in a particular Spanish city (where the trader, not the consumer, was based).

[47] Joined cases, *Océano Grupo Editorial* and *Salvat Editores*, n. 10.

Turning to the UK courts, the Court of Appeal *has* indicated that transparency does not necessarily legitimise where the term is sufficiently unfair in substance. Peter Gibson LJ cited the following comment by Hugh Beale:

> 'I suspect good faith has a double operation. First it has a procedural aspect. It will require the supplier to consider the consumer's interests. However, a clause which might be unfair if it came as a surprise may be upheld if the business took steps to bring it to the consumer's attention and to explain it. Secondly, it has a substantive content: some clauses may cause such an imbalance that they should always be treated as being contrary to good faith and therefore unfair.'[48]

However, the former House of Lords has not confirmed this beyond doubt. Lord Bingham has equated good faith with 'fair and open dealing'.[49] He said that 'openness' meant that terms should be 'expressed fully, clearly and legibly', not containing 'concealed pitfalls or traps', and being given 'appropriate prominence' where they might 'operate disadvantageously' to the consumer.[50] 'He said that 'fair' dealing: 'requires that the supplier should not, whether deliberately or unconsciously, take advantage of the consumer's necessity, indigence, lack of experience, unfamiliarity with the subject matter of the contract [or] weak bargaining position'.[51]

This may mean simply that consumers (as a class) are presumptively treated as suffering from the various weaknesses listed (i.e. these are weaknesses *relative* to the trader); and that traders are to be viewed as taking advantage of these if they use terms that are unduly detrimental in substance to consumer interests. In short, a reasonable level of fairness in substance is required for 'fair' dealing. If this is the case then, given that fair dealing is expressed as a *separate* requirement from 'open' dealing (fair *and* open), the suggestion would be that (for Lord Bingham) transparency *cannot* legitimise terms that are sufficiently unfair in substance. However, the difficulty is that it is far from clear that the above quotation *does* refer simply to unfairness in substance. It might be argued, for instance, that there is only 'advantage taking' where there is some positive procedural impropriety and/or the consumer is especially vulnerable in some way. In other words, it is not possible to say for sure

[48] From Beale, 'Legislative Control of Fairness', 245, cited in *Director General of Fair Trading* v. *First National Bank* [2000] 2 All ER 759 at 769.
[49] *Director General of Fair Trading* v. *First National Bank* [2001] 3 WLR 1297, at 1308.
[50] At 1308. [51] *Ibid.*

that Lord Bingham viewed fairness in substance as an entirely free-standing requirement.

Lord Steyn approved Lord Bingham's views as to good faith.[52] However, he also said that '[a]ny purely procedural or even predominantly procedural interpretation of the requirement of good faith must be rejected'.[53] This does not state explicitly, but does strongly suggest, that procedural fairness (including transparency) cannot legitimise a term that is sufficiently unfair in substance. However, there was no positive support from the other three judges for this. They did not reject any of Lord Steyn's judgment, but simply referred to their approval of the judgment of Lord Bingham.[54] In fact, the House of Lords was not required to answer the question as to the legitimising function of transparency, because it was not accepted that the term in question actually caused a significant (substantive) imbalance in rights and obligations[55] (so, whether unfairness in substance could be legitimised by transparency did not arise).

The position of lower courts is also unclear. Terms providing for substantial commission to be paid to an estate agent for minimal services in return have been held to be unfair by the High Court.[56] These were considered to cause a significant imbalance to the detriment of the consumer[57] (i.e. to be unfair in substance). It was also found that these commissions were not given sufficient prominence to satisfy the requirement of good faith.[58] The suggestion, certainly, is that a greater degree of prominence might have sufficed. Now, it does not necessarily follow from this that the court would take the view that *some* terms might *not* be able to be legitimised (via the good faith concept) by transparency. Equally, there was certainly no express indication of such a view.

It should also be noted here that the proposal of the English and Scottish Law Commissions to replace the good faith/imbalance test with a 'fair and reasonable' test[59] would not, in itself, resolve this question. This, as we have seen, is a question that arises because of the reference to good faith in the test. However, this being a test deriving from a

[52] At 1313. [53] *Ibid.*

[54] See the judgments of Lord Hope (1314–18), Lord Millett (1318–20) and Lord Rodger (1320–4)

[55] Lord Bingham at 1308, Lord Steyn at 1313–14, Lord Hope at 1316 and Lord Millett at 1319.

[56] *Office of Fair Trading* v. *Foxtons Ltd* [2009] EWHC 1681 (Ch).

[57] See paras. 90, 101 and 103. [58] See paras. 94, 101 and 106.

[59] Law Commissions, *Unfair Terms in Contracts*, Law Commission 292, Scottish Law Commission 199, at 3.84–96 and Draft Unfair Terms Bill, s. 4 (1).

European directive (the UTCCD), EU law requires that the national measures implementing the test be interpreted so as to give effect to its meaning.[60] In other words, good faith (whatever it means in terms of the role of transparency) must be read into any new UK test (whatever terminology it uses). Further, the proposed 'fair and reasonable' test would actually refer explicitly to transparency as a key factor to be taken into account.[61] It is true that the view of the Law Commissions is that the test be should be viewed as one under which a term can be sufficiently unfair in substance to be held to be unfair whatever the circumstances in which the agreement is made[62] (which we assume includes the question as to transparency). However, such a possibility is not provided for expressly in the test; so it would remain uncertain how the courts would approach the issue.

There must be a real risk that the Supreme Court could routinely accept transparency as a legitimising factor. Indeed, to return to the bank charges example, suppose that such charges ultimately can be tested for fairness under the general test. This might happen on the basis of the provision in the Consumer Rights Directive discussed above; that might suggest that 'price' should be understood more narrowly. Alternatively, there might be another way of arguing the case that might lead to the conclusion that bank charges were not excluded from the fairness test.[63] Either way, even if the charges were subject to the unfairness test, there is the possibility that the Supreme Court would hold that the general awareness of such terms rendered them transparent; that this satisfied the good faith requirement; and that, therefore, whether or not they caused significant imbalance/detriment, they were not unfair. In short, there is a chance that the Supreme Court

[60] *Marleasing SA* v. *La Commercialde Alimentacion* [1992] 1 CMLR 305; *Faccini Dori* [1995] All ER (EC) 1.

[61] *Unfair Terms in Contracts*; Draft Unfair Terms Bill, s. 4 (2)(1).

[62] Law Commissions, *Unfair Terms*, at 3.93.

[63] What is excluded from review under the unfairness test is the 'adequacy' of the price 'as against the goods or services supplied in exchange' (UTCCD, Art. 4(1), UTCCR, Reg. 6 (2)). This may refer only to whether the price is too high in relation to the goods or services received in exchange. It might, therefore be arguable that the exclusion does not apply at all where the complaint is not about adequacy, but about *equality*. The argument would be that those consumers being charged the various unauthorised borrowing fees were being unfairly discriminated against in that they were, to a disproportionate extent, cross-subsidising other customers, i.e. they were paying very high charges in order to save the majority of customers from relatively modest routine standing charges for banking services.

would carry over its 'assisted informed consent' approach into application of the general test on unfairness.

Such an approach would differ from that taken elsewhere. Certainly, the understanding in some civil law countries is that transparency is not necessarily a legitimising factor under the test in the UTCCD. One German scholar has strongly criticised what he views as an undue fixation with the procedural aspects of good faith at the expense of the substantive aspects.[64] Indeed, the German law implementing the UTCCD arguably emphasises that transparency is not necessarily a legitimising factor in two ways. First, there are separate provisions on 'surprising' terms (aimed at lack of transparency) and 'review of subject matter'.[65] The latter refers to whether the terms 'contrary to the requirement of good faith ... place the [consumer] at an unreasonable disadvantage'. (Given the separate provision on transparency, this seems to be focused principally on the impact of the term on the substantive interests of the parties.) Secondly, this latter test goes on to provide that an unreasonable disadvantage 'may *also* result from the fact that the provision is not clear and comprehensible'; indicating, surely, that an unreasonable disadvantage *may* be caused by unfairness in substance, irrespective of transparency.

So there may be a divergence between a tendency in UK courts to the 'assisted informed consent' model and the German model which appears to be more focused on solidarity (in the sense of protection from the impact of unfair substantive terms irrespective of transparency). This calls into question whether the UTCCD is successfully achieving the goal of a 'high level' of protection (certainly as far as the UK is concerned). The divergence between the UK and Germany also calls into question whether the UTCCD is successfully eradicating competitive distortions. It would, therefore, be extremely helpful if the UTCCD was amended so as to spell out that a term does not necessarily satisfy the requirement of good faith simply because it was transparent.

Transparency as a legitimising factor in relation to commercial practices

As already indicated, the UCPD is a more recent, and very important, extension of Europeanisation of consumer law. It is important, not least because of the huge range of behaviour it covers, i.e. any practice

[64] Micklitz, *The Politics of Judicial Co-operation in the EU*, 355–423.
[65] See, respectively, BGB, Art. 305c and BGB, Art. 307(1).

affecting consumer transactional decision-making carried out 'before, during or after' any 'commercial transaction'.[66] This means that, in relation to almost all conceivable goods or services, the regime applies from the stage of promoting and selling through to performance and enforcement. In doing so, it replaces well-known generally applicable domestic regimes, such as those on false trade descriptions and misleading pricing[67] while complementing more particular rules, e.g. those on harassment of debtors[68] and the regulatory rules on financial services.[69]

This broad coverage makes it especially important to pin down the general ethic of protection. Is it the 'assisted informed consent' model that allows transparency to legitimise practices, other unfairness notwithstanding? Or is it the more protective, solidarity-orientated ethic that requires more than transparency for fairness? As with unfair terms, this issue is important in determining whether the aim of a 'high level' of protection is achieved. Also, as with unfair terms, there is the risk that significant divergences in national interpretation will emerge (undermining the goal to eradicate competitive distortions) if we do not work towards a clear view as to the ethic of protection that is intended. Finally, the full harmonisation rule under the UCPD may make this issue especially significant.[70]

It is clear enough that the ethic is one of 'assisted informed consent' in the case of the 'misleading action' and 'misleading omission' concepts. Here, respectively, all the trader must do is avoid providing information that is likely to mislead the average consumer and provide information that is 'needed' by the average consumer to enable an 'informed' decision to be made.[71] It also seems fairly clear that the more protective ethic is intended in the case of the 'harassment' and 'coercion' limbs of the 'aggressive practice' concept.[72] Here, there is an aggressive practice if the harassment or coercion significantly restricts the 'freedom of choice' of the average consumer. It seems most likely that 'freedom of choice'

66 UCPD, Art. 3(1)/Consumer Protection from Unfair Trading Regulations (CPUTR) 2008, Reg. 2 (1).

67 These were the Trade Descriptions Act 1968 and the Consumer Protection Act 1987, Part III.

68 Administration of Justice Act 1970, s. 40.

69 In particular the powers of the Financial Services Authority under the Financial Services and Markets Act 2000.

70 It has certainly been held that national rules on commercial practices must be able to justify themselves under the tests in the UCPD (Joined cases *VTB-VAB NV* v. *Total Belgium NV* (C-261/07) and *Galatea BVBA* v. *Sanoma Magazines Belgium NV* (C-299/07)).

71 UCPD, Arts. 6 and 7; CPUTR, Regs. 5 and 6.

72 UCPD, Arts. 8 and 9; CPUTR, Reg. 7.

is restricted where the consumer is placed in a position where there are two or more substantively unreasonable alternatives, e.g. to go through an unnecessarily time consuming and burdensome complaints process or to abandon the complaint against the trader.[73] It does not seem that transparency is any type of defence in such cases. Indeed, the consumer will very often understand exactly what his options are, the problem being simply that these options are unreasonable.[74]

However, uncertainty as to the potentially legitimising role of transparency does arise in relation to the 'undue influence' limb of the aggressive practices concept[75] and under the general clause on professional diligence.[76] The problem is that, in both these cases, the requirement is that the practice should affect the ability of the consumer to take an 'informed decision'.[77] Now, it can certainly be rationalised that the informed decision-making of consumers can be so affected by a practice that formalised transparency (whether as to risks, the likelihood of the practice being carried out, etc.) will be unlikely to reinstate the possibility of a genuinely informed decision.[78] Nevertheless, the 'informed decision' concept undoubtedly leaves open the possibility of it being held that practices can always (or at least routinely) be legitimised by transparency. So, it would be better if the UCPD were amended so as to clarify that this will not necessarily be the case (or even that it will rarely be the case). This would clarify that these concepts are intended to provide a

[73] See, for example, the example of an aggressive practice on the 'always unfair' list: 'Requiring a consumer who wishes to claim on an insurance policy to produce documents which could not reasonably be considered relevant as to whether the claim was valid, or failing systematically to respond to pertinent correspondence, in order to dissuade a consumer from exercising his contractual rights' (UCPD, Annex, para. 27; CPUTR, Schedule 1, para. 27). This seems to be an example of the freedom of choice concept in action.

[74] See the discussion of this concept in C. Willett, 'Unfairness under the Consumer Protection from Unfair Trading Regulations', in J. Devenney, L. Fox-Mahoney and M. Kenny (eds.), *Conceptualising Unconscionability in Europe* (Cambridge University Press, 2010).

[75] UCPD, Arts. 8 and 9; CPUTR, Reg. 7.

[76] UCPD, Art. 5; CPUTR, Reg. 3(3). If a practice is not covered by the misleading action, misleading omission or aggressive practice general tests and is not on the 'always unfair' list, it may be caught by the general professional diligence clause, which seems to be aimed mainly at new practices that somehow are not covered by the misleading and aggressive concepts as currently defined (G. Howells, H. Micklitz and T. Wilhelmsson, *European Fair Trading Law: the Unfair Commercial Practices Directive* (Aldershot: Ashgate. 2006), 121).

[77] UCPD, Arts. 8 and 2 (j) and CPUTR, Reg. 7(3)(a) (undue influence); UCPD, Arts. 5 and 2 (e) and CPUTR, Regs. 3 (3) and 2(1) (professional diligence).

[78] See C. Willett, 'Fairness and Consumer Decision Making under the Unfair Commercial Practices Directive' (2010) *Journal of Consumer Policy*, 247.

reasonably high level of protection; that providing such a level of protection is not at risk from the full harmonisation rule; and it would potentially reduce the scope for divergent national approaches (divergences that will undermine the goal of eradicating competitive distortions).

Concluding comments

This chapter has considered the important question of the ethic of protection in EU consumer law and the extent to which it is restricted to an 'assisted informed consent' model. Certainly, it is not always so restricted. However, a key message has been that there is too often uncertainty as to whether this is the case, and key legislative provisions could be amended to make the position more certain. This is important in terms of the level of protection available in general; in terms of achieving the high level of protection goals of the directives; in achieving the goal of eradicating competitive distortions; and because of the full harmonisation context.

Finally, it may be that, in the absence of legislative clarification, regulators could have a key role to play in producing rigorous, research-based arguments that challenge the notion that transparency should routinely provide a 'defence'. Regulators, in practice, play a key role in unpacking the relevant concepts. Under both the unfair terms and unfair practices regimes, bodies such as the OFT and local trading standards authorities have powers to seek injunctions and enforcement orders against traders using unfair terms and practices.[79] However, for present purposes the key point is the regulatory element that partners these powers, this being the publication of guidance about the concepts and their application.[80] An enormous amount of work has been done since 1994 on unfair terms,[81] and guidance also now exists on practices.[82] This guidance is in a position to develop the concepts in ways that are strongly grounded in research work that demonstrates the limited capacity of transparency to genuinely inform consumers, and also the serious impact of terms and practices in a substantive sense. We should emphasise here that there

[79] UTCCR, Regs. 10–14; CPUTR, Reg. 26 and Enterprise Act 2002, s. 212.
[80] In the case of the UTCCR, there are specific duties to do this (UTCCR, Reg. 15).
[81] See OFT website on unfair contract terms.
[82] See OFT/BERR (2008), *Guidance on the Consumer Protection from Unfair Trading Regulations* (London: OFT/BERR), available at http://www.oft.gov.uk/shared_oft/business_leaflets/cpregs/oft1008.pdf.

is no implied criticism of the quality of argument adopted in previous OFT work or cases. The point is that an especially high degree of research-based rigour may be required, given the uncertainty as to the role of transparency and the possible innate inclination of the UK Supreme Court to the 'assisted informed consent' philosophy.

So, regulators, especially, the OFT, might draw heavily, for instance, on the behavioural economics research that consistently highlights the limitations of transparency in genuinely informing consumers.[83] This would strengthen the case for not allowing transparency to legitimise unfair terms and practices. This case might also be strengthened by drawing on research as to the economic and social impact on consumers of unfair substantive outcomes and risks.[84] A strong focus on this might influence courts to conclude that the 'assisted informed consent' model will often provide inadequate protection.

[83] See the literature cited at notes 18–24 above and see the related text. Note also that the European Commission has recently emphasised that the concepts in the UCPD should be interpreted in the light of this work (European Commission, Guidance on the Implementation/Application of Directive 2005/29/EC on Unfair Commercial Practices, SEC (2009) 1666. Brussels: European Commission, at 32).

[84] The OFT carries out extensive research on 'consumer detriment' (see, for example, www.oft.gov.uk/news/press/2006/detriment); and the point is that such research might be more rigorously built into guidance that unpacks the appropriate interpretations of the key unfairness concepts.

10

The best interests of the child and EU consumer law and policy: a major gap between theory and practice?

AMANDINE GARDE

Introduction

Children, who make up around a fifth of the EU population, are consumers in their own right in that they represent three markets:

- the primary market, as they have more and more buying power with their own money to spend;[1]
- the parental market, as they play a major role in influencing what their parents buy; and
- the future market, as it is likely that they will stick to the consumption habits which they have acquired as children when they grow older.[2]

Recent evidence suggests that, in the UK alone, overall spending on children (including childcare and education) amounts to around £100 billion per year.[3] It is therefore not surprising that children have received the increased attention of traders. First, they have become exposed to a growing number and range of commercial messages, which extend far

Senior Lecturer, Durham Law School.

[1] Recent estimates suggest that children now receive an average of £10 per week in pocket money and £16 in *ad hoc* hand-outs. D. Buckingham, *The Impact of the Commercial World on Children's Wellbeing* (Department for Children, School and Families and Department for Culture, Media and Sport, December 2009).

[2] In relation to food choices, for example, evidence emphasises the need to focus obesity prevention policies on children in light of the fact that an obese child is more likely to become an obese adult if he/she does not change his/her eating habits. Overweight children enter adulthood with a raised risk of adult obesity of up to seventeen-fold: H. Hauner, 'Transfer into Adulthood', in W. Kiess, C. Marcus and M. Wabtish (eds.), *Obesity in Childhood and Adolescence: Pediatrics and Adolescent Medicine*, vol. IX (S. Karger AG, 2004), 219.

[3] Buckingham, *The Impact of the Commercial World on Children's Wellbeing.*

beyond traditional media advertising and involve activities such as online marketing, sponsorship and peer-to-peer marketing.[4] Moreover, certain marketing techniques, including the use of cartoon or licensed characters, have been specifically developed to seduce young audiences.[5] Finally, companies are using 'integrated marketing communications', in which promotional activities range across different media platforms and which often blur the distinction between promotional and other content.[6] This commercialisation of childhood has raised significant concerns about harmful effects on children's well-being, and in particular on their mental and physical health.

The United Nations Convention on the Rights of the Child (often referred to as 'the UNCRC') has recognised that children form a vulnerable group of society requiring special protection from commercial exploitation.[7] More generally, Article 3(1) provides that 'in all actions concerning children, whether undertaken by public or private social welfare institutions, courts of law, administrative authorities or legislative bodies, the best interests of the child shall be a primary consideration'. At EU level, the best interests of the child principle is echoed in Article 24 of the EU Charter of Fundamental Rights and in the Commission Communication of 4 July 2006 establishing a long-term EU strategy to effectively promote and safeguard the rights of the child in EU policies and to support Member States' efforts in this field.[8] Moreover, the Lisbon Treaty, which recently entered into force, explicitly mentions the protection of the rights of the child as an objective of the European Union.

This chapter focuses on how the Union has taken the special vulnerability of children into account and ensured that they are sufficiently protected from harmful commercial practices when adopting and implementing EU consumer policy. It argues that there is indeed a significant gap between theory and practice in this area of EU competence. After

[4] *Ibid.*

[5] See in particular J. McGinnis, J. Gootman and V. Kraak, *Food Marketing to Children and Youth: Threat or Opportunity?* (Washington, DC: Institute of Medicine, 2006) and J. Harris, M. Schwartz and K. Brownell, 'Marketing Foods to Children and Adolescents: Licensed Characters and other Promotions on Packaged Foods in the Supermarket' (2009) 13 *Public Health Nutrition*, 409.

[6] Buckingham, *The Impact of the Commercial World on Children's Wellbeing.*

[7] Art. 36 mandates that states parties shall protect the child against all forms of exploitation prejudicial to any aspects of the child's welfare, while Art. 17(e) requires them to encourage the development of appropriate guidelines for the protection of the child from information and material injurious to his or her well-being.

[8] COM (2006) 367 final. The Commission Communication provides explicitly that the provisions of the UNCRC must be fully taken into account: at para. I.3.

focusing on the role which the best interests of the child principle should play in EU consumer law and policy, two case studies are presented: the first one on the regulation of product safety and the second one on the regulation of advertising to children. This chapter concludes with a few remarks on a possible way forward to ensure that theory and practice meet and that the best interests of the child are effectively upheld as a primary consideration in EU consumer policy.

The best interests of the child in EU consumer law and policy

Until a few years ago, EU law had paid hardly any attention to children's rights. The Treaty of Rome made no reference whatsoever to children. It is only following the adoption of the Treaty of Amsterdam that the first express reference to children was introduced in the EU Treaty, as Article K provided a basis for intergovernmental cooperation to tackle 'offences against children'. Nevertheless, this mention only concerned the cooperation of EU Member States in relation to such offences, without granting any new power of legislative harmonisation to the Union.[9] Moreover, the only secondary legislation affecting children which was adopted in the early days of the Community involved the extension of the right to education and social and tax advantages which workers benefited from to their children so as to facilitate their movement from one Member State to another.[10]

The gradual extension from Rome to Amsterdam of EU legislative competence, to areas such as consumer, environmental or employment protection has necessarily had an impact, either direct or indirect, on children. Moreover, the powers granted to the EU to support Member

[9] The Amsterdam Treaty contained other developments of relevance to children, even though they did not have children as their direct focus: Art. 13 EC introduced a non-discrimination clause empowering EU institutions to adopt legislation on various equality grounds, including age; Art. 137(j) EC introduced a legal basis for combating social exclusion, and tackling child poverty has become a key objective for EU action. More generally, Art. 6(2) TEU reaffirmed the EU's commitment to fundamental rights (which include children's rights). Following the entry into force of the Lisbon Treaty, Art. 13 EC, Art. 137 EC and Art. 6 TEU have been renumbered Art. 19 TFEU, Art. 153 TFEU and Art. 6 TEU respectively.

[10] See in particular Arts. 12 and 7(2) of Reg. 1612/68 ([1968] OJ L 257/2). Clare McGlynn has argued that children were seen as an obstacle to the proper functioning of the internal market, rather than as individuals in their own right: C. McGlynn, 'Rights for Children? The Potential Impact of the European Union Charter of Fundamental Rights' (2002) 8 *EPL* 387, at 388. See also H. Stalford, 'The Developing European Agenda on Children's Rights' (2000) 22 *Journal of Social Welfare and Family Law* 234.

States' action in fields such as public health, education or cultural policy also have the potential to affect children. In the 1980s and 1990s, the EU adopted certain measures of secondary legislation which more or less directly affected the legal position of children within the EU legal order.[11] Nevertheless, such legislation was adopted on an incremental basis and could not be regarded as constituting a coherent EU policy on children intended to promote their best interests. This prompted the formation of non-governmental organisations such as EURONET – the European Children's Network, which was founded in 1995 as a coalition of networks and organisations representing the interests of children in the Member States.[12] Their effective advocacy, together with the momentum created by the adoption in 1989 of the UNCRC, led to the recognition at EU level that the best interests of the child should become a primary consideration.

The EU Charter of Fundamental Rights

The proclamation by the Heads of the Member States of the EU Charter heralded a change of attitude towards children. The EU Charter is the first instrument giving some visibility to children's rights at EU level. Article 24 is entirely dedicated to 'the Rights of the Child':

> 1. Children shall have the right to such protection and care as is necessary for their well-being. They may express their views freely. Such views shall be taken into consideration on matters which concern them in accordance with their age and maturity.
> 2. In all actions relating to children, whether taken by public authorities or private institutions, the child's best interests must be a primary consideration.
> 3. Every child shall have the right to maintain on a regular basis a personal relationship and direct contact with both his or her parents, unless that is contrary to his or her interests.[13]

[11] This is particularly true of the Toy Safety Directive (Directive 88/378, discussed below) and the Young Workers Directive (Directive 94/33, [1994] OJ L 216/12). See also the Television Without Frontiers Directive (Directive 89/552, discussed below).

[12] For information, see www.crin.org/euronet/index.asp. See also the work carried out by Save the Children Europe: www.savethechildren.net/alliance/europegroup/europegrp_who.html.

[13] Several other articles of the EU Charter advance the situation of children at EU level. On the role which the EU Charter could play to give more prominence to children's rights in the EU legal order, see McGlynn, 'Rights for Children?', 387; see also H. Cullen, 'Children's Rights', in S. Peers and A. Ward (eds.), *The EU Charter of Fundamental Rights* (Oxford: Hart, 2004).

Article 24 incorporates several principles of the UNCRC, not least by requiring that the best interests of the child shall be considered across all policy areas relating to children (subject to the constitutional principle of conferral).[14] As the Commission noted, '*if fully implemented*, this represents a significant step towards "child-proofing" of EU legislation and policy'.[15]

This chapter is not the place to make a detailed presentation of the provisions of the UNCRC.[16] Suffice it to say that the UN General Assembly adopted the UNCRC on 20 November 1989; it entered into force on 2 September 1990.[17] The UNCRC has since been complemented by two optional protocols relating to the involvement of children in armed conflicts and to the sale of children, prostitution and child pornography.[18] The UNCRC contains two main sections: Articles 1 to 41 lay down the rights it guarantees to all human beings below the age of eighteen,[19] and Articles 42 to 54 deal with its entry into force and monitoring. The rights guaranteed can be divided into civil, political, economic, social and cultural rights, according to a traditional subdivision of human rights or, alternatively, into provision, protection and participation rights, to use the 3 Ps classification commonly relied upon in the context of children's rights.[20]

The Committee on the Rights of the Child – the body of independent experts that monitors the implementation of the Convention and its

[14] The EU Charter applies only to areas which fall within the scope of EU competence, as explicitly stated in Art. 51. Thus, the situation still is that major policy areas affecting children, including the administration of juvenile justice or the legality of corporal punishments, remain within the remit of Member States' powers and are not therefore directly affected by Art. 24. Nevertheless, Member States are all signatories to the UNCRC and, as such, are bound to uphold the best interests of the child principle laid down in Art. 3(1).

[15] Preliminary Inventory of EU Actions Affecting Children's Rights Commission, Staff Working Document Accompanying the Communication from the Commission Towards an EU Strategy on the Rights of the Child, SEC (2006) 889, at 3.

[16] For a detailed account, see G. Van Bueren, *The International Law on the Rights of the Child* (London: Save the Children, 1995).

[17] To date, the convention has been ratified by 193 states. Only two countries in the world are not parties to the UNCRC: the United States of America (!) and Somalia. Note that by signing the convention, the United States has signalled its intention to ratify, but it has yet to do so.

[18] Both protocols entered into force in 2002.

[19] The definition of a child is provided by Art. 1: 'for the purposes of the present Convention, a child means every human being below the age of eighteen years unless under the law applicable to the child, majority is attained earlier'.

[20] E. Verhellen, *Convention on the Rights of the Child*, 3rd edn (Leuven-Apeldoorn: Garant, 2000), 79.

protocols by state parties – has underlined four overarching provisions which constitute the guiding principles for interpreting other UNCRC articles:

- the obligation of states to respect and ensure the rights set forth in the convention to each child within their jurisdiction without discrimination of any kind (Article 2);
- the best interests of the child as a primary consideration in all actions concerning children, whether undertaken by public or private social welfare institutions, courts of law, administrative authorities or legislative bodies (Article 3);
- the child's inherent right to life and states parties' obligation to ensure to the maximum extent possible the survival and development of the child development (Article 6); and
- the child's right to express his or her views freely in all matters affecting the child, those views being given due weight (Article 12).[21]

As already mentioned, this chapter focuses on the principle of the best interests of the child. It is striking that there is little official guidance available on how this principle should be interpreted.[22] Its scope was not discussed at the drafting stage of the UNCRC and the *travaux préparatoires* do not contain any useful information on the matter.[23] This is all the more surprising in the light not only of the vagueness and the uncertainties in the wording of Article 3 UNCRC but also of the practical significance of the principle it lays down.

Several academic commentators have argued that the best interests principle should be given a broad scope as 'it has the advantage of operating as a principle to be considered in relation to each of the rights in the Convention and importantly, residually, to all actions concerning children'.[24] The wording of Article 3 UNCRC supports the view that

[21] Committee on the Rights of the Child, General Comments N.5 (2003), CRC/GC/2003/5, 4.

[22] Some information is available on the scope of Art. 3 UNCRC in the General Comments of the Committee on the Rights of the Child and in Country Specific Reports. Similarly, the Network of Independent Experts has provided some guidance on the scope of Art. 24 of the EU Charter, though rather little focuses on the best interest principle.

[23] On the drafting history of the UNCRC, see M. Freeman, 'Article 3: The Best Interests of the Child', in A. Alen *et al.* (eds.), *A Commentary on the United Nations Convention on the Rights of the Child* (Martinus Nijhoff, 2007), 44. See also P. Alston, 'The Best Interests Principle: Towards a Reconciliation of Culture and Human Rights' (1994) 8 *International Journal of Law and the Family* 1, at 10.

[24] Van Bueren, *The International Law on the Rights of the Child*, 46. See also Alston, 'The Best Interests Principle', 4.

the best interests of the child should be taken into consideration in all fields of policy, including consumer policy ('all areas of policy relevant to children'). So does the wording of Article 24 EU Charter ('all areas relating to children').[25] The Committee on the Rights of the Child does adopt a broad construction, referring to 'all legal revisions as well as in judicial and administrative decisions, and in projects, programmes and services which have an impact on children'.[26] This approach seems to have been upheld by EU institutions. The Commission has stressed in its Communication of July 2006 the importance of mainstreaming children's rights into all EU policy areas.[27] A dynamic interpretation of the principle is all the more warranted in light of the growing commercialisation of childhood and its impact on children's health and well-being. Nevertheless, while it is clear that the principle of the best interests of the child applies to all institutions and bodies of the Union, giving substance to the principle remains a difficult task. The determination of the best interests should be made on a case-by-case basis, bearing in mind that priority should be given not to any interests of the child but to his or her *best* interests, as discussed below.

Until the EU Charter became legally binding following the entry into force of the Lisbon Treaty in December 2009, there were limits to

[25] It has been noted that Art. 24(2) Charter and Art. 3 UNCRC are not identical to the extent that Art. 24(2) states that the best interest principle will apply in all actions 'relating' to children, whereas Art. 3 refers to all actions 'concerning' children. It is not clear whether this change is deliberate and how significant it might be in practice. Writing in 2002, Clare McGlynn argued that 'concerning' children may encompass many more indirect measures than the formulation 'relating to' children. If it seems clear that all policies, practices and other measures which have a direct impact on children will 'relate to' them, it is not so obvious for indirect measures. A measure may not have been adopted with children in mind, it might make no reference to children, but it might 'concern' children as it has an impact on them. Can it equally be said that the same measure 'relates' to children? A policy may be too general to be said to 'relate to' children, even if it is not child neutral: C. McGlynn, 'Rights for Children?', 396. The Commission Communication seems to imply, however, that the difference in wording should not bear any consequences and that a broad understanding of Art. 24 should be adopted, as it provides that 'it is important to ensure that all internal and external EU policies respect children's rights in accordance with the principles of EU law, and that they are fully compatible with the principles and provisions of the UNCRC and other international instruments', and that 'children's interests should be considered across all policy areas *relevant* to children' (Impact Assessment annexed to the Communication, at para. 3.2.1), which includes both direct and indirect measures – the degree of relevance being proportionate to the degree of directness of a given measure.

[26] Report on Benin in 1999, CR/C/15/Add. 106, at para. 14. Cited in Freeman, 'Article 3: The Best Interests of the Child', in 46.

[27] The concept of mainstreaming is discussed further below.

the practical significance of Article 24, as the EU Charter remained a political declaration only. If it had been invoked by both the EU legislature and the European Court, it could only offer them guidance. Moreover, the fact that the EU Charter does not expressly refer to the UNCRC (and Article 3 more specifically) raises the question of the extent to which EU institutions will feel bound by its provisions and by the recommendations and interpretative guidance of the Committee on the Rights of the Child. Recent judgments of the ECJ and the Commission's Communication may assist in answering this question.

The Court's judgment in Council *v.* Parliament (Family Reunification Directive)

The ECJ referred to the UNCRC for the first time in *Council* v. *Parliament (Family Reunification Directive)* in June 2006.[28] In this case, the European Parliament brought an action before the Court, challenging the legality of Council Directive 2003/86 on the right to family reunification by third-country nationals.[29] The directive provides that third-country nationals residing lawfully in the territory of the Member States are in principle entitled to the grant of authorisation by the host Member State allowing their children to join them. Nevertheless, it allows Member States to derogate from these rules. In particular, if a child is aged over twelve years and arrives independently from the rest of his or her family, the Member State may verify whether the child meets an integration condition provided by national law.[30] The European Parliament argued that this derogation violated the fundamental right to family life and ran counter to the best interests of the child principle. It therefore challenged the validity of the directive before the ECJ. The Court rejected the claim. It first pointed out that the right to respect for family life within the meaning of the European Convention on Human Rights was among the fundamental rights protected in EU law and that the UNCRC and the EU Charter also recognised this right.[31] Such a statement is significant, in that it is the first time that the ECJ has ruled that the UNCRC provides a source of the general principles of EU law.[32]

[28] Case C-540/03 *Parliament* v. *Council* [2006] ECR I-5769.

[29] [2003] OJ L 251/12. [30] Art. 4.

[31] *Parliament* v. *Council*, at paras. 35–9 and 57 and 58.

[32] Three Advocates General had referred to the UNCRC in their opinions prior to the Court's judgment in *Parliament* v. *Council*: AG Stix-Hackl on 13 September 2001 in Case C-459/99 *MRAX* [2002] ECR I-6591; AG Jacobs on 22 May 2003 in Case C-148/02 *Garcia Avello* [2003] ECR I-11613; and AG Kokott on 11 November 2004 in Case C-105/

The Court continued as follows:

> These various instruments stress the importance to a child of family life and recommend that States have regard to the child's interests but they do not create for the members of a family an individual right to be allowed to enter the territory of a State and cannot be interpreted as denying Member States a certain margin of appreciation when they examine applications for family reunification.[33]

On scrutinising the contentious provision at stake, the Court held that the EU legislature had sufficiently considered the best interests of the child:

> The content of Article 4(1) of the Directive attests that the child's best interests were a consideration of prime importance when that provision was being adopted and that it does not appear that its final subparagraph fails to have sufficient regard to those interests or authorises Member States which choose to take account of a condition for integration not to have regard to them. On the contrary ... Article 5(5) of the Directive requires the Member States to have due regard to the best interests of minor children.[34]

The fact that the directive mentions the best interests of the child and that EU institutions have referred explicitly to the UNCRC in the drafting process of the directive is not sufficient evidence that they have upheld the best interests of the child principle as a primary consideration. The reasoning of the ECJ fails to convince. In particular, its short statement that the UNCRC and the EU Charter 'recommend that States have regard to the child's interests' contains two flaws: first, these instruments contain a legal obligation on Member States ('shall' is much more obligatory than 'recommend'); secondly, they require that the *best* interests of the child should be a primary consideration (not any interests). As the EU Network of Independent Experts on Fundamental Rights wrote a few weeks before the Court upheld the validity of the Family Reunification Directive:

> States should avoid the separation of children from their parents due to immigration laws. It has already been mentioned that under Article 4(1)(d) of the Family Reunification Directive, a child's entry may be refused under certain circumstances, allowing the Member States to derogate from the rule on admission of children by the way of requiring the child to meet a condition for integration in case the child is over the age of 12 years and he or she has arrived independently from the rest of his or

03 *Criminal Proceedings Against Maria Pupino* [2005] ECR I-5285 and on 8 September 2005 in *Parliament* v. *Council*.

[33] *Parliament* v. *Council*, at para. 59.

[34] *Parliament* v. *Council*, at para. 73.

> her family. It should be recalled that the CRC imposes the obligation upon State parties to ensure that a child 'shall not be separated from his or her parents against their will' (Article 9(1) CRC). More importantly, Article 10(1) provides that 'applications by a child or his or her parents to enter or leave a State party for the purpose of family reunification shall be dealt with by State Parties in a positive, humane and expeditious manner'.[35]

It is indeed regrettable that the Court has mentioned the best interests of the child principle in passing rather than engaged with the balancing exercise between competing interests this principle requires. The best interests of the child principle is a fundamental legal principle of interpretation which should be relied upon, as such, to resolve the balancing of potentially competing rights by adding weight to a particular right. The use which the ECJ made of the UNCRC in *Parliament* v. *Council* fails to convince in terms of where the balance should lie between the state's security concerns and the best interests of the child to be reunited with his or her family. As Geraldine Van Bueren has noted, the best interests of the child may require that the ambit of a state's margin of appreciation be limited in order to incorporate the child's best interests.[36] Indeed, in situations where different interests compete or conflict with one another, the best interests principle becomes decisive, bearing in mind that consideration of the best interests of the child must embrace short- as well as long-term considerations for the child.[37]

The Commission Communication Towards a Strategy on the Rights of the Child and its Follow-up

The rejection of the Constitutional Treaty by the French and the Dutch peoples in 2005 prevented the insertion of the EU Charter into Part II of the Treaty. Notwithstanding this backlash, the Commission identified children's rights as one of its main priorities in its Communication on strategic objectives for 2005–2009.[38] In this context, the Group of

[35] EU Network of Independent Experts on Fundamental Rights, *Implementing the Rights of the Child in the EU*, Thematic Comment no. 4, 20 May 2006, 88.

[36] G. Van Bueren, *Child Rights in Europe* (Council of Europe Publishing, 2007), 30.

[37] EU Network of Independent Experts on Fundamental Rights, *Implementing the Rights of the Child in the EU*, 86.

[38] 'A particular priority must be effective protection of the rights of children, both against economic exploitation and all forms of abuse, with the Union acting as a beacon to the rest of the world': Commission Communication, Europe 2010: A Partnership for European Renewal, Prosperity, Solidarity and Security – Strategic Objectives 2005–2009, COM (2005) 12 final, at para. 2.3.

Commissioners on Fundamental Rights, Non-discrimination and Equal Opportunities launched a specific initiative, in April 2005, to advance the promotion, protection and fulfilment of children's rights in the internal and external policies of the EU. This was followed up in March 2006 by European Council Conclusions requesting EU Member States 'to take necessary measures to rapidly and significantly reduce child poverty, giving all children equal opportunities, regardless of their social background'. On 4 July 2006, the Commission adopted its Communication establishing a long-term EU strategy to effectively promote and safeguard the rights of the child in all the EU's internal and external policies and to support Member States' efforts in this field.[39]

The Commission Communication states explicitly that the provisions of the UNCRC must be fully taken into account[40] and acknowledges (at last) that 'the idea of creating children friendly societies within the EU cannot be separated from the need to further deepen and consolidate European integration'.[41] It goes on to recognise that an enormous gap exists between the good intentions of international treaties and the real-life conditions of poverty, neglect and exploitation that millions of children worldwide are forced to endure and that, in spite of progress achieved in some areas, much remains to be done,[42] stressing that the EU can bring essential and fundamental added value in the field of children's rights in both its internal and its external policies:

> there is thus an urgent need for a comprehensive EU strategy to increase the scale and effectiveness of EU commitments to improve the situation of children globally and to demonstrate real political will at the highest possible level to ensure that the promotion and protection of children's rights get the place they merit on the EU's agenda.[43]

The Commission Communication has increased the visibility of children as a group of citizens whose specific rights and interests must be recognised and protected at EU level. It has created an impetus reflected in the recent adoption of a range of measures which have the protection of children as their main focus (not least on cybercrime, sexual exploitation, child trafficking and child poverty and social inclusion),[44] and has recognised more generally that the EU does indeed have a role to play in promoting the best interests of the child in all its policies.

[39] COM (2006) 367 final. [40] Commission Communication, para. I.3.
[41] *Ibid.* para. I.2. [42] *Ibid.* para. I.4. [43] *Ibid.* para. II.1.
[44] For a discussion of these measures, see in particular H. Stalford and E. Drywood, 'Coming of Age? Children's Rights in the European Union' (2009) 46 *CMLRev* 143.

The Lisbon Treaty goes one step further. Not only does it give the same legal value as the Treaties to the Charter, but it also proclaims the respect for children's rights as one of the EU's main objectives. Article 3 TEU (ex Article 2 EC) provides as follows:

> 1. The Union's aim is to promote peace, its values and the well-being of its peoples ...
> 3. The Union shall establish an internal market ... It shall combat social exclusion and discrimination, and shall promote social justice and protection, equality between women and men, solidarity between generations and *protection of the rights of the child* ...
> 5. In its relations with the wider world, the Union shall uphold and promote its values and interests and contribute to the protection of its citizens. It shall contribute to ... *the protection of human rights, in particular the rights of the child*, as well as to the strict observance and the development of international law, including respect for the principles of the UN Charter.[45]

The combination of Article 3 of the TEU, Article 24 of the Charter and the Commission Communication of 2006 provides an excellent basis to develop policies at EU level which effectively take the best interests of the child into account as a primary consideration.

The best interest of the child and competing claims

The best interests principle is a welfarist principle which recognises that children need special protection due to their particular vulnerability. This being said, Article 3(1) of the UNCRC (and correspondingly Article 24(2) of the EU Charter) must be contrasted with Article 3 of the Declaration of the Rights of the Child of 1959 which stresses that the best interests of the child should be the primary consideration.[46] This change of wording from *the* primary consideration to *a* primary consideration raises the question of the potential conflict between children's rights and other competing claims.

[45] Emphasis added.

[46] Principle 2 states:

> The child shall enjoy special protection, and shall be given opportunities and facilities, by law and by other means, to enable him to develop physically, mentally, morally, spiritually and socially in a healthy and normal manner and in conditions of freedom and dignity. In the enactment of laws for this purpose, the best interests of the child shall be the paramount consideration.

See also Art. 4 of the African Charter on the Rights and Welfare of the Child: 'In all actions concerning the child undertaken by any person or Authority the best interests of the child shall be the primary consideration.'

Potentially competing interests have long been identified in the UNCRC context as including the interests of parents, the interests of families, the interests of the community at large or the interests of all children (as opposed to the interests of one child). These interests may also be relevant in the EU context, as the case of *Parliament* v. *Council (Family Reunification Directive)* discussed above has shown. In this particular context, however, one other fundamental principle comes into play which is absent from most other settings: namely, the principle of free movement underpinning EU internal market law.[47]

EU consumer policy has always been closely linked to the establishment and proper functioning of the internal market, this 'area without frontiers in which the free movement of goods, persons, services and capital is ensured in accordance with the provisions of the Treaties'.[48] As is well known, the rationale for the internal market is to stimulate competition by opening up frontiers so that consumers have a larger choice of goods and services and businesses benefit from larger markets and more opportunities to establish themselves abroad. Economic integration offers several advantages to the EU population, including EU children: for example, the free movement of toys allows for a wider range of toys being made available to them so that they can play creatively and better develop as a result. Nevertheless, economic integration may also create difficulties when the fundamental principle of free movement conflicts with other fundamental interests such as consumer, public health, environmental or employment protection. More specifically, the principle of free movement may not necessarily operate in the best interests of the child-consumer: the free movement of goods may cause concern in the absence of sufficiently rigorous EU product safety standards; similarly, the free movement of services may facilitate the dissemination of harmful materials, including violent and pornographic images or advertising for goods and services whose consumption

[47] Art. 3(3) TEU, quoted above, makes it very apparent that the internal market remains at the very core of the EU's objectives.

[48] Art. 26(2) TFEU (ex Art. 14(2) EC). Most EU consumer legislation is based on Art. 114(1) TFEU (ex Art. 95(1) EC). This clearly stems from both the wording of Art. 169 TFEU (ex Art. 153 EC), which explicitly refers to Art. 114 TFEU and the wording of Art. 114(3), which clearly provides for the obligation of EU institutions to ensure a high level of consumer protection when adopting harmonising measures on the basis of Art. 114(1). The mainstreaming provision previously contained in Art. 153(2) EC has become a provision of general application enshrined in Art. 13 TFEU: 'consumer protection requirements shall be taken into account in defining and implementing other Union policies and activities'.

by children should be either avoided altogether or limited (tobacco, alcohol, unhealthy food, medicinal products and treatments, as well as gambling services).

It is firmly established that the proper functioning of the internal market requires that certain non-commercial interests should be taken into account. Free movement has never been unlimited: both the EU legislature and the European Court of Justice have always recognised the existence of overriding requirements of public interest justifying that limits be set to free movement.

The *Dynamic Medien* case specifically involved the conflict between the free movement of goods and the protection of children.[49] In this case, the company Avides Media sold video and audio media by mail order via its internet site and an electronic trading platform. In particular, it imported Japanese cartoons from the UK into Germany. The cartoons were examined before importation by the British Board of Film Classification which checked the audience targeted, classified the cartoons in the category 'suitable only for 15 years old and over' and labelled them accordingly. Dynamic Medien, a competitor of Avides Media, applied for interim relief with a view to prohibiting Avides Media from selling such image storage media by mail order on the ground that the relevant German legislation prohibited the sale by mail order of image storage media which had not been examined in Germany in accordance with its provisions and which did not bear an age-limit label corresponding to a classification decision from a national competent authority. The national court referred the case to the ECJ and asked whether the prohibition in question constituted a measure having an equivalent effect within the scope of Article 28 EC (now Article 34 TFEU) and, if so, whether it could be justified.

The Court ruled that the Treaty provisions on the free movement of goods did not preclude the German rule at issue. To reach this conclusion, it insisted that the protection of the rights of the child was recognised by various international instruments which the Member States had cooperated on or acceded to, including the UNCRC, and which were among those concerning the protection of human rights of which it took account in applying the general principles of EU law.[50] It then stated that Article 17(e) provided that state parties were to

[49] Case C-244/06 *Dynamic Medien* [2008] ECR I-505.

[50] *Dynamic Medien*, para. 39. The Court explicitly relied on *Parliament* v. *Council (Family Reunification Directive)* [2006] ECR I-5769.

encourage the development of appropriate guidelines for the protection of children from information and material injurious to their well-being.[51] When assessing how the principle of free movement and the rights of the child were to be balanced against each other, the Court ruled that restrictions to free movement could only be justified if they were proportionate to the objective pursued: 'While it is true that it is for the Member States, in the absence of [EU] harmonisation, to determine the level at which they intend to protect the interest concerned, the fact remains that that discretion must be exercised in conformity with the obligations arising under [EU] law.'[52] It then noted that the German legislation at issue did not preclude all forms of marketing of unchecked image storage media and as such did not go beyond what was necessary to attain the objective pursued by Germany of protecting children against information and materials injurious to their well-being.[53] In its judgment, the Court did not discuss the fact that the British Board of Film Classification had already checked the cartoons. Instead, it stated the following:

> As regards the examination procedure established by the national legislature in order to protect children against information and materials injurious to their well-being, the mere fact that a Member State has opted for a system of protection which differs from that adopted by another Member State cannot affect the assessment of the proportionality of the national provisions enacted to that end. Those provisions must be assessed solely by reference to the objective pursued and the level of protection which the Member State in question intends to provide.[54]

This statement, coupled with the Court's reference to cases such as *Omega*,[55] suggests that Member States have indeed a broad margin of discretion (however, not unfettered) in deciding the level of protection they want to provide and the means they employ to do so. It is remarkable that the best interests principle was not mentioned at all either by the Court or by the Advocate General. This is all the more so as this principle has an important role to play in deciding whether a restriction on the free movement of goods imposed by a Member State to protect children's well-being is indeed proportionate. This seems to confirm the suspicion expressed above that the Court has so far failed to adopt a reasoned approach to arguments based on the best interests of the child. If in *Dynamic Medien*, the decision is rather child-friendly, the

[51] *Dynamic Medien*, para. 40. [52] *Ibid.*, para. 45. [53] *Ibid.*, para. 46.
[54] *Ibid.*, para. 49. [55] Case C-36/02 *Omega* [2004] ECR I-9609.

same cannot be said of the decision in *Parliament* v. *Council (Family Reunification Directive)* – admittedly not a free movement case, but none the less revealing of the Court's failure to determine where the best interests of the child should lie. As several authors have noted, 'the concept of the best interests of the child needs to be more than "raw judicial intuition"'.[56] Certain mechanisms should therefore be put in place to ensure the systematic assessment of the impact of all EU policies on children's rights at both the legislative and the monitoring stages of policy-making.

The mainstreaming of children's rights in all EU policies

As part of its strategy to improve the situation of children in the EU, the Commission has proposed to produce, among other things, a more comprehensive analysis of the needs and priorities and of the impact of relevant EU actions undertaken and more efficient mainstreaming of children's rights in EU policies:

> the EU's obligations to respect fundamental rights, including children's rights, implies not only a general duty to abstain from acts violating these rights, but also to take them into account *wherever relevant* in the conduct of its own policies under the various legal bases of the Treaties.[57]

The Commission has thus undertaken to mainstream children's rights 'when drafting [EU] legislative and non-legislative actions that may affect them'.[58] This reinforces the position that the best interests of the child principle should be given more prominence as a guiding principle of EU action.

Mainstreaming children's rights into all EU policies should involve a proactive approach rather than a reactive approach relying solely on the Court to review already adopted EU law and ensure that it complies with Article 24 of the EU Charter and Article 3 TEU. As Olivier De Schutter has remarked,

> mainstreaming should be seen as operating *ex ante* rather than *post hoc*: it influences the way legislation and public policies are conceived and different alternative paths compared to one another; it does not simply

[56] J. Wexler, 'Rethinking the Modification of Child Custody Decrees' (1985) 94 *Yale Law Journal* 757, at 784. See also Van Bueren, *The International Law on the Rights of the Child*, 46.

[57] Commission Communication, at para. I.3. The French version provides for 'la prise en compte systématique des droits de l'enfant dans les politiques européennes'.

[58] *Ibid.*

> require that such legislation and policies do not violate fundamental rights. It is pro-active, rather than reactive.[59]

More fundamentally, mainstreaming implies, at its core, that children's rights should not be promoted only via earmarked, distinct policies, but must be incorporated in all the fields of law – and policy-making: 'fundamental rights, thus, should be seen, as an integral part of all public policy making and implementation, not something that is separated off in a policy or institutional ghetto. Mainstreaming is transversal or horizontal.'[60] Assessing the impact of policies on children requires, in turn, that a careful balancing exercise is carried out between competing interests at every stage of the policy-making process, from the first Commission proposal, to the adoption by the Council and the European Parliament of the measure, to its implementation and application by all parties to which the measure in question is addressed. The practical difficulties involved in assessing where the best interests of the child lie do not mean, of course, that the best interests principle should not be fully upheld at EU level: the problem precisely is to design an effective and transparent mechanism to ensure that it is duly taken into account.

To assist the development of evidence-based policies and to better promote children's rights and protect their interests, the EU should rely more systematically on impact assessments. Monitoring the effectiveness of policies *ex post* is a valuable, even an essential, exercise. Nevertheless, anticipating the consequences of policies *ex ante* on the basis of solid integrated impact assessments will ensure that proposals are sustainable and therefore increase their chances of success at a much earlier stage. Consequently, all major policy initiatives with a potential economic, social and/or environmental impact require an integrated impact assessment. This applies in particular to most legislation (proposed directives or regulations) and to White Papers, action plans, expenditure programmes and negotiating guidelines for international agreements.[61] The Commission has published a series of impact assessment guidelines which are intended to give general guidance to the Commission services

[59] O. De Schutter, 'Mainstreaming Human Rights in the European Union', in P. Alston and O. De Schutter (eds.), *Monitoring Fundamental Rights in the EU: the Contribution of the Fundamental Rights Agency* (Oxford: Hart Publishing, 2005), 44.

[60] *Ibid.*, citing C. McCrudden, 'Mainstreaming Equality in the Governance of Northern Ireland' (1999) 22 *Fordham International Law Journal* 1696.

[61] The Commission has completed over four hundred impact assessments since 2002 when the impact assessment system was put in place. In 2008 alone, 135 were carried out: ec.europa.eu/governance/impact/ia_carried_out/ia_carried_out_en.htm.

for assessing the potential impacts of different policy options. The latest guidelines were issued in January 2009.[62]

Unfortunately, children's rights are not singled out: they fall within the three broad categories of economic, social and environmental impact. There is therefore a risk that a proposal with a broad range of impacts fails to consider specifically potential impacts on children.[63] The constitutional obligation of EU institutions to uphold the best interests of the child as a primary consideration in all policy areas supports the argument that children's rights should become a separate category for consideration, probably within the category of 'social impacts'. Moreover, it is necessary to ensure that impact assessments are used to inform policy decisions, rather than to justify a preferred policy option determined independently from the impact assessment process.[64] This is all the more important if policy is to rely on evidence rather than on assumptions.

As noted above, until the adoption of the Commission Communication of July 2006, the EU's approach to children's rights was incremental and could not be considered as coherent. Nearly four years later, the question remains whether the consideration of the best interests of the child has become more systematic and sufficient in EU policy-making. The Commission has undoubtedly taken a step in the right direction by committing itself to strengthening cooperation between the main stakeholders, not least by setting up a European Forum for the Rights of the Child, by promoting children's participation and by appointing a Commission coordinator for the rights of the child to increase the consistency and effectiveness of EU policies.[65]

As the EU legislature has repeatedly stated that citizens and not only businesses should reap the benefits of the internal market, several measures have been adopted which have as their explicit purpose an increased level of protection for consumers, including the youngest ones. The rest of this chapter focuses on two case studies which are intended

[62] ec.europa.eu/governance/impact/commission_guidelines/commission _guidelines_en.htm.

[63] One could draw an analogy with the EU's obligation to mainstream public health concerns into all EU policies, as laid down in Art. 168 TFEU (ex Art. 152 EC). A study conducted by the National Heart Forum found that in 2005 and 2006, 73 out of the 137 impact assessments carried out by the Commission did not mention the word 'health': R. Salay and P. Lincoln, *The European Union and Health Impact Assessments: Are They an Unrecognised Statutory Obligation?* (London: National Heart Forum, September 2008), 13.

[64] Information Note from the President to the Commission, 'Better Regulation and Enhanced Impact Assessment', 28 June 2007, SEC (2007) 926.

[65] Commission Communication, at para. III.

to demonstrate that Union institutions have neither sufficiently nor systematically upheld the best interests of the child as a primary consideration in EU consumer policy and that the Commission Communication has yet to play a meaningful role in EU policy-making in the interrelated policy areas of internal market, public health and consumer protection.

The regulation of toy safety

The proper functioning of the internal market requires that goods in free circulation are safe. As the younger children are, the more fragile they are to the presence of certain substances and the less careful with the goods they use they are likely to be, the EU has adopted a range of measures intended to increase the safety of goods specifically intended for children and goods likely to appeal to children. In the last couple of years alone, it has undertaken to set new safety standards for baby sleep products, for childcare products and for personal music players.[66]

Toys have been a particular EU concern, in so far as they are the category of goods giving rise to the highest number of notifications. In 2009, they accounted for 472 out of the 1993 notifications received (28 per cent) through the EU's rapid alert system for non-food dangerous products.[67]

The EU adopted Directive 88/378 on the safety of toys in 1988.[68] It lays down uniform rules to facilitate the free movement of toys while providing effective protection to consumers, especially children, against the hazards arising from them. Its key principle is that toys[69] may be

[66] The latest safety news is available from the Commission's website at: ec.europa.eu/consumers/safety/news/index_en.htm.

[67] This high percentage is in line with the situation observed in previous years: in 2008, toys accounted for 32 per cent of notifications; in 2007, for 31 per cent and in 2006, for 24 per cent. The RAPEX Reports are available at ec.europa.eu/consumers/reports/reports_en.htm. In 2009, market surveillance authorities in thirteen countries conducted a specific check on toy safety with a view to reducing the amount of unsafe toys on the EU market and to enabling Member States to gain experience in working together for better surveillance and enforcement of the safety rules: Results of the Joint Action on Toys, April 2010, ec.europa.eu/consumers/safety/news/report-joint-action-toys-15042010_en.pdf.

[68] [1988] OJ L 187/1, as amended by Directive 93/68, [1993] OJ L 220/1. The Toy Safety Directive was the first New Approach Directive ever adopted. New Approach means that the harmonising legislation only sets the essential safety requirements that goods placed on the EU market have to fulfil and that technical details are left to be fixed by standardisation organisations.

[69] A toy is defined as 'any product or material designed or clearly intended for use in play by children of less than 14 years of age' (Art. 1(1)). Annex I contains a list of products which shall not be regarded as toys for the purposes of the Toy Safety Directive (Art. 1(2)).

placed on the EU market[70] if they meet the essential safety requirements laid down by the Toy Safety Directive[71] and thus do not jeopardise the safety and/or health of users or third parties when they are used as intended or in a foreseeable way.[72] The essential safety requirements are laid down in Annex II to the directive. The first part of Annex II contains general principles,[73] whereas the second part deals with six particular risks: physical and mechanical properties, flammability, chemical properties, electrical properties, hygiene and radioactivity. Before being marketed, toys must bear the CE marking which indicates that they comply with the provisions of the Toy Safety Directive.[74] On the basis of these essential requirements, the European standardisation bodies have drawn up European harmonised standards.[75] These standards are not mandatory, but any toy complying with them is presumed to conform to the essential requirements laid down in the Toy Safety Directive,[76] and Member States may not impede their free movement.[77]

Nevertheless, certain shortcomings had been identified and new risks uncovered. It was decided that the Toy Safety Directive should be amended in particular to update the essential safety requirements it lays down (including rules on electrical properties and requirements on suffocation and choking hazards), in the first place, and to include newly identified hazards (such as requirements for noise, for laser, for activity toys, for speed limit and for chemicals), in the second place. On 18 June 2009, Directive 2009/48 (the 2009 Directive) was adopted.[78] It repeals and replaces the Toy Safety Directive of 1988.[79] Member States have until 20 January 2011 to adopt implementing measures and until 20 July 2011

[70] The expression 'placed on the market' covers both sale and distribution free of charge (Art. 2(3)).

[71] Art. 3. [72] Art. 2(1).

[73] In particular, the annex provides that 'the degree of risk present in the use of a toy must be commensurate with the ability of the users, and where appropriate their supervisors, to cope with it', particularly for 'toys which, by virtue of their functions, dimensions and characteristics, are intended for use by children of under 36 months', thus underlining the importance of adequate labelling (point I.2 and I.3).

[74] Art. 8(1)(a).

[75] The CEN has adopted Standard EN 71 applicable to toys and the CENELEC Standard EN 62115 applicable to electrical toys.

[76] Art. 5(1).

[77] Art. 4. On the Toy Safety Directive and its implementation in the United Kingdom, see S. Weatherill, 'Playing Safe: the United Kingdom's Implementation of the Toy Safety Directive', in T. Daintith (ed.), *Implementing EC Law in the United Kingdom – Structures for Indirect Rule* (Chichester: Wiley, 1995), 241.

[78] [2009] OJ L 170/1. [79] Art. 55.

to ensure that those measures are effectively applied (except for certain requirements which benefit from longer transitional periods, as discussed below).[80]

The 2009 Directive is a welcome step forward, in so far as it reinforces the essential safety requirements which all toys placed on the EU market must comply with and therefore improves the protection of children.[81] In particular, it limits the amounts of certain chemicals that may be contained in materials used for toys. It also bans the use of chemicals that are capable of provoking cancer, changing genetic information or harm reproduction – so-called carcinogenic, mutagenic or toxic for reproduction (CMR) substances – in accessible parts of toys. Similarly, the tolerable limit values of substances like nickel have been reduced and those heavy metals which are particularly toxic, such as lead or mercury, may no longer be intentionally used in toys. Furthermore, allergenic fragrances are either completely banned if they have a strong allergenic potential, or they have to be labelled on the toy if they are potentially allergenic for certain consumers. Finally, rules for toys in food have been introduced, so that toys which cannot be accessed without consuming the food itself are banned: toys must be packaged so that they are separated from the food, and that packaging should not present any choking hazard. It is revealing that the European Commission has translated the 2009 Directive into Chinese to facilitate cooperation with the main exporter of toys for the EU market.[82] The Commission has also produced an extended manual designed to facilitate its implementation and application by policy-makers and traders alike.[83]

Nevertheless, certain provisions of the 2009 Directive raise the question of the extent to which the EU has duly taken the best interest of

[80] Art. 54.

[81] Art. 10 and Annex II lay down these essential safety requirements. The Second Toy Safety Directive also improves the enforcement of the legislation and increases the visibility and understanding of warnings on toys.

[82] Asia is the leading supplier of toys with 97.6 per cent of the total import, China accounting for 90.7 per cent of all Asia imports (compared to 88.3 per cent in 2006 and 84.2 per cent in 2005). The total production of toys and games in the EU amounts to nearly 5 billion euro, of which 80 per cent is generated by France, Germany, Italy, Spain, the UK and Ireland. The EU has nearly two thousand manufacturers working in the toy and games sectors, directly employing nearly 100,000 people in the EU (half of whom work in production and half in research and development, marketing, sales, distribution and other services). See Toy Industries of Europe, Facts and Figures, July 2008, ec.europa.eu/enterprise/sectors/toys/files/tie_facts_figures2008_en.pdf.

[83] The Explanatory Guidance Document was published on 1 June 2010 and is available at: http://ec.europa.eu/enterprise/sectors/toys/files/tsd_explanatory_guidance_document_en.pdf.

the child into account as a primary consideration. For example, if it requires that toys which emit sound should not pose any hearing impairment risk to children,[84] it does not provide for a maximum safe level of sound (in decibels) for such toys. A noise limit remains to be defined by the competent standard bodies.[85] Similarly, it is regrettable that the essential safety requirements relating to the chemical properties of toys have not been drafted with the precautionary principle in mind. As stated above, if the directive provides that CMR substances shall not be used in toys,[86] this principle none the less contains certain exceptions, not least that CMR substances can be used when they are 'inaccessible to children in any form, including inhalation, when the toy is used as intended or in a foreseeable way, bearing in mind the behaviour of children'.[87]

This exception is worrying. If a child does not use the toy 'as intended or in a foreseeable way', he or she may be exposed to the presence of CMR substances contained in normally inaccessible parts of the toy. Should it not be accepted, in light of the severe detrimental impact such substances have on children's health, that the best interests of the child warrant their total prohibition in all parts of the toy whether these parts are accessible or not?[88] The preamble of the 2009 Directive acknowledges the limit of the system in place: 'The system established by this directive should also encourage, and in certain cases ensure, that dangerous substances and materials used in toys are replaced by less dangerous substances or technologies, where suitable economically and technically viable alternatives are available'.[89] A 'less dangerous substance' is not a substance which is not dangerous at all. Moreover, what could constitute 'suitable economically and technically viable alternatives'? The best interests of the child principle should arguably have been invoked to ensure that children's health was given an overriding priority over the financial interests of the toy industry. Admittedly, the toy industry is a sector which is largely composed of small and medium-sized enterprises which may consider regulation as a particular burden. Nevertheless, the toy

[84] Point I.10 of Annex II and Recital 27.

[85] See the comments issued jointly by ANEC and BEUC on the 2009 Directive, available at docshare.beuc.org/Common/GetFile.asp?ID=28605&mtd=ott&LogonName=GuestEN.

[86] Point 3 of Annex II. [87] Point 4(b) of Annex II and Art. 10(2).

[88] The requirement to bear in mind the behaviour of children admittedly increases the threshold, thus recognising that a child's behaviour may not be as predictable as an adult's. Nevertheless, it does not affect the thrust of the argument.

[89] At recital 26.

sector is also renowned for its capacity for innovation, with 60 per cent of toys representing new products on the market each year.[90]

Even if one accepts that a risk-free environment is inconceivable – and arguably undesirable – the failure to impose a total ban on the use of CMR substances in toys to cater for the economic interests of the toy industry constitutes a shortcoming of the EU's amended regulatory framework which becomes even more severe in light of the fact that the provisions of the 2009 Directive relating to chemical content benefit from a transitional period and are only due to enter into force on 20 July 2013.[91] Complexity is the reason put forward: the development of the harmonised standards which are necessary for compliance with the chemical requirements laid down in the 2009 Directive would require additional time.[92] Is it not arguable, however, that the complexity may well stem from the fact that CMR substances have not been banned altogether in the manufacturing of toys?

The revision process of the EU toy safety legislation reinforces the argument that the best interest of the child has not been a primary consideration. It is indeed most regrettable that EU rules on toy safety were only amended following the Mattel scandal in the summer of 2007, while the need to revise the Toy Safety Directive of 1988 had been identified many years earlier. In its Consumer Policy Strategy for the period of 2002 to 2006, the Commission had indicated that the Toy Safety Directive would be reviewed. Nevertheless, it was only in May 2007 that the Commission launched a public consultation.[93] The recall of some two million Mattel toys over the summer of 2007 seems to have prompted the Commission to publish a proposal for a directive alongside an impact assessment in January 2008. The directive was finally adopted some fifteen months later and published on 30 June 2009.[94]

[90] See Toy Industries of Europe, Facts and Figures, July 2008, ec.europa.eu/enterprise/sectors/toys/files/tie_facts_figures2008_en.pdf.

[91] Until this date, Part III of Annex II of the Toy Safety Directive of 1988 will continue to apply.

[92] Recital 47.

[93] In the meantime, DG Enterprise admittedly commissioned a study (published in October 2004) to assess the impact of the planned modifications for businesses (in particular small and medium-sized enterprises), consumers, public authorities, health and safety and the environment.

[94] More general questions also arise which relate not so much to the definition of essential toy safety requirements but to their enforcement: in particular, it has been argued that the fact that a toy bears the CE marking is not a reliable indicator that the toy in question is safe. Given the space constraints, these questions are not discussed here.

On the day the Commission published its proposal for a revised Toy Safety Directive, in January 2008, Vice-President Gunter Verheugen, who was then responsible for enterprise and industrial policy, stated:

> Health and safety of children is non-negotiable and cannot be subject to any compromises. That is why we have to ensure that toys put on the market in Europe are safe. The proposed new Directive which was adopted today incorporates the newest health and safety standards and improves the effectiveness and enforcement of the EU legal framework. Economic operators are now called to live up to their responsibilities to ensure that children can enjoy playing with toys without risks.[95]

EU toy safety legislation, and EU product safety legislation more generally, recognise that children are vulnerable consumers who do not generally show the same degree of care as the average adult user. Nevertheless, the 2009 Directive does strike a compromise; and if the need to protect the health of children is explicitly recognised in the impact assessment which the Commission published alongside its proposal for a revised directive, their best interests are not. Impact assessments must be more thorough and systematically address the balance between the principle of the best interests of the child and potentially competing interests. In particular, they must engage more convincingly with the balancing carried out between and the benefits to consumer health and the costs to industry, the latter being generally easier to quantify. It is only then that the Commission will be able to claim that the 2009 Directive is one of its achievements in promoting the rights and interests of children.[96]

The regulation of advertising to children

Children are subjected to extensive and pervasive commercial pressures. In particular, marketing to children raises a range of concerns which several stakeholders have highlighted. The major criticism encountered is that it is inherently unfair for the industry to use powerful and pervasive media to exploit children's inexperience and credulity for commercial gain and to insinuate consumerist values into childhood.[97]

[95] 'Safety first: Commission proposes new strict rules for toys', Brussels, 25 January 2008: IP/08/91.

[96] European Commission, 'Implementation of the European Union's Strategy on the Rights of the Child: State of Play', November 2009, ec.europa.eu/justice_home/fsj/children/docs/children_state_of_play_en.pdf.

[97] The impact of advertising on children is frequently discussed in academic literature. For a comprehensive and unsparing look at the demographic advertisers call 'the kid market', see the analysis of psychologist Susan Linn in S. Linn, *Consuming Kids:*

If media influence on children is sometimes presented positively, its influence tends to be rather negative, not least because the constant commercial pressure to which children are exposed as a result of the omnipresence of marketing may inhibit them from playing creatively, thus affecting their development.[98] Moreover, children often do not have the ability to distinguish between advertising and programmes until the age of eight and sometimes even much later. It is often not until the age of twelve that they fully understand the purpose of advertising. Nevertheless, such understanding is essential for them to develop a critical, questioning attitude to advertising and to distinguish between entertainment and commercial practices.[99]

The question therefore arises whether advertising to children should be permitted, and if so how it should be regulated. The EU was given an opportunity to engage with these issues and consider where the best interests of the child might lie during the revision process of Directive 89/552 (often referred to as the Television Without Frontiers Directive). Regrettably, however, Directive 2007/65, the amending directive which should have been implemented by all Member States by 19 December 2009, upholds the best interests of the child principle as an ancillary rather than a primary consideration. Directive 2010/13, which was adopted on 10 March 2010, repeals the 1989 Directive as subsequently amended.[100] The rest of this section relies on the numbering of the 2010 Directive, referred to as the Directive on Audiovisual Media Services (AVMS), except when references to the 1989 Television Directive are specifically warranted.

Marketing to children

The aim of the AVMS Directive is to promote the free movement of audiovisual media services. The Television Without Frontiers Directive covered only broadcasting services between the Member States,[101] but its

Protecting Our Children from the Onslaught of Marketing and Advertising (New York: Anchor, 2005).

[98] For a discussion of the links existing between play, creativity and health, see S. Linn, *The Case for Make Believe: Saving Play in a Commercialized World* (New York: The New Press, 2008).

[99] As regards adolescents, the issue may be more one of self-control and peer identification. On self-control, see D. Cutler, E. Glaeser and J. Shapiro, 'Why Have Americans Become More Obese?', Harvard Institute of Economic Research, Harvard University, January 2003.

[100] [2010] OJ L 95/21.

[101] The directive is based on Arts. 53 and 62 TFEU (ex Arts. 47 and 55 EC). On EU audiovisual policy, see O. Castendyk, E. Dommering and A. Scheuer (eds.), *European*

scope has been extended to other audiovisual media services, not least internet and video on-demand services. To this effect, the AVMS Directive relies on the state of establishment principle requiring Member States to allow the retransmission on their territory of audiovisual media services transmitted from other Member States provided that these services comply with the provisions of the directive.[102] Nevertheless, to ensure that free movement is acceptable to all EU Member States, the AVMS Directive also lays down a series of requirements intended to protect important objectives of public interest across the Union. Some of them regulate the timing and the content of marketing to children.[103] As regards timing, Article 20 of the AVMS Directive provides that children's programmes of less than thirty minutes may not be interrupted by television advertising or teleshopping. If their scheduled duration is thirty minutes or longer, they may be interrupted once for each scheduled period of at least thirty minutes. Moreover, Article 11 prohibits product placement in all children's programmes, irrespective of their duration.[104] Finally, Article 10(4) grants an option to Member States to prohibit the showing of a sponsorship logo during children's programmes. Nevertheless, these provisions imply that the AVMS Directive merely limits the amount of marketing children may be exposed to, without banning marketing to children as such.

As regards content, Article 9(1)(g) provides, after stating the general principle that 'audiovisual commercial communications shall not cause moral or physical detriment to minors', that:

- they shall not directly exhort minors to buy or hire a product or service by exploiting their inexperience or credulity;

Media Law (The Hague: Kluwer Law International, 2008); J. Harrison and L. Woods, *European Broadcasting Law and Policy* (Cambridge University Press, 2007); I. Katsirea, *Public Broadcasting Standards and European Law* (The Hague: Kluwer Law International, 2008); and A. Harcourt, *The European Union and the Regulation of Media Markets* (Manchester University Press, 2005).

[102] Art. 2. Nevertheless, 'each Member State shall ensure that all television broadcasts transmitted by broadcasters under its jurisdiction comply with the rules of the system of law applicable to broadcasts intended for the public in that Member State' (Art. 2(1)).

[103] The notion of 'audiovisual commercial communications' is defined as 'images with or without sound which are designed to promote, directly or indirectly, the goods, services or images of a natural or legal entity pursuing an economic activity. Such images accompany or are included in a programme in return for payment or for similar consideration or for self-promotional purposes'. The notion of 'audiovisual commercial communication' includes but is not limited to television advertising, sponsorship, teleshopping and product placement.

[104] One should note, however, that it does not ban product integration (i.e. when no remuneration or similar consideration is provided for).

- they shall not directly encourage minors to persuade their parents or others to purchase the goods or services being advertised;
- they shall not exploit the special trust minors place in parents, teachers or other persons; and
- they shall not unreasonably show minors in dangerous situations.

The wording of Article 9(1)(g), and in particular the use of the word 'directly', restricts its scope significantly. There are only very few examples of commercial communications which 'directly' call on children either to buy a specific product or to use their 'pester power' so that their parents buy this product for them. Marketing to children tends to be covert. This is even more so in light of the development of numerous marketing techniques specifically designed to attract the attention of children, such as host selling, character merchandising and the use of celebrities, as well as the integration of marketing into programmes (product placement or product integration), which all accentuate the difficulties for children to grasp the commercial intent of marketing practices. For example, just after winning eight gold medals at the 2008 Beijing Olympic Games, swimming champion Michael Phelps signed deals with two food industry giants: the first one with Kellogg's for the promotion of sugary breakfast cereals and the second one with McDonald's to serve as an ambassador actively recruiting Chinese children to become McDonald's customers.[105] Another instance is character merchandising which plays on children's fascination with a fantasy character, so as to induce them to buy or insisting on their parents buying the advertised good or service for them. Let us focus on McDonald's yet again: a Happy Meal often comes wrapped in a special box with scenes of the promoted film on it and usually containing a model of one of the characters. As there are several models which children can collect in one series, the incentive to eat regularly at McDonald's becomes even stronger.[106] Notwithstanding their effectiveness, such exhortations to buy are most likely to fall outside the scope of Article 9(1)(g) of the AVMS Directive.

During the revision process which led to the replacement of the Television Without Frontiers Directive by the AVMS Directive, the Hieronimy Report suggested that the scope of the directive should be extended to

105 See the McDonald's interview of the champion on 18 August 2008 after he had won eight gold medals, in which he stated that his favourite food was a double cheeseburger and fries: www.youtube.com/watch?gl=FR&v=pCWpkB45je0.

106 The problem is similar when characters such as Kellogg's Tony the Tiger are used by food operators to capture the imagination of children and make them want breakfast cereals with a sugar content of 37 per cent.

cover both direct and indirect exhortations to children.[107] Nevertheless, this suggestion was not taken up.

If the AVMS Directive is not particularly helpful in protecting children from harmful commercial practices at EU level, one may wonder whether any other legislative instruments could fill in the gap.

A directive of partial harmonisation

The AVMS Directive is a measure of partial harmonisation, to the extent that it does not cover all matters relating to the regulation of audiovisual commercial communications. In particular, it does not address the issue of how misleading and aggressive commercial practices should be regulated. The question therefore arises whether Directive 2005/29 on unfair commercial practices (the UCPD) could fill in the gap.

The UCPD introduces the first EU-wide ban on all unfair business-to-consumer commercial practices.[108] Member States should have adopted the necessary implementing measures by 12 June and ensured that they were fully complied with by 12 December 2007. Its key provision is Article 5 which prohibits all unfair business-to-consumer commercial practices. To be considered unfair, a practice must meet two criteria: it

[107] Amendment 68 (emphasis contained in the original text):

> Audiovisual commercial communications must not cause moral or physical detriment to minors. Therefore, it shall not directly *or indirectly* exhort minors to buy a product or service by exploiting their inexperience or credulity, directly *or indirectly* encourage them to persuade their parents or others to purchase the goods or services being advertised, exploit the special trust minors place in parents, teachers or other persons, *especially role models or persons exercising authority,* or unreasonably show minors in dangerous *or degrading* situations *unless justified for learning or training purposes.*

[108] Directive 2005/29, [2005] OJ L 149/22. The UCPD has been extensively commented upon. See, among others (in English): G. Howells, H. Micklitz and T. Wilhelmsson, *European Fair Trading Law: the Unfair Commercial Practices Directive* (Aldershot: Ashgate Publishing, 2006); H. Micklitz, N. Reich and P. Rott, *Understanding EU Consumer Law* (Antwerp: Intersentia, 2008); J. Stuyck, E. Terryn and T. van Dyck, 'Confidence Through Fairness? The New Directive on Unfair Business-to-Consumer Commercial Practices in the Internal Market' (2006) 31 *CMLRev* 107; S. Weatherill and U. Bernitz, *The Regulation of Unfair Commercial Practices under EC Directive 2005/29* (Oxford: Hart Publishing, 2007); A. Bakardjieva-Engelbrekt, *EU Marketing Practices Law in the Nordic Countries: Consequences of a Directive on Unfair Business-to-Consumer Commercial Practices* (Helsinki: The Nordic Council of Ministers Committee on Consumer Affairs, January 2005); A. Garde and M. Haravon, 'Unfair Commercial Practices: towards a Comprehensive European Consumer Policy?' (2006) 6 *European Journal of Consumer Policy,* 116.

must be contrary to the rules of professional diligence and it must materially distort or be likely to materially distort the economic behaviour of a consumer, that is 'to appreciably impair the consumer's ability to make an informed decision, thereby causing the consumer to take a transactional decision which he would not have taken otherwise'.[109] After laying down this broad prohibition, the UCPD identifies two main categories of unfair commercial practices: misleading and aggressive practices. Under Articles 6 and 7, a practice is misleading if it contains false information, omits material information or presents it in an unclear, unintelligible, ambiguous or untimely manner, or otherwise deceives or is likely to deceive the average consumer. Under Articles 8 and 9, a practice is aggressive if by harassment, coercion, including the use of physical force, or undue influence, it significantly impairs or is likely to significantly impair the average consumer's freedom of choice or conduct with regard to the product. In order to give a more concrete flavour to these general definitions, Annex I of the directive lists thirty-one commercial practices which are considered unfair in all circumstances. The list, which is applicable in all the Member States and can only be modified by revision of the directive, is not exhaustive;[110] however, if a consumer claims that his/her economic behaviour has been distorted as a result of a practice which is not listed, s/he will have to establish that the practice is indeed unfair. The list therefore reverses the burden of proof by laying down a presumption of unfairness. In other words, if Annex I is not exhaustive of all unfair commercial practices, it is exhaustive of the commercial practices which are presumed to be unfair.[111]

Before the adoption of the UCPD in May 2005, the Market Court in Finland held that a McDonald's commercial had violated the Finnish Consumer Protection Act by presenting Happy Meal Toys as the 'main message in spots, at the expense of the main product' (that is, the Happy Meal). In making the core of the commercial a toy and the main objective attracting children, McDonald's was deliberately taking consumer

[109] Art. 2(e). [110] Art. 5(5).

[111] This was confirmed by the ECJ in two preliminary rulings: in the *VTB-VAB* cases, the Court held that the UCPD precluded Belgium from imposing a general prohibition of combined offers made by a vendor to a consumer (Joined Cases C-261 and 299/07 *VTB-VAB* [2009] ECR I-2949); similarly, in the *Plus Warengesellschaft* case, the Court ruled that German law could not automatically prohibit promotional campaigns allowing consumers to take part in a lottery free of charge following a certain number of purchases as unfair commercial practices without taking the specific circumstances of individual cases into account (Case C-304/08 *Plus Warengesellschaft* [2010] ECR I-217.

attention away from the advertised product (the meal) and the commercial was thus deemed an 'inappropriate' form of advertising. The Market Court consequently ordered that the contentious commercial be withdrawn.[112] Nevertheless, it is arguable that the provisions of the UCPD, which is a measure of full harmonisation, are so restrictive that they may no longer allow a Member State to impose an outright ban on such marketing techniques. Not only does point 28 of the annex ban only 'direct exhortations', but the general unfairness clause contained in Article 5 of the directive provides that:

> Commercial practices which are likely to materially distort the economic behaviour only of a clearly identifiable group of consumers who are particularly vulnerable to the practice of the underlying product because of their mental or physical infirmity, age or credulity in a way which the trader could reasonably be expected to foresee, shall be assessed from the perspective of the average member of that group. This is without prejudice to the common and legitimate advertising practice of making exaggerated statements or statements which are not meant to be taken literally.[113]

The final sentence of this provision is striking. Could one not argue that it is precisely in the case of vulnerable groups – not least children – that exaggerations may be taken literally? This is particularly true when marketing techniques specifically aimed at children are used. Moreover, when is a message not to be taken literally? And from whose point of view should the exaggeration assessed? More generally, the wording of Article 5(3) is far too restrictive to warrant the claim that the best interests principle has become a guiding principle of EU legislative action. The group of consumers in question must not only be 'clearly identifiable' but also '*particularly* vulnerable'. That raises questions, not only as to what a clearly identifiable group is, but also as to how the threshold should be determined. For example, children of six years old are known to be particularly vulnerable to advertising as they are not able to distinguish it from other programmes and grasp its commercial intent. Children of more than twelve years of age are better equipped to do so. However, that does not mean that they are as able as adults to adopt the necessary critical stance towards the good or service advertised to them. Would they be taken as a 'particularly vulnerable' group within

[112] Reported in C. Hawkes, *Marketing Food to Children: the Global Regulatory Environment* (Geneva: WHO, 2004, updated in 2007), 7.

[113] See also recital 19 of the preamble. In any event, no assessment is required of 'each individual's circumstances, which would be unworkable' (Common Position of November 2004).

the meaning of Article 5(3)? Furthermore, the practice should materially distort the economic behaviour 'only' of the vulnerable consumer group. There may, however, be examples where a practice materially distorts the economic behaviour of both vulnerable consumers and, to a lesser extent, the public at large. For example, misleading advertising of diet food may well materially distort the economic behaviour of consumers suffering from obesity, as well as that of other consumers from the general public. What would the benchmark be in such circumstances: the average consumer from the vulnerable group or the average consumer in general?[114] It is therefore unlikely that the UCPD may offer much comfort. It certainly does not support the claim that the EU has treated the best interests of the child as a primary consideration.

Food marketing to children

The marketing of specific goods, whose consumption should either be prohibited or strictly regulated, has attracted specific criticisms. Consequently, the original version of the Television Without Frontiers Directive already banned tobacco advertising and the advertising of cigarettes and other tobacco products, as well as the advertising of medicinal products and medical treatments available only on prescription. It also banned the advertising of alcoholic beverages aimed specifically at minors. These restrictions have been extended to other audiovisual commercial communications following the entry into force of the AVMS Directive.[115]

Since the Television Without Frontiers Directive was first adopted, it has been recognised that the marketing of unhealthy food to children contributes to an 'obesogenic' environment, making healthy food choices more difficult, especially for children.[116] Consequently, in its Global Strategy on Diet, Physical Activity and Health, the WHO identified the regulation of the marketing of food to children as an area requiring further action and launched an extensive consultation process.[117] On 21 May 2010, the process culminated in the adoption, by the Sixty-third

[114] Bakardjieva Engelbrekt, *EU Marketing Practices Law in the Nordic Countries*, 29.

[115] See Art. 9(d), (e) and (f) applying respectively to tobacco products, alcoholic beverages and medicinal products and medical treatments available only on prescription.

[116] For a summary of existing evidence, see J. Harris *et al.*, 'A Crisis in the Marketplace: How Food Advertising Contributes to Childhood Obesity and What Can Be Done' (2009) 30 *Annual Review of Public Health* 211.

[117] *Global Strategy on Diet, Physical Activity and Health* (Geneva: WHO, May 2004):

World Health Assembly, of a set of recommendations calling on contracting parties to reduce both the exposure and the power of food marketing to children. (On 21 May 2010, the process culminated in the adoption of WHA Resolution 63.14 to reduce food marketing exposure to children.)

Reflecting (in part at least) these considerations, Article 9(2) of the AVMS Directive provides that:

> Member States and the Commission shall encourage media service providers to develop codes of conduct regarding inappropriate audiovisual commercial communication, accompanying or included in children's programmes, of foods and beverages containing nutrients and substances with a nutritional or physiological effect, in particular those such as fat, trans-fatty acids, salt/sodium and sugars, excessive intakes of which in the overall diet are not recommended.

This approach is in line with the position which DG SANCO adopted on the same issue in its Obesity Prevention White Paper of May 2007 and in which it stated its preference, at this stage, 'to keep the existing voluntary approach at EU level due to the fact that it can potentially act quickly and effectively to tackle rising overweight and obesity rates'.[118]

Nevertheless, the scope and effectiveness of Article 9(2) are limited in at least three ways. First, the wording is unclear. In particular, the phrase 'inappropriate audiovisual commercial communication' seems to invite the food industry to water down its obligation to limit unhealthy food advertising to children. If one can argue that all forms of commercial communication for unhealthy food directed at children are inappropriate, this is not what the wording of Article 9(2) suggests. On the contrary, it implies that there are appropriate and inappropriate unhealthy food adverts, thus putting the onus on the industry to tackle only the latter.

> food advertising affects food choices and influences dietary habits. Food and beverage advertisements should not exploit children's inexperience or credulity. Messages that encourage unhealthy dietary practices or physical inactivity should be discouraged, and positive, healthy messages encouraged. Governments should work with consumer groups and the private sector (including advertising) to develop appropriate multi-sectorial approaches to deal with the marketing of food to children, and to deal with such issues as sponsorship, promotion and advertising [para. 40(3)].

The WHO subsequently commissioned research and launched a consultation process. Information is available at: www.who.int/dietphysicalactivity/marketing-food-to-children/en/.

[118] COM (2007) 279 final, 6. On the EU's obesity prevention strategy, see A. Garde, *EU Law and Obesity Prevention* (Kluwer Law International, 2010).

One could imagine that using celebrities or cartoon characters would be viewed as inappropriate, as these techniques detract children's attention away from the actual product, whereas adverts that would not rely on such techniques would not be regarded as 'inappropriate'. Such an approach, apart from being ineffective, would be extremely cynical, as it would leave the industry with an extremely broad margin of discretion in relation to the content of its codes of conduct. The issue is made even worse bearing in mind that Article 9(2) only requires Member States and the Commission to 'encourage' media service providers to develop codes of conduct on the advertising of unhealthy food to children and to monitor the fulfilment of this obligation. There is no duty to ensure that such codes are indeed adopted. As the Commission stated, 'the co-regulatory and self-regulatory schemes have to be broadly accepted by main stakeholders in the Member States concerned and provide for effective enforcement. How these concepts of acceptability and effectiveness are interpreted can be decided at national level'; similarly for the interpretation of the terms 'encourage' and 'monitor'.[119]

Secondly, Article 9(2) only requires the industry to limit inappropriate unhealthy food advertising 'accompanying or included in children's programming'; but nowhere does the AVMS Directive define what is meant by 'children's programming'. The Hieronimy Report noted this shortcoming and suggested that, 'in the absence of a uniform EU-wide definition of "children" and "children's programmes" for the purposes of this directive', new recital 33A should be inserted in the preamble and provide that 'in order to reach an adequate level of protection of minors, the national regulatory authorities should determine time-zones for children and define the programmes aimed at children'.[120] This consideration is important in light of findings such as Ofcom's that 70 per cent of the time children spend watching television is outside designated children's viewing times.[121] The logical consequence therefore is that if too narrow a definition of the notion of 'children's programme' is adopted

[119] Minutes of the meeting of the EU Platform held on 19 November 2008 and whose afternoon was devoted to the role of the EU Platform on Diet, Nutrition and Physical Activity in relation to marketing and advertising: ec.europa.eu/health/ph_determinants/life_style/nutrition/platform/docs/ev_20081119_mi_en.pdf, at para. 8.

[120] Amendment 35.

[121] A programme of particular appeal to children under sixteen would be deemed to be one that attracted an audience index of 120 for this age group. If a programme attracts an under-sixteen audience in a proportion similar to that group's presence in the population as a whole, it is said to index at 100. So an index of 120 is an over-representation of that group by 20 per cent.

either by Member State legislation or, in the absence of legislative norms, by self-regulatory codes of conduct, children will not be sufficiently protected from the adverse effects of unhealthy food advertising.[122] Regrettably, the final version of the AVMS Directive does not acknowledge, let alone address, this important concern.

Finally, it is most unlikely that self-regulation is able to provide an appropriate mechanism to protect children effectively from exposure to unhealthy food marketing. If self-regulation has been praised for its flexibility and responsiveness, it does not guarantee that all food operators will abide by the relevant standards, self-regulation being, by definition, voluntary.[123] Some objections apply more specifically to the use of self-regulation in the area of food advertising to children. In particular, the coverage of the rules the food industry has set for its members is often too narrow. For example, while the industry has adopted certain measures to limit television and internet advertising to children, food operators have invested in new marketing techniques which fall outside the scope of the rules and which include advergames or mobile phone marketing.[124] More fundamentally, one may question whether the food industry should be required to 'shoot itself in the foot' and to stop using all the (legal) means at their disposal to increase their customer base in the absence of binding regulation obliging them to do so.

As stated above, the issue of the regulation of food marketing to children has given rise to debate both within and beyond the European Union in the light of growing childhood obesity rates worldwide. The set of recommendations endorsed by the Sixty-third World Health Assembly in May 2010 expressly call on contracting parties (including the European Union) to reduce both the exposure and the power of food marketing to children. Quite significantly, the recommendations acknowledge the central role of state authorities in policy making. In effect, recommendation 6 provides that

[122] The Recommendations for an International Code on Marketing of Foods and Non-Alcoholic Beverages to Children produced by the IOTF and Consumer International provide that 'both the absolute number of children likely to be watching or listening and the number of children as a proportion of the overall audience should be taken into account': www.iotf.org/documents/ConsumersInternationalMarketingCode.pdf, at Art. 5.1.

[123] The Inter-institutional Agreement on Better Lawmaking, adopted in 2003 by the European Parliament, the Council and the Commission, has defined self-regulation as 'the possibility for economic operators ... to adopt amongst themselves and for themselves common guidelines at European level': [2003] OJ C 321/1, para. 22.

[124] S. Dahl, L. C. Eagle and C. Baez, 'Analyzing Advergames: Active Diversions or Actually Deception', Middlesex University Working Paper, 2006: ssrn.com/abstract=907841.

> Government should be the key stakeholders in the development of policy and provide leadership through a multi-stakeholder platform for implementation, monitoring and evaluation. In setting national policy framework, governments may choose to allocate defined roles to other stakeholders, while protecting the public interest and avoiding conflict of interest.

If the recommendations do not go as far as prescribing the approach which Member States should adopt, they require that 'whole industry sectors' should abide by the standards they have adopted to regulate themselves. Moreover, the approach (which should be 'the most effective to reduce marketing to children of [unhealthy] foods') must be 'set within a framework developed to achieve the policy objectives', which suggests that Member States may not abdicate their overall responsibility. Finally, 'the policy framework should specify enforcement mechanisms and establish systems for their implementation', including 'clear definitions of sanctions' and 'a system for reporting complaints'. The recommendations therefore highlight how much more the European Union should do both in terms of standard setting and in terms of policy monitoring to ensure that the best interests of the child principle is effectively upheld.

Stricter national standards

Unlike the UCPD, the AVMS Directive is a measure of minimum harmonisation. Consequently, Member States are free to apply stricter requirements for audiovisual media service providers established on their territories, subject to the limits set by Treaty provisions, and Article 34 TFEU (ex Article 28 EC) on the free movement of goods and Article 56 TFEU (ex Article 49 EC) on the free movement of services more specifically.[125]

On this basis, several Member States have adopted measures intended to increase the level of protection provided to children from unhealthy food marketing. For example, the UK has adopted, following an extensive consultation process, measures that go further and are more likely to reduce the marketing pressure on children. These measures, which came into effect on a phased basis from April 2007 to 1 January 2009, include a total ban of unhealthy food advertising in and around all children's

[125] Art. 4: 'Member States shall remain free to require media service providers under their jurisdiction to comply with more detailed or stricter rules in the fields coordinated by this Directive provided that such rules are in compliance with Union law.'

television programming and on dedicated children's channels as well as in youth-oriented and adult programmes which attract a significantly higher than average proportion of viewers under the age of sixteen. In addition to general content rules requiring responsible advertising to all children at all times, Ofcom has also introduced new rules on the content of advertisements targeted at primary-school children which ban the use of celebrities and characters licensed from third parties (such as cartoons), promotional claims (such as free gifts) and health or nutrition claims.[126] This was followed by a first review intended to measure the effectiveness of the restrictions which had been introduced prior to 2009 (Phases I and II). Ofcom estimated that scheduling restrictions were achieving the objective of reducing significantly the number of food high in fat, salt or sugar (HFSS) product advertising impacts (i.e. each occasion when a viewer sees an advert) among children aged four to fifteen years: compared to 2005 estimates, children were exposed to 34 per cent less advertising for such foods in 2007/8.[127] This finding suggests that the UK regulatory framework is more protective of children's interests than the provisions laid down at EU level by the AVMS Directive. Nevertheless, Ofcom also found that advertisers had significantly increased the amount of HFSS advertising and sponsorship in periods outside children's airtime, at times when significant numbers of children might be watching.[128] These figures show that children were still seeing two-thirds of the advertising of HFSS foods, thus confirming the shortcomings of limiting the ban on unhealthy food advertising to children's programmes only.

In any event, however, the freedom which Member States have is strictly circumscribed, as it is conditional not only on their compliance with Union law,[129] but also on the state of establishment principle which obliges Member States to ensure freedom of reception without

[126] Details can be found on OFCOM's website: www.ofcom.org.uk/consult/condocs/foodads_new/.

[127] *Changes in the Nature and Balance of Television Food Advertising to Children: A Review of HFSS Advertising Restrictions* (London: OFCOM, 17 December 2008).

[128] *Ibid.*

[129] In matters of public health and lifestyle choices, it is likely that the Court would be reluctant, in the absence of EU harmonising measures, to curtail too drastically the discretion of national authorities to adopt measures supporting their obesity prevention strategies, subject to the principle of proportionality. For an analogy with the regulation of alcohol advertising, see Case C-405/98, *Gourmet International Products* [2001] ECR I-1795) (annotated by A. Biondi, (2001) 26 *ELR* 616) and Case C-429/02, *Bacardi France* [2004] ECR I-6613, where the ECJ refused to hold near total bans on alcohol advertising in breach of the principle of proportionality.

restricting the retransmission on their territory of audiovisual media services from other Member States for reasons which fall within the fields coordinated by the AVMS Directive. This was explicitly stated in the *De Agostini* judgment of the ECJ which confirmed that the state of establishment principle required that Member States were bound to accept broadcasts from other Member States, without having the possibility of applying the stricter national standards which they could only impose on the broadcasters established on their territories. Consequently, Sweden was prevented from applying to television broadcasts transmitted from the UK Article 11 of its Broadcasting Act banning advertising to children of less than twelve years old. On the other hand, Sweden could enforce its ban on children advertising for broadcasts emanating from its own territory, subject to its compliance with Treaty provisions on the free movement of goods and services. Applying this reasoning to the provisions of the AVMS Directive, one may therefore conclude that they strictly limit, though they do not negate, the freedom of Member States to implement coherent strategies aimed at protecting children from harmful marketing practices on their territories. This reinforces the need for an intervention at EU level, taking a high level of public health as a basis for action, as mandated by Articles 114(3) and 168(1) TFEU (ex Articles 95(3) and 152(1) EC).

One may hope that the review of the AVMS Directive which is due to take place in 2011 will acknowledge the shortcomings of its provisions relating to the marketing of goods and services to children. The best interests of the child principle requires a much stronger commitment of EU institutions, in the light of the existing evidence that marketing negatively affects children's consumption choices, health and development.

Conclusion

Notwithstanding Article 24 of the EU Charter, the Commission Communication on the Rights of the Child of July 2006 and new Article 3 TFEU, EU institutions have so far failed to consider the best interests of the child as a primary consideration in EU consumer policy.

As the Committee on the Rights of the Child has clearly stated, rhetorical statements that children's rights should be upheld cannot suffice. The means must be in place to ensure that they are effectively upheld:

> Ensuring that the best interests of the child are a primary consideration in all actions concerning children (Article 3(1)), and that all the provisions of the UNCRC are respected in legislation and policy development and delivery at all levels of government demands a continuous process of child impact assessment (predicting the impact of any proposed law, policy or budgetary allocation which affects children and the enjoyment of their rights) and child impact evaluation (evaluating the actual impact of implementation). This process needs to be built into government at all levels and as early as possible in the development of policy.[130]

Apart from systematic child impact assessments and child impact evaluation, a stronger involvement of children's rights advocates is also required. The mainstreaming of children's rights will only become a reality if children's rights organisations accept that they have to step outside their comfort zone and acquire the necessary expertise to influence the agenda in the interrelated fields of internal market, public health and consumer policy. All stakeholders should take ownership of the process and at least contribute to (if not prompt) the debate as to where the best interests of the child lie in all areas falling within the scope of EU competence. No policy is child neutral.[131]

There is no doubt that the political climate in the EU is much more favourable to children than it was a few years ago: we have witnessed a growing awareness of the need to mainstream children's rights into all areas of policy-making, and it is hoped that the strong commitment of EU institutions and all relevant stakeholders will reinforce this momentum. The Commission has recently adopted a new Communication on Children's Rights for the years 2011 to 2014 to further advance the EU Strategy on the Rights of the Child. It is regrettable, however, that it makes very little reference to the rights of the child-consumer. It nonetheless provides a timely opportunity to remind EU institutions of their commitment to mainstream children's rights into all the internal and external policies of the union.[132]

[130] Committee on the Rights of the Child, General Comments N.5 (2003), CRC/GC/2003/5, para. 45.

[131] S. De Vylder, 'Macroeconomic Issues and the Rights of the Child', in A. Weyts (ed.), *Understanding Children's Rights: Collected Papers Presented at the Seventh International Interdisciplinary Course on Children's Rights* (Ghent: Children's Rights Centre, University of Ghent, 2004), 431.

[132] Commission communication of 15 February 2011, An EU Agenda for the Rights of the Child, COM (2011) 60 final.

11

Protecting consumers of gambling services: some preliminary thoughts on the relationship with European consumer protection law

ALAN LITTLER

Introduction

Significant weight is attached to the role of the consumer and the protection that consumers as a class of economic actors receive in terms of achieving the completion of the internal market. In 2002 the European Commission noted that consumer policy 'at EU level has been the essential corollary of the progressive development of the internal market'.[1] Five years later and having noted that the internal market has delivered 'tangible benefits for EU citizens', the Commission opines that the internal market 'remains largely fragmented along national lines, forming 27 mini-markets'.[2] Fragmentation rather than integration of national markets characterises the provision of gambling services within the EU; substantial national markets remain largely foreclosed to competition and any legal cross-border movement. This is one area in which such tangible benefits have yet to be given any hint of an opportunity to materialise.

Within an approach based wholly upon negative integration national regulatory regimes regulating the supply of gambling activities have been on a collision course with the free movement principles since the *Schindler* decision of the ECJ in the early 1990s.[3] The debate as to how an internal market for gambling activities should shape up is far from over; indeed, considerable uncertainty prevails as to which measures and

Ph.D. (Tilburg), LL.M. (Leiden), LL.B. (Dundee). Post-doctoral researcher at the Tilburg Centre for Law and Economics, Tilburg University.

[1] European Commission, Consumer Policy Strategy 2002–2006, COM (2002) 208 final, 6.
[2] European Commission, EU Consumer Policy strategy 2007–2013, COM (2007) 99 final, 2.
[3] Case C-275/92, *Schindler*.

practices are compatible with the internal market.[4] Nevertheless, gambling is provided across all Member States in a multitude of forms, but in contrast to some other economic sectors a highly developed internal market is conspicuously absent. The case law of the ECJ provides Member States with a considerable margin of discretion within which measures restricting the cross-border movement of both gambling services and gambling service providers can be maintained. Consequently, consumers of gambling services are unable to avail themselves of the benefits of the internal market[5] which they are able to reap when engaging in other economic activities.

The cross-border consumption of gambling services can occur through one of three modes: first through the cross-border movement of the recipient, the consumer; secondly by the cross-border movement of the service provider; and thirdly upon the cross-border movement of the service itself. Examples of the first mode of supply include the fact that residents of a particular Member State may cross a nearby border to purchase lottery tickets from a neighbouring national lottery in the event of large jackpot,[6] or visit a casino while on holiday.[7] While EU law recognises the right of consumers to receive services when in other Member States, this mode of supply plays a rather limited role in the gambling sector.[8] Debate at the European level concentrates upon the second and third modes of supply, reflecting the scope of Articles 43 and 49 EC.[9]

[4] As discussed in A. Littler, *Member States versus the European Union: the Regulation of Gambling* (Leiden: Martinus Nijhoff, 2011).

[5] Benefits will only accrue to the extent that consumers are rational actors seeking to maximise the utility which is derivable from gambling services. Subsequent discussion will show that consumers cannot be relied upon to be rational actors in every type of transaction.

[6] Should they be fortunate enough to win, they will run the risk of receiving a rather hefty tax bill within their home Member State, this being the factual scenario which gave rise to case C-42/02, *Lindman*.

[7] Indeed, some Member States seek to capitalise upon an absence, or severely restricted supply, of a particular form of gambling in a neighbouring Member State. For example, Slovenia has a high concentration of casinos along its border with Italy, a Member State in which casinos are largely prohibited.

[8] Cases 286/82 and 26/83, *Luisi* and *Carbone*.

[9] With the entry into force of the Treaty of Lisbon the freedom of establishment is found in Art. 43 of the Treaty on the Functioning of the European Union (hereinafter the TFEU) and the free movement of services is encapsulated in Art. 56 TFEU. However, in the main body of the text, reference will be made to the article numbers as applicable following the Treaty of Amsterdam.

Two examples will be given from contemporary legal discourse to further conceptualise the nature of gambling services falling within the scope of these modes of free movement. Under the freedom of establishment of Article 43 EC the service provider rather than the service or service recipient is required to move; perhaps a casino operator established in one Member State will seek to enter the market of another. Such an attempt was made by a French operator with regard to the Dutch market; it ultimately failed in light of the monopoly held by the current operator in the Netherlands, namely Holland Casino.[10] In terms of Article 49 EC, with the advent of widespread internet usage, online gambling is a form which has great potential to bring different national policy choices into conflict with one another, and EU law, simultaneously. An example of such a form is the offering of sports-betting services by operators, established and licensed in Great Britain, to residents of other Member States.[11]

Consumer protection concerns can be relied upon by Member States to justify restrictive measures, and thus at present, legitimately hinder cross-border intra-Community trade. As will be illustrated in the brief discussion of the ECJ's case law, national concerns pertaining to consumer protection are only one of a basket of measures upon which Member States may restrict cross-border movement in this field. Furthermore, the ECJ has given relatively little consideration to what consumer protection in respect of consumers of gambling services could entail.

It is the object of this chapter to make some preliminary observations regarding the notion of consumer protection for consumers of gambling services in light of the more general debate on consumer protection and the thrust of this area of EU law. In essence this chapter represents the embryonic stages of an exercise in cross-fertilisation between two areas of Union law: that of the highly developed field of consumer protection with the less developed one of gambling regulation.

Three main steps form the basis of this embryo. First, the case law of the ECJ relating to measures restricting the cross-border movement of

[10] Raad van State, 14 March 1997, *Minister van Justitie en Holland Casino/Compagnie Financière Régionale B.V.*, LJN BA0670.

[11] The Gambling Act 2005 provides for a comprehensive regulatory regime for the regulation of nearly all forms of gambling within Great Britain, with the National Lottery constituting the principal exception. For example residents of the Netherlands cannot access all of the services of a well-known British brand, Ladbrokes, following an injunction obtained by the Dutch national operator of sports-betting services, De Lotto, in order to protect its monopoly status. See Hoge Raad, 18 February 2005, *Ladbrokes/De Nationale Sportstotalisator*, LJN AR4841.

gambling services will be considered, with attention to consumer protection issues. Secondly, attention will be paid to defining the notion of consumers for the purposes of gambling services with reference to national regulations and behavioural economic theory. Thirdly, in a broader perspective, mechanisms and practices which can loosely be referred to as 'responsible gambling' will be discussed so as to provide some linkage between protecting consumers of gambling services with protecting consumers of more general services. Conclusions will then be drawn as to how gambling represents an area of European consumer protection in practice.

An important element which this chapter does not delve into is that of the enforceability of contracts for gambling services. Whereas Great Britain has witnessed a reversal of the long-standing unenforceability of gambling contracts with the coming into force of the Gambling Act 2005,[12] and other Member States may do likewise,[13] the consequences of the status of such contracts within national law will not be analysed.[14] For the purposes of this chapter it is the nature of the activity in question and the interaction with the consumer which is paramount rather than the legal constructions which underpin gambling transactions. The consequences of this chasm cannot, and should not, be ignored in future work in this area.

Consumer protection in existing gambling case law

Arising from the cross-border mailing of lottery tickets, *Schindler* marked the start of a trickle of preliminary references concerning the justifiability

[12] Section 335(1) reads: 'The fact that a contract relates to gambling shall not prevent its enforcement.'

[13] From a global perspective see J. Kelly, 'Caught in the Intersection between Public Policy and Practicality: a Survey of the Legal Treatment of Gambling Related Obligations in the United States', (2002) 5 *Chapman Law Review* 87 and 'Appendix: An International Survey of Gambling Debt Enforcement Law' (2002) 5 *Chapman Law Review* 123 by the same author.

[14] For example, the legislative proposal in France by which parts of the national online gambling market will be opened to private operators recognises that contracts for gambling services amount to standard form contracts: 'Un joueur ou un parieur en ligne s'entend de toute personne qui accepte un contrat d'adhésion au jeu propose par un opérateur de jeux ou de paris en ligne.' See Art. 5(3) of the *Projet de loi relatif à l'ouverture à la concurrence et à la régulation du secteur des jeux d'argent et de hasard en ligne*, adopted by the *Assemblée nationale*, no. 384, 13 October 2009. For an analysis of the relationship between protection offered to consumers of online gambling services within the proposed legislation and consumer protection more generally, see A. Jouette Melchior, 'French Contract Law and Protection of the Internet Gambler in the New French Legislation', in C. Fijnaut, N. Hoekx and A. Littler (eds.), *Gambling Regulation in Europe* (Leiden: Martinus Nijhoff, 2010).

of measures restricting gambling services. Two year earlier, the European Commission had announced at the European Council's Edinburgh meeting that it was not intending to seek any harmonisation of national gambling regulations on the basis of the principle of subsidiarity.[15] Consequently, and moreover since gambling was removed from the scope of the Services Directive,[16] the ECJ has been the forum for considerable debate as to what Member States can do to restrict cross-border gambling services. Originally, in the proposal of the Commission gambling was included, subject to a transitional derogation, the removal of which was conditional upon a degree of harmonisation, a report and wide consultation.[17] Perhaps such harmonisation would have included matters concerning consumer protection. Ultimately, not only did the European Parliament alter the basis of the Services Directive by removing the country of origin principle, it also ensured that gambling received an absolute derogation. Seemingly the Parliament did this on the basis of supposed considerable diversity between Member States and a concern for consumer protection and public order.[18] This is reflected in recital 25 of the directive which refers to, but does not define, the 'specific nature' of 'gambling activities, including lottery and betting transactions' because they 'entail implementation by Member States of policies relating to public policy and consumer protection'.[19]

Nevertheless since the turn of this century, a healthy number of cases has developed in this vein, although it is not the purpose of this section to exhaustively analyse all aspects of each case.[20] Rather, attention will be

[15] European Council, Conclusions of the Presidency, Edinburgh 11 and 12 December 1992 (DOC/92/8, 13 December 1992). Annex 2 to Part A, Subsidiarity. Examples of the Review of Pending Proposals and Existing Legislation.

[16] Directive 06/123 on services in the internal market, [2006] OJ L 376/36.

[17] European Commission, Proposal for a Directive on services in the internal market, COM (2004) 2 final, Art. 40(1)(b).

[18] European Parliament, Committee on the Internal Market and Consumer Protection, Draft Report, Evelyn Gebhardt on the proposal for a directive on services in the internal market. Amendments 152–426 (PE 355.744v04.-00).

[19] Perhaps the exclusion of gambling, without any detailed consideration or extensive debate as to the content of national regulations pertaining to consumer protection, was part of a larger process in which the European Parliament, as described by Nicolaï and Schmidt, 'had to formally sacrifice mutual recognition at the altar of crude criticism which failed to understand that such recognition could be managed to address the extraterritorial tensions inherent in trade in services.' See K. Nicolaï and S.K. Schmidt, 'Mutual Recognition "on Trial": the Long Road to Services Liberalization', (2007) 14 *JEPP* 717–34, at 732.

[20] Case C-275/92, *Schindler*; C-124/97, *Läärä*; C-67/98, *Zenatti*; C-6/01, *Anomar*; C-42/02, *Lindman*; C-243/01, *Gambelli*; C-338/04, C-359/04 and C-360/04, *Placanica*; C-42/07, *Bwin* and C-153/08, *Commission* v. *Spain*.

focused upon the approach to consumer protection and whether any insight is given as to the characteristics of consumers of gambling services and the nature of their protection.

The ECJ in the first gambling specific decision of *Schindler* noted that lotteries had a 'peculiar nature' which justified Member States maintaining restrictive measures which might go so far as to prohibit forms of gambling.[21] This case arose following the prosecution of two brothers who attempted to import German lottery tickets into the United Kingdom at a time when there was a complete prohibition on large-scale lotteries in this jurisdiction. Prior to the introduction of the National Lottery in 1994 UK policy was based on objectives which included the prevention of crime, ensuring that gamblers were treated honestly, and avoiding the stimulation of demand in the gambling sector in light of the damaging social consequences of excessive gambling.[22] The ECJ's description of lotteries, and indeed the basis for a considerably wide margin of discretion, was based upon the following points:

- the moral, religious and cultural aspects of lotteries and other forms of gambling;
- the high risk of crime and fraud involved in lotteries due to the large amounts which can be staked and the commensurate high prizes;
- that lotteries (and other forms of gambling) are an incitement to spend which can have damaging consequences for both the individual and society as a whole; and
- that lotteries (and other forms of gambling) make a significant contribution to financing benevolent or public interest activities.[23]

Accordingly, these considerations, apart from the last because economic concerns cannot form an objective justification,[24] when taken together form a broad regulatory space within which Member States can restrict the cross-border movement of gambling services for 'the protection of the recipients of the service and, more generally, of consumers as well as the maintenance of order in society'.[25]

Seemingly the ECJ distinguishes between the recipients of a gambling service and consumers as a whole; but does this entail that in the view of

[21] *Schindler*, paras. 58–9. [22] *Ibid.*, para. 57. [23] *Ibid.*, paras. 60–1.
[24] Case C-325/84, *Bond van Adverteerders*, para. 34.
[25] *Ibid.*, para. 58. See A. Littler, 'Has the ECJ's Jurisprudence in the Field of Gambling Become More Restrictive when Applying the Proportionality Principle?', in A. Littler and C. Fijnaut (eds.), *The Regulation of Gambling: European and National Perspectives* (Leiden: Martinus Nijhoff, 2007), 15–40.

the ECJ a recipient of a gambling service is someone other than a consumer, as this latter concept is generally understood? In the subsequent decision of *Läärä* the notions of consumers and consumer protection were not developed beyond the analysis undertaken in *Schindler*; rather the ECJ reiterated the fact the protection of service recipients in general can justify restrictive measures. However, the ECJ does refer to the Finnish government's observation that the monopoly in question was necessary so as to 'limit exploitation of the human passion for gambling'.[26]

In the light of the ECJ's subsequent rulings this understanding appears to represent the general thrust of the Court. The decision in *Zenatti* was the first to arise out of national enforcement action against the cross-border provision of gambling services in light of the use the internet. A bookmaker established and licensed within the then prevailing British regulatory framework was offering services to Italian residents via a network of so-called 'data transmission centres' whereby local agents collected bets in contravention of the Italian legislation. Once again, the notion of consumers and consumer protection is not developed by the ECJ, but reference is made to Italy's objectives which, it is noted, are similar to those which prevailed in the UK before the introduction of the National Lottery.[27] Importantly, attention was given to the need for a genuine diminution of gambling opportunities and avoidance of the stimulation of demand through advertising; granting special or exclusive rights for the provision of gambling services was not acceptable if it was merely a means for the state to capture revenue.[28] The use of monopolies to confine the desire to gamble and to keep the exploitation of gambling within controlled channels had to be reflected by a genuine diminution of gambling opportunities.[29] While the notion of protecting consumers and society at large cannot be grounds for unduly restricting the development of the internal market, the ECJ makes no attempt to define the notion of consumer protection in this context.

Although the Italian regulatory regime underwent reform regarding the award of sports-betting licences two further cases arose following

[26] *Läärä*, paras. 32–3. The decision of the ECJ in *Anomar* did not offer any further insights into what could be encapsulated by the notion of consumer protection; in fact it only noted that all the Member States which had made written observations stressed the importance of this objective (Belgium, Finland, Germany, Portugal and Spain).

[27] *Zenatti*, paras. 30–1.

[28] See the Opinion of Advocate General Fennelly in *Zenatti*, delivered on 20 May 1999, para. 32.

[29] *Zenatti*, paras. 35–6.

Zenatti. The first was that of *Gambelli* which provides little insight into why gambling services may be limited to protect consumers.[30] The subsequent case of *Placanica*, however, represents a shift away from consumer protection in the arguments put before the ECJ, so as to concentrate upon combating crime and fraud.[31] This approach is further embodied by the *Bwin* decision,[32] although the rather blunt reasoning of the ECJ in that case can perhaps be offset by that which emerged in the context of a Commission infringement procedure against Spain regarding tax exemptions. In this latter case, the ECJ was perhaps its most critical of the justifications put forward by a Member State out of all the case law to date.[33] Of course, the nature of the proceedings against Spain in which the issues came to the ECJ's attention were fundamentally different from the earlier preliminary reference proceedings. Nevertheless this does little to diminish the understanding which the ECJ possesses of gambling.

Returning to *Gambelli* the ECJ opined that restrictions used to uphold imperative requirements, presumably including consumer protection, must be 'suitable for achieving those objectives, inasmuch as they must serve to limit betting activities in a consistent and systematic way'.[34] Thus, if a Member State feels that its public is endangered by the supply of gambling services and seeks to prevent the availability thereof from cross-border suppliers, it cannot likewise increase its domestic supply behind the veil of protection afforded by any restrictive measures. In written submissions to the ECJ Belgium noted that 'a common market for gambling can only incite consumers to waste more money and give rise to the damaging social consequences which that entails'.[35] Such an understanding negates the utility which consumers who do not spend

[30] *Gambelli* predates the introduction of the Gambling Act 2005. Reference should thus be made to the now repealed Betting, Gaming and Lotteries Act 1963 under which the operator Stanleybet was licensed by the relevant authorities of the city of Liverpool.

[31] As noted in N. Hoekx, 'Placanica: Combating Criminality vs. Reducing Gambling Opportunities as Grounds for Justification in the ECJ's Jurisprudence', in T. Spapens, A. Littler and C. Fijnaut (eds.), *Crime, Addiction and the Regulation of Gambling* (Leiden: Martinus Nijhoff, 2008), 69–92, and N. Hoekx, 'Kansspelen in Europa' (2007) 5 *Tijdschrijft voor Consumentenrecht en handelspratijken* 148–55.

[32] For a brief comment on this decision see A. Littler, 'Een Europese kijk op de voorgestelde wijziging van de Kansspelwet'/'Un point de vue européen sur la proposition d'amendement de la loi sur les jeux de hasard', in N. Hoekx and A. Verbeke (eds.), *Kansspelen in België/Les jeux de hazard en Belgique* (Ghent: Larcier, 2009), 3–19, 21–38.

[33] Given that the measure discriminated upon the basis of nationality, or rather place of establishment, then the grounds for justification were restricted to the narrowly interpreted grounds given in Art. 46 EC.

[34] *Gambelli*, para. 67. [35] *Ibid.*, para. 42.

beyond their means receive from gambling, while seemingly ignoring the scope for qualitative regulatory measures, including those upholding responsible gambling practices. These concerns are astutely noted by Advocate General Alber when observing that little reference is made to the 'dangerous effects that gambling might have on gamblers and their social environment'. In the absence of such elaboration he considers that fears of such dangers cannot form part of the protection of consumers as an overriding reason in the general interest.[36] Unfortunately, however, he does not proceed to define what the protection of consumers as a basis for upholding restrictions to Articles 43 and 49 EC could entail.[37]

As the latest instalment of the trio of Italian preliminary references, *Placanica* shifts the focus away from consumer protection and towards combating crime and fraud. Italy had claimed that an expansion of the market, while upholding barriers to market access, was necessary in order combat the illegal gambling market prevailing in Italy. The ECJ no longer makes any direct references to consumer protection forming an objective justification but to the 'objective of reducing gambling opportunities';[38] surely, though, protecting consumers from the dangers associated with gambling must go beyond limiting the supply of services so not to encourage excessive play? It would be surprising to think that the ECJ intended to exclude qualitative restrictions from the basket of measures which can ensure the protection of consumers and potentially restrict the free movement of gambling services. If Member States can only decide on the quantity of gambling services offered within their jurisdiction, then this would suggest that scope exists for positive harmonisation in terms of the quality of gambling services, in as far as their supply respects national decisions regarding the volume supplied.

The most recent case concerning non-discriminatory, or indistinctly applicable, restrictive measures arose in *Bwin*. Portugal had entrusted the organisation of lotteries and off-course betting to a single undertaking, the Santa Casa da Misericórdia, which had provided lottery services since 1783. In light of the advent of the internet and online gambling its monopoly was extended to the internet, foreclosing the opportunity

[36] In para. 127 the Advocate General states that 'what they [the Member States] fear most is the economic consequences of changes within the gambling sector'. Opinion of Advocate General Alber delivered on 13 March 2001, in *Gambelli, ibid.*

[37] Following the ruling in *Gambelli* the Italian *Corte Suprema di casszione* held that Italian policy was designed to expand supply with a view to increasing revenue, and that no justification could be found on the basis of consumer protection or limiting the propensity of consumers to gamble. See judgment no. 111/04 of 26 April 2004, *Gesualdi.*

[38] *Placanica*, paras. 52–3.

for private operators licensed elsewhere in the internal market to access the Portuguese market. Proceedings were initiated against such an operator licensed in Gibraltar and Austria which then sought to rely upon Article 49 EC to reach those residing in Portugal. Advocate General Bot aired a number of views regarding the role of competition and consumers of gambling services.[39] The Advocate General commenced by stating that 'Community law does not aim to subject games of chance and gambling to the laws of the market' which is true to the extent that Member States can restrict the supply of gambling services if they do so in a manner which is compatible with the free movement provisions.[40] Supremacy of these principles nevertheless prevails. Subsequently a normative statement was given to the effect that the benefits associated with competition such as higher quality at lower prices were inapplicable to gambling. Instead, only detriment would face consumers in a more open, integrated, internal market. Consequently, in the Advocate General's view, there would be an 'increasing share of household budgets spent on gaming' with the 'inevitable consequence, for most of them, of reducing their resources'.[41] Therefore, according to Advocate General Bot, restrictions imposed by Community law on national regulatory competences do not have the aim of establishing a common market and the liberalisation of gambling.[42]

Portugal sought to justify the restriction to the free movement of services on the basis of 'the fight against crime, more specifically the protection of consumers of games of chance against fraud on the part of operators'.[43] While consumers undoubtedly have to be protected against fraudulent practices initiated by gambling operators, such concerns can be distinguished from measures designed to protect consumers from the service itself. Avoiding the defrauding of consumers rests upon the probity of suppliers, and consequently upon the thoroughness of the procedure granting market access and subsequent supervision and enforcement by the relevant national authority. This particular aspect of gambling regulation does not control the structural characteristics of gambling services offered which are liable to endanger the welfare of individual consumers.[44] No comment is drawn from the ECJ as to the

[39] *Bwin*, Opinion of Advocate General Bot, delivered on 14 October 2008.

[40] *Ibid.*, para. 245. [41] *Ibid.*, para. 248.

[42] *Ibid.*, para. 258. [43] *Bwin*, para. 62.

[44] Two sets of characteristics can be used to describe offers of gambling services in relation to the attractiveness to consumers: first situational characteristics and secondly structural characteristics. The former mainly relate to the location of gambling opportunities, such

shift away from justifications on the basis of the need to protect consumers from the dangers of excessive gambling. Consequently attention is focused upon the efficacy of national licensing regimes and the denial of the need for any cross-border recognition by Member States receiving cross-border gambling services.[45] The only reference to consumers is the fact that, 'because of the lack of direct contact between consumer and operators, consumers of gambling services offered via the internet face 'different and more substantial risks of fraud by operators'.[46] With attention focused solely upon combating crime and fraud and an inherent shift for the time being away from measures specifically concerning consumer protection, the ECJ has not discussed in any of the decisions reviewed here the nature of the individuals who might benefit from consumer protection measures; are they rational, circumspect, or are they also vulnerable persons such as minors, and do such measures encompass 'professional gamblers'?

Moving to the infringement procedure against Spain, the ECJ delivered a judgment critical of the national regulations in question which concerned exemptions from the imposition of tax on winnings provided by public bodies and entities pursuing social or charitable non-profit-making activities. This exemption was only granted to eligible organisations established in Spain, and denied to comparable organisations established elsewhere in the internal market. Although the measure was ultimately found incompatible with Article 49 EC following the ECJ's dismissal of the grounds for justification advanced by Spain, the Court's response to the claim that the measure would combat gambling addiction is of particular interest. Attention was drawn to the fact that Spain did not provide any evidence to establish that addiction to gambling had 'reached the point amongst the population at which it could be considered to constitute a danger to public health'.[47] Addiction was not excluded from the scope of public health issues, which strongly suggests that preventing and combating gambling

as slot machines in fast-food take-aways, while the latter relates to the design of the gambling service in terms of how it encourages initial participation by an individual and then subsequently encourages the continuation of play, such short intervals between play and stakes being paid out. See M. Griffiths, A. Parke, R. Wood and J. Parke, 'Internet Gambling: An Overview of Psychosocial Impacts' (2006) 10(1) *UNLV Gaming Research and Review Journal* 27–39.

[45] *Bwin*, in particular para. 69. [46] *Ibid.*, para. 70.

[47] *Commission* v. *Spain*, para. 40. The ECJ also noted that exempting winnings from taxation was likely to encourage participation in forms of gambling enjoying such an exemption, and therefore such a measure was neither suitable nor coherent.

addiction reaches beyond the realm of consumer protection and into that of public health. Furthermore the ECJ appears to indicate that a threshold may exist before which addiction to gambling services could serve as a justification for a discriminatory measure restricting the movement of gambling services. Indeed, the ECJ did not note that Spain had failed to provide evidence illustrating that gambling addiction existed within Spain but that no evidence was adduced to show that it had reached a point at which it would be a danger to public health.[48] Unfortunately no indication was given as to the possible level of such a threshold. The consequences of gambling addiction thus cannot be ignored and nor should the prospect that 'gambling addicts' could fall beyond the bounds of any consumer protection measures. Potentially this could happen in two ways, first in terms of the justification of restrictive measures maintaining the fragmented internal market and secondly if there should be any future move towards positive harmonisation upon the basis of consumer protection.

In contrast to the case law which has been developed in the context of restrictions to the free movement of goods, the ECJ in these services cases at no point developed any sense of the characteristics of a consumer of gambling service. No reference consumer has emerged, even in an embryonic form; thus there is no reference to 'reasonably observant and circumspect' consumers of gambling services.[49] Furthermore, Unberath and Johnston note that in relation to the excessive consumption of certain foodstuffs 'the ECJ's "reference" consumer does not expect the State to regulate his diet in the safest way possible but merely to protect him against specific, well-established and serious health-risks'.[50] Such a poignant statement was made following their observation that even if a Member State proves that a particular food stuff poses a danger to health in cases of excessive consumption, the ECJ has not considered that such excessive consumption is a ground for prohibiting the marketing of such a good. Rather the existence of such dangers should be brought to the consumers' attention through labelling so that

[48] During the *Lindman* case, which also involved directly discriminatory taxation measures, the ECJ criticised the Member State concerned, Finland, for having failed to supply any evidence as to the gravity of risks connected to games of chance and 'the causal relationship between such risks and participation by nationals of the Member State concerned in lotteries organised in other Member States'. See para. 26 of *Lindman.*

[49] Case C-210/96, *Gut Springenheid GmbH and Rudolf Tusky*, para. 31; Case C-30/99, *Commission* v. *Ireland*, para. 32 and Case C-358/01, *Commission* v. *Spain*, para. 53.

[50] H. Unberath and A. Johnston, 'The Double-Headed Approach of the ECJ Concerning Consumer Protection' (2007) 44 *CMLRev* 1237–84, at 1252.

they can make up their own minds concerning how much they should consume.[51] While the dangers to society may differ between a high proportion of individuals becoming ill or overweight from a particular dangerous foodstuff compared to an excessive gambler the difference in the approach of the ECJ nevertheless remains stark.

Concurrently it can be concluded that the significant regulatory margin of discretion recognised by the ECJ permits Member States to maintain national preferences in terms of approaches and standards of consumer protection, which only serves to hinder negative harmonisation and perpetuate the fragmentation of the internal market. Such perpetuation is furthered by the lack of discussion as to the real nature of consumers of gambling services and the scope and purpose of consumer protection measures in this field. It is hoped that future gambling cases will seek to rule 'out certain national standards as being excessive',[52] although at the current stage of the game this is not the case.

Who are the consumers of gambling services?

The ECJ has alluded to the dangers of excessive spending and addiction which are associated with the provision of gambling services, but no insight has been provided as to the nature of consumers of gambling services. Although the dangers associated with gambling cannot and should not be ignored, for the vast majority of consumers of gambling services gambling does not endanger their well-being.

For example, the British Gambling Prevalence Survey of 2007 found that 68 per cent of the British adult population engaged in gambling activities in the year which the survey covered, which amounted to 32 million adults. While 10 million of these adults played just the National Lottery the survey also calculated the number of problem gamblers in the British adult population, which was calculated at between 236,000 and 284,000 adults, or 0.5 per cent to 0.6 per cent of the adult population.[53] This illustrates that for the vast majority of consumers of

[51] Case C-24/00, *Commission* v. *France*, para. 75.

[52] Unberath and Johnston, 'The Double-Headed Approach', at 1240.

[53] H. Wardle, K. Sproston, J. Orford, B. Erens, M. Griffiths, R. Constantine and S. Pigott, *British Gambling Prevalence Survey 2007* (National Centre for Social Research, 2007). Available at www.gamblingcommission.gov.uk/pdf/British%20Gambling%20Prevalence%20Survey%202007.pdf with an overview of the main findings on the website of the Gambling Commission (www.gamblingcommission.gov.uk). It should not be ignored that significantly higher rates of problem gambling may prevail in relation to consumers of particular forms of gambling and within certain sections of the community. Yet these

gambling services, the dangers of addiction and excessive gambling are not immediate concerns.

The aims of this section are threefold: first to distinguish consumers of gambling services who consume gambling services to an excessive degree from consumers who gamble within their financial means. Secondly, to gain a glimpse into the approach taken by Member States the regulatory regimes of France and the UK will be briefly reviewed in terms of the nature of natural persons their respective regulatory regimes aim to protect. Thirdly, given the general orientation of European consumer protection policies as being reliant upon the notion of the informed rational consumer, the appropriateness of this understanding will be considered in relation to gambling services.

Those who gamble to excess

Gamblers who play at excessive levels are referred to as either 'pathological gamblers' or 'problem gamblers'. Pathological gambling concerns 'persistent and recurrent maladaptive gambling behaviour that disrupts personal, family or vocational pursuits'.[54] This means that pathological gamblers suffer from addictive behaviour, whereby they 'have a frequent preoccupation with seeking out gambling', spend more money and time on gambling than they intend to and also become 'tolerant' in the sense that they have to increase their stakes to maintain a level of excitement.[55] More commonly used, although far less scientifically grounded in nature, is the term 'problem gambling', which has been defined as a 'more inclusive application applied to all patterns of gambling behavior which may compromise, disrupt or damage family, personal or vocational pursuits.

figures are relied upon to illustrate that for the vast majority of adults, gambling services are not a threat to their well-being.

[54] American Psychiatric Association, *Diagnostic and Statistical Manual of Mental Disorders* (Washington, DC: American Psychiatric Association, 2003), 671. There are various measures for establishing pathological gambling, such as the South Oaks Gambling Screen (SOGS) and the Canadian Problem Gambling Index (CPGI), with the latter being subject to some criticism; see E. Svetieva and M. Walker, 'Inconsistency between Concept and Measurement: the Canadian Problem Gambling Index (CPGI)' (2008) 22 *Journal of Gambling Issues* 157. See also N. Hoekx, 'De belangen van de speller: een delicaat evenwicht', in Hoekx and Verbeke, *Kansspelen in België*, 53–64.

[55] H. R. Lesieur and R. J. Rosenthal, 'Pathological Gambling: a Review of the Literature (Prepared for the American Psychiatric Association Task Force on DSM-IV Committee on Disorders of Impulse Control Not Elsewhere Classified) (1991) 7(1) *Journal of Gambling Studies* 5–40, at 8.

Problem gambling includes but is not limited to compulsive or pathological gambling.'[56]

The vast majority of consumers of gambling services do not face such problems but through having failed to consider the make-up of gambling service consumers the ECJ has lumped those who could perhaps derive a benefit from increased cross-border supplies together with those who are in danger from domestically supplied gambling services. Economic literature points towards consumer surplus, as conceptualising consumers' benefit from the increased supply of a certain good or service arising from greater competition within the (internal) market.[57] Such consumer surplus can be thought of in terms of the pleasure derived from gambling as a leisure good in addition to the increase in personal wealth which it can offer. However, there are challenges to the notion that in this respect the internal market has a role to play, namely that only detriment can arise from competition within the market for gambling services.[58] Such an understanding does not have any regard for the possibility that measures may be taken to qualitatively regulate gambling services on offer by imposing requirements within licensing conditions.

Approaches of Member States – whom do they seek to protect?

Earlier the ECJ was criticised for thinking about protecting players only in terms of the prevention of addiction and problem gambling, yet given the nature of the arguments submitted by Member States this is unsurprising. Although a detailed comparative analysis is required, dually in terms of general objectives and objectives specific to particular forms of gambling, it is probable that the majority of legislation in the Member States perceives consumer protection as primarily avoiding the individual and social problems associated with excessive gambling. Consumers who derive pleasure from gambling and gamble within their financial and temporal constraints are unlikely to be the main target of gambling-specific legislation.

[56] *Ibid.*, 7.

[57] For example, see D. Forrest, 'Consumer Interests and the Regulation and Taxation of Gambling', in T. Coryn, C. Fijnaut and A. Littler (eds.), *Economic Aspects of Gambling Regulation: EU and US Perspectives* (Leiden: Martinus Nijhoff, 2008), 103–17.

[58] Opinion of Advocate General Bot in C-42/07, *Bwin*, delivered on 14 October 2008, paras. 248–9. Advocate General Bot also voiced similar views in his Opinion delivered on 17 December 2009 in C-258/08, *Ladbrokes*, paras. 58–9.

The approaches of France and the United Kingdom will be briefly reviewed here, to provide an impression of the measures that Member States take regarding gambling regulation, with particular reference to the notions of consumer and consumer protection.

France

Domestically, attention is currently focused upon the impending opening up of part of the online sector to private operators. In general terms the French gambling market can be divided into three categories: first the sports-betting and lotteries sectors singularly supplied by the *Français de Jeux* (FDJ); secondly horse-race betting served by the *Pari Mutuel Urban* (PMU); and thirdly the casino sector in which the public sector has no presence. The two public operators, the FDJ and the PMU, currently enjoy an online presence to the exclusion of the casino operators and to all operators based elsewhere within the internal market. However, changes are afoot, and the online markets for sports-betting and horse-race betting will be opened up to competition, and the authorisation for skill-based games will permit the hitherto excluded casino operators to enter the online market.[59] Thus the PMU will lose the entirety of its online monopoly and the FDJ will lose its online sports-betting monopoly.

Through a brief analysis of selected provisions an understanding can be gained of current French thinking as to the nature of consumers of gambling services. Setting the backdrop to the regulatory regime is a statement that gambling is not an 'ordinary' economic activity and that it is necessary to establish a strict regulatory framework so as to secure public order, public security and the protection of health.[60] This is then

[59] See F. Trucy, *Rapport: Ouverture à la concurrence et à la régulation du secteur des jeux d'argent et de hasard en ligne.* Tome II: *Travaux de la commission, annexes et tableau comparatif*, No. 209 (Commission des Finances, Sénat, 2009–10). This document provides an oversight of the amendments made by the Senate to the original bill introduced in March 2009 (*Projet de loi relatif à l'ouverture à la concurrence et à la régulation du secteur des jeux d'argent et de hasard en ligne, no. 1549, 25 mars 2009*) and those of the lower chamber, *Projet de loi relatif à l'ouverture à la concurrence et à la régulation du secteur des jeux d'argent et de hasard en ligne* (*Assemblée nationale*, no. 384, 13 October 2009).

[60] *Ibid.*, Art. 1A. This reflects a statement previously made by the Minister of Finance upon the establishment of a body designed to add an element of independent oversight to the lottery products of the FDJ. The Minister stated: 'je pense que l'activité des jeux d'argent est une activité économique de nature très particulière'. See *Le Comité consultative pour l'encadrement des jeux et de jeu responsable* and see Ministère de l'Économie, des finances et de l'industrie, *Jean-François COPÉ a installé le Comité consultatif pour la mise en œuvre de la politique d'encadrement des jeux et de jeu responsable* (COJER) 27 June 2006. Indeed, one element the mandate of the consultative body, frequently referred to as 'COJER', is to

further enumerated by the need to limit and frame the offer and consumption of gambling services, with a view to four general aims and particularly that of preventing addiction and protecting minors. Reference is subsequently made to ensuring the integrity, reliability and transparency of gambling operations,[61] which can play an essential role in furthering the protection of consumers through upholding the quality of the service as a whole.

The protection of those who are deemed to be most vulnerable to the dangers of gambling services is elaborated on in Article 3 which seeks to exclude minors from the online gambling market; operators are prohibited from serving them and are obliged to require customers to enter their date of birth upon logging on to their site. Chapter V*bis* of the bill details obligations towards those not *a priori* excluded from gambling services, with these provisions forming the backbone of measures to combat addiction. Examples of such measures include requiring that players are able to self-exclude from the operators' services and the ability to set limits on the amount of money which can be lost. Yet, given its intervention in the regulation of this sector, the Senate has introduced an amendment which will require that operators inform consumers of the risk of addiction arising from their services.[62]

A further aspect of the proposed French regime is that it does not permit the online supply of forms of gambling which are more liable to generate problems regarding excessive gambling. Only those forms which rely to some extent upon players' skill are to be permitted, whereas games where the outcome is determined wholly by chance are excluded from the regime.[63] Thus, casino operators will be able to obtain a licence to offer poker online but will be excluded from offering well-established casino games such as roulette. Through excluding such games from the scope of the legislative proposals, short-odds gambling online will remain illegal in France.[64] Through limiting the liberalisation

help ensure that the products of the FDJ reflect the notion of responsible gambling and fight gambling addiction within this market.

[61] *Ibid.*, Art. 1 I(1) and (2) respectively. [62] *Ibid.*, Art. 20.

[63] Art. 1(2) refers to 'les jeux et les paris en ligne qui font appel au savoir-faire des joueurs et, s'agissant des jeux, font intervenir simultanément plusieurs joueurs'. The reference to gambling which involves numerous players simultaneously is to maintain the hitherto entrenched pari-mutuel form of gambling. See Trucy, *Rapport*, 61 in this regard. Consequently, and in contrast to other jurisdictions such as the United Kingdom, online spread betting and exchange betting remain prohibited. See *ibid.*, 81–5.

[64] Short-odds gambling is that in which there is a very short period of time between the consumer placing the stake and the outcome of the gamble being known, the dangers of

of the market to long-odds gambling, which inherently represent less of a risk, consumers are being protected from addiction through the prohibition of the most addictive forms of gambling. Concurrently this excludes would-be consumers from being able to take responsibility themselves and decide whether to engage with such forms of gambling while being able to benefit from the protection that responsible gambling techniques would otherwise afford them.

Seemingly the legislative proposal focuses attention upon consumers who are in danger of excessive gambling and the prevention of such levels being attained. Theoretically all consumers are potential excessive gamblers but the vast majority are likely only ever to be recreational gamblers, and for this class of consumer the protective measures introduced by this bill are more subtle, less pronounced than those designed to avoid addiction and likely to be reflected in concerns over integrity, reliability and transparency.

United Kingdom

Contemporary gambling regulation in the United Kingdom is upheld by a double-headed regime: those sectors regulated by the Gambling Act 2005 and supervised by the Gambling Commission with the National Lottery Act 1993 and the National Lottery Commission forming the second strand.[65]

The introduction of the Gambling Act 2005 in Great Britain represents a shift towards gambling being regulated as a leisure activity with three broad objectives which underpin the entire regulatory regime,

which are increased when any reward is received by the consumer instantaneously. Such an example would be slot machine gambling. In contrast, long-odds gambling has a longer period of time between the stake being placed and the outcome realised, for example, a weekly lottery draw. For information on how the structure of gambling products affects the propensity of that form to lead to excessive or addictive gambling, see M. Griffiths, 'Fruit Machine Gambling: the Importance of Structural Characteristics' (1993) 9 (2) *Journal of Gambling Studies* 101–20; M. Griffiths, 'Gambling Technologies: Prospects for Problem Gambling' (1999) 15(3) *Journal of Gambling Studies* 265–83; and M. Griffiths, A. Parke, R. Wood and J. Parke, 'Internet Gambling: an Overview of Psychosocial Impacts' (2006) 10(1) *UNLV Gaming Research and Review Journal.*

65 Most forms of gambling are regulated by the Gambling Act 2005, with the National Lottery forming the principal exception, as provided for by s. 15 of the 2005 Act. The other main exception being spread betting which is regulated by the Financial Services Authority under the Financial Services and Markets Act 2000, see s. 10(1) of the 2005 Act. Furthermore it should be noted that for all practical purposes the Gambling Act 2005 does not apply to Northern Ireland, but only England and Wales, and Scotland, according to s. 361(2).

constituting a move into the realm of 'free-market liberalisation'.[66] Two of these three objectives are liable to have a bearing upon consumer protection, namely ensuring that gambling is conducted in a fair and open way, and preventing gambling causing harm to or the exploitation of children and 'other vulnerable persons'.[67] The government proposals which gave rise to this legislation refer to 'deregulation', 'consumer choice' and 'consumer protection'; indeed the government went so far as to state that the Act would remove 'many provisions in the existing legislation that fetter the consumer's freedom to gamble'.[68] Indeed, a key aim of this contemporary regulation is to encourage the development of a competitive commercial market which will support such consumer choice.[69]

To protect 'vulnerable persons' in the parlance of the Gambling Act 2005 the notion of social responsibility has been established which requires the Gambling Commission to permit commercial gambling as far as it considers it reasonably consistent with the three objectives underlying the regulatory regime. In this regard the Gambling Commission is required to issue codes of practice for the provision of gambling services, which incorporate social responsibility provisions.[70] Consequently, responsible gambling requirements can be found in the Licence Conditions and Codes of Practice[71] which all holders of a licence issued under the 2005 Act must adhere to.[72] For example, all casino operators have to disclose information relating to the rules of each casino game

[66] R. Light, 'The Gambling Act 2005: Regulatory Containment and Market Control' (2007) 70(4) *MLR* 626–53, at 632.

[67] Section 1 Gambling Act 2005. The other objective being 'preventing gambling from being a source of crime or disorder, being associated with crime or disorder or being used to support crime'.

[68] Department for Culture, Media and Sport, Gambling and National Lottery Licensing Division, Draft Gambling Bill, Explanatory Notes, November 2003, 3.

[69] G. Reith, 'The Culture of Gambling in Great Britain: Legislative and Social Change', in Spapens *et al.*, *Crime, Addiction and the Regulation of Gambling*, 165–79.

Indeed, the government was perhaps a touch starry-eyed, thinking wishfully of a future in which 'well-informed adults will have greater freedom and choice to spend their leisure money on gambling if they want to. The law will, for the first time, treat them like grown ups.' Secretary of State's speech to the Business in Sport and Leisure Annual Conference, 19 November 2003, as quoted in Light, 'The Gambling Act 2005', at 634.

[70] Section 24(1) Gambling Act 2005.

[71] Gambling Commission, *Licence Conditions and Codes of Practice*, October 2008 (www.gamblingcommission.gov.uk/pdf/LCCP%20-%20Oct%202008.pdf).

[72] Further insight is gained from the Gambling Commission's Statement of principles for licensing and regulation (September 2009), which for example, notes in point 4.16 'The Commission will ensure that appropriate advertising codes continue to be in place to prevent consumers being misled.'

available in a venue,[73] and to exclude children as vulnerable persons from casinos, operators must have policies and procedures in place to prevent under-age gambling.[74]

Turning to the scope of protection offered by the regulation of the National Lottery, leaving aside those relating to the generation of revenues of good causes,[75] the core objectives of the regulatory regime are to generate net proceeds as high as possible while ensuring that the Lottery is run and promoted with 'all due propriety' and that the interests of every participant in the Lottery are protected.[76] The notion of 'every participant' is more inclusive than references to excessive gambling and gambling addiction and includes those playing within 'safe' boundaries.

Not all consumers of gambling services are addicts or individuals suffering from 'problem gambling' but to date the debate in the ECJ has failed to distinguish between these two categories. This situation is perhaps precipitated by the approach of national regulatory regimes, which seemingly concentrate upon regulating to prevent the worst-case scenario of gambling addiction, with less attention given to the protection of those who consume in moderation and gamble within their (financial) means. Consequently, it can be concluded that there is a tension at play between protecting the interests of recreational consumers of gambling services and those who are addicted to such services.

Who are the rational informed consumers of gambling services, if anyone?

Thus far this chapter has established that a chasm exists between the view of consumers of gambling services as held by the ECJ, in terms of vulnerable persons and the danger of excessive gambling, addiction and problem gambling with that generally held by EU policy which perceives consumers as informed individuals making rational decisions. This section seeks to offer an explanation as to how those who are not

[73] *Licence Conditions and Codes of Practice*, 45. [74] *Ibid.*, 24.

[75] It is conceivable that the generation of revenues for good causes is to the benefit of consumers to the extent that players benefit from the distribution of such revenues. Yet the scope of such benefits accrue to a group of persons which is not necessarily congruent with players; recipients of funding may or may not be players and furthermore such 'benefits' are not concerned with the protection of consumers.

[76] Section 4, National Lottery Act 1993. Accurately speaking the 1993 Act permits there to be more than one lottery under the National Lottery umbrella but that only one body may be licensed to run the National Lottery (see ss. 4 and 5). For the sake of simplicity reference in this chapter will be made solely to 'the National Lottery'.

a priori excluded, or deemed especially vulnerable, may nevertheless not fully reflect the informed and rational group of consumers active elsewhere within the internal market. Importantly this section does not attempt to offer an explanation of why some consumers more than others become addicted to gambling services, as this discourse is best covered by existing literature on the psychology of gambling addiction.

Early literature on the behaviour of economic actors considered why the notion of rational choice may constitute an oversimplification of how economic actors, such as consumers, behave. Rational choice assumes that economic actors are rational and seek to maximise their utility, which in turn is based upon a number of supporting assumptions. These include that such actors possess an 'impressively clear and voluminous' knowledge of their environment; have a 'well-organised and stable system of preferences'; and have 'a skill in computation that enables [them] to ... reach the highest attainable point on [their] preference scale'.[77] Indeed, in the 1950s it was understood that the notion of 'rational choice' sat uncomfortably alongside reality in which the 'organism's simplifications of the real world for purposes of choice introduce discrepancies between the simplified model and the reality'.[78] However, given that decisions taken by consumers frequently occur within complex environments, consumers cannot be guaranteed to constantly optimise their utility.[79] Reasons contributing to sub-optimal, or sub-rational, decision-making by consumers can be explained with particular reference to consumers of gambling services. Generally speaking the nature of gambling lends itself to consumers basing decisions on misunderstandings or incorrect views they hold of chance, and thus particular gambling products, which can be exacerbated by the degree of information asymmetry prevailing in this area.

Ultimately therefore this brief review will illustrate why national authorities may seek to protect consumers from the dangers associated with gambling services.[80] Rogers states that 'the most remarkable thing

[77] Quoting H. A. Simon, 'A Behavioral Model of Rational Choice' (1955) 69(1) *Quarterly Journal of Economics* 99–118, at 99.

[78] *Ibid.*, 114.

[79] H. A. Simons, 'Theories of Decision-Making in Economics and Behavioral Science' (1959) 49(3) *The American Economic Review* 253–83, where at 259 it is noted that 'the real world is so complicated that the theory of utility maximization has little relevance to real choices'.

[80] Although a question can be asked about the extent to which the public purse and good causes in general benefit from misunderstandings of how gambling products and services work, since their resident populations gamble more than they would otherwise do so and

about lotteries is why, given the low probabilities of winning and negative expected returns they offer, people actually play them at all'.[81] As a brief remark, failure to gamble in a utility-maximising manner may be in part due to subjective utility received by the player, which cannot be measured in terms of purely financial gains and losses. Roger suggest that such subjective utility may include excitement and social rewards.[82] Such considerations may further explain why consumer habits in this sector do not reflect utility maximisation in addition to those explanations offered in terms of consumers' lack of capacity to reach rational decisions.

One of the principal causes of sub-optimal decision-making is that consumers do not understand probabilities and notions of chance, which is partly responsible for the use of heuristics detailed below. Langer identifies the difficulties which consumers face as arising out of an inability to distinguish between skill and chance, with behaviour reflecting beliefs that 'chance events are subject to control'[83] and thereby failing to distinguish between controllable and uncontrollable events.[84] One such situation is that where consumers enjoy an element of choice, such as when selecting lottery numbers. The outcome of the lottery is wholly governed by chance and yet permitting individuals to select their own numbers mimics skill in a process devoid of skill.[85]

Closely related to this misplaced sense of control is what is known as the 'gambler's fallacy' in which consumers of gambling services overestimate the chances of winning through a rejection of scientific views of chance.[86] This has found expression in Tversky and Kahneman's observation that '[c]hance is commonly viewed as a self-correcting process in

in so doing contribute to the treasury or good causes. That said, some operators detail the probabilities of winning, and such transparency will be detailed subsequently in this chapter.

[81] P. Rogers, 'The Cognitive Psychology of Lottery Gambling: a Theoretical Review' (1998) 14(2) *Journal of Gambling Studies* 111–34, at 113.

[82] *Ibid.*, 115.

[83] E. J. Langer, 'The Illusion of Control' (1975) 32(2) *Journal of Personality and Social Psychology* 311–28, at 311.

[84] *Ibid.*, 313. [85] *Ibid.*, 316.

[86] See C. T. Clotfelter, and P. J. Cook, 'Notes: the "Gambler's Fallacy" in Lottery Play' (1993) 39 (12) *Management Science* 1521–5. See also G. S. Becker and K. M. Murphy, 'A Theory of Rational Addiction' (1988) 96 (4) *Journal of Political Economy* 675–700; P. J. Cook and C. T. Clotfelter, 'The Peculiar Scale of Economies of Lotto' (1993) 83 (3) *American Economic Review* 634–43; J. C. Handa, 'A Theory of Risk Preference in Gambling' (1971) 79 *The Journal of Political Economy* 1073–83; R. Rosett, 'Gambling and Rationality' (1965) 73(6) *The Journal of Political Economy* 595–607.

which a deviation in one direction induces a deviation in the opposite direction to restore the equilibrium'.[87]

In essence, where the probability of a particular outcome arising is wholly independent from one round to another, most gamblers will believe that the probability of a given outcome occurring will be reduced if it has recently occurred. A simple example of this fallacy is as follows; if a six is thrown on a die in the first round then because it has just occurred a six will not be thrown in the second round. Whether a six is thrown in the second round is entirely independent of the outcome of the first, yet research such as the work of Clotfelter and Cook in relation to state lottery play, shows that most gambling consumers do not fully appreciate this.[88]

This situation is exacerbated by bounded rationality and the use of heuristics by consumers.[89] The notion of bounded rationality reflects the fact that decision-makers make 'short cuts' in reaching a decision which negates the attainment of maximum utility.[90] One explanation rests upon the complexity of information provided to a decision-maker which goes beyond an individual's cognitive abilities. Additionally ambiguities can prevail in terms of information, where a consumer lacks the full range of information necessary to reach a decision which is optimal. Moreover, the consequences of taking a decision may not be clear. Where information does not prevail as to the structure of a particular game consumers may stake more money than if they knew the real chances of winning, while those moving towards excessive play may not appreciate the consequences of staking more money in more games.

Heuristics and biases frequently reduce the gain individuals may receive when making decisions, through a simplification of the decision-making process, which may mean that not all available information is processed. For example individuals may have an 'overconfidence bias', whereby they believe that 'good' things are more likely to happen, than 'bad'.[91] In this regard the gambler's fallacy prevails within this void

[87] A. Tversky and D. Kahneman, 'Judgment under Uncertainty: Heuristics and Biases' (1974) New Series, 185(4157) *Science* 1124–31, at 1125.

[88] In relation to pari-mutuel games offered by US state operators see D. Terrell, 'A Test of the Gambler's Fallacy: Evidence from Pari-mutuel Games' (1994) 8 *Journal of Risk and Uncertainty* 309–17. Although not uniquely related to gambling see M. Rabin, 'Inference by Believers in the Law of Small Numbers' (2002) 117 (3) *Quarterly Journal of Economics* 775–816.

[89] R. Korobkin and T. Ulen, 'Law and Behavioral Science: Removing the Rationality Assumption from Law and Economics' (2000) 88(4) *California Law Review* 1051–1144.

[90] *Ibid.*, 1075. [91] *Ibid.*, 1091.

created by the use of heuristics and biases. Given the existence of such limitations on the ability of consumers to process information and make reasoned, if not wholly rational, decisions, the mere provision of information is unlikely to amount to the adequate protection of consumers. However, this is not to suggest that no attention need be given to the manner in which information is framed and gambling services offered.

In their development of the notion of libertarian paternalism Sunstein and Thaler note the importance of framing upon the formation of preferences by an individual, specifically highlighting the relevance of context as determined by 'default rules, framing effects (that is, the wording of possible options), and starting points'.[92] They subsequently suggest that true preferences do not exist if the arrangement of alternative choices as presented to consumers has a 'significant effect on the selections the customers make'.[93] This could suggest that regulatory provisions pertaining to the design and organisation of gambling services in terms of their presentation to consumers could potentially have a significant impact upon the preferences formed by gambling consumers and eventual gambling habits, including the development or otherwise of excessive gambling patterns. As such, this could be used as a tool to encourage consumers to gamble in a way which is closer to a utility-maximising approach by limiting the impact of misunderstandings, heuristics and biases.

Consumer protection through responsible gambling measures

As suggested earlier, regulatory provisions can establish qualitative requirements which providers of gambling services are obliged to abide by, and it is at this juncture that consumer protection measures can contribute to the regulation of gambling. This section will attempt to broadly outline the nature of consumer protection measures in this sector. Initially measures which could be borrowed from the toolbox of more general consumer protection legislation will be reviewed before approaching the notion of responsible gambling, that is to say measures designed to prevent and reduce the harms associated with gambling, through discouraging excessive play.[94]

[92] C. Sunstein and R. Thaler, 'Libertarian Paternalism Is Not an Oxymoron' (2004) 70 (4) *University of Chicago Law Review* 1159–202, at 1161.

[93] *Ibid.*, 1164.

[94] G. Reith, *Research on the Social Impacts of Gambling* (Scottish Executive Social Research, 2006), 71. Available at www.scotland.gov.uk/Resource/Doc/143770/0036514.pdf.

General consumer protection toolbox

Techniques which prevail in protecting consumers can, and in some sectors do, play a role in protecting consumers of gambling services, particularly with regards to attempting to rectify the informational asymmetries which exist. Limitations abound regarding the ability of consumers to process information in a general sense,[95] and this ability is often further clouded in the gambling sector where misconceptions prevail. Consumer choice entails that the ultimate decision whether to gamble and how much to gamble rests with the consumer; yet to take such decisions, the consumer must be adequately informed about the nature of the gambling activity in question.[96] Providing information can be used to overcome informational asymmetries between consumers and operators,[97] but the presentation of information disclosed can also generate misunderstandings between consumers. One example of this would be the widespread difficulties which consumers have in comprehending probabilistic information which could undermine the value of requiring slot machine operators to display the cost of playing a particular machine in terms of payback percentages.[98]

Effective information disclosure, according to Eggert, should be based around a number of central concepts, such as simple and clear presentation; tailoring the information to the consumer (the possibility of which is enhanced by personal accounts with online operators); using a common industry format whereby standardisation would reduce confusion and allow for comparison of offers made by different operators; presentation in a manner which avoids misrepresentation by the operator; and avoidance of the use of probabilities.[99] Such methods are already reflected by existing regulatory regimes, for example in the United Kingdom. For example the conditions of the National Lottery operator's licence in the United Kingdom require that the operator provides the rules of the game, including the odds against winning,[100] and slot machines where the outcome is not

[95] G. K. Hadfield, R. Howse and M. J. Trebilcock, 'Information-Based Principles for Rethinking Consumer Protection Policy' (1998) 21 *Journal of Consumer Policy* 131–69, at 145.

[96] A. Blaszczynski, R. Ladouceur and H. J. Shaffer, 'A Science-Based Framework for Responsible Gambling: the Reno Model' (2004) 20 (3) *Journal of Gambling Studies* 301–17, at 311; K. Eggert, 'Truth in Gaming: Toward Consumer Protection in the Gambling Industry' (2004) 63 (2) *Maryland Law Review* 217, advances the notion that consumers could be better protected if the price of gambling disclosed in a casino environment.

[97] Hadfield *et al.*, 'Information-Based Principles', 141.

[98] As discussed by Eggert, 'Truth in Gaming', 266.

[99] *Ibid.*, 262–9.

[100] The requirements pertaining to the information included in *Player's Guide* are prescribed by the Conditions of the Third Licence to operate the National Lottery, granted under s. 5 of the National Lottery Act 1993 (www.natlotcomm.gov.uk/UploadDocs/

influenced by any degree of skill or intervention by the consumer must display a notice stating 'THIS MACHINE IS NOT RANDOM'.[101]

In addition to information disclosure, Eggert notes that any gambling industry advertising should not be misleading or misrepresent the chances of winning towards the wider public.[102] Within the British regulatory context, given that the Gambling Act 2005 permits for the first time the advertisement of gambling services, other than the National Lottery and including on television, stringent rules have been enacted which rein in the freedom of operators to prey on the weaknesses of consumers arising from misconceptions and informational asymmetries. These provisions show how the regulation of gambling touches those beyond players who conform to the notion of consumer in a purely contractual sense. Concepts applicable to protecting consumers of gambling services are also applicable to non-consumers and potential consumers, thus softening the boundaries of consumer protection in this regard.

If gambling operators track individual consumers' behaviour so as to offer individualised incentives for further play, in jurisdictions where advertising is permitted, then it would seem reasonable according to Eggert to use such information to discourage gambling by problem gamblers. Eggert, in the context of casino-based disclosure, argues that this would help 'gamblers understand how they consume gambling as a product, which will, in turn, make them better consumers of gambling services'.[103] Arguably such a form of disclosure would be beneficial for all consumers, not only those who experience problems with or because of their gambling behaviour. In this regard this example suggests a further blurring, between consumer protection and measures more akin to responsible gambling, which can be considered as consumer protection measures but mark a shift away from the prevailing European approach.

Gazing into the future, any EU harmonisation of mandatory information disclosure for gambling services would not harmonise the nature or substance of the transaction, i.e. the gambling service. In this sense, a parallel could be drawn with existing minimum harmonisation directives that seek to ensure transparency for consumers, while permitting

Contents/Documents/Third%20Licence%20as%20at%2004.02.10.pdf). Condition 7.22(b) requires that the Guide includes 'a statement as to the odds of winning the various prizes, and the likely proportion of the face value of tickets which is expected to be paid in prizes'. For further discussion on this in the context of the National Lottery, see D. Miers, *Regulating Commercial Gambling: Past, Present and Future* (Oxford University Press, 2004), 420.

[101] Gambling Commission, *Machine Standards Category A & B1*, June 2007.

[102] Eggert, 'Truth in Gaming', 312. [103] *Ibid.*, 273.

Member States to maintain national rules pertaining to the substance of contracts. Weatherill's observation regard the first directive on consumer credit that 'the substance of the bargain is in the main untouched, but the environment within which the bargain is made is adjusted by mandatory disclosure of particular types of information', would serve well in this regard.[104]

Responsible gambling

Responsible gambling takes the protection of consumers of gambling services beyond the disclosure of information, extending to more interventionist and paternalist measures given that the design of the gambling service is altered to minimise excessive play. Yet while being interventionist when thought of in terms of harm minimisation measures they should ensure 'protection against, and reduction of harm associated with, problem gambling' while having a minimum impact on recreational consumers.[105]

This approach goes beyond informing consumers but extends to altering the nature of a contract for gambling services. One commonly used mechanism is credit limits whereby daily or weekly limits on expenditure can be set by consumers when gambling online with individual operators.[106] Instances where national authorities set such limits represent the largest possible distance short of a complete prohibition, from the degree of consumer freedom inherent in protection based on

[104] Directive 97/102/EEC of 22 December 1986 for the approximation of the laws, regulations and administrative provisions of the Member States concerning consumer credit. S. Weatherill, *EU Consumer Law and Policy* (Cheltenham: Edward Elgar, 2005), 88.

[105] Australian Government Productivity Commission, *Gambling Draft Report*, October 2009. Available for consultation at www.pc.gov.au, in s. 3.6 referring to A. Blaszczynski, L. Sharpe, and M. Walker, *The Assessment of the Impact of the Reconfiguration on Electronic Gaming Machines as Harm Minimization Strategies for Problem Gambling.* Report for the Gaming Industry Operators Group Sydney (University of Sydney Gambling Research Group, 2001), 19.

[106] Self-regulation also prevails in this sector, see for example the European Gaming and Betting Association's (EGBA), *EGBA Standards: The Framework, Principles and Standards to Which EGBA Member Operators Annually Subscribe, Commit and Adhere*, October 2008 (www.egba.eu/pdf/EGBA_Standards_March_2009_EN.pdf) compliance with which is audited by eCOGRA (e-Commerce and Online Gaming Regulation and Assurance), a body whose mission statement shows that they intend to '[p]rotect players by addressing the need for fair gaming and responsible operator conduct' and '[s]et standards for the online gaming industry by providing an international framework of best operational and player practice standards (eGAP) for our growing list of global members and their licensed operators'. See www.ecogra.org.

the provision of information.[107] Other measures include the ability of players to self-exclude from the operator's site, the use of monetary currency rather than credits, and maintaining a timer on the screen so as to prevent disinhibition.[108] In essence the consumer is protected by eliminating or softening the most addictive elements of online gambling services. Further approaches can address issues such as the intensity of play,[109] the use of near misses which encourage further play and the use of self-exclusion mechanisms.[110] Examples from the British regulatory regime include the provision requiring bookmakers to provide consumers with the possibility of excluding themselves from an operator's services for a period of at least six months without a cooling-off period at the point when the consumer self-excludes. After the lapse of the exclusion period the consumer has to take positive steps to gamble again with the same operator, but before gambling recommences a cooling-off period applies, albeit of only a day.[111] Whereas in the Netherlands, which arguably can be said not to have an absolutely watertight prohibition on online gambling, permits sales for offline gambling via the internet sites of some incumbent operators and establishes a daily loss limit of 22.69 euro for such purposes.[112]

[107] One example being limits on daily losses on so-called e-commerce type gambling in the Netherlands, which is subsequently discussed.

[108] M. Smeaton and M. Griffiths, 'Internet Gambling and Social Responsibility: an Exploratory Study' (2004) 7 (1) *CyberPsychology and Behavior* 49 and C. Jawad and S. Griffiths, 'Preventing Problem Gambling on the Internet Through the Use of Social Responsibility Mechanisms', in T. Spapens *et al.*, *Crime, Addiction and the Regulation of Gambling*, 181–215.

[109] Australian Government Productivity Commission, *Gambling Draft Report*, October 2009. Available for consultation at www.pc.gov.au.

[110] Jawad and Griffiths, 'Preventing Problem Gambling', 207. However, there appears to be some tension in the literature as to the breadth of the notion of 'responsible gambling' for example, Jawad suggests that this covers harm minimisation and treatment while Blaszczynski, *et al.*, 'A Science-Based Framework', take a narrower approach based upon information. See also Griffiths *et al.*, 'Internet Gambling'.

[111] Gambling Commission, *Conditions and Codes of Practice Applicable to: Non-remote General Betting Licences*, December 2008. The United Kingdom regime distinguishes between ordinary code provisions and social responsibility code provisions which all licence holders are bound by. However, provisions of a responsible gambling nature can be found in both categories and no distinction shall be made for the purposes of this chapter. Regarding France secondary legislation will contain the exact standards of consumer protection measures commensurate with what is deemed here to be responsible gambling measures. Such legislation will only materialise once reform of the primary legislation is complete.

[112] One such example being the operation of the national sports-betting monopoly by De Lotto. See the terms of the authorisation granted by the Ministries of Justice, Public Health, Well-being and Sport; Beschikking van der Minister van Justitie en de Staatssecretaris van

Perhaps the more player intrusive measures under the umbrella of responsible gambling should not be thought of as elements of consumer protection but rather social law, as in the eyes of Stuyck.[113] Thinking in terms of a social-law approach Member States would pursue a public health-based approach to tackling negative consequences, which would permit restrictive measures both in relation to discriminatory restrictions but also on a more 'rule of reason' approach to Article 49 EC.[114] The possibility of relying upon a consumer protection approach would then prevail for non-problem gamblers and where gambling was truly a recreational activity.[115] Indeed, Stuyck subsequently professed the view that the 'protection of weak citizens and protection of the public at large against health and safety hazards should be appraised on their own merits, and are not an objective of "consumer" policy'.[116] Extrapolating such an approach to the gambling environment, this would mean that the protection of the 'vulnerable' in the parlance of British legislation would probably fall outside the scope any EU-wide gambling-consumer policy.

Would such a division advance the debate with regard to gambling? In theory it could alleviate some difficulties if attention was focused solely on those who are neither vulnerable nor problem gamblers. Yet to reflect such a division in practice would be immensely difficult in terms of regulation, regulatory compliance burdens, and the delivery of gambling services. It would, however, permit Member States to respond to issues of problem gamblers in a manner reflecting social preferences, while permitting 'regular' consumers to take advantage of the internal market. This would be a two-speed Europe of a novel nature: integration of the gambling market for those capable of looking after themselves while the vulnerable, and those who have demonstrated that they are unable to look after themselves, are

Volksgezondheid, Welzijn en Sport van 10 december 2004, no. L.O. 640/0073/0452482, *Houdende verlening van een vergunning tot het organiseren van sportprijsvragen, de lotto en cijferspel.* For a critique of the weaknesses of the prohibition of online gambling in the Netherlands see Littler, *Member States*.

[113] J. Stuyck, 'European Consumer Law After the Treaty of Amsterdam: Consumer Policy in or Beyond the Internal Market?' (2000) 37 *CMLRev* 367–400, at 375.

[114] D. Korn, R. Gibbins and J. Azmier, 'Framing Public Policy Towards a Public Health Paradigm for Gambling' (2003) 19 (2) *Journal of Gambling Studies* 235.

[115] This could be thought of in terms of both regulatory systems that reflect a policy choice which recognises that gambling in some forms may be recreational and also in respect of those for which gambling is merely a recreational activity.

[116] Stuyck, 'European Consumer Law', 400.

confined to national supplies and the conditions which Member States impose in a wholly internal, domestic setting.

At present, Member States are free to determine the underlying ideology behind the regulation of gambling, and more specifically the protection of consumers within their national market. Ultimately, consumer protection will reflect a balance of responsibilities for ensuring that responsible gambling prevails, with such responsibility being divided between the government, independent regulatory bodies, the gambling industry and consumers.[117] For as long as a form of gambling is not subject to a total prohibition, regulation could reflect the notion of libertarian paternalism in which regulatory regimes respect the notion of freedom of choice while placing boundaries around consumers which seek to uphold, and moreover perhaps promote, their welfare.[118]

To the extent that EU consumer protection policies rest upon informed consumer choices there could be some synergies between gambling regulation and general consumer protection. However, and this has been witnessed in relation to the responsible gambling measures described above, gambling regulation involves a considerable degree of state intervention into the realm of consumer sovereignty. Thus, policies and practices which may appear relatively libertarian in general consumer protection policy contexts may appear woefully inadequate in terms of protecting consumers of gambling services. Equally, regulatory regimes which place greater emphasis on consumers being responsible for their own (responsible) gambling behaviour may appear overly restrictive of an individual's freedom in comparison with more general consumer protection policies. Ideally any prevailing degree of paternalism, and therefore regulatory intervention, should reflect the fact that 'people do not behave in their own best interests'.[119] Moreover, paternalism can present costs if it prevents people from behaving in a manner which upholds their best interests. For certain classes of consumers this could hold true, such as skilled poker players, who gamble online as consumers but face a wall of mandatory requirements which the operator is required to implement, such as limits on the amount which

[117] Miers, *Regulating Commercial Gambling*, 484–5, for further elaboration of this division of responsibility.

[118] On libertarian paternalism see C. Sunstein and R. Thaler, 'Libertarian Paternalism', and on the closely related notion of 'asymmetric paternalism' see C. Camerer, S. Issacharoff, G. Loewenstein, T. O'Donoghue and M. Rabin, 'Regulation for Conservatives: Behavioural Economics and the Case for "Asymmetric Paternalism"', (2002–3) 151 *University of Pennsylvania Law Review* 1211–54.

[119] See Camerer *et al.*, 'Regulation for Conservatives', 1212.

they can stake or lose on a daily basis.[120] Such consumers would then be dissuaded from gambling with operators established within their home jurisdiction and therefore be more likely to gamble on sites located across borders, either within or beyond the European Union. Arguably, national policy choices should pay attention to the costs or burdens which will be placed upon those who are acting in a rational manner in a given gambling related environment, even if the majority of consumers cannot be assumed to act likewise. Ultimately, consumer protection provisions could be self-defeating if they drive some consumers to under regulated operators established in other jurisdictions.[121]

Furthermore, national discussions on consumer protection form part of a wider basket of gambling related policy and it would be perilous to ignore the relationship between consumer protection and other policy fields. Not only is this the case with regards to combating fraud and money laundering, or even public health, but with another policy bed-fellow, namely revenue generation. National gambling markets represent immense opportunities for national authorities, either through levying taxes on private operators or directly collecting revenue from public operators. To the extent that consumers gamble upon the basis of making errors of judgement any measures which are designed to improve the rationality of their decision-making may encourage them to reduce their consumption of gambling services.[122] In so doing this will reduce the margin that gambling operators, private and public a like, are able to derive from their consumers. If the impact of consumer protection measures were severe enough would it not be inconceivable that a decline in tax revenue could be witnessed? At a very fundamental level would national authorities be willing to forgo some revenue so as to secure the protection of their consumers against the services which they are offering to them, or at very least, legitimising?[123]

[120] Admittedly this would be a rather naive view of reality; such consumers would gamble with an operator located in another jurisdiction, either by travelling there in person or via the internet if payment transactions were not blocked by the financial services industry and online payment providers.

[121] Of course, one could argue that if professional players are wholly rational then perhaps they need not remain in the national market because they will be able to fend for themselves in the global market place. However, it must not be forgotten than in doing so they may well jeopardise other objectives of gambling regulation, such as anti-fraud and money laundering measures which fall beyond the remit of consumer protection.

[122] Reflecting Camerer *et al.*, 'Regulation for Conservatives', 1220.

[123] The impact on overall societal welfare in this regard would probably draw upon the distributional effects of gambling, and thus whether those sectors of society which pay the most in relative terms receive an equitable share of the supposed benefits. This a

In bringing this chapter around to the current ideas on maximum harmonisation in European consumer protection law, the main concern in the field of gambling regulation would probably be that it would squeeze out national policy preferences in relation to gambling.[124] This would prevent Member States from affording the level of protection that they feel is most appropriate for their consumers. Given that the ECJ considers that differences in gambling regulation between the Member States are a reflection of cultural differences, would this not lend weight to eventual arguments that it is inappropriate create a homogenous European consumer protection policy which prevails throughout this sector?[125] In order to preserve their competence to regulate gambling, it can readily be imagined that Member States would seek to exclude gambling contracts from the scope of a rigid European framework. Whether, and to what extent, an approach to consumer protection based upon maximum harmonisation would foreclose regulatory competence in this field would depend upon the nature of maximum harmonisation itself, and the scope of application of harmonising provisions of Union law.[126] Furthermore, maximum harmonisation is seen as a means to facilitate cross-border trade,[127] something which many Member States oppose in the gambling sector. Attempts at extending harmonisation of consumer protection provisions to gambling could face resistance in view of this, regardless of any benefits inherent in performing harmonisation exercises within this sector.

much broader question than that of consumer protection, but one in which consumer protection clearly has a place. In the paper by Camerer *et al.*, on the development of the notion of 'asymmetrical paternalism' overcoming the bounded rationality of consumers may 'lead to superior social outcomes even if individual firms are hurt'; *ibid.*, 1221.

124 M. W. Hesselink, 'European Contract Law: a Matter of Consumer Protection, Citizenship, or Justice?' (2007) 15 (3) *European Review of Private Law* 323–248, at 331. The review of the consumer *acquis* covers existing directives upholding consumer protection objectives and advances the notion of maximum harmonisation. Even if such harmonisation was targeted at the areas covered by the directives in question, gambling would not be affected, and in this regard, these comments are purely speculative in that there is no current policy review process which would bring gambling within any maximum harmonisation measures. See Green Paper on the review of the consumer *acquis* COM (2006) 744 final (8 February 2007).

125 To the knowledge of the author no research has been completed which shows how culture is reflected in contemporary gambling regulation and whether it necessarily leads to incompatible regulatory objectives and standards in a cross-border context.

126 For detailed thinking in this regard see V. Mak, 'Review of the Consumer Acquis: Towards Maximum Harmonization?' (2009) 17 *European Review of Private Law* 55–73.

127 *Ibid.*, 58.

Sight should not be lost of the other end of the harmonisation spectrum, namely minimum harmonisation. Even if an EU-based agreement were to be reached with regards to information disclosure, the chances of an agreement being reached upon some degree of minimum harmonisation for other requirements would be much less. Given the diversity between Member States in terms of approaches to protecting gamblers, as well as the precise standards which are imposed, minimum harmonisation of information disclosure would be a weak tool with which to bring the twenty-seven mini-markets together. However, any harmonisation of responsible gambling features would not deny Member States the competence to determine which forms of gambling were permitted within their jurisdiction. If a Member State wished to prohibit casinos, as in Ireland, then it would be able to do so; likewise if a Member State decided to prohibit a variant of a particular form of gambling, then this would remain feasible. For example in the field of sports-betting holders of licences granted under the Gambling Act 2005 are able to offer 'live sports-betting', whereas the licensing regimes of other jurisdictions do not, such as that proposed by France.[128] The competence of Member States to determine this constitutes an integral part of their competence to regulate their own national gambling markets.[129]

Conclusions

Given that it is the task of the EU to 'ensure that consumers are enabled to participate uninhibited in the market'[130] it may be surprising that more attention has not been directed to the nature of consumer protection in terms of gambling services, the existing degree of convergence between Member States' regulatory regimes and the possible contribution that some harmonisation or standardisation could make, so as to ensure that free market principles are upheld. Yet perhaps consumer protection has, thus far, fallen victim to the perceived uniqueness of the specific characteristics of the gambling market. Nevertheless, in order not to deprive consumers of gambling services from the benefits of the internal market, consumer protection measures could be subject to

[128] Project de loi *relatif à l'ouverture à la concurrence et à la régulation du secteur des jeux d'argent et de hasard en ligne, no. 1549 du 25 mars 2009.*

[129] A. Littler, 'Regulatory Perspectives on the Future of Interactive Gambling in the Internal Market' (2008) 33 (2) *European Law Review* 211–29.

[130] Unberath and Johnston, 'The Double-Headed Approach', 1244.

some degree of harmonisation. This would at least be in keeping with consumer protection policy at a more general level. However, where protecting consumers against the dangers of gambling becomes more a public health issue then these concerns should be separated from those of information disclosure and the less intrusive responsible gambling mechanisms such as the setting of credit limits. As indicated above this may be practically impossible and furthermore the regulation of gambling is frequently connected to other objectives, such as the eradication of crime and fraud. Once again it may not be feasible in practice to permit cross-border trade in gambling services on the basis of consumer protection if other objectives continue to justify restrictive measures. This may then hamper the development of the aforementioned two-speed Europe, with no discernible distinction arising between the market for recreational gamblers and that for problem or pathological gamblers, with no market perhaps arising in the first place.

In essence, there does not appear to be any real European notion of consumer protection in this field, notwithstanding the reliance which is placed on this principle before the ECJ and in other institutions. Furthermore, the theory and practice which exists elsewhere in the internal market has not spilt over to this sector, so from a European perspective the gambling sector could be said to be out step with both consumer protection theory and practice, and thus potentially to be an area ripe for a degree of European fertilisation.

PART III

Contextualising consumer protection in the EU

12

Consumer protection and overriding mandatory rules in the Rome I Regulation

CHRISTOPHER BISPING

Introduction

In cross-border transactions consumers arguably need more protection than in purely domestic situations: the other party, the language, the structure of the transaction and the law applicable to it might be foreign to the consumer. The conflict of law regime for contracts therefore provides that consumer contracts are generally governed by the law of the consumer's residence, or that a choice of law should not deprive the consumer of the protection afforded to him under that law. But not any situation which might be regarded as a consumer transaction under national law falls within the scope of the choice of law rule for consumer contracts. Moreover, the active consumer who ventures into foreign territories and enters into contracts while abroad is generally exempt from the special choice of law rule for consumer contracts. National courts have in the past nevertheless applied consumer protection legislation of the forum if that is also the country of the consumer's residence via the mechanism for mandatory provisions. After the reform of the European choice of law rules for contracts the concept of mandatory provisions has been more precisely defined and is now dealt with under the heading of overriding mandatory provisions in the Rome I Regulation.

The Rome Regulation on the Law Applicable to Contractual Obligations[1] lays down harmonised conflict of laws rules for contracts throughout the European Union. Harmonised conflict rules intend to safeguard uniformity of decision and to strengthen cross-border transactions by eliminating surprising results arising from obscure conflict of laws rules of Member States. As the outcome of a dispute should thus be the same

University of Leicester.

[1] Regulation (EC) no. 593/2008 of 17 June 2008, OJ L 1776/6 (commonly referred to as Rome I Regulation). It is successor to the Rome Convention [1980] OJ L 266.

throughout the EU, the risk of forum shopping is minimised.[2] In case of doubt a request for a preliminary ruling to the ECJ safeguards the uniform interpretation of the regulation.[3]

In this chapter I will discuss the position of national rules on consumer protection under the regulation. While these are given effect mainly by the article on consumer contracts,[4] it has been argued that in cases where the specific consumer protection mechanism does not apply, recourse can be had to the general notion of overriding mandatory provision.[5] This was the dominant view under the convention.[6] I will argue that this should not be maintained under the Regulation. I will also look at mandatory provisions of European origin, but not at those of third countries.[7]

Consumer protection under Rome I

The special consumer provision in Article 6 is an exception to the general principles of choice of law for contracts. Parties are generally free to choose the law applicable to their contract.[8] In the absence of a choice of law Article 4 lays down rules for the objective determination of the law applicable, which in most cases is the law of the habitual residence of the characteristic performer.[9] This puts consumers at a potential disadvantage as they will not normally be the party who is to render the characteristic performance. It would thus be the law of the professional that would apply by default to most consumer contracts.

The European legislator has acknowledged that the weaker party deserves protection 'by conflict-of-laws rules that are more favourable to their interests than the general rules'. Article 5 of the convention applied to certain types of consumer contracts only, namely the sale of goods and the provision of services. This was in line with the parallel

[2] M. Giuliano and P. Lagarde, 'Report on the Convention on the law applicable to contractual obligations' [1980] OJ C 282, 1, at 5.

[3] Art. 267 TFEU (ex Art. 234 TEC). [4] Art. 6. [5] Art. 9.

[6] A. Dicey, J. Morris and L. Collins on *The Conflict of Laws*, 14th edn (London: Sweet and Maxwell, 2006), vol. II, paras. 33–030/31; *contra*: D. Lasok and P. Stone, *Conflict of Laws in the European Community* (Abingdon: Professional Books, 1987), 385.

[7] Art. 9(3) has been reduced to such an extent that it now appears to be in line with the English position on illegality; see G. Cheshire, P. North and J. Fawcett, *Private International Law*, 14th edn (Oxford University Press, 2008), 740.

[8] Art. 3. In recital 11 the parties' freedom to choose the applicable law is described as a cornerstone of the choice of law rules for contracts.

[9] Art. 4 has undergone quite substantial changes compared to the Convention and now expressly determines the applicable law for a number of common types of contracts.

Brussels Convention.[10] The revised version in Article 6 Rome I Regulation brings the provision again in line with the revised jurisdiction rule under the Brussels I Regulation.[11] Article 6 now covers all contracts as long as they have been concluded in specified circumstances, subject to certain exceptions.

A relevant consumer contract under the Regulation is a contract concluded between a natural person for a purpose outside his trade or profession, the consumer, and a person acting in the exercise of his trade or profession, the professional. It is further required that the professional 'pursues his commercial or professional activities in the country where the consumer has his habitual residence' or 'by any means directs such activities to that country' and that 'the contract falls within the scope of such activities'.[12] This is in line with the provisions on jurisdiction in consumer cases under the Brussels I Regulation.[13] While the precise delimitation of the situational criteria of Article 6(1) is debated, in particular regarding contracts made via the internet,[14] it is certain that distance contracts where the professional has no physical presence at the consumer's residence are to be included;[15] equally, the mere possibility of accessing an internet site from a location does not trigger the operation of Article 6.[16] The website must be directed to the country of the consumer's residence, or at least not exclude custom from that country, and must allow for online contracting, or direct the consumer to other means of distance contracting (phone, fax, email, etc.).[17] Where, on the other hand, the contract was made in the country of the professional's residence, even earlier advertising of the products or services at the consumer's residence will not trigger the operation of Article 6.[18] This follows from the principle that for Article 6 to apply the contract should be closely connected to the consumer's residence.[19] The Regulation thus does not postulate a general rule that the law of the domicile of the

[10] Convention on Jurisdiction and the Enforcement and Recognition of Judgments ([1972] OJ L 299, 32) Arts. 13–15; on the UK's accession see the protocol [1978] OJ L 304, p. 50; the convention was implemented into UK law by the Civil Jurisdiction and Judgments Act 1982 (c 27).

[11] Regulation (EC) no. 44/2001, ([2001] OJ L 012, 1), Arts. 15–17.

[12] Art. 6(1).

[13] Cf. recital 24.

[14] The debate concerns mainly Arts. 15 *et seq.* Brussels I Regulation but is equally relevant to Art. 6(1) which is modelled after its jurisdictional counterpart. See the discussion in R. Plender and M. Wilderspin, *European Private International Law of Obligations*, 3rd edn (London: Sweet and Maxwell, 2009), para. 9–047ff.

[15] Recital 24.

[16] *Ibid.*

[17] Plender and Wilderspin, *European Private International Law of Obligations*, para. 9–056.

[18] *Ibid.*, para. 9–062.

[19] *Ibid.*

consumer will always apply. It only applies if there is a strong link to the consumer's country of residence. The holidaying consumer is still subject to the local law at his holiday destination.[20]

Article 6 does further not apply to a range of contracts, which for various reasons are explicitly excluded. It does not apply to service contracts where the services are to be provided exclusively in a country other than the consumer's residence,[21] for example the provision of hotel accommodation abroad: here the consumer cannot reasonably expect his or her own law to apply.[22] In line with the classic *lex situs* rule, contracts relating to a right *in rem* in, or a tenancy of, immovable property are excluded: here too the consumer cannot expect his or her own law to apply to contracts over land abroad.[23] The exclusions in Article 6(4)(d) and (e) concern financial instruments.[24] Excluded from the scope of Article 6[25] are finally all forms of carriage and insurance, for which provision is made separately.[26]

The consequence of a contract falling within Article 6 is twofold. First, in the absence of a choice by the parties, the law of the consumer's habitual residence will be applicable to the contract. The consumer thus benefits from being subject to the law he is deemed to be most familiar with. Second, if the contract is subject to another law by virtue of choice, then that choice will only be valid if it does not 'deprive the consumer of the protection afforded to him by provisions that cannot be derogated from by agreement'[27] under the law of the place of his residence. A choice of law is thus generally possible with the proviso that mandatory consumer protection provisions of the consumer's residence remain applicable. Where the chosen law appears to be more

[20] Unless the transaction was part of a package holiday deal (Art. 6(3)(b)).

[21] Art. 6(4)(a).

[22] Plender and Wilderspin, *European Private International Law of Obligations*, para. 9–074.

[23] Art. 6(4)(c). Timesharing agreements under Directive 94/47/EC are included as they only grant short-term rights of usage; see Plender and Wilderspin, *European Private International Law of Obligations*, paras. 9–076ff., who note the similarities to Art. 22 Brussels Regulation, and point out that a timeshare agreement which is mainly a service contract would be excluded under Art. 6(4)(a). A difference to Art. 22 Brussels Regulation must, however, be noted: short-term leases of foreign property are not excluded (these might come within the services exclusion though).

[24] Cf. F. Garcimartin Alferez, 'The Rome I Regulation: Exceptions to the Rule on Consumer Contracts and Financial Instruments' [2009] 5 *Journal of Private International Law* 85; Plender and Wilderspin, *European Private International Law of Obligations*, para. 9–078.

[25] Art. 6 operates '[w]ithout prejudice to Articles 5 and 7'.

[26] Art. 6(4)(b). There is a special choice of law rule for carriage contracts in Art. 5.

[27] Art. 6(2).

favourable to the consumer, the prevailing view is that the chosen law continues to apply.[28]

Limitations to the applicable law

The application of mandatory provisions of the consumer's residence by virtue of Article 6(2) limits the otherwise applicable law. This is not the only limitation in the Rome Regulation and it needs to be seen in the context of the Regulation's system of limiting the applicable law. The applicable law can be limited either by the operation of mandatory provisions or because its application breaches the forum's public policy.[29] Mandatory provisions can be broken down into two subcategories: (1) those provisions that cannot be derogated from by contract, and (2) overriding mandatory provisions.[30] The first category can be conveniently called (simple) mandatory provisions. They take precedence over the law chosen by the parties only; overriding mandatory provisions take precedence over any law that would otherwise apply to the contract. (Simple) mandatory provisions are those that in a purely domestic context are not open to party agreement; overriding mandatory provisions are those that even in an international case demand application. It is unclear when this is the case; the question is answered differently across Member States and in the academic debate.[31]

Before looking at overriding mandatory provisions in more detail, (simple) mandatory provisions deserve some further observation. Reference to those mandatory provisions can be found in Articles 3(3), 6(2), 8(1) and 11(5). The prototype is Article 3(3) which declares mandatory provisions applicable where a contract is a purely domestic one but for a choice of law. This is obvious as otherwise any mandatory provision of national law could always be avoided by choosing another law to apply to a contract which would render the idea of mandatory provisions

[28] G. Morse, 'The EEC Convention on the Law Applicable to Contractual Obligations' (1982) 2 *YEL* 107 at 136–7; A. Philip, 'Mandatory Rules, Public Law and Choice of Law', in North, *Contract Conflicts* (Amsterdam: North Holland, 1982), 81 at 99–100 (who advocates simultaneous application of both laws if they grant different favourable rights to the consumer, but application of the chosen law where this is more favourable); Plender and Wilderspin, *European Private International Law of Obligations*, para. 9–063.

[29] Art. 21.

[30] Note the welcome change in terminology. Under the convention both were termed 'mandatory provisions' in English. Other language versions more clearly differentiated the two types, e.g. in French *dispositions imperatives* and *lois de police*.

[31] See e.g. the discussion in Plender and Wilderspin, *European Private International Law of Obligations*, paras. 12–003ff.

meaningless. If a French consumer buys goods from a French professional, which are to be delivered and paid for in France, the parties cannot escape the application of French mandatory provisions by subjecting their contract to a foreign law. In Article 6 the same notion of mandatory provision prevails: the mandatory provisions of the consumer's law cannot be avoided by choice of another law.[32] Under Article 6(2), however, only those mandatory provisions that have as their main purpose the protection of consumers are applicable.[33] The consumer is thus protected to a similar extent as if he had entered into a purely domestic transaction.

Overriding mandatory provisions are applicable under the conditions set out in Article 9. The application of overriding mandatory provisions of the forum is not restricted in any way by the regulation.[34] Overriding mandatory provisions of the country where the contract is to be performed, if different from the forum, *may* be taken into account if they render performance of the contract unlawful.[35] In practical terms the overriding mandatory provisions of the forum are far more important as there is no reported case under the Convention where a mandatory provision of a third country was applied.[36] Overriding mandatory provisions are defined in Article 9(1) as:

> provisions the respect for which is regarded as crucial by a country for safeguarding its public interests, such as its political, social or economic organisation, to such an extent that they are applicable to any situation falling within their scope, irrespective of the law otherwise applicable to the contract.[37]

[32] Similar Art. 8 for employment contracts.

[33] Morse 'The EEC Convention', 107, at 136; Plender and Wilderspin, *European Private International Law of Obligations*, para. 9–063.

[34] Art. 9(2).

[35] Art. 9(3). The corresponding provision under the Convention (Art. 7(1)) was not in force in the UK and several other Member States. The departure from the earlier situation is however not as big as feared by some (A. Dickinson, 'Third-Country Mandatory Rules in the Law Applicable to Contractual Obligations: So long, Farewell, Auf Wiedersehen, Adieu?' [2007] 3 *Journal of Private International Law* 53–88; S. Dutson, 'A Misguided Proposal' (2006) 122 *LQR* 374 at 376–9) as the final wording of Art. 9(3) is limited to those overriding mandatory provisions that render performance unlawful. It is expected that under Art. 9(3) the English notion at common law will be continued, that a contract will not be enforced in an English court if its performance would be unlawful at the place of performance (see Plender and Wilderspin, *European Private International Law of Obligations*, para. 12–023 with references to case law).

[36] O. Lando and P. Nielsen, 'The Rome I Regulation' (2008) 45 *CMLRev* 1687, at 1722.

[37] This closely follows the definition given in a different context by the ECJ in *Criminal Proceedings against Jean-Claude Arblade* (Case C-369/96) [1999] ECR I-8453, paras. 30–31.

This is further illustrated in recital 37:

> Considerations of public interest justify giving the courts of the Member States the possibility, in exceptional circumstances, of applying exceptions based on ... overriding mandatory provisions. [That concept] should be distinguished from the expression 'provisions which cannot be derogated from by agreement' and should be construed more restrictively.

The Regulation places emphasis on three factors: (1) overriding mandatory provisions relate to public interests; (2) they are to be construed more narrowly than (simple) mandatory provisions; and (3) respect for them must be demanded by the country of whose law they form a part. The second of these criteria appears obvious, as a wide interpretation of what constitutes an overriding mandatory provision would bring about an unjustified interference with the underlying principles of party autonomy and decisional harmony. The first and third criteria are more difficult. It is not always easy to identify whether a provision protects a public or a private interest. In view of the wording of Article 9(1) and recital 37 some authors argue that provisions protecting purely private interests must be excluded.[38] Similarly, some European courts have not included those rules within the notion of mandatory provisions under Rome Convention Article 7. Most notably, the German *Bundesgerichtshof* (Federal Supreme Court) has ruled that consumer credit legislation aimed to protect private interests primarily and the protection of certain public interests, such as an orderly credit market, was only a reflex of the primary purpose, which did not justify the elevation of the legislation to the level of mandatory provision.[39] French courts, on the other hand, have followed a wider approach and have applied as mandatory provisions those rules that serve to protect a weaker party.[40] The third criterion, although mostly accepted without questioning, is equally cumbersome: how is it to be established whether a certain rule is internationally mandatory? When does a state demand the application of its law? There is consensus that if a statute states that it will apply irrespective of a choice of law this is sufficient to elevate it to the standing of an overriding mandatory provision.[41] But where the statute is silent on this point it will need to be interpreted with a view to

[38] Cheshire *et al.*, *Private International Law*, 738.

[39] BGH XI ZR 82/05, 13 December 2005 (2006) *NJW* 762.

[40] Cour de Cassation 1st Civil Chamber, 23 May 2006 (2006) *Bulletin des arrêts de la cour de cassation civil*, no. 258.

[41] Plender and Wilderspin, *European Private International Law of Obligations*, para. 12–007; T. Hartley, 'Mandatory Rules in International Contracts: the Common Law Approach'

establishing its desire to apply. Such interpretation is only required if it is clear that the statute is regarded as crucial to safeguard the country's public interests.[42]

Consumer protection as overriding mandatory provision

There are two views as to whether consumer protection provisions can be applied as overriding mandatory provisions.[43] The first view is that consumer protection is exhaustively covered by Article 6 and no recourse can be had to Article 9.[44] The second view is that where Article 6 does not apply recourse is possible to Article 9.[45] The number of cases where a consumer contract falls outside Article 6 is smaller than before as Article 5 of the convention was narrower. But a consumer contract, although coming *rationae materiae* under Article 6, can still not be covered by that article if the situational requirements are not met. If, for example, an English consumer travels to Spain and buys goods there, the situational requirements of Article 6 are lacking.[46] In such a situation it is also unlikely that an action would be brought at the consumer's residence: Brussels I Regulation Articles 15 and 16 do not apply for the same reason that Article 6 does not apply;[47] the place of performance according to Brussels I Regulation Article 5(1) is likely to be at the professional's residence. In such cases the consumer's home law does not apply and nor are his home courts called upon to adjudicate. A conflict between Articles 6(2) and 9(2) will not occur. It is further unlikely that the forum would take into account the protective consumer law via Article 9(3) as only overriding mandatory provisions of the country where performance is to be effected may be so taken into account. Only where the consumer is sued or, as the case may be, can sue, in his or her

(1997) 266 *Recueil des Cours*, 337, at 354–5; Dicey, Morris and Collins on *The Conflict of Laws*, paras. 1–036ff.

[42] Plender and Wilderspin, *European Private International Law of Obligations*, para. 12–008.

[43] A separate question is what happens if there is a conflict between a mandatory provision applicable under Art. 6(2) and an overriding mandatory provision under Art. 9(2). Plender and Wilderspin (*European Private International Law of Obligations*, para. 12–043) point out that this is very unlikely to arise, but if it did, suggest that Art. 9(2) should prevail.

[44] P. Stone, *EU Private International Law* (Cheltenham: Edward Elgar, 2006), 309; BGH VIII ZR 316/96, 19 March 1997 (1997) *Recht der Internationalen Wirtschaft* 875.

[45] Plender and Wilderspin, *European Private International Law of Obligations*, para. 12–040.

[46] *Ibid.*, para. 9–061.

[47] In this respect the assumption by Plender and Wilderspin (*European Private International Law of Obligations*, para. 12–035) that this situation may easily arise appears misconceived.

home country might a court consider consumer protection rules as overriding mandatory provisions where Article 6 is inapplicable.

Let us assume that an English consumer travels to Germany to buy goods there. If under the contract the goods had to be delivered at the consumer's residence in England, the consumer may bring an action for breach of contract against the seller in England.[48] Article 6 would not apply as the situational requirements are not met. The question is whether Article 9(2) would apply to give effect to English consumer rights. The Sale of Goods Act 1979, and the consumer protection provisions in section 48A–48F are silent as to their applicability irrespective of the choice of law by the parties. It is thus for the court to interpret whether the Act would apply. It seems doubtful that the consumer provisions of the Sale of Goods Act 1979, which operate only in addition to the regular remedies, would be considered overriding.[49] A German court would reach the same conclusion in this situation.[50]

The picture is quite different if one substitutes consumer credit for sale of goods. Let us assume that the English customer takes out a loan from an Italian lender in circumstances which are outside the scope of Article 6. As the Consumer Credit Act 1974 section 173(1) expressly prohibits contracting out, it is clear that the Act would qualify as a mandatory provision in the sense of Article 6(2) where that article applies. As the contract was made in circumstances where Article 6 does

[48] Under Art. 5(1)(a) Brussels I Regulation. The special rule on consumer jurisdiction is not applicable as the requirements for its application are not met, see above.

[49] In a domestic situation the consumer is protected by Unfair Contract Terms Act 1977 (ch. 50) s. 6(2) against contractual limitations of the seller's liability; but s. 26 exempts international supply contracts from the operation of UCTA 1977. The consumer rights under the Sale of Goods Acts can therefore not be regarded as overriding mandatory provisions. See Dicey, Morris and Collins on *The Conflict of Laws*, para. 33–054.

[50] A strange oddity would occur if the German court were to regard the German provisions on consumer sales as overriding mandatory provisions: under German law the consumer, as any other buyer, is limited to rights similar to those laid down in the Sale of Goods Act 1979 s. 48A–48F. There is no immediate right to rescission and damages under German law. The consumer's position is thus less favourable than his position under English law is, where he can exercise a right of rescission immediately without prior recourse to repair or replacement. Assuming a German court regarded consumer sales provisions as overriding mandatory provisions (which is unlikely given the reluctance to treat consumer law as mandatory in Germany, BGH XI ZR 82/05, 13 December 2005 (2006) *NJW* 762) these should then not be accessible to a *Günstigkeitsvergleich*, that is the assessment of which law is more favourable to the consumer. If German law regarded its consumer sales provisions as so important for its public interests then English law cannot take preference over them; see Plender and Wilderspin, *European Private International Law of Obligations*, para. 12–043.

not apply the question for an English court, if an action under the contract were brought in England, would be whether the Consumer Credit Act qualified as an overriding mandatory statute. The Act itself is silent on this matter but judicial *dicta* suggest that it might be so regarded.[51] An example often cited for the overriding mandatory character of consumer credit legislation is the pre-Convention case of *English* v. *Donnelly*[52] where it was held that the Hire Purchase and Small Debt (Scotland) Act 1954 applied to a transaction between an English hire-purchase dealer and a Scottish hirer despite a choice of English law. Lord Clyde described this Act as 'a piece of social legislation designed for the protection of certain persons, i.e. members of the public' which had to apply to any relevant contract made in Scotland. With respect, this cannot be used as an example for an overriding mandatory provision in the current sense. What Lord Clyde describes is much closer to a mandatory provision within the meaning of Article 6(2): if certain situational requirements are met (contract made in Scotland) then the Act applies either directly or despite a contrary choice of law. Although the language he uses is reminiscent of today's overriding mandatory provisions, it means something else. It is true that Lord Clyde concludes that if the Scottish Act applies 'the general rules of private international law are superseded by this express statutory provision'.[53] But this statement is to be read carefully: it was made in the context of a situation where one party to the transaction was domiciled in Scotland and the contract was made there. These circumstances today would give rise to the operation of Article 6. Lord Clyde's statement can thus without any pressure be taken to mean that the general rules of private international law give way to a specific choice of law rule for consumer contracts.

The Hire Purchase and Small Debt (Scotland) Act 1954 is a statute that might be regarded as containing a unilateral choice of law rule,[54] i.e. a 'choice of law rule that specifies the international application of the system of which it forms part, without indicating what law will apply if it does not'.[55] The choice of law rules under the regulation are multilateral choice of law rules that lay down general rules about which law applies in certain situations. In most areas multilateral choice of law rules have generally replaced unilateral choice of law rules, especially in harmonised

[51] *Office of Fair Trading* v. *Lloyds Bank TSB* [2007] UKHL 48; Lord Mance explicitly stated that the court had not been invited to rule on the international scope of the Act, but the gist of his speech suggests that the Act is of overriding mandatory nature.

[52] 1958 SC 494 (Court of Session, Scotland).

[53] *Ibid.*, at 499.

[54] Hartley (1997) 226 *Recueil* 339, at 347 and 354.

[55] *Ibid.*, at 354.

areas of law where decisional harmony is a prime objective.[56] Unilateral conflict of law rules are an obstacle to this aim as they bring about decisional disharmony. An English court might not have applied the Hire Purchase and Small Debt (Scotland) Act 1954 as it would not have been directed to apply it; an English court would have accepted the choice of law of the parties and would therefore not have paid attention to Scots law.

A further problem arises where the statute does not contain an explicit statement as to its international applicability, which then has to be established by way of construction of the statute. Interpretation requires looking at the purpose and background of the statute with a view to establishing what Parliament would have wanted had it given consideration to the matter.[57] This conflicts with the general presumption that statutes do not operate beyond the borders of the country.[58] It is also a step back to times that have been left behind in the conflict of laws, a return to statutist thinking. Statutists believed that the application of a statute could be determined by that statute's inherent desire to apply.[59] If there was no such desire a statute would not apply to an international situation. Interpretation of a statute could thus provide the answer as to its application to situations which had some foreign element.[60] A similar attitude is taken in modern American conflict of laws, where under various headings such as 'better law', 'interest analysis' and the like, despite many differences in detail, a basically statutist approach is taken: it is the law, statute or common law, that determines its applicability in international[61] situations. The current approach in Europe is fundamentally different and goes back to von Savigny,[62] who advocated that a legal relationship had its seat in a particular legal system. Von Savigny deducted the applicable law from the factual situation, not vice versa

[56] See recital 6.

[57] Dicey, Morris and Collins on *The Conflict of Laws*, para. 1–040.

[58] Bennion, *Statutory Interpretation*, 3rd edn (London: Butterworths, 2002) 306ff.; *Tomalin* v. *S Pearson & Son Ltd* [1909] 2 KB 61, 64 (CA).

[59] K. Lipstein, 'General Principles of Private International Law' (1972) 135 *Recueil* 99 at 113.

[60] As to the absurdity of the grammatical approach used by the statutists, see Bartolus' famous *questio Anglica*. Bartolus was regarded a jurist of extraordinary authority by later generations of lawyers and at one time it was thought *nemo jurist nisi bartolista* – only a follower of Bartolus was a true lawyer. See S. Vogenauer, 'Empire of Light' (2006) *OJLS* 627.

[61] And in the USA mainly interstate situations. It is of course of importance whether the choice is only between two systems within one political unit or whether it is between different political units.

[62] F. C. von Savigny, *Das heutige System des römischen Rechts*, vol. V (Berlin: Veit and Co., 1841).

as the statutists did. Article 9 introduces statutist thinking into the regulation by looking at whether a country *regards* the application of a provision as crucial for its interest. The will of the legislator is thus declared decisive.

The undesirability of unilateral choice of law clauses, and a general refusal to admit statutist thinking in European conflict of laws, does not imply that no unilateral choice of law rules exist, and that there might not be situations where they might be the lesser of two evils. Where there is a clear need and justification for giving effect to a provision this might be preferable to strict adherence to an abstract principle. But it is doubtful whether Article 9 is the best way to achieve this aim or whether public policy would provide the better basis for application of a norm where the outcome would otherwise be incompatible with fundamental principles of the forum. The question is then whether there is a need, or a justification, in policy terms for giving effect to consumer protection rules where Article 6 does not trigger their operation. The starting point has to be whether consumer protection rules serve to protect public interests, such as a country's political, social or economic organisation. Consumer protection might touch upon the social or economic organisation of a country. The second question is whether the reflexive protection of those interests is sufficient to trigger the applicability of Article 9 or whether these have to be a primary purpose of the statute in question.

In addressing the first question, Plender and Wilderspin point out that the ECJ has held that protection of workers[63] and consumer protection[64] are purposes that relate to the public interests of a state. The cases they quote in support of this view are about infringements of market freedoms by national legislation, an area where different considerations apply than in the conflict of laws. The national rules under investigation in these cases were true public law rules, concerning minimum wages, registration requirements for television signal standards, and labour legislation concerning social and labour documents. All these aspects have a strong regulatory nature. They were imposed by the respective states to safeguard the interests of the population as a whole: the proper functioning of the television system, and the proper operation of the labour market.

[63] *Criminal proceedings against Arblade* (Case C-369/96) [1996] ECR I-8453; *Infringement Proceedings against Portugaia Construcoes Lda* (Case C-164/99) [2002] ECR I-00787.

[64] *Canal Satélite Digital SL* v. *Administracion General del Estado, and Distribuidora de Television Digital SA (DTS)* (Case C-390/99) [2002] ECR I-00607.

Consumer protection does not equally protect the general public. Some aspects of consumer protection law might fall in this category of regulatory law. Registration requirements,[65] for example, would appear to be public and regulatory in nature; provisions regarding contracting and content of contracts are aspects of private law. The proper functioning of certain markets requires the market participants to have certain personal qualities and compliance is tested via registration. The mechanism of contracting and control of contract terms, on the other hand, protects primarily the consumer who is party to a regulated agreement. By regulating the agreement the overall consumer market is further regulated in that certain market practices are disallowed and certain standards of contracting upheld. But this effect on the consumer market is at best a reflex of the protection of the individual consumer. There are further systemic arguments to support the view that consumer protection provisions are not of overriding mandatory character.

It would appear contrary to principle to allow recourse to a general rule where a special rule exists: *lex specialis derogat legi generali.* Consumer protection is the role of Article 6. As consumer protection is effected via mandatory provisions, be they simple or overriding in nature, no recourse can be had to a general rule on overriding mandatory provisions. There are two main arguments against this reasoning: first, Article 9(2) says that 'nothing in this Regulation shall restrict the application of overriding mandatory provisions of the forum'. The application of these rules shall therefore not be excluded by virtue of Article 6(2).[66] But this interpretation is not necessarily the only possible one: the editors of Dicey, Morris and Collins rephrase the predecessor of Article 9(2) in a way suggesting that only the rules on the scope of the applicable law do not restrict the general applicability of the forum's overriding mandatory provisions.[67] This seems a logical approach, as these aspects are dealt with in the articles directly following Article 9. Article 9(2) would thus only apply to the provisions determining the scope of the applicable law, not the determination of the applicable law itself. The second argument against the *lex specialis* principle in this case is that Article 6(2) and Article 9(2) 'operate on a different basis and

[65] E.g. Consumer Credit Act 1974 s. 25.

[66] Plender and Wilderspin, *European Private International Law of Obligations*, para. 12–040.

[67] Dicey, Morris and Collins on *The Conflict of Laws*, rule 205(2) (para. 32R-131) refer only to rules 206–9, not, however, to rule 211 on consumer contracts. In para. 33–030 the editors take a different view and state that consumer protection provisions are applicable via Art. 7(2) Convention.

concern a different phenomenon'.[68] This cannot convince as mandatory provisions under the Regulation have a common core; they are mandatory and cannot be derogated from by contract. This is true for both simple and overriding mandatory provisions. All mandatory provisions take precedence over the parties' choice of law. Overriding mandatory provisions have some additional characteristics but this does not render them *sui generis*. By virtue of Article 3(3) or Article 6(2) both simple and overriding mandatory provisions supersede a choice of law made by the parties. Every overriding mandatory provision is also a (simple) mandatory provision. As Article 6(2) and 9(2) thus deal with rules of the same genus, the *lex specialis* principle should prevail.

Under the convention it has been argued that because of the limited scope of the consumer protection provision consumer protection rules can be given effect via what is now Article 9.[69] The Rome I Regulation introduces a much wider definition of relevant consumer contracts. All types of contract are now potentially covered by Article 6. Mandatory rules are therefore applicable via Article 6(2) in more cases. From this it can be deduced that Article 6 conclusively provides for all situations where the consumer needs protection.[70] In all exempt situations the consumer does not require or expect protection,[71] or is protected by special rules.[72] Where the situational requirements of Article 6 are missing, the professional has not been 'fishing'[73] for the consumer. It is a policy decision not to extend the protection to other situations.[74] In sum, the better arguments favour a restrictive approach towards Article 9(2).

European law and the ECJ

The unlucky emphasis on a country's desire for its law to apply can be addressed by giving the ECJ greater decisional force in this area. In order to demonstrate the role the ECJ could play in this area it is necessary to

68 Plender and Wilderspin, *European Private International Law of Obligations*, paras. 12–040/41.

69 Even the otherwise very restrictive German courts have held that 'such a preference does certainly in those situations not exist where [Art. 5(1)] is not applicable and therefore cannot expand preclusive effect'. BGH XI ZR 82/05, 13 December 2005 (2006) *NJW* 762 at 763 (para. 22).

70 Stone, *EU Private International Law*, 309.

71 See above in section on protection under Rome I.

72 Contracts of carriage and insurance, Arts. 5, 7.

73 P. Nielsen, comment on Art. 15 Brussels I Regulation, in U. Magnus and P. Mankowski, *Brussels I Regulation* (Munich: Sellier, 2007), Art. 15, para. 29.

74 Recital 25.

look at consumer protection provisions in European legislation, especially the planned directive on consumer rights.[75] While the idea of maximum harmonisation, which was an important part of the initial proposal, has been abandoned, the following discussion looks at the consequences such an approach would have had for the present question. It appears that maximum harmonisation would have rendered the present question less of a problem, at least where no third country is involved.

Rome I Regulation Article 3(4) disallows deviation from simple mandatory provisions of EU law by choosing a non-EU law where the situation is only connected to one or more Member States. This provision extends the protection afforded by Article 3(3) to the level of the EU. The parties cannot avoid the operation of consumer protection directives, even if Article 6 does not apply, where the situation is only linked to Member States. Whereas this rule might make sense if it referred to the standard required by EU law, it in fact looks at the implementation of the directive in question in the forum state.[76] In similarity to Article 9 (2) the forum is thus given a prominent role in determining the standard of protection applicable because under the current system of minimum harmonisation Member States can always exceed the level of protection. Article 3(4) thus provokes forum shopping.[77] An alternative would be to look at the implementation under the objectively determined law.[78] An even better rule would be to refer to the minimum standard required by the directive. This would not be a direct application of a directive as what is applied is the national legislation, albeit in a form reduced to the standard required by Community law.

Otherwise surprising results might occur: let us assume that a German labourer buys work clothes from a British supplier after being approached by the supplier in Britain at the home of a British friend. Article 6 would not apply, but the implementation of the Doorstep Selling Directive would.[79] If the contract contained a choice of a non-EU law Article 3(4) would require an assessment whether there are mandatory provisions

[75] Proposal for a Directive of the European Parliament and the Council on consumer rights, 8 October 2008, COM (2008) 614 final, 2008/0196 (COD).

[76] The issue does not arise for regulations as they are directly applicable.

[77] Plender and Wilderspin, *European Private International Law of Obligations*, para. 6–061.

[78] Max-Planck Institute for Comparative and International Private Law, Comments on the European Commission's Proposal for a Regulation of the European Parliament and the Council on the law applicable to contractual obligations (Rome I), (2007) 71 *Rabels Zeitschrift* 225 at 242, 246.

[79] Directive 85/577 [1985] OJ L 31.

of EU law that apply in this situation. The German implementation of the Doorstep Selling Directive[80] would cover this situation as German law has a wider notion of consumer that includes natural persons dealing for purposes that are attributable to their dependent professional activity.[81] The Cancellation of Contracts made in a Consumer's Home or Place of Work etc. Regulations 2008,[82] on the other hand, follow the European minimum standard and define a consumer as a person acting for purposes outside his trade or profession.[83] In this case the applicability of the consumer protection provisions depends on where the lawsuit takes place: a German court would apply the protective rules, an English court would not, and this despite the German court not attaching overriding mandatory character to the provisions in question. The misconception behind Article 3(4) is similar to the one behind Article 9(2) in that too much weight is placed on the law of the forum. This is at the expense of legal certainty and predictability.

The situation is aggravated by the fear that, in line with the *Ingmar* decision,[84] the ECJ might take a very generous view and regard most consumer protection provisions originating in EU law as having an overriding mandatory character.[85] This view would have become untenable had the proposed Consumer Directive been based on the idea of maximum harmonisation. One of the reasons for introducing the concept of maximum harmonisation in the original draft was the fact the conflict of laws rules in the Rome I Regulation do not address the issue of varying levels of protection under the current system of minimum harmonisation, causing 'a fragmented regulatory framework across the Community which causes significant compliance costs for businesses wishing to trade cross-border [and leading to] reluctance by businesses to sell cross-border to consumers which in turn reduces consumer welfare'.[86] Had it been implemented, the ECJ would have to guard against the uniform interpretation and application of the areas of law subject to maximum harmonisation. Any national attempt to increase the level of protection within the harmonised area would be in breach of

[80] § 312 BGB. [81] § 13 BGB. [82] SI 2008/1816. [83] SI 2008/1816, reg. 2(1).

[84] *Ingmar GB Ltd* v. *Eaton Leonard Technologies Inc.* (Case C-381/98) [2000] ECR I-9305).

[85] T. Pfeiffer, 'Die Entwicklung des Internationalen Vertrags-, Schuld- und Sachenrechts 1997–1999' (1999) *NJW* 3674, assumes this in particular with respect to the Doorstep Selling Directive; L. Bernardeau, 'Droit communautaire et lois de police: à la suite de l'arrêt Ingmar' (2001) *La semaine juridique*, ed. Gen. n. 24, 1158; Plender and Wilderspin, *European Private International Law of Obligations*, para. 12–050.

[86] Proposal for a Directive of the European Parliament and the Council on consumer rights, 8 October 2008, COM (2008) 614 final, 2008/0196 (COD), p. 2.

Community obligations. No state could then have attached overriding mandatory character to a rule in this area. And the European Commission did not attach such a quality to the Consumer Directive either. Article 43 of the proposal states '[i]f the law applicable to a contract is the law of a member state, consumer may not waive the rights conferred on them by this Directive.' While this might appear to indicate the overriding nature of the directive, recital 59 points to the opposite conclusion by referring to the Rome I Regulation in order to determine the law applicable to the contract. Were the proposed directive to be regarded as overridingly mandatory in character recital 59 would have to be explicit on this point. By referring the choice of law to the Rome I Regulation, however, it is obvious that the proposed directive would not override the law allocated under the Rome I Regulation. In so far the proposed directive would have been a very welcome clarification and rectification of the current situation.

Conclusion and outlook

Exempting provisions that protect individual consumers only from Article 9 does not render the consumer devoid of any protection. Article 6 covers those consumer situations where there is a need for protection. There are only a rather limited number of situations where potential hardship to a consumer could occur. The other party's interest in predictability and certainty of the law applicable requires restricting further exceptions. The relationship between Articles 6 and 9 is such that Article 6 constitutes an exhaustive regulation of consumer law which does not allow recourse to Article 9 where the situational requirements of Article 6 are not met. Its exclusive character extends to situations where Article 6 is inapplicable. Article 6 is *lex specialis* to Article 9.

Consumer protection provisions are not generally of internationally mandatory character as they do not serve to protect public interests. They primarily aim to protect private interests and public interests are affected as a reflex only. Earlier cases that have been mistakenly read to demonstrate the opposite in fact support this view.

The wording of Article 9 invests the national legislator with too much power to determine the international mandatory character of its legislation. A legislator could, in theory, declare any of its enactments internationally mandatory and thus prevent the operation of choice of law rules. A better approach would be to regard overriding mandatory provisions as exceptions to the general system of choice of law rules, the application of which require justification. The Rome I Regulation is a device to safeguard the proper functioning of the internal market[87] and deviations from its general scheme therefore require justification under, e.g. TFEU Article 36. *De lege ferenda* it would be desirable to change the wording of Article 9(1) to reflect these concerns. *De lege lata*, as has been shown, the same result follows from a proper construction of Article 9.

Any harshness to the consumer can be addressed by giving effect to specific consumer protection rules via the forum's notion of public policy[88] in exceptional circumstances. A foreign rule would then be disapplied if the application was manifestly incompatible with the public policy of the forum. Such incompatibility would be found where the outcome of the application of the foreign law was fundamentally different from the outcome under the forum's consumer protection rules. The advantage of this approach over the way via overriding mandatory provisions is that the test for public policy is much stricter: only where the application of the foreign rule 'would lead to a result wholly alien to fundamental requirements of justice as administered by an English court'[89] can the public policy exception operate. This represents a paradigmatic shift: it is no longer the national law's desire to apply that is decisive, it is the incompatibility of the operation of a foreign law with the forum's notion of justice. The deviation from national consumer protection rules could only then justify disapplying a foreign rule where the outcome of the application of that rule would lead to an outcome which was incompatible with the forum's notion of fairness and justice. The lacuna created by not applying the foreign law would need filling by recourse to the forum's law. Under the Brussels Regulation the ECJ has started to elaborate a common European *ordre public* as core of this concept.[90] It could play a similar role in substantive areas by elaborating the core of European law which applies irrespective to an otherwise applicable law. This approach would make sure that in – the rare – cases of unjustified hardship, the consumer is not left without protection.

[87] Recital 6. [88] Art. 21.

[89] *Kuwait Airways Corpn* v. *Iraqi Airways Co (Nos. 4 and 5)* [2002] AC 883, at para. 16.

[90] *Krombach* v. *Bamberski* (Case C-7/98) [2000] ECR I-1935.

13

Determining the applicable law for breach of competition claims in the Rome II Regulation and the need for effective consumer collective redress

LORNA GILLIES

Introduction

The last five years have witnessed a decrease in the parallelism between EU competition and consumer law policies. Recent policy and legislative developments in these politically distinct areas of EU law highlight that effective consumer protection and redress – where it does not currently exist at the level of Member States – will increasingly rely upon effective regulation and enforcement of anti-competitive business practices via EU competition law.[1] Indeed recital 7 of Regulation EC 1/2003 requires Member States to ensure that private individuals can pursue private redress mechanisms via national courts. Consequently, the increasing prevalence of private enforcement – namely private claims for damages – as a means of regulating market activity and enhancing consumer protection between the Member States necessitates reference to Community rules on private international law.[2] In 2002 Withers commented that the 'cause of action [for a claim in tort for breach of competition law] is very much at an incipient stage of development'.[3] The same could be said for analogous rules of EU private international law. Indeed, at the time Withers's valuable analysis of jurisdiction and applicable law rules

School of Law, University of Leicester. This chapter is dedicated to Rachael.

[1] For example, Regulation 1/2003 on the Implementation of the Rules on Competition Laid Down in Articles 81 and 82 of the Treaty, [2002], OJ 2002 L 1/1 (4 January 2003).

[2] C. Withers, 'Jurisdiction and Applicable Law in Antitrust Tort Claims' (2002) May *JBL* 250; B. Rodger, 'Private Enforcement and the Enterprise Act: an Exemplary System of Awarding Damages?' (2003) 24(3) *European Competition Law Review* 103, at 103–4; D. Fairgreave and G. Howells, 'Collective Redress Procedures – European Debates' (2009) 58(2) *ICLQ* 379, at 381.

[3] Withers, 'Jurisdiction'. Words added for syntax.

alluded to the need for many other significant 'additional procedural and evidential issues'[4] to be addressed to ensure the effectiveness of private enforcement as a remedy for victims of anti-competitive behaviour. Nevertheless, in accordance with Treaty obligations, the EU has continued to implement measures designed to facilitate private enforcement of competition laws. Furthermore it has also continued to implement measures pursuant to judicial cooperation in civil and commercial matters.[5] The most recent development connecting both measures is Regulation EC 864/2007 on the Law Applicable to Non-Contractual Obligations[6] (hereafter the Rome II Regulation), which provides rules to determine the applicable law of a non-contractual obligation. A key development offered by this new, communitarised private international law instrument is contained in Article 6. Article 6 of the Rome II Regulation determines the applicable law that will apply when private, final consumers or their representatives claim damages against businesses for anti-competitive practices or acts which have restricted competition, thereby impeding consumer choice.

The protection afforded to consumers by EU competition law can be distinguished by the duty owed to consumers,[7] the nature of the enforcement mechanism pursued (public or private), the type of the remedy sought (predominantly injunctions) and the location of the parties (whether domiciled or situated in the same or different jurisdictions). In general throughout the EU, public enforcement has been a – if not 'the' – prevalent redress mechanism, whether by way of proceedings pursued by the Commission[8] or by the individual Member States themselves. On the other hand, private enforcement of competition law has traditionally been limited to injunctive relief.[9] Such a remedy is premised on the objective of deterring businesses from acting in an anti-competitive

[4] *Ibid.*, 255; see further in response Rodger, 'Private Enforcement'.

[5] Art. 81 (ex Art. 65), TFEU.

[6] Regulation EC 864/2007 on the Law Applicable to Non-Contractual Obligations, (hereafter the Rome II Regulation) [2007] OJ L 199/40.

[7] Whether owed by the Member State or a business operating in the market.

[8] J. Fitchen, 'Choice of Law in International Claims Based on Restrictions of Competition: Article 6(3) of the Rome II Regulation' (2009) 5(2) *Journal of Private International Law* 337, at 338. See also specifically on Art. 6(3), Elena Rodriguez Pineau, 'Conflict of Laws Comes to the Rescue of Competition Law: the New Rome II Regulation' (2009) 5(2) *Journal of Private International Law* 311.

[9] Regulation EC 2006/2004 of the European Parliament and of the Councilof 27 October 2004 on Cooperation Between National Authorities Responsible for the Enforcement of Consumer Protection Laws (The Regulation On Consumer Protection Cooperation) [2004] OJ L 364/1; C. A. Jones, *Private Enforcement of Antitrust Law* (Oxford University Press, 1999).

manner either against their competitors or to protect private, end-user consumers.[10] Breach of either Articles 101 or 102 TFEU[11] (ex Articles 81 or 82 EC) also permits such victims of anti-competitive behaviour to claim damages. While the ability to claim damages will invariably also deter businesses contemplating anti-competitive practices, the purpose of damages in such instances is to provide 'victims' (essentially businesses or consumers) with compensation.[12] As far as private, final consumers are concerned, the ability to claim damages should provide them with increased protection against unscrupulous businesses and the effect of their commercial activities on the marketplace.[13]

First, it is necessary to consider what constitutes anti-competitive behaviour or business structures that have a detrimental effect on *consumers* in the marketplace. At this stage, it is worth clarifying the meaning of consumer. The prohibitions against anti-competitive behaviour or abuse of a dominant position in Articles 101 and 102 TFEU (ex Articles 81 and 82 EC) traditionally applied to 'any user'.[14] The articles in the most recent version of the Treaty refer in the majority to the effect of anti-competitive behaviour upon 'trading parties'.[15] Consumers are referred to in the context of such behaviour being permissible when it would be deemed to be 'fair'[16] to them, for example by improving competition and reducing prices. However, for the purposes of this chapter, it is necessary to focus on the protection to be given to the consumers in the 'restricted'[17] sense.

The restricted meaning of consumer applies in other recently enacted Community rules of private international law, including Article 15 of the Brussels I Regulation (on jurisdiction in civil and commercial matters) and Article 6 of the Rome I Regulation (on the law applicable to contractual obligations). In accordance with recital 21 of the Rome II Regulation, 'the conflict-of-law rule should protect competitors, *consumers* and the general public'.[18] The Rome II Regulation therefore distinguishes

[10] For example, the recent codified Directive 2009/22/EC on Injunctions for the Protection of Consumers' Interests [2009] OJ L 110/30.
[11] Both numberings will be provided.
[12] It is acknowledged that the definition of victim is developing as this area of law develops: see further on this Fitchen, 'Choice of Law'.
[13] Withers, 'Jurisdiction', 271.
[14] G. Howells and S. Weatherill, *Consumer Protection Law*, 2nd edn (Ashgate, 2005), 533.
[15] Art. 101(1) TFEU.
[16] Art. 101(3) TFEU (ex Art. 81(3)).
[17] C-89/91, *Shearson Lehmann Hutton* v. *TVB* [1993] ECR 1–139.
[18] Rome II Regulation, recital 21. Itallics added for emphasis. The French language version refers to *consommateurs*.

between other competitor businesses and consumers as private individuals (as well as the market as a whole). It would be fair to say that economic behaviour either horizontally between competitors or vertically between suppliers and competitors 'damage(s) … the consumer interest'[19] as a result of price-fixing arrangements/cartels which have the effect of limiting production in the marketplace 'to the prejudice of the consumer'[20] or ancillary conditions being imposed in contracts with consumers (for example, requiring consumers to enter into insurance or warranty agreements for the purchase of particular goods). Consumers may also be adversely affected by economic structures imposed by business activities such as monopolies and mergers. Such activities may constitute unfair commercial practices against consumers in the marketplace.

Second, it is necessary to consider where the parties are territorially located in order to determine the extent of business liability for breach of competition laws. The location of the parties is significant as far as competition law is concerned for, as Withers reminds us, '[e]ach … legal system … establishes a regime for the protection of effective competition … within their territorial jurisdiction'.[21] In accordance with *Courage*, such regimes are at the behest of 'safeguarding [individual] rights'[22] under EU competition law. Depending on where the parties are located, consumers may be exposed to anti-competitive behaviour either in the same Member State as the business or between Member States. It is the latter situation which this chapter is concerned. As technology continues to identify new consumer markets and competitors located in different Member States (and indeed beyond), the EU has recognised that the potential for cross-border anti-competitive practices has increased. EU competition policy aims to provide a coherent and consistent approach to the regulation of business activities and enforcement of competition laws for businesses operating in markets within and between the Member States. Until recent initiatives for the review of the consumer *acquis*[23] the same could not be said for consumer protection policy in

[19] Howells and Weatherill, *Consumer Protection Law*, 528. Words modified and removed for syntax.

[20] Art. 82 EC, observed by Howells and Weatherill as a 'rare explicit reference [in the Treaty] to the position of the consumer'; *ibid.*, 549–50. Words added for syntax.

[21] Withers, 'Jurisdiction'. Words removed for syntax.

[22] C-453/99, *Courage* v. *Crehan* [2001] ECR I-6297; [2002] QB 502, 522, 29E. Word added for syntax.

[23] European Commission, Green Paper on the review of the consumer *acquis*, COM (2006) 744.

the EU. The 'maximisation'[24] of consumer protection policy is now being pursued via proposals for, *inter alia*, a draft Directive on Consumer Rights[25] and an EU consumer collective redress mechanism.[26] When infringements of competition laws occur, different methods of enforcement or redress can be pursued depending on the nature of the breach and the location of the victims affected. As Jones attests, clearly defined communitarised rules of private international law and appropriate redress mechanisms will be required to facilitate private enforcement as an additional means of redress for breach of competition laws.[27]

While encapsulated in the Treaty, private enforcement of competition law has not traditionally been recognised and relied upon as an available (or implicitly preferred) option for resolving disputes in comparison to the established rules for anti-trust claims in the United States.[28] However, in order to safeguard the interests of other businesses, competitors and ultimately final consumers in the European marketplace, parties who have suffered loss or damage as a result of anti-competitive behaviour should be able to utilise (at least in theory) private means of redress via the ability to claim damages. In essence, the right is facilitated by the Treaty but the application is dependent, given the infancy of competition law,[29] upon measures[30] implemented by the Member States. For example, in the United Kingdom, the Enterprise Act 2002 permits consumer representatives to bring proceedings on behalf of consumers to the Competition Appeals Tribunal.[31] However, when parties are domiciled or located in different Member States, or the defendant's actions result in damage to the plaintiff who is situated in another jurisdiction, we have to turn to the rules of private international law[32] to determine three key elements.

[24] H. Micklitz and Norbert Reich, 'Crónica de una muerte anunciada: the Commission Proposal for a Directive on Consumer Rights' (2009) 46(2) *CMLRev* 471.

[25] European Parliament and Council, Proposal for a Directive on Consumers Rights, COM (2008) 614 final, 2008/0196 (COD).

[26] Green Paper on consumer collective redress COM (2008) 794 final 27 November 2008.

[27] Jones, *Private Enforcement*, 88–9, 91–2.

[28] On which see *ibid.*, 16 and generally; Withers, 'Jurisdiction', 250, 254 *et seq.*; Rodger, 'Private Enforcement', 103 *et seq.*; Fitchen, 'Choice of Law', 338.

[29] *Ibid.*, 340.

[30] Including measures for consumer collective redress: see Fairgreave and Howells, 'Collective Redress Procedures'.

[31] Enterprise Act 2002 Part 8.

[32] Acknowledged by Fitchen, 'Choice of Law', who then focuses his analysis of Art. 6(3) of Rome II on examination on the identity of the victim and the operation of current national remedies in his analysis of Art. 6(3).

First – assuming the dispute is a civil or commercial matter and the consumer has title to sue[33] – where can the aggrieved party sue (*lex fori*)? Second, once the *lex fori* has been established, what laws (*lex causae*) will apply? Finally, once a judgment has been obtained from the court, how and where can that judgment be recognised and enforced?[34] This chapter is concerned with recent developments in relation to the second matter – namely Community rules determining the applicable law – in the context of private redress for anti-competitive behaviour that has caused damage[35] to private, final (end-user) consumers. The new Rome II Regulation seeks to facilitate cross-border private enforcement of competition laws by stipulating the rules that will determine the applicable law for such claims. In seeking to make a (focused) contribution to the ongoing debate on this complex and contentious topic, this chapter considers the private international law perspective by examining the intrinsic value of EU communitarised applicable law rules for non-contractual obligations. The particular focus of this chapter is whether – in the context of the private enforcement of/claim for a breach of competition laws when a dispute occurs between consumers and businesses situated in different jurisdictions – the combination of the applicable law rules in the new Rome II Regulation and the proposals for an EU collective consumer redress mechanism can together provide a coherent basis for consumers and their representatives to seek damages for anti-competitive practices.

A number of the key issues and terms in the Rome II Regulation will be considered to highlight the practical challenges that consumers and their representatives will be required to assess before raising proceedings in the courts of a Member State. While the rules may, in theory at least, deter businesses from participating in cross-border anti-competitive practices, in practice, the consensus is that the content[36] and current lack of guidance on interpreting these new[37] law rules will render it even

[33] Akin to instituting proceedings for an injunction against a business; H. Micklitz, N. Reich and P. Rott, *Understanding EU Consumer Law* (Oxford: Intersentia/Hart, 2009), 356.

[34] In the private international law/conflict of laws sense, the term 'enforcement' is distinct from the 'enforcement' of (substantive) competition laws. The former is concerned with rules that permit enforcement of a judgment from the court of a Member State (or third state) in the courts of another Member State.

[35] Cf. Art. 15, Rome II, on which see M. Danov, 'Awarding Exemplary (or Punitive) Antitrust Damages in EC Competition Cases with an International Element – the Rome II Regulation and the Commission's White Paper on Damages' (2008) 29(7) *European Competition Law Review* 430.

[36] On which see generally A. Dickinson, *The Rome II Regulation: the Law Applicable to Non-Contractual Obligations* (Oxford University Press, 2008), ch. 6.

[37] As far as English conflict of laws is concerned.

more difficult for consumers and their representatives to pursue claims for damages as a means of private enforcement of competition laws. The effective application of Article 6 could therefore hinge upon either current collective procedures for private enforcement operating in the Member States (*where they already exist*)[38] or the proposed EU-led consumer collective redress mechanism (*if and when* it applies, and the form it will take).[39] What must be remembered is that despite justified concerns *vis-à-vis* the content and current limitations on the interpretation of Article 6 of Rome II, the (possibly indirect) deterrent[40] effect of these rules may prevent or facilitate the resolution of disputes without resorting to court proceedings, thereby improving competitive relations between businesses operating between the Member States for the benefit of all parties and specifically the protection of consumers.[41]

Going beyond *Courage*: Articles 101 and 102 TFEU and the collective consumer interest

According to Howells and Weatherill '(C)onsumer policy is a concealed aspect of competition policy and vice versa'.[42] The enforcement of competition law operates at a number of levels, all of which in theory should be open to a private consumer to utilise.[43] At an institutional level, the Commission's role in ensuring effective investigation of suspected infringements of competition law was affirmed in *Francesconi*[44] and *BEUC* v. *Commission*.[45] As Micklitz, Reich and Rott confirm:

> the powers have shifted. The Community may be authorised to order Community-wide measures and it may be required to comply with the duties to protect consumer's health and safety as set out in Articles 153, 95 and 30 EC. The Commission becomes increasingly more competent; however, it exposes itself to the risk of becoming subject to liability claims.[46]

The Court of First Instance in *Guerin Automobiles* v. *Commission*[47] permitted a complaint by an undertaking (Guerin) that 'had suffered damage as a result of restrictive practices [to] rely . . . on the rights conferred

[38] Rodger, 'Private Enforcement'. [39] Fitchen, 'Choice of Law', 338.
[40] Micklitz *et al.*, *Understanding EU Consumer Law*, 382. [41] *Ibid.*
[42] Howells and Weatherill, *Consumer Protection Law*, 519. Punctuation modified for syntax.
[43] *Ibid.*, 535. [44] C326/86, *Francesconi* [1989] ECR 2087.
[45] T-37/92, *BEUC* v. *Commission* [1994] ECR II-285.
[46] Micklitz *et al.*, *Understanding EU Consumer Law*, 340.
[47] C282/95, *Guerin Automobiles* v. *Commission*.

on it by Articles [81 and 82] . . . which produce direct effects in relations between individuals'.[48] The emphasis appears to rest on the exclusivity of power vested in the Commission to investigate such allegations.[49] At Member State level, the principles of equivalence and effectiveness place obligations upon Member States to ensure that Community competition rules and remedies (in particular damages)[50] are implemented for the benefit and protection of participants in the EU marketplace. Failure to do so risks the prospect of proceedings by private parties. Ever since *Courage* v. *Crehan*[51] and *Henkel*[52] there has been a specific ability (i.e. right) of businesses to be able to claim damages as a result of a breach of Article 101 or 102 TFEU (ex-Articles 81 or 82). The call is illustrative of the triple objective of competition law in protecting the marketplace, protecting competitors' interests and protecting competitors.

More recently, the Commission's White Paper on Actions for Damages for Breach of Anti-Trust Rules[53] proposes that businesses should be able to seek damages against competitors for breaches of competition law. Such remedies now extend to consumers. As Micklitz, Reich and Rott attest, Member States must ensure that they enact and implement EU laws to protect consumers or they will be liable for either a failure to act or a failure to properly implement measures[54] and would, therefore, as Withers confirms, be in breach of their statutory duty under the European Communities Act 1972. In terms of how competition law 'protects' consumers, the distinction can be made to some extent between substantive law and procedure. As Jones affirms, 'the Community provides the *substantive right* and the national court provides the *procedural means* of safeguarding that right *in the absence of Community legislation*'.[55] In accordance with the objectives of Regulation 1/2003 referred to earlier, it has always been the duty of Member States' national laws to 'protect . . . Community rights under competition rules . . . it is incumbent upon the Member States to provide remedies and procedures

[48] *Guerin Automobiles*, ibid. at 39; Jones, *Private Enforcement*, 78, words modified for syntax.

[49] T38/96, *Guerin Automobiles* v. *Commission* [1997] ECR II-1223 at paras. 25 *et seq.*

[50] See further Danov, 'Awarding Exemplary Damages'; Fitchen, 'Choice of Law'.

[51] *Courage.*

[52] C-167/00, *Verein für Konsumenteninformation* v. *Karl Heinz Henkel*, [2000] OJ C 192/11.

[53] The White Paper on 'Actions for breach of the EC anti-trust rules', Brussels, 2.4.2008, COM (2008) 165 final.

[54] Micklitz et al., *Understanding EU Consumer Law*, 321, 325; Withers, 'Jurisdiction' p. 252.

[55] Jones, *Private Enforcement*, 61, words italicised for emphasis.

suitable for the protection of those rights'.[56] The starting point for any claim for anti-competitive behaviour is Articles 101 and 102 (ex Articles 81 and 82 EC). According to Jones:

> Articles [81 and 82] create directly effective Community rights, and the right to damages is a necessary corollary of the principle of direct effect. The right of reparation arises equally with respect to loss and damage caused by private parties breaching Community law as it does from Member States breaching Community law.[57]

As a means of regulating the market and compensating victims of anti-competitive behaviour, there is clear justification for enabling *competitors* to pursue private damages claims against one another. Not surprisingly, however, there has been very limited quantitative evidence as to the ability and success of businesses claiming such damages via the courts. A recent study undertaken by Rodger of the position of private enforcement in the United Kingdom concluded that such actions (if they arise) tend to be resolved or settled out of court.[58] As far as *consumers* are concerned, two questions follow. First, to what extent can consumers benefit from equivalent protection? Second, following Withers's query of the need for a 'Euro tort',[59] to what extent it is necessary to have communitarised applicable law rules for such disputes? In respect of the first question the ability of consumers, in theory, to claim damages against businesses should improve market conditions, deter businesses from contemplating 'unfair commercial practices' and increase protection for consumers. In practice, it is a moot point to what extent the general take-up of private enforcement of claims for breach of competition will be by *individual* consumers – even less so when their dispute involves a business located in another Member State. It is submitted that the effectiveness of such protection provided by competition law could depend upon the enhancing the collective interest of consumers via an EU collective consumer redress mechanism. Such mechanisms currently operate to some extent across the Member States.[60] However, as a consequence of the principles of subsidiarity and proportionality, the approach is neither widespread nor consistent.[61] The potential for cross-border

[56] Arts. 3 and 11, reg. EC 1/2003; Jones, *ibid.*, 60. [57] *Ibid.*, 78.

[58] B. Rodger, 'Private Enforcement of Competition Law, The Hidden Story: Competition Litigation Settlements in the United Kingdom, 2000–2005' (2008) 29(2) *European Competition Law Review* 96–116, at 97.

[59] Withers, 'Jurisdiction', 253.

[60] See Fairgreave and Howells, 'Collective Redress Procedures'.

[61] Micklitz *et al.*, *Understanding EU Consumer Law*, 350, 361–2.

disputes between consumers and businesses as a result of anti-competitive behaviour renders both the applicable law rules governing such disputes and consequently the practical ability of consumers to raise such proceedings more acute. Therefore as regards the second question, a communitarised approach seeks to ensure that consumers in the Member States are provided with consistent, maximised protection against businesses operating in other Member States while at the same time the compatibility of jurisdiction and choice of law rules continue to be implemented in accordance with Treaty obligations.[62] Nevertheless, doubts have justifiably been raised regarding the basis and terms of Article 6 of the Rome II Regulation and – as is the invariable nature of communitarised private international law rules – a lack of current guidance from either the Commission or the Court of Justice of the European Union (CJEU) in defining the key provisions contained in the article.[63]

Accordingly the rest of this chapter is structured as follows. The next part will consider how Article 6 determines the applicable law of a non-contractual obligation in a claim for damages by consumers or their representatives. The specific aspects of Rome II that need to be addressed by the CJEU will be highlighted. The third part will consider collective redress traditionally, in terms of the consumer policy strategy and the Treaty. The fourth and final part will consider the treaty basis and competence for the EU consumer collective redress mechanism of the type proposed for consumers. The chapter will conclude by considering to what extent such a proposal can assist in the practical application of Article 6 of the Rome II Regulation.

The tort of unfair competition and the position of English private international law, then and now

As the next section of this chapter will consider, over the course of its inception and recent enactment, commentators, including Dickinson and Fitchen, have justifiably questioned the utility of the connecting factors in Article 6 in the Rome II Regulation with scepticism. Such views are meritorious. There is a certain novelty, as far as private international law is concerned, with applicable law rules for torts of this kind. English law has never had *specific* (in the sense of distinct) choice of law rules *per se* for anti-competitive behaviour or acts restricting

[62] Art. 81 TFEU (*ex* Art. 65).
[63] Dickinson, *The Rome II Regulation* and Fitchen, 'Choice of Law'.

competition. Therefore, it is worthwhile briefly reviewing how unfair competition previously constituted a tort for the purposes of private international law. Both jurisdiction and choice of law rules will be briefly considered as the latter are dependent upon the effective classification by the forum. The classification of what constitutes a tort for the purposes of private international law is dependent significantly upon first, which forum has jurisdiction over the dispute and secondly, the approach taken by the forum in classifying the tort in question.[64] It is worth remembering that the process of classification must be undertaken by the forum,[65] meaning that the 'cause of action' must have been capable of being recognised as a tort in itself[66] by the forum for the 'purposes of private international law'.[67]

It is necessary to determine where the defendant is situated before the English courts can assume jurisdiction, either via the 'traditional rules' or the Brussels I Regime. The outcome is the same – if the English court has jurisdiction, English law will apply as the *lex fori* to any claim for damages as a result of a tort. If the defendant business is not situated in a Member State, section IV of the Rules of Civil Procedure, Part B, paragraph 6.36(9)[68] applies where '(a) damage was sustained in within the jurisdiction; or (b) the damage sustained resulted from an act committed within the jurisdiction'. It is possible for the defendant business to argue that England is not the most appropriate forum on the grounds of *forum non conveniens* and that the English court should decline jurisdiction in favour of another more appropriate forum.[69] If the defendant business is situated in a Member State, the Brussels I Regime applies. Following its predecessor the Brussels Convention 1968, Regulation 44/2001 EC[70] (hereafter the Brussels I Regulation) requires that if the defendant business is not sued in the court of the Member State where it is situated (by virtue of Articles 2 and 60), then it can be sued in the courts of another Member State by virtue of Article 23 or one of the grounds of special jurisdiction in Article 5.

[64] P. M. North and J. J. Fawcett, *Cheshire and North's Private International Law*, 13th edn (Butterworths, 1999), 618ff. referring to the Private International Law (Miscellaneous Provisions) Act 1995 which has now been superseded by the Rome II Regulation.

[65] Dicey, Morris and Collins, *The Conflict of Laws*, 14th edn (Sweet and Maxwell, 2006), 1904.

[66] North and Fawcett, *Cheshire and North*.

[67] *Ibid.*, and at 629 on the Private International Law (Miscellaneous Provisions) Act; Dicey *et al.*, *Confict of Laws*, 1095–1096. Words italicised for emphasis.

[68] Previously para. 6.20(8) CPR. [69] Withers, 'Jurisdiction', 259.

[70] Regulation (EC) no. 44/2001 of 22 December 2000 on jurisdiction and the recognition and enforcement of judgements in civil and commercial matters [2001] OJ L 12/1 (hereafter the Brussels I Regulation).

Article 5(3) of the Brussels Convention 1968[71] provided that a claim in tort could be brought in the courts of the place where the tort, delict or quasi-delict occurred.[72] In line with the objectives of that convention,[73] an autonomous, Community[74] meaning was given to the definition of a tort. There is authority from *Garden Cottage Foods* v. *Milk Marketing Board*[75] in support that a claim for unfair competition constitutes the 'equivalent'[76] of a tort for the purposes of ascertaining jurisdiction under Article 5(3) of the Brussels Convention (and thereby its successor the Brussels I Regulation). The focus of the Brussels I Regulation in allocating jurisdiction is therefore on the *place* where the harmful event, or the act of unfair competition occurred, or may occur. This is significant as far as unfair competition is concerned for it will determine the territorial location of the market (or indeed part of the market), being the place where the consumer or competitor sustained damage, which justifies the allocation of special jurisdiction as an alternative to the defendant's domicile. In the English case *Provimi Ltd* v. *Avensis Animal Nutrition SA*,[77] the English High Court upheld a claim in tort for damages for breach of competition law under Article 5(3) of the Brussels Convention despite the existence of a jurisdiction clause in the contract between manufacturers, sellers and purchasers of vitamin tablets. Similar provisions in the Lugano Convention[78] were also considered in the Norwegian case *Saba Molnlycke AS* v. *Proctor and Gamble Scandinavia Inc.*[79]

In *Saba*, a case involving the alleged misleading advertising of nappies, the Norwegian Court of Appeal held that damage could include

[71] Convention on Jurisdiction and Recognition and Enforcement of Judgments in Civil and Commercial Matters, [1978] OJ L 304 (the Brussels Convention 1968).

[72] Unlike the Brussels I Regulation, it did not at that stage, apply to 'threatened wrongs'; North and Fawcett, *Cheshire and North* 215.

[73] *LTU* v. *Eurocontrol*, C-29/76 [1976] ECR 1541.

[74] *Kalfelis* v. *Schroeder*, C189/87 [1988] ECR 5565.

[75] *Garden Cottage Foods* v. *Milk Marketing Board* [1984] AC 130; see also North and Fawcett, *Cheshire and North*, 621 (despite the authors' acknowledgement that the Law Commission's 1984 Working Paper did not think it was clear whether unfair competition would be classified as tortious; *ibid.*).

[76] *Ibid.*

[77] *Provimi Ltd* v. *Avensis Animal Nutrition SA* [2003] EWCH 961 (Comm).

[78] A parallel convention to the 1968 Convention which operates between EFTA states; the Convention on Jurisdiction and the Enforcement of Judgments in Civil and Commercial Matters, done at Lugano, 16 December 1988 (the Lugano Convention) [1988] OJ L 319/9. The most recent version can be found at [2007] OJ L 339/3.

[79] *Saba Molnlycke AS* v. *Proctor and Gamble Scandinavia Inc* [1997] I L Pr 704; J. J. Fawcett and J. M. Carruthers, *Cheshire, North and Fawcett Private International Law*, 14th edn (Oxford University Press, 2007), 247.

'non-physical'[80] damage such as unfair – or as the court termed it 'improper or disloyal'[81] – competition irrespective of where the defendant company was situated. More recently, the English High Court held that as no damage had accrued in England, the English court could not take jurisdiction under Article 5(3) of the Brussels I Regulation. The court in *SanDisk Corp* referred to earlier authority from the European Court of Justice in *Dumez France SA* v. *Hessische Landesbank*[82] and the English High Court in *Domicrest* v. *Swiss Bank Corp.*[83] which both held that the place where the damage originated formed the basis of a claim under Article 5(3) of the Brussels Convention. In this respect, Withers's assessment of the 'place where the harmful event occurred' and his analogy with the ECJ's reasoning in *Shevill* v. *Press Alliance*[84] are instructive. Withers is correct in his view that it is the place where the anti-competitive behaviour *de facto* occurred that establishes jurisdiction as opposed to the place where any illicit agreement was entered into or adverse economic consequences occurred.[85] Withers considered that how the place where an agreement to undertake anti-competitive behaviour was colluded between competitors could often be a distinct place (or territory) from the place where the anti-competitive behaviour actually occurred. Furthermore, the anti-competitive behaviour alleged could occur in multiple jurisdictions – reflecting market conditions – a concern echoed by Dickinson and Fitchen in their assessments of Article 6 of the Rome II Regulation. Relying on *Shevill* – as Withers does 'by analogy'[86] – opens up the possibility for consumers to sue either where the business is situated or in the courts of the place where the harmful event occurred. However, the consequence of this approach is the fragmentation, or *Mosaikbetrachtung*,[87] of claims in different jurisdictions and the increased expense to consumers and their representatives in pursuing claims for damages in multiple jurisdictions.

Similar concerns have been echoed regarding classification and location of the tort for the purposes of ascertaining the applicable law. Prior to the Rome II Regulation, the applicable law rules for the majority of cross-border torts (excluding defamation) were to be found

[80] *Saba Molnlycke AS*, 709. [81] *Saba Molnlycke AS.*

[82] *Dumez France SA* v. *Hessische Landesbank (220/88)* [1990] ECR I-49 – most recently considered in a dispute alleging loss by unfair means of a licensing agreement in *Future Investments SA* v. *Federation Internationale de Football Association* [2010] EWHC 1019 (Ch).

[83] *Domicrest* v. *Swiss Bank Corp* [1999] QB 548.

[84] *Shevill* v. *Press Alliance SA* C-68/93 [1995] ECR I-415. [85] Withers, 'Jurisdiction', 261.

[86] *Ibid.* [87] See further on this Fitchen, 'Choice of Law'.

in the Private International Law (Miscellaneous Provisions) Act 1995, section 11 (as the general rule) and 12 (as the exception). Under section 11 of the 1995 Act, the applicable law was the law of the place where the tort occurred (whether in a single country (section 11(1)) or in different countries (section 11(2)[88]). Section 11(2)(c) applied 'the law of the country in which the most significant element or elements of those events occurred' to economic torts, including those 'unknown to English law'.[89] The concern as to how an English court was to consider the approach of a foreign law in classifying such a tort has not necessarily been removed by the introduction of Article 6 of Rome II. Furthermore, in the absence of guidance from the CJEU, it may be some time before the connecting factors in Articles 6(1) and (3) can be interpreted with certainty.

The Rome II Regulation

The communitarisation of choice of law rules for non-contractual obligations is the most recent illustration of Treaty objectives[90] for 'promoting the compatibility of the rules applicable in the Member States concerning the conflicts of laws and of jurisdiction'.[91] On 11 January 2009, Regulation 864/2007 on the Law Applicable to Non-Contractual Obligations (hereafter the Rome II Regulation) came into force across the Community (with the exception of Denmark). The Rome II Regulation provides freedom for the parties to select the applicable law governing a 'non-contractual obligation' that falls within the scope of the Regulation. However, such freedom is excluded from claims made under Article 6.[92] Stone regarded the Rome II Regulation proposal as a welcome development in regulating the 'three-dimensional function of competition law ... in a modern conflict-of-laws instrument.'[93]

Recital (6) of the Rome II Regulation states that:

> [t]he proper functioning of the internal market creates a need, in order to improve the predictability of the outcome of litigation, certainty as to the law applicable and the free movement of judgments, for the conflict-of-law

[88] Sec. 11(2)(c) for 'economic' torts such as unfair competition.

[89] North and Fawcett, *Cheshire and North*, 637.

[90] Arts. 61 and 65(b) EC. [91] Recital 2, Rome II Regulation.

[92] By virtue of Art. 6(4). Dickinson helpfully suggests that Art. 14 might still be able to apply in situations involving a specific competitor (i.e. by virtue of Art. 6(2) and Art. 4); *The Rome II Regulation*, 426. The CJEU's approach to Arts. 6(2) and (4) is awaited.

[93] P. Stone, *EU Private International Law* (Edward Elgar, 2006), 365.

rules in the Member States to designate the same national law irrespective of the Member State in which the claim is brought.[94]

In general, Article 3 specifies that the Rome II Regulation has universal application, which means that it applies regardless of the situation giving rise to the non-contractual obligation (the example given earlier about the place where the illicit agreement took place) and whether the obligation itself has any connection with an EU Member State. However, as will be seen with the specific rule for competition law, there has to have been an infringing act in the Member State, for example an act restricting competition in Article 6(3). This means there is no need for a party to be domiciled or resident in an EU Member State, the only connection for jurisdiction deemed necessary is that the dispute can be tried in a court of an EU Member State, which as we have seen could be either under Article 2 or (failing Article 23) Article 5 of the Brussels I Regulation.[95]

The Rome II Regulation applies to situations involving 'a conflict of laws, to non-contractual obligations in civil and commercial matters'. In determining what constitutes a conflict of laws (a dispute with a foreign element), the Rome II Regulation is to be given an autonomous interpretation. Under English law, foreign law must be pleaded and proved by the party wishing to rely on it.[96] The CJEU is authorised to give preliminary rulings on the interpretation of acts of the EU and, akin to the Brussels I Regulation and Rome I Regulation, this extends to preliminary rulings on the Rome II Regulation. The English courts must therefore act in accordance with either decisions from or principles set down by the CJEU. One of the key concepts is the meaning of 'non-contractual obligations'.[97] Before determining the applicable law under the Rome II Regulation, as we have seen briefly with jurisdiction, it is first necessary to characterise or classify the legal nature of the dispute according to whether the non-contractual obligation alleged to

[94] Recital 6, Rome II Regulation.

[95] Or alternatively, if there is more than one defendant, Art. 6.

[96] A challenge highlighted by Dickinson (*The Rome II Regulation* 418–26) when applying more than one applicable law under Art. 6(3) of the Rome II Regulation.

[97] If there was concurrent liability in contract and tort, it would be classified as a contractual liability; a point applied in the jurisdictional context in *Source* v. *TUV* [1998] QB 54. However, according to Cheshire and North the better approach, despite the recent introduction of the regulation and no authority in support, is that a tortuous classification is applied when operating the regulation since 'The Regulation envisages that there can be a tortious obligation in the situation where the parties have a pre-existing contractual relationship and there can be a tortious obligation to which there is a contractual defence'; Fawcett and Carruthers, *Cheshire, North and Fawcett*, 79.

have been breached is as a result of a breach of a tort, unjust enrichment, *negotiorum gestio* or *culpa in contrahendo*. Each Member State has its own definition of what constitutes a non-contractual obligation and it is therefore unfortunate that in recital 11 the Regulation offers limited guidance. Obligations that are non-contractual, and otherwise not excluded in Article 1(2), are to be defined in a positive way in the same way as Article 5(3) of the Brussels I Regulation.

Like Article 5(3) of the Brussels I Regulation, the Rome II Regulation also applies to threatened wrongs. Damage is defined under Article 2(1) as 'any consequence arising out of a tort/delict'. It has been suggested by Cheshire and North that this should be taken as direct damage, following a consistent approach with the Brussels I Regulation.[98] Furthermore, earlier concerns about what constitutes 'damage'[99] have – to some extent – been removed by Article 15 of the Rome II Regulation which determines, *inter alia*, the substance and procedural aspects of a non-contractual obligation including the basis of liability, grounds for exemption of liability, the assessment of damages and the remedy claimed. Danov maintains that irrespective of Article 15 the effect of both recital 32 and Article 21 may render invalid any claim for punitive or exemplary damages applicable under the *lex loci delicti* that would be incompatible with the public interest of the forum.[100] While the desire to ensure consistency and predictability via the applicable law will not be at the cost of offending the public policy of the forum, public policy is likely to be rarely invoked.

Recital 14 of the Rome II Regulation states that the connecting factors contained in the regulation 'are the most appropriate to achieve (the) objectives of legal certainty and justice in individual cases'.[101] It is these connecting factors that are crucial in determining the basis upon which Articles 4 and 6 operate and, indeed, interact with each other.

Article 4 – the general applicable law rule

The general choice of law rule in the regulation is provided in Article 4. Article 4 is designed to protect the individual party in a dispute where

[98] Ibid., 797–8. Cf. Dickinson, *The Rome II Regulation*, 397–8 who suggests that that the concept of damage under Art. 6(1) and 6(3) is distinct from Art. 5(3) of Regulation 44/2001 (the Brussels I Regulation) and, depending on the interpretation of recital 21, could lead to an inconsistent application of jurisdiction and applicable law rules in determining whether damage has occurred in an unfair competition case.

[99] See further Danov, 'Awarding Exemplary Damages'. [100] *Ibid.*, 432ff.

[101] Words modified and added for syntax.

a non-contractual obligation has been breached. It contains a general choice of law principle, an exception to that general principle and an escape clause, as follows. Article 4(1) states that the applicable law is the law of the country where the damage occurred. As with jurisdiction rules, the emphasis is to establish the *lex causae* of a territorial unit. Furthermore, the *lex causae* is not the law of the place where the indirect consequences of damage are felt. It is necessary therefore to determine the *lex loci delicti commissi* – specifically the *lex damni* – the place where the damage occurs, which can often be different from the place in which the event giving rise to the damage occurred. The exception is to be found in Article 4(2) which applies to 'internal' disputes, that is where both parties have the same habitual residence[102] when the dispute arises, that law will apply. The 'escape clause' is provided by Article 4(3) which requires a manifestly more closely connected country to be established for its laws to apply instead. Like Article 4(5) of the Rome Convention 1980, Article 4(3) is intended to take into account the law that reflects the 'centre of gravity' of the dispute. The 'high threshold'[103] required for the application of Article 4(3) was recently considered, and specifically rejected, by the English High Court in *Jacobs* v. *MIB*.[104]

Article 6 – the law applicable to unfair competition and acts restricting competition

Dickinson reminds us of the Commission's position on Article 6(1) and (2) when he states that the 'act of unfair competition, the defendant's conduct must have some impact upon relations between the participants in a particular market, whether horizontally (between competitors) or vertically (as against consumers collectively)'.[105] When considering Article 6, it is useful to take as a starting point recital 13 which states that, '[u]niform rules applied irrespective of the law they designate may avert the risk of distortions of competition between Community litigants'[106] and recital 19 which provides that '[s]pecific rules should be laid down for special torts/delicts where the general rule does not allow a reasonable balance to be struck between the interests at stake'.[107]

[102] Or, in the absence of a definition of where a business is located, its central administration.
[103] Fawcett and Carruthers, *Cheshire, North and Fawcett*, 799.
[104] *Jacobs* v. *Motor Insurers Bureau* [2010] EWHC 231 (QB); on the payment of compensation. See Court of Appeal [2010] EWCA Civ 1208 at para. 38.
[105] Dickinson, *The Rome II Regulation*, 403.
[106] Recital 13, Rome II Regulation.
[107] Recital 19, Rome II Regulation.

The Commission commented on the draft regulation to the effect that Article 6 was designed to correspond to the victim's expectations because:

> the rule generally designates the law governing their economic environment. But it also secures equal treatment for all operators on the same market. The purpose of competition law is to protect a market; it pursues a macro-economic objective.[108]

As Dickinson has observed *vis-à-vis* recital 21, 'the special rule in Article 6 is not an exception to the general rule in Article 4(1) but rather a clarification of it'.[109] The dual purpose of the 'effects test'[110] approach used to determine the applicable law rules for unfair competition is a 'market-orientated'[111] choice of law rule designed to provide protection for 'competitors, consumers and the general public'[112] and facilitate the proper economic functioning of the EU market. Dickinson maintains, however, that the net effect is that the applicable law rules in Article 6 are 'sufficiently independent of the general rule for torts to be characterized as special rules in their own right'.[113] Indeed, this would reflect the aim of the regulation to provide a 'flexible framework of conflict-of-laws rules [and] to enable the court seized to treat individual cases in an appropriate manner'.[114] With the aims of the regulation and recital 14 in mind, Article 6 provides the following choice of law rules:[115]

1. (T)he law applicable to a non-contractual obligation arising out of an act of *unfair competition* shall be the *law of the country where competitive relations or the collective interests of consumers are, or are likely to be, affected.*
2. Where an act of unfair competition affects exclusively the interests of a specific competitor, Article 4 shall apply.
3. (a) The law applicable to a non-contractual obligation arising out of a *restriction of competition* shall be the *law of the country where the market is, or is likely to be, affected.* Where the market is, or is likely to be, affected *in more than one country,* the person seeking compensation

108 EU Commission, cited by Stone, *EU Private International Law* 365 and Dickinson, *The Rome II Regulation* 412.

109 Recital 21, Rome II Regulation; Dickinson, *The Rome II Regulation*, 397.

110 Recital 22, Rome II Regulation refers to the 'law of the country where the market is, or is likely to be, affected in more than one country'. An approach endorsed by Withers, 'Jurisdiction'.

111 Dickinson, *The Rome II Regulation*, 405.

112 Recital 21, Rome II Regulation.

113 Dickinson, *The Rome II Regulation*, 397.

114 Recital 14, Rome II Regulation.

115 Words in italic for emphasis. Art. 6(2) is not considered here.

for damage who sues in the court of the domicile of the defendant, may instead choose to base his or her claim on the *law of the court seised*, provided that the market in that Member State is amongst those directly and substantially affected by the restriction in competition out of which the non-contractual obligation on which the claim is based arises; where the claimant sues, in accordance with the applicable rules on jurisdiction, more than one defendant in that court, he or she can only choose to base his or her claim on the law of that court if the restriction in competition on which the claim against each of these defendants relies directly and substantially affects also the market in the Member State of that court.

4. *The law applicable under this Article may not be derogated from by an agreement pursuant to Article 14.*[116]

Some of the key concepts of Article 6, namely 'unfair competition', the 'affected market', the effect on the market that justifies the application of Article 6(1) and the exception in Article 6(3), will now be considered. The lack of a clear definition of 'unfair competition' was acknowledged by the Wallis Report[117] during the drafting process of the regulation.[118] Essentially, as the Commission and Dickinson have both observed, the conduct must affect more than one participant in the marketplace (vis. 'participants') or the 'derogation'[119] in Article 6(2) will operate with the effect that the applicable law will instead be determined by Article 4.[120] While this may appear to provide a neat solution, the Commission acknowledged the lack of consistency in the connecting factors used in Articles 4 and 6.[121] Nevertheless, Dickinson has helpfully suggested that for the purposes of Article 6, unfair competition under English law could encompass the torts of 'passing off, malicious falsehood . . . in comparative advertising, and actions by a non-public body . . . under Part 8 of the Enterprise Act 2002'.[122] Of these, the first two could have a direct and detrimental impact upon consumers in the market.

Second, the objective of Article 6(1) is to protect claimants in the affected market. However a key criticism of the regulation is that it does not provide a definition of the 'affected market' as a connecting factor. It is submitted that it given the scope of application of Article 6 – horizontal

[116] Art. 6, Rome II Regulation. Words in italic for emphasis.
[117] Stone, *EU Private International Law*, 366.
[118] Dickinson, *The Rome II Regulation*, 403. Word italicised for emphasis.
[119] *Ibid.*, p.405. Words omitted for syntax. [120] *Ibid.*, 397.
[121] *Ibid.* [122] *Ibid.*, 404.

or vertical anti-competitive behaviour – a definition from the CJEU is essential for the effective operation of the Article. If it was defined, it must first be done for the purposes of private international law. Furthermore, it may have to be distinguished depending on the direction of the behaviour in dispute. In response, Dickinson has explored the narrower and wider meanings that could be attributed to the 'affected market', namely a market restricted to a single country or area (used more generally in competition law) or a wider concept of affected market where claims can be brought either by competitors or consumers.[123] Dickinson considers the potential application of a 'qualified affected market'[124] approach to encompass not just competitors but also consumers *and* their collective representatives who have been affected by anti-competitive behaviour within a particular area (as opposed to the entire marketplace).[125] By that it is assumed that the damage must be attributable to consumers or their representatives in a particular territorial unit or jurisdiction, for it is the law of that place which will apply in a claim brought in the court of a Member State under Article 6. Support for this approach was illustrated by analogous rules in the Brussels I Regulation considered earlier. Third, the required 'effect' on the market must be sufficiently, or causally, material to justify the application of Article 6. Dickinson has suggested, in line with earlier authority from the *Wood Pulp* case,[126] that the anti-competitive arrangement must have been 'implemented' within the Community, as opposed to quantifying a 'direct and sufficient effect' for the same purpose. Support for this view can also be drawn from Withers's analogy referred to earlier *vis-à-vis* distinguishing between the *lex causae* and the *lex damni* for the purposes of allocating jurisdiction for a cross-border tort. However the potential fragmentation of proceedings is increased as a result. Therefore, it must be shown that for Article 6 to apply anti-competitive behaviour and damage must have occurred in a particular territorial unit (jurisdiction) for the purposes of ascertaining the applicable law.

The applicable law rules for disputes as a result of a restriction of competition are contained in Article 6(3) and are deemed 'mutually exclusive' from the applicable law rules for unfair competition under Article 6(1).[127] A restriction of competition is defined in recital (23) as applying to:

[123] *Ibid.*, 413–4. [124] *Ibid.*, 414–15. [125] *Ibid.*, 414. [126] [1988] ECR 5193.

[127] Dickinson, *The Rome II Regulation*, 418. On Art. 6(3), see generally Fitchen, 'Choice of Law'.

> prohibitions on agreements between undertakings, decisions by associations of undertakings and concerted practices which have as their object or effect the prevention, restriction or distortion of competition *within a Member State or within the internal market*, as well as prohibitions on the abuse of a dominant position *within a Member State or within the internet market*, where such agreements, decisions, concerted practices or abuses are prohibited by Articles 81 and 82 of the Treaty or by the law of a Member State.[128]

The implications of more than one applicable law applying as a result of Article 6(3) are apparent, particularly where more than one national market is or is likely to be affected by the restrictive behaviour. A key challenge of the regulation will be to determine the 'affected market(s)' for the purposes of Article 6(3). As we have seen, the most effective starting point for the purposes of private international law is to determine the geographical location of the parties' activities in order to localise the dispute with a particular jurisdiction. Dickinson argues that while it may be necessary to consider a sub-category of connecting factors including, but not restricted to, such matters as national measures imposing barriers to trade, language and cultural differences, the views of market participants and differences in pricing,[129] such a 'legal-economic analysis of this kind . . . is one of the least satisfactory aspects of the Rome II Regulation',[130] and one that would probably have a prohibitive effect on litigation rather than facilitating predictability and certainty of result. In any event, an analogy with the European Commission's Statement on Article 15 and 73 of the Brussels I Regulation reminds us that language and currency were not deemed relevant considerations for the purposes of establishing whether a business directed its commercial activities towards a consumer's jurisdiction via a web site. However, perhaps Article 6(3) is concerned with distinguishing between disputes internal to each Member State,[131] disputes where agreement or collusion regarding anti-competitive behaviour originated outside the EU but the behaviour itself occurred in a Member State and disputes between parties situated in different Member States. In any event, the ethos of choice of law rules is to ascertain the system of law which will govern the dispute. Aside from determining the 'affected

[128] Recital 23, Rome II Regulation. Words in italic for emphasis.
[129] Dickinson, *The Rome II Regulation*, 422–3. [130] *Ibid.*
[131] Disputes between different parts of a Member State may still require reference to rules of private international law as they operate between those parts, e.g. a dispute between parties situated in England and Scotland.

market' for the purposes of Article 6(3), it will also be necessary to determine the point in time when the restriction of competition occurred in the marketplace.

As an alternative to the law(s) of the affected market(s), the claimant can select the law of the forum (*lex fori*) under Article 6(3) provided that more than one country is 'directly and substantially affected' by the implementation of the restrictive practice and the defendant is domiciled in the Member State of the *lex fori*. While at first hand this escape clause might seem advantageous to a claimant, the absence of a clear definition of what constitutes a 'direct and substantial' effect in the market of the *lex fori* could place an additional hurdle for the claimant to satisfy. A collective representative action on behalf of consumers could satisfy such a requirement. In any event the necessity for such a requirement is questioned given that if the claimant was to sue in the courts of the defendant's domicile under Article 2 of the Brussels I Regulation, the *lex fori* would apply. The defendant is already protected on the basis of *actor sequitur forum rei*, so the additional requirement appears unduly burdensome on a claimant.

The proposal for an EU consumer collective redress mechanism

In November 2008, the European Commission released a Green Paper on consumer collective redress.[132] The Green Paper outlines how the Commission seeks to consider 'options to close any gaps to effective redress' in both national and cross-border disputes with sellers especially when consumers are 'affected by the same legal infringement'.[133] According to Micklitz, Reich and Rott, the three bases for 'improv(ing) collective consumer protection [are] ... either ... internal market competence ... on Article 153(3)(b) in supporting Member States' measures ...[or]... the provisions of the Amsterdam Treaty on judicial cooperation in civil matters'.[134] As stated earlier, in accordance with *Courage* and *Manfredi*, the right to take action for breach of competition laws is permissible under Community law. Nevertheless, perhaps crucially, the 'procedural features, as well as the determination of the competent court, are subject to national law'.[135] Accordingly, the precursor to effective private enforcement for breach of competition law rules is the ability of consumers to be

[132] EU Commission, Green Paper on consumer collective redress, (COM 2008 794 final).
[133] *Ibid.*, 3, para. 4. [134] Micklitz *et al. Understanding EU Consumer Law*, 351.
[135] *Ibid.*, 337.

able to collectively take action via such a collective redress procedure facilitated by a Member State. When referring to collective redress, we are concerned here with an additional basis of private judicial redress by individuals and their representatives, not alternative dispute resolution (ADR).[136]

The inherent 'success rate' of Article 6 of Rome II, as Fitchen remarks, will depend upon the 'interaction, in the text, of competing policies which have influenced the Commission's desire [for] reform of private enforcement'.[137] As far as the EU consumer protection policy is concerned, the requirement for Member States to provide 'effective proceedings' has existed for over three decades.[138] As far as collective redress is concerned, Hodges has remarked that three key issues arise: (shared) competence, the capacity of representatives to take action and mutual recognition[139] leading towards effective enforcement. In accordance with Article 4 TFEU, the EU only has competence to take measures for collective redress – as Hodges correctly asserts – if the 'objectives [have not or] cannot be sufficiently achieved by the Member States'[140] (i.e. subsidiarity) and 'measures at EU level must not go beyond what is necessary to achieve the objects at which they are directed [proportionality].'[141] Furthermore, in the context of cross-border disputes, the Member States' 'procedural autonomy'[142] must also be respected, since Article 81 TFEU (ex Article 65 EC) 'requires evidence of cross-border matters and might . . . justify only cross-border measures'.[143]

In that regard, the current position of collective redress across the Member States is instructive. The legal basis as far as consumers are concerned is Article 115 TFEU (ex Article 95 EC) which requires consumers to be provided with a high level of protection. In accordance with Article 4 TFEU, the continued sharing of competence in the field of consumer protection will heavily affect any EU-wide collective redress mechanism.[144] A recent paper by Fairgreave and Howells highlights the

[136] Indeed, Micklitz, Reich and Rott confirm in their opinion that the Community does not have competence in the area of ADR; *ibid.* at 342. As traditional and Communitarised private international law provides rules for the determination of jurisdiction, choice of law and enforcement of foreign judgments, the use of ADR (however defined) as a means of facilitating collective consumer redress may be harder to justify.

[137] Fitchen, 'Choice of Law', 343.

[138] Micklitz *et al.*, *Understanding EU Consumer Law*, 342.

[139] C. Hodges, *The Reform of Class and Representative Actions in European Legal Systems* (Hart, 2008), 96.

[140] *Ibid.*, 93, 103; words in brackets added. [141] *Ibid.* [142] *Ibid.*

[143] *Ibid.*, 94. [144] See generally Fairgreave and Howells, 'Collective Redress Procedures'.

inherent challenges posed by shared competence. These authors suggest that 'national reform'[145] is the most likely outcome for claims already viable under national law. Alternatively, at best the mechanism could facilitate the resolution of otherwise 'non-viable consumer claims'[146] such as claims for damages for anti-competitive behaviour. Provided the Community has competence to instigate and enforce consumer collective redress in respect of the latter claims, the proposal would be a first, in that it would extend the principle of subsidiarity by providing the first cross-border basis for implementing, or enforcing,[147] collective redress via the Rome II Regulation. As far as consumer law is concerned, directives have traditionally facilitated consumer collective redress mechanisms by permitting Member States to implement such measures over and above the minimum required by EU law. The legal basis that a future collective redress mechanism will take (whether a regulation or directive) and its remit (that is, depending on the viability of the claim) are both crucial to achieving the objective of mutual recognition. If implemented as a regulation, and in combination with the 'maximisation' of consumer protection policy, such a collective redress mechanism would complement existing national collective redress procedures where they exist. A directive would not meet the objectives of maximising consumer protection across the Community.

The Green Paper considered four options for the development of collective redress at Community level: no action; cooperation between the Member States; a mix of policy instruments with a heavy reliance on ADR; and judicial collective redress. The first has been dismissed as it would not meet Treaty obligations in ensuring that consumers were provided with maximum protection. The second option is also not being pursued as the cooperation mechanism required between the Member States could be at odds with existing national measures and, in any event, top-down regulation would still be required. The third option has also been excluded, primarily because of the infancy of ADR and wider issues of competence.[148] Accordingly, the current status of the proposal for an EU collective redress mechanism has taken the fourth option, specifically a test case procedure in one Member State (i.e. by a consumer representative) followed up by individual action in other Member States. In practice, as currently proposed, it could be possible

[145] *Ibid.*, 379. [146] *Ibid.*
[147] Hodges, *Reform of Class Actions*, 103.
[148] See Micklitz *et al.*, *Understanding EU Consumer Law.*

for consumer representatives to sue via a test case procedure the offending business where the defendant is located (Article 2, Brussels I) in order that a claim for all of the damage (Article 6(1), Rome II) could be sought. Thereafter, consumers could sue in any of the places where damage occurred by virtue of Article 5(3) of Brussels I, thereby enabling the law of that place to apply in accordance with Article 6(1) of Rome II.

Conclusion

In 2002 Withers remarked that:

> [i]t remains uncertain whether the requisite elements (both procedural and substantive) of a claim for breach of Community competition rules are destined to be determined by Community law, rather than national law.[149]

This chapter has sought to briefly explore some of the issues raised by the specific applicable law rules for unfair competition and acts restricting free competition in the new Rome II Regulation on non-contractual obligations. Although the rules are drafted in such terms as to ensure that commercial entities and final end-user/private consumers (or their representatives) can claim damages for anti-competitive behaviour or an act restricting competition, a number of key concepts under Article 6 have not been sufficiently defined. Until such time that judicial guidance is provided by the CJEU, Article 6 will present challenges for private litigants who seek to utilise the EU's efforts to communitarise conflict of laws rules for anti-competitive behaviour and acts restricting competition. Furthermore, a key strength of Article 6 of Rome II is the ability of consumer representatives to claim damages on behalf of consumers. As far as Article 6 of the Rome II Regulation is concerned, the proposed EU consumer collective redress mechanism must therefore seek to address what Hodges identifies as the 'real issue' *vis-à-vis* effective collective redress namely 'first ... to deliver rectification of market imbalances: secondly, to deliver compensation when due; thirdly, [control] behaviour and; and fourthly, to enhance the economy'.[150]

[149] Withers, 'Jurisdiction', 253.
[150] Hodges, *Reform of Class Actions*, 248. Word added for syntax.

14

Horse sales: the problem of consumer contracts from a historical perspective

WARREN SWAIN

One anonymous reviewer writing in 1831 observed that:

> 'As full of diseases as a horse', says Shakespeare, and he might have made a comparison in another respect with equal truth, by saying 'as fruitful of law-suits as a horse'; for of all chattels, the purchase of one of this sort, is the most likely to be the purchase of a suit.[1]

Such remarks could have been made with equal force at any point in the last thousand years. Many horse sales fell within the modern definition of 'consumer contracts'[2] and, as a result, these transactions provide a valuable insight over a long period into some of the problems raised by the sale of defective goods to consumers.

Although most were far too poor to afford a horse, horse ownership had spread to men of quite modest means by the seventeenth century.[3] Until comparatively recently the horse played a vital role in English society.[4]

TC Beirne School of Law, the University of Queensland.

[1] Anon., 'Horse Causes' (1831) 5 *American Jurist and Law Magazine* 288.

[2] The term is of course anachronistic when applied before the twentieth century. English lawyers thought neither in terms of contract, as opposed to forms of action, nor consumers. Nevertheless, the modern definitions of a 'consumer' in its various guises fit the facts of most of the authorities very well: Unfair Contract Terms Act 1977, s. 25 (1); Unfair Terms in Consumer Contracts Regulations 1999 (SI 1999 no. 2083) R 3; Proposal for a Directive of the European Parliament and of the Council on Consumer Rights (2008/0196 (COD)) Ch 1, Art. 2.

[3] P. Edwards, *The Horse Trade of Tudor and Stuart England* (Cambridge University Press, 1988) 7–9, table 1 (a) shows that in Horbling, Lincolnshire, while 40 per cent of holdings were without a horse in 1636 this fell to 14.3 per cent between 1724 and 1742.

[4] T. J. Thirsk, *Horses in Early Modern England: for Service, for Pleasure, for Power* (University of Reading, 1978); P. Edwards, *Horse and Man in Early Modern England* (London: Hambledon Continuum, 2007).

As well as transporting goods and people[5] horses had important agricultural[6] and military[7] uses. By the eighteenth century horse-racing had become a plebeian as well as patrician pastime.[8]

Foreign visitors in the eighteenth century were struck by the relationship between the English and their horses. La Rochefoucauld wrote in his memoirs that the English possessed a 'natural affection for the horse'.[9] The American Quaker, John Woolman, was less impressed with what he had heard about the ill treatment of stage-coach horses.[10] But it was an Englishman Reverend Granger, who was most damning when in a sermon he described England as a 'Hell for Horses'.[11] There was an element of truth in both descriptions.[12] If not always well treated, horses were frequently admired. Horses were variously described as the 'noblest, strongest, swiftest, and most necessary of all the beasts'[13] and 'of all the unreasonable creatures upon the Earth are of the greatest understanding'.[14] Horses were portrayed as man's closest relation in the animal kingdom.[15] It was this insight which made for such biting satire in hands of Jonathan Swift.[16] Horses were fêted by such otherwise disparate

[5] Transportation include horseback, as pack horses, pulling carts and barges and coaches. Road transportation of goods and passengers greatly increased in the eighteenth century: S. Ville, 'Transport', in R. Floud and P. Johnson (eds.), *The Cambridge Economic History of Modern Britain* (Cambridge University Press, 2004), 294, at 296–9. For the preceding century, see J. A. Chartres, 'Road Carrying in England in the Seventeenth Century' (1977) 30 *Economic History Review* 73.

[6] Oxen were also used as draft animals: Edwards, *Horse and Man*, 183–6; G. E. Mingay, 'Farming Techniques', in G. E. Mingay (ed.), *The Agrarian History of England and Wales.* vol. VI, *1750–1850* (Cambridge University Press, 1989) 289.

[7] Edwards, *Horse and Man*, ch. 7. Henry Homer expressed concern in the 1760s that a decline in the number of horses would have a serious impact on England's military capabilities; H. Homer, *An enquiry into the means of preserving and improving the publick roads of this kingdom* (Oxford: 1767), 8.

[8] Edwards, *Horse and Man*, ch. 5; R. Malcolmson, *Popular Recreations in English Society 1700–1850* (Cambridge University Press, 1973), 50–1; H. Cunningham, *Leisure in the Industrial Revolution* (London: Croom Helm, 1980), 19–20.

[9] S. C. Roberts (trans.), F. de la Rochefoucauld, *A Frenchman in England* (Cambridge University Press, 1933), 74.

[10] J. Woolman, *The Works of John Woolman* (Philadelphia: 1774), vol. I, 230.

[11] J. Granger, *An apology for the brute creation, or abuse of animals censured* (London: 1772), 11.

[12] K. Thomas, *Man and the Natural World* (London: Penguin, 1984), 100–1.

[13] J. Worlidge, *Systema Agriculturae* (London: 1675), 160–1.

[14] *The Gentleman's Compleat Jockey* (London: 1715), 5.

[15] G. Buffon, *The Natural History of the Horse* (London: 1762). For further earlier examples see Edwards, *Horse and Man*, 22–3.

[16] P. Turner (ed.), J. Swift, *Gulliver's Travels* (Oxford University Press, 1998). The work was originally published in 1726. A similar sentiment is found in 'On Poetry: A Rapsody', which includes the line 'A founder'd horse will oft debate, Before he tries a five-barr'd Gate'; see

groups as medieval Welsh poets[17] and leading society figures who employed George Stubbs to immortalise their animals on canvas.[18] No doubt horse owners of all types, in every century, could feel sympathy with those unfortunate enough to purchase an animal which turned out to be defective. Horses were certainly susceptible to a wide range of diseases[19] and, as a potentially costly item,[20] often worth the trouble and expense of litigation.[21]

A brief history of horse sales from ancient Rome to seventeenth-century England

Writing in the century before the birth of Christ, Marcus Terentius Varro, in *De Re Rustica*,[22] described a formula used in horse sales which he attributed to the jurist Manilius.[23] Varro added that the terms appropriate for the sale of horses were similar to those of cattle and donkeys.[24] Cicero commented that a young man faced with the learning the poetry of Pacuvius or Manilius's conditions of sale would prefer the former.[25]

H. Davis (ed.), *Swift Poetical Works* (Oxford University Press, 1967), 569. According to Edward Stone, 'Swift's mock-serious device of presenting animals as equal or superior to human beings' reflected the popular theriophilistic literature of the day; see, E. Stone, 'Swift and the Horses: Misanthropy or Comedy?' in M. P. Foster (ed.), *A Casebook on Gulliver Among the Houyhnhnms* (New York: Thomas Cromwell, 1961), 184.

[17] B. Huws, 'Praise Lasts Longer than a Horse: Poems of Request and Thanks for Horses', in S. Davies and N. Jones (eds.), *The Horse in Celtic Culture: Medieval Welsh Perspectives* (Cardiff: University of Wales Press, 1997), 141.

[18] For examples see J. Egerton, *George Stubbs, Painter. Catalogue Raisonné* (Yale University Press, 2007), 36, 148–9, 214–15, 414. Stubbs also painted more humble horses and their owners; *ibid.*, 478.

[19] Shakespeare provides a particularly graphic description of ailments suffered by Petruchio's horse; see G. R. Hibbard, W. Shakespeare, *The Taming of the Shrew* (London: Penguin, 1968), Act 3, scene ii.

[20] For some figures on the cost of horses see, Edwards, *Horse Trade*, 14, appendix 2; Thirsk, *Horses in Early Modern England*, 24: 'All accounts of the horse trade of the later seventeenth century describe a highly differentiated demand for highly differentiated animals at a wide range of prices'. Thirsk gives an example of a horse selling for £200, which was an enormous sum in the 1660s.

[21] R. Boote, *An Historical Treatise of an Action or Suit at Law* (London: 1766), iii.

[22] W. D. Hooper and H. B. Ash (trans.), *Marcus Porcius Cato on Agriculture. Marcus Terentius Varro on Agriculture* (London: Heinemann, 1934).

[23] *Ibid.*, 2.7.6–7. A formula denotes used for convenience as opposed to a form which is required for validity; see B. Nicholas, 'Verbal Forms in Roman Law' (1991–1992) 66 *Tulane Law Review* 1605.

[24] Varro, *De Re Rustica*, 2.7.6–7. He goes into more detail about the sale of goats and sheep; *ibid.*, 2.3.5–6.

[25] E. W. Sutton (trans.), *Cicero De Oratore* (London: Heinemann, 1942), vol. I, 246–7.

Certainly Cicero's young man need not have possessed perfect recall. The precise wording was a matter for the parties.[26] This may have disadvantaged buyers in cases where the seller was a professional horse-dealer,[27] and market conditions were not in his favour.[28] Aside from the conditions of sale expressly agreed, the seller might still be liable on an *actio empti* for failing to disclose a known defect[29] or as a result of misdescribing the thing sold.[30] Latent defects did not generate liability. Special provisions for the sale of slaves in the market were introduced by an edict of the *aediles curules*[31] rendering the seller liable for latent defects for the first time. The edict was later extended to cattle.[32] Horses were not included.[33] But by around 500 AD, the law was transformed in the buyer's favour.[34] The seller was made liable for latent defects irrespective of the subject matter of the sale.[35]

The civilian legal systems of continental Europe continued in the Roman law tradition.[36] After the Norman Conquest at least,[37] English

[26] A. Watson, *The Law of Obligations in the Later Roman Republic* (Oxford University Press, 1965), 90.

[27] Horse dealing was a well established trade in the Roman World: A. Hyland, *Equus: The Horse in the Roman World* (Yale University Press, 1990), 71. Klaus-Dietrich Fischer (ed.), *Pelagonii Ars Veterinaria* (Leipzig: Teuber, 1981), I.6, I.5, II.24, II.27.

[28] J. A. C. Thomas, *Textbook of Roman Law* (Amsterdam: North-Holland Publishing, 1976), 287.

[29] A. Watson (ed.), *The Digest of Justinian* (University of Pennsylvania Press, 1998), D 19.1.4 pr.

[30] Waston, *Digest*, D 18.1.45.

[31] The *aediles curules* were magistrates charged with supervisions of activities in the market place; G. Mousourakis, *The Historical and Institutional Context of Roman Law* (Aldershot: Ashgate, 2003), 92–4.

[32] The earlier development of Greek law was very similar; see, F. Pringsheim, *The Greek Law of Sale* (Weimar: Hermann Böhlaus Nachfolger, 1950), 478–9.

[33] For brief descriptions of the operation of the Roman law of sale see: F. De Zulueta, *The Roman Law of Sale*, 2nd edn (Oxford University Press, 1949), 46–51; A. Rogerson, 'Implied Warranty Against Latent Defects in Roman and English Law', in D. Daube (ed.), *Studies in the Roman Law of Sale* (Oxford University Press, 1959), 112.

[34] Justinian's law was the law of the Eastern Empire. In the West the tendency was to restrict the seller's liability; see, P. Stein, 'Medieval Discussions of the Buyer's Actions for Physical Defects' in Daube, *Studies*, 102–3.

[35] Watson, *Digest*, D 21.1.pr.

[36] R. Zimmermann, *The Law of Obligations* (Oxford University Press, 1996), 322–5.

[37] The Saxon law codes may have recognised latent defects to some extent; G. Stone, 'Transaction of Sale in Saxon Times' (1913) 29 *Law Quarterly Review* 323, at 335 citing the law code of Ine rule 56 in F. Liebermann, *Die Gesetze Der Angelsachsen* (Halle: Max Niemeyer, 1903), vol. I, 114 which describes a sale of livestock which turns out to be defective. The buyer must return it within thirty nights and the seller must be prepared to swear that it was not defective at the time of the sale.

and Scots law was less friendly towards buyers in the absence of an undertaking that the horse was sound.[38] The law in Wales was totally different. The doctrine of *teithi* ensured that the horse was required to reach a minimum standard with certain additional conditions depending on the type of horse and irrespective of the terms of the sale.[39]

According to the author of the twelfth-century common law treatise, *Glanvill*, when a thing was sold as sound and turned out to be unsound it could be returned.[40] *Bracton* repeated the rule.[41] Both writers were concerned with the Royal Courts, though most of the surviving evidence comes from the local courts. In 1300 a friar bought a bay horse for 60 shillings and which the defendant 'asserted to be healthy and sound in its limbs'. On taking possession of the horse the friar alleged that the animal was maimed in the shoulders. The defendant denied warranting the horse but offered no defence and the London Mayor's Court found for the plaintiff.[42] The Exeter Borough Court twenty years earlier emphasised that the burden was on the buyer to prove that the animal was warranted sound. The animal was then examined to determine whether or not it was actually sound.[43]

A very early case of defective goods in the Royal Courts also involved a horse. The plaintiff, John de Ferrers, a nobleman, on his way to fight with the king against the Scots[44] purchased a horse from John, the vicar of Dodford in Northamptonshire. De Ferrers claimed that the horse was sold 'healthy in all its limbs and unmaimed' whereas in fact it was 'maimed and imperfect'.[45] As a result he was late arriving. The basis of the claim was 'trespass and deceit' and the fact that de Ferrers's

[38] For the law in Scotland in the Middle Ages see W. Gordon, 'Sale' in K. Reid and R. Zimmermann, *A History of Private Law in Scotland*. II: *Obligations* (Oxford University Press, 2000), 305, 306.

[39] D. Jenkins, 'The Horse in the Welsh Law Texts' in Davies and Jones, *The Horse in Celtic Culture*, 64, 69–71.

[40] G. D. G. Hall (ed.), *The Treatise on the Laws and Customs of the Realm of England Commonly Called Glanvill* (Oxford University Press, 1965), book X, 14.

[41] S. Thorne (ed.), *Bracton On the Laws and Customs of England* (Harvard University Press, 1968), f. 62, vol. II, 182.

[42] A. H. Thomas (ed.), *Calendar of Early Mayor's Court Rolls, 1298–1307* (Cambridge University Press, 1924), 68.

[43] M. Bateson (ed.), *Borough Customs*, vol. II (London: Selden Society, 1906), 182.

[44] M. Prestwich, *Plantagenet England 1225–1360* (Oxford University Press, 2005), 232–9.

[45] It was alleged that the horse was injured in its shoulder – a serious impediment on account of the weight of armour and weapons that the animal was expected to carry by this period; see R. H. C. Davis, *The Medieval Warhorse* (London: Thames and Hudson, 1989), 22–3.

enforced absence was a 'deceit of the king himself'. John the vicar simply denied having sold the horse. No outcome is recorded.

The precise form of words in the local courts varied. Sometimes the agreement (covenant) was emphasised and at other times the wrong done to the plaintiff by supplying defective goods (trespass).[46] In the Royal Courts a writ of trespass was used. The writ always alleged, 'with force of arms against the King's peace'. John de Ferrers was fortunate in this regard in having a plausible royal interest. Others may have obtained the same result by creative use of legal fictions.[47] By the end of the fourteenth century the emergence of the action of trespass on the case meant that neither a force of arms nor breach of the king's peace needed to be satisfied,[48] thereby making it easier to frame a claim.

Sir John de Aylesbury v. *John Watts*[49] may have been typical of the new sort of action.[50] The declaration alleged that Watts a horse-dealer:

> knowing that the horse was afflicted with blindness, by warranting him to be sound in eye and limb falsely and fraudulently sold him to aforesaid John de Aylesbury for a great sum of money, to the damage of the same John de Aylesbury of twenty pounds.

The writ of trespass on the case for deceit like trespass was a wrong-based action, ensuring that breach of warranty was fixed in tort rather than contract. There it would remain until the eighteenth century. The rule was *caveat emptor*.[51] The risk fell on the purchaser. As Fitzherbert explained, 'if he sells ... the horse without such a warranty, the other must buy it from him at his own risk, and his eyes ... should be judges in that case'.[52]

[46] S. F. C. Milsom, 'Sale of Goods in the Fifteenth Century' (1961) 77 *Law Quarterly Review* 257, 278.

[47] S. F. C. Milsom, 'Trespass from Henry III to Edward III' (1958) 74 *Law Quarterly Review* 195, 407, 561; J.H. Baker, *The Law's Two Bodies* (Oxford University Press, 2001), 41–2. None of Milsom's examples concerns horse sales.

[48] D. J. Ibbetson, *A Historical Introduction to the Law of Obligations* (Oxford University Press, 1999), 51–6.

[49] M. Arnold (ed.), *Select Cases of Trespass From the King's Courts 1307–1399*, vol. II (London: Selden Society, 1987), 447–8.

[50] For another example, *Thomas Saville* v. *John Ventrer* (1386) *ibid.* 448.

[51] The maxim was in use in Elizabethan times. Baker suggests that it may have been popularised by Coke; see J. H. Baker, 'Bezoar-Stones, Gall-Stones, and Gem-Stones: a Chapter in the History of the Tort of Deceit', in A. Burrows and Lord Rodger (eds.), *Mapping the Law Essays in Memory of Peter Birks* (Oxford University Press, 2006), 545, 550 n. 31.

[52] J. H. Baker, *Baker and Milsom Sources of English Legal History* (Oxford University Press, 2010), 386.

Although there were some variations in the standard formula the basic components changed little over the centuries from that used by John de Aylesbury. The central allegation was the existence of a warranty and a common defence was to deny that one had been given.[53] The count also alleged that the seller had knowledge of the defect. In practice the seller's state of mind was immaterial,[54] though it was sometimes suggested that a seller might be liable even in the absence of a warranty if he knew that the thing sold was defective.[55] Where the buyer could, despite the warranty, have identified the defect then the seller may have escaped liability.[56] Hankford J explained the consequences of this rule in the context of a horse sale:

> If a man sells me a blind horse and warrants it sound in all its parts, I shall not have an action of deceit against him afterwards, because I could have looked at it. But if it is sick inside its body, I shall have such action because I could not have known that illness.[57]

How jurors actually went about determining the factual question of the existence and content of a warranty can only be a matter of speculation,[58] but it seems unlikely that the actual term 'warranty' had to be used.[59] Sixteenth-century lawyers sometimes failed to draw a clear distinction between a warranty and a promise.[60] The issue would be resurrected in the eighteenth century when changes in pleading threw the question of whether the proper action was grounded in contract or tort into sharp focus.

Horse sales in eighteenth-century England

The century after 1750 was something of a golden age of horse-sale litigation, as a combination of judicial and jury activism, and a growth in legal and non-legal literature, thrust these transactions, which featured

[53] M. Arnold (ed.), *Select Cases of Trespass From the King's Courts 1307–1399* vol. I (London: Selden Society, 1984) lxxxiv; J. H. Baker, *The Oxford History of the Laws of England.* Vol. VI *1483–1558* (Oxford University Press, 2003), 772.

[54] Milsom, 'Sale of Goods', 280.

[55] Ibbetson, *Obligations*, 85; Baker, *Oxford History*, 771–2.

[56] Ibbetson, *Obligations*, 84; Baker, *Oxford History*, 772.

[57] *Drew Barantine's Case* (1411) YB M. 13 Hen IV f. 1 pl. 4 (Baker, *Sources*, 561). Also see *Anon* (1471) YB T. 11 Edw IV f. 6 pl. 10 (Baker, *Sources*, 563).

[58] For some speculation see Ibbetson, *Obligations*, 85.

[59] Baker, 'Bezoar-Stones', 549.

[60] Baker, *Oxford History*, 772–3.

in at least one popular novel of the time,[61] to prominence. The form of the claim also evolved. In *Stuart* v. *Wilkins*,[62] Ashhurst J, held that:

> Whatever may have been the old form, I believe it has been long settled that this form of action is right, and having been long established, I am of opinion that it ought to be supported.[63]

Buller J agreed that assumpsit for breach of warranty had existed 'ever since I have known anything of practice'.[64] There is an example in Dudley Ryder's notebooks from the 1750s[65] and an even earlier one in a leading abridgement in which this method of pleading was described as 'settled'.[66] Assumpsit as an action in contract[67] allowed a claim for breach of warranty and breach of contract to be combined in the same count without offending the rules against joinder.[68] Changes in the way that breach of warranty was framed provide no indication about the definition and operation of a warranty.

The purchase of a horse remained fraught with difficulty.[69] Veterinary medicine was still fairly primitive[70] and the inexperienced buyer was particularly at risk of being hoodwinked.[71] Henry Bracken warned that, 'in the art of horsemanship, the most difficult part is that of giving proper directions for the purchasing of a horse free from fault and blemish'.[72] The dice was not inevitably loaded in favour of the seller,

[61] A. Friedman (ed.), Oliver Goldsmith, *The Vicar of Wakefield* (Oxford University Press, 2006), 60. The novel was originally published in 1766.

[62] (1778) 1 Doug 18. [63] *Ibid.*, 21. [64] *Ibid.*, 21. Buller was called to the Bar in 1772.

[65] *Ross* v. *Edgar* (1754) LI Harrowby MS Doc. 13 f. 62 cited by M. Lobban, 'Contractual Fraud in Law and Equity' (1997) 17 *Oxford Journal of Legal Studies* 441, 460 n. 116.

[66] M. Bacon, *A New Abridgment of the Law* (London: 1736), vol. I, 52.

[67] *Assumpsit*, like deceit, had its origins in trespass on the case. For a potted history of the action see W. Swain, 'Assumpsit' in P. Cane and J. Conaghan (eds.), *The New Oxford Companion to Law* (Oxford University Press, 2008), 55–6.

[68] Bacon, *New Abridgment*, vol. I, 30. The rules against joinder prohibited contract and tort claims from appearing in the same count. For example in *Denison* v. *Ralphson* (1682) 1 Vent 365 an attempt to combine the old style of breach of warranty in the form of deceit and breach of contract was rejected. The great advantage of this new method of pleading was that the plaintiff could, in addition to, alleging breach of warranty recover the money paid for the defective goods in the same count: *Williamson* v. *Allison* (1802) 2 East 446, 451.

[69] E. R. Gent, *The Experienc'd Farrier or Farring Completed*, 4th edn (London: 1720), 63.

[70] The late eighteenth century nevertheless witnessed the origins of a distinct veterinary profession; see, L. Pugh, *From Farriery to Veterinary Medicine 1785–1795* (Cambridge: Heffer, 1962).

[71] W. Taplin, *The gentleman's stable directory: or, modern system of farriery* (London: 1778), 13.

[72] H. Bracken, *Ten Minutes Advice to Every Purchaser of a Horse out of a Dealer, jockey or groom's stable* (London: 1787), 1.

however. In *Hollingsworth* v. *Tattersall* an action for the breach of warranty of a horse,[73] one witness, Thomas Hull, described in Lord Mansfield's trial notes as a stable-keeper, and in a press report as a 'great-dealer in horses'[74] caused 'great laughter' from the assembled company when he:

> [t]old Lord Mansfield that it was now the mode among all the horse-dealers in the kingdom, though they knew the horse sound when sold, and sound when returned, yet rather than come before his Lordship, they always took the horse and returned the money, as they were of opinion his Lordship was, right or wrong, in favour of purchasers, and against the dealers.[75]

These events were sufficiently notorious to be included in Lord Eldon's *Anecdote Book* a quarter of a century later.[76] But the suggestion that Lord Mansfield was unsympathetic to horse-dealers was somewhat ironic in the circumstances given that the jury found for the plaintiff contrary to the Chief Justice's direction, which left him, 'much dissatisfied with the verdict' and shaking his head at the 'extraordinary conduct of the jury'.[77] James Oldham's analysis of the cases on horse sales in Lord Mansfield's notebooks has led him to conclude that after Mr Hull's intervention a verdict in the seller's favour was more likely than before.[78] Juries remained unpredictable, however.

Lord Mansfield enjoys a well-deserved reputation for his skilful use of special mercantile juries[79] even if, on occasions this meant that his directions lost all semblance of neutrality.[80] But mercantile jurors like those in *Holligsworth* v. *Tattersall* may also have been the most difficult to bully in this way.[81] Given the poor reputation for probity enjoyed by horse-dealers they were perhaps not a class of defendant likely to engender the sympathy of their fellow merchants. It was difficult

[73] (1778).The case is overlooked by the nominate reports. As a decision at Guildhall rather than *in banc* this is not surprising. Lord Mansfield's note of the trial survives: J. Oldham, *The Mansfield Manuscripts and the Growth of English Law in the Eighteenth Century* (Chapel Hill: University of North Carolina Press, 1992), vol. I, 332–3. Two different newspaper reports have also been located: *London Chronicle*, 30 May 1778; *Morning Post*, 1 June 1778.

[74] *London Chronicle, ibid.* [75] *Ibid.*

[76] A. Lincoln and R. McEwen (eds.), *Lord Eldon's Anecdote Book* (London: Stevens and Sons, 1960), [236].

[77] *Morning Post, ibid.*

[78] Oldham, *Mansfield Manuscripts*, vol. I, 232. [79] *Ibid.*, 82–99.

[80] For examples see W. Swain, 'Da Costa v. Jones', in C. Mitchell and P. Mitchell (eds.), *Landmark Cases in the Law of Contract* (Oxford: Hart, 2008), 118.

[81] *Capstack* v. *Williams* (1782), Oldham, *Mansfield Manuscripts*, vol. 1, 367.

to get such a verdict overturned provided the jury had addressed the correct matters.[82]

The first task of the jury was to determine whether or not a warranty had been given. The jury was only required to express an opinion on the existence of the warranty and it is possible that jurors might have been prepared to discover an express warranty on the slimmest pretext or even to imply one. There was sufficient sympathy for one buyer for the absence of an express warranty not to be fatal even though he knew all about the defect.[83] Implied warranties had become quite commonplace in maritime insurance contracts[84] and by the 1760s began to appear in horse sales as well. John Lawrence in *A Philosophical and Practical Treatise on Horses*[85] explained that where a horse was sold for more than ten pounds the law required the animal to be sound irrespective of whether the vendor gave an express warranty. He complained that this had the result of 'manifestly affording the purchaser an undue advantage'.[86] Lawrence was describing a version of the sound price doctrine whereby a horse that was sold for a sound or fair price carried an implied warranty of soundness. This sort of warranty attracted the attention of other legal writers. John Joseph Powell, in his *Essay Upon the Law of Contract*, argued that a purchaser would be taken not to have assented to contract, 'if a man sell a horse for a price, which it could not be worth unless it were sound, the contract will be void'.[87] The existence of such a far-reaching rule should be viewed with a degree of scepticism. Powell's work reflected his interest in first principles[88] and natural law theory[89] and is not always a very reliable guide of existing legal doctrine.[90] A different version of the sound price doctrine is found in Wooddeson's *Systematical View*, a work based on his Vinerian lectures of the 1770s, and which contrasted the earlier dominance of *caveat emptor*, with 'a more reasonable principle ... that a fair price implies a warranty'.[91]

[82] It was possible to argue that the jury reached a decision against the evidence on a motion for new trial but judges were reluctant to support such an argument; see J. Morgan, *Essays Upon the Law of Evidence, New Trials, Special Verdicts, Trials at Bar and Repleaders* (London: 1789), vol. II, 52–3.

[83] *Taylor* v. *Broderick* (1782) Oldham, *Mansfield Manuscripts*, vol. I, 372.

[84] Implied warranties were confined to fundamental matters like seaworthiness: *Eden* v. *Parkinson* (1781) 2 Doug 732, 735; *Schoolbred* v. *Nutt* (1782), Oldham, *Mansfield Manuscripts*, vol. I, 586.

[85] (London: 1796–98).

[86] Lawrence, *Treatise on Horses*, vol. II, 143.

[87] (London: 1790).

[88] *Ibid.*, vol. I, vi.

[89] *Ibid.*, vol. I, xliii.

[90] Most of the authorities cited by Powell pre-date 1750, T. Baloch, 'Law Booksellers and Printers as Agents of Unchange' (2007) 66 *Cambridge Law Journal* 389, at 416.

[91] *A Systematical View of the Laws of England* (London: 1792–93), vol. II, 415.

Twenty years before Woodeson, Blackstone in his *Commentaries on the Laws of England* made no mention of implying a warranty on payment of a fair price and merely reinforced the idea that a warranty of quality needed to be express.[92] His silence suggests that the idea may have gained currency after the mid-1760s. In 1778 in *Stuart* v. *Wilkins*,[93] Lord Mansfield explained that:

> [a] warranty extends to all faults known and unknown to the seller. Selling for a sound price without warranty may be a ground for assumpsit, but, in such a case, it ought to be laid that the defendant knew of the unsoundness.[94]

A manuscript report of the same judgment states that:

> The difference between an express warranty and where there is no warranty but the full price given as if sound, is, that in the case of an express warranty the law implies an assumpsit in all events, whether the unsoundness was in the knowledge of the defendant or not. But in the other case the law only implies the assumpsit if the defendant knew of it.[95]

A quarter of a century on, Grose J denied that Lord Mansfield had supported a sound price doctrine.[96] *Stuart* v. *Wilkins* was, strictly speaking, concerned with the question of whether assumpsit was the appropriate form of action. Lord Mansfield's obiter remarks can be treated as a mode of expression used in directing juries rather than a legal doctrine.[97] At the same time the bolder interpretation that Lord Mansfield was advocating a fully fledged sound price doctrine, would be entirely within character with a judge who was prepared to introduce a requirement of good faith in contracting.[98]

Lord Mansfield's version of the sound price doctrine was never as far reaching as Wooddeson's.[99] A sound price was not in itself enough to imply a warranty. A warranty would only be implied where there was a sound price and the seller knew of the defect. A genuine latent defect would not be covered. More than a decade before *Stuart* v. *Wilkins* at

[92] *Commentaries on the Laws of England* (Oxford: 1766), vol. II, 452.
[93] (1778) 1 Doug 18. [94] *Ibid.*, 20. [95] LI MS Hill 13 f. 258.
[96] *Parkinson* v. *Lee* (1802) 2 East 314, 318.
[97] A. W. B. Simpson, 'The Horwitz Thesis and the History of Contracts' (1979) 46 *University of Chicago Law Review* 533, at 581–3.
[98] *Carter* v. *Boehm* (1766) 3 Burr 1905, 1910; *Bexwell* v. *Christie* (1776) 1 Cowp 395.
[99] Horwitz accepts Wooddeson's definition at face value; M. Horwitz, 'The Historical Foundations of Modern Contract Law' (1973–74) 87 *Harvard Law Review* 917, at 926–7.

Hertford Assize,[100] the *London Chronicle* reported that Lord Mansfield made clear to those present, who included some jockeys, that 'if at any time they took a sound price for a horse they knew not to be sound, or concealed any defect, the not warranting him should not avail them at all'.[101]

Having established the existence of a warranty the next step, as Lord Mansfield explained to a jury in *Hopkins* v. *Hopkins*, was that:

> [t]hey had three things to consider; whether the beast was sound according to the engagement; whether she was returned in due time, according to the conditions; and, whether she was returned in reasonable time, according to the law.[102]

The horse in question had been sold with an express warranty of soundness. The jury heard witnesses on both sides as to the soundness of the horse and came to the conclusion that the horse was both unsound and returned as required by the conditions of sale.[103] Horse sales actually fell into three main categories. Horses were either sold with an express warranty as 'sound, free from vice or blemish, and quiet to ride or draw', 'sold without warranty to be taken with all faults'[104] or sold as sound with the exception of those faults which were highlighted.[105]

The sale of horses frequently came with conditions attached. In sales by auction at horse repositories the conditions were posted up for any buyer to read[106] thereby giving sufficient notice to incorporate the conditions into the sale.[107] One key term, at the well-known auction house Tattersall's, stated that:

> [t]he purchaser of any lot warranted in any way, and not answering the warranty given, must return the same on or before the evening of the

[100] The decision survives in Mansfield's notebook, *Worth* v. *Pank* (1764); Oldham, *Mansfield Manuscripts*, vol. I, 266.

[101] *London Chronicle*, 14 August 1764.

[102] As reported in the *Daily Advertiser*, 27 February 1778. For Lord Mansfield's trial note see Oldham, *Mansfield Manuscripts*, vol. I, 327–8. For similar instructions see *Cook* v. *Tattersall*, *Morning Chronicle*, 24 May 1777, cited by Oldham, *Mansfield Manuscripts*, vol. I, 233.

[103] The witnesses might prove unhelpful to the side that called them for example in *Neate* v. *Davis* (1764) Oldham, *Mansfield Manuscripts*, vol. I, 274–5 the witnesses for the defendant all gave evidence that the horse was unsound.

[104] (London: 1796–98), vol. II, 142.

[105] *Ibid.*, 144–5; *Redfern* v. *Tattersall* (1781), Oldham, *Mansfield Manuscripts*, vol. I, 235.

[106] *Hopkins* v. *Hopkins* (1778), Oldham, *Mansfield Manuscripts*, vol. I, 328. One of the witnesses, a clerk at the repository, said in evidence that 'the conditions of sale, all dealers know them. Plaintiff frequently buys and sells'.

[107] *Mesnard* v. *Aldridge* (1801) 3 Esp 271.

> second day from the sale, otherwise the purchaser shall be obliged to keep the lot with all faults.[108]

When a condition of this sort was used the warranty was only valid for a very short period. Without such a condition the seller who gave an express warranty was liable for an unsound horse irrespective of whether the horse was returned or the buyer even gave notice of the horse's condition.[109] There is some evidence that judges and juries were willing to ameliorate the effects of this sort of term. In *Hopkins* v. *Hopkins* the condition required the horse to be returned by the evening of the day following the sale. The horse had been retained for five days before being returned. Lord Mansfield rewrote the condition, directing the jury that the buyer was allowed to retain the horse for a reasonable period on the grounds that it was impossible to make a full discovery of latent defects in such a short period.[110] In *Buchanan* v. *Parnshaw*[111] a horse was sold warranted sound and six years old. A condition was attached that the horse be returned within two days if unsound. Lord Kenyon recognised the value of such a condition in public sales because of the risk of accident to the horse between the sale and the time when the horse might be returned. At the same time he held that while a condition was appropriate for unsoundness it did not apply when after ten days the horse was discovered to be twelve years old.

Procedural changes were as significant as changes in legal doctrine. The main business of the civil trial was conducted at *nisi prius*,[112] and overseen by a single judge who travelled on circuit. A verdict on the merits of the claim was reached by a jury having heard the evidence presented to them. Strictly speaking jurors were confined to deciding questions of fact.[113] In reality the boundary between law and fact was

[108] P. Mitchell, 'The Development of Quality Obligations in Sale of Goods' (2001) 117 *Law Quarterly Review* 645, 649, citing G. Oliphant, *The Law Concerning Horses* (London: 1847), 29.

[109] *Fielder* v. *Starkin* (1788) 1 H Bla 17.

[110] These remarks were contained in the press report in the *London Chronicle*, 27 February 1778.

[111] (1788) 2 TR 745.

[112] On the importance of this forum, see J. Oldham, 'Law-making at Nisi Prius in the Early 1800s' (2004) 25 *Journal of Legal History* 221. In London the court at Guildhall was the equivalent body.

[113] The distinction between fact and law emerged in the sixteenth century; see, B. Shapiro, *A Culture of Fact: England 1550–1720* (Cornell University Press, 2003), 10–11; M. S. Arnold, 'Law and Fact in the Medieval Jury Trial: Out of Sight, Out of Mind' (1974) 18 *American Journal of Legal History* 267.

difficult to draw.[114] Jury deliberations were not recorded and as some of Lord Mansfield's cases show juries enjoyed considerable room for manoeuvre. By the end of the eighteenth century, judges were making a conscious effort to place tighter controls on jury discretion and by the mid-nineteenth century, the power of the jury had been largely eroded. This shift had implications for disputes about horse sales.

Horse sales, legal formalism[115] and standard terms

Despite the coming of the railways[116] and the emergence of other new technology,[117] Thompson has estimated that there were over a million horses in 1811, a figure that had increased to 3 million a century later.[118] The reputation of dealers remained low,[119] but as the need for horses grew, the way horses were sold began to change.[120] The most expensive class of dealer still sold horses straight from country breeders. The horse repositories and fairs provided an opportunity to pick up a bargain but it came at a cost.[121] Sale by auction at the repositories did not afford a good opportunity to inspect the horse[122] and such sales were usually conducted using standard terms. The law was changing too. Perhaps the single most striking factor was the extent to which jurors had come to be supplanted by judges. This brought problems of its own.

In the introduction to his book, *The Horseman's Manuel*,[123] Robert Surtees[124] grumbled that:

[114] Sir J. Hawles, *The English-mans right a dialogue between a barrister at law and a jury-man* (London: 1680), 11.

[115] The idea is described in M. Horwitz, 'The Rise of Legal Formalism' (1975) 19 *American Journal of Legal History* 251. Formalism here is used in a descriptive sense without indorsing Horwitz's conclusions about cause.

[116] In 1830 there were a mere 157 km of railway track. By 1900 there were over 30,000 km; see B. R. Mitchell, *European Historical Statistics 1750–1975*, 2nd edn (London: Macmillan, 1981), 610, 612.

[117] J. Tann, 'Horse Power 1780–1880', in F.M.L. Thompson (ed.), *Horses in European Economic History* (Reading: The British Agricultural Society, 1983), 21.

[118] F. M. L. Thompson, 'Nineteenth-Century Horse Sense' (1976) 29 *Economic History Review* 60.

[119] G. Stephen, *The Adventures of a Gentleman in Search of a Horse* (London: Longmans, 1835), 141.

[120] J. Lawrence, *The Horse in all its Varieties* (London: 1829), 148–55.

[121] W. Youatt, *The Horse* (London: 1831), 369.

[122] *Ibid.*, 153.

[123] R. Surtees, *The Horseman's Manuel* (London: A. Miller, 1831).

[124] Surtees is best known for his novels on foxhunting featuring Mr Jorrocks but in his youth he had also been articled to several firms of solicitors: N. Gash, 'Surtees, Robert Smith', *Oxford Dictionary of National Biography.*

> [o]wing to the nature of their profession, the Judges have not those opportunities of acquiring information, or of ascertaining by experience the various peculiarities and qualifications of the horse ... But their ignorance of the economy of the horse is not the only disadvantage under which their Lordships labour ... The contradictory evidence, not to say perjury, and the stabularian and technical terms which are made use of, tend to heighten the embarrassment under which they are placed.[125]

Whether the agreement amounted to a warranty had become a question of law[126] eliminating the possibility of a sympathetic jury conjuring up the existence of a warranty.[127] Gibbs CJ described the question of soundness on the other hand as 'a question peculiarly fit for the consideration of a jury'.[128] He also made clear that the court *in banc* would not overturn a verdict simply because the trial judge came to a different conclusion from his jury. But this approach was already becoming dated. In *Broennenburgh* v. *Haycock*,[129] Burroughs J described unsoundness as 'compounded' of both fact and law. While the issue of whether the horse was in fact unsound remained a matter for the jury, the definition of unsoundness was unequivocally a matter for the judge.

Henry Jeremy wrote in 1825, that, 'it is to be regretted that the term (unsoundness) is not capable of more easy construction and definite meaning'.[130] Some judges did attempt a definition. Lord Ellenborough held that '[a]ny infirmity which renders a horse less fit for present use and convenience, is an unsoundness'.[131] Best CJ directed a jury that 'sound meant perfect'.[132] Nearly twenty years later in *Kiddell* v. *Burnard*, Parke B listed a series of conditions which rendered a horse unsound.[133]

Positive proof that the horse was unsound at the time of sale may not have been easy for a buyer. Mere suspicion was insufficient.[134] Where the value of the horse made the expense worthwhile, buyers were wise to follow Stephen's advice, that before returning the animal it was prudent to have it examined by two experts in horse ailments.[135] Even with

[125] Surtees, *Horseman's Manuel*, v-vi.
[126] *Dunlop* v. *Waugh* (1792) Peake 167; *Wood* v. *Smith* (1829) M & M 539.
[127] The firming up of the line between representation and warranty is a good example, see *Budd* v. *Fairmaner* (1831) 8 Bing 47; *Hopkins* v. *Tanqueray* (1854) 15 CB 130.
[128] *Lewis* v. *Peake* (1816) 7 Taunt 153, 154.
[129] (1817) Holt 630, 631.
[130] H. Jeremy, *The Laws Relating to Horses* (London: 1825), 23.
[131] *Elton* v. *Jordan* (1815) 1 Stark 127, 4 Camp 281.
[132] *Best* v. *Osborne* (1825) Ryan and Moody 290, 291.
[133] (1842) 9 M & W 668, 669–70.
[134] *Eaves* v. *Dixon* (1810) 2 Taunt 343.
[135] Stephen, *Adventures of a Gentleman*, 43.

expert evidence a buyer might still fail to convince a jury that the horse was unsound.[136] Because a warranty was a statement of existing fact, a dealer who was determinedly dishonest might simply lie about the condition of the horse at the time of sale with a view to establishing that the illness or injury occurred after the animal had left his hands.[137] Individual conditions came to be classified as a matter of law. Horses that were nerved,[138] suffered from bone stavin,[139] a cough,[140] or were short-sighted[141] were unsound; those with buck eyes,[142] a propensity to crib-biting,[143] were sound. It might be expected that this approach would have led to greater certainty but at various times roaring[144] and temporary injuries[145] fell within both categories.

Even where the horse was warranted sound and the condition fell within a definition or category of unsoundness the seller could still escape liability. Conditions of sale were increasingly sophisticated.[146] One term popular with dealers required the horse to be returned in two days along with a veterinary certificate that the horse was unsound.[147] Even on the assumption that the fault emerged in time,[148] terms of this type must have placed a heavy burden on buyers. Lord Mansfield had been prepared to rewrite a condition to ensure that it was reasonable. The sympathies of his nineteenth-century counterpart were equally obvious when, in *Bywater* v. *Richardson*[149] Denman CJ stated that:

> He (the seller) had every right to give such a limited warranty, and the plaintiff only was to blame if he did not avail himself of the time given to discover and object to the unsoundness.[150]

[136] *Eaves* v. *Dixon* (1810) 2 Taunt 343.

[137] This was perhaps a bigger threat once parties were competent witnesses in their own suit: (1833) 3 & 4 Will IV c 42 s 26, (1843) 6 & 7 Vict c 85, (1851) 14 & 15 Vict c 99 s 2.

[138] *Best* v. *Osborne* (1825) Ryan and Moody 290. Nerving involved cutting a nerve in a horse's leg, usually to relieve pain in a foot.

[139] *Watson* v. *Denton* (1835) 7 Car & P 85.

[140] *Coates* v. *Stephens* (1830) 2 M & R 157.

[141] *Holliday* v. *Morgan* (1858) 1 Ell & Ell 1.

[142] *Earle* v. *Patterson* reported from manuscript in Surtees, *Horseman's Manuel* 20–3.

[143] *Broennenburg* v. *Haycock* (1817) Holt 630; *Coates* v. *Stephens* (1838) 2 M & R 157.

[144] Roaring is a common respiratory disease of horses; see Surtees, *Horseman's Manuel*, 36–8; *Bassett* v. *Collis* (1810) 2 Camp 523; *Onslow* v. *Eames* (1817) 2 Stark 81.

[145] *Bolden* v. *Brogden* (1838) 2 M & Rob 113; *Coates* v. *Stephen* (1838) 2 M & Rob 157.

[146] Surtees, *Horseman's Manuel*, 78–94 and Stephen, *Adventures of a Gentleman*, 311–25 provides a range of examples from different dealers.

[147] This particular condition was used by Tattersall's and the Bazaar see, Stephen, *Adventures of Gentleman*, 312, 314.

[148] *Ibid.*, 138.

[149] (1834) 1 Ad & E 508.

[150] *Ibid.* 513.

Eighteenth-century buyers may have been able to draw some consolation from the sound price doctrine but this too had fallen out of favour.[151]

Horse sales and consumer contracts

Horse sales encapsulate some of the wider issues surrounding consumer contracts in the last century and a half. By the mid-nineteenth century the market in horses was complex. Despite the appalling reputation of horse-dealers as a class,[152] and a burgeoning literature, 'carelessness or ignorance' was still widespread.[153] The sound price doctrine was quietly retired. Jurors, whether motivated by commercial morality, a desire to punish dealers or to protect buyers, were no longer able to intercede on behalf of the consumer in the same manner as before. There was also considerable variation in the practice of dealers, as shown by a report of a House of Lords Committee on horses in 1873.[154] One dealer even suggested that 'you are obliged to give a warranty'.[155] Another said that he 'never gave a warranty' and that 'if the buyers are not able to judge for themselves, they may get the assistance of any professional men to help them judge'.[156] On account of his good reputation he claimed not to be short of customers. The same report also contains evidence that the law as it stood benefited large dealers[157] who sold horses cheaply without warranty, at the expense of smaller breeders who, unable to compete on price, felt compelled to give an express warranty. Smaller dealers feared that the cost of any resulting liabilities would drive them out of business.[158] Perhaps not surprisingly the dealers least likely to offer an express warranty and also selling on the most draconian terms contained in standard form contracts[159] were also the cheapest.

[151] *Jones* v. *Bowden* (1813) 4 Taunt 847, 851; *Gray* v. *Cox* (1824) 1 C & P 184, 185. Neither decision concerned a horse and in both the remarks that the sound price doctrine was 'long since exploded' came in the argument of counsel. See Stephen, *Adventures of a Gentleman*, 230.

[152] F. Taylor, *Recollections of a Horse Dealer* (London: 1861). In this respect they were rather like the secondhand car dealer of modern mythology.

[153] F. Lascelles, *Horse Warranty on the Purchase and Sale of Horses* (London: Reeves and Turner, 1877), i.

[154] *Report from the Select Committee of the House of Lords on Horses* (1873) (325) HC Papers vol. XIV.1.

[155] Evidence of Mr Shaw, 88. [156] Evidence of Mr Sheils, 114–15.

[157] Evidence of Colonel Kingscote, 181. [158] Evidence of Mr Shaw, 89.

[159] This somewhat undermines the view that standard form contracting 'was the natural outgrowth and was complementary to the mass produced product'; see G. Gluck, 'Standard Form Contracts: the Contract Theory Reconsidered' (1979) 28 *International*

Judicial reluctance to intervene need not be explained as 'a dramatic overthrow of an important element of the eighteenth century's equitable conception of contract'.[160] The sound price doctrine was a typical of the bold move that Lord Mansfield was sometimes capable of and just as short lived as some of his other attempts at reform.[161] The principle of *caveat emptor* was too well established. The idea that buyers of horses without an express warranty had no reason to complain was equally firmly within the common law tradition.[162] Just as importantly it was reflected in the way that horses were sold and the price that was paid. Whether this meant that the market worked effectively was another matter.[163] By the time that statute intervened to impose the same sort of implied warranties[164] as already found in the sale of some other types of goods[165] the internal combustion engine loomed large on the horizon.[166]

and Comparative Law Quarterly, 72, 73. Auction sales were another early example of standard form contracting. Because the bid was not accepted until the bringing down of the gavel, auctioneers began to include a condition of sale preventing a buyer from retracting once he had made his bid: R. Babington, *A Treatise on the Law of Auctions* (London: Butterworth, 1826), 30.

160 M. Horwitz, *The Transformation of American Law* (Harvard University Press, 1977), 180.

161 W. Swain, 'The Changing Nature of the Doctrine of Consideration 1750–1850' (2005) 26 *Journal of Legal History* 47.

162 Atiyah's suggestion that protection of buyers was not a common law tradition because 'few goods would have cost enough to justify a suit in the courts of Common law' fails to explain horse sales; see, P. Atiyah, *The Rise and Fall of Freedom of Contract* (Oxford University Press, 1979), 179.

163 G. Akerlof, 'The Market for "Lemons": Quality Uncertainty and the Market Mechanism' (1870) 84 *The Quarterly Journal of Economics* 488.

164 Sale of Goods Act (1893) 56 & 57 Vict c 71. Under the legislation the rule was still *caveat emptor.* Section 14 of the legislation stated that there was no general implied warranty of quality or fitness for purpose. There were several exceptions. The exceptions could be excluded by virtue of s. 55 as a result of agreement of the parties, a course of dealing or usage.

165 Mitchell, 'Quality Obligations', 650–6.

166 Mitchell, *European*, 670. There were 17,000 motor vehicles in 1904 in the UK rising to 260,000 at the start of the First World War.

15

The role of private litigation in market regulation: beyond 'legal origins'

AXEL HALFMEIER

Introduction

The problem of how consumer law is to be enforced has taken a new turn as a result of the development of the 'law and finance' or 'legal origins' theory propounded by leading American economists.[1] Although this theory mainly deals with corporate law, securities regulation and other financial matters, its basic findings can also be applied to consumer law in the broad sense. In this broad sense, a shareholder or an investor is also a consumer in the sense and ambit of European consumer law.[2] Indeed, the 'legal origins' theory claims to be applicable not only to narrow areas of corporate or financial regulation, but to the 'social control of economic life' in general.[3] Consumer law is certainly part of this wider concept of social regulation.

In this chapter an overview of the main features and current state of the 'legal origins' theory will be given. It proceeds to argue and explain that the legal origins theory must be put in a more historic perspective regarding the relationship between private and public law regulation. From this perspective, it will become clear that the legal origins theory

Professor of Private and Comparative Law, Leuphana University Lüneburg.

[1] For an overview on the 'legal origins' literature see, in particular, R. LaPorta, F. Lopez-de-Silanes and A. Shleifer, 'The Economic Consequences of Legal Origins' (2008) 46 *Journal of Economic Literature* 285–332; see also the critical appraisal by K. W. Dam, *The Law-Growth Nexus: the Rule of Law and Economic Development* (Brookings Institution, 2006). The 'legal origins' movement in economic literature was started mainly by R. LaPorta, F. Lopez-de-Silanes, A. Shleifer and R. Vishny, 'Legal Determinants of External Finance' (1997) 52 *Journal of Finance* 1131–50; R. LaPorta, F. Lopez-de-Silanes, A. Shleifer and R. Vishny, 'Law and Finance' (1998) 106 *Journal of Political Economy* 1113–55.

[2] See e.g. the decision of the German Federal Court (BGH) of 23 October 2001 (2002) 55 *NJW* 368 at 369.

[3] R. LaPorta *et al.*, 'The Economic Consequences of Legal Origins', 286.

does make a significant contribution to our understanding of regulatory strategies, but does not provide a substitute for policy decisions which need to be made by legislators and society in general.

The attempt here is not to undertake an internal criticism of the legal origins theory, in the sense that it must live up to its own economic standards and methods. This must be left to the economists themselves and has already been undertaken from such a purely economic perspective.[4] Instead, the question here is what consumer law discourse can gain from this discussion in the area of economics and also whether lawyers need to take a stand to defend the core business of law, by making reasonable value judgements within a given social context.

Current state of the 'legal origins' theory and internal criticism

Description of the basic theory

The 'legal origins' theory started in the late 1990s with certain articles by American economists on the relationship between the legal protection of investors, such as shareholders and third-party corporate creditors, and the economic success of certain countries.[5] It was later extended to securities regulation[6] and even to non-financial matters such as the regulation of labour markets,[7] military conscription[8] and government ownership of the media.[9]

The method was as follows: for a large number of countries, certain legal data were collected, such as the substantive and procedural protection of shareholders in that legal system;[10] these data were evaluated and coded usually on scales between zero and one, zero meaning that there was no protection at all and one meaning a maximum amount of protection. The aggregated data were then related to certain indicators

[4] See in particular H. Spamann, 'The "Antidirectors Rights Index" Revisited' (2010) 23 *Review of Financial Studies* 467–86; for an empirical test in the area of choice of law see S. Voigt, 'Are International Merchants Stupid? Their Choice of Law Sheds Doubt on the Legal Origin Theory' (2008) 5 *Journal of Empirical Legal Studies* 1–20.

[5] See the works cited above in n. 1.

[6] R. La Porta, F. Lopez-de-Silanes and A. Shleifer, 'What Works in Securities Laws?' (2006) 61 *Journal of Finance* 1–32.

[7] J. Botero *et al.*, 'The Regulation of Labor' (2004) 119 *Quarterly Journal of Economics*, 1339–82.

[8] C. Mulligan and A. Shleifer, 'Conscription as Regulation' (2005) 7 *American Law and Economics Review* 85–111.

[9] S. Djankov *et al.*, 'Who Owns the Media?' (2003) 46 *Journal of Law and Economics* 341–81.

[10] See e.g. La Porta *et al.*, 'What Works in Securities Laws?' at 5ff.

of the economic success of that country, such as the gross domestic product or the amount of stock market capitalisation. These relations were statistically analysed with econometric instruments: the idea here is that statistical methods can be used to determine whether a given correlation between certain data is only a coincidence or whether such correlations can be explained in terms of an economic model or whether we can even speak of relations between the figures in terms of causality. The findings of the 'legal origins' studies described seem to indicate that indeed there is something like a causal relationship between certain legal rules and economic success, so that one of the findings can and has been described simply as 'law matters': '[t]he measured differences in legal rules matter for economic and social outcomes'.[11]

However, the more controversial finding was that there is a noteworthy and significant difference between countries with common law legal origin and countries with civil law legal origin. The common law countries are described as relying mainly on private litigation to protect investor rights, while civil law tends more to what the authors describe as state intervention or bureaucratic regulation. Within the civil law family, the authors distinguished several sub-families, especially the German, French and Nordic sub-family, but found that the French civil law system is the one that relies most clearly on government regulation.[12]

The statistical methods used by these economists then show that not only does 'law matter' but also that the common law is superior in maximising social welfare, especially in comparison to systems originating in French civil law: the common law is described as 'associated with ... improved financial development, better access to finance and higher ownership dispersion'.[13] Accordingly, one of the main claims of the legal origins theory, illustrated with several examples, is that the common law is a tool for maximising social welfare superior to civil law or a more public regulatory style.

From the perspective of comparative law, it is interesting to note that this theory appears as a rebirth of the 'legal families' or *Rechtskreis* approach that was prevalent especially in traditional German comparative law textbooks.[14] At the end of the twentieth century, however, it seemed as if the distinction between legal families had lost much of its

[11] La Porta *et al.*, 'Economic Consequences of Legal Origins', 326.

[12] *Ibid.* 290. [13] *Ibid.*, 298.

[14] See, in particular, K. Zweigert and H. Kötz, *Introduction to Comparative Law* (Oxford: 1998); this seminal work of comparative law is cited by LaPorta *et al.*, 'Economic Consequences of Legal Origins', 286.

significance in view of the Europeanisation and even globalisation of law, worldwide law firms, legal transplants and other phenomena.[15] Nevertheless, the 'legal origins' economic theory uses this old comparative law concept as a cornerstone of its theory.

Internal criticism

It is not surprising that there has been a lot of criticism of the 'legal origins' theory. This criticism can be broadly classified into two groups: one concerns the assessment of the legal data and therefore the quality of the data input, and the other concerns its interpretation with the help of econometric methods. With regard to the legal data, it should be clear to everybody who has done some comparative legal research that a question such as 'how would you assess the level of shareholder protection in country X on a scale between 0 and 1?' is not easy to answer because it may depend on a complex interplay between written rules, case law, procedural rules and many other factors. It is therefore quite problematic whether 'numerical comparative law' as used in the legal origins theory is really a legitimate and meaningful method.[16]

Furthermore, it came to light that in some of the earlier studies these assessments were not even done by lawyers, so that their reliability is very low.[17] There are newer studies from 2007 and 2008 that try to check whether the data input is really reliable, and these more recent studies come to conclusions that are much less clear than the original claims regarding the superiority of the common law approach. One study that uses corrected data on the same subjects treated in the original 'law and finance' studies even comes to the conclusion that the corrected values for the 'anti-director rights index' (a quantitative measure of the level of shareholder protection in a given country) provide:

> no evidence that common law countries offer better investor protection than countries governed by civil law or that investor protection is positively

[15] For modern critiques of the 'legal families' concept see e.g. E. Örücü, 'A General View of "Legal Families" and of "Mixing Systems"', in E. Örücü and D. Nelken (eds.), *Comparative Law: a Handbook* (Oxford: 2007), 169–87; H. P. Glenn, 'Comparative Legal Families and Comparative Legal Traditions' in M. Reimann and R. Zimmermann (eds.), *The Oxford Handbook of Comparative Law* (Oxford: 2006), 421–39.

[16] See the critique by M. Siems, 'Numerical Comparative Law: Do We Need Statistical Evidence in order to Reduce Complexity?' (2005) 13 *Cardozo Journal of International and Comparative Law* 521–40.

[17] This is pointed out by Spamann 469; 'The "Antidirectors Rights Index" Revisited', for further critical evaluation of the 'legal data' input see Dam, *The Law-Growth Nexus*.

> correlated with ownership dispersion, larger equity markets or resilience to the Asian financial crisis.[18]

Furthermore, a recent empirical study regarding the relationship between shareholder protection and stock market development concluded that the differences between civil and common law jurisdictions declined over the period of 1995 to 2005 and failed to find any significant link between the level of shareholder protection and stock market development.[19] These corrections show that the empirical basis for the 'legal origins' theories must be viewed at least with scepticism.

The second criticism is even more complex since it questions the idea of a causal link between legal origin and financial or economic development. It is argued that the category of 'legal origin', in the sense of the common law or civil law origin of a legal system, is not the decisive factor, but that other factors such as culture, history and politics are more relevant.[20] This criticism is largely of a speculative nature and can hardly be evaluated here. However, the 'legal origins' authors remain confident that a legal tradition is not identical with cultural, historical or political developments or beliefs, but that it has a separate role as a causal factor in economic and social development.[21]

This must be seen as one of the lasting strong points of the legal origins theory: it gives empirical evidence to the relevance of law and legal tradition in social development. What has been, historically, described by Marxist theory as the 'relative autonomy of the superstructure' is now supported by econometric theory, or, as Friedrich Engels formulated in 1890: 'The economic situation is the basis, but the various aspects of the superstructure – political forms of class struggle and its results ... legal forms ... exert their influence on the development of the historic struggles and determine in many cases their form.'[22]

A third possible criticism that has not been fully explored is the impact of the financial crisis since 2007 on the findings of the legal origin theory. If it is argued that England and Wales, the USA, as the most important

[18] Spamann, 'The "Antidirectors Rights Index" Revisited', 483.

[19] J. Armour *et al.*, 'Shareholder Protection and Stock Market Development: an Empirical Test of the Legal Origins Hypothesis' (2009) 6 *Journal of Empirical Legal Studies* 343–80.

[20] For an overview of such criticism see LaPorta *et al.*, 'The Economic Consequences of Legal Origins, 310ff.; see also M. Siems, 'What does not Work in Comparing Securities Laws: a Critique on La Porta et al.'s Methodology' (2005) *International Company and Commercial Law Review* 300–5.

[21] LaPorta *et al.*, 'The Economic Consequences of Loyal Origins', 326.

[22] F. Engels, Letter to J. Bloch of 21 September 1890, *Marx Engels Werke*, vol. XXXVII, 462–3 (translated from German).

economies with common law legal origins, are also the most efficient in terms of financial development and guaranteeing social welfare, then why should one of the most striking financial crisis of the last decades have emerged precisely from these economies and legal systems? It was the ingenious common law-trained lawyer in English and American law firms who devised the 'sub-prime mortgages', 'asset-backed securities' and 'special purpose vehicles' which contributed to this crisis. In addition, the recent financial crisis shows that there was probably too little rather than too much government intervention in the financial sector.[23] The legal origins theory must give an explanation for this if it really wants to uphold the claim that the common law in combination with comparatively less government intervention is better for the economy.

Historic context of public and private regulation

Even before the advent of the legal origins theory it was obvious that law and legal systems can only be explained with reference to their historical development. It is therefore interesting that the 'legal origins' authors give a very specific historic explanation for the differences between civil and common law. They claim that in England during the seventeenth and eighteenth centuries, during the development of the capitalist economy, English lawyers were on the winning side of the Glorious Revolution and therefore worked together with property owners in order to protect property and freedom of contract with the common law system. On the other side of the Channel and much later, the French revolution was directed against the monarchy and against a monarchist judiciary so that the *Code Civil* aimed at constricting the power of the judges in pursuit of social goals.[24]

These and other specific historical explanations are very important, but one should also look beyond such historical contingencies: the contrast between private and public regulation is deeply embedded in social structures and paths of social evolution. Such a more structural view will be outlined here, beginning with ancient Roman law.

[23] See R. Stürner, 'Privatautonomie und Wettbewerb unter der Hegemonie der angloamerikanischen Rechtskultur?' (2010) 210 *AcP* 105 at 1/46.

[24] LaPorta *et al.*, 'The Economic Consequences of Legal Origins', 303; P. Mahoney, The Common Law and Economic Growth: Hayek might be Right' (2001) 30 *Journal of Legal Studies* 503–25 at 504–5.

Public actions in Roman law

Although it is often said that the civil law is based on Roman law, the ancient Roman law actually had important instruments of private litigation that are largely unheard of in today's civil law systems. In particular, in Rome there were many *actiones populares*, meaning actions that could be brought by any citizen, regardless of whether he was affected by the matter. Some of these actions related to the use of public roads, waterways and markets, but an action could also be brought by any citizen, not exclusively by an injured party, against somebody who poured liquids out of high buildings or who endangered the safety of the street by positioning dangerous objects on his balcony.[25] Variations of such 'popular actions' persisted, entering into medieval English law and are mentioned in Blackstone's *Commentaries*.[26] This ancient connection between Roman law and the common law styles of private litigation is often overlooked.

What does it mean with regard to regulatory style when we have a 'private' popular action that can be brought by any citizen in circumstances in which, today, we would rather see the police as competent to intervene? It surely does not mean that the Romans did not know of a distinction between private and public law,[27] but it means that they did not attribute the task of social regulation exclusively to the state and its authorities. Private and public competences were not strictly divided, and it was every citizen's right to intervene, and to get rewarded financially for such intervention with what we would today call punitive damages, in the interest of social goals such as functioning streets, secure cities and markets.

In ancient Roman society, public order was therefore seen as a legitimate private interest, unlike today, where public issues are assigned largely to the hands of the police and other government agencies. However, the legacy of popular actions is still existent in some legal systems and even the US class action or other similar instruments may be seen as distant relatives of these ancient instruments.

The Roman popular action therefore shows that the 'public regulation vs. private litigation' distinction drawn by the legal origins scholars does

[25] Dig. 9.3.1.pr, 9.3.5.5 (*actio de effusis vel deiectis*); Dig. 9.3.5.6; 9.3.5.13 (*actio de positis vel suspensis*); for a detailed account of the Roman popular actions see A. Halfmeier, *Popularklagen im Privatrecht* (Tübingen: 2006); see also F. Schulz, *Classical Roman Law* (Oxford University Press, 1951) 43.

[26] Blackstone, *Commentaries on the Laws of England*, II 437, IV 399.

[27] See Justinian's Institutions at 1.4.

not exist *per se*, but depends on specific social structures. While it was not much developed in Roman law, it returned as a much larger issue in modern times. In the Middle Ages and their feudal system, one could probably argue that everything was public law in a sense since relations between people, including many important economic relations, were based mainly on pre-defined status or other hierarchical relations.[28] The rise of modern private law in the context of the development of a market-based economy marks a clear break with such medieval traditions.

The private sphere as a central concept of modern capitalism

As a conscious departure from medieval times, the rise of capitalism meant that a 'private market sphere', a sphere which was supposed to be free of feudal intervention, was carved out of society. That sphere was supposed to be governed only by market forces, i.e. in legal terms by property rights and freely concluded contracts to exchange such rights.[29] This is what is meant by private law in today's sense and what the 'legal origins' theory defends as being not only in the interests of especially successful market participants, but also in the interests of society as a whole. The same argument was made by Adam Smith but, at his time, without any statistical or econometric evidence.[30] The liberal concept of private law is therefore closely linked to the idea of the market-driven regulation of society and thus to a focus on private litigation and the private enforcement of rights.

Although to some extent we take this concept of private law for granted in today's Western societies, it cannot be stressed enough how radically this liberal concept of private law broke with previous traditions and even with common sense. To take private property seriously means, *inter alia*, to free individual property owners from all social concerns and to separate most moral or social concerns from private law.[31] Whether your neighbour is needy or sick or has five children without shoes in the wintertime is of no concern to private law. Social

[28] In the sense of the famous phrase describing the movement 'from status to contract' by Henry Maine, *Ancient Law* (1861), 149.

[29] See the classical account of this idea by C. B. Macpherson, *The Political Theory of Possessive Individualism* (Oxford: 1962).

[30] A. Smith, *An Inquiry into the Nature and Causes of the Wealth of Nations* (1776; Oxford: 1998), 291.

[31] N. Luhmann, 'Zur Funktion der subjektiven Rechte', reprinted in N. Luhmann, *Ausdifferenzierungen des Rechts* (Frankfurt/Main: 1999), 360–73.

welfare would come about either spontaneously by the means of Adam Smith's invisible hand or, in so far as the market cannot guarantee sufficient welfare for everybody, alternatively, through taxes or other government intervention and redistribution, but not through private law or private litigation.

From today's perspective, this classical liberal model can be called extremist or fundamentalist, and it is not surprising that a strong counter-model evolved: during much of the late nineteenth and early twentieth century, socialism was regarded as the only viable alternative. Socialist legal and political thinking, at least in its classical version, clearly sought to undo the creation of the private economic sphere and to reintegrate the economic sphere into the public sphere: after the Russian October Revolution, Lenin made the famous statement that 'we do not acknowledge anything "private", but for us in the economic area everything is public law and not private'.[32] In this sense, the economy would become a matter of public concern again, which would thus open up the possibility of democratic control over the economic sphere. In this respect, socialist private law is something of a contradiction in itself.[33] In so far as it existed at all, it was regarded as a sector of minor importance; consequently, private litigation did not play a big role in socialist societies.

However, the idea of socialism plays a lesser role in today's discussions on European consumer law, and it is only included here to present a full sketch of the historical developments on which all strategies regarding the enforcement of consumer law have to build. In fact, socialism is used not as a strategy of legal or political theory anymore, but rather, as a dirty word to defame consumer law, for example when a well-known German professor of commercial law recently called the possibility of actions by consumer and environmental associations a result of 'neo-socialist theory'.[34] Such an outbreak only shows how carelessly this swearword is used, since a true socialist legal theory would call for the complete democratic and thus public regulation of the economy and not for giving associations the right to initiate private litigation.

[32] V. I. Lenin, Note for D.I. Kurski of 20 February 1922, reprinted in (German edn) *Werke*, vol. XXXVI, 550 (Berlin 1971); for a detailed account of the Russian discussion see N. Reich, *Sozialismus und Zivilrecht* (Frankfurt/Main: 1972), 22 and 133–6.

[33] But see Reich *Sozialismus und Zivilrecht passim*, for an extensive account of the theory and reality of 'socialist private law'.

[34] F. J. Säcker, *Die Einordnung der Verbandsklage in das System des Privatrechts* (Munich: 2006) at 43; see my book review in (2007) 120 *Zeitschrift für Zivilprozess* 393–7.

However, this vilification of private associations' litigation rights brings us to a curious dilemma: private enforcement is at once seen by the (mainly US American) free market proponents in the 'legal origins' theory as the ideal form of maximising social welfare; on the other hand it is viewed negatively by European conservatives as bringing society to the brink of socialism.

Access to justice in consumer law: a democratic ideal?

One of the reasons for this divided view seems to be that increasing private litigation to defend consumer rights historically has been a rather leftist strategy in the late twentieth-century Western world. In view of the failure of real socialism, progressive Western legal theory looked to new ways of increasing public control over the economic sector without advocating full-scale socialism, that is without demanding the expropriation of capitalist property and transferring it into the hands of the working class. Instead, these progressive scholars invented the consumer as, one might say, a new revolutionary subject. The consumer took the place of the working class which no longer seemed capable of bringing about revolution, let alone a better society. Where socialist theory tried to regulate production by replacing market forces with democratic decisions, the new consumer movement now accepted the capitalist mode of production, but tried to reform the economy and society from the other end by regulating consumption and not production.

This tendency was complemented by the 'access to justice' movement in the 1970s which argued for increased litigation possibilities in order to bring about social change through private litigation.[35] This had worked well in the American civil rights movement and was now expanded to consumer law, environmental law and other emerging social issues.

From the social reform through litigation perspective, private litigation to vindicate consumer and other individual rights was not only instrumental to achieving certain goals (such as maximising social welfare) but, in addition, participation through citizen suits, class actions or associations' actions and other forms of private litigation was seen as an end in itself in the sense of allowing for more participation in the regulation of the economy and society. If one looks at consumer law textbooks today, the vindication of consumer rights through private

[35] See, in particular, M. Cappelletti and B. Garth (eds.), *Access to Justice* (Sijthoff and Noordhott; 1978/9), vols. I–IV.

litigation is sometimes still glorified as a democratisation of society or a way to more participation of the part of the individual in society.[36]

It is the significant achievement of the 'legal origins' authors that they succeeded in putting such utopian ideas to an end. The cold hard view of these economists exposes the simple function of private litigation: it reallocates utility or, to put it more simply, shifts money from A to B.

In the American class action, probably the most powerful instrument of private litigation on this planet, this becomes crystal clear: while in theory consumer or other individual rights are vindicated through the class action, in fact it serves mainly to reallocate money from the defendant's deep pocket into the pockets of the plaintiffs' attorney and on the way there, it may leave some breadcrumbs for the actual holders of the right in question. This means that private litigation does not change the capitalist model of the economy at all. On the contrary, it is perfectly in line with Adam Smith and other proponents of free market: just as, according to Smith, the baker acts purely out of self-interest in making bread and still does something worthwhile for society as a whole, so does the entrepreneurial plaintiffs' attorney who acts in his own interest but also contributes to the ordering of the economy.

Even consumer associations cannot be seen as elements of democratic participation in any meaningful sense. At least in Germany, they hardly have any members, are financed by the government and are therefore only a form of quasi-government that disguises itself as a private initiative. In other countries, the main consumer advocates are state-appointed ombudsmen or other quasi-government agencies such as the Office of Fair Trading in the United Kingdom.

Outlook

The 'legal origins' theory as it has been described here may be controversial and in parts even faulty. Furthermore, it is unclear what will be left of it after the major financial crisis of the last two years which emanated mainly from the common law countries even though, under the theory, they should be the spearheads of superior financial markets, enhanced standards of protection and better economic development.

[36] See e.g. H. Micklitz, in *Münchener Kommentar zur Zivilprozessordnung*, 3rd edn (Munich, 2007), §3 UKlaG margin no. 5: the European rules on associations' actions are seen as a development of 'civil rights'.

Nevertheless, the 'legal origins' theory is an important contribution to the field of consumer and other regulatory law if we see it in its historical context: where public regulation has retreated and is still retreating from certain economic and social areas, a regulatory gap appears that can and must be filled with private litigation. However, such gap-filling through private litigation cannot be seen as an evolution of democracy or of participation in social matters, but is, rather, to be regarded mainly instrumental.

Private litigation therefore is a compensatory instrument that may work well under certain circumstances, especially if the actors are driven by their own greed or other selfish motives. In this reliance on individual vices to create public benefits, private litigation is largely based on the same principles as the capitalist economy itself. It therefore appears as the typical form of regulation in an age of deregulation and it is not a coincidence that the discussion on private litigation instruments has become so much stronger in Europe over the last decades.

In that respect, the 'legal origins' theory presents to us private litigation as a potentially efficient tool which is supported by economists precisely in view of this potential efficiency. For lawyers and legislators, however, efficiency cannot be the end of the story. If a certain goal is set, then an understanding of the efficiency parameters for the appropriate instruments as they have been studied in the 'legal origins' theory is certainly worthwhile. But to set a goal, value judgements are needed, especially by legislators and others involved in the law-making process. How acceptable do we find a model of society in which not only the economy in a strict sense but also many other areas, for example public transport, utilities, health, education, savings for retirement, are governed by private law in the sense that these areas are basically regulated by market transactions? These waves of deregulation and thus the increased hegemony of market-orientated and private law deserve critical appraisal and should not be taken as a natural evolution or the only possible form of governance.[37]

Nevertheless, in so far as deregulation has already taken place in European societies, the 'legal origins' theory shows that private litigation is a useful and necessary tool to achieve certain regulatory or social goals in such a context. Litigation rights, including class actions and similar

[37] For a German perspective and critique of purely market-based solutions see Stürner 'Privatautonomie', and even more extensively R. Stürner, *Markt und Wettbewerb über alles?* (Munich: 2007).

procedures, should therefore be extended and improved in all of these areas. For example, it seems no coincidence that the 'legal origins' theory deals extensively with investor protection given the context of a US scheme for retirement benefits which relies almost exclusively on private savings and investments. If people are forced to enter into market transactions even in this important area, the legal and social system must also give them the litigation tools necessary to achieve optimum outputs in terms of social welfare.

On the other hand, the 'legal origins' theory does not help us in deciding whether we actually want a society in which almost every area is regulated through market means and where private litigation is the cure for every illness. Even though Europe seems to lean in that direction today, this may well change in the future if scepticism regarding market-based solutions arises again. At this moment therefore, private litigation seems to be a very important part of the consumer law puzzle, but this may change according to future shifts in the public–private paradigm.

16

Advertising, free speech and the consumer

PAUL WRAGG

Introduction

In May 2008 the Consumer Protection from Unfair Trading Regulations 2008 ('the Consumer Regulations') and the Business Protection from Misleading Marketing Regulations 2008 ('the Business Regulations'; together, 'the regulations') came into force. These regulations implement the Unfair Commercial Practices Directive 2005/29 and the Misleading and Comparative Advertising Directive 2006/114. In particular, the Consumer Regulations prohibit unfair commercial practices (including advertising and marketing), aimed at consumers, relating to goods and services whereas the Business Regulations introduce measures relating to comparative advertising (both those aimed at consumers and those aimed at other businesses). Ervine, for example, describes the regulations as 'one of the most significant changes in consumer protection for a generation'.[1]

The aims of the regulations connect with broader and, as yet, largely unresolved issues relating to the potential scope of the freedom of expression clause contained within Article 10 of the European Convention on Human Rights ('the convention') to protect, or otherwise affect claims involving advertising. In general terms, UK case law demonstrates a fairly sporadic approach to the protection of freedom of expression under Article 10. As other commentators have noted,[2] the courts' approach seems to oscillate between extreme patterns of investigation into whether the interference with Article 10 is necessary or not so that in some cases the analysis is vigorous[3] and in others more markedly

University of Leeds.

[1] W. C. H. Ervine, 'The Consumer Protection from Unfair Trading Regulations 2008' (2008) *Scots Law Times* 147.

[2] See e.g. Eric Barendt, *Freedom of Speech,* 2nd edn (Oxford University Press, 2005); H. M. Fenwick and G. P. Phillipson, *Media Freedom under the Human Rights Act* (Oxford University Press, 2006).

[3] See e.g. *Redmond-Bate* v. *DPP* (1999) 7 BHRC 375.

lacklustre.[4] As will be shown, this pattern is evident in commercial expression cases as well. By surveying the few decided cases, it will become apparent that the UK judiciary's approach to commercial expression under Article 10 is less than fully formed. As a consequence of this, and the judiciary's rather erratic approach to the protection of free speech, the operation of the regulations may be affected to the extent that the protection of commercial expression impinges upon the realisation of its aims. Alternatively, the regulations may serve as a useful vehicle for clarifying the extent of the right to commercial expression in the UK. In either event, the courts' approach to the enforcement of the regulations should be significant.

Admittedly, since the regulations seek to prohibit misleading information being provided to traders and consumers alike, it may not be immediately apparent where the conflict with free speech principle will arise. Yet, it is submitted, such conflict could occur in two scenarios in particular: first, where the expression is treated as political speech by the courts despite being in the form of an advertisement; secondly, by virtue of the Article 10 claim being treated seriously, vigorous judicial scrutiny of the interference with expression may result in the regulations being enforced in narrower circumstances than were otherwise anticipated. In order to make these points some preliminary discussion of the courts' approach to freedom of commercial expression is required. Therefore, having set out the relevant features of the regulations, the discussion will introduce some of quirks and peculiarities about the judicial approach to commercial expression both in the UK and in the European Court of Human Rights ('ECHR').

The regulations

The regulations broadly seek to prohibit misleading information being provided to consumers or traders for the purposes of inducing sales. The Consumer Regulations specifically prohibit the use of 'unfair commercial practices'. Regulations 3(3) and 3(4) define a commercial practice as unfair if: it contravenes the requirements of professional diligence and it materially distorts the economic behaviour of the average consumer with regard to the product; it is a misleading action or omission; it is aggressive; or, if it is one of the commercial practices listed in Schedule 1

[4] See e.g. *R.* v. *Debnath* (2005) EWCA Crim 3472 or *Sanders* v. *Kingston* [2005] EWHC 1145 (Admin).

as unfair in all circumstances. It is an offence under the Consumer Regulations to engage in these prohibited activities, punishable by a fine and/or imprisonment of up to two years.[5] Commercial practice is defined as:

> any act, omission, course of conduct, representation or commercial communication (including advertising and marketing) by a trader, which is directly concerned with the promotion, sale or supply of a product to or from consumers, whether occurring before, during or after a commercial transaction (if any) in relation to a product.[6]

The Consumer Regulations adopt the ECJ standard of the 'average consumer' as the benchmark for determining whether a practice is misleading. This standard assumes that the average consumer is 'reasonably well informed, reasonably observant and circumspect'.[7] The Consumer Regulations further provide that where the commercial practice is directed to a particular group of consumers[8] or where a clearly identifiable group of consumers is particularly vulnerable to the practice or underlying product[9] then the reference to the average consumer should be read as a reference to the average member of that group. Regulation 2(6) does, however, explicitly recognise that this latter provision, aimed at vulnerable groups, is without prejudice to the common and legitimate advertising practice of making exaggerated statements that are not meant to be taken seriously.

The Business Regulations follow a similar format and specifically prohibit advertising which misleads traders and regulates comparative advertising so as to ensure that the advertisement accurately compares products without misleading or confusing traders or otherwise discrediting, denigrating or imitating competitors.[10] Regulation 2(1) defines advertising as 'any form of representation which is made in connection with a trade, business, craft or profession in order to promote the supply or

[5] Regs. 8–13. [6] Reg. 2(1).

[7] Reg. 2(2). See *Procter and Gamble* v. *Office for Harmonisation in the Internal Market (Trade Marks and Designs)*, C486–472/01P, [2004] *ETMR* 88; *Gut Springenheide and Tusky* v. *Oberkreisdirector des Kreises Steinfurt-Amt fur Lebensmiteluberwachung* [1999] 1 *CMLRev* 1383. See further J. Davis, 'Locating the Average Consumer: his Judicial Origins, Intellectual Influences and Current Role in European Trade Mark Law' (2005) 183 *Intellectual Property Quarterly.*

[8] Reg. 2(4).

[9] I.e. due to a mental or physical infirmity, age or credulity in a way which the trader could reasonably be expected to foresee and where the practice is likely to materially distort the economic behaviour only of that group, Reg. 2(5).

[10] Regs. 3 and 4.

transfer of a product'. It is an offence under the Business Regulations for a trader to engage in misleading advertising, punishable by fine and/or imprisonment for up to two years.[11]

A common feature of the regulations is that only those designated with enforcement responsibilities may initiate proceedings for breach of the regulations. This feature caused some consternation for the British Brands Group, among others, who had lobbied for affected companies to be able to initiate claims themselves.[12] Instead, the power to enforce is reserved for the Office of Fair Trading (OFT) and local authority trading standards services.[13] The regulations do encourage the enforcement authority to 'have regard to the desirability of encouraging control' of unfair commercial practices/advertising 'by such established means as it considers appropriate having regard to all circumstances', which in the case of advertising could be a referral to the Advertising Standards Agency (ASA) in the first instance.[14] This feature may explain why, so far, only two cases involving the regulations have been decided.[15] Both cases are High Court decisions although neither provides substantial insights into how the regulations will operate in practice and, indeed, neither was brought by the enforcement authorities: the first concerned permission to amend the claimant's case pleaded case to include alleged breaches of the regulations whereas in the second the claimant's allegation of a breach of the Consumer Regulations was dismissed on the basis

[11] Regs. 6 and 7.

[12] See questions put by Lorely Burt MP and Mark Prisk MP to Gareth Thomas, Parliamentary Under-Secretary of State for Business, Enterprise and Regulatory Reform when the First Delegated Legislation Committee considered the Draft Regulations on 6 May 2008; http://www.publications.parliament.uk/pa/cm200708/cmgeneral/deleg1/080506/80506s01.htm.

[13] The duty to enforce is to be found in Reg. 19 of the Consumer Regulations and Reg. 13 of the Business Regulations. 'Enforcement authority' is defined in Reg. 2 of both sets of regulations as the OFT and every local weights and measures authority in Great Britain. See also *Consumer Protection from Unfair Trading: Guidance on the UK Regulations (May 2008) implementing the Unfair Commercial Practices Directive* produced by the Office of Fair Trading (2008), 50.

[14] The ASA will investigate advertisements on radio and TV, in magazines and newspapers, posters (but not flyposters), leaflets, brochures, direct mail, cinema commercials, circulars, internet, commercial e-mail, SMS text message and advertisements on CD ROMS, DVDs, video and fax. The ASA adjudicates on breaches of the relevant advertising code (e.g. non-broadcast CAP code, Radio Advertising Standards Code, TV Advertising Standards Code) and, where such a breach occurs, will direct the offender to remedy the breach by, for example, discontinuing the practice. Where the offender refuses, the ASA can refer the matter to the OFT or OFCOM.

[15] *Tiscali UK Ltd* v. *British Telecommunications Plc* (2008) EWHC 3129 (QB); *McGuffick* v. *Royal Bank of Scotland Plc* (2009) EWHC 2386 (Comm).

that, as noted, the regulations do not confer any right of action upon individuals.[16]

As other commentators have noted,[17] the regulations make broad, sweeping changes that affect a range of pre-existing consumer protection measures. This was required by the Unfair Commercial Practices Directive 2005/29 in particular (which the Consumer Regulations implement). Since it is a maximum harmonisation directive, the government was burdened with the painstaking task of ensuring that any national law more stringent than the directive was repealed and replaced. Twenty-three laws were changed and thirty-one unfair sales practices created by the introduction of the regulations. Indeed, such was the scope of the changes that the introduction of the regulations had to be delayed by nearly two months.[18] When considering the draft regulations, the delegated legislation committee raised many questions, particularly as to how the regulations would operate in practice; how traders should be expected to cope with the extensiveness of the new laws; why the new laws do not permit consumers to escape bad bargains; and, moreover, why affected companies could not instigate proceedings for breach of the regulations.[19] In the context of a discussion that focused on these important central issues, it is unsurprising that no questions were raised about the potential free speech implications of enforcing the regulations. Indeed, the potential conflict with freedom of expression may not seem obviously pressing. After all, what free speech difficulties do the prohibition of misleading advertising or the regulation of comparative advertising actually present? Moreover, it may be wondered what advertising has to do with freedom of speech in any event.

Yet it is submitted that freedom of expression concerns are raised by the regulations and, while it is important not to exaggerate the potential conflicts that may arise, these issues may influence the development of the regulations. It will be argued that despite the lack of discussion about

[16] *McGuffick*, [87]–[91].

[17] See Ervine, fn. 1; G. Howells, 'The End of an Era – Implementing the Unfair Commercial Practices Directive in the United Kingdom: Punctual Criminal Law Gives Way to a General Criminal/Civil Law Standard' (2009) *JBL* 183; 'Unfair Competition and Comparative Advertising: New Regulations Criminalise Misleading Marketing and Unfair Commercial Practices and Regulate Comparative Advertising' (2008) *European Intellectual Property Review* 71; C. Cathcart and J. Williams, 'The Highly Detailed General Principles of the Consumer Protection from Unfair Trading Regulations 2008' (2009) *Scottish Law Gazette* 24; S. Singleton, 'The Consumer Protection from Unfair Trading Regulations' (2009) *Computer and Telecommunications Law Review* 77.

[18] See responses given by Mr Thomas, n. 12. [19] N. 12.

these free speech issues prior to implementation (and since), it remains important that both regulators and judges are aware of the possible issues since these issues, as they arise, will shape the manner in which the Regulations are enforced; section 3 of the Human Rights Act 1998 (the 'HRA') requires subordinate (and primary) legislation to be interpreted compatibly with the convention rights.[20] In order to fully explain those concerns, it is necessary to consider, first, the judicial approach to freedom of commercial expression post-HRA so that the place of advertising within the concept of free speech can be established, particularly since the connection between commercial expression and free speech may not be obvious to some. Having done so, and by reference to recent case law, it will be argued that in certain circumstances the effectiveness of the regulations may be affected either because the court treats the advertising as a form of political expression (and so affords it the maximum level of protection) or else, because it takes the free speech claim seriously, the court upholds the provisions of the regulations in narrower circumstances than might otherwise have been anticipated.

Judicial treatment of commercial expression in the UK and ECtHR: quirks and peculiarities

The right to freedom of expression under Article 10 of the convention was given further effect by the implementation of the HRA. Article 10(1) guarantees the right to freedom of expression[21] and Article 10(2) sets out the circumstances in which that right may be legitimately interfered with by the state.[22] Since the right to freedom of expression is not absolute, interferences with it are permissible so long as the restriction meets a 'pressing social need' and is proportionate to the achievement of that aim. While it is now easy enough to identify the source of the right

[20] For recent commentary on the use of s. 3 see P. Sales, 'A Comparison of the Principle of Legality and Section 3 of the Human Rights Act 1998' (2009) 125 *LQR* 598.

[21] Everyone has the right to freedom of expression. This right shall include freedom to hold opinions and to receive and impart information and ideas without interference by public authority and regardless of frontiers. This Article shall not prevent states from requiring the licensing of broadcasting, television or cinema enterprises.

[22] The exercise of these freedoms, since it carries with it duties and responsibilities, may be subject to such formalities, conditions, restrictions or penalties as are prescribed by law and are necessary in a democratic society in the interests of national security, territorial integrity or public safety, for the prevention of disorder or crime, for the protection of health or morals, for the protection for the reputation or rights of others, for preventing the disclosure of information received in confidence or for maintaining the authority and impartiality of the judiciary.

(prior to the HRA, the notion of a 'right' to free speech in the UK was highly contested),[23] identification of the concept governing the right proves to be much more elusive. In theory, the scope of a constitutional right to freedom of speech could be elucidated and defended in any number of ways.[24] It is a common complaint among academic commentators that the UK judiciary's approach to freedom of expression is generally under-theorised.[25] Several justificatory arguments have been advanced to defend the protection afforded freedom of speech and, by virtue of those arguments, define the parameters of the concept. There is a wealth of established academic commentary that synthesises and develops the more commonly used theories or else proposes new ones. Unfortunately, this rich vein remains largely untapped by the UK judiciary.[26] This is particularly significant because, notwithstanding that the very essence of the concept of free speech is often regarded as controversial (why *should* speech be free from state interference?),[27] the idea that the guarantee should extend beyond purely political speech to cover commercial expression is a constant source of academic disagreement.[28] Yet the controversy remains largely unrecognised by the UK judiciary and, similarly, is rarely discussed by UK academic commentators.[29]

[23] See discussion in Fenwick and Phillipson, *Media Freedom*, n. 2 for a concise history of the difficulties involved.

[24] Frederick Schauer's seminal work *Free Speech: a Philosophical Enquiry* (Cambridge University Press, 1982) remains an illuminating discussion of the philosophical issues surrounding the elucidation of the concept.

[25] See e.g. Ivan Hare, 'Crosses, Crescents and Sacred Cows: Criminalising Incitement to Religious Hatred' (2006) *Public Law* 521, 526.

[26] Notable exceptions include *Reynolds* v. *Times Newspapers* (2001) 2 AC 127 and *ex parte Simms* (2000) 2 AC 115 which makes *some* reference to these different theories of free speech.

[27] Furthermore P. Horton and L. A. Alexander, 'The Impossibility of a Free Speech Principle' (1983) 78 *Northwestern University Law Review* 319 and S. Fish, *There's No Such Thing as Free Speech and It's a Good Thing Too* (Oxford University Press, 1994) have questioned whether a satisfactory concept of free speech could ever be elucidated.

[28] See, for example, Eric Barendt, *Freedom of Speech* (Oxford University Press, 1985), who is fiercely opposed to it and, in favour of it, see, for example, Steven Shiffrin, 'The First Amendment and Economic Regulation: Away from a General Theory of the First Amendment' (1984) 78 *Northwestern University Law Review* 1212; Martin Redish, 'The First Amendment in the Marketplace: Commercial Speech and the Values of Free Expression' (1971) 39 *George Washington Law Review* 429, discussed below.

[29] But see Eric Barendt, *Freedom of Speech* (2005); C. Munro, 'The Value of Commercial Speech' (2003) *CLJ* 134; M. H. Randall, 'Commercial Speech under the European Convention on Human Rights: Subordinate or Equal?' (2006) *Human Rights Law Review* 53; and R. Caddell, 'Freedom of Commercial Speech and the UK Courts' (2005) *CLJ* 274 (case comment).

It seems peculiar that the UK judiciary does not engage with the rich vein of academic debate on the scope of freedom of speech particularly since – perhaps as a direct consequence of the failure to do so – the UK courts' normative stance on commercial expression is sketchy, at best, as demonstrated by the limited number of decisions cases involving such expression post-HRA. The first Article 10 case post-HRA to concern commercial expression, *R (on the application of British American Tobacco UK Ltd and others)* v. *Secretary of State for Health*,[30] suggested that the UK judiciary might adopt a conservative approach so that the Article 10 right in respect of commercial expression would be upheld only in narrow circumstances.[31] Briefly, the case concerned an application for judicial review by six companies involved in the tobacco industry challenging the legality of the Tobacco Advertising and Promotion (Point of Sale) Regulations 2004 on the basis that the ban on advertising tobacco products in the UK constituted a disproportionate restriction that impeded the 'very essence' of their freedom of commercial expression. In rejecting the application, McCombe J found that since 'freedom of commercial expression has been treated traditionally [in the ECHR] as of less significance than freedom of political or artistic expression'[32] it was not 'disproportionate to meet the objective of promoting health by restricting advertising at POS to a single advert of the type to be permitted'.[33]

However, the emergence of a more liberal approach to commercial expression can be found in the cases that followed *British American Tobacco* starting with the decision in *R (on the application of North Cyprus Tourism Centre Ltd)* v. *Transport for London*,[34] in which the claimant had sought judicial review of the decision of Transport for London to stop carrying advertisements promoting holidays in North Cyprus. The advertisements were removed following complaints that North Cyprus was not a country recognised by the UK government because it was illegally occupied by Turkey. It was not suggested by the claimant that the advertisements were a form of political expression (and, therefore, of particular significance): on the contrary, the claimant argued that the advertisements were wholly unconnected to the political landscape of the region (bearing only an innocuous strapline). Rather than find that the speech concerned was of limited significance in Article 10 terms and therefore capable of being readily interfered with, Newman J in

[30] (2004) EWHC 2493. [31] See Caddell, n. 29. [32] *Ibid.* [28].
[33] *Ibid.* [51]. [34] (2005) EWHC 1698.

the Divisional Court upheld the Article 10 claim on the basis that since the defendant had not sufficiently identified a legitimate aim in removing the advertisements[35] and nor had it sufficiently demonstrated a pressing social need for the interference,[36] there had been a violation. Thus the decision demonstrates a preparedness to scrutinise the necessity of the interference beyond something superficial and in a manner that is not influenced by any *ad hoc* assessment of the merits of the expression itself (which has been the criticism made in one high profile political expression case in particular).[37] In other words, it demonstrates a willingness to take the free speech claims of pure advertising seriously.

The Divisional Court decision in *Red Dot Technologies Ltd* v. *Apollo Fire Detectors Ltd*[38] and Court of Appeal decision in *Boehringer Ingelheim Ltd* v. *Vetplus Ltd*[39] provide further signs of a more liberal approach to commercial expression. Both cases involved comparative advertising. The case of *Boehringer* concerned an application for injunctive relief against Vetplus Ltd after it had threatened to publish an advertisement displaying its findings conducted on a dog care product made by Boehringer (which was similar to a product sold by Vetplus Ltd), which showed that the level of active ingredient present was far less than that advertised on the packaging. Part of the reasoning for rejecting Boehringer's injunctive relief claim centred on the 'important issues of free speech' at stake in the advertisement. In *Red Dot Technologies*, decided shortly after *Boehringer*, Richards J noted that 'comparative advertising is also a form of expression which, if fair and not misleading, is in the public interest'.[40]

Most recently, in the High Court decision in *Ajinomoto Sweeteners Europe SAS* v. *ASDA Stores Ltd (No. 2)*[41] the defendant supermarket raised a free speech defence to a malicious falsehood claim relating to the claimant's business of manufacturing and supplying 'aspartame', an artificial sweetener. The claim centred on ASDA's own brand product

[35] *Ibid.*, [93]. [36] *Ibid.*, [95]–[96].

[37] See the criticism levelled against the House of Lords and Lord Hoffmann in particular following the finding in *R. (on the application of ProLife Alliance)* v. *British Broadcasting Corporation* [2003] UKHL 23 that ProLife's political campaign had 'virtually nothing to do with the fact that a general election was taking place' [68], as part of his assessment that Article 10 had not been unduly interfered with. See Eric Barendt, 'Free Speech and Abortion' (2003) *Public Law* 580; Fenwick and Phillipson, *Media Freedom*, 586–92; I. Cram, *Contested Words: Legal Restrictions on Freedom of Expression in Liberal Democracies* (Ashgate, 2006).

[38] (2007) EWHC 1166 (Ch). [39] (2007) EWCA Civ 583.

[40] N. 38, [13]. [41] (2009) EWHC 1717 (QB).

range 'Good for you' which contained the statement 'No hidden nasties*', below which was the statement '*no artificial colours or flavours, no aspartame & no hydrogenated fat'. The claimants claimed that the inclusion of aspartame in this list implied that the artificial sweetener was a 'nasty' of the same magnitude as hydrogenated fat and, therefore, would scare customers into avoiding products containing aspartame. However, the court disagreed with that inference: it did not agree that the wording on the packaging meant that aspartame *was* potentially harmful or unhealthy but rather that if the consumer *thought* aspartame might be bad for them then this product was for them.[42] Of particular interest is that Tugendhat J distinguished between packaging that expressed information in 'severe black and upright fonts' and that which displayed it using 'what I call . . . cheerful and informal colours'. The former 'are to be understood seriously' and the latter 'are to be understood as mere advertising, with little, if any, content or endorsement from the advertiser. The function of these parts of the packaging would be reasonably understood as being to attract attention, rather than to inform.'[43] The implications of this decision on the operation of the regulations, if any, are discussed below.

The divergence in the level of treatment with which commercial expression claims are handled does raise issues about the normative position that the UK judiciary is aligned to when determining Article 10 cases. The courts' sketchy approach to these normative issues seems to contribute to the divergent standards of scrutiny that are to be applied when assessing the necessity of interference. For example, the lacklustre scrutiny in *British Tobacco* contrasts with a more rigorous investigation in *North Cyprus Tourism Centre Ltd.* Surveying this limited number of cases it seems that the court has largely embraced the ECHR approach to commercial expression, albeit without any serious scrutiny of the sufficiency, desirability or conceptual limits of the underlying rationale that may be said to accompany that approach.[44] The UK court's approach

[42] *Ibid.*, [63]–[85]. [43] *Ibid.*, [66].

[44] Section 2 of the HRA requires the UK judiciary to take ECtHR jurisprudence 'into account' when deciding convention rights cases. It is evident from leading case law that the judiciary treats s. 2 as an obligation to 'keep pace' with Strasbourg jurisprudence, see *R. (on the application of Ullah)* v. *Special Adjudicator* (2004) 2 AC 323 and, more recently, *Huang* v. *Secretary of State for the Home Department* (2007) 2 AC 167. There is a fascinating debate about whether the UK judiciary has interpreted this obligation too narrowly and should instead more actively scrutinise and develop the principles governing the Convention rights. See R. Masterman, 'Taking the Strasbourg Jurisprudence into Account: Developing a "municipal law of human rights" under the Human

mirrors, superficially at least, the ECHR's methodology for determining Article 10 claims, which is to examine the necessity of the interference with the expression at stake once satisfied that Article 10 is engaged. As its jurisprudence demonstrates, the ECHR applies a low threshold to the definition of expression;[45] thus it has been largely uncomplicated for litigants to establish that commercial expression is covered by Article 10. In determining the level of protection to be afforded, it has been observed that the most significant factor is the extent to which the expression connects with the democratic process.[46] Consequently, it has been said that the ECHR adopts a hierarchical approach to the process of scrutinising the necessity of interference so that while interferences with political expression are highly scrutinised, the level of examination where commercial expression is at stake is a lot less.[47]

To some extent this analysis is reflected in the Strasbourg jurisprudence where it is quite common for the commercial expression claim to be unsuccessful.[48] For example in *VgT* v. *Switzerland*, the ECHR emphasised that the exceptions to Article 10(2) must be narrowly construed and convincingly established 'particularly where the nature of the speech is political rather than commercial',[49] thus confirming the lesser standard of scrutiny required where commercial expression is at stake. To some extent this lesser standard results from the wide margin of appreciation that the ECHR affords to Member States to restrict commercial expression, particularly where competition[50] and advertising standards[51] are at stake. As noted above, this lesser standard of scrutiny is apparent in the UK court decision in *British American Tobacco*, in this case in the context of public health concerns.[52] However, as Fenwick and Phillipson argue,[53] there are inconsistencies in this hierarchical pattern of protection, particularly where the speech, although political in nature,

Rights Act' (2005) *ICLQ* 907 and 'Section 2(1) of the Human Rights Act 1998: Binding Domestic Courts to Strasbourg?' (2004) *PL* 725; see also J. Lewis, 'The European Ceiling on Human Rights' (2007) *PL* 720.

[45] Thus, for example, pornographic material is covered, see e.g. *Hoare* v. *UK* (1997) EHRLR 678, *Scherer* v. *Switzerland* (1994) 18 EHRR 276.

[46] L. Wildhaber, 'The Right to Offend, Shock or Disturb? Aspects of Freedom of Expression under the European Convention on Human Rights' (2001) 36 *The Irish Jurist* 17.

[47] D. J. Harris, M. O'Boyle and C. Warbrick, *Law of the European Convention of Human Rights* (Butterworths, 1995), 397.

[48] See e.g. *Casado Coca* v. *Spain* (1994) 18 EHRR 1.

[49] (2002) 34 EHRR 4, [66].

[50] *Jacubowski* v. *Germany* (1994) 19 EHRR 64.

[51] *Casado Coca* v. *Spain* (1994) 18 EHRR 1.

[52] See discussion above.

[53] Fenwick and Phillipson, *Media Freedom*, 50–72.

touches on religious sensibilities,[54] so that the usual high level of scrutiny is not always readily apparent. Likewise with commercial expression, some refinement to the analysis is required in light of recent Strasbourg jurisprudence where strong protection of commercial expression is apparent in the court's judgment. As the decision in *Krone Verlag GmbH* v. *Austria (No. 3)*[55] demonstrates, the conferment of this discretion to the Member State to determine how the right should be protected should not be taken to mean that the ECHR adopts an entirely dismissive approach to scrutinising the necessity of the interference with commercial expression. In *Krone*, a daily newspaper had published an advertisement comparing its own cost and quality with a competitor's newspaper. The competitor obtained an injunction, which required the newspaper to indicate differences in their coverage of foreign or domestic affairs, economy, culture, science, health, environmental issues and the law within that advertisement. Since this was a particularly onerous obligation, the ECHR held that Article 10 had been violated. In upholding the claim, the ECHR observed that there was a public interest at stake by the interference because 'advertising is a means of discovering the characteristics of services and goods offered to [citizens]'.[56]

Such a finding provokes debate about the meaning of 'public interest' and the extent to which a public interest is engaged by commercial expression, not least because that definition is particularly difficult to pin down. It is clear from UK case law that the judiciary has not yet settled upon a precise definition of the term, leaving some uncertainty about its parameters. While it seems relatively certain that the definition of 'public interest' is narrower than that which simply interests the public,[57] the debate is not yet fully resolved.[58] Indeed, the inclusion of commercial expression within the ambit of Article 10 broadens the scope of the term 'public interest', to some extent at least, since it ensures that

[54] For a recent example see *IA* v. *Turkey* (2007) 45 EHRR 30.

[55] (2006) 42 EHRR 28. [56] *Ibid.*, [31].

[57] See *Jameel (Mohammed) and another* v. *Wall Street Journal Europe Sprl* [2007] 1 AC 359; *Campbell* v. *MGN Ltd* [2004] 2 All ER 995; cf., *A* v. *B plc* [2003] QB 195.

[58] Likewise neither is the academic debate settled, see e.g. Robert Post, 'The Constitutional Status of Commercial Speech' (2000) 48 *UCLA Law Review* 1; Martin Redish, 'First Amendment Theory and the Demise of the Commercial Speech Distinction: the Case of the Smoking Controversy' (1997) 24 *Northern Kentucky Law Review* 553; Steven Shiffrin, 'The First Amendment and Economic Regulation: Away from a General Theory of the First Amendment,' (1984) 78 *Northwestern University Law Review* 1212; and C. Edwin Baker, *Human Liberty and Freedom of Speech* (Oxford University Press, 1989) on the difficulties of limiting the meaning of 'public interest' to the ambit of 'political speech'.

the term is not limited to that which directly relates to the democratic process. Instead, it would seem to open up the concept to include information that is directly relevant to private – and not simply public – decision-making.[59] The ECHR and UK courts' approach to advertising, particularly comparative advertising, emphasises the point; the courts seem concerned to protect such speech for its informational value.[60] Yet the constant theme within such decisions is the important caveat that the information provided in the advertisement must not be misleading if it is to be protected under Article 10. This is clear from the decisions in *Boehringer* and *Red Dot Technologies* in the UK and *Krone Verlag* in the ECHR. On that basis, the objectives of the regulations to prohibit advertising that *is* misleading would seem to present no conflict with Article 10.

However, while in general no conflict may arise, it is important to be aware of two quirks (in particular) in the way that Article 10 cases are decided since these may affect on the operation of the regulations. First, despite the fact that the expression is in the form of an advertisement, the court nevertheless may classify the expression as political rather than commercial, meaning that the expression would be entitled to the maximum level of protection. Secondly, if it is to take the free speech claim seriously then the court should scrutinise the necessity of interference beyond the superficial and so, for example, should concentrate its efforts on asking how seriously the average consumer would believe the alleged misleading advertisement rather than adopting a dismissive approach to the value of the free speech claim because the expression was commercial (e.g. as the court did in *North Cyprus Tourism Centre Ltd* as compared to *British American Tobacco*). These two issues are explored in greater detail in the following section.

Implications for the regulations

Classification as political expression

The notion that advertising may be classified as a form of political expression by the courts is not far-fetched. American commentators are familiar with the long-standing argument, first advanced in the 1970s by

[59] See Martin Redish, 'The Value of Free Speech' (1982) 130 *University of Pennsylvania Law Review* 591 who argues that information pivotal to private decision-making is just as vital as information limited to public decision-making within the concept of free speech.

[60] D. Feldman, 'Content Neutrality', in Ian Loveland (ed.), *Importing the First Amendment*, 2nd edn (Oxford University Press, 1998), 157.

Martin Redish,[61] that the distinction between commercial expression and political expression is unsustainable because the underpinning values advanced by both are not dissimilar enough to justify separate treatment. For example, Post observes that:

> underlying [the view that commercial speech may be of public interest] is the notion that citizens may acquire information from commercial speech that is highly relevant to the formation of democratic public opinion. Democratic public opinion, in turn, is the ultimate source of government decision making. If citizens learn from commercial advertising that pharmacy drugs are too expensive, for example, they might organize politically to advocate within public discourse for the creation of national health insurance.[62]

Alternatively, Post argues that 'visions of the good life articulated within commercial advertisements are relevant to [the political] process'.[63] Similarly, Kozinski and Banner, for example, argue that modern advertising does not typically contain the essential elements of a commercial transaction, such as price or purchase location.[64] Instead, advertisers tend to link their product to achievement of an image or ideal. It may be said that politicians do something similar by trying to sell an image or ideal to the voter and then linking a political party to its achievement.

As already noted, the corpus of UK and ECHR cases on commercial expression seem to support the view that the same value which underpins the protection of political expression under Article 10 (that freedom of expression upholds and furthers the democratic process) may also be evident in commercial expression as well. However, it is possible that the court may go further; instead of classifying the expression as commercial, the court could classify it as political despite it being presented in a commercial format (i.e. an advertisement). Such an approach is evident in the ECHR decision in *Open Door Counselling*.[65] In this case, concerning advertisements for abortion services, the ECtHR classified the expression as political, ignoring the format of the speech in the process.

[61] Martin Redish, 'The First Amendment in the Marketplace: Commercial Speech and the Values of Free Expression' (1971) 39 *George Washington Law Review* 429.

[62] Robert Post, 'The Constitutional Status of Commercial Speech' (2000) 48 *UCLA Law Review* 1, 11.

[63] *Ibid.*

[64] Alex Kozinski and Stuart Banner, 'Who's Afraid of Commercial Speech?' (1990) 76 *Virginia Law Review* 627, at 638–41.

[65] *Open Door Counselling and Dublin Well Woman* v. *Ireland* (1992) 15 EHRR 244.

Classification as political expression is different from the finding that although the expression is commercial the democratic process value is at stake for two reasons. First, where the expression is classified as political there is no debate about the level of protection that it ought to be afforded: the ECHR has stressed on a number of occasions that interferences with political expression must be afforded the highest level of scrutiny possible and, consequently, the necessity to interfere must be convincingly established.[66] Secondly, and perhaps more significantly, different normative considerations apply: whereas it seems readily accepted in both UK and Strasbourg jurisprudence that commercial expression may be interfered with where it is misleading,[67] even though the democratic process value is at stake, the notion of suppressing political expression because it is misleading is an imperiously weak argument in normative terms. This point is as evident in the classic argument for freedom of speech found in John Stuart Mill's argument from truth[68] as it is in the more contemporary arguments advanced by, for example, Alexander Meiklejohn (the argument from participation in a democracy),[69] Thomas Scanlon (the argument from autonomy)[70] and Martin Redish (the argument from self-fulfilment).[71] Although these philosophical and political arguments for the protection of free speech have been much discussed in the academic literature,[72] it is useful to refer to them briefly for the purposes of this discussion.

[66] *Lingens* v. *Austria* (1986) 8 EHRR 407.

[67] See comments of Richards J in *Red Dot Technologies*, discussed above. Similarly, in *Krone Verlag*, the ECtHR observed that advertising 'may sometimes be restricted, especially to prevent . . . untruthful or misleading advertising' [31].

[68] J. S. Mill, *On Liberty* [1859] (London: Routledge, 1991).

[69] Alexander Meiklejohn, *Free Speech and its Relation to Self-Government* (New York: Harper, 1948); 'The First Amendment is an Absolute' [1961] *Supreme Court Review* 245. Similar arguments can be found in Harry Kalven Jr, 'The New York Times Case: A Note on the Central Meaning of the First Amendment' [1964] *Supreme Court Review* 191; Robert Bork, 'Neutral Principles and Some First Amendment Problems' (1971) 47 *Indiana Law Journal* 1; and, Vincent Blasi, 'The Checking Value in First Amendment Theory' (1977) *American Bar Foundation Research Journal* 521 among others.

[70] Thomas Scanlon, 'A Theory of Freedom of Expression', in *The Philosophy of Law*, ed. R. M. Dworkin (Oxford University Press, 1977) and 'Freedom of Expression and Categories of Expression' (1979) *University of Pittsburgh Law Review* 519. See also Ronald Dworkin, 'Is there a Right to Pornography?' (1981) 1 *OJLS* 177.

[71] Martin Redish, 'The Value of Free Speech' (1982) 130 *University of Pennsylvania Law Review* 591. See also C. Edwin Baker, *Human Liberty and Freedom of Speech* (Oxford University Press, 1989) and Michael J. Perry, 'Freedom of Expression: an Essay on Theory and Doctrine' (1983) 78 *Northwestern University Law Review* 1139.

[72] See, for example, the discussion in Schauer, *Free Speech* and Barendt, *Freedom of Speech*.

In J. S. Mill's classic statement, freedom of speech ought to be protected so that the truth may be known. For that reason, Mill strongly argues against suppression of opinion because it is held to be false since to do so would be an assumption of infallibility:[73] 'We can never be sure that the opinion we are endeavouring to stifle is a false opinion; and if we were sure, stifling it would be an evil still'[74] because the suppressed opinion may turn out to be true[75] or it may be false but falsehood has value in providing a 'livelier impression' of the truth.[76] Furthermore, rational discourse requires a proper understanding of the arguments for and against the 'truth'. Holding a true opinion is not equivalent to understanding it.[77] Meiklejohn's argument similarly defends against the suppression of speech where it relates to the democratic process on the basis that the state lacks the power to interfere with such speech. He argues that speech 'must have a freedom unabridged by our agents. Though they govern us, we, in a deeper sense, govern them. Over our governing, they have no power. Over their governing, we have sovereign power.'[78] Scanlon makes a similar point, albeit from a different perspective (individual autonomy), by arguing that 'a legitimate government is one whose authority citizens can recognize while still regarding themselves as equal, autonomous, rational agents'.[79] He explains that 'to regard himself as autonomous . . . a person must see himself as sovereign in deciding what to believe and in weighing competing reasons for action'. Therefore, 'an autonomous person cannot accept without independent consideration the judgment of others as to what he should believe or what he should do'.[80] Finally, Redish argues that freedom of speech fosters self-rule, which permits 'control of [one's] own destiny through making life-affecting decisions'.[81] He illustrates his point with the following example:

> [Suppose] an individual wishes to . . . vote for a candidate because the candidate looks good with his tie loosened and his jacket slung over his shoulder, who are we to tell him that these are improper acts? We may prefer that he make his judgments . . . on more traditionally 'rational' grounds . . . [b]ut in these areas society has left the ultimate right to

[73] Mill, n. 68, 29. [74] *Ibid.*, 28. [75] *Ibid.*, 75. [76] *Ibid.*, 34. [77] *Ibid.*, 56.

[78] Meiklejohn, 'The First Amendment is an Absolute', 257.

[79] Scanlon, 'A Theory of Freedom of Expression', 161.

[80] *Ibid.*, 163. Though Scanlon did later reconsider the soundness of his argument, see Thomas Scanlon, 'Freedom of Expression and Categories of Expression'. Irrespective, it remains an important theory, as Barendt notes, *Freedom of Speech*, 17–18.

[81] *Ibid.*

> decide to the individual, and this would not be much of a right if we prescribed how it was to be used.[82]

Although premised on very different rationales, the unifying theme of these arguments is that political expression should not be suppressed because it is considered untrue or misleading. Indeed, the ECtHR seems to have explicitly recognised this point. In a case concerning political expression, it observed that Article 10:

> as such does not prohibit discussion or dissemination of information received even if it is strongly suspected that this information might not be truthful. To suggest otherwise would deprive persons of the right to express their views and opinions about statements made in the mass media and would thus place an unreasonable restriction on the freedom of expression set forth in Article 10.[83]

However the expression is classified, once the court accepts that Article 10 is engaged the regulations must be applied in a manner that is compatible with Article 10. Where the speech is classified as political, any interference with the expression must be convincingly established and, consequently, the claim that the speech should be interfered with because it is misleading may fail if the court is to ensure compatibility with Article 10. In such a case, the court may ignore the format of the expression, as the ECHR did in *Open Door Counselling*. Given the rising prominence of environmental issues in the news, it is not surprising that there is a noticeable growing trend of adverts emphasising the benefits to society of the advertised product or service and it may be that difficult cases which engage these issues may arise in this context.

Likewise, the case could concern the health benefits of a product.[84] Such a case may exhibit parallels with *Hertel* v. *Switzerland*,[85] which concerned a journal article that attacked microwaves as unsafe for human health. In *Hertel*, the legislative provision extended beyond misleading commercial practices by economic agents to include any conduct by any person

[82] Redish, 'The Value of Free Speech', 619.

[83] *Salov* v. *Ukraine* (2007) 45 EHRR 51 [113].

[84] Indeed, the ASA recently censured Tetley GB Ltd for a TV advert depicting a young lady, dressed ready for jogging, abandoning her pursuit of exercise in favour of drinking Tetley's own brand green tea instead against the backdrop of a voice-over which said 'For an easy way to help look after yourself pick up Tetley green tea. It's full of anti-oxidants.' In its adjudication, the ASA decided that the advertisement was misleading because it implied that Tetley green tea had greater health benefits than it actually did; http://www.asa.org.uk/asa/adjudications/public/TF_ADJ_47670.htm.

[85] *Hertel* v. *Switzerland* (1999) 28 EHRR 534.

considered 'deceptive or in any other way offends the principle of good faith and ... affects relations between competitors or between suppliers and customers'. Furthermore, it stated that 'a person acts unfairly if he ... denigrates others or the goods, work, services, prices or business of others by making inaccurate, misleading or unnecessarily wounding statements'. However, because the ECHR had determined that the expression contributed to a debate of general public interest, the expression was afforded the high level of protection provided to political expression and, therefore, it did not matter that the opinion was a minority one or even that it may be devoid of merit since 'in a sphere in which it is unlikely that any certainty exists, it would be particularly unreasonable to restrict freedom of expression only to generally accepted ideas'.[86] A similar scenario could potentially arise under the Consumer Regulations where a trader wrote an article in a trade journal, for example, in connection with a product being sold by that trader, particularly where unresolved scientific or medical issues existed.

There is, however, scope for arguing that the court will find there has been no violation of Article 10 notwithstanding that the expression is classified by the court as political in circumstances where the advertisement appears on the broadcast media. In such circumstances, the advertisement would fall within the ambit of the Communications Act 2003, which prohibits political advertising on the broadcast media. The House of Lords recently found in *Animal Defenders International (ADI)*[87] that the blanket prohibition on political advertising on television and radio was compatible with Article 10 due to 'the greater immediacy and impact of television and radio advertising'[88] in conjunction with the finding that the rights of others exception contained within Article 10(2) includes 'a right to be protected against the potential mischief of partial political advertising'.[89] It should be said, however, that this finding is not entirely in keeping with Strasbourg jurisprudence. In a case involving a similar legislative provision, the ECHR observed that while the effect of the broadcast media may be an important factor in the consideration of the proportionality of the interference, any interference with political expression calls for the closest scrutiny and alternatives to, for example, blanket bans must be considered.[90] Thus, if

[86] *Ibid.*, [50].
[87] *R. (on the application of Animal Defenders International)* v. *Secretary of State for Culture, Media and Sport* (2008) UKHL 15.
[88] *Ibid.*, [30]. [89] *Ibid.*, [28].
[90] *TV Vest AS & Rogaland Pensjonistparti* v. *Norway* (app no. 211332/05).

the court is to keep pace with Strasbourg then the approach evident in *ADI* needs to soften. Consequently, the justification for interfering in these circumstances is not as strong as it was. However, the point remains that classification of the advertisement as political in these circumstances changes the applicable legislative framework from the regulations to the Communications Act.

Another prominent issue in this regard is the sustainability of the argument that political and commercial expression ought to be treated differently when the democratic process value is at stake. Besides the obvious difficulties of defining 'commercial expression' with sufficient precision to justify the distinction in standards of protection,[91] there is also the normative issue of justifying the distinction. In this regard, the arguments outlined above are clearly relevant. It is also worth noting the arguments advanced to say that commercial expression ought not to be covered by the free speech guarantee. There is the dismissive approach which bluntly asserts that it is 'intuitive' that commercial expression is excluded from the realm of free speech[92] since inclusion would 'trivialise'[93] the concept and there is the more reasoned argument that 'purely commercial speech plays little role in the exposition and debate of political ideas, (political speech might be *about* commercial matters, but it does more than propose a commercial transaction)'.[94] The intuitive approach has been defended on the basis that there is an 'intuitive belief that commercial speech is somehow more akin to conduct than are other forms of speech'; that 'it is a prelude to and therefore becomes integrated into, a contract, the essence of which is the presence of a promise'.[95] Consequently, since 'a promise is an undertaking to ensure that a certain state of affairs takes place, promises obviously have a closer connection with conduct than with self-expression'.[96] On this basis, 'false advertisements are indistinguishable from unfulfilled contractual promises'.[97]

[91] See, for example, Barendt, *Freedom of Speech*, 395–9.

[92] See discussion of this view in R. Shiner, *Freedom of Commercial Expression* (Oxford University Press, 2003).

[93] As the Attorney General of Quebec argued unsuccessfully in *Ford* v. *Attorney General of Quebec* [1988] 2 SCR 712, [53]; see also Geoffrey Marshall, Case Comment, 'Taking Rights for an Override: Free Speech and Commercial Expression' (1989) *PL* 4.

[94] John Valauri, 'Smoking and Self-Realization: a Reply to Professor Redish' (1997) 24 *Northern Kentucky Law Review* 585, 587.

[95] D. Farber, 'Commercial Speech First Amendment Theory' (1979) 4 *Northwestern University Law Review* 372, 389.

[96] *Ibid.* [97] *Ibid.*, 390.

However, the type of expression contemplated for this discussion is not only that which simply proposes a commercial transaction but also that for which a public interest exists. Once this core value is identified, the definition of speech as 'commercial' or 'political' becomes nothing more than a transparent means of preventing one speaker expressing himself as easily as another.[98] Yet the eventual finding that one is more important than the other appears to be a fallacy. What is really being said is that the expression of an individual or company is of lesser value because the speaker clearly has a financial incentive in mind when speaking. Yet it is well established in the academic literature that this profit motive argument is flawed. As Barendt observes, on that basis, the free speech claims made by all publishers, authors and, even, many (if not all) politicians seeking election would seem to be precarious.[99] Consequently, the finding that one type of expression should be suppressed because it is considered misleading but the other definitely not seems difficult to justify. If, as seems to be the case, both categories of speech are entitled to Article 10 protection due to the important societal interest being advanced by providing information of benefit to the public at large then the justification for treating the two differently seems obscure. If the same democratic process value is at stake then why is commercial speech not the equal of political speech? As yet the case law contains no real solution to the quandary.

Taking the free speech claim seriously

The second scenario arises because recent cases demonstrate a willingness on the part of the judiciary to take the Article 10 claims of commercial expression seriously so that submissions that the actual or desired interference with the expression is justified are scrutinised beyond a superficial assessment. It may seem strange to raise this as a concern for the operation of the regulations, not least because the court is obliged by the HRA to investigate the necessity of an interference with

[98] Although Redish, for example, dismisses this view as snobbery: 'most of these attacks [on free speech protection for commercial speech] – much like similar attacks against obscenity protection – may be deconstructed into little more than a result-orientated attempt to stifle advocacy of a particular ideological perspective or point of view'; 'First Amendment Theory and the Demise of the Commercial Speech Distinction: the Case of the Smoking Controversy' (1997) 24 *Northern Kentucky Law Review* 553, 556.

[99] Barendt, *Freedom of Speech* 24.

expression in *every* Article 10 claim, not just those involving what observers might categorise as 'important' speech, such as political speech. Yet, in the context of an approach to Article 10 that oscillates between rigorous and lacklustre scrutiny of the necessity of interference, the point is significant. As other commentators have observed,[100] in some cases decided under the HRA, the finding that the interference with Article 10 is justified has resembled more of an assertion than a reasoned and considered opinion. Consequently, where an unsophisticated approach is taken to the Article 10 claim, the extent of the coverage given in the decision to defending the necessity of interference is likely to be minimal and perhaps limited to a few observations that since commercial expression is not highly regarded by the ECHR in Article 10 cases and since there is an identifiable interest at stake, i.e. the consumer rights of others,[101] then any interference with Article 10 generated by the regulations is justified.

Yet, as noted above, more recent commercial expression cases in the UK suggest the distinct possibility of a more inquisitive approach to the necessity of the potential interference such that the focus of the court's decision is on the standard applied to the process of deciding that expression is 'misleading'. In the context of comparative advertising, the court may focus on how onerously the restrictions are applied.[102] As noted in section 2, the regulations apply the standard of the 'average consumer' for the purposes of determining if the commercial practice is misleading. Where Article 10 is engaged, the court may apply the provision narrowly. To some extent, the definition within the regulations of the 'average consumer' being well informed and circumspect makes this approach easier since it prompts the submission that the average consumer is unlikely to be fooled easily. In this regard, the court may readily accept submissions that the prosecuted expression would not be taken seriously by the average consumer and so therefore cannot be said to be misleading. As *Ajinomoto Sweeteners Europe*[103] demonstrates, such an approach may generate findings that raise questions about the sensitivity of the court to consumer-orientated concerns and/or the court's view

[100] See, for example, H. M. Fenwick, 'Clashing Rights, the Welfare of the Child and the Human Rights Act' (2004) 67(6) *MLR* 889.

[101] See *ADI*, and *ProLife*, for illustrative examples of how flexibly the concept of 'rights of others' has been interpreted for accommodating rights that are 'not strictly legal' (see Lord Scott, *ProLife*, [91], the reference in Art. 10(2) to the 'rights of others': 'need not be limited to strictly legal rights').

[102] As in *Krone Verlag*. [103] See n. 41.

of consumer habits (i.e. the suggestion that consumers do not take information displayed on packaging all that seriously if it is in a playful font). Thus, in such circumstances, the absence of a public interest to support the Article 10 claim may be immaterial.

Furthermore, it is worth reiterating the point that judicial recognition of advertising as a form of free speech means that all infringements must be justified by reference to Article 10. Companies defending claims under the regulations will be encouraged to plead not only that Article 10 is at stake but also that the expression involves a public interest since where such a potential contribution can be established the task of suppressing the speech becomes harder. Geraint Howells has predicted that 'injunctions should play a major role in the future [of the regulations]'.[104] Yet advertisers will be further encouraged to advance free speech-based arguments where injunctive relief is sought following the decision in *Boehringer*.[105] In that case, the Court of Appeal was referred to section 12(4), HRA, which states, *inter alia*, that when the court is deciding whether to award injunctive relief particular regard should be had to the importance of the convention right to freedom of expression and the extent to which the proceedings concern material that is or appears to be journalistic, literary or artistic and, furthermore, the extent to which it is, or would be, in the public interest for the material to be published. The court was then referred to the decision in *Cream Holdings*,[106] in which the House of Lords had interpreted section 12(4) as requiring the courts to be 'exceeding slow' to grant interim restraint orders where an applicant had not satisfied the court that he would probably, as in 'more likely than not', succeed at trial. A lesser standard than this might be applied in cases where the adverse consequences of publication might be extremely serious. This approach clearly differs from the lower standard imposed by the usual *American Cyanamid* test which requires the applicant to demonstrate a 'real prospect of success'.[107] Thus, if the injunction is intended to be used more readily by those enforcement agencies designated by the Regulations then such a weapon may well be blunted where the free speech argument is raised.

[104] Howells, 'The End of an Era – Implementing the Unfair Commercial Practices Directive in the United Kingdom: Punctual Criminal Law Gives Way to a General Criminal/Civil Law Standard' (2009) *JBL* 183, at 194.

[105] See n. 39. [106] *Cream Holdings* v. *Banerjee* (2004) UKHL 44.

[107] *American Cyanamid* v. *Ethicon* (1975) AC 396.

Conclusion

The objectives of the regulations are not going to be undone by the operation of Article 10 in this area. Since only designated enforcement agencies can enforce the regulations – rather than individual consumers or affected businesses – it may be that only the more serious and significant examples of misleading advertisements or comparative advertisements in breach of the business regulations are litigated and that, consequently, the free speech issues outlined above hardly figure. Allied to this point is the fact that the regulations require enforcement agencies to have regard to the desirability of encouraging control of unfair commercial practices by such established means as it considers appropriate, which in an advertising context translates to referring the matter to the ASA in the first instance. This would seem to reinforce the prospect that many cases may never reach court. Nevertheless these conclusions do not detract from the significance of the points advanced above. Indeed, it is important that enforcement agencies are aware of these potential hurdles before they initiate what could otherwise become very expensive injunction applications that may fail due to the uncertain status freedom of commercial expression currently holds.

Furthermore, given the impression gained from the limited number of cases decided, it is likely that the ECHR and UK courts' approach to commercial expression so far will have some impact in shaping the regulators' approach to enforcing the regulations. Where these free speech issues do arise in court, the UK judiciary may be presented with a stark choice: to either clarify the theoretical basis of commercial speech protection by adopting the liberal approach highlighted above and so strengthen the position of commercial expression or else retreat into the wide margin of appreciation afforded Member States and so, for example, restrict the protection of commercial expression to that which demonstrates an acute contribution to the democratic process value (narrowly defined). Thus, it is not the case that the activity of Article 10 in the field of commercial expression will defeat the consumer-orientated ambitions of the regulations. It may be that the value of the regulations from a free speech perspective is the clarification that decided cases bring to the position of commercial expression in an Article 10 context. This would be particularly welcomed from both a free speech and consumer law perspective.

17

Are consumer rights human rights?

MONIKA JAGIELSKA AND MARIUSZ JAGIELSKI

Introduction

Over the last two decades, consumer rights have increasingly appeared in certain, usually newly adopted, constitutional acts, most often in provisions listing catalogues of human/fundamental rights and in EU primary law.[1] In this chapter we ask whether consumer rights can be classified as human/fundamental rights, and look to the role they play in consumer protection. We go on to question the role of constitutional courts in this field and ask whether consumer protection can be achieved by other fundamental/human rights. Finally we turn to EU law, pointing out the similarities between national and EU developments in consumer rights, and discussing what the national constitutional experience means for establishing the level and means of consumer protection in the EU.

Consumer provisions in national constitutions

Rules on consumer protection are present in several national Constitutions of European and non-European countries. They are expressed in various manners and in a range of contexts. They usually appear in newly adopted Constitutions (for example in Poland or Lithuania) or are introduced into the text of 'old' acts (for example in Mexico). It is sometimes unclear whether these rules will play an important role in consumer protection, or whether they are a mere declaration of the legislator's goodwill, words that look impressive but have little solid meaning. We take the view that the 'truth' is somewhere in the middle; on the one hand it is a kind of declaration, but on the other it represents the more general tendency of constituting social rights.

University of Katowice.

[1] S. Weatherill, *EC Consumer Law and Policy* (New York: 1997), 3–19.

Elements of various states' policies

The general approach treats consumer protection as one of many state aims and policies and it is presented together with others, usually in the context of ensuring proper market functioning. According to Article 19 of the Bulgarian Constitution, 'the state must establish and guarantee equal legal conditions for economic activity to all citizens and corporate entities by preventing any abuse of a monopoly status and unfair competition, and by protecting the consumer'. Sometimes consumer protection is mentioned in connection with specific rights that need protecting, as in Article 64 of the Cambodian Constitution: 'The State will ban and severely punish anyone who imports, manufactures or sells illicit drugs or counterfeit and expired goods that affect the health and life of consumers.' Meanwhile, Article 78 of the Colombian Constitution provides: 'Anyone who, in the production and marketing of goods and services, may jeopardise the health, safety, and adequate supply to consumers and users will be held liable in accordance with the law.'

Such rules constitute an element of state policy indicating the development and interpretation of various legal provisions and statutory legislation. They do not play a single role; they take their place in an array of instruments aimed at protecting differentiated targets. Additionally, they do not constitute consumer rights; instead their role is limited to shaping state policy.

One of a number of values protected

Consumer protection is also treated as one of a number of protected values, for example in the Paraguayan Constitution, which speaks, in Article 38, about the right to defend common interests:

> Everyone has the right, either individually or within a group, to demand that public officials adopt measures to defend the environment, the preservation of the habitat, public health, national cultural heritage, the interests of consumers, and other areas that, due to their legal nature, concern the community and are related to the quality of life and to property belonging to the community.

It is not possible to talk about consumer rights under this approach either; rather these are certain interests which have to be taken into account in the course of state activities. They also do not constitute a single value, but belong to a catalogue of interests of varied nature, which should be observed by the state, although probably at a low level of enforcement.

Single protected value

However, for this analysis, more interesting are those constitutional rules that are devoted solely to consumer protection. Some of these simply declare the state's intention to protect consumers, for example, in Article 46 of the Lithuanian Constitution: 'The State will defend the interests of consumers.' Similarly in Article 90 of the Serbian Constitution: 'The Republic of Serbia will protect consumers'; Article 5 of the Brazilian Constitution: 'The State will provide, as set out in the law, for the defence of consumers'; or Article 57 of the Thai Constitution: 'The right of a person as a consumer will be protected as provided by law'.

It is worth noting that these provisions use different legal formulae to describe what is protected: interests, rights or simply consumers. From a theoretical point of view, such differences may have legal consequences, especially in the context of rights in opposition to interests. It may nevertheless be questioned whether in practice there will be a difference in the forms of protection in such cases.

Protected rights

Some other constitutions recognise particular consumer 'rights'. Section 53 of East Timor's Constitution reads, '[C]onsumers have the right to goods and services of good quality, to truthful information and the protection of their health, safety and economic interests, as well as to reparation for damages.' The Portuguese Constitution states: '[C]onsumers have the right to good quality goods and services consumed, to training and information, to the protection of health, safety and their economic interests, and to reparation for damages' (Article 60).

This construction seems to be the furthest reaching and most protective. It uses a notion of right that is the furthest reaching approach (in comparison to interests or policies) and may probably be treated as a sole basis of a claim. In addition, there are no limits on the protection that should be afforded.

Rights protected in a way prescribed by law

Lastly there are Constitutions that invoke consumer rights, but clearly state that the sphere of protection should be prescribed by law. The Spanish Constitution declares that:

> the public authorities will guarantee the defence of consumers and users, protecting their safety, health, and legitimate economic interests through effective procedures ... Within the framework of the provisions of these

> paragraphs, the law will regulate domestic commerce and the system of licensing commercial products.

Section 42 of the Argentinian Constitution guarantees that

> [A]s regards consumption, consumers and users of goods and services have the right to the protection of their health, safety, and economic interests; to adequate and accurate information; to freedom of choice and equitable and reliable treatment. The authorities will provide for the protection of these rights.

Finally, Article 76 of the Polish Constitution provides that

> [P]ublic authorities will protect consumers, customers, hirers or lessees against activities threatening their health, privacy and safety, as well as against dishonest market practices. The scope of such protection will be specified by statute.

This approach seems to be the most balanced. It not only lists the areas of protection but also clearly shows the intentions of the legislator to limit the scope of protection to these situations which are acknowledged to be worth protecting by statute.

Declarations or norms?

As we can see from the above examples, the idea of consumer protection appears in different manners in different Constitutions and, at first sight, it may play various roles. In the theory of constitutional law, the character of constitutional norms is fiercely discussed. Under prevailing opinion, all constitutional provisions, largely because they were adopted in a special constitutional procedure and were purposely introduced into the text of the constitution, have a normative character, i.e. public authorities are bound by them, even if they were prescribed in a vague manner.[2] When trying to evaluate the nature of consumer-related constitutional provisions we should, therefore, first distinguish three types of constitutional provisions: principles, subjective rights and programme norms. This distinction will be useful for determining the actual role of constitutional consumer protection provisions.

[2] B. Banaszak, *Porównawcze prawo konstytucyjne współczesnych państw demokratycznych* (Wolters Kluwer, 2007), 110.

Principles, subjective rights or 'programme' norms?

'The principle of constitution' is a legal concept representing a fundamental idea of the political, social or economic order of the state.[3] It is questionable whether the constitutional principles are of a normative character. The Polish Constitutional Tribunal, for example, decided that 'the principles are binding legal norms' which 'can and should be taken into account as the base for evaluating the conformity of legal provisions with the Constitution'.[4] However, it is doubtful whether such a principle can constitute the sole basis for the court's findings in a particular situation. It can have an indirect effect when the provision is combined with another principle, such as, for example, a provision that embodies a subjective right. It may be assumed that the constitutional consumer protection provisions listed above can be treated as such principles.[5]

Subjective rights constitute a type of norm created in the form of a person's claim directed towards the state. Their normative importance results from two factors. First, they are enforceable, which means they can be invoked in court proceedings and can constitute a sole basis for court findings.[6] Secondly, they are constitutionally protected, which means they must be respected by public authorities.[7] The constitutional theory, created by national constitutional courts and the ECHR, drew up principles limiting the possibility of constraining constitutional rights. The limitations must be statutory, proportional and necessary in a democratic society, and cannot restrain the essence of a right.[8] The constitutional consumer protection provisions listed above can rarely or even never, as emerges from constitutional court findings (below), be treated as subjective rights.

Finally, programme norms (guidelines, directive principles, legislative commands or policies) are something between constitutional principles

[3] A. Eide, C. Krause and A. Rosas (eds.), *Economic, Social and Cultural Rights: a Textbook*, (Dordrecht, Boston, London: 2001).

[4] Court judgment on 30 November 1988, K 1/88, *Orzecznictwo Trybunału Konstytucyjnego w 1988* (Warsaw 1990), 97.

[5] K. Wojtyczek, 'Formy konstytucjonalizacji zasad konstytucyjnych', in P. Sarnecki (ed.), *Konstytucjonalizacja zasad i instytucji ustrojowych* (Wydawnictwo Sejmowe, 1997), 28ff.

[6] B. Banaszak, *Outline of Polish Constitutional Law* (Wydawnictwo Uniwersytetu Wrocławskiego, 2005), 80.

[7] P. Tuleja, *Normatywna treść praw jednostki w ustawach konstytucyjnych RP* (Wydawnictwo Sejmowe, 1997), 36ff.

[8] A. Łabno, 'Ograniczenia wolności i praw człowieka na podstawie art. 31 Konstytucji III RP', in B. Banaszak and A. Preisner (eds.), *Prawa i wolności obywatelskie w Konstytucji RP* (C. H. Beck, 2002), 701ff.

and subjective rights. They constitute a type of constitutional provision determining, in a general way, the goals, directions and tasks of the state in specific areas. They do not give rise to subjective rights that can be directly enforced in the courts and must be provided for in legislation in order to become enforceable. They are still binding on public authorities, in the sense that they are obliged to take them into account in the course of their activities.[9] Clearly, consumer constitutional provisions may play a role as such guidelines.

Constitutional Court findings

In spite of these stipulations, we assume that consumer rights contained in a Constitution can have an indirect effect and serve as an aid to interpretation.[10] To take some examples from Polish Constitutional Court judgments dealing with Article 76 of the Polish Constitution, the Court states that Article 76 should be treated as an interpretational directive at least, even if it does not create constitutional rights.[11] Consumer protection is regarded by the Court as a 'constitutional value', but only as far as it is prescribed by a statute. The requirement of consumer protection arising out of Article 76 does not create any direct personal rights for the citizens,[12] but must be taken into consideration as a potential basis for interpretation. This means that all exceptions from general rules of law that can be disadvantageous for consumers must be interpreted strictly.[13] Although Article 76 does not embody a subjective right, it formulates state obligations that must be elaborated through statute. In this regard not only Polish legislation but also the *acquis communautaire* are relevant in evaluating the provision of consumer protection.[14] The scope of consumer protection is outlined at a statutory

[9] T. Gizbert-Studnicki and A. Grabowski, 'Normy programowe konstytucji' in *Charakter i struktura norm konstytucji* (Wydawnictwo Sejmowe, 1997), 97ff.

[10] For more on Art. 76 of Polish Constitution see E. Łętowska, 'Konstytucyjne i wspólnotowe uwarunkowania rozwoju prawa konsumenckiego', C. Mik (ed.), *Konstytucja Rzeczypospolitej Polskiej z 1997 r. a członkostwo Polski w Unii Europejskiej* (Torun: 1999), 373–385; M. Jagielska and M. Jagielski, 'Możliwości interpretacyjne art.76 Konstytucji RP w świetle europejskiego prawa ochrony konsumenta', in *Konstytucja Rzeczypospolitej*, 407–426; R. Stefanicki, 'Konstytucjonalizacja ochrony konsumenta na tle standardów prawa wspólnotowego' (2008) *Państwo i Prawo* 3, 5–19.

[11] Court judgment P 10/04 OTK no. 1A/2005, poz. 7.

[12] Court judgment on 12 January 2000, sygn. P. 11/98, OTK ZU no. 1/2000, poz. 3.

[13] Court judgment on 26 January 2005, OTK-A 2005/1/7.

[14] Court judgment on 21 April 2004 K 33/03, OTK ZU no. 4/A/2004, poz. 31.

level, but this does not mean that the legislature is completely free in shaping it. The Constitutional Tribunal may evaluate whether the means adopted are appropriate (proportional) for the aims of consumer protection.[15] The obligations imposed on the state are not purely formal; and whether the proposed solution is effective and able, in the prevailing market situation. to bring about the expected results needs to be examined.[16]

In its judgments, the Polish Constitutional Tribunal not only established a general rule for the application of Article 76 of the Constitution, but also gave some hints regarding certain more detailed issues. First of all it dealt with the problem of the notion of the consumer used in the provision. It declared that this notion cannot be understood in its precise, private law meaning according to Article 22^1 of the Polish Civil Code. Under that provision, a consumer is a natural person concluding a contract not directly connected with the consumer's business activity. Therefore, consumers can act within the scope of their business, but not directly connected with their professional activities.[17] Explaining its position, the Tribunal pointed out that the notions used in the Constitution have their own autonomous meaning, which should not be determined by statute.[18] The aim and the substance of this provision is to ensure protection to those who create autonomous relations where they are in a (usually economically) weaker position compared with the other party. *Inter alia* this means that this rule can be used to ensure protection to employees in their relations with employers. According to the Tribunal, consumer protection should allow consumers to act freely in making their choice. Consumers' participation in the market must be shaped in such a way that they can freely, on the basis of given knowledge and information and in accordance with their own interests, satisfy their appreciated needs.[19] Many of the Court's rulings based on Article 76 of the Constitution focused on the issue of information given to consumers. It clearly stated that insufficient or opaque information is an infringement of Article 76. Consumers' right to obtain clear and complete information is one of the guarantees needed to allow them to play their role on the market safely and consciously.

[15] Court judgment on 21 April 2004 K 33/03 OTK ZU 2004 no. 3A.
[16] Court judgment on 26 January 2004 P 10/04 OTK ZU 2005 no. 10A.
[17] Court judgment on 20 April 2005, sygn. K 42/02 OTK ZU no. 4/A/2005.
[18] Court judgment on 2 December 2008 K 37/07 OTK-A 2008/10/172.
[19] Court judgment on 13 September 2005 K 38/04 OTK-A 2005/8/92.

Denial of a subjective right

Article 76 does not constitute a subjective human right, but, rather, empowers public authorities to take actions aimed at accomplishing special objectives. A consumer is not granted a direct right to bring a claim in court. Likewise, this provision does not establish grounds to bring a constitutional claim.[20] On the other hand, consumers are able to turn to the Polish Ombudsman for assistance in protecting their freedoms or rights and, if applicable, have the right to claim compensation for damage caused by the actions of a public body that are contrary to the law (Article 77 of the Constitution). This is also an instrument of directing and shaping the activities of public authorities. It can be used as an interpretational tool by the judiciary, as it contains a general rule to be used in the process of creating and applying the law. Therefore, principles included in Constitutions that refer to consumers can only be treated as indirect instruments of consumer protection. They do not constitute subjective rights.

Consumer human/fundamental rights

By 'human/fundamental rights' we understand all the rights and freedoms that are safeguarded by national Constitutions or international human rights documents.[21] According to the classical, liberal concept of human rights, rights are innate and are derived from the individual nature of a human, rather than being 'granted'. This emphasises a person's individual responsibility for his or her own life and treats human rights as safeguards against the wilfulness of the state. The 'positive' role of the state is confined to being a guarantor of natural rights and, in order to achieve this goal, it can apply commands and prohibitions.[22] In relation to the market, the state plays a very restrained, protective role; it ensures market freedom, order and rules, while refraining from interfering in relations between participants. In this concept of human/fundamental rights there is no place for consumer rights.

Nowadays, the liberal concept of human/fundamental rights is supplemented by the 'social state' concept. According to this concept, the purpose of the state is to direct the processes of social development

[20] Court judgment on 8 May 2000, SK 22/99 OTK ZU 2000 no. 4.

[21] As defined by C. Mak, 'Harmonising Effects of Fundamental Rights in European Contract Law' (2007) 1 *Erasmus Law Review* 60.

[22] Banaszak, *Outline of Polish Constitutional Law*, 67.

and to ensure the fair and just distribution of benefits. The state is obliged to ensure opportunities for individual development in society. To reach these aims, the state can apply a wide spectrum of measures, including those affecting relations between social subjects. This changes the character of human/fundamental rights. Besides the protection of individuals they also have important social functions, namely protecting the interests of individuals and serving the common good. Due to this they can be treated as an instrument of social order. On the basis of the 'social state' concept of human rights, new types of rights have been created; especially important among those rights are social rights.[23]

Fundamental rights and private law

The growing influence of fundamental rights on relationships between private parties under contract law makes it possible to speak about the tendency towards the constitutionalisation of contract law, and shows that the world of fundamental rights and the world of contract law no longer exist in isolation from each other.

The question now is not whether fundamental rights may affect relationships between private parties at different phases of the life of a contract, but rather to what extent this will occur. The next question is whether fundamental rights are directly binding only on the public authorities, or also on private parties.[24] Is it possible to say that they are directly bound as formulated on a constitutional level, or that they are only indirectly addressed and should be taken into account in the process of interpreting and applying the law? In fact, national legal systems have developed various ways of giving effect to fundamental rights in contract law. Under the first approach, fundamental rights in contractual relationships are held to give effect in the same way as in state–citizen relationships (direct effect). Meanwhile, the second approach takes the view that judges cannot and should not do more than draw

[23] *Ibid.* at 68.

[24] C. Mak, *Fundamental Rights in European Contract Law: a Comparison of the Impact of Fundamental Rights on Contractual Relationships in Germany, the Netherlands, Italy and England* (Kluwer Law International, 2008); C. Mak, 'Harmonising Effects', 61–2; O. Cherednychenko, *Fundamental Rights, Contract Law and the Protection of the Weaker Party: a Comparative Analysis of the Constitutionalisation of Contract Law, with Emphasis on Risky Financial Transactions* (Munich: 2007); O. Cherednychenko, 'The Harmonisation of Contract Law in Europe by Means of the Horizontal Effect of Fundamental Rights?' (2007) 1 *Erasmus Law Review* 39–41; M. Safjan, 'Efekt horyzontalny praw podstawowych w prawie prywatnym: autonomia woli a zasada równego traktowania' (2009) 2 *Kwartalnik Prawa Prywatnego* 298.

inspiration from the fundamental rights when interpreting the rules of contract law (indirect effect).[25] From this perspective, fundamental rights serve as an inspiration for the solution of contractual disputes in which values protected by these rights are at stake. The fundamental rights in question may be seen as representing political choices for the protection of certain values in society, but at the same time they constitute enacted rules that may be invoked to enforce the protection of the interests they represent. Fundamental rights may, therefore, in practice form the basis for challenges to the validity of certain contractual terms. They import new values that were not previously recognised in private law.[26]

Yet this view may be questioned. Fundamental rights are hardly suitable for the direct regulation of relationships between private parties in various phases of the contract's life and, in particular, for protecting the weaker party against risky financial transactions in the private law courts. The interests of the weaker party can be protected not simply by a single fundamental right, but by several. There is a danger of arbitrary choices between constitutional rights being made by judges guided primarily by their own views. In certain cases, one and the same fundamental right can be used to support the diametrically opposing claims of the parties. As a result, the courts must resolve the conflict arising between two fundamental rights. In the absence of a hierarchy between fundamental rights, the only way of doing this is through balancing the two competing rights against each other.

It is important to note that the application of fundamental rights does not usually have a real effect, as private law provisions can lead to the same results. In contrast to fundamental rights, contract law is much better equipped to address the issue of the imbalance in power in contractual relationships and to provide a basis for an open debate on the extent of the protection of the weaker party at a European level.

Constitutional Court findings

The German *Bundesverfassungsgericht* adopted an indirect influence approach to fundamental rights through the general clauses of private law, rather than proclaiming the direct applicability of these rights between private parties. In the *Handelsvertreter* case in 1990,[27] the Court invalidated a non-competition clause in a contract between a commercial

[25] See also Safjan, 'Efekt', 299–310.

[26] C. Mak, 'Fundamental Rights and the European Regulation of Consumer Contracts' (2008) 31 *Journal of Consumer Policy* 429–30.

[27] Court judgment on 7 January 1990, *BVerfGE* 81, 242.

agent and his principal on the grounds that it was contrary to the agent's constitutional right of freedom to exercise a profession guaranteed by Article 12 (1) of the Constitution (GG). It is worth underscoring that the Court said that private-law courts are obliged to protect constitutional rights in cases where a 'structural inequality in bargaining power' has led to a situation in which a contract is exceptionally onerous for the weaker party. Private-law courts are obliged to protect the constitutional right to private autonomy of this party by intervening within the framework of general clauses.[28] In the light of the constitutionally protected principles of private autonomy (Article 2 GG) and the social state (Articles 20 and 28 GG), the German *Bundesverfassungsgericht* has ruled that courts in civil cases must intervene where a structural imbalance or inequality of power between the contracting parties has resulted in a contract weighing extraordinarily heavily (exceptionally onerous) on the weaker party.[29] Similarly, in the *Parabolantenne* case,[30] the Court developed a method of reading specific provisions of law, mostly general clauses, in the light of constitutionally protected rights. The Italian Supreme Court has applied this method to the general clause of 'good faith', determining that the principle of solidarity, safeguarded by Article 2 of the *Costituzione*, requires the civil courts to make sure that contracting parties have been able to contribute substantively to the content of their contract.[31] It flows from the Constitutional Court case law that fundamental rights are used as a tool in balancing the tension between party autonomy and the protection of the weaker party to the contract.

Role of consumer human/fundamental rights

As we can see, treating consumer protection rules as human/fundamental rights does not necessarily mean much. From a constitutional theory perspective, consumer protection provisions should be treated as constitutional principles or programme norms.[32] They are used to protect the weaker party to a contract, although only in a limited scope. Moreover, such norms are not directly targeted at consumers but rather at workers or sureties. It is highly questionable whether such provisions can be used, for example, to protect the economic interests of consumers. However, they are not meaningless and it is worth noting that, because

[28] See *Bürgschaft* judgment of 19 October 1993, *BVerfGE* 89, 214.

[29] Cherednychencko, 'The Harmonisation of Contract Law', 46–8.

[30] Court judgment on 9 February 1994, *BVerfG* 90, 27.

[31] Mak, 'Harmonising Effects', 64–6. [32] See above p. 340.

of the inclusion of consumer provisions into constitutional catalogues of human/fundamental rights, some legal instruments designated for subjective rights' protection have been used in the area of consumer law (especially the principles of proportionality and the essence of right)[33] or have obtained a constitutional basis.

Protection through other rights

In our opinion consumers can obtain constitutional protection through the application or interpretation of certain recognised subjective rights, especially civil or political rights. This type of application of subjective civil and political rights to protect non-subjective rights is recognised by some Constitutional Courts and takes place in the area of economic and social rights.[34] Similarly, the Polish Constitutional Court has not only used Article 76 of the Constitution to protect consumers, as described above, but has also granted protection on the basis of other constitutional provisions (Article 32 on equality,[35] Article 54 on information,[36] or Article 2 on legislation).[37]

EU dimension

EU 'primary' law

The European dimension of consumer protection has existed for over thirty-five years.[38] The original EEC Treaty of 1957 did not foresee any specific powers in the field of consumer policy. Although the word 'consumer' appears several times in the text of the Treaty, each time

[33] Court judgment on 21 April 2004, K 33/03, 31/4A/2004 and court judgment on 2 December 2008 K 37/07 OTK-A 2008/10/172.

[34] I.Hare, 'Verticality Challenged: Private Parties, Privacy and the Human Rights Act' (2001) *EHRLR* 526–540.

[35] Court judgment on 13 September 2005, K 38/04 92/8/A/2005.

[36] Court judgment on 21 April 2004, K 33/03, 31/4A/2004.

[37] Court judgment on 13 September 2005, K 38/04 92/8/A/2005.

[38] T. Bourgoignie, 'European Community Consumer Law and Policy: from Rome to Amsterdam' (1998) *Consumer Law Journal* 440ff.; T. Bourgoignie, 'Droit et politique communautaires de la consommation: de Rome á Amsterdam' (1997) *Revue européenne de droit de la consommation* 195ff.; S. Chillon, 'Le droit communautaire de la consommation après les traités de Maastricht et d'Amsterdam: un droit emancipé?' (1998) *Revue européenne de droit de la consommation* 265ff.; H. Micklitz, and S. Weatherill, 'Consumer Policy in the European Community: Before and After Maastricht' (1993) *Journal of Consumer Policy*, 285–321; D. Stuyck, 'European Consumer Law after the Treaty of Amsterdam: Consumer Policy in or beyond the Internal Market?' (2000), *CMLRev* 37.

it is connected to a different EC policy, such as the protection of competition, health or the environment. In 1973 the Council of Europe approved a European Charter of Consumers. According to the Charter's provisions, consumers have the right to protection and assistance, understood as protection against physical injury caused by unsafe products and protection against damage to their economic interests. The Charter went on to specify a number of consumer rights: to redress, to information, to education and to representation and consultation.[39] In 1975, the European Community recognised the relevance of consumer protection to the operation of the common market for the first time, in a resolution concerning consumer rights and interests.[40] The rights established by the resolution concern consumer health and safety, the protection of consumer economic interests, advice and the right to damages, information and education and the consultation and representation of consumers.

The Second Action Programme of 1981 went on to lay down five fundamental consumer rights: the protection of life, health and safety, the protection of economic interests, the right to compensation, education and information and finally the right to be represented. The Council Resolution of 23 June 1986 stressed the need for a high level of consumer protection and underlined the value of consumer information and education.

In 1987, the Single European Act recognised consumer protection as an autonomous policy aim connected to the internal market. The general developments that took place in the 1990s gradually shifted the emphasis from market and economic considerations to a wider synthesis between economic and social issues.[41] P. Lagarde used a very convincing concept of a theatre performance to describe the evolution of consumer protection in EU law.[42] In the first act of this play, the consumer was absent. In the second, he appeared as a passive member that should be protected against the market, and, in the third, he became an active actor with his own role to play in creating the market. The same phases of evolution can be observed on the level of primary law in the sphere of

[39] Also S. Weatherill, *EU Consumer Law and Policy*, 7–10.

[40] Council Resolution (EC) No. 92/1, Preliminary Programme of the European Economic Community for a Consumer Protection and Information Policy, 1975 OJ (C 92).

[41] Also H. Micklitz, N. Reich and P. Rott, *Understanding EU Consumer Law* (Intersentia, 2009).

[42] P. Lagarde, 'Le consommateur en droit international privé' in *Ludwig Boltzmann Institut für Europarecht: Vorlesungen und Vorträge*, h.4 (Vienna, 1999).

granting rights to consumers. An important step was taken with the Treaty of Maastricht of 1992. It inserted a new Chapter XI on Consumer Protection into the EC Treaty and added 'a contribution to the strengthening of consumer protection' to the list of the Community's activities. According to Article 129a(1) EC (now 169 TFEU), the Community will contribute to reaching a high level of consumer protection through measures adopted pursuant to Article 114 TFEU in the context of the completion of the internal market, specific action supporting and supplementing the policy pursued by the Member States to protect the health, safety and economic interests of consumers and to provide adequate information to consumers.

The Treaty of Amsterdam introduced some changes to Article 129a, also renumbering it as Article 153 (now 169 TFEU). According to these changes, the Community will contribute to protecting the health, safety and economic interests of consumers, as well as to promoting their right to information, education and to organise themselves in order to safeguard their interests. As alluded to above, though Article 169 TFEU lists consumer interests and rights, the question remains whether this provision has direct effect and can be used by consumers as a legal basis for their claims. It must be noted that Article 169 TFEU is mainly directed towards EU bodies and imposes an obligation on them to ensure a high level of consumer protection. It empowers them to undertake suitable activities, but it does not create any obligation on Member States, or individuals. Special attention should be focused on the right of information. This is the only sphere of protection in Article 169 TFEU that is named as a 'right', which in fact means that it can be directly horizontally applicable.[43]

Role of Article 169 TFEU

In *Rivero*, the ECJ stated that the scope of Article 129a (now 169 TFEU) was limited. The provision provides that the Community has a duty to contribute to achieving a high level of consumer protection and creates Community powers on a consumer protection policy, without laying down any obligation on Member States or individuals. More importantly, according to the ECJ:

> Article 129a cannot justify the possibility of clear, precise and unconditional provisions of directives on consumer protection that have not been transposed into Community law within the prescribed period being

[43] Also Micklitz *et al.*, *Understanding EU Consumer Law*, 22.

> directly relied on as between individuals. In the absence of measures implementing the directive within the prescribed period, a consumer may not, even in view of Article 129a of the Treaty, base a right of action on the directive itself against a lender who is a private person.[44]

Article 169 TFEU cannot, therefore, be treated as a separate and individual base for consumer claims and does not possess direct effect. It must be complemented by provisions of secondary law. Such rules already exist.[45] One may wonder the extent to which these provisions really play a protective role. Without going into detail, it may be assumed that EU secondary consumer legislation is not actually targeted at protecting consumers, but rather at the proper operation of the market. These observations are much more grounded if we deeply examine the scope of the draft directive on consumer rights. In many fields, and especially in the framework of consumer sales, given that the directive adopts a total harmonisation approach, it gives consumers less protection than they already have on the basis of current legislation.

It must be noted that consumer protection is also mentioned in the European Charter of Fundamental Rights, approved in Nice in 2000. According to Article 38 of this charter, 'Union policies must ensure a high level of consumer protection'. In this way consumer protection was acknowledged as a fundamental right in the EU.[46]

Parallel development

The evolution of consumer protection in EU law discloses parallels to the evolution of constitutional provisions: first treated as one of various factors influencing other policies; later as one of those policies; and, at last, as a separate provision. The Single European Act confirmed this and recognised consumer protection as a legitimate goal of the Community within the context of the internal market. The Treaty of Maastricht, in contrast, provided for a *distinct* legal basis for specific Community measures in consumer protection. Accordingly, consumer protection has moved up to the rank of a fundamental constitutional value of EU law. What does this mean for consumer protection?

The evaluation should be carried out in compliance with national experiences of consumer protection constitutionalisation. This means that evolution of the provisions of the European Charter of Fundamental

[44] 7 March 1996, *El Corte Inglés SA* v. *Cristina Blázquez Rivero*, Case C-192/94, I-01281.

[45] For example: Directives 93/13, 85/577, 97/7, 90/314, 99/44, 2008/48, 2008/12.

[46] J. Barcz, *Fundamental Rights Protection in the European Union* (Warsaw 2009), para. 27 XII.

Rights and the TFEU can be compared to parallel provisions contained in national constitutions. Therefore they may have an indirect effect, which has been acknowledged in ECJ case law. In this regard, one cannot anticipate that the line accepted in *Rivero* would be changed. Furthermore, in a number of cases the Court interpreted EU legislation in the light of fundamental rights under existing EU law. It has stated that the content of fundamental rights must be respected when adopting and implementing ECU law and that national law must be interpreted and applied in a way that is compatible with fundamental rights. The ECHR and the ECJ should determine an appropriate level of protection to be granted to a particular weaker party on the basis of fundamental rights prescribed in the ECHR.[47] We assume that this is the direction of development of consumer protection on the primary level, together with the principles of proportionality or the core of right concept.[48]

Protection by other rights

At EU level as much as in constitutional law, consumer protection will be developed through reference to EU fundamental rights where they are acknowledged as subjective rights.[49] The consumer may refer to such rights as privacy (Article 8, ECHR), non-discrimination (Article 14, ECHR) and, possibly, the freedom to receive information (Article 11(1), Charter of Fundamental Rights of the EU). The probable direction of development will be parallel to the evolution of constitutional law; incidental, but rather high in special spheres of protection. It may even be achieved in an easier manner (in comparison with national legislation), as some grounds already exist in EU law. For example the right to protection of privacy, as a fundamental right, constitutes part of the European Charter of Fundamental Rights, and can thus serve as a foundation of consumer protection.[50] It may be even better observed in those rights that are protected in EU secondary legislation. For example, taking the example of data protection law, consumers may, in some areas, be protected by general EU data protection instruments and specific instruments

[47] D. Kornobis-Romanowska, *Europejska konwencja praw człowieka w systemie prawa wspólnot europejskich* (Dom Wydawniczy ABC) 97 *et seq.*

[48] I. Justyńska, *Zasada poszanowania praw człowieka w europejskim prawie wspólnotowym* (Toruń: 2009), 258ff.

[49] S. Douglas-Scott, *Constitutional Law of the European Union* (London: Longman, 2002).

[50] Compare judgments of ECJ in J. Braciak, *Prawo do prywatności* (Wydawnictwo Sejmowe, 2004) 104–5.

relating directly to consumers. They give persons the right to be informed, to have access to data, to object to automated processes and provide administrative and judicial remedies. The Data Protection Directive may, therefore, be treated as an important consumer protection instrument in relation to processes of consumer information.[51]

Protection through other rights can be especially important if the development of EU consumer protection goes in a direction traced by the draft directive on consumer rights.[52] If the total harmonisation approach is maintained,[53] then sometimes it may be better for a consumer to seek protection either through other rules, or even not to be treated as a consumer.[54]

Conclusions

The 'fundamentalisation' of consumer rights is developing along parallel lines with regard to national constitutional and EU law. This parallel development brings with it new values and possibilities in elaborating consumer protection. Nevertheless, the catalyst for this process should be continue to be found in secondary legislation (usually consumer protection is 'specified by statute').

Introducing consumer protection into the catalogue of fundamental rights does not presuppose their direct effect or the possibility of formulating a claim solely on the basis of fundamental rights. The recognition of consumer protection as a fundamental value will be of importance in the process of interpreting and applying the law.

The introduction of consumer protection into a 'supra-statute' law (catalogues of human/fundamental rights) means that it is becoming part of the constitutional order. As a result, these rights are submitted to constitutional protective instruments, such as the principal of proportionality and the core of right.

[51] L. A. Bygrave, *Data Protection Law: Approaching its Rationale, Logic and Limits*, (Kluwer Law International, 2002), 97ff.; C. Kuner, *European Data Protection Law: Corporate Compliance and Regulation* (Oxford University Press, 2007), 63ff.

[52] Proposal for a Directive of the European Parliament and of the Council on consumer rights/* COM/2008/0614 final – COD 2008/0196.

[53] Among others see also H. Micklitz and N. Reich, 'Crónica De Una Muerte Anunciada: the Commission Proposal for a "Directive On Consumer Rights"', (2009) 46 *CMLRev* 493ff.; T. Wilhelmsson 'Full Harmonisation of Consumer Contract Law?' (2008) 2 *ZEuP* 228–9.

[54] As it sometimes happens, for example in Polish law in the issue of non-conformity, when it is in some areas better for a consumer to seek protection not in consumer-orientated rules (Consumer Sales Law of 2002) but in the provisions of the Civil Code.

Finally, consumer protection can be achieved through other subjective rights, already approved of and detailed in secondary legislation. This way of proceeding may even ensure a higher level of protection, especially when compared to secondary consumer law, and especially in comparison with the proposed directive on consumer rights, which in fact places consumer law on the outskirts of civil law.

18

Consumer protection in a normative context: the building blocks of a consumer citizenship practice

JIM DAVIES

Introduction

There has been a transformation of the consumers' role in the EU since the 1980s: a transformation that has seen the consumer of the internal market[1] evolve from the feeble agent of market economics requiring rights-based protection into the *potentially* confident, informed and empowered 'motor of economic change'.[2] This chapter examines the developing notion of a consumer citizenship practice associated with this transformation. It draws attention to the institutional structures for individual and collective agency and reflect movements in decision-making power away from the Member States: upwards to the EU; outwards to independent regulatory agencies and enforcement authorities; and downwards to individual consumers. It has been argued that the move to regulatory agencies has produced a weakening of the state-*qua*-central actor although at the same time it could be seen as *a strengthening of public action* and effective governance for the people'.[3] Agencies and regulatory authorities are thus forming networks of self-supporting epistemic communities for the sharing of new ideas and best practices.

Specifically, this chapter discusses the normative influences that shape individual consumer behaviour and argues that, while the networks of

Department of Law, University of Northampton. This chapter reproduces Chapter 5 from Jim Davies's book *The European Consumer Citizen in Law and Policy* published 2011, (Palgrave Macmillan) reproduced with the permission of Palgrave Macmillan.

[1] For the sake of consistency, the terms EU and internal market are used throughout.

[2] Commission, 2007, EU Consumer Policy Strategy 2007–2013 – Empowering consumers, enhancing welfare, effectively protecting them (Communication) COM (2007) 99 final, 13 March 2007, 2.

[3] V. Schmidt, 'The EU and its Member States: from Bottom up to Top down', in D. Phinnemore and A. Warleigh-Lack (eds.), *Reflections on European Integration: 50 Years of the Treaty of Rome*. (Basingstoke: Palgrave Macmillan, 2009), 205.

self-supporting epistemic communities provide platforms for a *theoretical* application of consumer citizenship practice, individual and structural barriers limit its practical application. Normative orientations of consumer citizenship practice are located in the enforcement and empowerment aspects of consumer protection; state, civil society and market sources of consumer information; individual and structural aspects of capability; and the individualistic and solidaristic aspects of motivation. A model hierarchy of these normative orientations is introduced outlining the features or enablers of such a consumer citizenship practice. A practice that is capable of policy and market shaping through the transactional, post-transactional and extra-transactional consumer behaviours that are developing with the encouragement of the EU institutions but that are limited by the barriers that challenge the effectiveness of these normative influences.

EU consumer protection: law and policy, development and integration

Prior to the 1970s there was little recognition of the consumer at the Community level and consumer protection measures were left to develop separately within the Member States. This began to change following the Paris Summit in 1972 where the heads of state and government emphasised, under the development of the social policy, that they attached much importance to strengthening and coordinating measures of consumer protection.[4] Explicit recognition that the status of the consumer was about to change came in the 1975 preliminary programme for a consumer protection and information policy.[5] Albeit a modest start, the consumer was no longer to be the stereotypical utility-maximising model of micro-economic theory.[6] No longer to be seen merely as a purchaser and user of goods and services for personal, family or group purposes, the consumer was to be recognised 'as a person concerned with the various facets of society which may affect him either directly or indirectly as a consumer'.[7] The effects of globalisation were also affecting the consumer, who in the

[4] Bulletin of the European Communities, Statement from the Paris Summit October 1972, no. 10, last accessed at www.ena.lu/statement-paris-summit-19–21-october-1972–020002284.html on 20 January 2010.

[5] Preliminary programme of the European Economic Community for a consumer protection and information policy [1975] OJ C 92/2.

[6] See S. Drakopoulos, 'Keynes' Economic Thought and the Theory of Consumer Behaviour' (1992) 39, *Scottish Journal of Political Economy* 318.

[7] *Ibid.*, item 3.

past had constituted 'an individual purchaser in a small local market, [but had now] become *merely a unit in a mass market*, the target of advertising campaigns and of pressure by strongly organized production and distribution groups'.[8] The consumer was recognised as having lost power in a changing market environment and was to be protected at the Union level by positive harmonisation and the introduction of consumer rights.[9]

Consumer protection became a policy focus in the Community, built on a set of rights with the potential to check the power of capital and restore market efficiency. It was, however, made clear that these rights were to be addressed through 'action under specific Community policies such as the economic, common agricultural, social, environment, transport and energy policies as well as by the approximation of laws'.[10] Then, the Single European Act 1986 significantly altered the relationship between consumer policy and the process of approximation of laws as it affected the functioning of the internal market. In particular, the addition of Article 114 TFEU (Article 95 EC) required the institutions to 'take as a base a high level of protection' in proposals concerning 'health, safety . . . and consumer protection' and procedurally introduced qualified majority voting for adoption in Council, although it did not provide a specific legal base for consumer legislation.[11] Legislative development of the consumer *acquis* was soon to follow in a number of priority areas through which the Council sought proposals from the Commission for harmonisation of consumer protection measures. Confirmation to pursue these priorities came with the second programme for a consumer protection and information policy and marked the beginning of a limited and fragmented expansion in consumer protection measures of minimum harmonisation.[12]

[8] *Ibid.*, item 6, emphasis added.

[9] J. Davies, *The European Consumer Citizen in Law and Policy* (Palgrave MacMillan, 2011), 26.

[10] S. Weatherill, 'Consumer Policy', in P. Craig and G. de Búrca (eds.), *The Evolution of EU Law* (Oxford University Press, 1999), 694.

[11] J. Stuyck, 'European Consumer Law after the Treaty of Amsterdam: Consumer Policy in or beyond the internal Market?' (2000) 37 *CMLRev* 367, at 378.

[12] Limited proposals included directives: to protect the consumer in respect of contracts which have been negotiated away from business premises; relating to the approximation of the laws, regulations and administrative provisions of the Member States concerning misleading and unfair advertising; relating to the approximation of the laws, regulations and administrative provisions of Member States concerning liability for defective products and a directive relating to the approximation of the laws, regulations and administrative provisions of the Member States concerning consumer credit.

This was also a period in which the ECJ 'played a major role in moving the Community along a continuum from Market towards State'[13] and in which the process of EU integration developed manifold, complex and at times contradictory relationships between the economic and political levels, as well as in the legal sphere of structures, institutions and norms.[14] As with other areas, norm creation in the consumer sphere is marked by legal elements that play a dual role in which 'they are both the object and the agent of integration'.[15] Dehousse and Weiler also point out that legal and institutional factors largely condition the evolution of the integration process through an influence that is often indirect, but that 'can directly affect the substance of the policies pursued by the various actors'.[16] They assert that any attempt to review the legal patterns of integration 'should encompass the relationships between all actors interested by this phenomenon', both public and private actors, and that 'private actors can play a semi-normative role in drafting integration instruments'.[17] Both formal and informal channels now exist for such public and private actors, including the individual consumer, to influence the development of centralised consumer policy through the exercise of behaviours that define consumer citizenship practice.[18]

The internal market does not, however, offer uniform opportunities and, within the confines of consumer policy, the broader issues and complexities of EU integration, associated with geographic and functional expansion, have produced systemic inconsistency at the Member State level. Such inconsistency challenges any traditional notion of a Kelsenian or Hartian legal order as a hierarchical structure of norms in the EU.[19] Instead, new governance techniques of benchmarking, identification

[13] H. Micklitz, T. Roethe, and S. Weatherill (eds.), *Federalism and Responsibility: a Study on Product Safety Law and Practice in the European Community* (London: Graham and Trotman, 1994), 12 and 14. Attention is drawn to the inevitable process of change in the Community's legal order whereby 'The executive force of Community law cannot vary from one State to another in deference to subsequent domestic laws, without jeopardising the attainment of the objectives of the Treaty', explained by the Court as early as 1964 in Case 6/64, *Costa* v. *ENEL* [1964] ECR 585.

[14] R. Dehouss, and J. Weiler, 'The Legal Dimension', in W. Wallace (ed.), *The Dynamics of European Integration* (London: Royal Institute of International Affairs, 1990), 242.

[15] *Ibid.*, at 243. [16] *Ibid.*, at 247. [17] *Ibid.*, at 249.

[18] Davies, *The European Consumer Citizen*, 8.

[19] S. Weatherill, 'On the Depth and Breadth of European integration' (1997) 17 *OJLS*, 537; N. Walker, 'Legal Theory and the European Union: a 25th Anniversary Essay' (2005) 25 *OJLS* 581, at 592.

of 'best practice' and non-binding cooperation are employed to promote the integration process and add to the policy-making process.[20] The growth in the number of Member States acceding to the EU since the 1990s has seen the theoretical debates over European integration develop into an analysis of the process of Europeanisation, raising questions of how the EU's supranational institutions have affected the institutions of the Member States and how the policies of the EU affect national policy.[21] In setting out the parameters for locating consumer citizenship practice within such a polycentred structure of political authority this chapter identifies, in the context of the theory and practice of consumer protection, what Walker suggests should be encouraged: that is,

> a new commitment to a bottom-up democratic experimentalism ... in which coherence is ... a ... matter of forward-looking mutual learning and synergy between different problem-solving micro-communities in which the norm-application distinction dissolves in a process of continuous reflection, adaptation and recognition.[22]

Transforming boundaries: transforming roles

While the geographic boundaries of the internal market have been transformed with the accession of new Member States so too have broad sectors of the internal market been transformed from state-based monopolies into liberalised markets of services of general interest. Prior to the mid-1980s, the traditional bilateral private law relationship, based on freedom to contract between the customer and the merchant, had been superseded in those sectors that became state monopolies. The incumbent service provider was obliged to contract with the customer and the legal relationship between the state monopoly and the customer switched to a public law setting in which price was often determined by political subsidy. Subsequent privatisation and liberalisation introduced new dynamics into the customer/service provider relationship. Privatisation brought with it the concept of the universal service obligation that reached 'beyond the limits set to the freedom of contract via standard terms legislation' [23] and introduced a guarantee of 'access to all, irrespective of the economic, social or geographical situation, at a specified quality and

[20] G. Majone, *Dilemmas of European Integration* (Oxford University Press, 2005) 59.
[21] Schmidt, 'The EU', 194. [22] Walker, 'Legal Theory', 594.
[23] H. W. Micklitz, 'Universal Services: Nucleus for a Social European Private Law', EUI Working Paper, Law 2009/12, last accessed at http://cadmus.eui.eu/dspace/bitstream/1814/12238/1/LAW_2009_12.pdf on 24 September 2009, 10.

an affordable price'.[24] While privatisation was accompanied by rules to prevent social exclusion, liberalisation introduced competition to the provision of services and choice of service provider for the consumer. The essential nature of this marketisation of public services attracted an amalgam of developing normative processes that influenced market dynamics and brought about a hybridisation of public and private law in a public services sector that yielded the conflated concept of the consumer citizen.[25]

With liberalisation came the establishment of regulatory agencies operating between the state and the new consumer citizen; these agencies have created a framework through which the Commission appears to express an aspiration for an active and participatory consumer citizenship practice and in which the regulatory agencies act as 'representatives' of the consumer citizen interest, reinforcing the opportunities and extending the capabilities for consumers:

> to take up their rights, especially their right of access, often requires the existence of independent regulators with appropriate staff and clearly defined powers and duties. These include powers of sanction, in particular the ability to monitor the transposition and enforcement of universal service provisions. These also require provisions for the *representation and active participation of consumers and users* in the definition and evaluation of services, the availability of appropriate redress and compensation mechanisms, and the existence of a review clause allowing requirements to be adapted over time to reflect new social, technological and economic developments.[26]

Yet, as Micklitz points out, there is no legal obligation in the secondary legislation for the regulatory agencies to uphold the rights of consumer citizens, although '[t]here is a gradual movement of [EU] secondary law into that direction which might overcome ... the still existing discrepancies between the role and function of the regulatory agencies in the Member States'.[27]

For the individual consumer, the normative orientations that support the consumer's ability to actively participate in market shaping may be

[24] E. Szyszczak, *The Regulation of the State in Competitive Markets in the EU* (Oxford: Hart, 2007), 244–5.

[25] Micklitz, 'Universal Services', 9, although Micklitz uses the reverse and hyphenated form 'citizen-consumer'.

[26] Commission, 2007, 'Services of general interest, including social services of general interest: a new European commitment' (Communication) COM (2007) 725 final, 20 November 2007 at 10–11, emphasis added. See also Micklitz, 'Universal Services', 16.

[27] *Ibid.* at 16.

drawn together and assembled into a hierarchical framework. It is a framework that can be used as a tool in assessing the functioning of any particular market sector, or in the formulation of strategy: a framework in which the inherent barriers to the normative influences highlight the practical limitations of consumer citizenship practice. It is also a tool that provides for the assessment of the extent to which consumers have the protection, information, capability and motivation to pursue their aspirations, if they have any, as market agents. This hierarchical model, depicted in Table 18.1, identifies normative influences that are interlinked and interrelated so that the effectiveness of each level has dependencies contingent on both its subordinate and superior levels. While closely interlinked and interrelated, the separate levels of this hierarchy are also distinct in their normative dimensions.

In its normative dimension European consumer protection law addresses the issues of how legal rules can be formulated to complete the internal market, to protect vulnerable consumers or to provide mechanisms for redress with regard to faulty or damaged goods or services. This is the legal base in the hierarchy of consumer citizenship practice that, at a minimum, makes available to individuals a framework of consumer rights to which they can appeal.[28] The second level comprises normative sources of information that are a necessary adjunct to consumer empowerment, even if their effect is limited.[29] At the third level, capability is used within the dual context of Amartya Sen's capability approach that gives normative priority to the existential features of functionings[30] and Rawlsian principles of social justice: social justice that is dependent on structural policies to alleviate poverty, inequality and unemployment, and that Echávarri discusses in the context of social capability and the individuals' access to the capability for being self-sufficient, the capability for self-respect and the capability for agency.[31] Finally, at the highest level of the normative hierarchy, motivation is used as a label for consumer behaviour that can be understood in the

[28] See generally N. MacCormick, *Institutions of Law: an Essay in Legal Theory* (Oxford University Press, 2007).

[29] G. Howells, 'The Potential and Limits of Consumer Empowerment by Information' (2005) 32 *Journal of Law and Society* 349, at 357.

[30] D. Gasper, 'What is the Capability Approach? Its Core, Rationale, Partners and Dangers' (2007) 36 *The Journal of Socio-Economics* 335, at 337.

[31] See R. Echávarri, 'Development Theories and Development as Social Capability Expansion', Working Paper 0305, Departamento de Economía – Universidad Pública de Navarra, last accessed at ftp://ftp.econ.unavarra.es/pub/DocumentosTrab/DT0305.PDF on 4 December 2009.

Table 18.1. *Normative hierarchy of consumer citizenship practice*

Level	Normative hierarchy			Features/enablers	Barriers/consequences
4	Motivation	Solidaristic and communitarian		Self-responsibility; altruism; ethical and sustainable consumption; communal interest; perceived effectiveness of action; wealth; trustworthiness of information source; 'good guilt' social trends	Capability barriers; dependency on education and/or capability factors; unwilling to act; cost; attitude–behaviour gap; information overload
		Individualistic		Self-responsibility; personal safety; demand for quality and reduced cost; self-interest; perceived effectiveness of action; wealth	Capability barriers; dependency on education and/or capability factors; unwilling to act; cost; attitude–behaviour gap
3	Capability	Structural	Market	Open markets and free competition; absolute and comparative monitoring of consumer behaviours/outcomes (e.g. scoreboard and eurobarometer); access to national consumer agencies; product design; soft law in the form of industry standards and voluntary codes of quality; corporate social responsibility; non-discriminatory dignity and respect	Market distortion and market failure; competition and policy deficit; market power; inadequate unbundling in network sectors; lack of operational transparency; general consumer detriment; product design; generic delivery and consumer interface models

Table 18.1. (*cont.*)

Level	Normative hierarchy			Features/enablers	Barriers/consequences
			Social	Access to primary social goods (rights, liberties, opportunities, powers and income and wealth); perceived individual responsibility; future focused; able to take action; no/few personal needs conflicts with action; access to informed fora and/or social groups	Cultural barriers; little/no sense of individual responsibility; cost driven choice/no choice; present focused; unacceptable or unfeasible goals
		Individual	Cognitive	The exercise of informed, educated and reasoned, value guided choice; learned experience	Individual consumer detriment; mistake; false perceptions of consumer welfare; limited access to education
			Physical	Active and communicative; confidence and self-assuredness; switching; complaining	Vulnerability through disability, age, language and deprivation; individual consumer detriment
			Financial	The means to choose not limited to price	Limitation of means; financial vulnerability; consumer detriment
2	Information	Product labelling and branding		Origin and content data; safety information; energy efficiency ratings; 'green' labelling; brand identification; product differentiation; informed choice	Technical terminology; pace of life; accessibility of information; dependency on education and/or capability; globalised e-commerce

		Education and public information	Market functioning indicators (scoreboard data); consumer agency awareness; confident consumers; informed choice; school's curriculum	Insufficient education opportunity and/or capability barriers; information overload
		National consumer organisations	Product comparison; representative action; popular awareness and media presence; informed choice; promotion of consumer interests	Insufficient education and/or capability to exploit information; lack of conformity between Member States
1	protection	Empowerment	Consumer rights and redress mechanisms; guarantees and obligations in standard term contracts; consumer voice and influence; consumer agency in policy development; universal/ public service rights; informed choice; trust in national consumer agencies; transparency of contract terms	Consumer irrationality and inconsistency; narrow interpretation of subsidiarity; different national laws of contract; lack of understanding and/or acceptance of self-responsibility
		Enforcement	Effective public enforcement and regulatory agencies; guarantees and obligations in standard term contracts; universal/public service obligations; transparent redress mechanisms; ADR provisions; competition authorities	Competition enforcement deficit; access to (competition) evidence; cost; globalised e-commerce; lack of awareness of enforcement processes

context of the intrinsic motivation directed by the individual consumer's sense of compliance with, and commitment to, personal and social norms, and the consumers' identification with the social groups that they associate themselves with.[32]

The protected, informed, capable and motivated consumer assumes the role of the consumer citizen, the embodiment of the effective and empowered market agent that appears to be the central goal of EU consumer policy.[33] This is the consumer policy strategy that recognises empowered consumers as the 'motor of economic change'; that through information and education empowered consumers will assume civic duties as market agents, asserting their rights and adopting behaviours that will exercise a normative influence in encouraging suppliers to improve the quality, competitiveness and the sustainability of their goods or services. Encouragement of such agency can be found in the Commission's consumer policy strategy for 2007–2013 where the objective of shifting the focus of regulation 'towards citizen-focused outcomes', is based on the provision of market tools to 'empower citizens, as consumers, to make sustainable environmental choices'.[34] A policy that extends the normative influences on consumer behaviour into the fourth motivational level of the hierarchy that embraces ethical choice.

The Commission's approach is to encourage empowerment *and* personal development through inclusive policies aimed at reducing dependence and supporting the autonomy and self-reliance of people so that they will be able to adopt greater responsibilities.[35] It is an approach that links the empowerment aspect of consumer protection with both the information and motivation levels in the normative hierarchy by seeking to ensure that consumers can make 'informed, environmentally and socially responsible choices on food, the most advantageous products and services, and those that correspond most to their lifestyle objectives'.[36]

[32] For a discussion of the normative aspect of intrinsic motivation, see A. Lam and J. Lambermont-Ford, 'Knowledge Creation and Sharing in Organisational Contexts: A Motivation-based Perspective', School of Management, Royal Holloway University of London, Working Paper Series SoMWP-0801, last accessed at http://eprints.thul.ac.uk/727/3/Lam-LF_0801.pdf on 2 November 2009.

[33] Commission, A single market for 21st century Europe (Communication) COM (2007) 724 final, 20 November 2007, 6.

[34] *EU Consumer Policy Strategy*, 3.

[35] Commission, 2001, Draft joint report on social inclusion (Communication) COM (2001) 565 final, 10 October 2001; see also EU Consumer Policy Strategy.

[36] Commission, 2005, Healthier, safer, more confident citizens: a health and consumer protection strategy (Communication) COM (2005) 115 final, 6 April 2005 at s. 4.2.4.

At the information level, consumer empowerment is supported by product information, branding and labelling that the Court recognises contain a mechanism for achieving consumer protection, although empowerment through information has already been identified as a 'contrivance of limited effect' and 'wasted on many'.[37] Physical access to product information may be a necessary prerequisite for acquiring empowering information but it needs to be complemented with intellectual and social access in order to realise its full potential.[38] As Howells has identified, busy lives and the frequent need to seek out information result in few consumers taking any notice of the information provided. Although some do and, he suggests, some of those may have more reason to than others, for those that do form a 'margin of active information seeking consumers [who] can have a healthy impact on the market'.[39] This is a margin with the cognitive capability to exercise value guided and informed choice to push up standards for all and that connect the information, capability and motivation levels of consumer citizenship practice. It is a margin where information is empowering for the consumer, where information can be absorbed, and where the individual is motivated and able to act on the information.

Howells, however, also identifies limitations on the normative value of information for those with busy lives and the frequent need to seek out information, and suggests that choice for all, but particularly for the poor, may merely be illusory.[40] Consumers do not, or cannot, always make rational and fully informed choices: consequentially, personal or individual consumer detriment impinges on normative aspects of motivation and capability and justifies the introduction of consumer protection measures. In contrast, Scammell provides a far more positive commentary. She sees possibilities for information and choice effectively transforming the market and the power of the consumer, relative to that of the producer, such that '[i]ncreasingly producers will have to find products for consumers, not customers for pre-designed products'.[41]

For European policy-makers, Europe Economics has provided a detailed report that both analyses the issues of personal and structural consumer detriment and identifies its potential use as a policy tool. Structural consumer detriment is identified as an economics-based concept that

[37] Howells, 'The Potential and Limits', 352 and 357.

[38] *Ibid.*, at 357. [39] *Ibid.* [40] *Ibid.*, at 358.

[41] M. Scammell, 'Citizen Consumers: towards a New Marketing of Politics?' LSE, last accessed at http://depts.washington.edu/gcp/pdf/citizenconsumers.pdf on 10 December 2009 at 5.

focuses on the loss of consumer welfare due to market or regulatory failure and that has the potential to apply across an entire market or sector.[42] In its analysis of structural detriment, the report suggests that the Commission might use the concept in the context of competition law, citing mergers, cartels and abuse of dominant position investigations; and in the '[i]mpact assessment of policies designed to improve outcomes for consumers by addressing market or regulatory failures'.[43]

In contrast, Europe Economics associate the concept of personal consumer detriment with a focus on negative outcomes for individual consumers, relative to some benchmark such as expectations or reasonable expectations, and the idea that some aspects of this type of detriment depend on the psychology of the person concerned. With regard to consumer welfare, the report identifies a number of aspects of personal detriment, providing examples of 'things which could constitute a "negative outcome" for a consumer' which include: financial loss, inconvenience, loss of time, stress, low quality products and reduced real choice. Such examples are then categorised as financial or non-financial detriment and take the form of a psychological damage that is revealed through negative feelings of anger, worry or regret, feelings, that may be associated with the counterfactual benchmark of consumer expectations (actual or reasonable), and in which 'personal detriment becomes almost identical to widely accepted definitions of consumer dissatisfaction'. The report also highlights the complexities that may be associated with the use of 'expectations' as a counterfactual in an EU context: it draws attention *inter alia* to the lower level of consumer expectation that may be found in the newer Member States, as compared to the EU15, who may as a consequence 'appear to suffer lower detriment even if, objectively measured, consumer outcomes are actually worse'.[44]

While acknowledging the complex and diverse range of barriers that stand in the way of the consumers' opportunity to exercise influence as a 'motor of economic change', the central argument of this chapter calls for a more holistic approach to the development of consumer agency in the internal market, an approach that, if adopted, would see greater focus placed on the relationships between, and the consequential effects of, the normative influences in the primary categories of consumer

[42] Europe Economics, '*An analysis of the issue of consumer detriment and the most appropriate methodologies to estimate it*' Report for DG SANCO, 2007, last accessed at http://ec.europa.eu/consumers/strategy/docs/study_consumer_detriment.pdf on 23 November 2009, at 40–1.

[43] *Ibid.*, at 66. [44] *Ibid.*, at 47–50.

citizenship practice that encompass consumer protection, information, capability and motivation.

Normative influences of consumer protection

Consumer protection is positioned as the foundation level in a hierarchy of consumer citizenship practice based on normative orientations. It is a stratum of normative influence characterised by the provisions of the EU's consumer *acquis* and other legislative initiatives that provide for the paradigms of consumer empowerment and enforcement. These are the twin channels of consumer protection that have been identified as underpinning EU consumer policy and are identified with the 'smooth functioning of markets',[45] a 'smooth functioning' that is monitored at the EU level by the Consumer Markets Scoreboard through a screening of consumer markets and detailed analysis of those sectors that are then suspected of malfunctioning.[46] Such monitoring measures the consumer behaviours associated with complaints, prices, satisfaction, switching and safety, and provides for national benchmarking data focused on enforcement. This is consumer behaviour predicated on the the five basic consumer rights, introduced in the preliminary programme for a consumer protection and information policy,[47] on the normative effects of the contractual documentation obligations of the consumer *acquis*, and on the normative consequences stemming from the involvement of consumer organisations and the introduction of regulatory bodies within structures of new governance.[48]

The basic rights introduced in the preliminary programme provided the normative context that was to be reflected in the consumer *acquis* and that embraced the right to protection of health and safety; the right to protection of economic interests; the right of redress; the right to information and education; and the right of representation (the right to be heard). Examples of contractual documentation obligations with normative effect appear through a variety of obligations placed on the

[45] Commission, Second consumer markets scoreboard (Staff Working Document) SEC (2009) 76, (Part 3), 28 January 2009, at 1.

[46] Commission, Consumer Markets Scoreboard website, http://ec.europa.eu/consumers/strategy/facts_en.htm#background.

[47] Preliminary programme of the European Economic Community for a consumer protection and information policy [1975] OJ C 92/2, para. 3.

[48] See generally Davies, *The European Consumer Citizen*, Chapter 3.

seller in the subsequent consumer protection legislation and appear *inter alia* as: warranty periods and guarantees over the rights within which the consumer is entitled to a free repair of the goods or services, or to their replacement, or to a refund of money paid;[49] the right to withdraw from or cancel the contract (cooling off);[50] fairness in standard term contracts;[51] and the use of plain language.[52] Yet, at this foundation level, application of the consumer *acquis* provides only 'a fragmentary harmonisation ... and, since the national laws of contract are different, it causes problems when it needs to be adjusted to the various national laws'.[53] In the liberalised areas of services of general economic interest, it is universal and public service obligations that give a normative orientation to the provision of services which may be uneconomic but that are recognised as socially essential. Member States are obliged to ensure a geographic universal service of specified quality and at an affordable price in the telecommunications,[54] postal[55] and electricity markets.[56] Such obligations also provide the normative impetus for transparent consumer complaint procedures.[57]

Reinforcing the normative potential of consumer protection measures and enforcement mechanisms at this foundation level are the regulatory bodies, consumer organisations and the dispute mediation bodies of the EU and the Member States' new governance networks for consumer policy. These form the complex infra-national governance structures that embrace civil society, provide a platform for consumer citizenship practice and support consultation and the representation of consumers' interests.[58]

[49] Directive (EC) 99/44 on certain aspects of the sale of consumer goods and associated guarantees [1999] OJ L 171/12, Arts. 3 and 6.

[50] For example, Directive (EEC) 85/577 to protect the consumer in respect of contracts negotiated away from business premises [1985] OJ L 372/31, Arts. 4 and 5; Directive (EC) 97/7 on the protection of consumers in respect of distance contracts [1997] OJ L144/19, Art. 6.

[51] Directive (EEC) 93/13 on unfair terms in consumer contracts [1993] OJ L95/29, Arts. 3, 4 and 6.

[52] *Ibid.*, Arts. 4 and 5.

[53] O. Lando, 'Liberal, Social and "Ethical" Justice in European Contract Law' (2006) 43 *CMLRev* 817, at 818.

[54] Directive (EC) 2002/22 universal services directive, Art. 11.

[55] Directive (EC) 2008/6 full accomplishment of community postal services, Art. 1(16).

[56] Directive (EC) 2003/54 electricity common rules, Art. 3(3).

[57] For example, Directive (EC) 2002/22 universal services directive, Art. 34.

[58] For a detailed analysis of the networks and structures of new governance in the consumer arena see Davies, *The European Consumer Citizen*, Chapter 3.

Normative aspects of information provision

Standardised, normative, documentation of sell-by dates, best-before dates, contents lists, nutritional values, energy efficiency labelling and recycling information are familiar to all. The strategy of empowering consumers through information and education has already been recognised as having the dual objective of both providing consumers with the means to protect themselves and the consequential drive towards quality improvement and competition for goods and services in the market. As such, consumer empowerment has been explicitly linked to a healthier economy such that 'the rationale for consumer protection becomes in part the health of the economy'.[59] It is in this vein that, in the United Kingdom, the then Department of Trade and Industry (DTI) has suggested that:

> [e]mpowering consumers benefits not only the individuals concerned, but consumers and markets as a whole. Competitive markets are driven by empowered consumers because people who vote with their feet prompt businesses to improve, and to offer even better deals to their customers. Empowering consumers is therefore central to our strategy for improving Britain's consumer regime.[60]

One of the desired outcomes of such a policy approach is to bring about change in the manner in which individuals act when engaged as consumers. In seeking to empower consumers through the normative channels of education and information such a policy extends the role of the consumer to one more akin to that of a citizen. In the case of the United Kingdom, through the auspices of the DTI, there is an express desire 'to see consumers who understand that they have responsibilities as well as rights'.[61] British consumer law does not, however, stand alone: it is strongly influenced by EU consumer policy and its preference for providing information rather than interventionist norms.[62] As Howells identifies, this approach is epitomised in a Commission Communication that includes an action point for the development of better informed and educated consumers whereby:

> consumers, through better information, are able to make informed, environmentally and socially responsible choices on food, the most

[59] Howells, 'The Potential and Limits', 350.
[60] DTI, 2005, Extending competitive markets: empowered consumers, successful businesses, last accessed at http://www.berr.gov.uk/files/file23787.pdf on 10 December 2009, para. 5.2.
[61] *Ibid.* [62] Howells, 'The Potential and Limits', 351.

> advantageous products and services, and those that correspond most to their lifestyle objectives thus building up trust and confidence.[63]

An action that was reflected, in the context of its focus, in the DTI publication some two months later that introduced a new government service, Environment Direct:

> which will provide consumers with information and advice on how to reduce the environmental impact of the goods and services they buy and use. This will raise awareness of the collective effects of individual consumption decisions, but will also help empower consumers to take personal responsibility through more informed choices.[64]

and, in the context of its scope, by the DTI's objective that:

> [we] not only want to empower consumers shopping in Britain, we also want consumers to have the confidence to shop across national borders. The Government may have a role to play in helping consumers get advice or redress in cross-border cases as it may be hard for them to do so on their own. We will push for our vision of the empowered and responsible consumer, with appropriate protection for vulnerable consumers, to become the norm in the EU consumer regime.[65]

Analysis of contemporary consumption suggests, however, that any simplistic notion of the consumer is misplaced and choice, a reality for most consumers, also has important limitations. While acknowledging the essential nature of information as a precursor to real choice such analysis identifies 'the vital unpredictability which characterizes some of our actions and experiences as consumers, both singly and collectively'.[66] This is an analysis identifying that, as consumers, individuals can be just as irrational, incoherent and inconsistent as they can be rational, planned and organised; we may act in an individualistic way or follow social norms and expectations; we may seek out risk and excitement or look for comfort and security; and we may, or may not, be fettered by moral considerations. In the context of a succession of portraits of the consumer it is an analysis that discusses the fragmentations and contradictions of consumer definition and behaviour and suggests that such complexities 'should be recognised as core features of contemporary

[63] Healthier, safer, more confident citizens: a health and consumer protection strategy, at s. 4.2.4.
[64] DTI, Extending competitive markets, para. 5.6. [65] *Ibid.* at para. 5.7.
[66] Y. Gabriel, and T. Lang, *The Unmanageable Consumer: Contemporary Consumption and its Fragmentations* (London: Sage, 1954), 4.

consumption': complexities that give pertinence to the idea of the unmanageable consumer.[67]

The intrinsic complexity of consumer behaviour is compounded by the external influence of intensified and sophisticated marketing practices that bring an ever-increasing flow of information and advertising to consumers, which consumers need to be able to evaluate in terms of the claims made for products, including the environmental and ethical aspects of the good or service. The challenges presented by these changes stimulated a response, sponsored by the Commission's Education 2010 scheme, which sought, through the school curriculum, to develop the analytical capability and critical awareness in children and young people to manage their personal finances and to relate to economic developments in the wider society: to develop the capability to choose lifestyles that are in harmony with the requirements for sustainable consumption and a sustainable development in general.[68] This is an initiative in which the concept of consumer citizenship has gained increasing attention and that has led to a definition of consumer citizenship practice whereby:

> the individual, in his/her role as a consumer, actively participates in developing and improving society by considering ethical issues, diversity of perspectives, global processes and future conditions. It involves taking responsibility on a global as well as regional, national, local and family scale when securing one's own personal needs and well-being.[69]

Normative aspects of capability

Where social rights manifest themselves as immediate claims on resources they can be seen as 'the equivalent of commodities which individuals can convert into potential or actual functionings';[70] functionings that, in this context equate to the concept of individual capability, and that the Supiot Report argued (in the context of labour market participation) would help to provide a basis for a real freedom of

[67] *Ibid.* at 4 provide portraits of the consumer as chooser, communicator, explorer, identity-seeker, hedonist or artist?, victim, rebel, activist and citizen.

[68] Davies, *The European Consumer Citizen*, 103–104.

[69] V. Thoresen, Consumer education and teacher training: developing consumer citizenship, Comenius 2.1 Project 2001–2004, conference and progress report, last accessed at http://fulltekst.bibsys.no/hihm/oppdragsrapport/2003/03/opprapp03_2003.pdf on 18 January 2010.

[70] S. Deakin, 'The "Capability" Concept and the Evolution of European Social Policy', in M. Dougan and E. Spaventa (eds.), *Social Welfare and EU Law* (Oxford: Hart, 2005) 22.

choice.[71] The concept of 'capability', developed by Amartya Sen,[72] provides a 'broad normative framework for the evaluation and assessment of individual well-being and social arrangements, the design of policies and proposals about social change in society'.[73] It is a tool within which such phenomena as poverty, inequality or well-being can be conceptualised and evaluated through a 'focus on what people are effectively able to do and to be'.[74] At its core the capability approach provides a focus on individual potential, it:

> offers a response, based on the market-creating function of the rules of social law. In order to participate effectively in a market order, individuals require more than formal access to the institutions of property and contract. They need to be provided with the economic means to realise their potential.[75]

The capability concept also recognises *inter alia* that economic resources alone are not sufficient for individuals to be able to exercise their ability to achieve a particular set of functionings. Effective participation in the market, in the context of consumer citizenship, can be improved with a relevant knowledge of consumer rights and individual consumer responsibilities. The foundations of this knowledge are being established through formal consumer education, and specifically consumer education of the young which, as a policy objective of the Commission, has become a social norm, entrenched within the school curriculum, in all Member States.[76] It is, however, perceptions of the welfare effects of the market that appear significant in influencing customer citizenship practice in the increasingly complex consumer environment in which consumers, differentiated by individual and structural capability parameters and motivational drivers, have to take ever more responsibility and where education 'is only partly a solution due to the functional illiteracy of even educated people in dealing with some of the complexities involved and information overload'.[77]

[71] A. Supiot (ed.), *Au delà de l'emploi: transformations du travail et l'avenir du droit du travail en Europe* (Paris: Flammarion, 1999); Deakin, 'The "Capability" Concept', 3.

[72] A. Sen, *Commodities and Capabilities* (Amsterdam: North Holland, 1985); A. Sen, *Development as Freedom* (Oxford University Press, 1999); Deakin, 'The "Capability" Concept', 3.

[73] I. Robeyns, 'The Capability Approach: a Theoretical Survey' (2005) 6 *Journal of Human Development* 94.

[74] *Ibid.* [75] Deakin, 'The "Capability" Concept, 6–7.

[76] Davies, *The European Consumer Citizen*, 87.

[77] M. Kuneva, A blueprint for consumer policy in Europe: making markets work with and for people (Lisbon Council e-brief) last accessed at http://ec.europa.eu/consumers/docs/kuneva_consumer_blueprint_en.pdf on 4 January 2010, at 2.

Capability barriers are not limited to characteristics of the individual consumer and issues of structural capability highlight a tension between the market and the social values that are related to individualistic and solidaristic aspects of motivation and to social aspects of individual capability. Ugur's perspective of the European network industries illustrates aspects of a general consumer detriment that he attributes to the persistence of market distortions within the liberalised sectors. Market dominance, inadequate unbundling[78] and lack of transparency, coupled with the low demand and supply elasticities characteristic of networked industries, is conducive to increased mark-ups that, he suggests, 'may persist even if prices fall after market opening'.[79] This analysis highlights the effect of a general consumer detriment resulting from impaired structural capability with consequences for the consumer similar to those that may result from the market distortions produced by breaches of the competition rules.

Normative aspects of motivation

Motivation, as a normative orientation of consumer citizenship practice, embraces both individualistic and solidaristic acts that may result in improved market conditions for other consumers. For the purposes of this essay the consequences of the individual benefit sought in the *Watts* case[80] are of interest. Mrs Watts's daughter had been denied authorisation from her local health authority for her mother to receive treatment abroad on the ground that treatment could be provided without undue delay, within the context of the way in which the United Kingdom National Health Service dealt with waiting lists in managing health care provision. Mrs Watts, however, took the position that, for her, the delay was too long and so she *chose* to undergo the necessary hip replacement in France for which she paid £3,900. On her return, Mrs Watts continued with an application for permission to apply for judicial review the health authority's refusal decision and claimed in addition reimbursement of the medical fees she had incurred in France. Through her choosing

[78] See, for a very recent judgment, Case C-522/08, *Telekomunikacja Polska SA w Warszawie* v. *Prezes Urzędu Komunikacji Elektronicznej*, judgment of 11 March 2010, not yet reported.

[79] M. Ugur, 'Liberalisation in a World of Second Best: Evidence on European Network Industries', MPRA Paper no. 17873, last accessed at http://mpra.ub.uni-muenchen.de/17873/1/MPRA_paper_17873.pdf on 25 October 2009, 4.

[80] C-372/04, *R on the application of Yvonne Watts* v. *Bedford Primary Care Trust and Secretary of State for Health* [2006] ECR I-4325, para. 91.

to travel to France for her treatment and through her pursuit of the judicial review, options for other UK patients have been improved. The consideration of undue delay is now decided by reference to objective (international) medical standards instead of institutional norms and, suggests Davies, '*Watts* almost establishes a right to adequate medical care . . .[t]his is not a right written into many constitutions, and it is controversial whether the Community should be the source of it, but nor is it something that is easy to reject'.[81]

In contrast, solidaristic and communitarian acts of consumer citizenship practice provide for an extension of Lewis's 'moral concept of the market in which individuals' behavioural changes are 'motivated by the internalisation of particular normative orientations'.[82] This is the exercise of the choice to change one's lifestyle or pattern of consumption in the belief that it is the right thing to do: an act of citizenship 'understood as a mediating practice which connects the individual and the institutional levels of society [and provides]... a common identity which links otherwise disparate individuals together as a collectivity with common interests'.[83] What makes this citizenship dimension of consumer behaviour important is that the state, as defined at any level, cannot do everything, an assertion that is particularly relevant in the context of the Commission's need for us all to 'move towards more sustainable patterns of consumption'.[84] While environmental concerns have been acknowledged as important in influencing people's behaviour, it is financial cost, rather that environmental cost, that has been identified as the strongest motivator within the context of energy saving. GDP is also recognised as positively correlating with ethical buying at the national level so that 'higher income levels enable consumer decisions to be influenced more by value-based concerns, rather than purely monetary ones'.[85] Even so, consumer knowledge and attitudes about environmental issues frequently fail to be translated into behavioural changes but remain as a (motivational) attitude–behaviour gap that 'could be

[81] G. Davies, 'The Effect of Mrs Watts' Trip to France on the National Health Service' (2007) 8 *Kings Law Journal* 158, at 166.

[82] J. Barry, 1996. 'Sustainability, Political Judgement and Citizenship: Connecting Green Politics and Democracy', in B. Doherty and M. de Geus (eds.), *Democracy and Green Political Thought* (London: Routledge, Kias), 122.

[83] *Ibid.*, at 123.

[84] Commission, 2008, On sustainable consumption and production and sustainable industrial policy action plan (Communication) COM (2008) 397 final, 16 July 2008, at 2.

[85] Logica, CMG (no date). Turning concern into action: energy efficiency and the European consumer, last accessed at http://www.logica.com/file/8243 on 12 December 2009, 7.

described as one of the greatest challenges facing the public climate change agenda'.[86] Within this environmental sphere, Boström and Klintman provide an example of a link between this attitude–behaviour gap and the notion of consumer citizenship practice discussed in this chapter. They identify that many people express a willingness 'to make dramatic changes in their everyday lives in order to decrease their ecological footprint', a social goal they suggest that can be partly accomplished through the citizen expressing 'political concerns through more active consumer choices' even where such 'green choices do not always represent the most inexpensive option' and the consumer who wants to boycott will often pay more.[87]

A rise in such political consumption is confirmed through recent empirical research, and historical examples, which identify 'that a growing number of citizens are turning to the market to express their political and moral concerns' and that 'political consumer activism can be an effective way of changing both corporate and governmental policy and behaviour'.[88] Political consumers 'choose particular producers or products because they want to change institutional or market practices. They make their choices based on considerations of justice or fairness, or on an assessment of business and government practices'.[89] Identified through the lens of political science, these are the choice behaviours of consumer citizenship practice, behaviours that are shaped by the choice of producers and products based on political and/or ethical considerations.

Conclusions

The internal market has been transformed over the past thirty or forty years through expansion and technological change, through market liberalisation and through the accompanying development of regulation with new normative orientations. Once separate private law and public law relationships have become hybridised and the once weak consumer has been transformed, at least in policy, into an empowered agent of economic change, an agency aligned with a civic duty to actively participate

[86] *Ibid.* 10.

[87] M. Boström and M. Klintman, *Eco-Standards, Product Labelling and Green Consumerism* (Basingstoke: Palgrave Macmillan, 2008), 2.

[88] D. Stolle, M. Hooghe and M. Micheletti, 'Politics in the Supermarket: Political Consumerism as a Form of Political Participation' (2005) 26 *International Political Science Review* 245, at 248.

[89] *Ibid.*, at 246.

in developing and improving society. The behaviours that define this agency, and that are suggested to be capable of market shaping, are being encouraged at the EU and Member State level through the express desires of policy and regulatory institutions. Behaviours that explain consumer citizenship as the deliberate, active and informed participation in making buying choices, and in pursuing consumer rights, with due cognisance of the wider ethical issues; of the diversity of perspectives, of global processes and of future conditions on a global, regional, national, local and family scale.

For consumers to be able to exhibit sufficient of the behaviours necessary for this consumer citizenship practice to be effective as the paradigm through which they can exercise influence in the market as the 'motor of economic change', there is a need to minimise the complex and diverse range of barriers that stand in the way. The hierarchy of consumer citizenship practice introduced in this chapter helps to expose the normative orientations that exist in the areas of consumer protection, information, capability and motivation that comprise the paradigm. It also helps to identify the relationships between the levels and the barriers to effective consumer citizenship practice associated with each level. At the foundation level, consumer protection is positioned as a stratum of normative influence characterised by the provisions of the EU's consumer *acquis* and other legislative initiatives that provide a basic, if limited and fragmented, framework for consumer rights and remedies. It is also the level at which contractual documentation requirements with normative effect appear in a variety of obligations placed on the seller that seek to protect vulnerable consumers and establish grounds for redress.

Normative sources of information that are a necessary element of consumer empowerment, even if their effect is limited, are accommodated at the second level of the hierarchy. This is a level where sell-by dates, best-before dates, contents lists, nutritional values, energy efficiency labelling and recycling information are complemented by the further product information, branding and labelling that the Court has recognised as containing mechanisms for achieving consumer protection. It is the level at which consumers are provided with information and advice through which, if capable and motivated, they are encouraged, for example, to reduce the environmental impact of the goods and services they buy and use and to take personal responsibility in exercising informed choice.

At the third normative level in the hierarchy of consumer citizenship practice, existential aspects of individual capability linked to features of human functionings and principles of social justice are positioned alongside aspects of structural capability associated with the access to primary social goods and effective markets free from distortion. It is at this level that social policy and the welfare effects of the market, or the perceived welfare effects of the market, interact to influence the degree to which consumers will experience individual and/or structural consumer detriment. Financial, physical or cognitive problems may lead to a diminished capability and resultant personal consumer detriment for the individual, but structural issues of market failure or distortion, of competition infringement, or of restricted market opening lead to a general consumer detriment with its limitation of the agency capability central to the exercise of consumer citizenship practice.

Motivation, as the fourth normative level in the hierarchy of consumer citizenship practice, is used as a label for consumer behaviour that can be understood in the context of the intrinsic motivation directed by the individual consumer's sense of compliance with, and commitment to, personal (individualistic) and social or environmental (solidaristic) norms. It is the level at which the focus of normative influence can switch from bearing on the consumer, as it has done in the orientations found at the levels of consumer protection, information and capability: it is the level at which the motivated consumer can exert a normative influence on the market and where consumer choice can be predicated on market efficiency or political or ethical considerations.

The normative orientations that give explanation to the model of consumer citizenship practice developed in this chapter have been drawn together and assembled into a framework that can be used as a tool in assessing the functioning of any particular market sector, or as a tool that may assist in the balancing of competing strategic objectives. It is also a tool that provides for the assessment of the extent to which consumers have the protection, information, capability and motivation to pursue their aspirations, if they have any, as market agents and a framework in which the barriers to normative influence highlight the practical limitations of consumer agency and consumer citizenship practice.

19

Recommended changes to the definitions of 'auction' and 'public auction' in the proposal for a directive on consumer rights

CHRISTINE RIEFA

Introduction

For many years, auctions were the reserve of only a handful of specialists present in the auction room but they are now within the grasp of the general public via the television and the internet. In particular, online auctions have in recent years developed exponentially and eBay, born in the late 1990s, is now the largest online auction provider on the globe. The popularity of online auctions for the sale of consumer goods is unprecedented and is set to continue in years to come. Yet to this date in Europe there is no clear legal regime regulating the activities of businesses using auction processes to sell their products to consumers.

Indeed, Directive 97/7/EC of 20 May 1997 on the protection of consumers in respect of distance contracts (the Distance Selling Directive, DSD), which offers a right to information and a right to withdraw as its main features, excludes 'contracts concluded at an auction' from its scope.[1] A literal and hasty interpretation of the DSD and in particular of its Article 3(1) could therefore lead to the conclusion that the DSD does not apply to online auctions organised on eBay and similar sites.[2] Indeed, Article 3(1) DSD does not define 'auctions' and this lack of definition[3]

Brunel Law School, Brunel University.

[1] [1997] OJ L144 19. See Art. 3(1).

[2] For example, this is the view of P. S. Atiyah, J. Adams and H. McQueen (in *The Sale of Goods*, 11th edn (Longman, 2005), 58); G. Howells and S. Weatherill (in *Consumer Protection Law*, 2nd edn (Ashgate, 2005), 370); or B. W. Harvey and F. Meisel in *Auctions Law and Practice* (Oxford University Press 2006), 17 no. 1.41). *Contra*, see Christine Riefa, 'To Be or Not to Be an Auctioneer? Some Thoughts on the Legal Nature of Online "eBay" Auctions and the Protection of Consumers' (2008) 31 *Journal of Consumer Policy* 167–94.

[3] Alongside the fact that Directive 97/7/EC is a minimum harmonisation directive enabling Member States to maintain or introduce more stringent protective measures.

has undeniably been a contributing factor to the discrepancies between Member States' implementation of the directive.[4]

To rectify the fragmentation that followed, the European Commission suggests reforming the current regime via the proposal for a Directive on Consumer Rights. The proposed directive attempts to provide the legal certainty that is lacking in the absence of an authoritative definition of auctions and suggests to create a new system which no longer exclude contracts concluded at an auction from the scope of the directive, but instead defines the terms 'auction' and 'public auctions' respectively in Articles 2(15) and 2(16) of the directive.

For the auction sales that are caught by the directive, a new regime will also be enacted. It broadly includes information requirements[5] as a trade-off for an absence of a right to withdraw from auctions.[6] This proposed new regime has already been strongly criticised[7] for initiating a dangerous erosion of consumer rights.[8] However, the purpose of this chapter is not to reiterate criticisms regarding the regime, and in particular the absence of a right to withdraw from online auction sales, but rather to focus on the backbone of this new regime: the legal definitions of auction and public auction.

This chapter starts by reviewing why the introduction of definitions and in particular a distinction between auctions and public auctions, is a welcomed initiative in trying to alleviate fragmentation. Those definitions will form the backbone of the new regime for auctions in the proposed directive and they therefore need to be reliable legal concepts for Member States to use. This is particularly important since the directive

[4] Indeed, the Working Document of the Commission on the responses to the consultation on the Distance Selling Directive 97/7/EC contained in Communication 2006/514/EC recognized that the 'definition of auctions causes problems' (no other references – see answer to question 9 in the document available online: http://ec.europa.eu/consumers/cons_int/safe_shop/dist_sell/sum_responses_consultations_en.pdf). Also, the Communication on the implementation of Directive 97/7/EC of the European Parliament and of the Council of 20 May 1997 on the protection of consumers in respect of distance contracts clearly acknowledged the 'need to look at the meaning of "auction" in national laws' (COM (2006) 514 final, 7).

[5] Under Arts. 5 and 7 as well as 9 and 11 for distance sales.

[6] Art. 19 which lists the exceptions from the right of withdrawal indicates that 'in respect of distance contracts, the right of withdrawal shall not apply as regards ... (h) contracts concluded at an auction'.

[7] Christine Riefa, 'A Dangerous Erosion of Consumer Rights: the Absence of a Right to Withdraw from Online Auctions', in Geraint Howells and Reiner Schultze (eds.), *Modernising and Harmonising Consumer Contract Law* (Sellier, 2009), 177–88.

[8] *Ibid.*

is currently being devised as a maximum harmonisation directive, leaving Member States little room for manoeuvre. The chapter also focuses on the finer detail of the reform and puts forward some essential changes: the need for a clearer terminology acknowledging the differences between public auctions and auctions and secondly, the necessary changes to the wording of the definitions in the proposed directive.

The definitions of 'auctions' and 'public auctions' in the directive: a welcomed initiative

The absence of a definition of the term auction in the Distance Selling Directive has lead to a series of problems, and in particular to the creation of a fragmented regime for the protection of consumers buying on online auction sites. The formulation of definitions therefore appears a welcomed initiative although a perilous one.

Defining 'auctions' and 'public auctions': an impossible task?

Across Europe, some Member States do possess a definition of the term auction and/or public auction but there is no authoritative definition at European level and the concepts, even when defined by national law, vary significantly according to local legal culture as well as the objectives set for the legislation in place. Indeed, auction law may try and control the way contracts are concluded[9] or protect buyers from frauds and other abuses,[10] or simply be a remnant of Member States wanting to protect their revenues through the sale of offices.[11]

In addition many types of auctions coexist, making it difficult to capture the essence of this notion in one uniform definition.[12] Some auctions are English, using ascending bids, others are Dutch using descending bids. Some are Japanese, Scottish even Yankee auctions. They are conducted by candle or via sealed bids. Some are public auctions

[9] One example is found in the German law, §156 BGB, under which a sale by auction is concluded by the fall of the hammer. In England, see Sale of Goods Act 1979, s. 57(2).

[10] See for example, in England the Mock Auctions Act 1961.

[11] One such regime was first established in France, but amended in 2000 to comply with freedom of movement of services in the EU, which the auctioneers' monopoly was contrary to. For more details, see Laurence Mauger-Vielpeau, *Les ventes aux enchères publiques* (Economica, 2002), 3–6.

[12] For a study of these different types of auctions, see Christina Ramberg, *Internet Marketplaces: the Law of Auctions and Exchanges Online* (Oxford University Press, 2002), 36–43, no. 4.01 to 4.32. Also see Brian W. Harvey and Franklin Meisel, *Auctions Law and Practice*, 3rd edn (Oxford University Press, 2006), 3–4, no. 1.02 to 1.04.

organised by auctioneers, others are judicial auctions ordered by a court. Some are voluntary auctions, others are forced. Some are concluded at the fall of a hammer, others at the expiry of a time limit, or any other customary manner. Some occur with the parties present in the auction room, while others are taking place online or use a mixture of both physical presence and distance bids.[13]

This wide variety of auction processes really begs the question as to whether or not defining the term auction is actually an impossible task. In fact, as Christina Ramberg notes 'the question of how to define an auction in the legal sense cannot generally be solved.'[14] She adds: 'It is not possible, nor advisable, to give a single legal definition of the term auction'.[15] But if defining uniformly what an auction is appears impossible, this is not necessarily an obstacle to the use of a tailored definition for a particular purpose. Indeed, according to Harvey and Meisel, being unable to define precisely the notion of auction, or the role of eBay as an auctioneer, for example, does not preclude being able to determine whether certain types of auction sales can be subjected to the Distance Selling Regulations in the UK.[16] It is true that one may not necessarily need to know what an auction is 'universally' in order to define which types of auction will be subject to specific legislation. In our case, the purpose is to define at a European level, concepts that can be used by Member States to determine the protection granted to consumers buying goods and services using auctions and public auctions. This is particularly pressing since the absence of a clear definition in the DSD of the term 'auction' clearly yielded inopportune consequences (as we will see below), so much so that regardless of how difficult the exercise may be, it appears necessary for the proposed Consumer Rights Directive to define the concepts of 'auction' and 'public auction' and precisely to define the contours of consumer protection in this area.

[13] See for example, auctions on eBay that are totally dematerialised as well as auctions for the sale of virtual land in MMPORGs (Massively Multi-Players Online Role-Playing Games) such as Second Life or Entropia. By contrast, auctions on the www.salesroom.com are all auctions taking place in physical auction rooms, but where internet bids can be placed following the auction live on the internet via audio and even video links.

[14] Ramberg, *Internet Marketplaces*, 58, no. 4.97. [15] *Ibid.*, 59, no. 4.98.

[16] Harvey and Meisel, *Auctions Law and Practice*, 17, no. 1.41. The authors argue that 'even if Internet auction sites such as eBay are not auctioneers in the traditional sense with the concomitant duties and rights . . ., this does not mean that the sales effected by them are not auctions for the purposes of the Distance Selling Regulations'. The Distance Selling Regulations are in the UK the direct implementation of the DSD and include the exclusion of 'sales concluded at an auction'.

Defining 'auctions' and 'public auctions': a necessary step to avoid fragmentation

This indeed seems to be the best way to avoid the fragmentation caused by the fact that Article 3(1) DSD excluded 'auctions' from the scope of the directive, without giving a precise definition of what types of auctions were in fact excluded, i.e. public auctions or all types of auction. One can loosely distinguish four groups of Member States, all proceeding with the implementation of the DSD in different ways on this particular aspect, resulting in very unequal protection for consumers buying on online auction sites across Europe.

A first group of Member States such as France and Luxembourg have legal definitions of the notions of both 'public auctions', requiring the intervention of an auctioneer, and 'online brokered auctions' characterised by the absence of adjudication and intervention of a third party in the conclusion of the sale.[17] Only public auctions are excluded from the scope of the DSD and online auctions as practised on eBay are subject to the distance selling rules, providing consumers with a right to withdraw. In Spain also the notion of a public auction is defined by law but it is in the DSD that a distinction is made between auctions and online auctions, the latter being subject to the distance selling rules in their entirety.[18]

In the second group of Member States, namely Belgium and Greece, this distinction is simply superfluous since the directive is fully applicable to all online auctions because Article 3(1) was not implemented

[17] In Luxembourg, Art. 50bis of *loi du 14 août 2000 sur le commerce électronique* (Electronic Commerce Act 2000), inserted by *loi du 5 Juillet 2004* is the text of reference. The law in Luxembourg is directly inspired by French law and makes a distinction between public auctions and online brokered auctions. Only public auctions are excluded from the scope of the distance selling provisions, resulting in consumers buying on eBay being protected by a right to withdraw. In France, see *loi no. 2000–642 du 10 juillet 2000, portant règlementation des ventes volontaires de meubles aux enchères publiques* (Voluntary Public Auctions and Auction Brokerage Act 2000), J.O., 11 juillet 2000, no. 159, 10474. This Act introduced new articles in the French commercial code including that of an online brokered auction in Art. L 321–3 para. 2 which states: 'Brokerage operations in computerised auctions, characterised by the absence of an adjudcation and intervention by a third party in the conclusion of the sale of an item of property between the parties, shall not constitute a sale by public auction'.

[18] See *Ley 7/1996* (LOCM) and Royal Decree 1/2007 on the defence of consumers (titulo III, Art. 92–106). Art. 93 (1b) of the decree excludes contracts concluded at auction from the scope of the legislation but not online auctions. The law clearly indicates that online auctions are subject to the distance selling rules.

at all.[19] As a result, auctions are caught by the implementing legislation and consumers are entitled to information and a right to withdraw.

In a third group of EU Member States, such as Germany and Austria, online auctions were caught by the directive but without a right to withdraw.[20] However, in those countries case law has subsequently drawn a distinction between online auctions and public auctions and in effect reinstated the right to withdraw from purchases made on eBay. Indeed, in Germany, the *Bundesgerichtshof* (BGB) settled the delicate question of the legal classification of online auctions practised on eBay, subjecting such sales to the distance selling legislation in its entirety and differentiating them from traditional auctions. Back in 2004, a decision of the German Supreme Court[21] concerning the sale of diamond bracelet on eBay decided that traditional auctions in German law required the 'fall of the hammer' in order to conclude an auction sale in accordance with paragraph 156 of the BGB. In the absence of such event, no adjudication was to take place and the sale was therefore subject to the distance selling rules according to the court, allowing the unsatisfied consumer to return the bracelet he had received. The Austrian position is perhaps a little more disputed as the two decisions which did give consumers a right to withdraw from eBay sales are from lower courts and to this date there has been no decision from the Austrian Supreme Court.[22] Nevertheless, it is striking to note that even where the legislator has excluded auctions from a right to withdraw without distinguishing between the types of auctions, case law has come to make such distinction, significantly reinforcing consumer rights in this group of Member States.

Finally in the last group of Member States, Article 3(1) was fully implemented and consumers do not have a right to information or to

[19] Greece and Belgium were the only two Member States not to implement Art. 3(1). While protective of consumers, the lack of implementation may mean that all type of auctions (public and online) are caught by the directive if they occur at a distance. Belgium does not have a legal definition of auctions, but *loi du 14 juillet 1991 sur les pratiques du commerce et sur l'information et la protection du consommateur*, Arts. 69 to 75 regulate sales by public auctions. In Greece, the rules applicable to auctions are defined in the Civil Code (Arts. 513–61 and 199) and the Civil Procedure Code (Art. 1021 on voluntary sales). The notion of auction is defined in a decision from the Ministry of Culture (voy. 34674/2008).

[20] In Germany see §312 BGB and, in particular, §312 d (4) and (5). In Austria, see para. 5b point 4 of the Austrian Consumer Code, which excludes online auctions from the scope of the right to withdraw.

[21] *Bundesgerichtshof* VIII ZR 375/03, 3 November 2004.

[22] See *Wiener Neustadt* 15 May 2006, 2C569 and *Wiener Neustadt* 31 October 2006, 17R 274/06z. Both decisions considered that the expression auction sale in para. 5b Z4 of the Consumer Code did not include online 'eBay'-type auctions.

withdraw; but some strong voices are being heard to the contrary. For example, in the Netherlands, Jac Hjma argues that 'eBay-type' auctions should be included within the scope of the distance selling provisions, since their exclusion is primarily based on the idea that vendors would be disadvantaged by the cost and effort required to proceed with a second auction if buyers were allowed to withdraw from an adjudicated sale. Yet he contends, the sales on eBay are sufficiently simple to dispense with this protection for sellers.[23] In the UK the legal classification of online eBay auctions also remains uncertain. In the absence of any authoritative definition of an 'auction' in English law, whether statutory or anchored in common law, it is unclear whether the DSD can apply to such sales. Eminent authors such as Atiyah, Adams and McQueen[24] or Howells and Weatherill[25] have argued that eBay auctions are excluded from the scope of the DSD, making no distinction between public auctions and online auctions on eBay. Harvey and Meisel have a more developed view suggesting that eBay can be considered 'as acting as auctioneers, albeit to a limited extent'.[26] However, other authors consider that eBay is in no way a traditional auctioneer and as a result advocate that consumers should be protected by the distance selling provisions, including the right to withdraw, since what the UK regulations excludes are in fact public auctions and not online 'eBay-type' auctions.[27]

Whatever position one feels is most appropriate and whatever national interpretation appears most judicious, it is clear that the discrepancies in the definition of the scope of the directive with regard to the inclusion or non-inclusion or even partial inclusion of auctions creates regrettable differences in the protection of consumers, not to mention the barriers to competition between businesses in the internal market. A definition of the notion of auctions and public auctions appears therefore to be a necessary exercise in order to avoid such undesirable consequences. The annexes to the Commission staff working document accompanying the proposed Consumer Rights Directive[28] reveal that the inclusion of the afore-mentioned definitions is intended

[23] Jac Hjma, in *C. Asser's handleiding tot de beoefening van het Nederlands burgerlijk recht*, Deel 5-I. Koop en ruil, 7th edn (Deventer: Kluwer, 2007).

[24] Atiyah *et al.*, *The Sale of Goods*, 58.

[25] Howells and Weatherill, *Consumer Protection Law*, 370.

[26] Harvey and Meisel, *Auctions Law and Practice*, 17, no. 1.41.

[27] Riefa, 'To Be or Not to Be an Auctioneer?', 167–94.

[28] Commission staff working document accompanying the proposal for a directive of the European Parliament and of the Council on Consumer Rights, SEC (2008) 2547, Annexes, 167.

to avoid fragmentation between Member States which, according to the Commission, has led to a rise in consumer complaints in respect of online auctions. It is also intended to avoid legal uncertainty in the absence of an authoritative definition of an auction.

While we doubt that fragmentation between Member State legislation is the direct source of the rise in consumer complaints (since very few consumers actually do purchase cross-border), it is nevertheless agreed that under the DSD, implementations at national level have led to much uncertainty and different levels of protection for consumers and that a definition of the concept of 'auction' at European level is a welcomed initiative.

Distinguishing between an auction and a public auction: the backbone of the new legal regime in the proposed directive

Perhaps more crucially, it is not the definition of auction and public auction that is most useful, but the distinction drawn between them. The definitions of auctions and public auctions, in Articles 2(15) and 2(16) of the proposed Consumer Rights Directive, are therefore the backbone of the new proposed legal regime.

Article 2(16) of the directive defines a public auction as:

> a method of sale where goods are offered by the trader to consumers, who attend or are given the possibility to attend an auction in person, through a competitive bidding procedure run by an auctioneer and where the highest bidder is bound to purchase the goods.

By contrast, under Article 2(15) an auction is:

> a method of sale where goods or services are offered by the trader through a competitive bidding procedure which may include the use of means of distance communication and where the highest bidder is bound to purchase the goods or the services. A transaction concluded on the basis of a fixed-price offer, despite the option given to the consumer to conclude it through a bidding procedure is not an auction.

What is important at this stage is to notice the differences and resemblances between the two concepts. According to Article 2(15) and 2(16), a 'public auction' and an 'auction' share a number of characteristics but also differ on a number of others.

First, a competitive bidding procedure is being used in both types of auction. But in a public auction, this procedure is being run by an auctioneer, a requirement that is absent from the definition of an auction. Secondly, both are methods of sale where goods are offered by the trader. But there are variations as to the parties and the object of the transactions. In a public auction, the target is a clearly defined consumer, a term that is missing from the definition of an auction. In addition, a public auction can only concern goods whereas an auction includes services. Third, the highest bidder is bound to purchase the goods on both types of auctions. However, the way in which the sale is organised differs drastically, since in a public auction consumers need to attend or be given the possibility to attend the competitive bidding in person, whereas in an auction a means of distance communication can be used. Finally, the definition of an auction acknowledges that fixed price sales can run alongside bidding procedures, a modality that is not envisaged in the definition of a public auction.

Because the definitions are the backbone of the new legal regime, it is vital to define concepts that can apply uniformly across the Member States and be future proof. This chapter will now put the definitions to the test and identify where improvements may be necessary and recommended.

The need for clearer terminology acknowledging the differences between auctions and public auctions

For something so important, the distinction between auction and public auctions in the proposed directive is actually confusing and a change in terminology may be necessary, not only to facilitate comprehension and avoid confusion but also to reflect legal realities.

Distinguishing between the mechanics of auctions and the legal consequences of auctions

In previous work[29] I discussed at length the legal classification of online eBay auctions and the fact that they are not traditional (or public) auctions, despite sharing many similarities in the processes employed. A three-prong test was used to determine the legal classification of online auctions by opposition to public/traditional auctions and showed that three main factors were normally present in the identification of a public auction across the definitions generally adopted by Member States:

- the sale is organised by public competition;
- the sale involves a relationship of agency (it is run by an auctioneer with the legal authority to commit the parties); and
- the sale goes to the best bidder.

[29] Riefa, 'To Be or Not to Be an Auctioneer?', 167–94. Note that this article was written before the introduction of the proposed directive.

The relationship of agency was identified as being the key differentiating factor between public auctions and online eBay auctions. This is because the concept of auctions can be broken down into two elements: the auction process, i.e the mechanics of the sale, and the legal consequences of the sale. Public competition and the sale going to a best bidder are mechanical elements, while the legal powers granted to the auctioneer to commit the parties to the sale engender specific legal consequences which would be absent from another type of sale, even if it used the same mechanics.

The absence of a relationship of agency and the intervention of the auctioneer mean that while sales on eBay may look like auctions, they are only auctions in name but not if subject to thorough legal analysis. Continuing to call them 'auctions' in the proposed directive may therefore be confusing. Some authors, including myself, have chosen to call them online 'eBay' auctions to mark the difference clearly, but it is obvious that this is not a strategy that can easily be used in legislation. It is clear also from the preparatory materials that the Commission is not only hoping to deal adequately with online auctions, especially those concluded on eBay or other similar sites but also, although to a lesser extent, with auctions organised on television.[30] Consequently, 'online' can no longer adequately describe both types of sales and a more generic term ought to be adopted. One could think of calling them distance auctions, but this could also be confusing should a 'public auction' take place at a distance, although under the current regime this may not be possible.[31] One solution may be to follow the lead of a number of jurisdictions in Europe[32] where the legislator has made a clear distinction between the two types of auctions by focusing on the legal construction of the sales rather than their mechanical workings.

For example in France, Article L321–3 of the Commercial Code[33] refers to the 'act of offering an item of property at a distance via electronic

[30] Commission staff working document accompanying the proposal for a directive of the European Parliament and of the Council on Consumer Rights, Annexes, SEC (2008) 2547, 167. Note that I have not studied television auctions in detail and I am therefore unable to assess the impact that the directive may have on them. This chapter purely focuses on online auctions as conducted on eBay and similar websites.

[31] Note that in its current wording, Art. 2(16) defining public auctions does not make any express references to public auctions being organised using means of distance communications. This is problematic, as we will see further below in this chapter.

[32] See Luxembourg and France for example.

[33] The translation is our own (preferred to the official translation available on legifrance.gouv.fr). The French original version states more elegantly:

means, by acting as the owner's agent, in order to sell this item to the best bidder' by comparison with the notion of *courtage aux enchères* akin to brokerage, which is characterised by 'the absence of an "adjudication" and intervention by a third party in the conclusion of the sale of an item of property'. However the use of 'brokerage' as a terminology is not completely useful, as it encompasses different legal notions depending on which Member States one looks at, thus potentially further complicating the task of defining auctions uniformly across Europe for the purpose of the proposed directive.

Recasting auctions as bidding procedures

Although it is not a perfect description, one could favour the term 'bidding procedure' because a bidding procedure as opposed to a public auction would at the very least better convey the difference between the two modes of sale and make it clearer to consumers that the legal regime attached to both sales was also different. This expression is also a good contender since it is already being used by the Commission. Indeed, the Commission is not oblivious to this distinction between mechanics and legal consequences, since alongside the term public auction and auction in the proposed directive, it uses the notion of 'competitive bidding procedures', thus acknowledging that alongside the legal classification of a sale as an auction it is possible to isolate its technicalities and identify that an auction is a procedure under which parties bid competitively. The bidding procedure is even opposed to fixed-price sales and Article 2(15) states that a 'transaction concluded on the basis of a fixed-price offer, despite the option given to the consumer to conclude it through a bidding procedure is not an auction'.

Better clarity is necessary on this last point, however, because if one looks at the French version of the definition of an auction, what is described as a 'bidding procedure' in the English version of Article 2(15) of the directive, is in fact a 'tender procedure' in the French version, both again having slightly different legal meanings in different Member States:

> Le fait de proposer, en agissant comme mandataire du propriétaire, un bien aux enchères publiques à distance par voie électronique pour l'adjuger au mieux-disant des enchérisseurs constitue une vente aux enchères publiques au sens du présent chapitre.
>
> Les opérations de courtage aux enchères réalisées à distance par voie électronique, se caractérisant par l'absence d'adjudication et d'intervention d'un tiers dans la conclusion de la vente d'un bien entre les parties, ne constituent pas une vente aux enchères publiques.

It is clear that the variety of legal systems in place in the EU, and the number of autonomous definitions in place, render the process of defining an EU concept thorny. Ultimately what the new definitions ought to focus on is the fact that public auctions are different from the bidding procedures used on eBay and other auction platforms because the latter are in fact private treaty sales that use the mechanics of the auction process to determine the parties and the price, but do not engender the traditional legal consequences of a sale by auction.[34] The main key difference is really anchored in the role of the auctioneer and the definitions adopted by the proposed directive should be amended in order to provide a clear and effective way to test which sales are caught by it.

Necessary changes to the wording of the definitions of auction and public auction in the proposed directive

There are three main areas to focus on in order to produce reliable definitions for both the concept of auction and that of a public auction.[35] The proposed directive needs definitions that adequately reflect the legal construction of public auctions and bidding procedures. As a result, some changes in the wording are necessary. Further, definitions should be technology and product neutral, prompting further changes. Finally, tighter definitions of the parties to an auction sale or a bidding procedure may also be required.

The need for definitions that adequately reflect the legal construction of public auctions and bidding procedures

First, if one wants to reflect the legal construction of public auctions and bidding procedures adequately, the term 'highest bidder' should be

[34] For example, see below the discussions regarding the fact that the bidding procedures do not engender 'final' sales to which a highest or best bidder is bound. They also are not conducted by auctioneers mandated to affect the legal relationships of the parties as well as committed by law to ascertaining the authenticity of the goods advertised for sale amongst other legal consequences of sale by public auctions. For more on this point, also see Riefa, 'To Be or Not to Be an Auctioneer?', 167–94.

[35] Note that in the current wording, both sales are subject to a slightly different legal regime under the directive and we are hoping that as the text is discussed by Member States it will be altered even more significantly in order to create two separate regimes, one for public auctions and one for 'auctions', or bidding procedures as we prefer to call them, the latter enabling consumers to withdraw from sales of consumer products.

changed to 'best bidder'.[36] This reference is problematic indeed because only in what is technically called an English auction (ascending bids), does one find a highest bidder. By contrast, in a Dutch auction, bids decrease as opposed to increase and, in some other auctions, the winning bid will be the lowest unique bid, meaning that the person having won the auction may not be the one having bid the highest or even lowest amount of money. By referring to a highest bidder, the Commission runs the risk of limiting the scope of the directive to English auctions. This may have the rather unfortunate consequence of pushing auction organisers to running only auctions using decreasing or other modes of bidding in order to evade the application of the directive.[37] Therefore, the use of the term 'best bidder' may be preferred as it would allow for other types of auctions to be represented and caught by the directive.

It also seems essential to remove the reference to the fact that the highest (or best) bidder is 'bound to purchase the goods' in the definition of an auction in Article 2(15). This common characteristic of both auctions and public auctions is not an accurate reflection of the legal realities of a transaction concluded using an online bidding procedure.

In traditional forms of auction (public auctions) the law normally determines the moment and manner of the conclusion of the contract. The direct consequence of such rules is that at the close of the auction, one knows with certainty the identity of the buyer and the price at which the goods are to be purchased (provided that in a reserve auction, the reserve price has been met).[38] No bid can be withdrawn after the auctioneer has accepted it, because the auctioneer, acting as an agent,

[36] See Riefa, 'To Be or Not to Be an Auctioneer?', 167–194, at 171.

[37] Or in the current wording of the directive, if an auction organiser wanted to guarantee the absence of a right to withdraw he could run English auctions exclusively, as other types of auctions would presumably not be caught.

[38] For example, in the UK, s. 57(1) of the Sale of Goods Act 1979 (SGA 1979) indicates that 'a sale by auction is complete when the auctioneer announces its completion by the fall of the hammer or any other customary manner'. It is understood that under this section, the auctioneer formulates an invitation to treat and that each competitive bid constitutes an offer that the auctioneer will accept at the close of the sale, thus forming the contract. However, when the sale is made with a reserve, s. 57(3) SGA 1979 suggests that each bid converts into a conditional offer. The condition is that, should the reserve price be met, the sale has to go to the highest bidder. In the event that the reserve price is not met, the auctioneer is under no obligation to sell and is free to reject any bids made as he was for sales under s. 57(1) SGA 1979. Similar rules are applicable across Europe to determine the conclusion of a contract of sale at auctions. For example, in Germany, under §156 of the BGB, the contract is concluded only at the fall of the hammer when the auctioneer declares the winning bid and closes the sale.

has the legal authority to commit seller and buyer to the transaction.[39] As a result, the use of the expression 'bound to purchase' in the definition of public auctions is accurate.

However, it stops being relevant for sales concluded under Article 2(15), the so-called auctions or bidding procedures. Indeed, in sales concluded on eBay, the best bidder is not bound by law to make the purchase. While online auction sites terms and conditions mimic the rules of public auctions and include clauses to the same effect, the obligation imposed on the parties to conclude the contract at the close of the auction sale is only a contractual one and does not find its source in statute or case law. As a result, it is arguable that the contractual obligation to conclude the sale is only actionable between the online auction site and the user but not directly between users.

It is even possible for bidders to retract their bids in situations where it would not normally be possible to do so at public auction. Indeed, bidders are able to withdraw a bid if they have accidentally entered a wrong bid amount, if the description of an item they have bid on has changed significantly or if the bidder cannot reach the seller either by phone or email after the close of the sale.

Worse, in some situations, the best bidder not only will not be bound to purchase, but he will purely and simply be prevented from doing so. There are two situations in which this can occur on eBay. The seller may, on the one hand, refuse to complete the transaction with the highest bidder if for example, a buyer fails to meet the conditions of a seller's listing (such as payment method or geographical zone for delivery) or if the buyer cannot authenticate the buyer's identity.[40] In such situations what are known as second chance offers can often take place, and the seller, having failed to complete the sale with the original highest bidder, will select the under-bidder of his choice and offer to sell the item for the price stipulated in the bid of this particular individual.

On the other hand, the practice of auction sales running alongside fixed-price sales opened for the duration of the auction often results in the best bidder not being the party with whom the sale is in fact concluded. Indeed, while the auction runs, it is possible for the seller to offer the same product for sale at a fixed price. During the auction process anyone can select this option and buy the product for a fixed

[39] Riefa, 'To Be or Not to Be an Auctioneer?', 167–194, at 180.

[40] Note for those unfamiliar with eBay that such occurrences are not rare since the parties remain anonymous during the bidding process and their true identities only gets revealed once the sale has ended.

price, thus putting an end to the auction. The person making a fixed-price purchase before the end of the auction automatically closes the auction and sidelines the best bidder in the process.[41] Interestingly the Commission is aware of this practice and we have already seen that it clearly acknowledges it in Article 2(15) of the directive stating that 'a transaction concluded on the basis of a fixed-price offer, despite the option given to the consumer to conclude it through a bidding procedure is not an auction'. While fixed-price sales are clearly not auctions, they are not the 'bidding procedures' defined as auctions in Article 2(15) either. It is therefore inaccurate to define 'eBay-type' auctions as method of sale where the highest (or best) bidder is bound to purchase the goods. To persist in this description of the sale may mean that sales on auction platforms are outside the scope of the directive since the current definition is in our view an inaccurate definition of what an online bidding procedure actually is. This state of affairs would clearly be contrary to what the Commission is trying to achieve. Indeed, it is clear from the Working Document of the Commission on the responses to the consultation on the DSD contained in Communication 2006/514/EC that 'generally speaking the emphasis seems to be on the need to cover auctions conducted on so called online auction platforms. . . . Overall it seems, as most Member states feel, at least online auction platform should be covered.'[42]

The need to adopt technology and product neutral definitions

The definition of an auction refers to both goods and services, while that of a public auction only mentions goods. As a result, a reading of the proposed directive could be that public auctions cannot concern services. This discrepancy needs to be addressed. Indeed, the bidding process with or without the intervention of an auctioneer is the factor that makes those sales different from private treaty sales and not the goods or services they concern. It does not seem wise to differentiate between auctions or bidding procedures and

[41] Interestingly, if this is the case, under the new regime defined by the directive, the buyer would have a right to withdraw from the fixed price sale, whereas if he or she ends up being the best bidder and the auction running its course, then this buyer would not be able to withdraw from the sale. This is clearly an anomaly that needs to be addressed and we do so further below. Note that the process seems to have recently changed on eBay.co.uk.

[42] See answer to question 9 in the document available online: http://ec.europa.eu/consumers/cons_int/safe_shop/dist_sell/sum_responses_consultations_en.pdf.

public auctions on the grounds of the products being sold, although we acknowledge that certain types of products or services could be banned or restricted from being sold using such a sale technique for a variety of reasons (*ordre public* being one of them), but this would then be as a derogation. Where the emphasis needs to be put is clearly on the legal consequence of the sale, which differ dramatically if conducted by an auctioneer or a principal using a 'bidding procedure' to conclude the sale, to borrow once again the expression contained in Article 2(15).

In addition, the definitions ought to be technology neutral. This can be done by levelling the differences in the requirements of a physical presence or the use of means of distance communications in both definitions. In its current wording, Article 2(16) defining public auctions does not make any express references to public auctions being organised by means of distance communications. Instead Article 2(16) requires that they be conducted in a physical environment with consumers being given at least the possibility of attending the sale in person. For auctions, however, the requirement of a physical presence disappears but it is replaced by the fact that the competitive bidding procedure may include the use of means of distance communications. We infer from the definitions in Articles 2(15) and (16) that while an auction may also be conducted with the physical presence of the bidders, a public auction cannot be conducted at a distance.[43] This is problematic. Primarily what gives the sale its legal nature (i.e. public auction or bidding procedure) is not the technology employed to organise the sale, but the intervention or not of a third party, the auctioneer, in the direction of the sale. As a result, we feel that this artificial distinction in the proposed directive is superfluous. Indeed, auctioneers have already organised 'distance only' auctions,[44] and while current practice for traditional auctions is still to combine auctions taking place in the auction room, with bidders present as well as bidders following online or on the phone,[45] an artificial restriction in the definition risks barring future development in the practice of public auctions without any convincing case being put forward for doing so.

[43] This would explain why all references to public auctions is absent from the parts of the directive defining the rights of consumers in distance contracts.

[44] See for example, *Chambre nationale des Commissaires priseurs and Another* v. *Société NART SAS and Another, Tribunal de Grande Instance* (District Court) Paris, 3 May 2000, [2001] ECC 24.

[45] See for example, www.the-saleroom.com.

The need for a tighter definition of the parties to an auction sale or a bidding procedure

Only sales between a trader and a consumer (B2C) are caught by the proposed directive.[46] As a result, consumer to consumer (C2C) as well as business to business (B2B) sales will remain outside the scope of the directive. It is important to have clarity on what sales are caught. The current absence of a direct reference to consumers in the definition of an auction is therefore inconvenient. In the definition of a 'public auction', the recipient of the sale is identified as being a 'consumer', whereas in the definition of an 'auction', consumers are not mentioned directly. Only the latter part of Article 2(15) pDCR makes an indirect reference by discussing the option given to the consumer to conclude a sale through a bidding procedure. The fact that the sales make different references to consumers raises some questions as to why the Commission decided to draw such a distinction. One could assume that the Commission may have wanted to see auctions (bidding procedures) have a wider scope than public auctions and potentially be addressed to businesses also. However, given that Article 1 clearly frames the proposed directive as being concerned with contracts between consumers and traders, we feel that this is unlikely. The differences in the definitions may only be the result of an oversight but further precision is necessary.

Another and more important challenge concerns the absence of a discussion about the fact that the legal classification of actors selling via online auctions (bidding procedures) is not as straightforward as the directive seems to make out. It proposes to consolidate the definitions of trader and consumers, in Articles 2(1) and (2) pDCR, and therefore the auctions and public auctions caught within the scope of the directive will have to take place between 'any natural person who, in contracts covered by this Directive, is acting for purposes which are outside his trade, business, craft or profession' and 'any natural or legal person, who in contract covered by this Directive is acting for purposes relating to his trade, business, craft or profession and anyone acting in the name of or on behalf of the trader'.

However, online activity has blurred the essential binary distinction that used to exist between consumers and professionals. Starting up an online web-based business no longer requires major capital investment or sophisticated infrastructure. Individuals who do not conceive of themselves as commercial entrants may find themselves sometimes

[46] Art. 1 of the proposed directive.

unexpectedly making money in the online world. Many eBay users, for example, end up using eBay as a source of second income, selling regularly on the site. Those 'hybrid consumers'[47] are an emerging category of electronic commerce actors. They are individuals who have, often unknowingly or unwillingly, displayed the characteristics of a business. While we are not suggesting that a new category of actors be defined in the directive, we would welcome guidance from the Commission as to where the threshold between 'consumer' and 'trader' can be found.[48] Without a more harmonised way at looking at this threshold, the maximum harmonisation approach in the directive may be defeated, as it is completely possible that even if Member States were to implement the directive 'word for word', they would still be able to introduce a variable leading to fragmentation, i.e. when sales move from being C2C to B2C on online auction sites and vice and versa. Clearly such classification has an important impact on the legal regime that needs to apply to auction sales since auctions between two consumers or two businesses will remain outside the scope of the directive, while sales between a trader and a consumer will be caught.

A clear approach in this area is even more important because to preserve the business model adopted by online auction platforms, the identity of the parties is not fully revealed until the close of a sale and it may therefore be difficult for consumers to know who they are contracting with and, as a result, what rights are associated with such transaction.

Conclusion

Defining auctions and public auctions even within the confine of the application of the proposed directive is a difficult exercise. Yet it appears a necessary one to combat fragmentation. The situation arising from the DSD had led to a variety of implementation and major discrepancies between the ways consumers are protected if buying on online auction

[47] For more on the notion of 'hybrid consumers', see Christine Riefa, 'The Reform of Electronic Consumer Contracts in Europe: towards an Effective Legal Framework?' (2009) 14(2) *Lex Electronica* 17.

[48] Short of defining this by law it may be possible to envisage an industry code of practice whereby online auction sites agree to define this threshold and apply it to their users. eBay in France, for example, already uses criteria to classify sellers as professional seller: individuals whose turnover is over €2,000 for three consecutive months must identify themselves as professionals or risk being barred from using the site. See eBay news, http://actualites.ebay.fr/showitem&id=437, last consulted 22 March 2010.

sites. The first attempt made by the Commission to define those notions in the proposed new directive requires many amendments, but the definitions already contain the key distinction between the two notions, i.e. the intervention or non-intervention of an auctioneer in the sale process. Because the use of terminology such as 'auction' and 'public auction' can be confusing, the use of the term 'bidding procedure' may be preferred for sales where an auctioneer does not participate to the conclusion of the sale. Indeed, in those cases, the auction process is only a mechanical tool that does not engender any legal consequences. The notion of bidding procedure therefore adequately, if not perfectly, reflects the reality. To draw such clear distinction would then allow differentiating between legal regimes applicable to consumers.

One notable improvement on the DSD, would have been to conclude that only public auctions were excluded from the directive and grant consumers a right to withdraw in bidding procedures. However, the Commission went a different way and decided to subject all public auctions and auctions to a right to information (although with some special dispensations for public auctions) but to bar all types of auction sales from a right to withdraw. As previously noted, this is a dangerous state of affairs which also represents a significant attrition of consumer rights in Member States where a distinction between public auctions and bidding procedures has already been made either by legislation or case law. One can only hope that having proceeded with some essential changes to the definitions, the Commission and the Member States will go further and review the legal regimes applicable to online auctions aiming to achieve a high level of consumer protection, and grant a right to withdraw from bidding procedures, albeit limited in certain instances.[49]

[49] For more on this proposal, see Riefa, 'A Dangerous Erosion', 177–88.

We are happy to report that since writing this article, the proposal for a Directive on Consumer Rights was amended and the final version of the Directive defines 'public auction' and only excludes those sales from the right to withdraw. Some recommended changes to the definition of public auctions have taken place, addressing many of the concerns expressed in this chapter.

20

Consumer law regulation in the Czech Republic in the context of EU law: theory and practice

BLANKA TOMANČÁKOVÁ

Introduction

In 2004 the European Union accepted ten new countries, which on 1 May became full members of the 'European family'. For most of the countries this meant a complete change in their national legal systems because the Member States had to introduce new legal measures in order to establish a European market along with a competitive environment.

The area of EU consumer law is mainly covered by the directives. Each Member State has an obligation to adopt, in its national legal system, all possible measures to ensure that the directives are fully effective in accordance with the objectives which they pursue. Member States may, in the area covered by the directives, adopt or retain stricter provisions which grant a higher degree of protection to consumers. The nature and the scope of the obligations imposed on the Member States by the EU are usually determined by the content, scope and characteristics of the directives (minimum or maximum harmonisation), which the Member States are required to transpose with their national legislation. The Member States may also implement some of them in some other way. Member States are obliged to establish for that purpose a specific legal framework in the area of consumer protection. The legal position of consumers under national law must be suitably precise and clear. Given that consumers are of various nationalities (especially in cross-border transactions) and are normally unfamiliar with the principles of legal orders other than that of their own country, it is important that the individuals affected are, for reasons of legal certainty, aware of all their rights and be able to assert them before the national courts. However as the ECJ held in several of its rulings:

Law Faculty of Palacký University Olomouc, Czech Republic.

> The transposition of a directive into domestic law does not necessarily require that its provisions be incorporated formally and verbatim in express and specific legislation. Thus, the existence of general principles of constitutional or administrative law may render implementation by specific legislation superfluous. Depending on the content of the directive, a general legal context may suffice provided that it effectively guarantees the full application of the directive in a sufficiently clear and precise manner. Should the directive be intended to create rights for individuals, the persons concerned must also be in a position to know the full extent of their rights in order that they may, if necessary, rely on them before the national courts.[1]

Clearly, this is particularly important with directives which guard the rights of individuals in various Member States.

On 17 November 2009 the Czech Republic celebrated the twentieth anniversary of the Velvet Revolution which brought an end to the communist regime in the Czech Republic. However, the beginning of a new political system brought with it a new legislative challenge, particularly in the regulation of private law. These were controversial mainly because the legal system had for so long been influenced by the law of the Soviet Union, with an accent on the socialist principles dictated by the *nomenklatura*. The main problem was that most of the private law institutions and terms known to normal private law societies were absent; they had either been omitted from the Civil Code in the mid-1970s, or their meaning has been realigned, revised or twisted to comply with Communist Party orthodoxy. In 1989 it was practically impossible to call together legal experts who would be able to draft a Civil Code, because there was neither the time nor the experience to engage in such law reform.

After the Velvet Revolution it was decided that the 1964 Civil Code would be used, that the dysfunctional communist provisions would be taken away and within a few years a new, more appropriate Civil Code should be prepared. That was the original idea. Unfortunately, twenty years after the revolution, we are still using the same dysfunctional Civil Code, resulting in enormous practical problems due to gaps in its coverage and the ideologically twisted provisions of the code. Fortunately, a new recodified Civil Code has now been prepared and will be approved by the Czech Parliament.

The recodification process of the private law was very difficult. It was not only the Civil Code which required recodification; a new Act on

[1] Case C-478/99, *Commission of the European Communities* v. *Kingdom of Sweden* [2002] ECR I-4147.

Business Corporations (Business Act) and an Act on International Private Law were also needed. There were only a few experts who could deal with such a massive recodification of the Czech private law and, in addition, the unstable political environment did not help. The enactment of any legal Act is not only about specialised work done by experts, it is also about the political will to pass it.

The new Czech Civil Code is called Codex for Life, codex Inspired by Life.[2] The official Recodification Commission of the Ministry of Justice led by Professor Karel Eliáš worked on the new Civil Code for more than eight years. The process of the Civil Code Act preparation was unique; the draft of the Civil Code was distributed for informal 'remark proceedings' (public discussions) in summer 2007. It was distributed both to the legal community and the general public and all groups were given the opportunity to read the proposal and give their remarks and proposals on individual problems. Over three thousand suggestions came out of the public 'remark proceedings'.

The new Civil Code returns Czech private law to the standards of the European legal culture and national legal traditions which were rejected after the revolution in 1948 when the Communist Party came to power. The new Civil Code represents a definite break with the totalitarian conception of the civil law as a means of controlling society in the interests of the *nomenklatura*. The new Civil Code grants greater freedom to the individual, emphasising respect for the will of the individual; this enables people to act in private law relationships as they really wish. There is a focus on party autonomy; the proposal of the new Civil Code abandons the idea of the current Code, which is to regulate all aspects of normal human life.

The Civil Code grants a reasonable level of protection to the vulnerable. While everyone is responsible for their actions and the new Civil Code accepts a natural inequality of the parties it will in some cases protect those who are in a weaker position (children, old people, consumers, etc.). The new Civil Code strengthens the position of private law, unifies private law regulation (several civil law Acts, such as the Business Act, are included in this codex) and gives priority to personal rights. Within this Code the position of an owner is reinforced and a unified regulation of the law of obligations is introduced. There is an improved regulation of inheritance law (with a new emphasis on the

[2] The final version of draft available at: http://obcanskyzakonik.justice.cz/tinymce-storage/files/Vladni_navrh_obcanskeho_zakoniku_LRV_090430_final_s%20obsahem.pdf.

will of the deceased person), regulation of consumer protection and regulation of tort liability.

The new terminology and taxonomy of the new Civil Code are among the greatest improvements.[3] When drafting a legal instrument terminology and systematicity are among the most important issues: the wrong terminology may cause significant problems. This must be borne in mind especially when drafting EU Acts, which require transposition in all Member States. Few are aware that communist legal regulation in some of the accession states (among which the Czech Republic) changed traditional legal terminology according to the Soviet pattern (instead of one-word terms communist legal regulation used multi-word terms which are unintelligible not only for lawyers but, more importantly, for ordinary people).

In the new Civil Code there is a completely new set of rules of interpretation. Notwithstanding the fact that national law must ensure that the result intended by consumer directives is actually achieved, one of the biggest problems in Czech consumer practice nowadays is very poor or non-existent case law.[4] The EU anticipates that the rights given to consumers under the directives will be formulated clearly and transparently, and that their effective enforcement will be available through the competent national courts.

In some of the post-communist courts, judges remain unaware of the conventional democratic principles according which cases should be judged and which are binding upon them in their decisions. Under the Soviet model, where provisions were uncertain, the judges stuck to the formal interpretation of the provision without examining its real purpose. This is, however, contrary to the rulings of the ECJ:

> Where, under national legislation, any uncertainty subsists as to whether the provisions of a directive which seeks to grant rights to individuals have been complied with, such uncertainty cannot be dispelled by invoking the possibility of the schematic interpretation of the provisions in question, or of their interpretation by national judicial authorities in such a way as to ensure conformity with the directive in question. As the Court has held, it is particularly true in the field of consumer protection that, even where the settled case-law of a Member State interprets the

[3] For more on taxonomy in law see for example P. Birks (ed.), *The Classification of Obligations* (Oxford: Clarendon Press, 1997); P. Birks, 'Equity in Modern Law' (1996) 26 *Western Australia Law Review* 1, at 4.

[4] For more on case law in consumer contracts see J. Grygar, 'The Judiciary and Consumer Protection', in H. Schulte-Nölke and L. Tichý (eds.), *Perspectives for European Consumer Law* (Munich: Sellier, 2010), 99–108.

> provisions of national law in a manner deemed to satisfy the requirements of a directive, that cannot achieve the clarity and precision needed to meet the requirement of legal certainty.[5]

In the new Civil Code there are basic rules for an interpretation of a person's will; if it is impossible to interpret such a will with the given rules, it is necessary to use analogy, that is to use a rule which is the closest possible to the given case.[6] There can be cases when analogy cannot be used, then the basic rule is that the court will decide on the basis of the principle of equity. What may sound familiar to the traditional civil law regulations in most EU countries is almost unknown to the Czech courts (except for the Constitutional Court) because the Czech courts are strictly formal in their decisions. According to the new Civil Code if a judge wants to give a ruling different from the former case law, he has to give profound reasoning for such a result.[7]

Law of Obligations and consumer protection

The chapters on the Law of Obligations belong to the most important parts of any code of private law and cover the law of contract, tort and restitution. The Law of Obligations is a category of law concerned with legal claims between individual legal subjects.[8] The taxonomy and other theoretical questions became important especially in connection with the harmonisation of private law in the EU and with the efforts to consolidate European private law. Although European private law remains largely independent from traditional national private legal orders, European private law and national private laws are mutually interrelated.[9]

The current chapters of the Czech Law of Obligations are not unified and the meaning of most of the institutions is simplified or misinterpreted. In the proposal of the new Civil Code the part on the Law of Obligations has been changed completely. The biggest benefit for the legal system is unification; there will only be one Code which will deal

[5] Case C-144/99, *Commission* v. *Netherlands* [2001] ECR I-3541, para. 21.

[6] F. Melzer, *Metodologie nalézání práva* (Prague: C.H. Beck, 2009).

[7] Art. 10 of the new Civil Code.

[8] G. Samuel, *Law of Obligations and Legal Remedies* (London: Cavendish Publishing Limited, 2001), 2.

[9] H. Micklitz, *The Visible Hand of European Private Law. Outline of a Research Design.* At http://www.eui.eu/Documents/DepartmentsCentres/Law/Professors/Micklitz/VisibleHand.pdf.

with the law of obligations. Nowadays there are two codes: the Civil Code and the Commercial Code, both of which contain rules for contracts, tort and quasi-delict,[10] which cause a hindrance to dispute solving in practice.

Consumer contracts in general

Under EU law, most of the directives on consumer law must be binding as to the result to be achieved; the national authorities, however, remain competent to determine the choice of the form and methods of implementation. In general we can say that consumer law regulation in the Czech Republic has several problems which will be solved by the proposal of the new Civil Code. This will be done, principally, by including the correct translations of the directives, taking into consideration all nuances of Czech private law and interpreting the most recent ECJ case law in the field of the consumer protection.

The problem of incorrect translation in consumer protection has been resolved in the new Civil Code by correct translation of the directives.[11] This has resulted in clear and efficient consumer protection provisions which are included in the proposal of the new Civil Code. It is interesting that these proposed provisions are nowadays used to interpret the wrong translation of the consumer protection provisions in the current Civil Code.

Substantive changes have been made to purchase contract provisions, mainly with the aim of defining what a purchase contract is and how it differs from a contract for work. This is a big problem in practice due to the different warranty period provisions of these contracts. The current problem with Czech purchase-contract regulation is that it contains two different sets of rules on warranty. One set of rules concerns the conformity with the contract, pursuant to Directive 1999/44/EC the other comes from the time when the Civil Code did not include the rules on conformity with the contract as laid down in the directive. In this sense we can say that we have a liability for defects in a narrow sense (liability for the conformity with the contract, Article 616 CC) and a liability for defects in a wide sense (legal warranty, Article 619 CC); however, both of them contain very similar rules and cause misinterpretation.

[10] V. Bednář, in J. Fiala and M. Kindl *et al.*, *Občanský zákoník, Komentář* (Prague: I.díl. 1.vyd. Wolters Kluwer ČR, 2009), 67.

[11] Cf. the English, German and French versions.

Definition of a consumer

The definition of a consumer has been discussed many times, not only by the legal experts but also in the ECJ. Most of the experts, as well as the ECJ, have come to the conclusion that the term 'consumer', as referring to someone who concludes a consumer contract, must be interpreted as referring solely to natural persons.[12] The main reason for this protection of natural persons is because legal persons and companies do not generally find themselves in a weaker position. There is no reason to grant them protection which, as an exception to contractual freedom, must, moreover, be strictly interpreted.

The notion of a consumer being a natural person seems to be confirmed by the objective of the Community legislation as well, because the intention to protect a category of persons in a weak position, and only that category of persons, is confirmed in many of the consumer protection directives. As the Court noted in *Océano*:

> The system of protection introduced by the Directive [93/13] is based on the idea that the consumer is in a weak position vis-à-vis the seller or supplier, as regards both his bargaining power and his level of knowledge. This leads to the consumer agreeing to terms drawn up in advance by the seller or supplier without being able to influence the content of the terms.[13]

In *Di Pinto*, the ECJ interpreted the term 'consumer' as it arose in Directive 85/577/EEC on Doorstep Selling; the consumer was defined by the court as being a natural person who, in the transactions covered by the directive, is acting for purposes which can be regarded as outside his trade or profession.[14]

A consumer in the Czech Civil Code was (until 30 June 2010) defined as a person someone who, when concluding a contract, does not act within the scope of the business or other entrepreneurial activity.[15] Within this definition the consumer was simply defined as a person, without specification as to whether s/he was a private (natural) or a legal person. This definition thus invoked an idea that consumers can be both private and legal persons when not acting within the scope of their business or other entrepreneurial activity. Such an extensive interpretation

[12] Judgment of the Court (Third Chamber) of 22 November 2001. *Cape Snc* v. *Idealservice Srl* (C-541/99) and *Idealservice MN RE Sas* v. *OMAI Srl* (C-542/99) [2001] ECR I-9049.

[13] Joined cases C-240/98 to C-244/98 [2000] ECR I-4941.

[14] Criminal proceedings against *Patrice Di Pinto*, Case C-361/89 [1991] ECR I-1189.

[15] Art. 52 CC.

was, however, in violation of both the object of the consumer protection and the recent case law of the ECJ.[16]

As a result of the current ECJ case law and the pressure applied by consumer protection advocates in the Czech Republic, the Czech Parliament has adopted an amendment[17] according to which a consumer is defined as a natural person who, when concluding and performing a contract, is acting for purposes which can be regarded as outside his or her trade or profession.

The proposal of the new Civil Code states that a consumer is a *man* (a natural person) who concludes or negotiates a consumer contract outside the scope of any business or entrepreneurial activity. Legal persons (especially those who do not run business, such as non-governmental organisations or foundations) receive a certain level of protection within the general provisions included in the general part of the law of obligations.

Under the current provisions when a consumer concludes a contract with a person who is an entrepreneur's representative, he or she is not protected under the consumer law provisions. The proposal of the Civil Code would tackle this and grant protection to consumers who conclude contracts with persons who are not entrepreneurs themselves but act as their representatives. The same applies to the contracts concluded with persons who under the Czech law do not hold the status of an entrepreneur (e.g. persons running public services, such as hospitals).

It is a question whether, in accordance with the new proposal on the directive on consumer protection,[18] protection of a consumer who negotiates with a professional, who represents another consumer, should not be included. Under the directive proposal, this consumer is not covered by this legal regulation because, prior to the conclusion of the contract, the intermediary must disclose to the consumer that he is acting in the name of or on behalf of another consumer. The contract that has been concluded will not be regarded as a contract between the consumer and the trader but rather as a contract between two consumers and, as such, falling outside the scope of this directive.

Unfair terms

Various EU programmes for consumer protection and information policy[19] have underlined the importance of safeguarding consumers

[16] C-541 and 542/99 *Cape Snc.* v. *Idealservice Srl* and *Idealservice MN RE* v. *OMAI Srl* [2001] ECR I-9049.

[17] Act no. 155/2010 Coll. [18] Art. 7.

[19] OJ C 92, 25 April 1975, 1 and OJ C 133, 3 June 1981, 1.

in the matter of unfair terms in contracts. That is why the Council adopted Directive 93/13/EEC on unfair terms in consumer contracts. The directive is intended not only to facilitate the establishment of the internal market but also to ensure protection for consumers when they purchase goods or services. This directive has been adopted on grounds of ensuring effective market integration. The legal systems of different Member States relating to the unfair terms in contracts between an entrepreneur and a consumer show many disparities. This means that the national markets for the sale of goods and services to consumers differ from each other and that distortions of competition arise among the sellers and suppliers, especially when we are dealing with cross-border trade.

The directive brings a regulation of unfair terms, which are contractual terms which have not been individually negotiated. Such terms are regarded as unfair if, contrary to the requirement of good faith, they cause a significant imbalance in the parties' rights and obligations to arise under the contract, to the detriment of the consumer. Although the directive contains certain general rules for the assessment of an unfair term, it will be for the national court, having regard to all the relevant factors in the individual case, to ascertain whether the contractual terms in question are unfair in reality.

I have previously mentioned the most visible problem of the current consumer protection provisions in the Czech Civil Code: the inaccurate translation of the consumer protection directives. This is also typical for the unfair terms provisions in Articles 55 and 56 CC. The current provisions state that consumer contracts must not contain terms that are contrary to the requirement of good faith and produce a considerable inequality in rights and duties of the parties to the detriment of the consumer. However, Czech private law does not distinguish between subjective and objective good faith.[20] Good faith in Czech law is connected to a different institution, mainly the right of possession and is thus perceived as a subjective good faith. The proposal of the new Civil Code changes this by stating the obligation to act within the scope of objective good faith which is defined as an obligation to set up a claim and fulfil objective duties while abiding by good morals faithfully and respecting good practice in public life.[21] This means

[20] P. Tégl, '*Některé teoretické problémy nabývání od neoprávněného*' (2009) 17(10) *Právní rozhledy*, 343–52.

[21] Art. 1671 of the new Civil Code.

that good faith in this context will be examined as would *Treu und Glauben* in the German legal system.[22]

The old provisions on unfair terms (in force until 30 June 2010) set down that when a contract or its provision was in conflict with these clauses on unfair terms, the consumer had the right to appeal for its invalidity (so called relative invalidity of legal conduct).[23] This Civil Code provision was clearly in conflict with both the object of the consumer protection and the ECJ case law.[24] The principle of the relative invalidity of conduct is that the legal conduct remains valid until the other person appeals for its invalidity. The limitation period relevant for relative invalidity is three years, and after this period the right to appeal for the relative invalidity of the conduct becomes statute barred.[25] Thus it is the consumer who has to decide whether he will appeal for the invalidity of the unfair term. However, this assumes that the consumer knows what a relative invalidity is and knows his or her rights to appeal. This is contrary to Directive 93/13/EEC on unfair terms in consumer contracts, which does not mention anything about relative invalidity. It states that the Member States must specify that unfair terms used in a contract concluded with a consumer by a seller or supplier should not be binding on the consumer and that the contract will continue to bind the parties upon those terms if it is capable of continuing in existence without the unfair terms. According to the principle of minimum harmonisation the Member States can lay down stricter conditions than those in the directives. The relative invalidity could be hardly considered to be stricter that the absolute invalidity[26] because the consumer does not know what the relative invalidity is or how to appeal on it. In this sense we can also interpret some of the ECJ case law.[27] Due to this fact, the Czech Parliament passed an amendment[28] according to which relative invalidity was changed to absolute invalidity.

[22] See S. Whittaker, and R. Zimmermann, *Good Faith in European Contract Law* (Cambridge University Press, 2000).

[23] Art. 55 CC.

[24] M. Hulmák, in J. Švestka, *et al.*, *Občanský zákoník. Komentář. Díl I (§ 1 – 459)*. 1. vyd (Prague: C. H. Beck, 2008), 483.

[25] Although you may find different opinions on the fact that this right does not become statute barred – P. Bezouška, in Fiala and Kindl *et al.*, *Občanský zákoník. Komentář*, 235.

[26] Which means that the legal conduct is invalid from the beginning without the necessity of appealing the invalidity.

[27] C-240/98 to C-244/98 *Oceáno Grupo Editorial SA* v. *Roció Muricano Quintero*; C-473/00 *Cofidis SA* v. *Jean-Loius Fredout* [2000] ECR I-4941.

[28] Act No. 155/2010 Coll.

The proposed new Civil Code is in compliance with EU law and gives consumers a reasonable level of protection. It states that the unfairness of a contract term should be assessed, taking into account the nature of the goods or services for which the contract was concluded and by referring, at the time of conclusion of the contract, to all the circumstances attending to the conclusion of the contract and to all the other contract terms or the terms of another contract on which the contract in question is dependent. In practice this means that first of all it is necessary to assess the rights and duties of the parties. If these rights and duties are not balanced it is necessary to assess whether this imbalance is detrimental to the consumer and whether this imbalance is tolerable. The assessment, according to the general criteria chosen of the unfair character of terms, in particular in sale or supply activities of a public nature providing collective services which take account of solidarity among users, must be supplemented by a means of making an overall evaluation of the different interests involved. Particular regard must be given to the strength of the bargaining positions of the parties, whether the consumer had an inducement to agree to the term and whether the goods or services were sold or supplied to the special order of the consumer. Assessment of the unfair nature of the terms must relate neither to the definition of the main subject matter of the contract nor to the adequacy of the price and remuneration. These terms must be in plain intelligible language.

The consumer protection regulation in the new Czech Civil Code lists only examples of unfair terms or, more precisely, lists the most common examples of unfair terms. These can be divided into several groups. The first group is represented by terms which exclude or limit the legal liability of an entrepreneur in the event of the death of a consumer or personal injury to the latter resulting from an act or omission of the seller or supplier. The second group concerns the performance itself or performance where the consumer is not aware of the obligations he is supposed to fulfil. The third group covers terms relating to the changes or termination of the obligation by authorising the seller or supplier to dissolve the contract on a discretionary basis where the same facility is not granted to the consumer, or permitting the seller or supplier to retain sums paid for services not yet supplied where it is the seller or supplier who dissolves the contract. This also covers terms enabling the seller or supplier to terminate a contract of indeterminate duration without reasonable notice except where there are serious grounds for doing so. The fourth group comprises terms which provide for the price of goods to be determined at the time of delivery or allow a seller of goods or supplier of services to increase their price without, in both cases, giving the consumer the corresponding right to cancel the contract if the final price is too high in relation to the price agreed when the contract was concluded.

Last but not least, the fifth group is represented by terms which exclude or hinder the consumer's right to take legal action or exercise any other legal remedy, particularly by requiring the consumer to take disputes exclusively to arbitration not covered by legal provisions. Thus unduly restricts the evidence available to him or imposes on him a burden of proof which, according to the applicable law, should lie with another party to the contract. These arbitration clauses remain one of the biggest problems within Czech consumer law. Arbitration as a means of dispute settlement is, in the Czech legal system, enacted by a regulation which is mainly used for business to business relationships.[29] The same legal regulation is applied to business to consumer relationships, which sometimes causes problems for dispute resolution and Czech consumer protection, mainly because arbitrators are economically linked to the entrepreneur and tend to give rulings in favour of the entrepreneur.[30]

Ancillary contracts

As proposed in the directive on consumer rights, if the consumer exercises his right of withdrawal from a distance or an off-premises contract, any ancillary contracts shall be automatically terminated, without any costs for the consumer. The Member States have to lay down detailed rules on the termination of such contracts.[31] The current Czech consumer protection regulation does not effectively regulate these ancillary (dependent) contracts. The provision on dependent contracts sets out that if one of the contracts is terminated, the other contract terminates or loses its binding force. This is used mainly for contracts where the performance is covered by consumer credit.

[29] Act No. 216/1994 Coll., on arbitration proceedings and on the enforcement of arbitration awards.

[30] M. Hulmák, and B. Tomančáková, 'Rozhodčí řízení jako vhodný prostředek řešení sporů mezi dodavatelem a spotřebitelem (1. část)' (2010) *Obchodněprávní revue*, č. 6., M. Hulmák, and B. Tomančáková, 'Rozhodčí řízení jako vhodný prostředek řešení sporů mezi dodavatelem a spotřebitelem (2. část)' (2010) *Obchodněprávní revue*, 2010, č. 7.

[31] Art. 18.

The current regulation includes a provision on ancillary/dependent contracts in Article 62 CC, a provision regulating timeshare agreements.[32] While protection of the timeshare consumer is not as effective as it should be, Article 62 covers cases of withdrawal from the contract when the payment, which the consumer makes for exercising his right to use the timesharing property, has been partly or fully paid under a credit agreement concluded between the vendor (as a creditor) and consumer (as a debtor), or a credit agreement concluded between a third party (as a creditor) and the vendor (as a debtor). This establishes a direct right of on the part of the consumer to receive the money from the creditor. The provision protects both parties from possible complications when cancelling the consumer credit agreement when the price is covered by a credit granted by the vendor or by a third party. The meaning and purpose of this provision is to allow cancellation of a credit contract from the beginning. The provision covers cases when the consumer withdraws from the contract for reasons stipulated by law but also for the reasons stated in the timeshare agreement as provided for under Article 48.[33] The regulation does not deal with cases in which the payment is provided on the basis of a credit contract concluded between a third party (as a creditor) and a consumer (as a debtor), or cases in which the payment is paid by a third party on behalf of the consumer.

The current timeshare legislation in the Czech Civil Code explicitly states that the credit contract shall be cancelled, without any sanction either on the part of the vendor or the third party. Although the article does not define the term 'sanction', it is necessary to interpret it from its legal context (usually a fine or another penalty). When interpreting the sanction it is necessary to evaluate in each case not only the type of claim but also the circumstances under which the claim arose. Thus, regardless of the legal form, the sanction is any performance which relates (directly or indirectly) to the cancellation of the credit agreement.

The draft of the new Civil Code proposes that this provision on dependent contracts be applicable on all consumer contracts. The regulation explicitly states that when the price is paid under a consumer credit contract and the consumer withdraws from the contract, the

[32] Art. 62 CC.

[33] §48 (1) of the Czech Civil Code: The participant may withdraw from the agreement in cases stipulated in this Act or agreed by the participants. (2) Withdrawal from the agreement shall result in cancellation of the agreement *ex tunc* unless an act or an agreement of the participants stipulate otherwise.

effects of the withdrawal will apply to the consumer credit contract as well as the main contract. That means that the consumer does not have to negotiate on the consumer credit contract or withdraw from this dependent contract; instead the contract is terminated automatically.

Travel contract and the loss of joy

One of the fields affected by consumer protection is that of the travel contract. The current provisions in the Czech Civil Code are nothing more than a simple transposition of the Directive 90/314/EEC on package travel, package holidays and package tours. However, the new Civil Code includes provisions on 'loss of joy' when consumers have the right to sue for damages caused by the loss of joy, for example, because they did not enjoy the holiday due to a change in the contract provisions.

According to the current regulation the travel agent is liable *vis-à-vis* the customer for violation of obligations arising under the concluded travel agreement regardless of whether these obligations are to be performed by the travel agent or by other suppliers of travel services provided in the framework of the trip.[34] This means that if a travel agent is obliged to accommodate a consumer in a five-star hotel and on arrival the consumer finds out that this is a three-star hotel, the consumer can only ask for the difference in the price.

Under the current Czech regulation of the travel contract there are no special provisions for 'loss of joy'.[35] The only possibility under the current regulation is to sue the travel agent for the breach of provisions on protection of personhood according to which the consumer is entitled, in particular, to demand that unlawful violation of his/her personhood be abandoned, that consequences of this violation be removed and that a adequate satisfaction be given to him/her. The consumer in this case also has a right to pecuniary satisfaction of the immaterial detriment. The amount of the satisfaction has to be specified by the court with regard to intensity and circumstances of the infringement which has arisen.[36]

Conclusions

The regulation of consumer protection via EU law has passed significant milestones. Nowadays there is a relatively complex regulatory framework

[34] 852i CC.
[35] See M. Hulmák, 'Ztráta radosti z dovolené' (2009) 17(2) *Právní rozhledy* 52–4.
[36] Arts. 11–15 CC.

which provides adequate consumers protection for, though problems remain which need to be addressed.

The Member States are free to choose the form and methods for the purpose of achieving the result pursued by most of the consumer protection directives. The Czech Republic, like all the EU Member States, was supposed to transpose the consumer protection rules accurately into its legal system. However there are severe practical problems attributable to imperfect implementation, mainly caused by an incorrect translation and transposition of terms and definitions into the national legal system.

The current Civil Code of the Czech Republic, which includes the private law framework for consumer protection, dates back to 1964. It is an obsolete Code based on a socialist understanding of private law relationships. Within the recodification process, which started in 2001, many professional bodies, academics, practitioners, judges, non-governmental organisations and the public were asked to make comments on the proposal of the new Civil Code. The proposal represents an entirely new legal regulation which highlights the social values of the modern society. The basic principle is the protection of human beings, not of the state; at the same time central to the proposal is the freedom of the individual it expresses, which plays the most important role. The proposal includes an improved regulation of consumer law, addressing and resolving the practical, real-world problems. Apart from other positives, it returns Czech private law to the standards of European legal culture and national legal traditions which were rejected after the revolution in 1948 when the Communist Party came into power.

21

Resistance towards the Unfair Terms Directive in Poland: the interaction between the consumer *acquis* and a post-socialist legal culture

RAFAŁ MAŃKO

Introduction

This chapter aims to present the interaction between the consumer *acquis* and post-socialist legal culture in Poland as exemplified by the rules on unfair terms in consumer contracts. It will focus on resistance towards Directive 93/13/EC among Polish legislators, scholars and judges, attempting to link this resistance to the background elements of the socialist legal tradition still present in Polish legal culture. The chapter will analyse two specific areas of resistance: the general test of unfairness and the abstract review of standard terms.

It will be argued that the general test of unfairness has been implemented in Poland in a way which departs from the directive – 'good faith' was substituted by 'good customs' and 'significant imbalance' was substituted by a 'gross violation of interests' of the consumer. It will be submitted that the implementing provisions are actually more lenient towards the trader than the directive requires. The interpretation of the implementing provisions within scholarship and case law is very often detached from the text of the directive and leads to conclusions hard to reconcile with the intent of the Community legislator. Judges and scholars tend to assimilate the 'good customs' clause with the socialist general clause of 'principles of social coexistence', still present within the Polish Civil Code, rather than exploring the meaning of 'good faith' in the directive.

Secondly, it will be argued that the rules on abstract review were implemented by the legislator in a piecemeal manner without providing

Lawyer Linguist, Court of Justice of the European Union, Luxembourg. The views expressed in this chapter are exclusively those of the author and should not be attributed to the Court of Justice of the European Union.

specific guidance to the courts on how to perform this novel type of review. Many scholars, paying insufficient attention to the directive, have pronounced themselves against any form of abstract review and its third-party effects. There is also evidence within the case law showing that judges have virtually abstained from performing abstract review, resorting to concrete review instead and refusing to recognise the third-party effects of judgments condemning a given term as unfair. This anti-European entrenchment has however been reversed by a landmark decision of the Supreme Court.

Historical background

It must be kept in mind that Poland (just like the other Central European countries that joined the European Union in 2004) has had a different experience with regard to consumer protection from Western European Member States. The difference of experience is a result of the political and socio-economic system prevalent in Poland (and Central Europe) between 1944 and 1989, which is often referred to as 'real or state-socialism'. While consumer protection played an important role within the mechanism of the market welfare state in Western Europe (as evidenced in the emergence of consumer protection law in the 1970s in France, Germany and the UK), in state socialist Poland this issue was not viewed as one of primary importance at the time. This was due to the fact that the vast majority of the economy was 'socialised' (i.e. owned by the state *de iure* or at least *de facto*);[1] thus, at least on the theoretical level, it belonged to the entire society.[2] However, consumer protection is based on a paradigm of opposition of interests between the consumer and the trader; therefore, in the system of a 'socialised economy' this opposition was difficult to uphold on the theoretical level.

As a result, the Civil Code enacted in 1964 contained neither a definition of a consumer[3] nor a distinct body of consumer protection

[1] Formally, the 'socialised economy' was comprised, on the one hand, of *de iure* state property (state enterprises) and, on the other hand, of cooperative property (which *de iure* was not state property). However, in the light of the centralisation of the cooperative movement in communist Poland and the effective control of the state over cooperatives one can say that cooperative property was *de facto* state property.

[2] Both the Constitution of 1952 and the Civil Code of 1964 made it clear that the notion of 'state property' was a synonym for 'property of the whole nation' (*mienie ogólnonarodowe*).

[3] The notion of a consumer was inserted to the Civil Code only in 2000 when the Unfair Terms Directive was implemented. See for more details below.

rules.[4] Quite ironically, in relationships between consumers and 'units of socialised economy' the Civil Code was actually based on the principle of freedom of contract.[5] This allows us to speak of a structural deficit of consumer protection in state socialist Poland.

This does not, however, imply that the Western European notions of consumer protection did not permeate into the Polish legal scholarship of that period. As a matter of fact, both the notion of consumer and the need to create a body of consumer law was appreciated by a number of scholars.[6]

Furthermore, the ever-deepening economic crisis in state socialist Poland, particularly acute in its terminal decade of existence (1980–9), leading to shortages of basic consumer goods (including everyday foodstuffs) placed the issue of consumer protection on a different level: the interest of the consumer became primarily focused on *obtaining* consumer goods rather than worrying about legal entitlements. It was not so much the fairness of the transaction that mattered but the the *conclusion* of the transaction as such. As a matter of fact, this led to the creation of peculiar consumer rights, e.g. the duty of the shop to display all goods for sale, rather than keep them 'under the counter' for sale only to selected consumers.[7]

The transformation from a centralised and state-owned economy to a capitalist economy, which occurred essentially between 1988 and 1990, led to an instant improvement in the market of consumer goods (without, however, avoiding poverty, hyperinflation and high unemployment). Furthermore, another obstacle to the development of consumer law, i.e. the lack of opposition of interests between

[4] The state socialist legislator did not see the need to create such a body of rules (see E. Łętowska, 'Kształtowanie się odrębności obrotu mieszanego' [The Emergence of the Distinct Character of Mixed Transactions] in E. Łętowska (ed.), *Tendencje rozwoju prawa cywilnego* [Trends in Development of Civil Law] (Warsaw: Zakład Narodowy im. Ossolińskich and Wydawnictwo Polskiej Akademii Nauk, 1983), 418–19.

[5] *Ibid.*, 425.

[6] See e.g. the definitions coined by E. Łętowska, 'Ochrona konsumenta z punktu widzenia polityki prawa' [Consumer Protection from the Point of View of Legal Policy] (1978) 4 *Państwo i Prawo* 16; C. Żuławska, *Obrót z udziałem konsumenta. Ochrona prawna* [Consumer Transactions: Legal Protection] (Warsaw: 1987), 17; S. Włodyka, *Prawo gospodarcze. Zarys systemu. Część ogólna* [Economic Law. Outline of a System: General Part] (Warsaw: 1982), vol. II, 72. Cf. M. Rejdak, 'Definicja konsumenta w rozumieniu kodeksu cywilnego (art. 22[1] k.c.)' [The Definition of a Consumer Within the Meaning the Civil Code (Art. 22[1] CC)] (2006) 16(1) *Rejent* 118ff., at 126.

[7] Para. 6(2) General Terms of Contracts of Retail Sale of Goods and General Terms of Warranty (Monitor Polski 1983 No. 21, item 118) and para. 6 Regulation of Internal Commerce and Service of 14 February 1983 (Dziennik Ustaw, PRL No. 8, item 46).

the consumer and the 'socialised economy', was finally removed with the emergence of a private sector and the privatisation of the state sector, especially in the field of commerce. The argument that the consumer, as citizen, was theoretically the owner of the 'socialised' retail company could no longer be upheld. Nevertheless, attempts at introducing consumer protection in Poland were difficult and not always succesful; legislative enactments were of doubtful quality and the attitude of the courts was far from being pro-consumer. It was pointed out that the courts lacked sensitivity towards the protection of consumer rights;[8] thus, regardless of the quality of the law-in-the-books, the law-in-action was certainly limping.[9]

Europeanisation of Polish consumer law

Without any delay, after the transformation from a centrally planned and state-owned economy towards a capitalist economy and parliamentary democracy the Polish ruling elites opted for European integration as the country's goal. Therefore, in 1991 Poland signed an Association Agreement with the European Communities.[10] Article 68 of the Agreement imposed upon Poland the duty to (gradually) adapt its legal system to Community standards.[11] The actual nature of that duty was, however, the object of dispute. According to one group of authors, Article 68 merely imposed an obligation of best endeavours and not an obligation of result, whereby timetable and methodology would be left, *de iure* at least, to the Polish authorities.[12] According to another group of authors,

[8] E. Łętowska, *Prawo umów konsumenckich* [Consumer Contract Law] (Warsaw: C. H. Beck, 1999), 244.

[9] See e.g. E. Łętowska, 'Ochrona konsumenta jako problem legislacyjny okresu transformacji' [Consumer Protection as a Legislative Problem in the Period of Transformation] (1994) 1690 *Acta Universitatis Wratislaviensis* 91.

[10] The Accession Agreement, signed on 16 December 1991, entered into force on 1 February 1994.

[11] Cf. C. Mik, *Europejskie prawo wspólnotowe. Zagadnienia teorii i praktyki* [European Community Law: Theoretical and Practical Issues] (Warsaw: C. H. Beck, 2000), vol. II, 788; A. Łazowski, *Adaptation of the Polish Legal System to European Union Law: Selected Aspects*, SEI Working Paper no. 45 (Sussex: 2001); Z. Brodecki and E. Gromnicka, *Układ Europejski z komentarzem* [The Europe Agreement with a Commentary] (Warsaw: Lexis Nexis, 2001); A. Łazowski, 'Approximation of Laws', in A. Ott and K. Inglis (eds.), *Handbook on European Enlargement: a Commentary on the Enlargement Process* (The Hague: T.M.C. Asser Press, 2002), 631ff.

[12] S. Sołtysiński, 'Dostosowanie prawa polskiego do wymagań Układu Europejskiego' [The Adaptation of Polish Law to the Requirements of the Europe Agreement] (1996) 4–5 *Państwo i Prawo* 31, at 33; B. Nowak, 'Implementation of Directives into Domestic Legal

Article 68 was the source of an obligation of result from the time at which Poland filed a request for full Community membership on the basis of Article 49 EU – to the extent that the implementation of Community law was possible.[13] Regardless of that dispute it must be added that following signature of the accession treaty,[14] Poland undertook to implement[15] and apply the entire existing *acquis communautaire* by 30 April 2004, i.e. the last day prior to accession.[16]

Although consumer law was only a very small element of the entire *acquis* that was to be implemented, it has been noted that the European Commission, which was charged with the monitoring of Poland's implementation progress, excercised rigorous scrutiny with that regard during the period directly preceding Poland's accession to the EU.[17] Well-informed scholars (and insiders at the same time) have remarked that 'the Commission wanted Polish legislators to transfer the literal wording of directives into the national law'.[18] According to their account, the Commission's scrutiny took the form of a mechanical comparison of the English text of the relevant directive with an English translation of the Polish implementing measure which, as has been pointed out,

System: the Case of Poland' (2005) 9 *Yearbook of Polish Legal Studies* 67ff., at 67. This view was also presented by N. Reich, 'Transformation of Contract Law and Civil Justice in the New EU Member Countries' (2005) 23 *Penn State International Law Review* 587, at 599. See also Brodecki and Gromnicka, *Układ Europejski*, 100–1, who state that it is up to Poland to organise the harmonisation of the legislation.

[13] E. Piontek, 'Central and Eastern European Countries in Preparation for Membership in the European Union: a Polish Perspective' (1997) 1 *Yearbook of Polish European Studies* 73. Cf. A. Łazowski, 'Wybrane prawne aspekty rozszerzeń Unii Europejskiej w 2004 r. i 2007 r.' [Selected Legal Aspects of the Enlargments of the European Union in 2004 and 2007], in M. M. Kenig-Witkowska (ed.), *Prawo instytucjonalne Unii Europejskiej* [The Institutional Law of the European Union], 3rd edn (Warsaw: C. H. Beck, 2007), 422ff. at 435.

[14] Signed on 13 December 2003 in Athens.

[15] Some authors define the term 'implementation' as meaning both the legislative (transposition) and judicial (application) dimension of conforming to directives (see e.g. Nowak, 'Implementation', 67 n. 1). However, I will use the term 'implementation' as a synonym of the French transposition, thus referring exclusively to the legislative stage of respecting directives by the Member States.

[16] E. Łętowska and A. Wiewiórowska-Domagalska, 'The Common Frame of Reference: the Perspective of a New Member State' (2007) 2 *European Review of Contract Law* 277ff., at 282.

[17] E. Łętowska, M. Jagielska, K. Lis, P. Mikłaszewicz and A. Wiewiórowska-Domagalska, 'Implementation of Consumer Law in Poland' (2007) 6 *European Review of Private Law* 873ff., at 878 and 881.

[18] Łętowska and Wiewiórowska-Domagalska, 'The Common Frame', 290. To the same effect see Łętowska *et al.*, 'Implementation', 882.

often led to misunderstandings.[19] Any departure by the Polish legislator from the literal wording of the directive was said to have caused suspicion and criticism from the side of the Commission,[20] whose officials were – goes the account – not keen on understanding the intricacies of the structure and operation of the Polish legal system.[21]

As to the Polish side, it should be mentioned that in 1994, the Legislative Council (a governmental advisory body on legislative matters) adopted an official position in which it expressed scepticism and concern regarding the dangers posed to national legal culture by EC law and stated that implementation of Community law:

> may not lead to the loss of the specific and distinct character of the Polish legal system and to the imposition of alien conceptions and legislative approaches, not in conformity with this system ... [T]he reform of Polish law may not be subject to a general slogan of adaptation to Community law.[22]

Similar concerns were also raised by certain scholars.[23] This distrust towards Community legal culture is indeed perplexing if one considers that the specific character of Polish law is said to lie only in a mixture of foreign ingredients.[24]

Bearing in mind the Legislative Council's approach, it is easier to understand why it took a decade for the first provisions of European private law directives to be implemented into Polish law. Although as of

[19] Łętowska and Wiewiórowska-Domagalska, 'The Common Frame', 291; Łętowska *et al.*, 'Implementation', 883. In this context one can wonder about the quality of the translations the Commission used during the screening process.

[20] Łętowska *et al.*, 'Implementation', 878.

[21] Łętowska and Wiewiórowska-Domagalska, 'The Common Frame', 291; Łętowska *et al.*, 'Implementation', 880.

[22] Stanowisko Rady, 'Legislacyjnej w sprawie dostosowania prawa polskiego do systemu prawa Unii Europejskiej' [Position of the Legislative Council of 25 March 1994 with regard to the adaptation of Polish law to the legal system of the European Union] (1994) 3 *Kwartalnik Prawa Prywatnego* 743ff., at 747.

[23] M. Nawrocka, 'Ochrona konsumenta przed nieuczciwymi klauzulami umownymi w Unii Europejskiej i w Polsce' [The Protection of the Consumer From Unfair Contractual Clauses in the European Union and in Poland] (1998) 6, *Monitor Prawniczy* 216ff., at 223.

[24] T. Giaro, 'Moderniesierung durch Transfer: Schwund ostorpeaischer Rechtstraditionen', in T. Giaro (ed.), *Modernisierung durch Transfer im 19. und fruhen 20. Jahrhundert* (Frankfurt am Main: Vittorio Klosermann, 2006), 275ff., at 319ff. Cf. R. Mańko, 'Unifikacja europejskiego prawa prywatnego z perspektywy społeczeństwa polskiego – przyczynek do dyskusji' [The Unification of European Private Law from the Perspective of Polish Society] (2007–8) 11 *Nowa Europa* 35ff., at 47–52; R. Mańko, 'The Unification of Private Law in the European Union from the Perspective of Polish Legal Culture' (2007–8) 11 *Yearbook of Polish European Studies* 109ff., at 115–25.

1994, when the Europe Agreement entered into force, there were already six private law directives requiring implementation,[25] not to mention numerous directives in the field of company law,[26] it was not until 2000 that the Polish legislator made any progress in this direction, fuelling the concern of the scholarly community with regard to the slow pace of implementation.[27]

During the 1990s it had not been decided which model to following when transposing the consumer *acquis* into the Polish legal system. Three options were envisaged: implementation within multiple statutes (symmetrically to the directives); implementation within a single consumer act (something akin to the French *code de la consommation*); or implementation within the existing Civil Code of 1964. In 1999 the competent parliamentary committee proposed a bill for a single consumer act that was to consist of a general part with definitions and certain general principles and a specific part covering unfair terms, contracts concluded outside business premises, distance contracts, product safety, product liability, consumer credit, consumer arbitration and consumer organisations.[28] Eventually the government opted for the approach suggested by the Commission for the Codification of Civil Law. This approach was characterised by dualism: some issues (product liability and unfair terms) were to be regulated within the Civil Code, while other issues (distance contracts and contracts concluded outside business premises were) to be regulated in a separate statute.

It is worth noting that the Codification Commission proposed restraining legislative activity to the minimum levels of protection granted by the directives and rejected an extension of consumer rights beyond the scope explicitly required by the Community, claiming that this approach would 'better serve the harmonisation of law understood . . . [as] the acceptance of the "philosophy" of the European directives'.[29]

[25] The Product Liability Directive 1985 (85/374); the Doorstep Selling Directive 1985 (85/577); the Commercial Agency Directive 1986 (86/653); the Consumer Credit Directive 1987 (87/102); the Package Travel Directive 1990 (90/314) and the Unfair Terms Directive 1993 (93/13). Soon afterwards the Timesharing Directive 1994 (94/47) was also adopted.

[26] Among these typically private law directives are the First, Second, Third, Sixth and Twelfth Company Directives (dated 1968, 1976, 1978, 1982, 1989).

[27] E. Łętowska, 'Ochrona konsumenta. Wprowadzenie' [Consumer Protection: An Introduction] (1996) 5:(2) *Kwartalnik Prawa Prywatnego* 383ff., at 390.

[28] 'Poselski projekt ustawy o ochronie konsumentów' [Parliamentary Draft Consumer Protection Act] (1999) 8(3) *Kwartalnik Prawa Prywatnego* 611ff.

[29] See Draft Doorstep and Distance Contracts Act 1998, 351.

Currently, the Commission for the Codification of Civil Law under the presidency of Professor Zbigniew Radwański[30] is preparing a new draft Civil Code.[31] As of early 2012, only book I of the draft was available (which had been published in 2008).[32] It was the intent of the Codification Commission to publish the remaining books of the draft by 2010; however, those optimistic plans were not executed.[33] As a matter of fact, in 2010 judges of the Civil Chamber of the Supreme Court have pronounced negatively with regard to the draft book I and, in general, have been against the enactment of a new Civil Code.[34] The Codification Commission[35] seems to have abandoned the idea of a new Civil Code.

The implementation and application of the general prohibition of unfair terms

Legislative transposition

The good faith clause contained in the general prohibition of unfair terms certainly constitutes the core of Directive 93/13; the good faith clause has been the source of certain controversy between scholars, some of whom regard it as a 'legal irritant' from the point of view of Anglo-Saxon legal culture.[36] It is therefore worth scrutinising how the Polish legislature dealt with this centrepiece of the Unfair Terms Directive. And this is where the comparative lawyer must admit to

[30] Biography at http://pl.wikipedia.org/wiki/Zbigniew_Radwa%C5%84ski (accessed 1 March 2010).

[31] Z. Radwański (ed.), *Zielona księga. Optymalna wizja kodeksu cywilnego w Rzeczypospolitej Polskiej* [Green Paper: Optimal Vision of the Civil Code in the Republic of Poland] (Warsaw: Oficyna Wydawnicza Ministerstwa Sprawiedliwości, 2006).

[32] Księga pierwsza Kodeksu cywilnego. Projekt z uzasadnieniem [book I of the Civil Code: a Draft With Motives] (Warsaw: 2008); available online at: http://www.ms.gov.pl/kkpc/proj080227.rtf (accessed 1 March 2010).

[33] M. Domagalski, 'Nowy kodeks nie teraz' [New Code Not Now], *Rzeczpospolita*, online edition www.rp.pl, accessed 22 March 2010. See also M. Domagalski interviewing Z. Radwański, 'Nowy kodeks cywilny trudniejszy niż sądzono' [New Civil Code More Difficult than it Was Thought], *Rzeczpospolita*, online edition www.rp.pl, accessed 22 March 2010.

[34] Projekt Kodeksu cywilnego. Księga pierwsza. Sprawozdanie z dyskusji przeprowadzonej w Izbie Cywilnej Sądu Najwyższego [Draft Civil Code. Book I. Minutes of the Discussion in the Civil Chamber of the Supreme Court] (2010) 10, *Przegląd Sądowy*, 104–23.

[35] Domagalski, 'Nowy kodeks'.

[36] G. Teubner, 'Legal Irritants: Good Faith in British Law or How Unifying Law Ends Up in New Differences' (1998) 61 *MLR* 11ff.

being surprised by the Polish solution, for the good faith (*bona fides*) clause has been substituted by another general clause, also originating from Roman law, but quite different in its scope and significance[37] – the immorality clause.[38] One could argue that the latter clause is more favourable towards businesses, given that *bona fides* encompasses more than *contra bonos mores*, including the subjective and psychological elements of the contractual relationship. The drafters responsible for the elimination of *bona fides* in the Polish transposition measure have defended their choice by the alleged necessity of avoiding the confusion between *bona fides* in its objective and subjective sense.[39]

Another crucial concept contained in the directive's prohibition of unfair terms is the requirement that the incriminated contractual term cause a significant imbalance in the contractual relationship between the trader and the consumer. With regard to that requirement, the Polish legislature once again opted to depart from the wording chosen by the Community law-makers. Thus, instead of referring to an 'essential' or 'significant' (and unjustified) disproportion or imbalance between the rights and duties of the parties to a consumer contract, Polish law uses a concept unknown to the directive, namely that of a 'gross violation of the consumer's interests'. It has been argued that the 'gross violation' test is more lenient to the economic operator than the 'significant imbalance' test within the directive, pointing out that this modification can be qualified as an infringement of EU law.[40]

[37] The general clauses of 'good faith' (*bona fides*) and 'good customs' (*contra bonos mores*) may not be placed on an equal footing because they refer to different criteria of evaluation (M. Pilich, 'Zasady współżycia społecznego, dobre obyczaje czy dobra wiara? Dylematy nowelizacji klauzul generalnych prawa cywilnego w perspektywie europejskiej' [Principles of Social Coexistence, Good Customs or Good Faith? Dilemmas of Amending the General Clauses of Civil Law in a European Perspective], in M. Pazdan *et al.* (eds.), *Europeizacja prawa prywatnego* [The Europeanisation of Private Law] (Warsaw: Oficyna a Wolters Kluwer Business, 2008), vol. II, 179.

[38] The Civil Code in its Art. 3851 §1 sentence 1, provides as follows: 'The terms of a contract concluded with a consumer, not negotiated individually, are not binding upon him, if they shape his rights and duties in a manner contrary to good customs and grossly violate his interests (prohibited contractual terms).'

[39] Cf. Z. Radwański and M. Zieliński, 'Uwagi *de lege ferenda* o klauzulach generalnych w prawie prywatnym' [*De Lege Ferenda* Remarks on General Clauses in Private Law] [2001] 2 *Przegląd Legislacyjny* 11ff., at 24.

[40] Pilich, 'Zasady współżycia', 178.

The legislature, when choosing to opt for a 'gross violation of interests' instead of a 'significant imbalance', was probably inspired by the formulation of the prohibition of unfair terms as introduced in 1990 into Article 385^2 of the Civil Code.[41] However, despite its prima facie pro-consumer character, this provision did not prove to be an effective means of reviewing standard terms. It was criticised by scholars for various reasons[42] and it was virtually not applied by the court in practice.[43] In this light the choice of the same expression as in the ineffective and dead-letter rules of 1990 could be seen as an indication to the courts that a 'gross violation of consumer's interests' was something extremely rare and extraordinary, rather than a frequent practice of economic operators which must be eliminated by the courts as part of their everyday duties.

The two modifications of the normative content of the directive – the substitution of *bona fides* by *contra bonos mores* and the 'significant imbalance' test by the 'gross violation of interests' test – should be linked together. The *bona fides* standard is strictly connected to the idea of contractual equilibrium; thus there is a conceptual correlation between the violation of good faith and significant imbalance. On the other hand, the *contra bonos mores* standard is, arguably, more lenient towards the contracting party acting dishonestly, and is not connected to the lack of contractual equilibrium but rather to a violation of basic Community standards. An obvious correlation between the *contra bonos mores* standard and contractual equilibrium seems be lacking; hence the legislature coupled it with the standard of a 'gross violation of interests' which is linked (in its terminology) with the standard of 'gross negligence'.

[41] Art. 385^2 of the Civil Code in its version of 1990 provided that:

> §1. Where the general conditions of contracts, model contracts and regulations result in grossly unjustified benefits accruing to the party who relies thereupon, the other party may request the court to declare their application ineffective. However, this may not take place later than one month following performance of the contract.
>
> §2. The entitlement contemplated by the above section shall not extend to persons concluding contracts within the sphere of their economic activity.

[42] W. Popiołek in K. Pietrzykowski (ed.), *Kodeks cywilny. Komentarz. Tom I* [Civil Code: a Commentary. Vol. I] (Warsaw: C. H. Beck, 1997), 711; M. Bednarek, *Wzorce umów w prawie polskim* [Standard Terms in Polish Law] (Warsaw: C. H. Beck, 2005), p. 48.

[43] Łętowska, 'Ochrona', 91; P. Podrecki and F. Zoll, 'Odpowiedzialność podmiotów świadczących usługi' [The Liability of Subjects Providing Services], in E. Traple and M. du Vall, *Ochrona konsumenta. Część I. Opracowanie analityczne* [Consumer Protection. Part I: Analytical Elaboration] (Warsaw: Urząd Komitetu Integracji Europejskiej, 1998), 132.

In light of the above it seems that on the law-in-the-books level the choices effected by the Polish legislature while transposing the Unfair Terms Directive could constitute a departure from the minimum standards of the directive, in favour of economic operators but to the detriment of consumers. However, the actual meaning of the black-letter rules of the Civil Code is a matter of interpretation performed by scholars and judges who carve out the actual law-in-action. In the following sections I shall discuss this aspect.

Doctrinal interpretation and judicial application

While the legislature substituted *contra bonos mores* for *bona fides*, it seems that the doctrine of private law has moved even further away from the letter and spirit of the Community instrument, proposing to interpret the *contra bonos mores* clause in the light of the general clause of 'principles of social coexistence' (*zasady współżycia społecznego*). The latter general clause was introduced into the Polish legal system back in 1950 as a transplant from the laws of the Soviet Union.[44] At the time of their transposition into Polish law, the 'principles of social coexistence' were viewed as the expression of the new, socialist morality, as opposed to the bourgeois general clauses of the capitalist legal system, such as equity (*aequitas*), good faith (*bona fides*) and good customs (*boni mores*).[45] The 'principles of social coexistence' permeated the entire Civil Code ousting all the traditional general clauses. Quite remarkably, after 1990 they were retained and were still used in new legislative enactments. Since 1999, however, new legislative instruments have not employed this socialist general clause but resorted to 'equity' or 'good customs' instead. This led to a dualism of general clauses in Polish private law which perplexed the doctrine and judiciary, who came up with various interpretations of this cohabitation.

Without, therefore, going into the details of this discussion it is necessary to point out here the specific features of the principles of

[44] The law of the Soviet Union knew a general clause of 'principles of socialist coexistence', contained both in the Constitution and in civil law legislation; this model was exported to other countries belonging to the socialist legal family (A. Wolter, *Prawo cywilne. Część ogólna* [Civil Law: the General Part] (Warsaw: Państwowe Wydawnictwo Naukowe, 1955), 62–3; T. Justyński, *Nadużycie prawa w polskim prawie cywilnym* [Abuse of Right in Polish Civil Law] (Cracow: Zakamycze, 2000), 97.

[45] S. Szer, *Prawo cywilne* [Civil Law], 2nd edn (Warsaw: 1962), 25; J. Nowacki, 'Niektóre zagadnienia zasad współżycia społecznego' [Certain Issues Regarding the Principles of Social Coexistence] (1957) 12 (7–8) *Państwo i Prawo* 99ff., at 107.

social coexistence which have been developed by the doctrine and judiciary of the socialist period and which have, as a rule, been upheld until now. First of all, the principles are considered to be a synthesis of the actual views of society rather than an equitable solution found by the judge on his own responsibility. Hence the judge is formally speaking reduced to the role of a spokesperson of the ethical views of society, a social scientist in a judicial gown. Secondly, the judge applying the principles is supposed to single out and identify a concrete principle of social coexistence that she or he is applying to the facts of the case. A mere reference to the principles of social coexistence in general and in the plural is not sufficient. Thirdly, the principles of social coexistence are objective in character. Unlike the good faith clause, they are not supposed to encompass the subjective intent of the parties. A judge applying the principles of social coexistence is expected to evaluate the parties' conduct only on the basis of their external behaviour, and not their subjective motivation. Fourthly, the principles of social coexistence were originally intended as a uniform general clause. The principles displaced a variety of general clauses (such as good faith, equity, good customs, fair dealing) thus substituting a variety of standards with one uniform standard. Thus the differentiation of standards as between the more demanding *Treu und Glauben* standard and the less demanding *gute Sitten* standard (as in the German BGB) was not known to the Polish Civil Code.

Taking this context into account, scholarly interpretations according to which the *contra bonos mores* standard (found in the Polish provisions implementing the Unfair Terms Directive) is 'similar, or even identical to, the clause on principles of social coexistence' (Skory) is not without impact upon the judicial application of that standard. In fact, following the tradition of case law during the socialist period, where concrete (singled out) principles of social coexistence had to be pleaded (as opposed to the notion of principles of social coexistence in general), Skory advocates the same approach in relation to good customs. What is characteristic in Skory's approach is that, in analysing the content of the 'good customs' concept, he does not regard it as an implementation of the directive's good faith requirement (which is defined in the directive's preamble) but analyses it quite independently of the directive, resorting either to pre-war Polish definitions of good customs or to the socialist notion of principles of social coexistence. There is no reference to objective good faith in Skory's analysis, despite its presence as a general clause in pre-socialist legislation (as one of the general clauses in the

Code of Obligations). This indicates how strong the intellectual link remains between socialist legal culture and its principles of social coexistence and, conversely, how weak is the cultural impact of Europeanisation.

In the context of unfair terms Łętowska also assumed the indistinguishable character of 'good customs' and 'principles of social coexistence',[46] seeing no difference in the functioning of good faith, good customs and the principles of social coexistence. It is therefore no wonder that scholars such as Małgorzata Bednarek[47] consider that, when interpreting the clause of 'good customs', courts and scholars refer to case law concerning the principles of social coexistence (a similar approach is implicitly taken by Podrecki and Zoll).[48] This approach of interchangeability of general clauses deprives them of any individual character; they are treated as synonymous expressions of the legal language and, as a consequence, they entail the same methodology and the same standard.

However, it is not only scholars who tend to equate 'good customs' and the 'principles of social coexistence'. There is a host of case law (also regarding unfair terms) which indicates that courts feel entitled to use the two concepts interchangeably[49] and actually go so far as to identify the specific 'principle of good customs' [sic!] applicable in the case.

[46] E. Łętowska, *Ochrona niektórych praw konsumentów. Komentarz* [The Protection of Certain Rights of Consumers: a Commentary], 3rd edn (Warsaw: C. H. Beck, 2001), 104: 'As regards the technique of applying general clauses, the reform introduced is of no significance: every general clause ultimately rests upon the evaluation of the judge and his axiological feeling, determined by objective and subjective criteria which ought to be explicitly stated in the judgment.'

[47] Bednarek, *Wzorce*, 180.

[48] P. Podrecki and F. Zoll, 'Odpowiedzialność podmiotów świadczących usługi' [The Liability of Subjects Providing Services], in Traple and du Vall. *Ochrona konsumenta*, 140: 'the precise phraseology deployed (whether principles of social coexistence, good custom, good faith in the objective sense, requirements of loyalty) is essentially a matter of legislative elegance'.

[49] See e.g. the judgment of the Court of Appeal in Łódź of 22 April 1992 in case I ACr 132/92, *Dom Mody Nestor* v. *Przedsiębiorstwo Gospodarki Mieszkaniowej*, OSA 1993/5/34: 'The principles of social coexistence are rules of conduct which are closely linked to moral and customary norms. Beyond doubt good customs [*boni mores*] which are binding in legal transactions are part of them.' See also judgment of the Supreme Court of 6 May 1998 in case II CKN 734/97, *Przedsiębiorstwo Produkcyjno-Usługowe E.* v. *Przedsiębiorstwo Produkcyjno-Handlowe E.-B.*, OSNC 1999/2/25; judgment of the Supreme Court of 22 April 2004 in case I CK 547/03, *Halina G.* v. *Grażyna T. and Jan T.*, M. Spół, 2005/3/67: 'The principles of social coexistence also referred to as good customs are a general clause.' The same phrase was later repeated by the Supreme Court in its judgment of 23 April 2004 in case I CK 548/03 *Ryszard G.* v. *Grażyna T. and Ewa R.*, LEX no. 334983 and in a judgment of the same day in case I CK 550/03 *Jerzy Z.* v. *Grażyna T. and Ewa R.*, LEX no. 188472.

The Supreme Court is making efforts to change this attitude of the lower courts. In a judgment of 3 February 2006,[50] explicitly invoking the directive as its source of inspiration, that Court remarked that:

> It is impossible to agree with the appellant's submissions that the court is under a duty to specify which particular 'good custom' was violated *in casu.* The appellant's view is based on the premise that the normative system to which the general clause of good customs refers is a closed catalogue . . . The lower courts ought to have comprehensively justified the reasons for finding a particular term to be unlawful, invoking the ethical rules of honest and loyal dealing in transactions. They were not, however, under a duty to point to a concrete principle.

Another issue is the relationship between the *contra bonos mores* clause and the gross violation of the consumer's interests. Are these two separate and cumulative premises of unfairness which have to be fulfilled jointly to trigger the sanction of ineffectivess ('not binding') or are they just two sides of one standard? According to Maciej Skory the first interpretation is right, i.e. the shaping of rights and duties in contravention of good customs and the gross violation of the consumer's interest are two independent and separate conditions of unfairness.[51] What is more, the violation of good customs should, according to Skory, be treated as remaining in a causal link with the violation of the consumer's interest (as its cause).[52]

As a matter of fact, this view has even been adopted by the Supreme Court in its judgment of 6 April 2004,[53] in which it pointed out that there were four separate premises of unfairness, among which a violation of *boni mores* and a gross violation of the consumer's interests were two separate premises which had to be fulfilled jointly. Therefore, according to the Supreme Court, it is possible for a particular term to violate good customs and to violate the interests of the consumer, although in a less than flagrant way (Skory)[54] or that one could imagine a truly gross violation of the consumer's interest which would not violate good

However, in a judgment of 26 January 2006 (case II CK 378/05, *V* v. *J*, LEX no. 172222, Wokanda 2006/6/8) the Supreme Court stated that the good customs were *a part* of a wider general clause, i.e. the principles of social coexistence.

[50] Case I CK 297/05 *UPC Polska*, LEX no. 179741, Wokanda 2006/7–8/18.

[51] M. Jagielska, 'Niedozwolone klauzule umowne' [Prohibited Contractual Terms], in E. Nowińska and P. Cybula, *Europejskie prawo konsumenckie a prawo polskie* [European Consumer Law and Polish Law] (Cracow: Zakamycze, 2005), 57ff., at 83.

[52] M. Skory, *Klauzule abuzywne w polskim prawie ochrony konsumenta* [Unfair Terms in Polish Consumer Protection Law] (Cracow: Zakamycze, 2005), 173.

[53] Case I CK 472/03, LEX no. 125052. [54] Skory, *Klauzule*, 177.

customs (Popiołek).[55] The introduction of the need for a causal link between the violation of good customs and the violation of the consumer's interest creates additional issues, especially as regards the nature of that causal link.[56]

In my opinion this represents the introduction of a new element into the test of unfairness, one not found in the directive itself, which lowers the standard imposed upon the trader and, as a consequence, lowers the protection afforded to the consumer. Ultimately, this creates a situation in which a particular term may be regarded as violating good customs but, at the same time, not violating the consumer's interests flagrantly (Skory).[57] Such an interpretation of the Polish provision – perfectly correct within the limits of its text (Pecyna)[58] – runs counter to the spirit and even letter of the directive. Furthermore, as I already indicated above, the use of the term 'grossly' (*rażąco*) in the Polish Code may be interpreted otherwise than 'significant' in the directive, since this adjective is already present in numerous articles of the Civil Code. Indeed some scholars, such as Skory, encourage resort to the literature and case law regarding those articles in order to interpret the term 'grossly' in the provisions implementing the directive. Thus, instead of interpreting the notion of 'gross violation' in the spirit of the directive's 'significant imbalance', Polish scholars and judges are invited to resort to national standards, which were developed in areas of the law other than unfair terms, such as the law of delict and its concept of gross negligence.[59]

In its judgment of 3 February 2006[60] the Supreme Court ruled in favour of a pro-Community interpretation of the relevant rules of the Civil Code and established a clear and direct link between the notion of 'violation of interests' (in Polish law) and the notion of 'imbalance of rights and duties' (in European law). A similar link was established by the Supreme Court between the notions of 'gross' (in Polish law) and 'essential' (in European law). In this judgment the Polish implementing

[55] W. Popiołek, in K. Pietrzykowski (ed.), *Kodeks cywilny*, 4th edn (Warsaw: C. H. Beck 2005), 987.

[56] Skory, *Klauzule*, 174. [57] *Ibid*., 175.

[58] M. Pecyna, *Kontrola wzorców poza obrotem konsumenckim* [Control of Model Contracts in Non-Consumer Transactions] (Cracow: Zakamycze, 2003), 141–2.

[59] Arts. 14 §2 (gross injury to an incapacitated party to a contract), 202 (juridical act grossly violating the principles of sound management of common property), 303 (gross infringement of holder of a servitude), 371, 388, 484, 685, 757, 777, 781, 788 (as indicated by Skory, *Klauzule*, 178 n. 323).

[60] Case I CK 297/2005, *Miejski i Powiatowy Rzecznik Konsumentów w L.* v. *U*, LexPolonica no. 399979, LEX no. 179741, Biul.SN 2006/5/12, Wokanda 2006/7–8/18.

measure, however distant its wording may be from that of the directive, was clearly linked to the latter instrument, ensuring an effectively pro-Community interpretation of the national rules. However, one can wonder whether the Supreme Court's reasoning is not an example of *praeter legem* interpretation, necessary to ensure Poland's compliance with its duties under the Unfair Terms Directive despite the legislature's extravagancies.

The implementation of abstract review of unfair terms

Legislative transposition

Within European law, the rules pertaining to the abstract review of unfair terms are to be found both in Article 7 of the Unfair Terms Directive and in the Injunctions Directive (98/27).[61] The latter directive permits the use of injunctions to protect the collective interests of the consumer; the Member States may permit injunction petitions to be brought by independent public bodies or by consumer organisations. The Injunctions Directive also explicitly deals with the collective interests of consumers covered by the Unfair Terms Directive.

The rules regarding abstract review have been transposed by the Polish legislature exclusively within the Code of Civil Procedure, while no corresponding substantive-law rules have been provided for.[62] Exclusive jurisdiction in those cases has been vested in the Competition and Consumer Protection Court in Warsaw (*Sąd Ochrony Konkurencji i Konsumentów*, hereinafter referred to as 'Consumer Court').[63] *Locus standi* has been granted to a wide range of claimants, including people who, in the light of the defendant's offer, may have entered into a contract containing an unfair term; a Polish or EU consumer organisation; a district or town Consumer Ombudsperson; the President of the Office for the Protection of Competition and Consumers; any prosecutor; the (national) Ombudsperson.[64] The actions become time barred

[61] Directive 98/27/EC of the European Parliament and of the Council of 19 May 1998 on injunctions for the protection of consumers' interests ([1998] OJ L 166 51–55).

[62] Cf. Skory, *Klauzule*, 287ff.; Flaga-Gieruszyńska in *Kodeks*, 2006, 1401. Supreme Court judgment of 11 October 2007 in Case III SK 19/07 *DK* v. *Telekomunikacja Polska SA*, LEX no. 496411, para. 3.

[63] Article 479[36] of ustawa z dnia z dnia 17 listopada 1964 r. – Kodeks postępowania cywilnego [Act of 17 November 1964 – Code of Civil Procedure] (Dz.U. no. 43, item 296 with further amendments, hereinafter referred to as Code of Civil Procedure).

[64] Art. 479[38] Code of Civil Procedure.

after the expiry of a six-month deadline following the performance (or expiry) of the contract but they may be brought throughout the period of applicability of a standard-form contract containing an unfair term.[65]

From the perspective of the third-party effects of a judicial decision pronouncing that a particular contractual term is unlawful one should point above all to Article 479^{43} of the Code of Civil Procedure which provides that a 'judgment having the force of *res judicata* is binding upon third parties from the moment at which the term found to be unlawful is entered into the register [of unfair terms]'.

Judgments having the force of *res judicata* are published both in a dedicated Register of Unfair Terms and in the *Judicial and Economic Monitor*.[66] Two issues remain open as regards a literal interpretation of the legislative provisions. First of all, the procedural provisions do not explicitly establish the actual standard of unfairness (test of unfairness) that ought to be applied by the courts,[67] i.e. whether this should be the same standard as in the concrete review of unfair terms (defined in Article 385^{1} of the Civil Code) or whether this standard should be applied *mutatis mutandis* or by way of analogy only, or indeed be entirely replaced with a different test. Secondly, the rule concerning the third-party effects of a judgment (Article 479^{43} of the Code of Civil Procedure) is extremely succinct and fails to define the scope of this rule (i.e. whether it applies only to the particular unfair term, other similar unfair terms, or any terms having the same or similar purpose or effect). On the level of black-letter rules, the two issues remain unresolved and require a doctrinal and judicial creative interpretation. The latter could either be inspired by the relevant EU instruments or be an autonomous interpretation, based only on sources of national law. The latter case could open the door to a negation of the very concept of abstract review and attempts at reinterpreting it as a form of concrete review. In the following sections I will show that such attempts – which may be qualified as resistance towards EU law – have actually taken place.

Doctrinal and judicial interpretation

Certain Polish authors have negated the third-party effects of judicial decisions declaring a particular term to be unfair. One such author, M. Skory, expressed the view that the third-party effect was synonymous

[65] Art. 479^{39} Code of Civil Procedure. [66] Art. 479^{44} Code of Civil Procedure.
[67] Cfr Skory, *Klauzule*, 287ff.; Flaga-Gieruszyńska in *Kodeks*, 1401.

with the fact that anyone may invoke the judgment, although the prohibition itself was, according to him, binding exclusively on the defendant and not on other economic operators.[68] In my view such an interpretation completely deprives the third-party effect provided for in Article 479[13] of the Code of Civil Procedure of any real content. Such a reading of this provision would allow other economic operators to continue using a standard term which had already been ruled unlawful. Characteristically, in his argumentation in support of the narrow interpretation, Skory fails to mention the Unfair Terms Directive even once[69] and bases his entire reasoning solely on Polish transposition measures. M. Skory's view gained support in the writings of M. Jagielska.[70]

In order to support their interpretation, the members of the doctrine opposing the abstract review of unfair terms have relied upon two types of argument. The first argument (which may be dubbed 'pragmatic' or 'practical') rests upon the assumption that an unfair term could actually be fair if used by a different economic operator, in a different sector of the economy or in a different type of contract.[71]

The second argument (which can be dubbed as 'ideological') rests upon the fear of giving judges law-making powers.[72] It must be kept in

[68] Skory, *Klauzule*, 306. [69] *Ibid.*, 298–308.

[70] M. Jagielska, 'Niedozwolone klauzule umowne' [Prohibited Contractual Terms] in E. Nowińska and P. Cybula, *Europejskie prawo konsumenckie a prawo polskie* [European Consumer Law and Polish Law] (Cracow: Zakamycze, 2005), 57ff., at 95–6: '[A] judgment having the force of *res judicata* is effective only "unilaterally": towards consumers and not other traders ... [I]f the term is used in a different standard-form contract by a different trader, it will be necessary to review it once again'.

[71] Skory, *Klauzule*, 291–3, 295, 296–7, 304–6; I. Wesołowska, 'Niedozwolone postanowienia umowne' [Prohibited Contractual Terms], in C. Banasiński (ed.), *Standardy wspólnotowe w polskim prawie ochrony konsumenta* (Warsaw: Prawo i Praktyka Gospodarcza, 2004), 196; Jagielska, 'Niedozwolone', 95–7.

[72] Skory, *Klauzule*, 306–8:

> A further argument to support the position outlined above may be found when analysing the provisions from the perspective of the conformity of the legal norms derived from those provisions with the fundamental rules governing the functioning of the state, as expressed in the Constitution. To accept that ... registration of the judgment of the Court for the Protection of Competition and Consumers would entail a prohibition upon use of such terms by all subjects and in all conditions would be tantamount to establishment of a general and abstract legal norm by the court ... This would mean that the Court for the Protection of Competition and Consumers is entitled to create the law, whereas the creation of law is constitutionally guaranteed as being within the exclusive competence of legislative bodies and not bodies applying the law. Accordingly, this would violate ... the Constitution. Jagielska, 'Niedozwolone', 96:

mind that a rigid negation of judicial law-making was a charactersitic feature of state-socialist legal scholarship; therefore its presence in the Polish debate on abstract review of unfair terms may be seen as an instance of the interaction of the post-socialist elements in legal culture on the one hand and European elements on the other.

Similar resistance towards abstract review can be found in the case law. In a judgment of 11 June 2003[73] the Consumer Court also adopted a narrow view, limiting third-party effects solely to the trader who was actually party to the proceedings. In numerous cases the Consumer Court recondemned unfair terms which had already been entered into the Register of Unfair Terms even in situations where the terms were identically phrased.[74] As a result, one single term was entered into the Register as many as five times, the only difference being the name of the economic operator using the term (which was not always mentioned).[75] The Consumer Court explicitly rejected the view that an unfair term condemned during abstract review could not be used by other economic operators (even if copied literally).[76] It also ruled that only those consumers who actually entered into a contract with the rogue economic

> The consequence of applying Article 479[43] [Code of Civil Procedure 1964] as the basis for issuing judgments effective 'bilaterally' – both vis-à-vis all consumers and all traders – raises doubts of a constitutional nature. The registration of a clause has the same effect as the addition of a new term to the list of prohibited terms in Article 385[3] of the Civil Code. The actions of a court, an adjudicating body, would become law-making actions and the court's judgment would need to be treated as a source of law which contradicts Article 84 of the Constitution of the Republic of Poland.

[73] Case XVII Amc 46/02.

[74] Cf. Jagielska, 'Niedozwolone', 95.

[75] 'In situations unforeseen by this contract, decision shall be taken by [trader's name] in the form of an ordinance' – see Register of Unfair Terms [*Rejestr Klauzul Niedozwolonych* – www.uokik.gov.pl (as of 1 June 2008), terms nos. 22, 37, 46, 52 and 75. Two pairs of terms are identical even as to the name of the trader; thus they are exactly identical.

[76] Consumer Court judgments: of 7 February 2005 in case XVII Amc 108/03, *Prezes UOKiK* v. *Oasis Tours*, MSiG 2006/243/15393; of 22 August 2005 in case XVII Ama 21/05, *Kredyt Bank* v. *Prezes UOKiK*, Dz.Urz.UOKiK 2005/3/45, Wokanda 2006/5/52. In the latter judgment we read:

> The view that the application of an abusive clause entered into the register of forbidden clauses on the basis of a judgment pronounced against a different operator is forbidden also *vis-à-vis* other operators is wrong. First of all, those judgments forbid the application of the aforementioned terms of a model contract only *vis-à-vis* a concrete operator. Secondly, the declaration of abusiveness occurs in the context of the entire model and with regard to the legal relationships that it regulates.

operator could invoke the entering of the standard term into the Register of Unfair Terms *vis-à-vis* that operator.

However, stating that Polish scholars and judges have been resisting the abstract review of unfair terms *en masse* certainly would not do justice to Polish legal culture. It must therefore be emphasised that from the outset there were also scholars who advocated a pro-Community interpretation of the Polish transposing measures. Thus, E. Łętowska can be viewed as a pioneer in countering anti-European resistance strategies. In her commentary on the Consumer Protection Act 2000 she emphatically endorsed the full third-party effects and rejected the reservations of those viewing judgments as a new source of law.[77] A similar position was also adopted by M. Bednarek[78] followed by I. Wesołowska.[79] According to the latter author, the third-party effects of a judgment extend to all natural and legal persons, both economic operators and consumers, and prohibit anyone from including such a term in any standard-form contract;[80] this prohibition extends not only to the literal meaning of the term but also to any other term which effectively employs the same content, albeit expressed in different words.[81]

The pro-Community interpretation endorsing full third-party effects gained the support of the Office for the Protection of Competition and Consumers (*Urząd Ochrony Konkurencji i Konsumenta*, the Polish administrative agency in charge of competition law and consumer protection, hereinafter reffered to as the 'Consumer Office'). The Consumer Office thus interpreted the third-party effects of a judgment condemning unfair terms as extending to all economic operators (but not to all natural and legal persons) and to terms which, despite having a different wording, had the same actual content (the same meaning). This situation led to a clash between the views of the Consumer Office on the one hand (supporting a pro-Community interpretation) and the Consumer Court on the other hand (resisting the third-party effects). Thanks to the fact that judgments of the Consumer Court may be attacked before the Supreme Court, it was the latter jurisdiction's task to resolve the dispute between the administrative agency and the specialised court in charge of consumer protection.

It was in its judgment of 13 July 2006[82] that the Supreme Court finally gave its support to the pro-Community interpretation. The highest

[77] Łętowska, *Ochrona*, 173. [78] Bednarek, *Wzorce*, 218.
[79] Wesołowska, 'Niedozwolone', 199. [80] *Ibid.*, 203. [81] *Ibid.*
[82] Case III SZP 3/06, *Towarzystwo Finansowo-Inwestycyjne Spółka z o.o.* v. *Prezes UOKiK* [2006] 3–4 *Transformacje Prawa Prywatnego* 113.

judges of the country referred in their decision to the relevant Community instruments, treating them as as a guideline for the construction of the national transposing measures. The Supreme Court judges rejected the approach of the Consumer Court and advocated a wide understanding of the third-party effects of judgments condemning unfair terms and entering them in the Register. According to the Supreme Court's judgment, a standard term entered into the Register is not only prohibited *vis-à-vis* the same economic operator but also *vis-à-vis* other operators. This also includes situations where an economic operator uses a similar term having the same practical consequences, even if it is not literally identical. The Supreme Court elucidated that its ruling represented a *praeter legem* interpretation of the Polish transposing measures, which was nevertheless justified in light of Poland's EU obligations as interpreted by the European Court of Justice. It should be pointed out that in rejecting the case law of the Consumer Court, the Supreme Court condemned it for not having taken any account of EU law, and specifically for not having fulfilled the duty of taking into account the Injunctions Directive and the Unfair Terms Directive when interpreting national measures. The Supreme Court explicitly referred to the EU legal order as the justification for its approach and *praeter legem* interpretation giving full effect to the directives.

Conclusions

The implementation of the Unfair Terms Directive in Poland has led to a clash of two legal cultures: the (Western) European legal culture and the post-socialist (post-communist) legal culture in Poland. I decided to analyse this clash by referring to two specific areas: the general prohibition of unfairness with its general clause of *bona fides* and the abstract control of unfair terms and the third-party effects of judgments issued as a result of such control. In both areas I identified a certain degree of resistance towards the novelties of the EU instrument; the resistance was identified at all three levels of legal culture – legislation, scholarship and adjudication. I do not wish to argue that the resistance towards the Unfair Terms Directive in Poland is an isolated case; I am fully aware of the difficulties that this directive has faced in other Member States, including the 'old' Member States of the Western part of the Union. However, in my chapter I have tried to show that at least some of the arguments and methods of resistance could in one way or another be linked to the peculiarities of Polish legal culture and specifically its state-socialist heritage. Resorting to a post-socialist general clause (the 'principles of social coexistence') instead of the directive's 'good faith' clause is one example. The resistance towards third-party effects for fear of judicial law-making (condemned by state-socialist legal scholarship) is another. Remaining fully aware that resistance towards certain elements of the *acquis communautaire* among the actors of national legal cultures is by no means a Polish idiosyncrasy, I wished to draw attention to some specific aspects of that resistance which seem to be linked to certain state-socialist characteristics still present in Polish legal culture.

PART IV

Conclusions

22

European consumer protection: theory and practice

MEL KENNY AND JAMES DEVENNEY

This volume has analysed European consumer protection law in its theoretical and practical dimensions: an analysis set in the broader context of consolidation and codification initiatives exemplified *inter alia* in the review of the consumer *acquis*, the publication of the Draft Common Frame of Reference and the proposal for an EU Consumer Rights Directive. The issues explored by the contributors to this volume are even more relevant and important today given, for example, the revisions to the proposed Consumer Rights Directive, the Commission's appointment of an Expert Group on a Common Frame of Reference in the area of European contract law,[1] and the Commission's 2010 Green Paper on policy options for progress towards a European Contract Law for consumers and businesses.[2]

Norbert Reich provocatively set the scene for our analysis with his critique of the 'new approach' to targeted, 'full' harmonisation in EU consumer protection,[3] initiatives aimed at preventing Member States from maintaining or adopting more protective provisions of consumer law in the harmonised field. While seeking to remedy the fragmentation of consumer protection attributed to minimum harmonisation, this approach is contradicted by the principle of 'home country' protection otherwise adopted under the new Regulation 593/2008 (Rome I).[4] Reich argues that the 'new approach' is inappropriate for promoting consumer

[1] See Commission Decision 2010/233/EU; (2010) OJ L 105/109.

[2] See European Commission, Green Paper from the Commission on policy options for progress towards a European Contract Law for consumers and businesses, COM (2010) 348 final, 1 July 2010.

[3] Targeted full harmonisation: Art. 4, Proposed Consumer Rights Directive COM (2008) 614 final. See also H. Micklitz and N. Reich, 'Cronica de una muerta anunciada: the Commission Proposal on a Directive of Consumer Rights' (2009) 46 *CMLRev* 471–519.

[4] [2008] OJ L 176/6.

confidence, threatening unpredictable legal fragmentation in the patchwork of national private law systems, downgrading the importance of consumer protection and failing to respect the principle of proportionality in EU law-making.[5] As a compromise Reich advocates a strategy of 'half harmonisation': allowing full harmonisation for imperative reasons relating to the internal market, yet otherwise respecting minimum harmonisation, in particular where constitutional traditions need to be respected in line with the principles of proportionality and subsidiarity. Reich is critical of Commissioner Reding's proposal to limit full harmonisation to online transactions, but welcomes any softening of the 'new approach' that this may represent, a development which may allow a broader role for the optional instrument (blue button) in cross-border transactions.

In the first part of this collection, with contributions from Twigg-Flesner, Mak, Poncibò, Rott and Barral-Viñals, a critical eye was cast over EU consumer protection strategies and mechanisms, with particular emphasis on the rationales for EU consumer protection law; the concept of effective enforcement; the broader modernisation agenda in European private law; the post-Lisbon policy matrix; and the constitutionalisation of consumer protection.

Christian Twigg-Flesner argued that EU consumer law has reached a watershed: that what once seemed the inexorable progress of directive-led, legal harmonisation of national law has been halted. Twigg-Flesner attributes this to two main factors: first, institutional politics and Commissioner Reding's commitment to setting priorities in EU consumer law; and, second, the resumption of work on the Common Frame of Reference. Discourse has been promoted in particular by the Commission's 2010 Green Paper, announcing that piecemeal harmonisation has run its course. The Green Paper restricts the scope of EU consumer law to the cross-border situation and spurns the adoption of further directives, restricting the form of EU consumer law to the regulation. Moreover, by switching to a regulation, Twigg-Flesner argues that a model will be created for the development of a transnational consumer law applicable beyond the borders of the EU.

Vanessa Mak questioned the systematicity of EU private law and the place of consumer protection within that body of law. Mak observes a contradiction in EU consumer law: while the processes of positive and negative integration have produced a lack of coherence in EU consumer

[5] Art. 5(4) TEU.

law with further fragmentary effects for national legal systems, simultaneously attempts at introducing consolidating directives, such as the proposed Consumer Rights Directive, have fought to improve the very coherence of EU consumer law. Mak makes the case that more systematicity is required, and focuses, in her survey, on financial services and rejects maximum harmonisation. Mak distinguishes between cross-border and purely domestic transactions, transactions of a different nature which may none the less require regulation on the basis of a common standard of consumer protection, adjustment to national measures being possible along *Cassis de Dijon* lines. Mak argues that in the case of cross-border transactions of central importance for the internal market a higher standard of consumer protection is required than in domestic transactions, transactions which would be addressed by national measures in accordance with the principles of subsidiarity and proportionality.

Cristina Poncibò examined whether the modernisation of competition law enforcement can serve as a template for the modernisation of EU consumer law. To this end Poncibò focuses on the role of enforcement, co-regulation and the role of private parties in ensuring consumer protection. More specifically, the representation of consumers' interests in the European standardisation bodies and the emergence of private collective enforcement procedures in national legal orders are held up to scrutiny. While casting her analysis in less dramatic terms than Twigg-Flesner, Poncibò shares the view that consumer protection has entered a new phase. However, Poncibò observes that important caveats attach to the modernisation agenda; in particular the reality of consumer behaviour, as disclosed by behavioural sciences' analysis, casts doubt on the emergence of the 'new', 'empowered consumer'. None the less, Poncibò argues that important steps need to be taken to better incorporate consumers' interests in standard-setting, steps to ensuring adequate standards which can, in turn, be buttressed by collective enforcement proceedings.

Peter Rott took a more sceptical view on the privatisation agenda, focusing on the effective enforcement of EU consumer law, an area which has remained within national competence. Drawing distinctions between national approaches, between those states relying on private enforcement supplemented by collective proceedings (Germany) and those relying on a mixture of criminal and/or public law/regulatory responses (Belgium, UK and Scandinavia), Rott dissects national and EU overreliance on private law mechanisms, illuminating the limits of private enforcement and collective proceedings and elaborating criteria on the extent to which public and criminal law sanctions are necessary to ensure the effective enforcement of EU consumer law. In situations such as cold calling, Rott argues that fines and criminal sanctions are the *only* ways in which consumers can be protected. Rott advocates a Member State specific approach to the use of public and criminal sanctions, it being for each Member State to assess, in the light of the particular national impediments to effective enforcement, which public/criminal measures would fill the gaps. Finally, Rott argues that specialised agencies such as consumer authorities and ombudsmen, rather than competition authorities or prosecutors, should play the lead role in ensuring effective enforcement.

In her survey of new rationales in EU consumer law faced with the new challenges of e-commerce, Barral-Viñals argued that traditional consumer protection solutions were inappropriate; that in the internet age, we require a high level of protection and that enforcing e-consumers' rights remains problematic. The chapter draws attention to the future challenges facing consumer protection in e-commerce.[6] Barral-Viñals argues both that the concept of the consumer in e-commerce is broader than the traditional, 'offline' consumer, with implications for the EU information paradigm, and that, given the technological opportunities offered by the internet, online dispute resolution (ODR) needs to play a more central role in building consumer confidence and developing a practical approach to dispute resolution.

What emerges from these contributions is of EU consumer law having arrived at a watershed at which, as Twigg-Flesner puts it, some redefinition of its form (regulation v. directive) and scope (cross-border v. internal dimension) is required. Similarly, Mak and Reich point to this moment in consumer protection and advocate the rejection the maximum or 'full' harmonisation approach, and its replacement with more subtle models of harmonisation – models which, as Mak observes, require higher standards of consumer protection in the cross-border situation. Meanwhile, Poncibò applies the competition enforcement template to consumer law, but raises important caveats on the utility of privatised consumer law. This point is deepened in Rott's contribution in which he argues that, selectively, public enforcement mechanisms and criminal penalties may be the only means by which effective consumer protection

[6] Future Challenges Paper 2009–2014; Communication on EU consumer policy strategy 2007–2013, COM (2007) 99 final, both available at: http://ec.europa.eu.

can be ensured. Meanwhile, Barral-Viñals makes the point that a higher level of consumer protection is required in the light of the introduction of new technology, a point reinforced by Rott's analysis of the cold-calling cases. Finally, in their approaches, Barral-Viñals and Poncibò emphasise the difficulty with real-world consumer behaviour, both arguing that the new, empowered consumer has not emerged and that, as a result, the information paradigm is not an appropriate, and should certainly not be seen as the only mechanism for consumer protection.

Part II dealt with concepts of vulnerability in the context of consumer protection and critically explored responses to vulnerability in this context. With contributions from Schüller, Willett, Morgan-Taylor, Garde and Littler this section illuminated and sought to resolve key questions about the proper scope of European consumer protection law.

Bastian Schüller revisited the definition of the consumer in EU law, questioning whether, as the EU moves towards becoming an increasingly political Union, the definition of the consumer needs to be updated. Schüller reflects on whether the definition of the consumer needs to be upgraded from that of a legal person acting for purposes outside his business, trade or profession so as to reflect more closely the acts and behaviour which truly characterise the consumer. Echoing Poncibò's and Barral-Viñals's earlier analyses, Schüller questions the rationality of consumer decisions and goes on to examine the persuasiveness of common demarcations drawn, for example, between consumers and professionals. As a result the information paradigm, so heavily promoted in the development of EU consumer law, is questioned. Buttressing his case with behavioural studies research, Schüller argues that effective consumer protection has to distinguish different situations in order to strike a balance between protection and an inflation of transaction costs. Finally, with the advent of full harmonisation, Schüller advocates the case for redefining the consumer in terms of his/her actual behaviour rather than instrumentalising the consumer for political purposes.

Linking criticism of the information paradigm in EU consumer law with the assumption of the arrival of the new, empowered consumer, Chris Willett and Martin Morgan-Taylor turned to the Unfair Terms in Consumer Contracts Directive and reflected on the role of contract transparency. To this end Willett and Morgan-Taylor focused on the extent to which transparency has been and should be seen as a legitimising factor in EU consumer protection, this being of importance given both the scale of EU harmonisation and the moves towards measures of maximum harmonisation. The contributors dissect the limits of transparency, pointing out the need for solidarity in certain transactions, 'assisted informed consent' notwithstanding, and that there are situations in which transparency fails to produce any certainty. In such situations we may need to reject transparency as a legitimising factor. Given these constraints Willett and Morgan-Taylor argue that regulators such as the Office of Fair Trading in the UK need to refer to behavioural research on the limits of transparency in genuinely informing consumers.

Amandine Garde drew our attention to another underrepresented group in consumer discourse, and another gap between theory and practice: children. She analyses the protection of children both quantitatively and in terms of the markets to which they are relevant: as a primary market; as a crucial influence on the parental market; and as future consumers. While the commercialisation of childhood has become increasingly sophisticated and concerns have arisen about its mental and physical impact, the EU response has remained muted. Despite the UN Convention on the Rights of the Child and the EU Charter of Fundamental Rights,[7] the EU has largely failed to integrate the special interests of the child in the elaboration of EU consumer protection. Garde argues that child impact assessments and evaluations need to be involved in policy formulation, and that children's rights' advocates need to be brought more explicitly into the EU policy-and law-making processes. To paraphrase Garde, stakeholders need to take ownership of the promotion of children's rights. As Garde concludes, while the commitments to advancing the EU strategy on children's rights make no reference to the child as a consumer, the policy goal should be that children are heard as well as seen in the EU.

Alan Littler turned to another special case in EU consumer protection: that of gambling, an area still dominated by national restraints foreclosing the market from competition and cross-border trade. As Littler observes, the case law provides Member States with a considerable margin of discretion within which restrictions on free movement of gambling services and gambling service providers can be maintained. Yet while this freezes the consumer of gambling services out of the internal market, the advent of online gambling has expanded the area of potential conflict between Member States *inter se* and between national and EU law. While consumer protection may justify national restrictions to the fundamental freedoms, Littler identities a blind spot in the ECJ's approach to what consumer protection in respect of

[7] Art. 36 UNCRC, Art. 24 EU Charter of Fundamental Rights.

gambling entails, arguing that consumer protection has fallen victim to the unique characteristics of gambling. Littler advocates harmonisation playing a greater role so long as a distinction is drawn between recreational and pathological gamblers, the latter being subject to justified national restrictions. Though it remains a field which is out of step with consumer protection theory and practice, Littler is sceptical as to whether the EU will be able to accommodate such a distinction.

The scope of consumer law which emerges from these contributions remains highly contested. While Schüller points to the need to revisit the consumer definition in the light of the new political dimensions of the Union, Willett and Morgan-Taylor highlight the limits of contractual transparency as a legitimising factor in EU consumer protection, given situations in which solidarity rather than information is needed and situations in which transparency fails to produce legal certainty. Meanwhile Garde's analysis of consumer protection and the rights of the child, and Littler's analysis of gambling and gambling services, point to under-represented constituencies in consumer protection discourse.

Part III contextualised various aspects of European consumer protection law, integrating in the process a broad church of perspectives: private international law; historical analysis of consumer protection in action; critical analysis of the role of private litigation in market regulation; public law influences on consumer protection standards; the experience of the accession states in adjusting their private law to the Europeanisation process; and the citizenship implications of consumer protection. In so doing, intriguing insights were offered on aspects of consumer protection in individual Member States. With contributions from a range of national and comparative perspectives from Bisping, Gillies, Swain, Halfmeier, Wragg, Jagielska, Jagielski, Davies, Riefa, Tomančáková and Mańko this part was the most expansive.

On the conflict of law dimension to consumer protection, Christopher Bisping elaborated on how the new Regulation 593/2008 (Rome I) seeks to harmonise the rules so as to strengthen cross-border contracting. In particular, Bisping is concerned with the cases where a transaction might not be deemed to fall within the scope of the choice of law rules, or situations in which the active consumer is held to be exempted from those rules. In such cases, where specific consumer protection does not apply, resort has traditionally been made to the notion of overriding mandatory requirements; here Bisping argues against interventionism. What would emerge would be a very narrow and not uncontested margin of consumer protection, balancing consumer protection with the countervailing rights of the counterparty. Nevertheless, as Bisping concedes, in exceptional cases relief could be extended to the consumer.

Lorna Gillies addressed the Communitarisation of choice of law rules for non-contractual obligations provided for in Regulation 864/2007 (Rome II). Given the privatisation of competition law enforcement promoted under the new Regulation 1/2003/EC,[8] Gillies focuses on the application of the regulation to the choice of law in unfair competition and restrictions of competition cases,[9] and the need for effective collective redress alluded to in the Commission's 2008 Green Paper.[10] Gillies places Rome II in the context of the Commission's attempts to promote judicial cooperation in civil and commercial matters. However, Gillies observes that a number key concepts under Article 6 of Rome II remain unclear: what is 'unfair competition' under the regulation? How should the 'affected market' as a connecting factor be defined? Such lack of clarity, until resolved by the ECJ, represents a real challenge for private litigants. More positively, a key step taken in the Rome II regulation is the recognition of the role of collective redress in rectifying market failures and providing compensation, a recognition which now requires elaboration in the 2008 proposed consumer collective redress mechanism.

Warren Swain in his *tour de force* on horse-trading in the eighteenth and nineteenth centuries supplied a cautionary tale on seeking effective consumer protection in its historical perspective. Among the hurdles to effective protection identified by Swain are, first, that reliance on the judicial approach and case-law innovation can be difficult to sustain; that the complexity of markets can condition poor protective standards; that, in the common law jurisdiction, the market tends to favour the cheaper dealer with the lower standard of consumer protection; and, finally, that attempts at reform have themselves invariably been overtaken by new technology.

Axel Halfmeier looked to the investor or shareholder as a consumer of financial services and the applicability and significance of the US 'legal origins' theory in shaping regulatory strategy. The thesis put forward by 'legal origins' theory concerns the strength of protection it attributes to the private litigation model in common law systems as compared to the public regulatory model promoted in civil law systems. Halfmeier points

[8] Recital 7, Reg. 1/2003 on the implementation of the Rules of Competition, 16 December 2002 ((2002) OJ L 1/1 of 4 January 2003).

[9] Arts. 6(1) and 6(3) Rome II, Reg. 864/2007/EC on the law applicable to non-contractual obligations [2007] OJ L 199/40.

[10] Commission's Green Paper on collective consumer redress (COM (2008) 794 final).

out the controversial aspects of this theory and questions its capacity to withstand the current financial crisis. Nevertheless, Halfmeier argues that legal origins theory makes an important contribution to discourse on regulation, noting that: 'where public regulation has retreated and is still retreating from certain economic and social areas, a regulatory gap appears that can and must be filled with private litigation'. Simultaneously, however, he notes that deregulation and the private litigation response may not always be appropriate where public goods are concerned, which forces us to question an overreliance on the market mechanism and private litigation.

Paul Wragg juxtaposed the interplay of national regulations on unfair commercial practices and misleading and comparative advertising with Article 10 ECHR on the freedom of expression. The national regulations in question, the Consumer Protection from Unfair Trading and the Business Protection from Misleading Marketing Regulations (both 2008) respectively transpose the Unfair Commercial Practices Directive 2005/29 and the Misleading and Comparative Advertising Directive 2006/114. Mapping out the boundary between the unfair or misleading commercial practice and freedom of commercial expression may prove, as Wragg argues, to have significant implications for enforcement agencies and may leave national judges facing stark choices between strengthening the scope of commercial free speech or widening the discretion of the Member States to restrict freedom of commercial expression to a narrow band of cases in which democratic processes are at stake.

Jagielska and Jagielski examined the interplay between consumer and human rights, and question whether a 'fundamentalisation' of consumer rights has been set in motion. The chapter studied the different ways in which consumer protection has been incorporated into national constitutions: as an element of national policy; as one of a number of values to be promoted; as a value in itself; as explicitly recognised individual rights; and, finally, as consumer rights invoked in constitutions, the level of practical protection being determined by private law. The rights involved in these cases conform to one of three types: principles, subjective rights and an intermediate category of 'programme' norms. Having mapped out these classifications, the scope of constitutionalised consumer protection is assessed, as are the broader implications of constitutionalising consumer rights. Jagieslka and Jagielski argue that the importance attributed to consumer protection via the constitution will continue to influence the interpretation and application of the law and that this means that provisions of consumer protection need to be interpreted in the light of fundamental principles such as proportionality. Finally, there is the development of subjective rights in consumer protection, a development potentially eclipsing the role of consumer protection foreseen, for example, in the proposed Consumer Rights Directive.

Against the background of otherwise sceptical positions on consumer empowerment (*inter alia* Poncibò, Halfmeier, Rott), Jim Davies mapped out the transformation of consumer protection over the last forty years; the consumer changing from: 'feeble agent of market economics . . . into the *potentially* confident, informed and empowered "motor of economic change"'. This development, Davies argues, was accompanied by the rearrangement of decision-making power away from Member States and towards the EU, independent regulatory agencies, enforcement authorities and individual consumers. Consequentially, a new consumer citizenship practice – a deliberate, active and informed participation of the consumer – became possible. Davies identifies the levels of consumer protection contributing to this model of 'consumer citizenship practice' and the relationships between the levels and obstacles to this practice; a survey which helps to identify problems in ensuring effective protection. The model is comprised of four levels of consumer protection:

1. first, the basic framework supplied by the consumer *acquis*, the legislative framework and contractual documentation aimed at protecting the vulnerable consumer and providing redress;
2. second, the more explicit level of product information and labelling requirements, encouraging the exercise of personal responsibility and informed choice, a product information level which only works where consumers are motivated and capable;
3. third, a level linking aspects of individual and structural capability and determining whether the consumer faces individual problems (financial, physical or cognitive) or structural detriment (market failure). Obstacles at this level frustrate effective consumer citizenship;
4. finally, the motivational level of consumer citizenship at which the individualistically or solidaristically motivated consumer exerts influence on the market.

By specifying the protection, information, capability and motivation levels of consumer protection, a template by which we can measure the true extent of consumer empowerment and assess the obstacles to effective consumer citizenship practice is supplied.

Christine Riefa's chapter expanded this survey to another category of contracts and consumer protection issues frequently underrepresented in consumer protection discourse: the auction. The context of this is provided by the increasing resort to auctions as a sales method, a trend accelerated by the emergence of TV auction platforms and the advent of the online auction. Riefa deals with the need to address the confusion caused by the Distance Selling Directive, a directive which excluded contracts 'concluded at an auction', and critically evaluates the line taken in the proposed Directive on Consumer Rights and the definitions it produces of the auction and the public auction. Riefa places the bidding procedure at the centre of her thesis for supplying a reliable demarcation and necessary differentiation between the situations without producing further fragmentation. Riefa criticises in particular the reliance on informational rights and the rejection of a right to withdraw from all types of auction.

Finally, two chapters dealt with the perspective of the new accession states. First, Blanka Tomančáková explored the recodification of Czech private law following the 1989 Velvet Revolution. She analysed recodification as part of a broader exercise in legal reform which also necessitated new interpretational rules, a new Act on Business Corporations and an Act on International Private Law. While acknowledging that transposition of EU law does not require verbatim incorporation in specific legislation,[11] Tomančáková observes that until recodification poor translation of EU texts had been a cause of difficulty. More significance for the future development of Czech private law is attributed by Tomančáková to the collective dialogue of stakeholders in the recodification process, a process which returns the Czech Republic to the European legal tradition from which it was separated after 1948. Meanwhile, Rafał Mańko's analysis focused on the Unfair Terms Directive and the clash of the EU model with post-communist legal culture in Poland. Mańko identified a degree of resistance in Poland to the EU instrument and a questioning as much of the directive itself as of the legal scholarship and case law accompanying it. These problems with the reception of EU law are neither idiosyncratic nor unique to Poland, but can be attributed to the peculiarities of Polish legal culture and its post-socialist antecedents.

The final part of this volume thus integrates a variety of perspectives and a welter of considerations into our analysis. From the conflict perspective questions are raised by Bisping on the proper extent of consumer protection in cross-border transactions while Gillies points to gaps in Rome II, in the context of non-contractual obligations,

[11] Case C-478/99, *Commission* v. *Sweden* [2002] ECR I-4147.

underscoring the importance of collective redress explicitly recognised in the 2008 proposal. From a historical, common law perspective Swain supplies a provocative and challenging assessment of the pitfalls of ensuring consumer protection via case law and judicial initiative. Meanwhile, Halfmeier elaborates ideas on the relative strengths of the public/private dichotomy (regulatory v. privatised approach) with his critical analysis of legal origins theory and assessment of the role of private litigation in market regulation. Similarly, Wragg extends our analysis with a juxtaposition of unfair commercial practices, misleading and comparative advertising with the human rights dimension of free commercial expression. Wragg argues that this interplay may potentially lead us to a stark choice between strengthening commercial free speech and widening national discretion to restrict commercial expression. Meanwhile, Jagielska and Jagielski expanded on the constitutional rights aspect of consumer protection, forcefully observing the need to interpret consumer protection in the light of fundamental principles such as proportionality and the emergence of a new category of subject rights in consumer protection, a catalogue of rights eclipsing the consumer protection model foreseen in the proposed Consumer Rights Directive. Amid the general scepticism attaching to the notion of the empowered consumer Davies, in a fascinating analysis, supplied a template through which the strength and obstacles to effective consumer citizenship practice can be assessed and, potentially, addressed. Meanwhile, Riefa further expands our survey to the important, yet underrepresented area of sales via auction. These types of sale, especially with the evolution of multimedia platforms and the advent of web-based auctioneers, are increasingly popular. Finally, Tomančáková and Mańko in their analyses supply important observations on the reception of EU consumer protection in the legal cultures of the accession states of Central and Eastern Europe.

The contributions to this volume point to a new moment in European consumer protection. The tension which emerges at this watershed between those favouring legislative or judicial harmonisation bears witness to how essentially contested EU consumer protection discourse has become. Meanwhile, while all agree that consumer protection has been transformed over the last forty years, the extent to which a new, empowered consumer has emerged, and, if so, on which markets s/he is to be found, is open to dispute. Together, the contributors to this volume have presented a rich, multi-dimensional discourse on consumer protection, and have exposed some of the complex demarcation lines between ensuring consumer protection and other policy goals; elaborating levels of consumer protection in a plethora of consumer contexts; and integrating conflict, constitutional and accession state perspectives. Controversially, this is a discourse whose sophistication outstrips the discourse currently taking place within auspices of the Commission's vehicle: the Expert Group on a Common Frame of Reference. What emerges is a refined model of polycontextual EU consumer protection law, of a model which rejects the assumptions contained in the Commission's 2010 Green Paper and questions the coordinates of the revised proposed Consumer Rights Directive. Instead, this model argues for the adoption of incremental, flexible processes of selective legislative harmonisation and pragmatic, spontaneous harmonisation through judicial collaboration.

INDEX

access to justice under 'legal origins' theory 309–10
acquis see 'consumer *acquis*'; financial services
advertising *see also* commercial expression
  to children *see* children's rights
  of gambling services, control of 227
  as political expression 325–32
aggressive practices
  prohibition by Unfair Commercial Practices Directive 45
alternative dispute resolution (ADR) *see also* online dispute resolution
  legal framework 89–92
  use of 72
ancillary contracts in Czech law 408–10
anti-competitive behaviour *see also* unfair commercial practices
  definition of 259–60
  Rome II Regulation provision 273–8
  Treaty basis for claims of 265
applicable law to contract terms *see* Rome I Regulation
Argentina
  constitutional consumer rights 339
assisted informed consent model
  transparency issues 148–9
auction
  bidding procedure
    auction as 388–94
    definition as to legal construction of 389–92
    definition of parties to 394–5
  Consumer Rights Directive definition
    difficulties 380–1
    necessary changes to 389–95
    necessity 382–5
    neutrality as to technology and product 392–3
    provision 379
    public auction distinguished 385–6
    terminology issues 386
    usefulness 380
  exclusion from Distance Selling Directive 378
  growth of online auctions 378
  operation and legal consequences distinguished 386–8
'average (typical) consumer' concept 24, 36, 38–41, 45, 118 *see also* 'empowered consumer' concept; rational informed consumer

banking
  Icelandic crisis 23, 37
behavioural studies insights as to consumers *see* consumer
bidding procedure *see* auction
blacklisted contract terms 151–2
Brazil
  constitutional consumer rights 338
Bulgaria
  constitutional consumer rights 337
Business Regulations
  coming into force 313
  and ECHR Article 10 335
  and freedom of expression issues 313–14
  provisions generally 314–18

Cambodia
  constitutional consumer rights 337
capability as empowered consumer
  individual capability 371–2
  as normative influence 360, 371–3
  structural capability impairment and general consumer detriment 373
case law
  children's rights 171–3, 177–9
  competition law enforcement 263–4, 269
  constitutional consumer rights 341–52
  definition of consumer 125–6
  freedom of expression 318–34
  gambling services 205–14
  human/fundamental rights 345–6
Cassis de Dijon test 23, 24, 25
chapter summaries 437–49
Charter of Fundamental Rights provision
  children's rights provision *see* EU Charter of Fundamental Rights
children's advertising, regulation of
  food marketing 194–8
  marketing to children 188–91
  Member State Law, strengthening of 198–200
  partial harmonisation 191–4
  rationale for 187–8
  and Unfair Commercial Practices Directive (UCPD) 191–4
children's rights
  advertising *see* children's advertising, regulation of
  advertising to 164–5
  Commission strategy document 173–5
  competing interests to 175–9
  as consumers 164
  Dynamic Medien judgment 177–9
  EU Charter of Fundamental Rights provision 167–71
  EU consumer law and policy development 166–82
  Family Reunification Directive judgment 171–3
  and internal market 175–9, 181
  legislative coherence as to 167
  non-governmental organisations (NGOs) 167
  prioritising in EU policies 179–82
  toy safety regulation 182–7
  Treaty provision as to 166, 175, 177, 198, 200
  UN Convention *see* United Nations Convention on the Rights of the Child (UNCRC)
choice-of-law rules
  and Rome I Regulation 250
class action and 'legal origins' theory 310
collective enforcement *see* group actions
Colombia
  constitutional consumer rights 337
commercial expression
  see also advertising
  free speech claims as to 332–4
  freedom of expression jurisprudence 318–25
Common Frame of Reference (CFR) *see* Draft Common Frame of Reference (DCFR) for Contract Law
competence *see* legislative competence
competition law
  breaches of, provision against *see* Rome II Regulation
  case law as to enforcement 263–4
  consumer protection under 258–9
  link with consumer law 257–8, 263
  private enforcement
    issues as to 265
    possibility for 261–3
    proposals for 264–6
    tort of unfair competition 266–70
  self-regulation 48
conferral principle
  Treaty basis of 14–15
conflict of laws rules *see* Rome I Regulation
constitutional consumer rights *see* consumer rights as human rights
constitutional courts
  consumer rights jurisprudence 341–52

constitutional courts (cont.)
denial of subjective rights 343
human/fundamental rights judgments 345–6
constitutional provisions
constitutional principles as norms 340
parallel developments in EU law 350–1
programme norms
nature of 340–1
types of 340–1
subjective rights as norms 340
see also subjective rights
types of 339–41
consumer *see also* consumer citizenship; consumer rights as human rights; normative influences of consumer protection
acceptance of internal market 45, 127
'average consumer' concept 24, 36, 38–41, 45
behavioural studies insights
anchoring and adjustment heuristic 135–6
availability heuristic 134–5
bounded rationality 130–1
bounded self-interest 131–2
bounded willpower 131
context of choice situations 136–7
general observations 129–30
importance for consumer regulation 142
linking to economic theory 139–41
overconfidence bias 136
prospect theory 138–9
representativeness heuristic 132–3
child as *see* children's rights
collective enforcement *see* group actions
competition law protection 258–9
confidence in internal market 3
definition of
Czech law 403–4
e-commerce 83–6
detriment *see* consumer detriment
'empowered consumer' concept 45
gamblers *see* gambling services
human rights *see* consumer rights as human rights
information *see* information provision and consumer empowerment
investor or shareholder as 300
legal definition of
in consumer legislation 124
Consumer Rights Directive *see* Consumer Rights Directive
importance of 123
as natural person 124
rational informed consumers 221–5
understanding of contract terms, assisted informed consent model 148–9
'consumer *acquis*'
Green Paper on review of 9–10
review of 3, 9–10, 22
consumer citizenship *see also* normative influences of consumer protection
concept of 354–5
and development of consumer protection 355–8
'empowered consumer' 364
and transformation of internal market 358–67
consumer credit
expansion of cross-border market, regulatory effect of 30–1
maximum harmonisation 33
right of cancellation 34–5
Consumer Credit Directive
maximum harmonisation 30, 33
revision of 33
consumer detriment
concept of 365
financial/non-financial 366
general 373
personal 365–6
structural 365–6
consumer fraud
criminal sanctions against 79
consumer law *see also entries at* consumer credit

access to justice under 'legal origins' theory 309–10
clash with free movement regulation 24–6
co-regulation *see* co-regulation
consumer protection development generally 355–8
cross-border-only regulation *see* cross-border-only regulation
directives *see* directives
enforcement *see* enforcement
harmonisation *see* harmonisation
historical development 7–10
and internal market 7
and 'legal origins' theory *see* 'legal origins' theory
legislative competence 29–31
level of protection under 36–41
link with competition law 257–8, 263
as 'mandatory law' 7
national constitutional provisions *see* consumer rights as human rights
New Legislative Framework 50–5
proliferation of laws 9, 21
responsibility for 6
self-regulation *see* self-regulation
as social regulation 300
transparency *see* transparency as legitimising factor
Treaty basis 7–8, 14–15

consumer organisations
and 'legal origins' theory 310
participation in standards setting *see* standards

Consumer Protection Co-operation Regulation (CPC Regulation) 60–2

consumer protection networks 58–62

Consumer Regulations
coming into force 313
and ECHR Article 10 335
and freedom of expression issues 313–14
provisions generally 314–18

consumer rights as human rights *see also* subjective rights
Constitutional Court jurisprudence 341–52
as constitutional norms or principles 339–41
denial by constitutional court 343
European Charter of Consumers 348
European Charter of Fundamental Rights 350
human/fundamental rights
concepts of 343–4
Constitutional Court jurisprudence 345–6
and private law 344–5
role of 346–7
and 'social state' concept 343–4
issue of 336
Member State policies 337
national constitutional provisions 336–9 *see also* constitutional provisions
and other protected rights 337
parallel developments in EU law and national constitutions 350–1
protection via other kinds of rights
EU law 351–2
national constitutional provisions 347
rights protection with prescribed limits 338–9
rules protecting specific rights 338
Second Action Programme 348
Treaty provision 347–51

Consumer Rights Directive
auctions *see* auction; public auction
critiques of 44–5
definition of 'auction' and 'public auction' *see* auction; public auction
definition of consumer
and harmonisation 124–5, 128–9
judicial grounds 125–6
political grounds 126–8
full harmonisation under 44
limitations of 11
proposal for 3, 10, 18, 22, 27, 39, 43

contract law
Green Paper *see* Green Paper on European Contract Law
horse sales *see* horse sales
policy options for 11–12
scope for application of 12–13
Contract Law Directive
proposal for 12
Contract Law Green Paper *see* Green Paper on European Contract Law
Contract Law Regulation
proposal for 12
contract terms
'always unfair' (blacklisted) terms 151–2
applicable law *see* Rome I Regulation
consumer understanding of *see* consumer; transparency as legitimising factor
transparency as legitimising factor *see* transparency as legitimising factor
co-regulation
as complement to public enforcement 50
concept of 47–8
encouragement of 49–50
goals for 48
increased use of 46
and New Legislative Framework 50–5
self-regulation distinguished 47–8
Court of Justice of the European Union (ECJ) *see also* case law
and financial services law 34–5
reference to UNCRC 171–3
role in European State development 357
and Rome I Regulation 252–5
CPC Network 60–2
criminal law enforcement *see also* Germany
relationship with private law and public law 67–8
sanctions 76–81
and unfair competition law 80–1
use of 64–5
cross-border-only regulation
as alternative to directive 15–17
as alternative to harmonisation 13–14
arguments for 17–20
automatic application of 18
as complement to national regimes 19–20
and Green Paper on *acquis* review 18
right of cancellation 35
Treaty considerations 14–15
cross-border transactions
and 'average consumer' 38–41
consumer interests in 36–8
legal definition of 17–18
level of protection for 36
Czech Republic
ancillary contracts 408–10
consumer contracts generally 402
definition of consumer 403–4
New Civil Code 398–401
travel contracts, damages for loss of joy 410
unfair terms provisions 404–8

Denmark
definition of consumer 124
DG Justice
consumer law responsibility 6
directives *see also* Consumer Credit Directive; Consumer Rights Directive; Distance Selling Directive; Doorstop Selling Directive; Television Directives
adoption of 8
definition of consumer 128
list of 8
transposition of 8, 9, 15–16, 124
Distance Selling Directive (DSD)
exclusion of auctions from 378
domestic transactions
consumer interests in 36–8
harmonisation applied to 25–7, 30
level of protection for 36
Doorstep Selling Directive
right of cancellation under 34

Draft Common Frame of Reference (DCFR) for Contract Law
CFR interface with Member States' law 112
collective enforcement provisions 116–18
content of 99
cross-border transactions provision 5
development of CFR from 100, 110–11, 119–20
Expert Group 10, 100
information duties provision 41
publication of 99
purpose of 99–100
resumption of work on 6
review of effect of provisions 114
unfair terms provisions 100–1, 116–18
unfairness test 101
Dynamic Medien judgment
children's rights 177–9
e-commerce *see also* online dispute resolution (ODR)
confidence building 88–9, 92–4
consumer protection issues 82–3
definition of consumer 83–6
mass contracting 87
non-experts, protection of 86–7
East Timor
constitutional consumer rights 338
'empowered consumer' concept 45, 354, 364 *see also* 'average consumer' concept; consumer citizenship; rational informed consumer
empowered consumership
capability for *see* capability for empowered consumership
motivation for *see* motivation for empowered consumership
enforcement *see also* criminal law enforcement; private law enforcement; public law enforcement
choice of sanctions 67–8
effective enforcement principle 66
to ensure fair competition 67
and 'legal origins' theory *see* 'legal origins' theory
Member States' approaches to 64–5 *see also* Germany
need for 66–7
networks 58–62
by private actors *see* co-regulation; private actors; self-regulation
relationship between private law, public law and criminal law 67–8
EU Charter of Fundamental Rights
children's rights provision 167–71
EU private law
as 'multi-level system' 21
European Charter of Consumers
rights provisions 348
European Charter of Fundamental Rights
consumer protection under 350
European Civil Code
proposal for 12
European Competition network (ECN) 58
European Consumer Centers Network (ECC-Net) 60
European Convention on Human Rights (ECHR)
freedom of expression provision (Article 10) 313–14, 318–25, 326–7, 329, 330–1, 332–4, 335
freedom of expression judgments 318–34
European Court of Justice *see* Court of Justice of the European Union (ECJ)
European Standards Organisations (ESOs)
and New Legislative Framework 51, 53
European state
development of market into 357
Europeanisation *see* harmonisation

Family Reunification Directive
ECJ judgment 171–3
FIN-Net 60

financial services
  acquis, limitations of 33
  approaches to regulation 23
  and Court of Justice of the European Union (ECJ) 34–5
  EU regulatory framework 32
  level of consumer protection 36–41
  maximum harmonisation 27–9
  minimum harmonisation, arguments for 29–33
  problems of regulation 22–3
  twin-level regulatory approach 35
Finland
  gambling services regulation 208
food marketing to children, regulation of 194–8
four freedoms of EU Treaty
  negative harmonisation by 21, 24
France
  French Revolution and civil law development 305
  gambling services operation 204
  gambling services regulation 217–19, 234
  mandatory provisions 244, 245
fraud actions
  consumer fraud 79
  limitations of 79–80
  offers disguised as bills 77
  premium number frauds 77–8
  subscription traps 78–9
free movement regulation
    see also internal market
  'average consumer' concept 24
  Cassis de Dijon test 23, 24
  and children's rights 175–9
  clash with consumer law 24–6
  clash with Member State law 202–3
  clash with other regulatory priorities 32
  Dynamic Medien judgment 177–9
  regulatory approach 23
freedom of expression
  advertising, jurisprudence 318–25
  claims for commercial expression 332–4
  commercial expression as political expression 325–32
  and consumer protection
    Consumer Regulations and Business Regulations 313–14
  ECHR provisions 313–14
fundamental human rights
    see consumer rights as human rights

gambling services
  advertising control 227
  case law 205–14
  consumer protection measures 225–34
  consumers, nature of 214–15
  excessive gamblers, regulatory approach to 215–16
  fragmentation of national markets 202
  information disclosure, consumer protection via 225–8
  Member State approaches to regulation
    France 217–19
    prevention of addiction 216–17
    United Kingdom 219–21
  Member State restriction of 204
  modes of cross-border consumption 203
  national regulation and free movement 202–3
  rational informed consumers 221–5
  responsible gambling, measures to promote 228–34
  Treaty provisions 203
Germany 79
  children's rights judgment 177–8
  constitutional consumer rights 345–6
  enforcement
    consumer fraud 79
    criminal law and unfair competition law 80–1
    criminal law sanctions 76–81
    criminal law, use of 64–5
    experience generally 74–5
    fraud actions, limitations of 79–80
    group actions 64, 73

individual actions *see* individual enforcement actions
offers disguised as bills 77
premium number frauds 77–8
private law 64–5
public law, perspectives on 81
public law sanctions 75–6
public law, use of 64–5
subscription traps 78–9
gambling services operation 207
mandatory provisions 245
unfair contract terms provisions 159
Green Paper on European Contract Law
alternatives to harmonisation within 13
policy options within 11–12
publication of 6, 10
purpose of 10
scope of 11, 12–13
Green Paper on review of 'consumer *acquis*'
approach to regulation in 18
publication of 9–10
group actions
consumer collective redress, proposals for 278–81
DCFR provisions 116–18
effectiveness of provisions for 115–19
issues as to current regime for 118–19
limitations of 72–4
support for 57–8
use of 64

harmonisation
alternatives to 6, 13
arguments for 7
cross-border-only regulation as alternative to 13–14
and definition of consumer 124–5, 128–9
by directives 3–4, 8, 13–14, 15–16, 21, 22, 24, 25, 26, 27–9, 30, 111
and domestic transactions 25–6
by four freedoms 21, 24
full (maximum) harmonisation 3–4, 11, 23, 27–9, 30, 33, 44, 80–1, 123, 128–9, 143, 145, 146, 156, 160, 162, 233
'*half harmonisation*' theory 4
minimum harmonisation 3, 4, 12, 29, 101, 142, 145, 198, 227–8, 234
negative harmonisation 21, 24, 214
networks 59
New Approach 51
non-legislative harmonisation 103–4, 107, 115
partial harmonisation 191–4
Poland 415–19
positive harmonisation 21, 24, 210, 213
question of scope of 26–7
strategies (table) 5
and subsidiarity principle 12, 206
transparency issues 144–7
horse sales
as consumer contracts 299
defective horse, risk of purchasing 282, 284
eighteenth-century jurisprudence 288–95
horse ownership, social importance of 282
liability for defects, historical development 284–8
medieval jurisprudence 285–8
nineteenth-century legal developments 295–8
teithi, Welsh doctrine of 286
human rights *see* consumer rights as human rights

Icelandic banking crisis 23, 37
individual enforcement actions
alternative dispute resolution (ADR) *see* alternative dispute resolution (ADR); online dispute resolution
emphasis on 64
high-value claims 70–1
lack of evidence precluding 69
limitations to 68–72
low-value claims 69–70
psychological barriers to 71
situations precluding 69
time lapse precluding 69

individuals *see* private actors
information provision and consumer empowerment 360, 365, 369–71
internal market *see also* free movement regulation
  barriers to 103
  and children's rights 175–9, 181
  consumer acceptance of 45, 88, 127
  consumer confidence 3
  consumer law tied to 7
  Contract Law Green Paper proposals 11, 12–13
  development into European state 357
  ECJ's role as to 3
  inconsistent regulatory application 24–5, 358
  and legislative competence 29–30
  New Strategy report 19
  promotion of 27, 32, 45, 56
  strategy for consumer protection 3
  transformation of 358–67
  Treaty provision 256
  uniform rules and standards 3, 4, 12
International Consumer Protection and Enforcement Network (ICPEN) 59
investor as consumer 300
Italy
  constitutional consumer rights 346
  gambling services regulation 208–10

judicial group action *see* group actions

legal norms *see* constitutional provisions
'legal origins' theory
  application of 301
  basic theory 301–3
  critiques of 303–5
  development of 300
  differences between common law and civil law systems
    historical explanation for 305
    observations of 302–3
    Roman Law origins 306–7
  historical context of law, importance for theory 305
  methodology 301–2
  outlook for 310–12
  private law, importance for capitalism 307–9
legislative competence
  and internal market policy 29–30
  Treaty basis of 29
lex specialis principle
  and Rome I Regulation 251–2
Lithuania
  constitutional consumer rights 336, 338
loss of joy, damages for 410

'mandatory law'
  EU consumer law as 7
market integration *see* free movement regulation; internal market
Member State Law *see also specific jurisdictions e.g.* United Kingdom
  accession of new members 397
  children's advertising provisions, strengthening of 198–200
  constitutional consumer rights *see* constitutional provisions; consumer rights as human rights
  cross-border-only regulation as complement to 19–20
  definition of consumer 128–9
  enforcement, approaches to 64–5
  and free movement regulation 202–3
  interface with CFR 112
  pre-emption of *see* pre-emption of Member State law
  proliferation of consumer laws 9
  transposition of consumer directives 8
Mexico
  constitutional consumer rights 336
misleading practices
  prohibition by Unfair Commercial Practices Directive 45
motivation for empowered consumership
  as normative influence 360–4, 373–5

national law *see* Member State law
natural person
consumer as 124
Netherlands
gambling services regulation 204
networks for consumer protection 58–62
New Approach to harmonisation 51
New Legislative Framework 50–5
non-governmental organisations (NGOs)
children's rights 167
normative influences of consumer protection
capability (third level) *see* capability for empowered consumership
hierarchical framework 359–64
information provision (second level) 360, 365, 369–71
legislative basis of hierarchy (first level) 360
motivation (fourth level) *see* motivation for empowered consumership
operation of 367–8
norms, constitutional *see* constitutional provisions
Norway
definition of consumer 124

online auction *see* auction
online dispute resolution (ODR)
adaptability of 94
adaption of traditional ADR 95
automated negotiation systems 96–8
change from ADR to 92–4
Electronic Consumer Dispute Resolution (ECODIR) 96
establishment of efficient system of 94
role in building confidence in online transactions 88–9, 92–4
typology 94–5
online transactions *see* e-commerce

Paraguay
constitutional consumer rights 337
plain language in contract terms 152–4
Poland
constitutional consumer rights 336, 339, 340, 341–3, 347
harmonisation 415–19
and Unfair Terms Directive
historical background 413–15
implementation issues 412–13
implementation of abstract review of unfair terms 427–32
jurisprudence 422–7, 428
legislative transposition 419–22, 427–8
political expression
advertising as 325–32
Portugal
constitutional consumer rights 338
gambling services regulation 210–12
pre-emption of Member State law
doctrine of 3
limits to 4
private actors *see also* consumer organisations; individual enforcement actions; non-governmental organisations (NGOs)
collective enforcement by 55–8
competition law enforcement by 261–3
directive provisions for 48–9
enforcement networks 58–62
enforcement role of 43
judicial group action 57–8
private international law
competition law enforcement *see* competition law
private law
importance for capitalism under 'legal origins' theory 307–9
private law enforcement *see also* Germany
class action and 'legal origins' theory 310
limitations of 68–74
relationship with public law and criminal law 67–8
use of 64–5
proportionality principle
application of 4, 12
Treaty basis of 4, 14–15, 30

public auction *see also* auction
  Consumer Rights Directive
      definition
    adequacy 389–92
    auction distinguished 385–6
    difficulties 380–1, 382–5
    neutrality as to technology and
      product 392–3
    provision 379
    terminology issues 386, 389–95
    usefulness 380
public authorities
  consumer protection network 58
public interest or safety
  and applicability of Rome I
      Regulation 250–1
public law enforcement
      see also Germany
  perspectives on 81
  relationship with private law and
      criminal law 67–8
  Roman Law 306–7
  sanctions 75–6
  use of 64–5

rational informed consumer 221–5
'reference consumer' *see* 'average
      consumer' concept
regulation, cross-border-only *see*
      cross-border-only regulation
Regulation no. 593/2008 *see* Rome
      I Regulation
Regulation no. 864/2007 *see* Rome II
      Regulation
rights of the child *see* children's rights
Roman Law
  horse sales, liability for defects
      284–5
  public actions 306–7
Rome I Regulation
  adoption of 4
  consumer protection provisions
      240–3
  harmonised conflict rules 239–40
  overriding mandatory provisions
    applicable law limitations 243–6
    choice-of-law rules 250
    CJEU's role as to 252–5
    concept of 239
    consumer protection as 246–52
    and *lex specialis* principle 251–2
    public interest or safety as triggers
      for application of 250–1
    scope of relevant contracts 252
Rome II Regulation
  application of 270
  coming into force 257–8, 270
  consumer collective redress 278
  general applicable law provision
      (Article 4) 272–3
  location of parties, importance
      of 260–1
  private enforcement of competition
      law, key issues 262–3
  provisions generally 257–8
  unfair competition and anti-
      competitive acts provision
      (Article 6) 273–8

Second Action Programme
  fundamental consumer rights 348
self-regulation
  co-regulation distinguished 47–8
  competition law 48
  as complement to public
      enforcement 50
  critiques of 46
  directive provisions for 48–9
  encouragement of 49–50
  increased use of 46
  Report on 47
Serbia
  constitutional consumer rights 338
shareholder as consumer 300
single market *see* internal market
social regulation
  consumer law as 300
'social state' concept
  and human/fundamental rights 343–4
Spain
  constitutional consumer rights 338–9
  gambling services regulation 209,
      212–13
standards
  consumer organisations'
      organisation for dealing with 54

consumer participation
funding 55
recognition 54–5
lack of awareness of role in consumer protection 53–4
New Legislative Framework 50–5
subjective rights
as constitutional norms 340
denial by constitutional court 343
subsidiarity principle
and harmonisation 12, 206
Treaty basis of 14–15, 30
suretyship contracts
comprehensive approach to consumer protection 112–15
Sweden
children's advertising provisions, strengthening of 200

Television Directives
children's advertising provisions 187–200
minimum harmonisation 198
partial harmonisation 191–4
Thailand
constitutional consumer rights 338
tort of unfair competition 266–70
Towards a Strategy on the Rights of the Child' (Commission Communication) 173–5
toy safety regulation 182–7
transparency as legitimising factor
'always unfair' (blacklisted) terms 151–2
approaches to 147–51
assisted informed consent model 148–9
bank charges 152–4
commercial practices 159–62
and harmonisation 144–7
importance for consumer regulation 144
key issues 143–4
meaning of transparency 147–8
plain language in contract terms 152–4
rejection of 149–51
and unfairness test 154
travel contracts, damages for loss of joy 410
Treaty freedoms
negative harmonisation by 21, 24
Treaty provision
anti-competitive behaviour claims 257–8, 265, 279
children's rights 175, 177, 198, 200
conferral principle 14–15
consumer collective redress 278
consumer human rights 347–51
consumer law generally 7–8, 14–15
consumer protection 356
gambling services 203
internal market 256
as to legislative competence 29
private enforcement of competition law 261
proportionality principle 14–15, 30
subsidiarity principle 14–15, 30
'typical consumer' *see* 'average (typical) consumer' concept

Unfair Commercial Practices Directive (UCPD)
and 'average consumer' concept 45
and children's advertising regulation 191–4
prohibition of misleading practices and aggressive practices 45
self-regulation provision 50
transparency issues 145–7
unfair competition
Rome II Regulation provision 273–8
tort of 266–70
unfair terms
and 'average consumer' concept 25
collective enforcement against 115–19
Czech Republic 404–8
DCFR provisions 100–1
Directive 3, 4, 8, 30, 66, 67, 116
unfairness test 101
Unfair Terms on Consumer Contracts Directive (UTCCD)
and Polish law *see* Poland
transparency issues 144–5, 146–7
United Kingdom
application of future CFR 112

United Kingdom (cont.)
children's advertising provisions, strengthening of 198–200
children's rights judgment 177
consumer information provision 369–70
enforcement, approaches to 64
freedom of expression 313–14, 318–25, 332–4
gambling services operation 204, 208
gambling services regulation 205, 207, 219–21, 227, 229, 234
Glorious Revolution and common law development 305
horse sales *see* horse sales
judicial group action 57–8
mandatory provisions 247–9
private enforcement of competition law 261–2, 265, 275
tort of unfair competition 266–70
unfair contract terms provisions 151, 156–60
unfairness test 101
United Nations Convention on the Rights of the Child (UNCRC)
balancing of competing interests under 175–6
ECJ reference to 171–3
provisions 165, 168–71
United States
conflict of laws rules 249
'legal origins' theory
and class action 310
development of 300, 301

Lightning Source UK Ltd.
Milton Keynes UK
UKOW051331250413

209764UK00001B/10/P